Toyota RAV4
Owners Workshop Manual

by Bob Henderson and Andy Legg

Models covered

(4750 - 7AV1 - 400)

RAV4 models, two-wheel-drive and four-wheel-drive, including special/limited editions

Petrol: 1.8 litre (1794cc) & 2.0 litre (1998cc)

Diesel: 2.0 litre (1995cc)

Does NOT cover new RAV4 range introduced Feb 2006

© Haynes Group Limited 2016

ABCDE
FGHIJ

A book in the **Haynes Owners Workshop Manual Series**

All rights reserved. No part of this book may be reproduced or transmitted in any form or by any means, electronic or mechanical, including photocopying, recording or by any information storage or retrieval system, without permission in writing from the copyright holder.

ISBN **978 1 78521 018 1**

British Library Cataloguing in Publication Data
A catalogue record for this book is available from the British Library.

Printed in India

Haynes Group Limited
Sparkford, Yeovil, Somerset BA22 7JJ, England

Haynes North America, Inc
2801 Townsgate Road, Suite 340, Thousand Oaks, CA 91361, USA

Disclaimer

Contents

LIVING WITH YOUR TOYOTA RAV4

Safety first!	Page	0•5
About this manual	Page	0•6
Introduction to the Toyota RAV4	Page	0•6

ROADSIDE REPAIRS

If your car won't start	Page	0•7
Jump starting	Page	0•8
Wheel changing	Page	0•9
Identifying leaks	Page	0•10
Towing	Page	0•10

WEEKLY CHECKS

Introduction	Page	0•11
Engine oil level	Page	0•11
Coolant level	Page	0•12
Windscreen washer fluid level	Page	0•13
Battery electrolyte level	Page	0•13
Brake and clutch fluid level	Page	0•13
Power steering fluid level	Page	0•14
Automatic transmission fluid level	Page	0•14
Tyre and tyre pressure checks	Page	0•15

Lubricants and fluids	Page	0•16

MAINTENANCE

Routine maintenance and servicing

Petrol models	Page	1A•1
Servicing specifications	Page	1A•2
Maintenance schedule	Page	1A•4
Maintenance procedures	Page	1A•7
Diesel models	Page	1B•1
Servicing specifications	Page	1B•2
Maintenance schedule	Page	1B•3
Maintenance procedures	Page	1B•5

Contents

REPAIRS AND OVERHAUL

Engine and associated systems
Petrol engines – 2000 and earlier   Page **2A•1**
Petrol engines – 2001 and later   Page **2B•1**
Diesel engines   Page **2C•1**
Engine removal and overhaul procedures   Page **2D•1**
Cooling, heating and air conditioning systems   Page **3•1**
Fuel and exhaust systems – petrol engines   Page **4A•1**
Fuel and exhaust systems – diesel engines   Page **4B•1**
Engine electrical systems   Page **5•1**
Emissions and engine control systems – petrol engines   Page **6A•1**
Emissions and engine control systems – diesel engines   Page **6B•1**

Transmission
Manual transmission   Page **7A•1**
Automatic transmission   Page **7B•1**
Clutch and driveshafts   Page **8•1**

Brakes and Suspension
Brakes   Page **9•1**
Suspension and steering systems   Page **10•1**

Body equipment
Body   Page **11•1**
Chassis electrical system   Page **12•1**
Wiring diagrams   Page **12•22**

REFERENCE

Dimensions and weights   Page **REF•1**
Conversion factors   Page **REF•2**
General repair procedures   Page **REF•3**
Vehicle identification numbers   Page **REF•4**
Buying spare parts   Page **REF•5**
Jacking and vehicle support   Page **REF•5**
Tools and working facilities   Page **REF•6**
MOT Test Checks   Page **REF•8**
Troubleshooting   Page **REF•12**

Index
Index   Page **REF•19**

Advanced driving

Many people see the words 'advanced driving' and believe that it won't interest them or that it is a style of driving beyond their own abilities. Nothing could be further from the truth. Advanced driving is straightforward safe, sensible driving - the sort of driving we should all do every time we get behind the wheel.

An average of 10 people are killed every day on UK roads and 870 more are injured, some seriously. Lives are ruined daily, usually because somebody did something stupid. Something like 95% of all accidents are due to human error, mostly driver failure. Sometimes we make genuine mistakes - everyone does. Sometimes we have lapses of concentration. Sometimes we deliberately take risks.

For many people, the process of 'learning to drive' doesn't go much further than learning how to pass the driving test because of a common belief that good drivers are made by 'experience'.

Learning to drive by 'experience' teaches three driving skills:

☐ Quick reactions. (Whoops, that was close!)
☐ Good handling skills. (Horn, swerve, brake, horn).
☐ Reliance on vehicle technology. (Great stuff this ABS, stop in no distance even in the wet...)

Drivers whose skills are 'experience based' generally have a lot of near misses and the odd accident. The results can be seen every day in our courts and our hospital casualty departments.

Advanced drivers have learnt to control the risks by controlling the position and speed of their vehicle. They avoid accidents and near misses, even if the drivers around them make mistakes.

The key skills of advanced driving are **concentration**, effective all-round **observation, anticipation** and **planning.** When **good vehicle handling** is added to

these skills, all driving situations can be approached and negotiated in a safe, methodical way, leaving nothing to chance.

Concentration means applying your mind to safe driving, completely excluding anything that's not relevant. Driving is usually the most dangerous activity that most of us undertake in our daily routines. It deserves our full attention.

Observation means not just looking, but seeing and seeking out the information found in the driving environment.

Anticipation means asking yourself what is happening, what you can reasonably expect to happen and what could happen unexpectedly. (One of the commonest words used in compiling accident reports is 'suddenly'.)

Planning is the link between seeing something and taking the appropriate action. For many drivers, planning is the missing link.

If you want to become a safer and more skilful driver and you want to enjoy your driving more, contact the Institute of Advanced Motorists at www.iam.org.uk, phone 0208 996 9600, or write to IAM House, 510 Chiswick High Road, London W4 5RG for an information pack.

Working on your car can be dangerous. This page shows just some of the potential risks and hazards, with the aim of creating a safety-conscious attitude.

General hazards

Scalding

• Don't remove the radiator or expansion tank cap while the engine is hot.
• Engine oil, automatic transmission fluid or power steering fluid may also be dangerously hot if the engine has recently been running.

Burning

• Beware of burns from the exhaust system and from any part of the engine. Brake discs and drums can also be extremely hot immediately after use.

Crushing

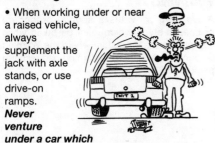

• When working under or near a raised vehicle, always supplement the jack with axle stands, or use drive-on ramps. *Never venture under a car which is only supported by a jack.*
• Take care if loosening or tightening high-torque nuts when the vehicle is on stands. Initial loosening and final tightening should be done with the wheels on the ground.

Fire

• Fuel is highly flammable; fuel vapour is explosive.
• Don't let fuel spill onto a hot engine.
• Do not smoke or allow naked lights (including pilot lights) anywhere near a vehicle being worked on. Also beware of creating sparks (electrically or by use of tools).
• Fuel vapour is heavier than air, so don't work on the fuel system with the vehicle over an inspection pit.
• Another cause of fire is an electrical overload or short-circuit. Take care when repairing or modifying the vehicle wiring.
• Keep a fire extinguisher handy, of a type suitable for use on fuel and electrical fires.

Electric shock

• Ignition HT voltage can be dangerous, especially to people with heart problems or a pacemaker. Don't work on or near the ignition system with the engine running or the ignition switched on.

• Mains voltage is also dangerous. Make sure that any mains-operated equipment is correctly earthed. Mains power points should be protected by a residual current device (RCD) circuit breaker.

Fume or gas intoxication

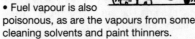

• Exhaust fumes are poisonous; they often contain carbon monoxide, which is rapidly fatal if inhaled. Never run the engine in a confined space such as a garage with the doors shut.
• Fuel vapour is also poisonous, as are the vapours from some cleaning solvents and paint thinners.

Poisonous or irritant substances

• Avoid skin contact with battery acid and with any fuel, fluid or lubricant, especially antifreeze, brake hydraulic fluid and Diesel fuel. Don't syphon them by mouth. If such a substance is swallowed or gets into the eyes, seek medical advice.
• Prolonged contact with used engine oil can cause skin cancer. Wear gloves or use a barrier cream if necessary. Change out of oil-soaked clothes and do not keep oily rags in your pocket.
• Air conditioning refrigerant forms a poisonous gas if exposed to a naked flame (including a cigarette). It can also cause skin burns on contact.

Asbestos

• Asbestos dust can cause cancer if inhaled or swallowed. Asbestos may be found in gaskets and in brake and clutch linings. When dealing with such components it is safest to assume that they contain asbestos.

Special hazards

Hydrofluoric acid

• This extremely corrosive acid is formed when certain types of synthetic rubber, found in some O-rings, oil seals, fuel hoses etc, are exposed to temperatures above 400°C. The rubber changes into a charred or sticky substance containing the acid. *Once formed, the acid remains dangerous for years. If it gets onto the skin, it may be necessary to amputate the limb concerned.*
• When dealing with a vehicle which has suffered a fire, or with components salvaged from such a vehicle, wear protective gloves and discard them after use.

The battery

• Batteries contain sulphuric acid, which attacks clothing, eyes and skin. Take care when topping-up or carrying the battery.
• The hydrogen gas given off by the battery is highly explosive. Never cause a spark or allow a naked light nearby. Be careful when connecting and disconnecting battery chargers or jump leads.

Air bags

• Air bags can cause injury if they go off accidentally. Take care when removing the steering wheel and/or facia. Special storage instructions may apply.

Diesel injection equipment

• Diesel injection pumps supply fuel at very high pressure. Take care when working on the fuel injectors and fuel pipes.

⚠️ *Warning: Never expose the hands, face or any other part of the body to injector spray; the fuel can penetrate the skin with potentially fatal results.*

Remember...

DO

• Do use eye protection when using power tools, and when working under the vehicle.

• Do wear gloves or use barrier cream to protect your hands when necessary.

• Do get someone to check periodically that all is well when working alone on the vehicle.

• Do keep loose clothing and long hair well out of the way of moving mechanical parts.

• Do remove rings, wristwatch etc, before working on the vehicle – especially the electrical system.

• Do ensure that any lifting or jacking equipment has a safe working load rating adequate for the job.

DON'T

• Don't attempt to lift a heavy component which may be beyond your capability – get assistance.

• Don't rush to finish a job, or take unverified short cuts.

• Don't use ill-fitting tools which may slip and cause injury.

• Don't leave tools or parts lying around where someone can trip over them. Mop up oil and fuel spills at once.

• Don't allow children or pets to play in or near a vehicle being worked on.

Its purpose

The purpose of this manual is to help you get the best value from your vehicle. It can do so in several ways. It can help you decide what work must be done, even if you choose to have it done by a dealer service department or a garage; it provides information and procedures for routine maintenance and servicing; and it offers diagnostic and repair procedures to follow when trouble occurs.

We hope you use the manual to tackle the work yourself. For many simpler jobs, doing it yourself may be quicker than arranging an appointment to get the vehicle into a garage and making the trips to leave it and pick it up. More importantly, a lot of money can be saved by avoiding the expense the garage must pass on to you to cover its labour and overhead costs. An added benefit is the sense of satisfaction and accomplishment that you feel after doing the job yourself.

Using the manual

The manual is divided into Chapters. Each Chapter is divided into numbered Sections, which are headed in bold type between horizontal lines. Each Section consists of consecutively numbered paragraphs.

The reference numbers used in illustration captions pinpoint the pertinent Section and the paragraph within that Section. That is, illustration 3.2 means the illustration refers to Section 3 and paragraph (or Step) 2 within that Section.

Procedures, once described in the text, are not normally repeated. When it's necessary to refer to another Chapter, the reference will be given as Chapter and Section number. Cross-references given without use of the word 'Chapter' apply to Sections and/or paragraphs in the same Chapter. For example, 'see Section 8' means in the same Chapter.

References to the left or right side of the vehicle assume you are sitting in the driver's seat, facing forward.

This manual is not a direct reproduction of the vehicle manufacturer's data, and its publication should not be taken as implying any technical approval by the vehicle manufacturers or importers.

We take great pride in the accuracy of information given in this manual, but vehicle manufacturers make alterations and design changes during the production run of a particular vehicle of which they do not inform us. No liability can be accepted by the authors or publishers for loss, damage or injury caused by errors in, or omissions from, the information given.

NOTE

A **Note** provides information necessary to properly complete a procedure or information which will make the procedure easier to understand.

CAUTION

A *Caution* provides a special procedure or special steps which must be taken while completing the procedure where the Caution is found. Not heeding a Caution can result in damage to the assembly being worked on.

WARNING

A *Warning* provides a special procedure or special steps which must be taken while completing the procedure where the Warning is found. Not heeding a Warning can result in personal injury.

Introduction to the Toyota RAV4

Toyota RAV4 models are available in three- and five-door body styles.

The transversely mounted inline four-cylinder engines used in these vehicles are equipped with electronic fuel injection.

The engine drives the front wheels through either a five-speed manual or a four-speed automatic transmission with independent driveshafts. On 4WD models, drive to the rear wheels is through a propeller shaft, rear differential, and two rear driveshafts.

Suspension is independent at all four wheels, MacPherson struts being used at the front end and trailing arms, control arms, coil springs and telescopic shock absorbers at the rear. The rack-and-pinion steering unit is mounted on the suspension crossmember.

The brakes are disc at the front and either drums or discs at the rear, according to model. Power assistance is standard. Some models are equipped with an optional Anti-lock Brake System (ABS).

Acknowledgements

We are grateful for the help and co-operation of the Toyota Motor Corporation for their assistance with technical information and certain illustrations. Technical writers who contributed to this project include Jeff Kibler, Rob Maddox, John Wegmann and Jamie Sarté.

The following pages are intended to help in dealing with common roadside emergencies and breakdowns. You will find more detailed fault finding information at the back of the manual, and repair information in the main chapters.

If your car won't start and the starter motor doesn't turn

☐ If it's a model with automatic transmission, make sure the selector is in P or N.
☐ Open the bonnet and make sure that the battery terminals are clean and tight.
☐ Switch on the headlights and try to start the engine. If the headlights go very dim when you're trying to start, the battery is probably flat. Get out of trouble by jump starting (see next page) using a friend's car.

If your car won't start even though the starter motor turns as normal

☐ Is there fuel in the tank?
☐ Is there moisture on electrical components under the bonnet? Switch off the ignition, then wipe off any obvious dampness with a dry cloth. Spray a water-repellent aerosol product (WD-40 or equivalent) on ignition and fuel system electrical connectors like those shown in the photos. (Note that diesel engines don't usually suffer from damp).

a) Check the condition and security of the battery connections.
b) Check the fuses in the fusebox.
c) Check the wiring to the ignition coil at the front of the engine (petrol models only).
d) Check that the ECM wiring is secure.
e) Check that the fuel lines are secure and no air in the system.
f) Check that electrical connections are secure (with the ignition switched off) and spray them with a water-dispersant spray like WD-40 if you suspect a problem due to damp

Jump starting

When jump-starting a car using a booster battery, observe the following precautions:

✔ Before connecting the booster battery, make sure that the ignition is switched off.

✔ Ensure that all electrical equipment (lights, heater, wipers, etc) is switched off.

✔ Take note of any special precautions printed on the battery case.

✔ Make sure that the booster battery is the same voltage as the discharged one in the vehicle.

✔ If the battery is being jump-started from the battery in another vehicle, the two vehicles MUST NOT TOUCH each other.

✔ Make sure that the transmission is in neutral (or PARK, in the case of automatic transmission).

 HAYNES HiNT *Jump starting will get you out of trouble, but you must correct whatever made the battery go flat in the first place. There are three possibilities:*

1 *The battery has been drained by repeated attempts to start, or by leaving the lights on.*

2 *The charging system is not working properly (alternator drivebelt slack or broken, alternator wiring fault or alternator itself faulty).*

3 *The battery itself is at fault (electrolyte low, or battery worn out).*

1 Connect one end of the red jump lead to the positive (+) terminal of the flat battery

2 Connect the other end of the red lead to the positive (+) terminal of the booster battery.

3 Connect one end of the black jump lead to the negative (-) terminal of the booster battery

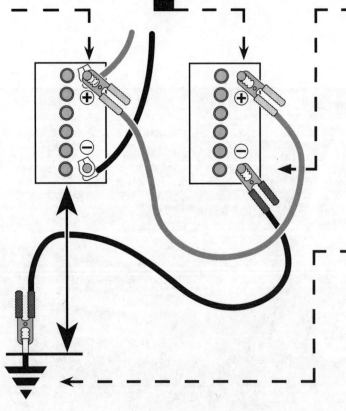

4 Connect the other end of the black jump lead to a suitable metal part of the engine on the vehicle to be started

5 Make sure that the jump leads will not come into contact with the fan, drive-belts or other moving parts of the engine.

6 Start the engine using the booster battery and run it at idle speed. Switch on the lights, rear window demister and heater blower motor, then disconnect the jump leads in the reverse order of connection. Turn off the lights etc.

Wheel changing

Note: *Some of the details shown here will vary according to model.*

⚠️ *Warning: Do not change a wheel in a situation where you risk being hit by other traffic. On busy roads, try to stop in a lay-by or a gateway. Be wary of passing traffic while changing the wheel – it is easy to become distracted by the job in hand.*

Preparation

☐ When a puncture occurs, stop as soon as it is safe to do so.
☐ Park on firm level ground, if possible, and well out of the way of other traffic.
☐ Use hazard warning lights if necessary.

☐ If you have one, use a warning triangle to alert other drivers of your presence.
☐ Apply the handbrake and engage first or reverse gear (or Park on models with automatic transmission).

☐ Chock the wheel diagonally opposite the one being removed – a couple of large stones will do for this.
☐ If the ground is soft, use a flat piece of wood to spread the load under the jack.

Changing the wheel

1 The jack is stored beneath the driver's seat. Move the driver's seat fully to the rear and unscrew the adjustment rod to release the jack.

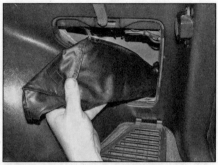

2 The tools are stored behind a flap on the right-hand side of the luggage compartment. Open the flap and remove the tools.

3 Remove the spare wheel from the back door. To do this, first remove the cover (a full cover is secured with a toggle clip, and a half cover is secured with a nut). Unscrew the nuts and lift the spare wheel from the back door.

4 Use the wheel brace to slacken each wheel nut by half a turn only.

5 Locate the jack below the lifting point for the wheel to be removed (see *Jacking and vehicle support* in the *Reference* chapter for jacking points). Turn the jack handle clockwise until the wheel is raised clear of the ground.

6 Unscrew the wheel nuts and remove the wheel. An adapter will be required for the locking wheel nut.

7 Fit the spare wheel, and screw on the nuts. Lightly tighten the nuts with the wheel brace then lower the vehicle to the ground.

8 Securely tighten the wheel nuts in the sequence shown.

Finally . . .

☐ Stow the punctured wheel inside the luggage compartment or on the back door until repaired.
☐ Remove the wheel chocks.
☐ Stow the jack and tools in their correct locations.
☐ Check the tyre pressure on the wheel just fitted. If it is low, or if you don't have a pressure gauge with you, drive slowly to the nearest garage and inflate the tyre to the correct pressure.
☐ Tighten the wheel nuts to the specified torque at the earliest possible opportunity.

Identifying leaks

Puddles on the garage floor or drive, or obvious wetness under the bonnet or underneath the car, suggest a leak that needs investigating. It can sometimes be difficult to decide where the leak is coming from, especially if the engine bay is very dirty already. Leaking oil or fluid can also be blown rearwards by the passage of air under the car, giving a false impression of where the problem lies.

Warning: Most automotive oils and fluids are poisonous. Wash them off skin, and change out of contaminated clothing, without delay.

 The smell of a fluid leaking from the car may provide a clue to what's leaking. Some fluids are distinctively coloured. It may help to clean the car carefully and to park it over some clean paper overnight as an aid to locating the source of the leak.
Remember that some leaks may only occur while the engine is running.

Sump oil

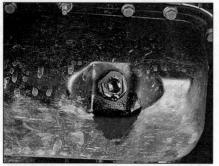

Engine oil may leak from the drain plug...

Oil from filter

...or from the base of the oil filter.

Gearbox oil

Gearbox oil can leak from the seals at the inboard ends of the driveshafts.

Antifreeze

Leaking antifreeze often leaves a crystalline deposit like this.

Brake fluid

A leak occurring at a wheel is almost certainly brake fluid.

Power steering fluid

Power steering fluid may leak from the pipe connectors on the steering rack.

Towing

When all else fails, you may find yourself having to get a tow home – or of course you may be helping somebody else. Long-distance recovery should only be done by a garage or breakdown service. For shorter distances, DIY towing using another car is easy enough, but observe the following points:

☐ Use a proper tow-rope – they are not expensive. The vehicle being towed must display an ON TOW sign in its rear window.

☐ Always turn the ignition key to the 'On' position when the vehicle is being towed, so that the steering lock is released, and the direction indicator and brake lights work.

☐ Only attach the tow-rope to the towing eyes provided. The front towing eyes are located beneath the right- and left-hand end of the front bumper. The rear towing eye is located beneath the left-hand side of the rear bumper.

☐ Before being towed, release the handbrake and select neutral on the transmission. On models with automatic transmission, do not exceed 30 mph and do not tow for more than 30 miles. If in doubt, do not tow, or transmission damage may result.

☐ Because the power steering will not be operational, greater-than-usual steering effort will be required.

☐ Note that greater-than-usual pedal pressure will be required to operate the brakes, since the vacuum servo unit is only operational with the engine running.

☐ The driver of the car being towed must keep the tow-rope taut at all times to avoid snatching.

☐ Make sure that both drivers know the route before setting off.

☐ Only drive at moderate speeds and keep the distance towed to a minimum. Drive smoothly and allow plenty of time for slowing down at junctions.

Introduction

There are some very simple checks which need only take a few minutes to carry out, but which could save you a lot of inconvenience and expense.

These *Weekly checks* require no great skill or special tools, and the small amount of time they take to perform could prove to be very well spent, for example:

☐ Keeping an eye on tyre condition and pressures, will not only help to stop them wearing out prematurely, but could also save your life.

☐ Many breakdowns are caused by electrical problems. Battery-related faults are particularly common, and a quick check on a regular basis will often prevent the majority of these.

☐ Fluids are an essential part of the lubrication, cooling, brake, clutch and other systems. Because these fluids gradually become depleted and/or contaminated during normal operation of the vehicle, they must be periodically replenished. **Note:** *The vehicle must be on level ground before fluid levels can be checked.*

☐ If your car develops a brake fluid leak, the first time you might know about it is when your brakes don't work properly. Checking the level regularly will give advance warning of this kind of problem.

☐ If the oil or coolant levels run low, the cost of repairing any engine damage will be far greater than fixing the leak, for example.

Engine oil level

1 The engine oil level is checked with a dipstick located at the front side of the engine **(see illustration)**. The dipstick extends through a metal tube from which it protrudes down into the engine sump.

2 The oil level should be checked before the vehicle has been driven, or about five minutes after the engine has been shut off. If the oil is checked immediately after driving the vehicle, some of the oil will remain in the upper engine components, producing an inaccurate reading on the dipstick.

3 Pull the dipstick from the tube and wipe all the oil from the end with a clean rag or paper towel. Insert the clean dipstick all the way back into its metal tube and pull it out again. Observe the oil at the end of the dipstick. At its highest point, the level should be between the L and F marks or between the two dimples **(see illustrations)**.

4 It takes one litre of oil to raise the level from the L mark to the F mark (or the lower dimple and the upper dimple) on the dipstick. Do not allow the level to drop below the L mark (or the lower dimple) or oil starvation may cause engine damage. Conversely, overfilling the engine (adding oil above the F mark or upper dimple) may cause oil fouled spark plugs, oil leaks or oil seal failures.

5 Remove the threaded cap from the valve cover to add oil **(see illustration)**. Use a funnel to prevent spills. After adding the oil, refit the

filler cap hand tight. Start the engine and look carefully for any small leaks around the oil filter or drain plug. Stop the engine and check the oil level again after it has had sufficient time to drain from the upper block and cylinder head galleys.

6 Checking the oil level is an important preventive maintenance job. A continually dropping oil level indicates oil leakage through damaged seals, from loose connections, or past worn rings or valve guides. If the oil looks milky in colour or has water droplets in it, a cylinder head gasket may be blown. The engine should be checked immediately. The condition of the oil should also be checked. Each time you check the oil level, slide your thumb and index finger up the dipstick before wiping off the oil. If you see small dirt or metal particles clinging to the dipstick, the oil should be changed (see Chapter 1A or 1B).

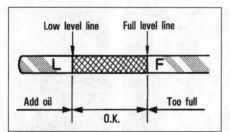

The engine oil dipstick is located at the front of the engine

Where the dipstick has Full and Low level marks, the oil level should be at or near the F mark – if it isn't, add enough oil to bring the level to near the F mark (it takes approximately 1 litre to raise the level from the L to the F mark)

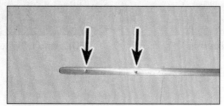

Where the engine oil dipstick has two dimples – keep the oil level at or near the upper dimple

The threaded oil filler cap is located on the valve cover – always make sure the area around the opening is clean before unscrewing the cap to prevent dirt from contaminating the engine

Coolant level

⚠️ *Warning: Do not allow antifreeze to come in contact with your skin or painted surfaces of the vehicle. Flush contaminated areas immediately with plenty of water. Don't store new coolant or leave old coolant lying around where it's accessible to children or pets – they're attracted by its sweet smell and may drink it. Ingestion of even a small amount of coolant can be fatal. Wipe up garage floor and drip pan spills immediately. Keep antifreeze containers covered and repair cooling system leaks as soon as they're noticed.*

1 All petrol models covered by this manual are equipped with a coolant recovery system where the reservoir is at atmospheric pressure. A white coolant reservoir located in the left

The coolant reservoir is located in the left front corner of the engine compartment – make sure the level is between Low and Full marks on the reservoir – 2000 and earlier models shown here . . .

front corner of the engine compartment is connected by a hose to the base of the radiator filler neck **(see illustrations)**. As the coolant heats up during engine operation, coolant can escape through a pressurised filler cap, then through a connecting hose into the reservoir. As the engine cools, the coolant is automatically drawn back into the cooling system to maintain the correct level.

2 All diesel models are equipped with an expansion tank (located on the engine compartment front crossmember) which holds a reserve of coolant. The radiator and expansion tank are both pressurised by a pressure cap located on the top of the tank. As the engine heats up and cools, coolant is allowed to expand into and out of the expansion tank.

3 The coolant level should be checked regularly. It must be between the Full and Low lines on the tank **(see illustration)**. The level will vary with the temperature of the engine. When the engine is cold, the coolant level should be at or slightly above the Low mark on the tank. Once the engine has warmed-up, the level should be at or near the Full mark. If it isn't, allow the fluid in the tank to cool, then remove the cap from the reservoir and add coolant to bring the level up to the Full line.

4 Use only ethylene/glycol type coolant and water in the mixture ratio recommended by your owner's manual. Do not use supplemental inhibitor additives. If only a small amount of coolant is required to bring the system up to the proper level, water can be used. However, repeated additions of water will dilute the

recommended antifreeze and water solution. In order to maintain the proper ratio of antifreeze and water, it is advisable to top-up the coolant level with the correct mixture. Refer to your owner's manual for the recommended ratio.

5 If the coolant level drops within a short time after replenishment, there may be a leak in the system. Inspect the radiator, hoses, engine coolant filler cap, drain plugs, air bleeder plugs and water pump. If no leak is evident, have the radiator cap pressure tested by a service station.

⚠️ *Warning: Never remove the radiator cap or the coolant recovery reservoir cap when the engine is running or has just been shut down, because the cooling system is hot. Escaping steam and scalding liquid could cause serious injury.*

6 If it is necessary to open the radiator cap, wait until the system has cooled completely, then wrap a thick cloth around the cap and turn it to the first stop. If any steam escapes, wait until the system has cooled further, then remove the cap.

7 When checking the coolant level, always note its condition. It should be relatively clear. If it is brown or rust-coloured, the system should be drained, flushed and refilled. Even if the coolant appears to be normal, the corrosion inhibitors wear out with use, so it must be renewed at the specified intervals.

8 Do not allow antifreeze to come in contact with your skin or painted surfaces of the vehicle. Flush contacted areas immediately with plenty of water.

. . . 2001 and later models look like this

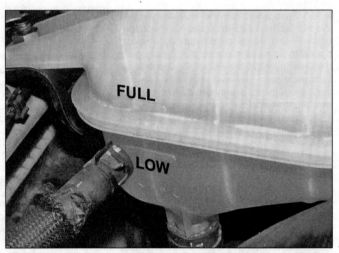

FULL and LOW level marks on the coolant expansion tank

Windscreen washer fluid level

1 Fluid for the windscreen (and rear window) washer system is stored in a plastic reservoir which is located on the right-hand side of the engine compartment **(see illustration)**. **Note:** *On 2000 and earlier models the fluid level is checked with a small dipstick, located next to the reservoir filler neck.*

2 In milder climates, plain water can be used to top-up the reservoir, but the reservoir should be kept no more than two-thirds full to allow for expansion should the water freeze. In colder climates, the use of a specially-designed windscreen washer fluid, available at your dealer and any car accessory store, will help lower the freezing point of the fluid. Mix the solution with water in accordance with the manufacturer's directions on the container. Do not use regular antifreeze; it will damage the vehicle's paint.

The windscreen/rear window washer fluid reservoir is located in the right-hand front corner of the engine compartment

Battery electrolyte level

1 On models not equipped with a sealed battery, unscrew the filler/vent cap and check the electrolyte level. It must be between the upper and lower levels. If the level is low, add distilled water. Refit and securely retighten the cap. *Caution: Overfilling the cells may cause electrolyte to spill over during periods of heavy charging, causing corrosion or damage.*

Brake and clutch fluid level

1 The brake master cylinder is mounted on the front of the brake vacuum servo unit in the engine compartment. The clutch master cylinder used on vehicles with manual transmissions is located next to the brake master cylinder.

2 The brake master cylinder and the clutch master cylinder share a common reservoir. To check the fluid level of either system, simply look at the MAX and MIN marks on the brake

The brake fluid level should be kept between the MIN and MAX marks on the translucent plastic reservoir

fluid reservoir **(see illustration)**. The level should be at or near the maximum fill line.

3 If the level is low, wipe the top of the reservoir cover with a clean rag to prevent contamination of the brake or clutch system before lifting the cover.

4 Add only the specified brake fluid to the reservoir (refer to *Lubricants and fluids* at the end of this chapter or to your owner's manual). Mixing different types of brake fluid can damage the system. Fill the brake master cylinder reservoir only to the dotted line – this brings the fluid to the correct level when you put the cover back on.

⚠ *Warning: Use caution when filling the reservoir – brake fluid can harm your eyes and damage painted surfaces. Do not use brake fluid that has been opened for more than one year (even if the cap has been on) or has been left open. Brake fluid absorbs moisture from the air. Excess moisture can cause a dangerous loss of braking.*

5 While the reservoir cap is removed, inspect the master cylinder reservoir for contamination. If deposits, dirt particles or water droplets are present, the fluid in the brake system should be changed (see Chapter 1A or 1B for the brake fluid renewal procedure or Chapter 8 for the clutch hydraulic system bleeding procedure).

6 After filling the reservoir to the proper level, make sure the lid is properly seated to prevent fluid leakage and/or system pressure loss.

7 The brake fluid in the master cylinder will drop slightly as the brake pads at each wheel wear down during normal operation. If the master cylinder requires repeated replenishing to keep it at the proper level, this is an indication of leakage in the brake or clutch release system, which should be corrected immediately. Check all brake and clutch release lines and connections, along with the brake and clutch master cylinders, brake calipers, wheel cylinders and clutch release cylinder (see Chapter 1A or 1B for more information).

8 If, upon checking the master cylinder fluid level, you discover the reservoir empty or nearly empty, the brake system or clutch release system must be diagnosed immediately (see Chapters 8 and 9).

Power steering fluid level

1 Unlike manual steering, the power steering system relies on fluid which may, over a period of time, require replenishing.

2 The fluid reservoir for the power steering pump is mounted on the left-hand side strut tower **(see illustration)**.

3 For the check, the front wheels should be pointed straight-ahead and the engine should be off.

4 Use a clean rag to wipe off the reservoir cap and the area around the cap. This will help prevent any foreign matter from entering the reservoir during the check.

5 Twist off the cap and check the temperature of the fluid at the end of the dipstick with your finger.

6 View the level of power steering fluid through the translucent reservoir. At no time should the fluid level drop below the upper mark for each heat range.

7 If additional fluid is required, pour the specified type directly into the reservoir, using a funnel to prevent spills.

8 If the reservoir requires frequent fluid additions, all power steering hoses, hose connections, the power steering pump and the rack-and-pinion assembly should be carefully checked for leaks.

The power steering fluid reservoir is located on the right side of the engine compartment, mounted to the strut tower – the fluid level is checked by looking through the plastic reservoir

Automatic transmission fluid level

1 The level of the automatic transmission fluid should be carefully maintained. Low fluid level can lead to slipping or loss of drive, while overfilling can cause foaming, loss of fluid and transmission damage.

2 The transmission fluid level should only be checked when the transmission is hot (at its normal operating temperature). If the vehicle has just been driven over 10 miles, the transmission is hot.

Caution: If the vehicle has just been driven for a long time at high speed or in city traffic in hot weather, or if it has been pulling a trailer, an accurate fluid level reading cannot be obtained. Allow the fluid to cool down for about 30 minutes.

3 If the vehicle has not just been driven, park the vehicle on level ground, set the handbrake and start the engine. While the engine is idling, depress the brake pedal and move the selector lever through all the gear ranges, beginning and ending in Park.

4 With the engine still idling, remove the dipstick from its tube **(see illustration)**. Check the level of the fluid on the dipstick **(see illustration)** and note its condition.

5 Wipe the fluid from the dipstick with a clean rag and reinsert it back into the filler tube until the cap seats.

6 Pull the dipstick out again and note the fluid level. If the transmission is cold, the level should be in the COLD or COOL range on the dipstick. If it is hot, the fluid level should be in the HOT range. If the level is at the low side of either range, add the specified automatic transmission fluid through the dipstick tube with a funnel.

7 Add just enough of the recommended fluid to fill the transmission to the proper level. It takes about one pint to raise the level from the low mark to the high mark when the fluid is hot, so add the fluid a little at a time and keep checking the level until it is correct.

8 The condition of the fluid should also be checked along with the level. If the fluid at the end of the dipstick is black or a dark reddish brown colour, or if it emits a burned smell, the fluid should be changed (see Chapter 1A or 1B). If you are in doubt about the condition of the fluid, purchase some new fluid and compare the two for colour and smell.

The automatic transmission dipstick (arrowed) is located in a tube which extends forward from the transmission toward the radiator

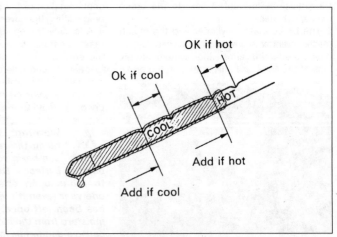

If the automatic transmission fluid is cold, the level should be between the two lower notches; if it's at operating temperature, the level should be between the two upper notches

Tyre and tyre pressure checks

1 Periodic inspection of the tyres may spare you from the inconvenience of being stranded with a flat tyre. It can also provide you with vital information regarding possible problems in the steering and suspension systems before major damage occurs.

2 Normal tread wear can be monitored with a simple, inexpensive device known as a tread depth indicator **(see illustration)** available from car accessory shops or service stations. When the tread depth reaches the specified minimum, renew the tyre(s).

3 Note any abnormal tread wear **(see illustration)**. Tread pattern irregularities such as flat spots or more wear on one side than the other are indications of front end alignment and/or balance problems. If any of these conditions are noted, take the vehicle to a tyre dealer or service station to correct the problem.

4 Look closely for cuts, punctures and embedded nails or tacks. Sometimes a tyre will hold its air pressure for a short time or leak down very slowly even after a nail has embedded itself into the tread. If a slow leak persists, check the valve stem core to make sure it is tight. Examine the tread for an object that may have embedded itself into the tyre. If a puncture is suspected, it can be easily verified by spraying a solution of soapy water onto the puncture area **(see illustration)**. The soapy solution will bubble if there is a leak. If the puncture is inordinately large, a tyre dealer can usually repair the punctured tyre.

5 Carefully inspect the inner sidewall of each tyre for evidence of brake fluid leakage. If you see any, inspect the brakes immediately.

6 Correct tyre air pressure adds miles to the lifespan of the tyres, improves mileage and enhances overall ride quality. Tyre pressure cannot be accurately estimated by looking at a tyre, particularly if it is a radial. A tyre pressure gauge is therefore essential. Keep an accurate gauge in the glovebox. The pressure gauges fitted to the nozzles of air hoses at service stations are often inaccurate.

7 Always check tyre pressure when the tyres are cold. 'Cold', in this case, means the vehicle has not been driven over a mile in the three hours preceding a tyre pressure check. A pressure rise of four to eight psi is not uncommon once the tyres are warm.

A tyre tread depth indicator should be used to monitor tyre wear

8 Unscrew the valve cap protruding from the wheel or hubcap and push the gauge firmly onto the valve **(see illustration)**. Note the reading on the gauge and compare this figure to the recommended tyre pressure shown on the tyre placard on the left door. Be sure to refit the valve cap to keep dirt and moisture out of the valve stem mechanism. Check all four tyres and, if necessary, add enough air to bring them up to the recommended pressure levels.

9 Don't forget to keep the spare tyre inflated to the specified pressure (consult your owner's manual). Note that the air pressure specified for a compact spare is significantly higher than the pressure of the regular tyres.

Shoulder Wear

Underinflation (wear on both sides)
Under-inflation will cause overheating of the tyre, because the tyre will flex too much, and the tread will not sit correctly on the road surface. This will cause a loss of grip and excessive wear, not to mention the danger of sudden tyre failure due to heat build-up.
Check and adjust pressures
Incorrect wheel camber (wear on one side)
Repair or renew suspension parts
Hard cornering
Reduce speed!

Centre Wear

Overinflation
Over-inflation will cause rapid wear of the centre part of the tyre tread, coupled with reduced grip, harsher ride, and the danger of shock damage occurring in the tyre casing.
Check and adjust pressures

If you sometimes have to inflate your car's tyres to the higher pressures specified for maximum load or sustained high speed, don't forget to reduce the pressures to normal afterwards.

Uneven Wear

Front tyres may wear unevenly as a result of wheel misalignment. Most tyre dealers and garages can check and adjust the wheel alignment (or "tracking") for a modest charge.
Incorrect camber or castor
Repair or renew suspension parts
Malfunctioning suspension
Repair or renew suspension parts
Unbalanced wheel
Balance tyres
Incorrect toe setting
Adjust front wheel alignment
Note: *The feathered edge of the tread which typifies toe wear is best checked by feel.*

This chart will help you determine the condition of your tyres, the probable cause(s) of abnormal wear and the corrective action necessary

Spray a soapy water solution onto the tread – leaks will cause bubbles to appear

Check the pressure at least once a week with a gauge (don't forget the spare!)

Note: *Listed here are manufacturer recommendations at the time this manual was written. Manufacturers occasionally upgrade their fluid and lubricant specifications, so check with your local dealer for current recommendations.*

Engine oil:
Petrol engines .... Multigrade engine oil, viscosity SAE 5W/30 to 20W/50, to API SL or SM

Diesel engines .... Multigrade engine oil, viscosity SAE 5W/30 to 20W/50, to API CF-4, CF (also CE or CD)

Manual transmission oil .... API GL-5 SAE 75W-90 gear oil

Automatic transmission fluid:
2WD models .... DEXRON III automatic transmission fluid

4WD models .... Toyota automatic transmission fluid Type T or T-IV, or equivalent

Transfer case lubricant (4WD models):
Above -18°C .... API GL-5 SAE 90 or 85W-90 hypoid gear oil

Below -18°C .... API GL-5 SAE 80W or 80W-90 hypoid gear oil

Rear differential lubricant (4WD models):
Above -18°C .... API GL-5 SAE 90 hypoid gear oil

Below -18°C .... API GL-5 SAE 80W or 80W-90 hypoid gear oil

Brake fluid .... DOT 4 brake fluid

Clutch fluid .... DOT 4 brake fluid

Engine coolant .... 50/50 mixture of ethylene glycol-based antifreeze and distilled water (Toyota Super Long Life Coolant recommended)

Power steering system .... DEXRON III automatic transmission fluid

Chapter 1 Part A:
Routine maintenance and servicing – petrol models

Contents

	Section number
Air filter element renewal	15
Automatic transmission fluid and filter change	30
Auxiliary drivebelt check, adjustment and renewal	9
Battery check, maintenance and charging	8
Brake check	14
Brake fluid change	23
Clutch pedal freeplay check and adjustment	7
Cooling system check	11
Cooling system servicing (draining, flushing and refilling)	27
Driveshaft boot check	20
Engine oil and oil filter change	5
Evaporative emissions control system check	28
Exhaust system check	29
Fuel filter renewal (2000 and earlier models)	24
Fuel system check	16
Introduction	1
Major services	4
Manual transmission lubricant change	31

	Section number
Manual transmission lubricant level check	17
Minor services	3
Pollen filter renewal (2001 and later models)	22
Positive Crankcase Ventilation (PCV) valve and hose check and renewal	34
Rear differential lubricant change (4WD models)	33
Rear differential lubricant level check (4WD models)	21
Seat belt check	13
Servicing – general information	2
Spark plug check and renewal	25
Spark plug lead, distributor cap and rotor check and renewal	26
Steering and suspension check	19
Transfer case lubricant change (4WD models)	32
Transfer case lubricant level check (4WD models)	18
Tyre rotation	12
Underbonnet hose check and renewal	10
Valve clearance check and adjustment	35
Windscreen wiper blade inspection and renewal	6

Degrees of difficulty

| **Easy,** suitable for novice with little experience | 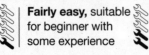 | **Fairly easy,** suitable for beginner with some experience | 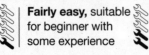 | **Fairly difficult,** suitable for competent DIY mechanic | 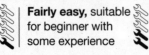 | **Difficult,** suitable for experienced DIY mechanic | 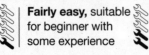 | **Very difficult,** suitable for expert DIY or professional | |

Capacities*

Engine oil (including filter):
1.8 litre models . . . . 3.7 litres
2.0 litre models:
  1996 . . . . 3.9 litres
  1997 to 2000 . . . . 4.1 litres
  2001 and later . . . . 4.2 litres
Coolant:
1996 to 2000 models:
  Manual transmission . . . . 8.0 litres
  Automatic transmission . . . . 7.7 litres
2001 and later models:
  Manual transmission . . . . 6.3 litres
  Automatic transmission . . . . 6.6 litres
Transmission:
Manual:
  1996 to 2000 models:
    2WD . . . . 3.9 litres
    4WD . . . . 5.0 litres
  2001 and later models:
    2WD . . . . 1.9 litres
    4WD . . . . 3.4 litres
Automatic (drain and refill):
  1996 models . . . . Up to 3.3 litres
  1997 models:
    2WD . . . . Up to 3.3 litres
    4WD . . . . Up to 7.0 litres
  1998 to 2000 models . . . . Up to 3.3 litres
  2001 and later models:
    2WD . . . . Up to 3.3 litres
    4WD . . . . Up to 3.9 litres
Transfer case (4WD models):
  1996 to 2000 models . . . . 0.7 litres
  2001 and later models . . . . 0.9 litres
Rear differential (4WD models) . . . . 0.9 litres
All capacities approximate. Add as necessary to bring up to appropriate level.

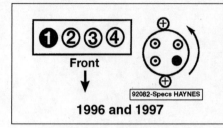

1996 and 1997

Cylinder location and distributor rotation

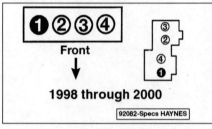

1998 through 2000

Cylinder and coil terminal locations

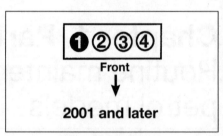

2001 and later

Cylinder locations

Ignition system

Spark plug type and gap:
Type:
  1997 and earlier . . . . NGK BKR6EP-11 or equivalent
  1998 to 2000 . . . . NGK BKR6EKB-11 or equivalent
  2001 and later:
    1.8 litre models . . . . Denso K16R-U11 or equivalent
    2.0 litre models . . . . NGK IFR6A11 or equivalent
Gap . . . . 1.1 mm
Spark plug lead resistance (maximum) . . . . 25 000 ohms
Engine firing order 1-3-4-2

Valve clearances (engine cold)

1.8 litre models:
  Inlet valve . . . . 0.15 to 0.25 mm
  Exhaust valve . . . . 0.25 to 0.35 mm
2.0 litre models:
  2000 and earlier:
    Inlet valve . . . . 0.18 to 0.28 mm
    Exhaust valve . . . . 0.28 to 0.38 mm
  2001 and later:
    Inlet valve . . . . 0.18 to 0.30 mm
    Exhaust valve . . . . 0.30 to 0.40 mm

Cooling system

Thermostat rating:
  Starts to open . . . . 80 to 84°C
  Fully open . . . . 95°C

Auxiliary drivebelt tension (with Burroughs or Nippondenso tension gauge)

2000 and earlier models
Used belt (a belt which has been used more than 5 minutes):
  Alternator:
    With air conditioning .... 110 +/- 10 lbf (equivalent to 12.0 mm deflection)
    Without air conditioning .... 95 +/- 20 lbf
  Power steering pump .... 80 +/- 20 lbf
New belt (a belt that has been used less than 5 minutes):
  Alternator:
    With air conditioning .... 165 +/- 25 lbf (equivalent to 10.0 mm deflection)
    Without air conditioning .... 125 +/- 25 lbf
  Power steering pump .... 120 +/- 25 lbf

2001 and later models
Fitted with an automatic drivebelt tensioner.

Clutch pedal
Freeplay .... 5 to 15 mm
Height:
  2000 and earlier .... 162 to 172 mm
  2001 and later .... 169 to 179 mm

Brakes
Disc brake pad lining thickness (minimum) .... 4.7 mm
Drum brake shoe lining thickness (minimum) .... 1.6 mm
Handbrake adjustment .... 6 to 8 clicks

Suspension and steering
Steering wheel freeplay limit .... 25.6 mm
Balljoint allowable movement .... 0 mm

Torque wrench settings

	lbf ft	Nm
Automatic transmission:		
Sump bolts:		
1996 and 1997	4	5
1998 to 2000:		
2WD	4	5
4WD	6	8
2001 and later	6	8
Filter bolts	7	10
Drain plug:		
1996 to 2000	13	18
2001 and later	35	47
Differential case drain plug (2001 and later 2WD models)	40	54
Auxiliary drivebelt tensioner (2001 and later models):		
Nut	44	60
Bolt	44	60
Engine oil drain plug:		
2000 and earlier	27	37
2001 and later	18	24
Fuel filter banjo bolt (2000 and earlier models only)	21	29
Manual transmission drain and level/filler plugs	36	49
Rear differential drain and level/filler plugs	36	49
Seat bolts/nuts	27	37
Spark plugs:		
2000 and earlier	13	18
2001 and later	15	20
Transfer case drain and level/filler plugs	29	39
Wheel nuts	76	103

The maintenance intervals in this manual are provided with the assumption that you, not the dealer, will be doing the work. These are the minimum maintenance intervals recommended by the factory for vehicles that are driven daily. If you wish to keep your vehicle in peak condition at all times, you may wish to perform some of these procedures even more often. Because frequent maintenance enhances the efficiency, performance and resale value of your car, we encourage you to do so.

Note

If the vehicle is operated under severe conditions, perform all maintenance indicated with an asterisk (*) at half the indicated intervals. Severe conditions exist if you mainly operate the vehicle:

In dusty areas.
Towing a trailer or caravan.
Idling for extended periods.
Driving at low speeds when outside temperatures remain below freezing and most trips are less than four miles long.

When the vehicle is new, it should be serviced by a dealer service department (or other workshop recognised by the vehicle manufacturer as providing the same standard of service) in order to preserve the warranty. The vehicle manufacturer may reject warranty claims if you are unable to prove that servicing has been carried out as and when specified, using only original equipment parts or parts certified to be of equivalent quality.

Caution 1: These models are equipped with an anti-theft radio. Before performing a procedure that requires disconnecting the battery, make sure you have the proper activation code.

Caution 2: Disconnecting then reconnecting the battery can cause driveability problems that require a scan tool to remedy. See Chapter 5, Section 1, for the use of an auxiliary voltage input device (or 'Memory-saver') before disconnecting the battery.

Every 250 miles or weekly, whichever comes first

☐ Refer to *Weekly checks*

Every 5000 miles or 6 months, whichever comes first

☐ Renew the engine oil and oil filter (Section 5)

Note: *Toyota recommends that the engine oil and filter are changed every 10 000 miles or 12 months. However, oil and filter changes are good for the engine, and we recommend that the oil and filter are renewed more frequently, especially if the car is used mainly for short journeys.*

Every 10 000 miles or 12 months, whichever comes first

☐ Inspect (and renew, if necessary) the windscreen wiper blades (Section 6)*
☐ Check the clutch pedal for proper freeplay (Section 7)
☐ Check and service the battery (Section 8)
☐ Check and adjust if necessary the engine auxiliary drivebelts (Section 9)*
☐ Inspect (and renew if, necessary) all underbonnet hoses (Section 10)
☐ Check the cooling system (Section 11)
☐ Rotate the tyres (Section 12)
☐ Check the seat belts (Section 13)
☐ Inspect the brake system (Section 14)*
☐ Check and renew, if necessary, the air filter (Section 15)*
☐ Inspect the fuel system (Section 16)
☐ Check the manual transmission lubricant level (Section 17)
☐ Check the transfer case lubricant level (4WD models) (Section 18)
☐ Inspect the suspension and steering components (Section 19)*
☐ Check the driveshaft boots (Section 20)
☐ Check the rear differential lubricant level (4WD models) (Section 21)
☐ Renew the pollen filter (2001 and later models) (Section 22)*

Every 20 000 miles or 2 years, whichever comes first

All items listed above plus:
☐ Renew the brake fluid (Section 23)
☐ Renew the fuel filter (2000 and earlier engines) (Section 24)
☐ Check (and renew, if necessary) the conventional, non-platinum or non-iridium type spark plugs (Section 25)
☐ Inspect (and renew, if necessary) the spark plug leads, the distributor cap and rotor (Section 26)
☐ Service the cooling system (drain, flush and refill) (Section 27) – Note: Not Long Life coolant
☐ Inspect the evaporative emissions control system (Section 28)
☐ Inspect the exhaust system (Section 29)
☐ Change the automatic transmission fluid and filter (Section 30)
☐ Change the manual transmission lubricant (Section 31)
☐ Change the transfer case lubricant (4WD models) (Section 32)
☐ Change the rear differential lubricant (4WD models) (Section 33)
☐ Check and renew if necessary the PCV valve (Section 34)

Every 40 000 miles or 4 years, whichever comes first

All items listed above plus:
☐ Renew the air filter element (Section 15)*

Every 60 000 miles or 6 years, whichever comes first

☐ Renew the platinum or iridium type spark plugs (Section 25)
☐ Check and adjust the valve clearances (Section 35)
☐ Renew the timing belt (where applicable) (Chapter 2A or 2C)*

Typical engine compartment components – 2000 and earlier models

1 Brake fluid reservoir (LHD shown)
2 Fuse/relay block
3 Air filter housing
4 Relay block
5 Distributor
6 Coolant reservoir
7 Radiator hose
8 Radiator cap
9 Engine oil dipstick
10 Auxiliary drivebelt
11 Windscreen washer fluid reservoir
12 Power steering fluid reservoir
13 Spark plug
14 PCV valve
15 Engine oil filler cap
16 Battery (LHD shown)

Typical engine compartment components – 2001 and later models

1 Brake fluid reservoir (LHD shown)
2 Fuse/relay block
3 Coolant reservoir
4 Automatic transmission fluid dipstick
5 Radiator cap
6 Upper radiator hose
7 Air filter housing
8 Spark plug
9 Engine oil filler cap
10 Engine oil dipstick
11 Auxiliary drivebelt
12 Windscreen washer fluid reservoir
13 Power steering fluid reservoir
14 PCV valve
15 Battery (under cover) (LHD shown)

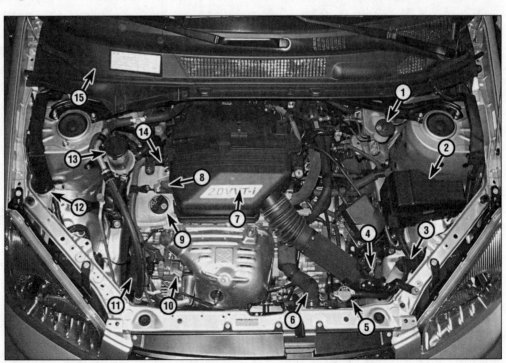

Typical engine compartment underbody components

1 Engine oil filter
2 Front suspension strut unit
3 Automatic transmission drain plug
4 Engine oil drain plug
5 Front disc brake caliper
6 Driveshaft boot
7 Steering gear boot
8 Balljoint

Typical rear underbody components

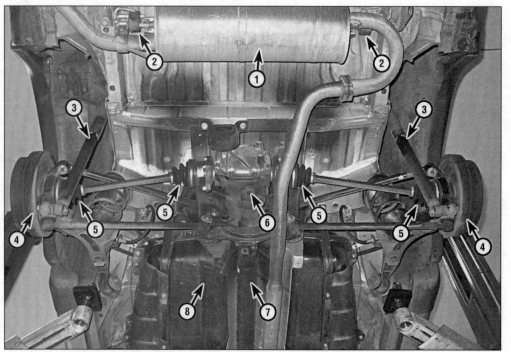

1 Silencer
2 Exhaust system mounting
3 Shock absorber
4 Rear drum brake assembly
5 Driveshaft boot
6 Differential
7 Propeller shaft
8 Fuel tank

1 Introduction

This chapter is designed to help the home mechanic maintain the Toyota RAV4 for peak performance, economy, safety and long life.

Included is a master maintenance schedule, followed by sections dealing specifically with each item on the schedule. Visual checks, adjustments, component renewal and other helpful items are included. Refer to the accompanying illustrations of the engine compartment and the underside of the vehicle for the location of various components.

Servicing your vehicle in accordance with the mileage/time maintenance schedule and the following Sections will provide it with a planned maintenance program that should result in a long and reliable service life. This is a comprehensive plan, so maintaining some items but not others at the specified service intervals will not produce the same results.

As you service your RAV4, you will discover that many of the procedures can – and should – be grouped together because of the nature of the particular procedure you're performing or because of the close proximity of two otherwise unrelated components to one another.

For example, if the vehicle is raised for any reason, you should inspect the exhaust, suspension, steering and fuel systems while you're under the vehicle. When you're rotating the tyres, it makes good sense to check the brakes and wheel bearings since the wheels are already removed.

Finally, let's suppose you have to borrow or hire a torque wrench. Even if you only need to tighten the spark plugs, you might as well check the torque of as many critical nuts and bolts as time allows.

The first stage of this maintenance program is to prepare yourself before the actual work begins. Read through all sections pertinent to the procedures you're planning to do, then make a list of and gather together all the parts and tools you will need to do the job. If it looks as if you might run into problems during a particular segment of some procedure, seek advice from your local dealer parts department.

2 Servicing – general information

The term servicing is used in this manual to represent a combination of individual operations rather than one specific procedure that will maintain an engine in proper tune.

If, from the time the vehicle is new, the routine maintenance schedule is followed closely and frequent checks are made of fluid levels and high-wear items, as suggested throughout this manual, the engine will be kept in relatively good running condition and the need for additional work will be minimised.

More likely than not, however, there may be times when the engine is running poorly due to lack of regular maintenance. This is even more likely if a used vehicle, which has not received regular and frequent maintenance checks, is purchased. In such cases, an engine service will be needed outside of the regular routine maintenance intervals.

The first step in any service or diagnostic procedure to help correct a poor-running engine is a cylinder compression check. A compression check (see Chapter 2D) will help determine the condition of internal engine components and should be used as a guide for tune-up and repair procedures. If, for instance,

the compression check indicates serious internal engine wear, a conventional service won't improve the performance of the engine and would be a waste of time and money. Because of its importance, the compression check should be done by someone with the right equipment and the knowledge to use it properly.

3 Minor services

The following procedures are those most often needed to bring a generally poor-running engine back into a proper state of tune.
a) Check all engine related fluids (Weekly checks).
b) Clean, inspect and test the battery (Section 8).
c) Check and adjust the auxiliary drivebelts (Section 9).
d) Check all under bonnet hoses (Section 10).
e) Check the cooling system (Section 11).
f) Renew the air filter (Section 15).
g) Renew the spark plugs (Section 25).
h) Inspect the spark plug leads, distributor cap and rotor as applicable (Section 26).

4 Major services

In addition to those items listed in Section 3 (Minor services) add the following items:
a) Check the fuel system (Section 16).
b) Renew the spark plug leads, distributor cap and rotor (Section 26).
c) Check the ignition system (Chapter 5).
d) Check the charging system (Chapter 5).

Every 5000 miles or 6 months

5 Engine oil and oil filter change

1 Frequent oil changes are the best preventive maintenance the home mechanic can give the engine, because ageing oil becomes diluted and contaminated, which leads to premature engine wear.
2 Make sure that you have all the necessary tools before you begin this procedure (see illustration). You should also have plenty of rags or newspapers handy for mopping-up any spills.
3 Access to the underside of the vehicle is greatly improved if the vehicle can be lifted on a hoist, driven onto ramps or supported by axle stands.

⚠️ Warning: Do not work under a vehicle which is supported only by a hydraulic or scissors-type jack.

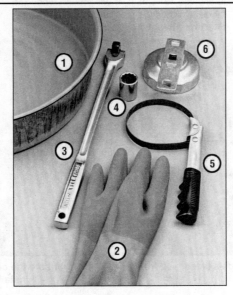

5.2 These tools are required when changing the engine oil and filter
1 **Drain pan** – It should be fairly shallow in depth, but wide in order to prevent spills
2 **Rubber gloves** – When removing the drain plug and filter, it is inevitable that you will get oil on your hands (the gloves will prevent burns)
3 **Socket bar** – Sometimes the oil drain plug is very tight and a long socket bar is needed to loosen it
4 **Socket** – To be used with the socket bar or a ratchet (must be the correct size to fit the drain plug)
5 **Filter removal strap** – This is a metal band-type strap, which requires clearance around the filter to be effective
6 **Filter removal tool** – This type fits on the bottom of the filter and can be turned with a socket bar (different sizes are available for different types of filters)

5.7 Use a proper size spanner or socket to remove the oil drain plug and avoid rounding it off

5.13a Oil filter location – 2000 and earlier models (accessed from above)

4 If this is your first oil change, get under the vehicle and familiarise yourself with the location of the oil drain plug. The engine and exhaust components will be warm during the actual work, so try to anticipate any potential problems before the engine and accessories are hot.

5 Park the vehicle on a level spot. Start the engine and allow it to reach its normal operating temperature (the needle on the temperature gauge should be at least above the bottom mark). Warm oil and sludge will flow out more easily. Turn off the engine when it's warmed-up. Remove the filler cap in the rear cam cover.

6 Raise the vehicle and support it on axle stands.

⚠ **Warning: To avoid personal injury, never get beneath the vehicle when it is supported by only by a jack. The jack provided with your vehicle is designed solely for raising the vehicle to remove and renew the wheels. Always use axle stands to support the vehicle when it becomes necessary to place your body underneath the vehicle.**

7 Being careful not to touch the hot exhaust components, place the drain pan under the drain plug in the bottom of the sump and remove the plug **(see illustration)**. You may want to wear gloves while unscrewing the plug the final few turns if the engine is really hot.

8 Allow the old oil to drain into the pan. It may be necessary to move the pan farther under

the engine as the oil flow slows to a trickle. Inspect the old oil for the presence of metal shavings and chips.

9 After all the oil has drained, wipe off the drain plug with a clean rag. Even minute metal particles clinging to the plug would immediately contaminate the new oil.

10 Clean the area around the drain plug opening, refit the plug and tighten it securely.

11 Move the drain pan into position under the oil filter.

12 If you're working on a 2000 or earlier model, remove all tools, rags, etc, from under the vehicle, being careful not to spill the oil in the drain pan, then lower the vehicle. On 2001 and later models the filter is accessed from underneath.

13 Loosen the oil filter **(see illustrations)** by turning it anti-clockwise with the filter removal strap. Any standard filter removal strap should work. Once the filter is loose, use your hands to unscrew it from the block. Just as the filter is detached from the block, immediately tilt the open end up to prevent the oil inside the filter from spilling out.

⚠ **Warning: The engine exhaust manifold may still be hot, so be careful.**

14 With a clean rag, wipe off the mounting surface on the block. If a residue of old oil is allowed to remain, it will smoke when the block is heated up. It will also prevent the new filter from seating properly. Also make sure

that the none of the old gasket remains stuck to the mounting surface. It can be removed with a scraper if necessary.

15 Compare the old filter with the new one to make sure they are the same type. Smear some engine oil on the rubber gasket of the new filter and screw it into place **(see illustration)**. Because overtightening the filter will damage the gasket, do not use a filter removal strap to tighten the filter. Tighten it by hand until the gasket contacts the seating surface. Then seat the filter by giving it an additional 3/4-turn. If you're working on a 2001 or later model, lower the vehicle now.

16 Add new oil to the engine through the oil filler cap in the valve cover. Use a spout or funnel to prevent oil from spilling onto the top of the engine. Pour three litres of fresh oil into the engine. Wait a few minutes to allow the oil to drain into the pan, then check the level on the oil dipstick (see *Weekly checks* if necessary). If the oil level is at or near the F mark, refit the filler cap hand tight, start the engine and allow the new oil to circulate.

17 Allow the engine to run for about a minute. While the engine is running, look under the vehicle and check for leaks at the sump drain plug and around the oil filter. If either is leaking, stop the engine and tighten the plug or filter slightly.

18 Wait a few minutes to allow the oil to trickle down into the pan, then recheck the level on the dipstick and, if necessary, add enough oil to bring the level to the F mark.

19 During the first few trips after an oil change, make it a point to check frequently for leaks and proper oil level.

20 The old oil drained from the engine cannot be re-used in its present state and should be discarded. Check with your local refuse disposal company, disposal facility or environmental agency to see if they will accept the oil for recycling. Don't pour used oil into drains or onto the ground. After the oil has cooled, it can be drained into a suitable container (capped plastic jugs, topped bottles, milk cartons, etc) for transport to one of these disposal sites.

5.13b Oil filter location – 2001 and later models (accessed from below)

5.15 Lubricate the oil filter gasket with clean engine oil before installing the filter on the engine

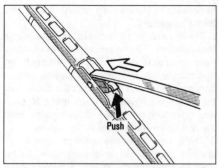

6.5 Push on the release lever and slide the wiper assembly down out of the hook in the end of the wiper arm

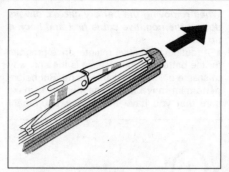

6.6 After detaching the end of the element, slide it out of the end of the frame

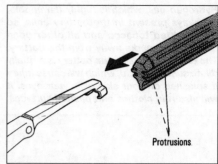

6.7 Insert the end of the element with the protrusions in first

Every 10 000 miles or 12 months

6 Windscreen wiper blade inspection and renewal

1 The windscreen wiper and blade assembly should be inspected periodically for damage, loose components and cracked or worn blade elements.
2 Road film can build up on the wiper blades and affect their efficiency, so they should be washed regularly with a mild detergent solution.
3 The action of the wiping mechanism can loosen nuts and bolts, so they should be checked and tightened, as necessary, at the same time the wiper blades are checked.
4 If the wiper blade elements are cracked, worn or warped, or no longer clean adequately, they should be renewed.
5 Remove the wiper blade assembly from the arm by pushing on the release lever, then sliding the assembly down and out of the hook in the end of the arm (see illustration).
6 Detach the blade insert element and pull it out of the right end of the wiper frame (see illustration).
7 Insert the new element end with the small protrusions into the right side of the wiper frame (see illustration). Slide the element fully into place, then seat the protrusions in the end of the frames to secure it.

7 Clutch pedal freeplay check and adjustment

1 Press down lightly on the clutch pedal and, with a ruler, measure the distance that it moves freely before the clutch resistance is felt (see illustration). The freeplay should be within the specified limits. If it isn't, it must be adjusted.
2 Loosen the locknut on the pedal end of the clutch pushrod (see illustration).
3 Turn the pushrod until pedal freeplay and pushrod freeplay are correct.
4 Tighten the locknut.
5 After adjusting the pedal freeplay, check the pedal height.
6 If pedal height is incorrect, loosen the locknut and turn the stopper bolt until the height is correct. Tighten the locknut.

8 Battery check, maintenance and charging

⚠ *Warning: Certain precautions must be followed when checking and servicing the battery.*

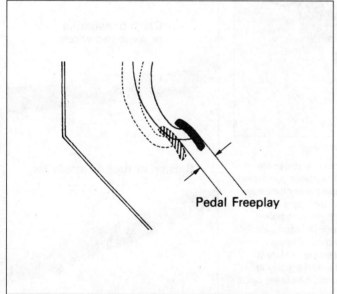

7.1 To check clutch pedal freeplay, measure the distance between the natural resting place of the pedal and the point at which you encounter resistance

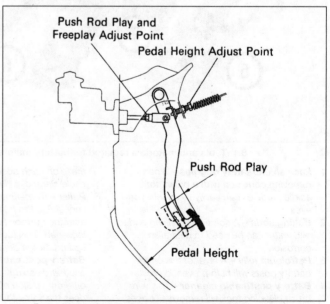

7.2 The clutch pedal pushrod play, pedal height and freeplay adjustments are made by loosening the locknut and turning the appropriate threaded adjuster

Hydrogen gas, which is highly flammable, is always present in the battery cells, so keep lighted tobacco and all other open flames and sparks away from the battery. The electrolyte inside the battery is actually dilute sulphuric acid, which will cause injury if splashed on your skin or in your eyes. It will also ruin clothes and painted surfaces.

When removing the battery cables, always detach the negative cable first and hook it up last.

1 A routine preventive maintenance program for the battery in your vehicle is the only way to ensure quick and reliable starts. But before performing any battery maintenance, make sure that you have the proper equipment necessary to work safely around the battery (see illustration).

2 There are also several precautions that should be taken whenever battery maintenance is performed. Before servicing the battery, always turn the engine and all accessories off and disconnect the cable from the negative terminal of the battery. **Note:** *If you're working on a 2001 or later model, raise the cowl cover for access to the battery.*

3 The battery produces hydrogen gas, which is both flammable and explosive. Never create a spark, smoke or light a match around the battery. Always charge the battery in a ventilated area.

4 Electrolyte contains poisonous and corrosive sulphuric acid. Do not allow it to get in your eyes, on your skin on your clothes. Never ingest it. Wear protective safety glasses when working near the battery. Keep children away from the battery.

5 Note the external condition of the battery. If the positive terminal and cable clamp on

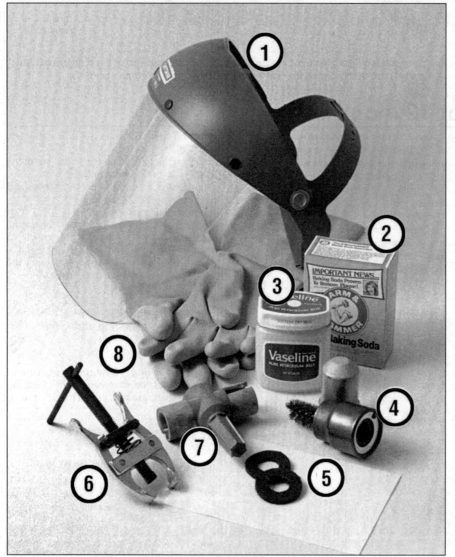

8.1 Tools and materials required for battery maintenance

1 *Face shield/safety goggles – When removing corrosion with a brush, the acidic particles can easily fly up into your eyes*
2 *Baking soda – A solution of baking soda and water can be used to neutralise corrosion*
3 *Petroleum jelly – A layer of this on the battery posts will help prevent corrosion*
4 *Battery post/cable cleaner – This wire brush cleaning tool will remove all traces of corrosion from the battery posts and cable clamps*
5 *Treated felt washers – Placing one of*

these on each post, directly under the cable clamps, will help prevent corrosion
6 *Puller – Sometimes the cable clamps are very difficult to pull off the posts, even after the nut/bolt has been completely loosened. This tool pulls the clamp straight up and off the post without damage*
7 *Battery post/cable cleaner – Here is another cleaning tool which is a slightly different version of number 4 above, but it does the same thing*
8 *Rubber gloves – Another safety item to consider when servicing the battery; remember that's acid inside the battery*

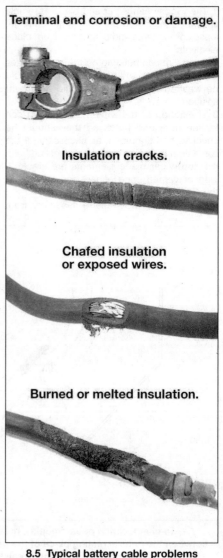

Terminal end corrosion or damage.

Insulation cracks.

Chafed insulation or exposed wires.

Burned or melted insulation.

8.5 Typical battery cable problems

8.6a Battery terminal corrosion usually appears as light, fluffy powder

8.6b Removing a cable from the battery post with a wrench – sometimes a pair of special battery pliers are required for this procedure if corrosion has caused deterioration of the nut hex (always remove the earth (-) cable first and hook it up last)

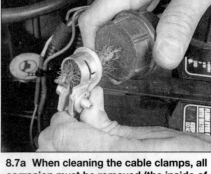

8.7a When cleaning the cable clamps, all corrosion must be removed (the inside of the clamp is tapered to match the taper on the post, so don't remove too much material)

8.7b Regardless of the type of tool used to clean the battery posts, a clean, shiny surface should be the result

8.8 Make sure the battery hold-down clamps are tight

your vehicle's battery is equipped with a rubber protector, make sure that it's not torn or damaged. It should completely cover the terminal. Look for any corroded or loose connections, cracks in the case or cover or loose hold-down clamps. Also check the entire length of each cable for cracks and frayed conductors (see illustration).

6 If corrosion, which looks like white, fluffy deposits (see illustration) is evident, particularly around the terminals, the battery should be removed for cleaning. Loosen the cable clamp bolts with a spanner, being careful to remove the earth cable first, and slide them off the terminals (see illustration). Then disconnect the hold-down clamp bolt and nut, remove the clamp and lift the battery from the engine compartment.

7 Clean the cable clamps thoroughly with a battery brush or a terminal cleaner and a solution of warm water and baking soda (see illustration). Wash the terminals and the top of the battery case with the same solution but make sure that the solution doesn't get into the battery. When cleaning the cables, terminals and battery top, wear safety goggles and rubber gloves to prevent any solution from coming in contact with your eyes or hands. Wear old clothes too – even diluted, sulphuric acid splashed onto clothes will burn holes in them. If the terminals have been extensively corroded, clean them up with a terminal cleaner (see illustration). Thoroughly wash all cleaned areas with plain water.

8 Make sure that the battery tray is in good condition and the hold-down nut and bolt are tight (see illustration). If the battery is removed from the tray, make sure no parts remain in the bottom of the tray when the battery is refitted. When refitting the hold-down clamp bolt or nut, do not overtighten it.

9 Information on removing and refitting the battery can be found in Chapter 5. Information on jump starting can be found at the front of this manual.

Cleaning

10 Corrosion on the hold-down components, battery case and surrounding areas can be removed with a solution of water and baking soda. Thoroughly rinse all cleaned areas with plain water.

11 Any metal parts of the vehicle damaged by

corrosion should be covered with a zinc-based primer, then painted.

Charging

 Warning: When batteries are being charged, hydrogen gas, which is very explosive and flammable, is produced. Do not smoke or allow open flames near a charging or a recently charged battery. Wear eye protection when near the battery during charging. Also, make sure the charger is unplugged before connecting or disconnecting the battery from the charger.

12 Slow-rate charging is the best way to restore a battery that's discharged to the point where it will not start the engine. It's also a good way to maintain the battery charge in a vehicle that's only driven a few miles between starts. Maintaining the battery charge is particularly important in the winter when the battery must work harder to start the engine and electrical accessories that drain the battery are in greater use.

13 It's best to use a one or two-amp battery charger (sometimes called a 'trickle' charger). They are the safest and put the least strain on the battery. They are also the least expensive. For a faster charge, you can use a higher amperage charger, but don't use one rated more than 1/10th the amp/hour rating of the battery. Rapid boost charges that claim

to restore the power of the battery in one to two hours are hardest on the battery and can damage batteries not in good condition. This type of charging should only be used in emergency situations.

14 The average time necessary to charge a battery should be listed in the instructions that come with the charger. As a general rule, a trickle charger will charge a battery in 12 to 16 hours.

9 Auxiliary drivebelt check, adjustment and renewal

Check

1 The alternator, power steering pump and air conditioning compressor auxiliary drivebelts, also referred to as simply 'fan' belts, are located at the right end of the engine. The good condition and proper adjustment of the alternator belt is critical to the operation of the engine. Because of their composition and the high stresses to which they are subjected, auxiliary drivebelts stretch and deteriorate as they get older. They must therefore be periodically inspected.

2 On 2000 and earlier models, multiple belts are used; one belt transmits power from the crankshaft to the alternator, one drives the

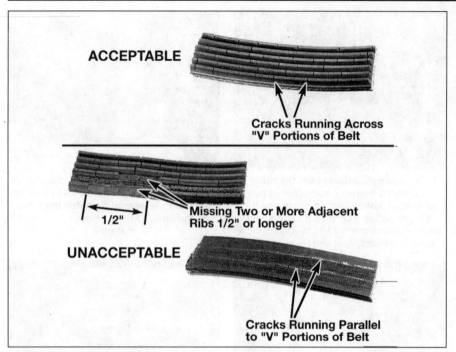

ACCEPTABLE

Cracks Running Across "V" Portions of Belt

1/2"

Missing Two or More Adjacent Ribs 1/2" or longer

UNACCEPTABLE

Cracks Running Parallel to "V" Portions of Belt

9.3 Check the multi-ribbed belt for signs of wear like these – if the belt looks worn, renew it

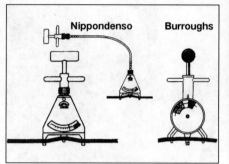

Nippondenso   Burroughs

9.4 If you are able to borrow either a Nippondenso or Burroughs belt tension gauge, this is how it's installed on the belt – compare the reading on the scale with the specified drivebelt tension

air conditioning compressor (if equipped), and one drives the power steering pump. On 2001 and later models, a single 'serpentine' auxiliary drivebelt is used.

3 With the engine off, open the bonnet and locate the auxiliary drivebelt(s). With an electric torch, check each belt for separation of the adhesive rubber on both sides of the core, core separation from the belt side, a severed core, separation of the ribs from the adhesive rubber, cracking or separation of the ribs, and torn or worn ribs or cracks in the inner ridges of the ribs (see illustration). Also check for fraying and glazing, which gives the belt a shiny appearance. Both sides of the belt should be inspected, which means you will have to twist the belt to check the underside. Use your fingers to feel the belt where you can't see it. If any of the above conditions are evident, renew the belt (go to Paragraph 9).

4 Belt tension on 2000 and earlier models must be manually adjusted (on 2001

and later models the tension is adjusted automatically). To check the tension of each belt in accordance with factory specifications, use either a Nippondenso or Burroughs belt tension gauge on the belt (see illustration). Measure the tension in accordance with the manufacturer's instructions and compare your measurement to the specified auxiliary drivebelt tension for either a used or new belt. Note: A 'used' belt is defined as any belt which has been operated more than five minutes on the engine; a 'new' belt is one that has been used for less than five minutes.

5 If you don't have either of the above tools, and cannot borrow one, the following rule of thumb method is recommended: Push firmly on the belt with your thumb at a distance halfway between the pulleys and note how far the belt can be pushed (deflected) (see illustration). The belt should deflect approximately 6 mm if the distance from pulley centre to pulley centre is 30 cm or less; the belt should deflect about 12 mm if the distance from pulley centre to pulley centre is greater then 30 cm.

Adjustment

2000 and earlier models

6 To adjust the alternator/air conditioning compressor belt, loosen the alternator pivot bolt and the adjusting lockbolt (models with air conditioning) or the adjusting bolt (models without air conditioning) at the alternator bracket. On models with air conditioning, turn the adjusting bolt and measure the belt tension in accordance with one of the above methods. On models without air conditioning, lever the alternator up in its bracket. When the proper

tension is achieved, tighten the lockbolt and pivot bolt securely (see illustration).

7 Adjust the power steering pump belt by loosening the pivot bolt and the lockbolt that secures the pump to the slotted bracket, then pivot the pump (away from the engine to tighten the belt, toward it to loosen it) until the proper tension is reached. When the proper tension is achieved, tighten the lockbolt and pivot bolt securely.

2001 and later models

8 Auxiliary drivebelt tension on 2001 and later models is adjusted automatically by a spring-loaded tensioner.

Drivebelt renewal

2000 and earlier models

9 To renew a belt, follow the above procedures for auxiliary drivebelt adjustment but slip the belt off the crankshaft pulley and remove it. If you are renewing the power steering pump

9.5 Firmly push on the drivebelt and check how much it deflects – 2000 and earlier models only

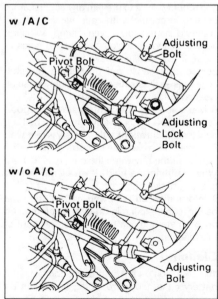

w /A/C

Adjusting Bolt

Pivot Bolt

Adjusting Lock Bolt

w/o A/C

Pivot Bolt

Adjusting Bolt

9.6 After loosening the lockbolt, turn the adjusting bolt to tension the alternator/air conditioning compressor drivebelt

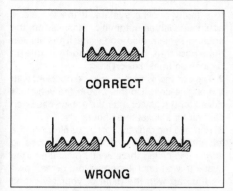

CORRECT

WRONG

9.11 When installing a multi-ribbed belt, make sure that it is centred – it must not overlap either edge of the pulley

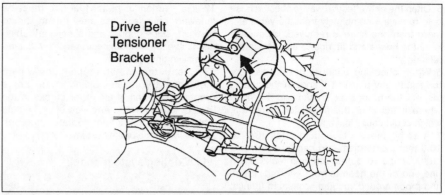

Drive Belt Tensioner Bracket

9.13 To release the tension on the drivebelt, place a long spanner or socket and ratchet on the hex-shaped boss, then turn the tensioner clockwise – 2001 and later models

belt, you will have to remove other belts first because of the way they are arranged on the crankshaft pulley. Because belts tend to wear out more or less together, it is a good idea to renew all belts at the same time. Mark each belt and its appropriate pulley groove so the new belts can be fitted in their proper positions.

10 Take the old belts to the parts department in order to make a direct comparison for length, width and design.

11 After renewing the auxiliary drivebelt, make sure that it fits properly in the ribbed grooves in the pulleys **(see illustration)**. It is essential that the belt be properly centred.

12 Adjust the belt(s) in accordance with the procedure outlined above.

2001 and later models

13 Rotate the belt tensioner clockwise to release the tension, then slip the belt off the pulleys **(see illustration)**. Slowly release the tensioner.

14 Route the new belt over the pulleys **(see illustrations)**, again rotating the tensioner to allow the belt to be fitted, then release the belt tensioner.

15 Make sure the belt is properly centred in the pulleys.

Automatic tensioner renewal

 Warning: Disconnect the cable from the negative terminal of the battery before performing this procedure.

16 To renew a tensioner that does not properly tension the belt, or one that exhibits binding or a worn-out bearing/pulley, remove the auxiliary drivebelt (see Paragraph 13) then unscrew the mounting bolt and nut **(see illustration)**.

17 Refitting is the reverse of the removal procedure. Tighten the nuts and bolts to the torque values listed in this Chapter's Specifications.

18 Refit the auxiliary drivebelt (see paragraphs 14 and 15).

10 Underbonnet hose check and renewal

Caution: Renewal of air conditioning hoses must be left to a dealer service department or air conditioning specialist that has the equipment to depressurise the system safely. Never remove air conditioning

components or hoses until the system has been depressurised.

General

1 High temperatures in the engine compartment can cause the deterioration of the rubber and plastic hoses used for engine, accessory and emission systems operation. Periodic inspection should be made for cracks, loose clamps, material hardening and leaks.

2 Information specific to the cooling system hoses can be found in Section 11.

3 Some, but not all, hoses are secured to the fittings with clamps. Where clamps are used, check to be sure they haven't lost their tension, allowing the hose to leak. If clamps aren't used, make sure the hose has not expanded and/or hardened where it slips over the fitting, allowing it to leak.

Vacuum hoses

4 It's quite common for vacuum hoses, especially those in the emissions system, to be colour-coded or identified by coloured stripes moulded into them. Various systems require hoses with different wall thickness, collapse resistance and temperature resistance. When renewing hoses, be sure the new ones are made of the same material.

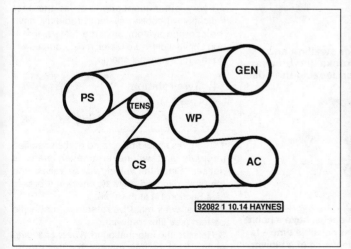

9.14 Drivebelt routing diagram – 2001 and later models

9.16 The drivebelt tensioner on 2001 and later models is retained by a nut and a bolt

5 Often the only effective way to check a hose is to remove it completely from the vehicle. If more than one hose is removed, be sure to label the hoses and fittings to ensure correct refitting.

6 When checking vacuum hoses, be sure to include any plastic T-fittings in the check. Inspect the fittings for cracks and the hose where it fits over the fitting for distortion, which could cause leakage.

7 A small piece of vacuum hose (8.0 to 10.0 mm inside diameter) can be used as a stethoscope to detect vacuum leaks. Hold one end of the hose to your ear (but not in) and probe around vacuum hoses and fittings, listening for the 'hissing' sound characteristic of a vacuum leak.

⚠ *Warning: When probing with the vacuum hose stethoscope, be very careful not to come into contact with moving engine components such as the auxiliary drivebelts, cooling fan, etc.*

Fuel hose

⚠ *Warning: Fuel is extremely flammable, so take extra precautions when you work on any part of the fuel system. Don't smoke or allow open flames or bare light bulbs near the work area, and don't work in a garage where a gas-type appliance (such as a water heater or a clothes dryer) is present. Since fuel is carcinogenic, wear fuel-resistant gloves when there's a possibility of being exposed to fuel, and, if you spill any fuel on your skin, rinse it off immediately with soap and water. Mop-up any spills immediately and do not store fuel-soaked rags where they could ignite. The fuel system is under constant pressure, so, if any fuel lines are to be disconnected, the fuel pressure in the system must be relieved first. When you perform any kind of work on the fuel system, wear safety glasses and have a Class B type fire extinguisher on hand.*

8 Check all rubber fuel lines for deterioration and chafing. Check especially for cracks in areas where the hose bends and just before fittings, such as where a hose attaches to the fuel filter.

9 High quality fuel line, specifically designed for fuel injection systems, must be used for fuel line renewal.

⚠ *Warning: Never use anything other than the proper fuel line for fuel line renewal.*

10 Spring-type clamps are commonly used on fuel lines. These clamps often lose their tension over a period of time, and can be 'sprung' during removal. Renew all spring-type clamps with screw clamps whenever a hose is renewed.

Metal lines

11 Sections of metal line are often used for fuel line between the fuel pump and fuel injection unit. Check carefully to be sure the line has not been bent or crimped and that cracks have not started in the line.

12 If a section of metal fuel line must be renewed, only seamless steel tubing should be used, since copper and aluminium tubing don't have the strength necessary to withstand normal engine vibration.

13 Check the metal brake lines where they enter the master cylinder and brake proportioning unit (if used) for cracks in the lines or loose fittings. Any sign of brake fluid leakage calls for an immediate thorough inspection of the brake system.

11 Cooling system check

1 Many major engine failures can be attributed

Check for a chafed area that could fail prematurely.

Check for a soft area indicating the hose has deteriorated inside.

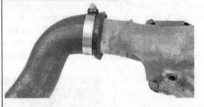
Overtightening the clamp on a hardened hose will damage the hose and cause a leak.

Check each hose for swelling and oil-soaked ends. Cracks and breaks can be located by squeezing the hose.

11.4 Hoses, like drivebelts, have a habit of failing at the worst possible time – to prevent the inconvenience of a blown radiator or heater hose, inspect them carefully as shown here

to a faulty cooling system. If the vehicle is equipped with an automatic transmission, the cooling system also cools the transmission fluid and thus plays an important role in prolonging transmission life.

2 The cooling system should be checked with the engine cold. Do this before the vehicle is driven for the day or after the engine has been shut off for at least three hours.

3 Remove the radiator cap by turning it to the left until it reaches a stop. If you hear a hissing sound (indicating there is still pressure in the system), wait until it stops. Now press down on the cap with the palm of your hand and continue turning to the left until the cap can be removed. Thoroughly clean the cap, inside and out, with clean water. Also clean the filler neck on the radiator. All traces of corrosion should be removed. The coolant inside the radiator should be relatively transparent. If it's rust-coloured, the system should be drained and refilled (see Section 27). If the coolant level isn't up to the top, add additional antifreeze/coolant mixture (see *Weekly checks*).

4 Carefully check the large upper and lower radiator hoses along with the smaller diameter heater hoses that run from the engine to the bulkhead. Inspect each hose along its entire length, renewing any hose which is cracked, swollen or shows signs of deterioration. Cracks may become more apparent if the hose is squeezed **(see illustration)**. Regardless of condition, it's a good idea to renew hoses every two years.

5 Make sure that all hose connections are tight. A leak in the cooling system will usually show up as white or rust-coloured deposits on the areas adjoining the leak. If wire-type clamps are used at the ends of the hoses, it may be a good idea to renew them with more secure screw-type clamps.

6 Use compressed air or a soft brush to remove bugs, leaves, etc, from the front of the radiator or air conditioning condenser. Be careful not to damage the delicate cooling fins or cut yourself on them.

7 Every other inspection, or at the first indication of cooling system problems, have the cap and system pressure tested. If you don't have a pressure tester, most garages will do this for a minimal charge.

12 Tyre rotation

1 The tyres should be rotated at the specified intervals and whenever uneven wear is noticed. Since the vehicle will be raised and the tyres removed anyway, check the brakes (see Section 14) at this time.

2 Radial tyres must be rotated in a specific pattern **(see illustrations)**.

3 Refer to the information in *Wheel changing* at the front of this manual for the proper procedures to follow when raising the vehicle and changing a tyre. If the brakes are to be checked, do not apply the handbrake as stated. Make sure the tyres are blocked to prevent the vehicle from rolling.

4 Preferably, the entire vehicle should be raised at the same time. This can be done on a hoist or by jacking up each corner and then lowering the vehicle onto axle stands placed beneath the underbody. Always use four axle stands and make sure the vehicle is firmly supported.

5 After rotation, check and adjust the tyre pressures as necessary and be sure to check the nut tightness.

6 For further information on the wheels and tyres, refer to Chapter 10.

13 Seat belt check

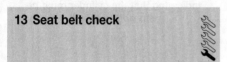

1 Check the seat belts, buckles, latch plates and guide loops for obvious damage and signs of wear. Seat belts that exhibit fraying along the edges should be renewed.

2 Where the seat belt stalk bolts to the floor of the vehicle, check that the bolts are secure.

3 See if the seat belt reminder light comes on when the key is turned to the Run or Start position. A chime should also sound.

14 Brake check

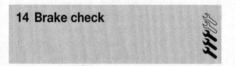

⚠️ **Warning: Dust created by the brake system is harmful to your health. Never blow it out with compressed air and don't inhale any of it. An approved filtering mask should be worn when working on the brakes. Do not, under any circumstances, use petroleum-based solvents to clean brake parts. Use brake system cleaner only.**

Note: *For detailed photographs of the brake system, refer to Chapter 9.*

1 In addition to the specified intervals, the brakes should be inspected every time the wheels are removed or whenever a defect is suspected. Any of the following symptoms could indicate a potential brake system defect: The vehicle pulls to one side when the brake pedal is depressed; the brakes make squealing or dragging noises when applied; brake travel is excessive; the pedal pulsates (this may be the ABS system); brake fluid leaks, usually onto the inside of the tyre or wheel.

2 The disc brake pads have built-in wear indicators which should make a high-pitched squealing or scraping noise when they are worn to the renewal point. When you hear this noise, renew the pads immediately or expensive damage to the discs can result.

3 Loosen the wheel nuts.

4 Raise the vehicle and place it securely on axle stands.

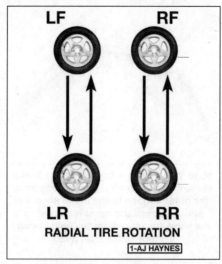

12.2a Four-tyre rotation pattern

5 Remove the wheels (see *Wheel changing* at the front of this book, or your owner's manual, if necessary).

Disc brakes

6 There are two pads – an outer and an inner – in each caliper. The inner pads are visible through small inspection holes in each caliper **(see illustration)**. The outer pads are more easily viewed a the edge of the caliper.

7 Check the pad thickness by looking at each end of the caliper and through the inspection hole in the caliper body. If the lining material is less than the thickness listed in this Chapter's Specifications, renew the pads. **Note:** *Keep in mind that the lining material is riveted or bonded to a metal backing plate and the metal portion is not included in this measurement.*

8 If it is difficult to determine the exact thickness of the remaining pad material by the above method, or if you are at all concerned about the condition of the pads, remove the caliper(s), then remove the pads for further inspection (see Chapter 9).

9 Once the pads are removed from the calipers, clean them with brake cleaner and remeasure them.

10 Measure the disc thickness with a

14.6 You will find an inspection hole like this in each caliper through which you can view the thickness of remaining friction material for the inner pad

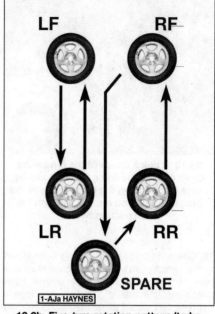

12.2b Five-tyre rotation pattern (to be used only if the spare tyre is the same as the other four)

micrometer to make sure that it still has service life remaining. If any disc is thinner than the specified minimum thickness, renew it (refer to Chapter 9). Even if the disc has service life remaining, check its condition. Look for scoring, gouging and burned spots. If these conditions exist, remove the disc and have it resurfaced (see Chapter 9).

11 Before refitting the wheels, check all brake lines and hoses for damage, wear, deformation, cracks, corrosion, leakage, bends and twists, particularly in the vicinity of the rubber hoses at the calipers.

12 Check the clamps for tightness and the connections for leakage. Make sure that all hoses and lines are clear of sharp edges, moving parts and the exhaust system. If any of the above conditions are noted, repair, reroute or renew the lines and/or fittings as necessary (see Chapter 9).

Rear drum brakes

13 To check the brake shoe lining thickness without removing the brake drums, remove the rubber plug from the backing plate and use an electrric torch to inspect the linings **(see illustration)**. For a more thorough brake inspection, follow the procedure below.

14 Refer to Chapter 9 and remove the rear brake drums.

15 Note the thickness of the lining material on the rear brake shoes **(see illustration)** and look for signs of contamination by brake fluid and grease. If the lining material is within 1.6 mm of the recessed rivets or metal shoes, renew the brake shoes. The shoes should also be renewed if they are cracked, glazed (shiny lining surfaces) or contaminated with brake fluid or grease. See Chapter 9 for the renewal procedure.

14.13 A quick check of the remaining drum brake shoe lining material can be made by removing the rubber plug in the backing plate and looking through the inspection hole

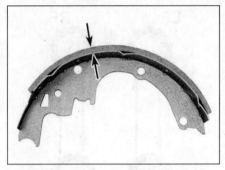

14.15 If the lining is bonded to the brake shoe, measure the lining thickness from the outer surface to the metal shoe, as shown here; if the lining is riveted to the shoe, measure from the lining outer surface to the rivet head

14.17 Carefully peel back the wheel cylinder boot and check for leaking fluid indicating that the cylinder must be renewed or rebuilt

16 Check the shoe return and hold-down springs and the adjusting mechanism to make sure they're refitted correctly and in good condition. Deteriorated or distorted springs, if not renewed, could allow the linings to drag and wear prematurely.

17 Check the wheel cylinders for leakage by carefully peeling back the rubber boots **(see illustration)**. If brake fluid is noted behind the boots, the wheel cylinders must be renewed (see Chapter 9).

18 Check the drums for cracks, score marks, deep scratches and hard spots, which will appear as small discoloured areas. If imperfections cannot be removed with emery cloth, the drums must be resurfaced by an engine reconditioner (see Chapter 9 for more detailed information).

19 Refit the brake drums.

20 Refit the wheels and nuts.

21 Remove the axle stands and lower the vehicle.

22 Tighten the wheel nuts to the torque listed in this Chapter's Specifications.

Brake vacuum servo check

23 Sit in the driver's seat and perform the following sequence of tests.

24 With the brake fully depressed, start the engine – the pedal should move down a little when the engine starts.

25 With the engine running, depress the brake pedal several times – the travel distance should not change.

26 Depress the brake, stop the engine and hold the pedal in for about 30 seconds – the pedal should neither sink nor rise.

27 Restart the engine, run it for about a minute and turn it off. Then firmly depress the brake several times – the pedal travel should decrease with each application.

28 If your brakes do not operate as described above when the preceding tests are performed, the brake vacuum servo has failed. Refer to Chapter 9 for the renewal procedure.

Handbrake

29 Slowly pull up on the handbrake and count the number of clicks you hear until the handle is up as far as it will go. The adjustment is correct if you hear the specified number of clicks. If you hear more or fewer clicks, it's time to adjust the handbrake (refer to Chapter 9).

30 An alternative method of checking the handbrake is to park the vehicle on a steep hill with the handbrake set and the transmission in Neutral (be sure to stay in the vehicle for this procedure). If the handbrake cannot prevent the vehicle from rolling, it is in need of adjustment (see Chapter 9).

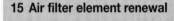

15 Air filter element renewal

1 On 2000 and earlier models, the air filter is located inside a housing at the left-hand side of the engine compartment, however on 2001 and later models it is located directly on top of the engine.

2 To remove the air filter, release the spring clips that keep the two halves of the air filter housing together, then pull the cover away and, noting how the filter is fitted, remove the air filter element **(see illustrations)**.

3 Inspect the outer surface of the filter element. If it is dirty, renew it. If it is only moderately dusty, it can be re-used by blowing it clean from the back to the front surface with compressed air. Because it is a pleated paper type filter, it cannot be washed or oiled. If it cannot be cleaned satisfactorily with compressed air, discard and renew it. While the cover is off, be careful not to drop anything down into the housing.

Caution: Never drive the vehicle with the air cleaner removed. Excessive engine wear could result and backfiring could even cause a fire under the bonnet.

4 Wipe out the inside of the air filter housing.

15.2a On 2000 and earlier models, release these clips to lift off the top of the air filter housing

15.2b On 2001 and later models, release these clips . . .

15.2c . . . pull the cover out of the way and lift the element out

5 Place the new filter element into the air cleaner housing, making sure it seats properly.
6 Refitting of the cover is the reverse of removal.

16 Fuel system check

16.2 Use a small screwdriver to carefully lever out the old gasket – take care not to damage the cap

16.5 Inspect the filler hose for cracks and make sure the clamps are tight

 Warning: Fuel is extremely flammable, so take extra precautions when you work on any part of the fuel system. Don't smoke or allow open flames or bare light bulbs near the work area, and don't work in a garage where a gas-type appliance (such as a water heater or a clothes dryer) is present. Since fuel is carcinogenic, wear fuel-resistant gloves when there's a possibility of being exposed to fuel, and, if you spill any fuel on your skin, rinse it off immediately with soap and water. Mop-up any spills immediately and do not store fuel-soaked rags where they could ignite. When you perform any kind of work on the fuel system, wear safety glasses and have a fire extinguisher on hand. On all petrol models, the fuel system is under constant pressure, so, before any pipes are disconnected, the fuel system pressure must be relieved (see Chapter 4A).

1 If you smell fuel while driving or after the vehicle has been sitting in the sun, inspect the fuel system immediately.
2 Remove the fuel filler cap and inspect it for damage and corrosion. The gasket should have an unbroken sealing imprint. If the gasket is damaged or corroded, remove it and fit a new one **(see illustration)**.
3 Inspect the fuel feed and return lines for cracks. Make sure that the threaded flare-nut type connectors which secure the metal fuel lines to the fuel rail and, on 2000 and earlier models, the banjo bolt that secures the banjo fitting to the in-line fuel filter are tight.
4 Since some components of the fuel system – the fuel tank and part of the fuel feed and return lines, for example – are underneath the vehicle, they can be inspected more easily with the vehicle raised on a hoist. If that's not possible, raise the vehicle and support it securely on axle stands.
5 With the vehicle raised and safely supported, inspect the fuel tank and filler neck for punctures, cracks and other damage. The connection between the filler neck and the tank is particularly critical. Sometimes a rubber filler neck will leak because of loose clamps or deteriorated rubber **(see illustration)**. These are problems a home mechanic can usually rectify.

 Warning: Do not, under any circumstances, try to repair a fuel tank (except rubber components).

6 Carefully check all rubber hoses and metal lines leading away from the fuel tank. Check

for loose connections, deteriorated hoses, crimped lines and other damage. Carefully inspect the lines from the tank to the fuel injection system. Repair or renew damaged sections as necessary (see Chapter 4A).
7 The evaporative emissions control system can also be a source of fuel odours. The function of the system is to store fuel vapours from the fuel tank in a charcoal canister until they can be routed to the intake manifold where they mix with incoming air before being burned in the combustion chambers.
8 The most common symptom of a faulty evaporative emissions system is a strong odour of fuel. If a fuel odour has been detected, and you have already checked the areas described above, check the charcoal canister, and the hoses connected to it.

17 Manual transmission lubricant level check

1 The manual transmission does not have a dipstick. To check the fluid level, raise the vehicle and support it securely on axle stands, then remove the underbody splash shield. On the front side of the transmission housing, you will see a plug **(see illustration)**. Remove it. If the lubricant level is correct, it should be up to the lower edge of the hole.
2 If the transmission needs more lubricant (if the level is not up to the hole), use a syringe or

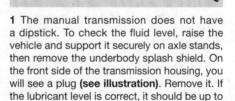
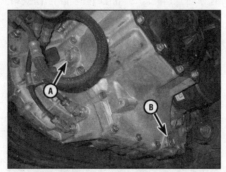

17.1 Remove the check/fill plug and use your finger as a dipstick to check the manual transmission lubricant level

A   Check/fill plug   B   Drain plug

a gear oil pump to add more. Stop filling the transmission when the lubricant begins to run out the hole.
3 Refit the plug and tighten it securely. Drive the vehicle a short distance, then check for leaks.

18 Transfer case lubricant level check (4WD models)

1 Raise the vehicle and support it securely on axle stands.
2 Using the appropriate spanner, unscrew the plug from the transfer case.
3 Use your little finger to reach inside the housing to feel the lubricant level. The level should be at or near the bottom of the plug hole. If it isn't, add the recommended lubricant through the plug hole with a syringe or squeeze bottle.
4 Refit and tighten the plug. Check for leaks after the first few miles of driving.

19 Steering and suspension check

Note: *For detailed illustrations of the steering and suspension components, refer to Chapter 10.*

With the wheels on the ground

1 With the vehicle stopped and the front wheels pointed straight-ahead, rock the steering wheel gently back-and-forth. If freeplay **(see illustration)** is excessive, a front wheel bearing, steering shaft universal joint or lower arm balljoint is worn or the steering gear is out of adjustment or broken. Refer to Chapter 10 for the appropriate repair procedure.
2 Other symptoms, such as excessive vehicle body movement over rough roads, swaying (leaning) around corners and binding as the steering wheel is turned, may indicate faulty steering and/or suspension components.
3 Check the shock absorbers by pushing down and releasing the vehicle several times at each corner. If the vehicle does not come

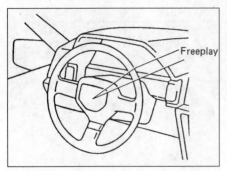

19.1 Steering wheel freeplay is the amount of travel between an initial steering input and the point at which the front wheels begin to turn (indicated by a slight resistance)

19.7 To check a balljoint for wear, try to lever the control arm up-and-down to make sure there is no play in the balljoint (if there is, renew it)

19.8 Push on the balljoint boot to check for damage

back to a level position within one or two bounces, the shocks/struts are worn and must be renewed. When bouncing the vehicle up-and-down, listen for squeaks and noises from the suspension components. Additional information on suspension components can be found in Chapter 10.

Under the vehicle

4 Raise the vehicle with a jack and support it securely on axle stands. See *Jacking and vehicle support* at the back of this book for the proper jacking points.
5 Check the tyres for irregular wear patterns and proper inflation. See *Weekly checks* for information regarding tyre wear and Chapter 10 for the wheel bearing renewal procedures.
6 Inspect the universal joint between the steering shaft and the steering gear housing. Check the steering gear housing for grease leakage or oozing. Make sure that the dust seals and boots are not damaged and that the boot clamps are not loose. Check the steering linkage for looseness or damage. Check the tie-rod ends for excessive play. Look for loose bolts, broken or disconnected parts and deteriorated rubber bushings on all suspension and steering components. While an assistant turns the steering wheel from side-to-side, check the steering components for free movement, chafing and binding. If the steering components do not seem to be reacting with the movement of the steering

wheel, try to determine where the slack is located.
7 Check the balljoints for wear by trying to move each control arm up-and-down with a lever **(see illustration)** to ensure that its balljoint has no play. If any balljoint does have play, renew it. See Chapter 10 for the balljoint renewal procedure.
8 Inspect the balljoint boots for damage and leaking grease **(see illustration)**. Renew the balljoints if they are damaged (see Chapter 10).
9 At the rear of the vehicle, inspect the suspension arm bushings for deterioration.

20 Driveshaft boot check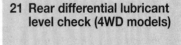

1 The driveshaft boots are very important because they prevent dirt, water and foreign material from entering and damaging the constant velocity (CV) joints. Oil and grease can cause the boot material to deteriorate prematurely, so it's a good idea to wash the boots with soap and water. Because it constantly pivots back-and-forth following the steering action of the front hub, the outer CV boot wears out sooner and should be inspected regularly.
2 Inspect the boots for tears and cracks as well as loose clamps **(see illustration)**. If there is any evidence of cracks or leaking

lubricant, they must be renewed as described in Chapter 8.

21 Rear differential lubricant level check (4WD models)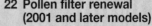

1 Raise the vehicle and support it securely on axle stands.
2 Using the appropriate spanner, unscrew the plug from the rear differential **(see illustration)**.
3 Use your little finger to reach inside the housing to feel the lubricant level. The level should be at or near the bottom of the plug hole. If it isn't, add the recommended lubricant through the plug hole with a syringe or squeeze bottle.
4 Refit and tighten the plug. Check for leaks after the first few miles of driving.

22 Pollen filter renewal (2001 and later models)

1 Open the glovebox door, push in on the sides and allow the door to hang down (see Chapter 11 if necessary).
2 Pull the filter element straight out of the case **(see illustration)**.
3 Refitting is the reverse of removal.

20.2 Flex the driveshaft boots by hand to check for cracks and/or leaking grease

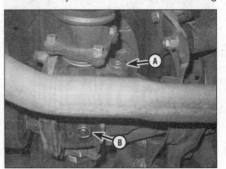

21.2 Location of the rear differential check/fill plug (A) – B is the drain plug (4WD models)

22.2 The pollen filter is retained in the blower case by clips on each side

Every 20 000 miles or 2 years

23 Brake fluid change

⚠ **Warning: Brake fluid can harm your eyes and damage painted surfaces, so use extreme caution when handling or pouring it. Do not use brake fluid that has been standing open or is more than one year old. Brake fluid absorbs moisture from the air. Excess moisture can cause a dangerous loss of braking effectiveness.**

1 At the specified intervals, the brake fluid should be drained and renewed. Since the brake fluid may drip or splash when pouring it, place plenty of rags around the master cylinder to protect any surrounding painted surfaces.

2 Before beginning work, purchase the specified brake fluid (see *Lubricants and fluids*).

3 Remove the cap from the master cylinder reservoir.

4 Using a hand-held suction pump or similar device, withdraw the fluid from the master cylinder reservoir.

5 Add new fluid to the master cylinder until it rises to the line indicated on the reservoir.

6 Bleed the brake system as described in Chapter 9 at all four brakes until new and uncontaminated fluid is expelled from the bleeder screw. Be sure to maintain the fluid level in the master cylinder as you perform the bleeding process. If you allow the master cylinder to run dry, air will enter the system.

7 Refill the master cylinder with fluid and check the operation of the brakes. The pedal should feel solid when depressed, with no sponginess.

⚠ **Warning: Do not operate the vehicle if you are in doubt about the effectiveness of the brake system.**

24 Fuel filter renewal (2000 and earlier models)

⚠ **Warning: Fuel is extremely flammable, so take extra precautions when you work on any part of the fuel system. Don't smoke or allow open flames or bare light bulbs near the work area, and don't work in a garage where a gas-type appliance (such as a water heater or a clothes dryer) is present. Since fuel is carcinogenic, wear fuel-resistant gloves when there's a possibility of being exposed to fuel, and, if you spill any fuel on your skin, rinse it off immediately with soap and water. Mop-up any spills immediately and do not store fuel-soaked rags where they could ignite.**

When you perform any kind of work on the fuel system, wear safety glasses and have a fire extinguisher on hand. On all petrol models, the fuel system is under constant pressure, so, before any pipes are disconnected, the fuel system pressure must be relieved (see Chapter 4A).

Note: *The fuel filter on 2001 and later models is integral with the fuel pump module in the fuel tank; there is no routine maintenance interval for fuel filter renewal on these models.*

1 Relieve the fuel system pressure (see Chapter 4A). Disconnect the negative battery cable.

2 The canister filter is mounted in a bracket on the bulkhead under the air filter housing and fuse/relay block.

3 Remove the air filter housing and fuse/relay block.

4 Using a spanner to steady the filter, remove the banjo bolt at the top and, using a flare-nut spanner, if available, loosen the fitting at the bottom of the fuel filter **(see illustration)**.

5 Remove both bracket bolts from the bulkhead and remove the old filter and the filter support bracket assembly.

6 Note that the inlet and outlet pipes are clearly labelled on their respective ends of the filter and that the flanged end of the filter faces down. Make sure the new filter is fitted so that it's facing the proper direction as noted above. When correctly fitted, the filter should be positioned so that the outlet pipe faces up and the inlet pipe faces down.

24.4 The fuel filter is mounted to the left strut tower – 2000 and earlier models

7 Connect the threaded fitting to the bottom of the filter and tighten it securely. Using new sealing washers, connect the banjo fitting to the top of the filter and tighten the banjo bolt to the torque listed in this Chapter's Specifications.

8 The remainder of refitting is the reverse of the removal procedure.

25 Spark plug check and renewal

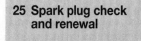

Note: *See maintenance schedule for service intervals.*

1 Spark plug renewal requires a spark plug socket which fits onto a ratchet bar. This socket is lined with a rubber grommet to protect the porcelain insulator of the spark plug and to hold the plug while you remove it from the spark plug hole. You will also need a wire-type feeler

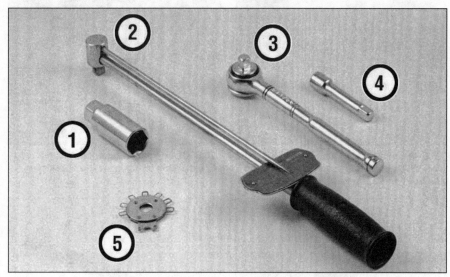

25.1 Tools required for changing spark plugs

1 Spark plug socket – *This will have special padding inside to protect the spark plug porcelain insulator*

2 Torque wrench – *Although not mandatory, use of this tool is the best way to ensure that the plugs are tightened properly*

3 Ratchet – *Standard hand tool to fit the plug socket*

4 Extension – *Depending on model and accessories, you may need special extensions and universal joints to reach one or more of the plugs*

5 Spark plug gap gauge – *This gauge for checking the gap comes in a variety of styles. Make sure the gap for your engine is included*

25.4a Spark plug manufacturers recommend using a wire-type gauge when checking the gap – if the wire does not slide between the electrodes with a slight drag, adjustment is required

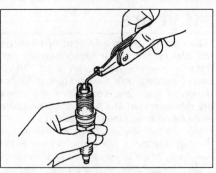

25.4b The spark plugs on 1998 to 2000 models have two earth electrodes – check the gap between each ground electrode and the centre electrode

25.4c To change the gap, bend the side electrode only, as indicated by the arrows, and be very careful not to crack or chip the porcelain insulator surrounding the centre electrode

gauge to check and adjust the spark plug gap and a torque wrench to tighten the new plugs to the specified torque **(see illustration)**.

2 If you are renewing the plugs, purchase the new plugs, adjust them to the proper gap and then fit each plug one at a time. **Note:** *When buying new spark plugs, it's essential that you obtain the correct plugs for your specific vehicle. This information can be found in the Specifications Section at the beginning of this Chapter.*

3 Inspect each of the new plugs for defects. If there are any signs of cracks in the porcelain insulator of a plug, don't use it.

4 Check the electrode gaps of the new plugs. Check the gap by inserting the wire gauge of the proper thickness between the electrodes at the tip of the plug **(see illustrations)**. The gap between the electrodes should be identical to that listed in this Chapter's Specifications or in your owner's manual. If the gap is incorrect, use the notched adjuster on the feeler gauge body to bend the curved side electrode slightly **(see illustration)**.

Caution: The spark plugs on 2001 and later models use iridium-coated electrodes. Don't attempt to adjust the gap on a used iridium-coated plug.

5 If the side electrode is not exactly over the centre electrode, use the notched adjuster to align them.

Caution: If the gap of a new plug must be adjusted, bend only the base of the earth electrode – do not touch the tip.

Removal

6 To prevent the possibility of mixing up spark plug leads, work on one spark plug at a time. On 2000 and earlier models, remove the lead and boot from one spark plug. Grasp the boot – not the cable – as shown, give it a half twisting motion and pull straight up **(see illustration)**. On 2001 and later models, remove the ignition coils (see Chapter 5).

7 If compressed air is available, blow any dirt or foreign material away from the spark plug area before proceeding.

8 Remove the spark plug **(see illustration)**.

Refitting

9 Prior to refitting, it's a good idea to coat the spark plug threads with anti-seize compound **(see illustration)**. Also, it's often difficult to insert spark plugs into their holes without cross-threading them. To avoid this possibility, fit a length of snug-fitting rubber hose over the end of the spark plug **(see illustration)**. The flexible hose acts as a universal joint to help align the plug with the plug hole. Should the plug begin to cross-thread, the hose will slip on the spark plug, preventing thread damage. Tighten the plug to the torque listed in this Chapter's Specifications.

10 On 2000 and earlier models, attach the plug lead to the new spark plug, again using a twisting motion on the boot until it is firmly seated on the end of the spark plug. On 2001 and later models, refit the ignition coil.

11 Follow the above procedure for the remaining spark plugs, refitting them one at a time to prevent mixing up the spark plug leads.

25.6 When removing the spark plug leads on 2000 and earlier models, pull only on the boot and use a twisting/pulling motion

25.8 Use a spark plug socket with a long extension to unscrew the spark plug

25.9a Apply a thin coat of anti-seize compound to the spark plug threads

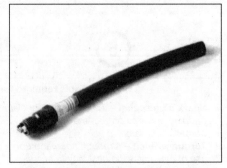

25.9b A length of close-fitting rubber hose will save time and prevent damaged threads when fitting the spark plugs

26 Spark plug lead, distributor cap and rotor check and renewal

Note: *Only 1996 and 1997 models are equipped with distributors. 1998 to 2000 models have a distributorless ignition system. All 2000 and earlier models have spark*

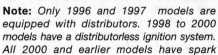

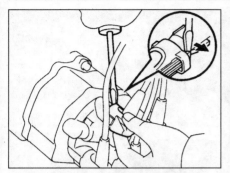

26.8 Use a small screwdriver to lift the lock claw up when detaching the spark plug boot from the distributor

plug leads, but 2001 and later models have 'coil over plug' ignition systems, where the ignition coils fit directly over the spark plugs. Therefore, this procedure does not apply to 2001 and later models.

1 The spark plug leads should be checked whenever new spark plugs are fitted.

2 Begin this procedure by making a visual check of the spark plug leads while the engine is running. In a darkened garage (make sure there is ventilation) start the engine and observe each plug lead. Be careful not to come into contact with any moving engine parts. If there is a break in the lead, you will see arcing or a small spark at the damaged area. If arcing is noticed, make a note to obtain new leads, then allow the engine to cool and check the distributor cap and rotor.

3 The spark plug leads should be inspected one at a time to prevent mixing up the order, which is essential for proper engine operation. Each original plug lead should be numbered to help identify its location. If the number is illegible, a piece of tape can be marked with the correct number and wrapped around the plug lead.

4 Disconnect the plug lead from the spark plug. A removal tool can be used for this purpose or you can grasp the rubber boot, twist the boot half a turn and pull the boot free. Do not pull on the lead itself.

5 Check inside the boot for corrosion, which will look like a white crusty powder.

6 Push the lead and boot back onto the end of the spark plug. It should fit tightly onto the end

26.11a Remove the screws (upper screw shown, lower screw not visible) and detach the distributor cap

of the plug. If it doesn't, remove the lead and use pliers to carefully crimp the metal connector inside the lead boot until the fit is snug.

7 Using a clean rag, wipe the entire length of the lead to remove built-up dirt and grease. Once the lead is clean, check for burns, cracks and other damage. Do not bend the lead sharply, because the conductor might break.

8 Disconnect the lead from the distributor cap (1997 and earlier models) or coil pack (1998 to 2000 models), using a small screwdriver to lift up on the lock claw, if equipped **(see illustration)**. Check for corrosion and a tight fit. Reconnect the lead.

9 Inspect the remaining spark plug leads, making sure that each one is securely fastened at the distributor or coil pack and spark plug when the check is complete.

10 If new spark plug leads are required, purchase a set for your specific engine model. Pre-cut lead sets with the boots already fitted are available. Remove and renew the leads one at a time to avoid mix-ups in the firing order.

11 On 1997 and earlier models, detach the distributor cap by removing the retaining screws **(see illustration)**. Look inside it for cracks, carbon tracks and worn, burned or loose contacts **(see illustration)**.

12 Remove the screws and pull the rotor off the distributor shaft **(see illustration)**. Examine it for cracks and carbon tracks **(see illustration)**. Renew the cap and rotor if any damage or defects are noted.

26.11b Inspect the distributor cap for carbon tracks, charred or eroded terminals and other damage (if in doubt about its condition, install a new one)

13 It is common practice to fit a new cap and rotor whenever new spark plug leads are fitted, but if you wish to continue using the old cap, check the resistance between the spark plug leads and the cap first **(see illustration)**. If the indicated resistance is more than the maximum value listed in this Chapter's Specifications, renew the cap and/or leads.

14 When fitting a new cap, remove the leads from the old cap one at a time and attach them to the new cap in the exact same location – do not simultaneously remove all the leads from the old cap or firing order mix-ups may occur.

27 Cooling system servicing (draining, flushing and refilling)

⚠️ *Warning: Do not allow engine coolant (antifreeze) to come in contact with your skin or painted surfaces of the vehicle. Rinse off spills immediately with plenty of water. Antifreeze is highly toxic if ingested. Never leave antifreeze lying around in an open container or in puddles on the floor; children and pets are attracted by its sweet smell and may drink it. Check with local authorities on disposing of used antifreeze. Many communities have collection centres which will see that antifreeze is disposed of safely. Antifreeze is flammable under*

26.12a The rotor is secured by two screws

26.12b Check the rotor for damage, wear and corrosion (if in doubt about its condition, buy a new one)

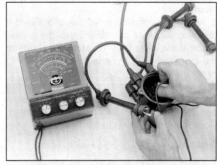

26.13 Measure the resistance value of the distributor cap and the spark plug HT leads – if it exceeds the specified maximum value, renew either the cap, or the leads, or both

27.4 On most models you will have to remove a cover for access to the radiator drain fitting located at the bottom of the radiator – before opening the valve, push a short section of 10 mm ID hose onto the plastic fitting (arrowed) to prevent the coolant from splashing

27.5 On 2001 and later models, attach a length of tubing to the spigot on the engine block drain, then loosen the drain bolt and allow the block to drain

certain conditions – be sure to read the precautions on the container.
Note: *Coolant renewal at this interval applies to Standard Coolant (Red/Green only) and not to Long Life Coolant (Pink).*
1 Periodically, the cooling system should be drained, flushed and refilled to replenish the antifreeze mixture and prevent formation of rust and corrosion, which can impair the performance of the cooling system and cause engine damage. When the cooling system is serviced, all hoses and the radiator cap should be checked and renewed if necessary.

Draining

2 Apply the handbrake and block the wheels. If the vehicle has just been driven, wait several hours to allow the engine to cool down before beginning this procedure. Where necessary, remove the engine undertray.
3 Once the engine is completely cool, remove the radiator cap.
4 Move a large container under the left-hand side of the radiator to catch the coolant. Attach a 10 mm inner diameter hose to the drain fitting to direct the coolant into the container (some models are already equipped with a hose), then open the drain fitting (a pair of pliers may be required to turn it) **(see illustration).**
5 After the coolant stops flowing out of the radiator, move the container under the engine block drain plug **(see illustration).** Loosen the plug and allow the coolant in the block to drain.
6 While the coolant is draining, check the condition of the radiator hoses, heater hoses and clamps (refer to Section 11 if necessary). Renew any damaged clamps or hoses.

Flushing

7 Once the system is completely drained, remove the thermostat from the engine (see Chapter 3). Then refit the thermostat housing without the thermostat. This will allow the system to be thoroughly flushed.
8 Tighten the radiator drain plug. Turn your

heating system controls to Hot, so that the heater core will be flushed at the same time as the rest of the cooling system.
9 Disconnect the upper radiator hose from the radiator, then place a garden hose in the upper radiator inlet and flush the system until the water runs clear at the upper radiator hose **(see illustration).**
10 In severe cases of contamination or clogging of the radiator, remove the radiator (see Chapter 3) and have a radiator repair facility clean and repair it if necessary.
11 Many deposits can be removed by the chemical action of a cleaner available at car accessory stores. Follow the procedure outlined in the manufacturer's instructions.
Note: *When the coolant is regularly drained and the system refilled with the correct antifreeze/water mixture, there should be no need to use chemical cleaners or descalers.*
12 Remove the overflow hose from the coolant

Garden hose → / Upper hose expels water → / Radiator →

27.9 With the thermostat removed, disconnect the upper radiator hose and flush the radiator and engine block with a garden hose

recovery reservoir. Drain the reservoir and flush it with clean water, then reconnect the hose.

Refilling

13 Close and tighten the radiator drain. Refit and/or tighten the block drain plug. Refit the thermostat (see Chapter 3).
14 Place the heater temperature control in the maximum heat position.
15 Slowly add new coolant (a 50/50 mixture of water and antifreeze) to the radiator until it's full. Add coolant to the reservoir up to the lower mark.
16 Leave the radiator cap off and run the engine in a well-ventilated area until the thermostat opens (coolant will begin flowing through the radiator and the upper radiator hose will become hot).
17 Turn the engine off and let it cool. Add more coolant mixture to bring the level back up to the lip on the radiator filler neck.
18 Squeeze the upper radiator hose to expel air, then add more coolant mixture if necessary. Renew the radiator cap.
19 Start the engine, allow it to reach normal operating temperature and check for leaks. Where removed, refit the engine undertray.

28 Evaporative emissions control system check

1 The function of the evaporative emissions control system is to draw petrol vapours from the fuel tank and fuel system, store them in a charcoal canister and then burn them during normal engine operation.
2 The most common symptom of a fault in the evaporative emissions control system is a strong fuel odour in the engine compartment (2000 and earlier models) or from under the vehicle (2001 and later models). If a fuel odour is detected, inspect the charcoal canister. On 2000 and earlier models it's located in the left rear corner of the engine compartment **(see illustration).** On 2001 and later models

it's located under the vehicle on the left side, forward of the fuel tank **(see illustration)**. Check the canister and all hoses for damage and deterioration.

3 The evaporative emissions control system is explained in more detail in Chapter 6A.

29 Exhaust system check

1 With the engine cold (at least three hours after the vehicle has been driven), check the complete exhaust system from its starting point at the engine to the end of the tailpipe. This should be done on a hoist where unrestricted access is available.

2 Check the pipes and connections for evidence of leaks, severe corrosion or damage. Make sure that all brackets and hangers are in good condition and tight.

3 At the same time, inspect the underside of the body for holes, corrosion, open seams, etc, which may allow exhaust gases to enter the passenger compartment. Seal all body openings with silicone or body putty.

4 Rattles and other noises can often be traced to the exhaust system, especially the mountings and supports. Try to move the pipes, silencer and catalytic converter. If the components can come in contact with the body or suspension parts, secure the exhaust system with new mountings **(see illustration)**.

5 Check the running condition of the engine by inspecting inside the end of the tailpipe. The exhaust deposits here are an indication of engine state-of-tune. If the pipe is black and sooty or coated with white deposits, the engine is in need of a tune-up, including a thorough fuel system inspection.

30 Automatic transmission fluid and filter change

Note: Some filters are not actually 'filters', but fine-mesh screens which can be cleaned with solvent instead of being renewed.

1 At the specified time intervals, the automatic transmission fluid should be drained and renewed.

2 Before beginning work, purchase the correct transmission fluid (see *Lubricants and fluids*).

3 Other tools necessary for this job include axle stands to support the vehicle in a raised position, spanners, drain pan, newspapers and clean rags.

4 The fluid should be drained immediately after the vehicle has been driven. Hot fluid is more effective than cold fluid at removing built-up sediment.

⚠ **Warning: Hot fluid can scald – wear protective gloves.**

5 After the vehicle has been driven to warm-up the fluid, raise it and support it on axle stands

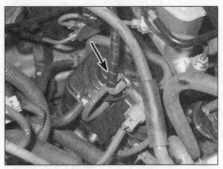

28.2a Check the evaporative emissions control canister for damage and the hose connections for cracks and damage – 2000 and earlier models shown

for access to the transmission and differential drain plugs.

6 Move the necessary equipment under the vehicle, being careful not to touch any of the hot exhaust components.

7 Place the drain pan under the drain plug in the transmission sump and remove the drain plug with the Allen key **(see illustration)**. Be sure the drain sump is in position, as fluid will come out with some force. Once the fluid is drained, refit the drain plug securely. On 2001 and later 2WD models there's also a drain plug on the transmission's differential housing. Remove the plug and allow the fluid to drain **(see illustration)**. After the fluid has drained, refit the plug (using a new gasket) and tighten it to the torque listed in this Chapter's Specifications.

8 Remove the front transmission sump bolts, then loosen the rear bolts and carefully lever

30.7a Remove the automatic transmission drain plug with a hex key

30.8a After loosening the front bolts, remove the rear transmission sump bolts and . . .

28.2b On 2001 and later models, the EVAP canister is located under the vehicle on the left side, forward of the fuel tank (cover removed)

29.4 Be sure to check each exhaust system rubber mounting for damage

the sump loose with a screwdriver and allow the remaining fluid to drain **(see illustrations)**. Once the fluid had drained, remove the bolts and lower the sump.

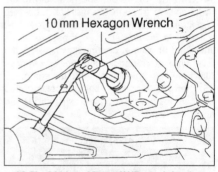

30.7b 2001 and later 2WD models also have a drain plug on the differential case

30.8b . . . allow the remaining fluid to drain out

30.9 Remove the filter bolts and lower the filter (be careful, there may be some residual fluid)

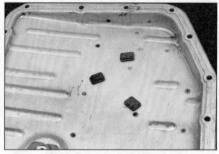

30.11 Noting their locations, remove any magnets and wash them and the sump in solvent before refitting them

32.2 Transfer case drain plug

9 Remove the filter retaining bolts, disconnect the clip (some models) and lower the filter from the transmission **(see illustration)**. Be careful when lowering the filter as it contains residual fluid.

10 Place the new (or cleaned) filter in position, connect the clip (if equipped) and insert the bolts. Tighten the bolts to the torque listed in the Specifications Section at the beginning of this Chapter.

11 Carefully clean the gasket surfaces of the fluid sump, removing all traces of old gasket material. Noting their location, remove the magnets, wash the sump in clean solvent and dry it with compressed air. Be sure to clean and refit any magnets **(see illustration)**.

12 Fit a new gasket, place the fluid sump in position and refit the bolts in their original positions. Tighten the bolts to the torque listed in this Chapter's Specifications.

13 Lower the vehicle.

14 With the engine off, add new fluid to the transmission through the dipstick tube (see *Lubricants and fluids* for the correct type). Use a funnel to prevent spills. It is best to add a little fluid at a time, continually checking the level with the dipstick (see *Weekly checks*). Allow the fluid time to drain into the sump.

15 Start the engine and shift the selector into all positions from P to L, then shift into P and apply the handbrake.

16 With the engine idling, check the fluid level. Add fluid up to the Cool level on the dipstick.

31 Manual transmission lubricant change

1 Raise the vehicle and support it securely on axle stands, then remove the engine undertray.

2 Remove the drain plug(s) and drain the lubricant **(see illustration 17.1)**.

3 Refit the drain plug(s) and tighten to the torque listed in this Chapter's Specifications.

4 Add new lubricant until it is even with the lower edge of the filler hole (Section 17). See *Lubricants and fluids* for the correct type.

32 Transfer case lubricant change (4WD models)

1 Raise the vehicle and support it securely on axle stands.

2 Remove the drain plug and drain the lubricant **(see illustration)**.

3 Refit the drain plug and tighten it to the torque listed in this Chapter's Specifications.

4 Add new lubricant until it is even with the lower edge of the filler hole (see Section 18). See *Lubricants and fluids* for the correct type.

33 Rear differential lubricant change (4WD models)

1 Raise the rear of the vehicle and support it securely on axle stands.

2 Remove the drain plug and drain the lubricant **(see illustration 21.2)**.

3 Refit the drain plug and tighten it to the torque listed in this Chapter's Specifications.

4 Add new lubricant until it is even with the lower edge of the filler hole (see Section 20). See *Lubricants and fluids* for the specified lubricant type.

34 Positive Crankcase Ventilation (PCV) valve and hose check and renewal

1 The PCV valve and hose is located in the valve cover. On 2000 and earlier models it's mounted in a grommet on the valve cover **(see illustration)**. On 2001 and later models it's threaded into the left-hand end of the valve cover **(see illustration)**.

34.1a On 2000 and earlier models the PCV valve is mounted in a rubber grommet in the valve cover (location on the cover may vary)

34.1b On 2001 and later models the PCV valve is threaded into the valve cover

2 Remove the PCV valve from the cover. On 2000 and earlier models, grasp the valve firmly and pull it out of its grommet. On 2001 and later models, detach the hose, unscrew the valve from the cover, then reattach the hose.
3 With the engine idling at normal operating temperature, place your finger over the end of the valve. If there's no vacuum at the valve, check for a plugged hose or valve. Renew any plugged or deteriorated hoses.

4 Turn off the engine. Remove the PCV valve from the hose. Connect a clean piece of hose and blow through the valve from the valve cover (cylinder head) end. If air will not pass through the valve in this direction, renew it **(see illustration)**.
5 When purchasing a new PCV valve, make sure it's for your particular vehicle and engine size. Compare the old valve with the new one to make sure they're the same.

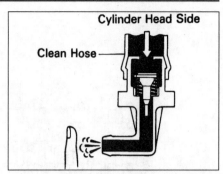

34.4 To check the PVC valve, first attach a clean section of hose to the cylinder head side of the valve and blow through it – air should pass through easily – then blow through the intake manifold side of the valve and verify that air passes through with difficulty

Every 60 000 miles or 6 years

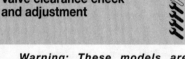

35 Valve clearance check and adjustment

⚠️ **Warning: These models are equipped with airbags. Always disable the airbag system before working in the vicinity of any airbag system component to avoid the possibility of accidental deployment of the airbag(s), which could cause personal injury (see Chapter 12).**

Note: *If you're working on a 1997 or earlier model, the following procedure requires the use of a special valve lifter tool if the adjustment is to be carried out leaving the camshafts in position. The alternative is to remove the camshafts after making the following check.*

Check

1 Disconnect the negative cable from the battery.
2 Remove the valve cover as described in Chapter 2A or 2B, then remove the spark plugs.
3 Position the number 1 piston at TDC on the compression stroke as described in Chapter 2A or 2B, then measure the clearances of the indicated valves with feeler blades **(see illustrations)**. Record the measurements which are out of specification. They will be used later to determine the required new shims (2000 and earlier models) or followers (2001 and later models).
4 Now, turn the crankshaft one complete revolution and realign the timing marks. Measure the remaining valve clearances **(see illustration)**.

Adjustment

Note: *2000 and earlier models use renewable adjustment shims that ride on top of the followers. 2001 and later models don't have shims; instead, they use followers of different thickness to provide the correct valve clearance.*

2000 and earlier models

5 If any of the valve clearances were out of specification, turn the crankshaft pulley until the camshaft lobe above the first valve which you intend to adjust is pointing upward, away from the shim.
6 Position the notch in the valve follower toward the centre. Then depress the valve follower with the special valve lifter tools **(see illustration)**. Place the special valve lifter tool in position as shown, with the longer jaw of

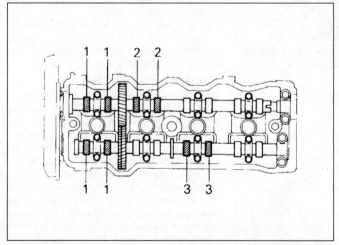

35.3a When the no. 1 piston is at TDC on the compression stroke, the valve clearance for the no. 1 and no. 3 cylinder exhaust valves and the no. 1 and no. 2 cylinder inlet valves can be measured – 2000 and earlier models shown, later models similar

35.3b Check the clearance for each valve with a feeler gauge of the specified thickness – if the clearance is correct, you should feel a slight drag on the gauge as you pull it out

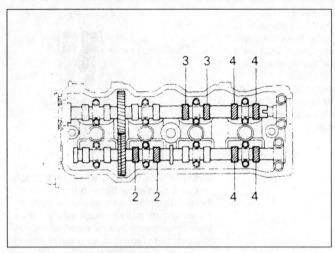

35.4 When the no. 4 piston is at TDC on the compression stroke, the valve clearance for the no. 2 and no. 4 exhaust valves and the no. 3 and no. 4 intake valves can be measured

35.6a Install the valve lifter tool as shown and squeeze the handles together to depress the valve follower, then hold the follower down with the smaller tool so the shim can be removed

the tool gripping the lower edge of the cast follower boss and the upper, shorter jaw gripping the upper edge of the follower itself. Depress the valve follower by squeezing the handles of the valve lifter tool together, then hold the follower down with the smaller tool and remove the larger one. Remove the adjusting shim with a small screwdriver or a pair of tweezers **(see illustrations)**. Note that the wire hook on the end of some valve lifter tool handles can be used to clamp

both handles together to keep the follower depressed while the shim is removed.

2001 and later models

7 If any of the valve clearances were out of adjustment, remove the camshaft(s) from over the follower(s) that was/were out of the specified clearance range (see Chapter 2B).

All models

8 Measure the thickness of the shim or follower with a micrometer **(see illustrations)**.

To calculate the correct thickness of a new shim or follower that will place the valve clearance within the specified value, use the following formula:

N = T + (A – V)

T = Thickness of the old shim or follower.
A = Valve clearance measured.
N = Thickness of the new shim or follower.
V = Desired valve clearance (see this Chapter's Specifications).

9 Select a shim or follower with a thickness as close as possible to the valve clearance calculated. The shims are available in several sizes as shown **(see illustration)**. The followers on 2001 and later models are available in 35 sizes in increments of 0.020 mm, and range in size from 5.060 mm to 5.740 mm **(see illustration)**. **Note:** *Through careful analysis of the shim sizes needed to bring the out-of-specification valve clearance within specification, it is often possible to simply move a shim that has to come out anyway to another location requiring a shim of that particular size, thereby reducing the number of new shims that must be purchased. Followers must not be moved around in this way, as it will increase wear.*

2000 and earlier models

10 Place the special valve lifter tool in position **(see illustration 35.6a)**, with the longer jaw of the tool gripping the lower edge of the cast follower boss and the upper, shorter jaw gripping the upper edge of the follower itself, press down the valve lifter by squeezing the handles of the valve lifter tool together and fit the new adjusting shim (note that the wire hook on the end of one valve lifter tool handle can be used to clamp the handles together to keep the follower depressed while the shim is inserted. Measure the clearance with a feeler gauge to make sure that your calculations are correct.

11 Repeat this procedure until all the valves which are out of clearance have been corrected.

35.6b Keep pressure on the follower with the smaller tool and remove the shim with a small screwdriver . . .

35.6c . . . a pair of tweezers or a magnet as shown here

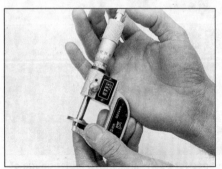

35.8a Measure the shim thickness with a micrometer – 2000 and earlier models

35.8b On 2001 and later models, measure the thickness of the follower head with a micrometer

2001 and later models

12 Fit the proper thickness follower(s) in position, making sure to lubricate them with camshaft installation grease first. **Note:** *Apply the lubricant to the underside of the follower where it contacts the valve stem, the walls of the follower and the face of the follower.*

13 Refit the camshaft(s) (see Chapter 2B).

All models

14 Refit the valve cover and remaining components using a reversal of the removal procedure.

New shim thickness   mm (in.)

Shim No.	Thickness	Shim No.	Thickness
1	2.500 (0.0984)	10	2.950 (0.1161)
2	2.550 (0.1004)	11	3.000 (0.1181)
3	2.600 (0.1024)	12	3.050 (0.1201)
4	2.650 (0.1043)	13	3.100 (0.1220)
5	2.700 (0.1063)	14	3.150 (0.1240)
6	2.750 (0.1083)	15	3.200 (0.1260)
7	2.800 (0.1102)	16	3.250 (0.1280)
8	2.850 (0.1122)	17	3.300 (0.1299)
9	2.900 (0.1142)		

35.9a Valve adjusting shim thickness chart – 2000 and earlier models

New lifter thickness   mm (in.)

Lifter No.	Thickness	Lifter No.	Thickness	Lifter No.	Thickness
06	5.060 (0.1992)	30	5.300 (0.2087)	54	5.540 (0.2181)
08	5.080 (0.2000)	32	5.320 (0.2094)	56	5.560 (0.2189)
10	5.100 (0.2008)	34	5.340 (0.2102)	58	5.580 (0.2197)
12	5.120 (0.2016)	36	5.360 (0.2110)	60	5.600 (0.2205)
14	5.140 (0.2024)	38	5.380 (0.2118)	62	5.620 (0.2213)
16	5.160 (0.2031)	40	5.400 (0.2126)	64	5.640 (0.2220)
18	5.180 (0.2039)	42	5.420 (0.2134)	66	5.660 (0.2228)
20	5.200 (0.2047)	44	5.440 (0.2142)	68	5.680 (0.2236)
22	5.220 (0.2055)	46	5.460 (0.2150)	70	5.700 (0.2244)
24	5.240 (0.2063)	48	5.480 (0.2157)	72	5.720 (0.2252)
26	5.260 (0.2071)	50	5.500 (0.2165)	74	5.740 (0.2260)
28	5.280 (0.2079)	52	5.520 (0.2173)		

35.9b Valve follower thickness chart – 2001 and later models

Notes

Chapter 1 Part B:
Routine maintenance and servicing – diesel models

Contents

	Section number
Air filter element renewal	33
Air filter renewal	15
Automatic transmission fluid and filter change	27
Auxiliary drivebelt check, adjustment and renewal	9
Battery check, maintenance and charging	8
Brake check	14
Brake fluid change	24
Clutch pedal freeplay check and adjustment	7
Cooling system check	11
Cooling system servicing (draining, flushing and refilling)	25
Driveshaft boot check	20
Engine oil and oil filter change	5
Exhaust system check	26
Fuel filter renewal	32
Fuel system check	16
High-pressure fuel pipes renewal	36
High-pressure fuel pump renewal	37
In-tank fuel filter renewal	34
Introduction	1

	Section number
Major services	4
Manual transmission lubricant change	28
Manual transmission lubricant level check	17
Minor services	3
Pollen filter renewal	22
Positive Crankcase Ventilation (PCV) hose check and renewal	31
Rear differential lubricant change (4WD models)	30
Rear differential lubricant level check (4WD models)	21
Seat belt check	13
Servicing – general information	2
Steering and suspension check	19
Timing belt renewal	35
Transfer case lubricant change (4WD models)	29
Transfer case lubricant level check (4WD models)	18
Tyre rotation	12
Underbonnet hose check and renewal	10
Valve clearance check and adjustment	23
Windscreen wiper blade inspection and renewal	6

Degrees of difficulty

Easy, suitable for novice with little experience	**Fairly easy,** suitable for beginner with some experience	**Fairly difficult,** suitable for competent DIY mechanic	**Difficult,** suitable for experienced DIY mechanic	**Very difficult,** suitable for expert DIY or professional

Capacities*

Engine oil (including filter)	6.4 litres
Coolant	7.6 litres

Transmission:

Manual:

2WD	1.9 litres
4WD	3.4 litres

Automatic (drain and refill):

2WD	Up to 3.3 litres
4WD	Up to 3.9 litres
Transfer case (4WD models)	0.9 litres
Rear differential (4WD models)	0.9 litres

* All capacities approximate. Add as necessary to bring up to appropriate level.

Valve clearances (engine cold)

Inlet valve	0.20 to 0.30 mm
Exhaust valve	0.35 to 0.45 mm

Cooling system

Thermostat rating:

Starts to open	80 to 84°C
Fully open	95°C

Auxiliary drivebelt tension (with Burroughs or Nippondenso tension gauge)

Note: *The alternator drivebelt is fitted with an automatic tensioner, however, the power steering pump/air conditioning compressor drivebelt has manual adjustment.*

Used belt (a belt which has been used more than 5 minutes)	80 ± 20 lbf (equivalent to 10.0 mm deflection)
New belt (a belt that has been used less than 5 minutes)	120 ± 25 lbf (equivalent to 10.0 mm deflection)

Clutch pedal

Freeplay	5 to 15 mm

Height:

2000 and earlier	162 to 172 mm
2001 and later	169 to 179 mm

Brakes

Disc brake pad lining thickness (minimum)	4.7 mm
Drum brake shoe lining thickness (minimum)	1.6 mm
Handbrake adjustment	6 to 8 clicks

Suspension and steering

Steering wheel freeplay limit	25.6 mm
Balljoint allowable movement	0 mm

Torque wrench settings

	lbf ft	Nm
Automatic transmission:		
Sump bolts	6	8
Filter bolts	7	10
Drain plug	25	34
Differential case drain plug	40	54
Auxiliary drivebelt tensioner:		
Nut	44	60
Bolt	44	60
Engine oil drain plug	18	24
Manual transmission drain and level/filler plugs	36	49
Rear differential drain and level/filler plugs	36	49
Seat bolts/nuts	27	37
Transfer case drain and level/filler plugs	29	39
Wheel nuts	76	103

The maintenance intervals in this manual are provided with the assumption that you, not the dealer, will be doing the work. These are the minimum maintenance intervals recommended by the factory for vehicles that are driven daily. If you wish to keep your vehicle in peak condition at all times, you may wish to perform some of these procedures even more often. Because frequent maintenance enhances the efficiency, performance and resale value of your car, we encourage you to do so.

Note

If the vehicle is operated under severe conditions, perform all maintenance indicated with an asterisk (*) at half the indicated intervals. Severe conditions exist if you mainly operate the vehicle:

> In dusty areas.
> Towing a trailer or caravan.
> Idling for extended periods.
> Driving at low speeds when outside temperatures remain below freezing and most trips are less than four miles long.

When the vehicle is new, it should be serviced by a dealer service department (or other workshop recognised by the vehicle manufacturer as providing the same standard of service) in order to preserve the warranty. The vehicle manufacturer may reject warranty claims if you are unable to prove that servicing has been carried out as and when specified, using only original equipment parts or parts certified to be of equivalent quality.

Caution 1: These models are equipped with an anti-theft radio. Before performing a procedure that requires disconnecting the battery, make sure you have the proper activation code.

Caution 2: Disconnecting then reconnecting the battery can cause driveability problems that require a scan tool to remedy. See Chapter 5, Section 1, for the use of an auxiliary voltage input device (or 'Memory-saver') before disconnecting the battery.

Every 250 miles or weekly, whichever comes first

- [ ] See *Weekly checks*

Every 5000 miles or 6 months, whichever comes first

- [ ] Renew the engine oil and oil filter (Section 5)

Note: *Toyota recommends that the engine oil and filter are changed every 10 000 miles or 12 months. However, oil and filter changes are good for the engine, and we recommend that the oil and filter are renewed more frequently, especially if the car is used mainly for short journeys.*

Every 10 000 miles or 12 months, whichever comes first

- [ ] Inspect (and renew, if necessary) the windscreen wiper blades (Section 6)*
- [ ] Check the clutch pedal for proper freeplay (Section 7)
- [ ] Check and service the battery (Section 8)
- [ ] Check and adjust if necessary the engine auxiliary drivebelts (Section 9)
- [ ] Inspect (and renew if, necessary) all underbonnet hoses (Section 10)
- [ ] Check the cooling system (Section 11)
- [ ] Rotate the tyres (Section 12)
- [ ] Check the seat belts (Section 13)
- [ ] Inspect the brake system (Section 14)*
- [ ] Check and renew, if necessary, the air filter (Section 15)*
- [ ] Inspect the fuel system (Section 16)
- [ ] Check the manual transmission lubricant level (Section 17)
- [ ] Check the transfer case lubricant level (4WD models) (Section 18)
- [ ] Inspect the suspension and steering components (Section 19)*
- [ ] Check the driveshaft boots (Section 20)
- [ ] Check the rear differential lubricant level (4WD models) (Section 21)
- [ ] Renew the pollen filter (Section 22)*
- [ ] Check and adjust the valve clearances (Section 23)

Every 20 000 miles or 2 years, whichever comes first

All items listed above plus:

- [ ] Renew the brake fluid (Section 24)
- [ ] Service the cooling system (drain, flush and refill) (Section 25) – **Note:** *Not Long Life coolant*
- [ ] Inspect the exhaust system (Section 26)
- [ ] Change the automatic transmission fluid and filter (Section 27)
- [ ] Change the manual transmission lubricant (Section 28)
- [ ] Change the transfer case lubricant (4WD models) (Section 29)
- [ ] Change the rear differential lubricant (4WD models) (Section 30)
- [ ] Check and renew if necessary the PCV hoses (Section 31)

Every 40 000 miles or 4 years, whichever comes first

All items listed above plus:

- [ ] Renew the fuel filter (Section 32)*
- [ ] Renew the air filter element (Section 33)*

Every 50 000 miles or 5 years, whichever comes first

All items listed above plus:

- [ ] Renew the in-tank fuel filter (Section 34)

Every 60 000 miles

- [ ] Renew the timing belt* (Section 35)
- [ ] Renew the Long Life coolant (Section 25)

Every 90 000 miles

- [ ] Renew the high-pressure fuel injector pipes and fuel inlet pipe (Section 36)

Every 180 000 miles

- [ ] Renew the high-pressure fuel pump (Section 37)

Underbonnet view

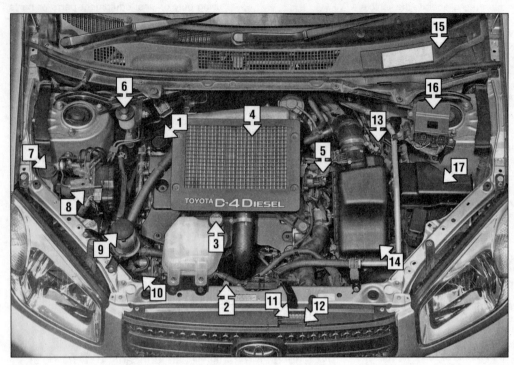

1 Engine oil filler cap
2 Engine oil dipstick
3 Coolant expansion tank
4 Intercooler
5 Brake vacuum pump
6 Brake fluid reservoir
7 Windscreen washer fluid reservoir
8 Brake ABS hydraulic unit
9 Power steering pump hydraulic fluid reservoir
10 Power steering pump
11 Radiator
12 Air conditioning condenser
13 Fuel filter
14 Air cleaner and filter element
15 Battery (under cover)
16 Electronic driving unit (EDU)
17 Fusebox and relays

Front underbody view

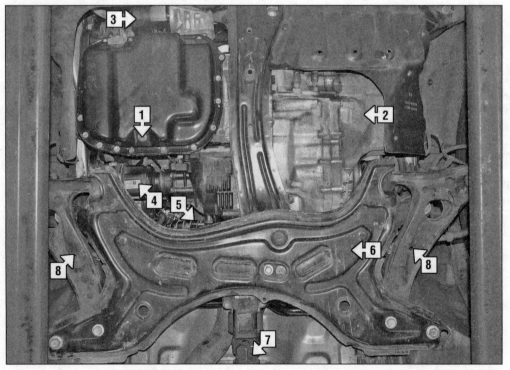

1 Engine oil drain plug
2 Manual transmission
3 Engine oil filter
4 Driveshaft
5 4WD transfer case
6 Front suspension crossmember
7 4WD propeller shaft
8 Front suspension lower control arms

Typical rear underbody components

1 Silencer
2 Exhaust system mounting
3 Shock absorber
4 Rear drum brake assembly
5 Driveshaft boot
6 Differential
7 Propeller shaft
8 Fuel tank

Maintenance procedures

1 Introduction

This chapter is designed to help the home mechanic maintain the Toyota RAV4 for peak performance, economy, safety and long life.

Included is a master maintenance schedule, followed by sections dealing specifically with each item on the schedule. Visual checks, adjustments, component renewal and other helpful items are included. Refer to the accompanying illustrations of the engine compartment and the underside of the vehicle for the location of various components.

Servicing your vehicle in accordance with the mileage/time maintenance schedule and the following Sections will provide it with a planned maintenance program that should result in a long and reliable service life. This is a comprehensive plan, so maintaining some items but not others at the specified service intervals will not produce the same results.

As you service your RAV4, you will discover that many of the procedures can – and should

– be grouped together because of the nature of the particular procedure you're performing or because of the close proximity of two otherwise unrelated components to one another.

For example, if the vehicle is raised for any reason, you should inspect the exhaust, suspension, steering and fuel systems while you're under the vehicle. When you're rotating the tyres, it makes good sense to check the brakes and wheel bearings since the wheels are already removed.

Finally, let's suppose you have to borrow or hire a torque wrench. Even if you only need to tighten the spark plugs, you might as well check the torque of as many critical nuts and bolts as time allows.

The first stage of this maintenance program is to prepare yourself before the actual work begins. Read through all sections pertinent to the procedures you're planning to do, then make a list of and gather together all the parts and tools you will need to do the job. If it looks as if you might run into problems during a particular segment of some procedure, seek advice from your local dealer parts department.

2 Servicing – general information

The term servicing is used in this manual to represent a combination of individual operations rather than one specific procedure that will maintain an engine in proper tune.

If, from the time the vehicle is new, the routine maintenance schedule is followed closely and frequent checks are made of fluid levels and high-wear items, as suggested throughout this manual, the engine will be kept in relatively good running condition and the need for additional work will be minimised.

More likely than not, however, there may be times when the engine is running poorly due to lack of regular maintenance. This is even more likely if a used vehicle, which has not received regular and frequent maintenance checks, is purchased. In such cases, an engine service will be needed outside of the regular routine maintenance intervals.

The first step in any service or diagnostic

procedure to help correct a poor-running engine is a cylinder compression check. A compression check (see Chapter 2D) will help determine the condition of internal engine components and should be used as a guide for tune-up and repair procedures. If, for instance, the compression check indicates serious internal engine wear, a conventional service won't improve the performance of the engine and would be a waste of time and money. Because of its importance, the compression check should be done by someone with the right equipment and the knowledge to use it properly.

3 Minor services

The following procedures are those most often needed to bring a generally poor-running engine back into a proper state of tune.
a) *Check all engine related fluids (Weekly checks).*
b) *Clean, inspect and test the battery (Section 8).*
c) *Check and adjust the auxiliary drivebelt (Section 9).*
d) *Check all under bonnet hoses (Section 10).*
e) *Check the cooling system (Section 11).*
f) *Renew the air filter (Section 15).*
g) *Renew the glow plugs (Chapter 5).*

4 Major services

In addition to those items listed in Section 3 (Minor services) add the following items:
a) *Check the fuel system (Section 16).*
b) *Check the charging system (Chapter 5).*

Every 5000 miles or 6 months

5 Engine oil and oil filter change

1 Frequent oil changes are the best preventive maintenance the home mechanic can give the engine, because ageing oil becomes diluted and contaminated, which leads to premature engine wear.
2 Make sure that you have all the necessary tools before you begin this procedure **(see illustration)**. You should also have plenty of rags or newspapers handy for mopping-up any spills.
3 Access to the underside of the vehicle is greatly improved if the vehicle can be lifted on a hoist, driven onto ramps or supported by axle stands.

⚠️ *Warning: Do not work under a vehicle which is supported only by a hydraulic or scissors-type jack.*

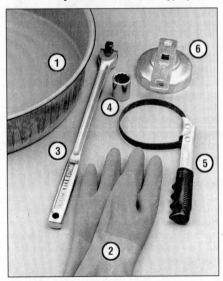
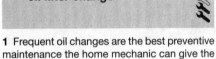

4 If this is your first oil change, get under the vehicle and familiarise yourself with the location of the oil drain plug. The engine and exhaust components will be warm during the actual work, so try to anticipate any potential problems before the engine and accessories are hot.
5 Park the vehicle on a level spot. Start the engine and allow it to reach its normal operating temperature (the needle on the temperature gauge should be at least above the bottom mark). Warm oil and sludge will flow out more easily. Turn off the engine when it's warmed-up. Remove the filler cap in the rear cam cover.
6 Raise the vehicle and support it on axle stands.

⚠️ *Warning: To avoid personal injury, never get beneath the vehicle when it is supported by only by a jack. The jack provided with your vehicle is designed solely for raising the vehicle to remove and renew the wheels. Always use*

5.2 These tools are required when changing the engine oil and filter

1 **Drain pan** – *It should be fairly shallow in depth, but wide in order to prevent spills*
2 **Rubber gloves** – *When removing the drain plug and filter, it is inevitable that you will get oil on your hands (the gloves will prevent burns)*
3 **Socket bar** – *Sometimes the oil drain plug is very tight and a long socket bar is needed to loosen it*
4 **Socket** – *To be used with the socket bar or a ratchet (must be the correct size to fit the drain plug)*
5 **Filter removal strap** – *This is a metal band-type strap, which requires clearance around the filter to be effective*
6 **Filter removal tool** – *This type fits on the bottom of the filter and can be turned with a socket bar (different sizes are available for different types of filters)*

axle stands to support the vehicle when it becomes necessary to place your body underneath the vehicle.
7 Being careful not to touch the hot exhaust components, place the drain pan under the drain plug in the bottom of the sump and remove the plug. You may want to wear gloves while unscrewing the plug the final few turns if the engine is really hot.
8 Allow the old oil to drain into the pan. It may be necessary to move the pan farther under the engine as the oil flow slows to a trickle. Inspect the old oil for the presence of metal shavings and chips.
9 After all the oil has drained, wipe off the drain plug with a clean rag. Even minute metal particles clinging to the plug would immediately contaminate the new oil.
10 Clean the area around the drain plug opening, refit the plug and tighten it securely.
11 Move the drain pan into position under the oil filter.
12 The oil filter is located on the front of the engine, and may be accessed from above **(see illustration)**. If you prefer to access the filter from below, you will have to raise and support the front of the vehicle and remove the engine undertray.

5.12 The oil filter is located on the front of the engine

13 Loosen the oil filter (see illustration) by turning it anti-clockwise with the filter removal strap. Any standard filter removal strap should work. Once the filter is loose, use your hands to unscrew it from the block adapter. Just as the filter is detached from the block, immediately tilt the open end up to prevent the oil inside the filter from spilling out.

⚠️ **Warning: The engine exhaust manifold may still be hot, so be careful.**

14 With a clean rag, wipe off the mounting surface on the block. If a residue of old oil is allowed to remain, it will smoke when the block is heated up. It will also prevent the new filter from seating properly. Also make sure that the none of the old gasket remains stuck to the mounting surface. It can be removed with a scraper if necessary.

15 Compare the old filter with the new one to make sure they are the same type. Smear some engine oil on the rubber gasket of the new filter and screw it into place (see illustration). Because overtightening the filter will damage the gasket, do not use a filter removal strap to tighten the filter. Tighten it by hand until the gasket contacts the seating surface. Then seat the filter by giving it an additional 3/4-turn. Where applicable, lower the vehicle now and refit the undertray.

16 Add new oil to the engine through the

5.13 Unscrew the oil filter from the adapter/housing on the front of the engine

oil filler cap in the valve cover. Use a spout or funnel to prevent oil from spilling onto the top of the engine. Pour three litres of fresh oil into the engine. Wait a few minutes to allow the oil to drain into the pan, then check the level on the oil dipstick (see *Weekly checks* if necessary). If the oil level is at or near the F mark, refit the filler cap hand tight, start the engine and allow the new oil to circulate.

17 Allow the engine to run for about a minute. While the engine is running, look under the vehicle and check for leaks at the sump drain plug and around the oil filter. If either is leaking, stop the engine and tighten the plug or filter slightly.

18 Wait a few minutes to allow the oil to

5.15 Fitting the new oil filter

trickle down into the pan, then recheck the level on the dipstick and, if necessary, add enough oil to bring the level to the F mark.

19 During the first few trips after an oil change, make it a point to check frequently for leaks and proper oil level.

20 The old oil drained from the engine cannot be re-used in its present state and should be discarded. Check with your local refuse disposal company, disposal facility or environmental agency to see if they will accept the oil for recycling. Don't pour used oil into drains or onto the ground. After the oil has cooled, it can be drained into a suitable container (capped plastic jugs, topped bottles, milk cartons, etc) for transport to one of these disposal sites.

Every 10 000 miles or 12 months

6 Windscreen wiper blade inspection and renewal

1 The windscreen wiper and blade assembly should be inspected periodically for damage, loose components and cracked or worn blade elements.

2 Road film can build up on the wiper blades and affect their efficiency, so they should be washed regularly with a mild detergent solution.

3 The action of the wiping mechanism can loosen nuts and bolts, so they should be checked and tightened, as necessary, at the same time the wiper blades are checked.

4 If the wiper blade elements are cracked, worn or warped, or no longer clean adequately, they should be renewed.

5 Remove the wiper blade assembly from the arm by pushing on the release lever, then sliding the assembly down and out of the hook in the end of the arm (see illustration).

6 Detach the blade insert element and pull it out of the right end of the wiper frame (see illustration).

7 Insert the new element end with the small protrusions into the right side of the wiper frame (see illustration). Slide the element fully into place, then seat the protrusions in the end of the frames to secure it.

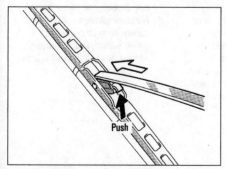

6.5 Push on the release lever and slide the wiper assembly down out of the hook in the end of the wiper arm

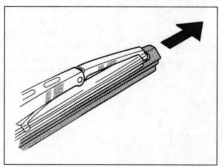

6.6 After detaching the end of the element, slide it out of the end of the frame

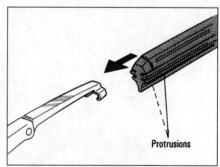

6.7 Insert the end of the element with the protrusions in first

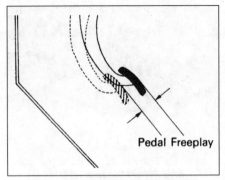

7.1 To check clutch pedal freeplay, measure the distance between the natural resting place of the pedal and the point at which you encounter resistance

7 Clutch pedal freeplay check and adjustment

1 Press down lightly on the clutch pedal and, with a ruler, measure the distance that it moves freely before the clutch resistance is felt (see illustration). The freeplay should be within the specified limits. If it isn't, it must be adjusted.
2 Loosen the locknut on the pedal end of the clutch pushrod (see illustration).
3 Turn the pushrod until pedal freeplay and pushrod freeplay are correct.
4 Tighten the locknut.
5 After adjusting the pedal freeplay, check the pedal height.
6 If pedal height is incorrect, loosen the locknut and turn the stopper bolt until the height is correct. Tighten the locknut.

8 Battery check, maintenance and charging

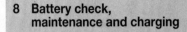

⚠️ *Warning: Certain precautions must be followed when checking and servicing the battery. Hydrogen gas, which is highly flammable, is always present in the battery cells, so keep lighted tobacco and all other open flames and sparks away from the battery. The electrolyte inside the battery is actually dilute sulphuric acid, which will cause injury if splashed on your skin or in your eyes. It will also ruin clothes and painted surfaces. When removing the battery cables, always detach the negative cable first and hook it up last.*

1 A routine preventive maintenance program for the battery in your vehicle is the only way to ensure quick and reliable starts. But before performing any battery maintenance, make sure that you have the proper equipment necessary to work safely around the battery (see illustration).
2 There are also several precautions that should be taken whenever battery maintenance is performed. Before servicing the battery, always turn the engine and all accessories off and disconnect the cable from the negative terminal of the battery. Note: *Raise the cowl cover for access to the battery.*
3 The battery produces hydrogen gas, which is both flammable and explosive. Never create a spark, smoke or light a match around the battery. Always charge the battery in a ventilated area.

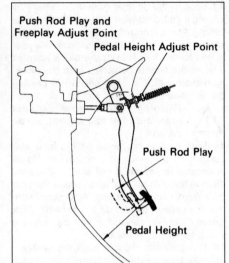

7.2 The clutch pedal pushrod play, pedal height and freeplay adjustments are made by loosening the locknut and turning the appropriate threaded adjuster

4 Electrolyte contains poisonous and corrosive sulphuric acid. Do not allow it to get in your eyes, on your skin on your clothes. Never ingest it. Wear protective safety glasses when working near the battery. Keep children away from the battery.
5 Note the external condition of the battery. If the positive terminal and cable clamp on your vehicle's battery is equipped with a rubber protector, make sure that it's not torn or damaged. It should completely cover the terminal. Look for any corroded or loose

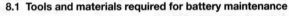

8.1 Tools and materials required for battery maintenance

1 *Face shield/safety goggles – When removing corrosion with a brush, the acidic particles can easily fly up into your eyes*
2 *Baking soda – A solution of baking soda and water can be used to neutralise corrosion*
3 *Petroleum jelly – A layer of this on the battery posts will help prevent corrosion*
4 *Battery post/cable cleaner – This wire brush cleaning tool will remove all traces of corrosion from the battery posts and cable clamps*
5 *Treated felt washers – Placing one of these on each post, directly under the cable clamps, will help prevent corrosion*
6 *Puller – Sometimes the cable clamps are very difficult to pull off the posts, even after the nut/bolt has been completely loosened. This tool pulls the clamp straight up and off the post without damage*
7 *Battery post/cable cleaner – Here is another cleaning tool which is a slightly different version of number 4 above, but it does the same thing*
8 *Rubber gloves – Another safety item to consider when servicing the battery; remember that's acid inside the battery*

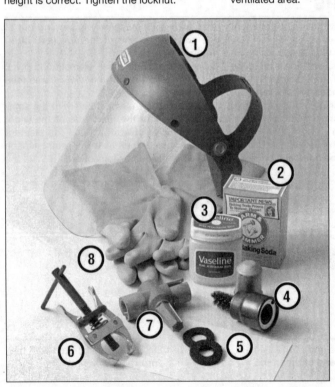

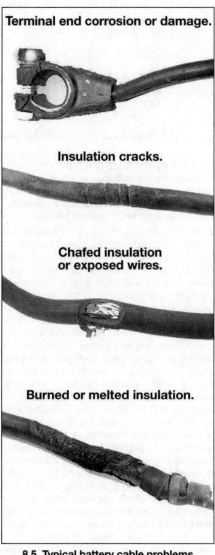

Terminal end corrosion or damage.

Insulation cracks.

Chafed insulation or exposed wires.

Burned or melted insulation.

8.5 Typical battery cable problems

8.6a Battery terminal corrosion usually appears as light, fluffy powder

8.6b Removing a cable from the battery post with a spanner – sometimes a pair of special battery pliers are required for this procedure if corrosion has caused deterioration of the nut hex (always remove the earth (-) cable first and hook it up last)

connections, cracks in the case or cover or loose hold-down clamps. Also check the entire length of each cable for cracks and frayed conductors **(see illustration)**.

6 If corrosion, which looks like white, fluffy deposits **(see illustration)** is evident, particularly around the terminals, the battery should be removed for cleaning. Loosen the cable clamp bolts with a spanner, being careful to remove the earth cable first, and slide them off the terminals **(see illustration)**. Then disconnect the hold-down clamp bolt and nut, remove the clamp and lift the battery from the engine compartment.

7 Clean the cable clamps thoroughly with a battery brush or a terminal cleaner and a solution of warm water and baking soda **(see illustration)**. Wash the terminals and the top of the battery case with the same solution but make sure that the solution doesn't get into the battery. When cleaning the cables, terminals and battery top, wear safety goggles and rubber gloves to prevent any solution from coming in contact with your eyes or hands. Wear old clothes too – even diluted, sulphuric acid splashed onto clothes will burn holes in them. If the terminals have been extensively corroded, clean them up with a terminal cleaner **(see illustration)**. Thoroughly wash all cleaned areas with plain water.

8 Make sure that the battery tray is in good condition and the hold-down nut and bolt are tight **(see illustration)**. If the battery is removed from the tray, make sure no parts remain in the bottom of the tray when the battery is refitted. When refitting the hold-down clamp bolt or nut, do not overtighten it.

9 Information on removing and refitting the battery can be found in Chapter 5. Information on jump starting can be found at the front of this manual.

Cleaning

10 Corrosion on the hold-down components, battery case and surrounding areas can be removed with a solution of water and baking soda. Thoroughly rinse all cleaned areas with plain water.

11 Any metal parts of the vehicle damaged by corrosion should be covered with a zinc-based primer, then painted.

Charging

⚠️ *Warning: When batteries are being charged, hydrogen gas, which is very explosive and flammable, is produced. Do not smoke or allow open flames near a charging or a recently charged battery. Wear eye protection when near the battery during charging. Also, make sure the charger is unplugged before connecting or disconnecting the battery from the charger.*

12 Slow-rate charging is the best way to restore a battery that's discharged to the point where it will not start the engine. It's also a good way to maintain the battery charge in a vehicle that's only driven a few miles between

8.7a When cleaning the cable clamps, all corrosion must be removed (the inside of the clamp is tapered to match the taper on the post, so don't remove too much material)

8.7b Regardless of the type of tool used to clean the battery posts, a clean, shiny surface should be the result

8.8 Make sure the battery hold-down clamps are tight

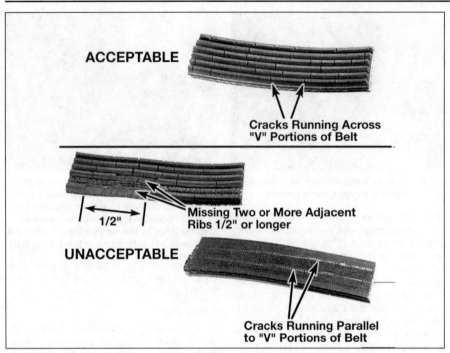

ACCEPTABLE

Cracks Running Across "V" Portions of Belt

1/2"

Missing Two or More Adjacent Ribs 1/2" or longer

UNACCEPTABLE

Cracks Running Parallel to "V" Portions of Belt

9.3 Check the multi-ribbed belt for signs of wear like these – if the belt looks worn, renew it

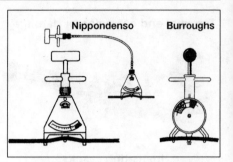

Nippondenso   Burroughs

9.4 If you are able to borrow either a Nippondenso or Burroughs belt tension gauge, this is how it's installed on the belt – compare the reading on the scale with the specified drivebelt tension

starts. Maintaining the battery charge is particularly important in the winter when the battery must work harder to start the engine and electrical accessories that drain the battery are in greater use.

13 It's best to use a one or two-amp battery charger (sometimes called a 'trickle' charger). They are the safest and put the least strain on the battery. They are also the least expensive. For a faster charge, you can use a higher amperage charger, but don't use one rated more than 1/10th the amp/hour rating of the battery. Rapid boost charges that claim to restore the power of the battery in one to two hours are hardest on the battery and can damage batteries not in good condition. This type of charging should only be used in emergency situations.

14 The average time necessary to charge a battery should be listed in the instructions that come with the charger. As a general rule, a trickle charger will charge a battery in 12 to 16 hours.

9 Auxiliary drivebelt check, adjustment and renewal

Check

1 The alternator, power steering pump and air conditioning compressor auxiliary drivebelts, also referred to as simply 'fan' belts, are located at the right end of the engine. The good condition and proper adjustment of the alternator belt is critical to the operation of the engine. Because of their composition and the high stresses to which they are subjected, auxiliary drivebelts stretch and deteriorate as they get older. They must therefore be periodically inspected.

2 On all diesel models, two belts are used; one belt transmits power from the crankshaft to the alternator, and the other drives the air conditioning compressor and power steering pump.

3 With the engine off, open the bonnet and locate the auxiliary drivebelt(s). With an electric torch, check each belt for separation of the adhesive rubber on both sides of the core, core separation from the belt side, a severed core, separation of the ribs from the adhesive rubber, cracking or separation of the ribs, and torn or worn ribs or cracks in the inner ridges of the ribs (see illustration). Also check for fraying and glazing, which gives the belt a shiny appearance. Both sides of the belt should be inspected, which means you will have to twist the belt to check the underside. Use your fingers to feel the belt where you can't see it. If any of the above conditions are evident, renew the belt (go to Paragraph 7).

4 The alternator drivebelt is fitted with an automatic tensioner, however, the power steering pump/air conditioning compressor drivebelt has manual adjustment. To check the tension of the PAS/AC belt in accordance with factory specifications, use either a Nippondenso or Burroughs belt tension gauge on the belt (see illustration). Measure the tension in accordance with the manufacturer's instructions and compare your measurement to the specified auxiliary drivebelt tension for either a used or new belt. Note: *A 'used' belt is defined as any belt which has been operated more than five minutes on the engine; a 'new' belt is one that has been used for less than five minutes.*

5 If you don't have either of the above tools, and cannot borrow one, the following rule of thumb method is recommended: Push firmly on the belt with your thumb at a distance halfway between the pulleys and note how far the belt can be pushed (deflected). The belt should deflect approximately 6 mm if the distance from pulley centre to pulley centre is 30 cm or less; the belt should deflect about 12 mm if the distance from pulley centre to pulley centre is greater then 30 cm.

Adjustment

6 To adjust the power steering pump/air conditioning compressor drivebelt, first loosen the lockbolt in the centre of the idler pulley, then turn the adjustment bolt located at the front of the adjustment pulley bracket (see illustrations). On completion of the adjustment, tighten the lockbolt.

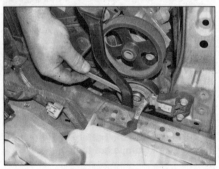

9.6a Loosen the lockbolt in the centre of the idler pulley . . .

9.6b . . . then turn the adjustment bolt as required

9.7 Removing the power steering pump/compressor drivebelt

9.8 Rotate the tensioner clockwise and remove the alternator drivebelt

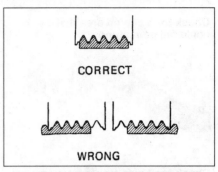

9.9 When installing a multi-ribbed belt, make sure that it is centred – it must not overlap either edge of the pulley

Drivebelt renewal

7 To renew the power steering/air conditioning compressor drivebelt, follow the procedures for adjustment as described above, then slip the belt from the pulleys **(see illustration)**. Fit the new belt, and adjust as described previously.

8 To renew the alternator drivebelt, rotate the belt tensioner clockwise to release the tension, then slip the belt off the pulleys **(see illustrations)**. Slowly release the tensioner. Fit the new belt, again rotating the tensioner to allow the belt to be fitted, then release the belt tensioner.

9 Make sure the belt is properly centred in the pulleys **(see illustration)**.

Automatic tensioner renewal

 Warning: Disconnect the cable from the negative terminal of the battery before performing this procedure.

10 To renew a tensioner that does not properly tension the belt, or one that exhibits binding or a worn-out bearing/pulley, remove the auxiliary drivebelt then unscrew the mounting bolt and nut.

11 Refitting is the reverse of the removal procedure. Tighten the nuts and bolts to the torque values listed in this Chapter's Specifications.

12 Refit the auxiliary drivebelt as previously described.

10 Underbonnet hose check and renewal

Caution: Renewal of air conditioning hoses must be left to a dealer service department or air conditioning specialist that has the equipment to depressurise the system safely. Never remove air conditioning components or hoses until the system has been depressurised.

General

1 High temperatures in the engine compartment can cause the deterioration of the rubber and plastic hoses used for engine, accessory and emission systems operation. Periodic inspection should be made for cracks, loose clamps, material hardening and leaks.

2 Information specific to the cooling system hoses can be found in Section 11.

3 Some, but not all, hoses are secured to the fittings with clamps. Where clamps are used, check to be sure they haven't lost their tension, allowing the hose to leak. If clamps aren't used, make sure the hose has not expanded and/or hardened where it slips over the fitting, allowing it to leak.

Vacuum hoses

4 It's quite common for vacuum hoses, especially those in the emissions system, to be colour-coded or identified by coloured stripes moulded into them. Various systems require hoses with different wall thickness, collapse resistance and temperature resistance. When renewing hoses, be sure the new ones are made of the same material.

5 Often the only effective way to check a hose is to remove it completely from the vehicle. If more than one hose is removed, be sure to label the hoses and fittings to ensure correct refitting.

6 When checking vacuum hoses, be sure to include any plastic T-fittings in the check. Inspect the fittings for cracks and the hose where it fits over the fitting for distortion, which could cause leakage.

7 A small piece of vacuum hose (8.0 to 10.0 mm inside diameter) can be used as a stethoscope to detect vacuum leaks. Hold one end of the hose to your ear (but not in) and probe around vacuum hoses and fittings, listening for the 'hissing' sound characteristic of a vacuum leak.

 Warning: When probing with the vacuum hose stethoscope, be very careful not to come into contact with moving engine components such as the auxiliary drivebelts, cooling fan, etc.

Fuel hose

 Warning: Diesel fuel isn't as volatile as petrol, but it is flammable, so take extra precautions when you work on any part of the fuel system. Don't smoke or allow naked flames or bare light bulbs near the work area. Don't work in a garage or other enclosed space where there is a gas-type appliance (such as a water heater or clothes dryer). Avoid direct skin contact with diesel fuel – wear protective clothing, safety glasses and gloves when handling fuel system components and have a fire extinguisher on hand. Ensure that the work area is well ventilated.

8 Check all rubber fuel lines for deterioration and chafing. Check especially for cracks in areas where the hose bends and just before fittings, such as where a hose attaches to the fuel filter.

9 High quality fuel line, specifically designed for fuel injection systems, must be used for fuel line renewal.

Warning: Never use anything other than the proper fuel line for fuel line renewal.

10 Spring-type clamps are commonly used on fuel lines. These clamps often lose their tension over a period of time, and can be 'sprung' during removal. Renew all spring-type clamps with screw clamps whenever a hose is renewed.

Metal lines

11 Sections of metal line are often used for fuel line between the fuel pump and fuel injection unit. Check carefully to be sure the line has not been bent or crimped and that cracks have not started in the line.

12 If a section of metal fuel line must be renewed, only seamless steel tubing should be used, since copper and aluminium tubing don't have the strength necessary to withstand normal engine vibration.

13 Check the metal brake lines where they enter the master cylinder and brake proportioning unit (if used) for cracks in the lines or loose fittings. Any sign of brake fluid leakage calls for an immediate thorough inspection of the brake system.

11 Cooling system check

1 Many major engine failures can be attributed to a faulty cooling system. If the vehicle is equipped with an automatic transmission, the cooling system also cools the transmission fluid and thus plays an important role in prolonging transmission life.

Check for a chafed area that could fail prematurely.

Check for a soft area indicating the hose has deteriorated inside.

Overtightening the clamp on a hardened hose will damage the hose and cause a leak.

Check each hose for swelling and oil-soaked ends. Cracks and breaks can be located by squeezing the hose.

11.4 Hoses, like drivebelts, have a habit of failing at the worst possible time – to prevent the inconvenience of a blown radiator or heater hose, inspect them carefully as shown here

2 The cooling system should be checked with the engine cold. Do this before the vehicle is driven for the day or after the engine has been shut off for at least three hours.

3 Remove the radiator cap by turning it to the left until it reaches a stop. If you hear a hissing sound (indicating there is still pressure in the system), wait until it stops. Now press down on the cap with the palm of your hand and continue turning to the left until the cap can be removed. Thoroughly clean the cap, inside and out, with clean water. Also clean the filler neck on the radiator. All traces of corrosion should be removed. The coolant inside the radiator should be relatively transparent. If it's rust-coloured, the system should be drained and refilled (see Section 25). If the coolant level

isn't up to the top, add additional antifreeze/coolant mixture (see *Weekly checks*).

4 Carefully check the large upper and lower radiator hoses along with the smaller diameter heater hoses that run from the engine to the bulkhead. Inspect each hose along its entire length, renewing any hose which is cracked, swollen or shows signs of deterioration. Cracks may become more apparent if the hose is squeezed **(see illustration)**. Regardless of condition, it's a good idea to renew hoses every two years.

5 Make sure that all hose connections are tight. A leak in the cooling system will usually show up as white or rust-coloured deposits on the areas adjoining the leak. If wire-type clamps are used at the ends of the hoses, it may be a good idea to renew them with more secure screw-type clamps.

6 Use compressed air or a soft brush to remove bugs, leaves, etc, from the front of the radiator or air conditioning condenser. Be careful not to damage the delicate cooling fins or cut yourself on them.

7 Every other inspection, or at the first indication of cooling system problems, have the cap and system pressure tested. If you don't have a pressure tester, most garages will do this for a minimal charge.

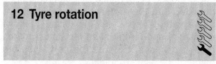

12 Tyre rotation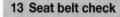

1 The tyres should be rotated at the specified intervals and whenever uneven wear is noticed. Since the vehicle will be raised and the tyres removed anyway, check the brakes (see Section 14) at this time.

2 Radial tyres must be rotated in a specific pattern **(see illustrations)**.

3 Refer to the information in *Wheel changing* at the front of this manual for the proper procedures to follow when raising the vehicle and changing a tyre. If the brakes are to be

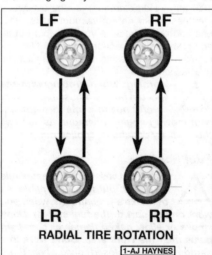

12.2a Four-tyre rotation pattern

checked, do not apply the handbrake as stated. Make sure the tyres are blocked to prevent the vehicle from rolling.

4 Preferably, the entire vehicle should be raised at the same time. This can be done on a hoist or by jacking up each corner and then lowering the vehicle onto axle stands placed beneath the underbody. Always use four axle stands and make sure the vehicle is firmly supported.

5 After rotation, check and adjust the tyre pressures as necessary and be sure to check the nut tightness.

6 For further information on the wheels and tyres, refer to Chapter 10.

13 Seat belt check

1 Check the seat belts, buckles, latch plates and guide loops for obvious damage and signs of wear. Seat belts that exhibit fraying along the edges should be renewed.

2 Where the seat belt stalk bolts to the floor of the vehicle, check that the bolts are secure.

3 See if the seat belt reminder light comes on when the key is turned to the Run or Start position. A chime should also sound.

14 Brake check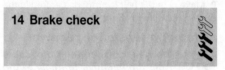

⚠ **Warning: Dust created by the brake system is harmful to your health. Never blow it out with compressed air and don't inhale any of it.**

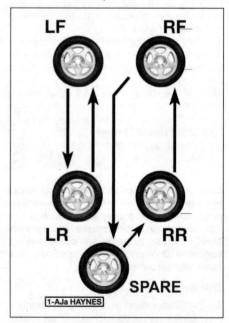

12.2b Five-tyre rotation pattern (to be used only if the spare tyre is the same as the other four)

14.6 You will find an inspection hole like this in each caliper through which you can view the thickness of remaining friction material for the inner pad

14.13 A quick check of the remaining drum brake shoe lining material can be made by removing the rubber plug in the backing plate and looking through the inspection hole

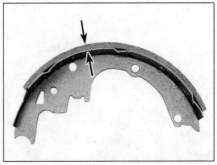

14.15 If the lining is bonded to the brake shoe, measure the lining thickness from the outer surface to the metal shoe, as shown here; if the lining is riveted to the shoe, measure from the lining outer surface to the rivet head

An approved filtering mask should be worn when working on the brakes. Do not, under any circumstances, use petroleum-based solvents to clean brake parts. Use brake system cleaner only.

Note: *For detailed photographs of the brake system, refer to Chapter 9.*

1 In addition to the specified intervals, the brakes should be inspected every time the wheels are removed or whenever a defect is suspected. Any of the following symptoms could indicate a potential brake system defect: The vehicle pulls to one side when the brake pedal is depressed; the brakes make squealing or dragging noises when applied; brake travel is excessive; the pedal pulsates (this may be the ABS system); brake fluid leaks, usually onto the inside of the tyre or wheel.

2 The disc brake pads have built-in wear indicators which should make a high-pitched squealing or scraping noise when they are worn to the renewal point. When you hear this noise, renew the pads immediately or expensive damage to the discs can result.

3 Loosen the wheel nuts.

4 Raise the vehicle and place it securely on axle stands.

5 Remove the wheels (see *Wheel changing* at the front of this book, or your owner's manual, if necessary).

Disc brakes

6 There are two pads – an outer and an inner – in each caliper. The inner pads are visible through small inspection holes in each caliper **(see illustration)**. The outer pads are more easily viewed a the edge of the caliper.

7 Check the pad thickness by looking at each end of the caliper and through the inspection hole in the caliper body. If the lining material is less than the thickness listed in this Chapter's Specifications, renew the pads. **Note:** *Keep in mind that the lining material is riveted or bonded to a metal backing plate and the metal portion is not included in this measurement.*

8 If it is difficult to determine the exact thickness of the remaining pad material by the above method, or if you are at all concerned

about the condition of the pads, remove the caliper(s), then remove the pads for further inspection (see Chapter 9).

9 Once the pads are removed from the calipers, clean them with brake cleaner and remeasure them.

10 Measure the disc thickness with a micrometer to make sure that it still has service life remaining. If any disc is thinner than the specified minimum thickness, renew it (refer to Chapter 9). Even if the disc has service life remaining, check its condition. Look for scoring, gouging and burned spots. If these conditions exist, remove the disc and have it resurfaced (see Chapter 9).

11 Before refitting the wheels, check all brake lines and hoses for damage, wear, deformation, cracks, corrosion, leakage, bends and twists, particularly in the vicinity of the rubber hoses at the calipers.

12 Check the clamps for tightness and the connections for leakage. Make sure that all hoses and lines are clear of sharp edges, moving parts and the exhaust system. If any of the above conditions are noted, repair, reroute or renew the lines and/or fittings as necessary (see Chapter 9).

Rear drum brakes

13 To check the brake shoe lining thickness without removing the brake drums, remove the rubber plug from the backing plate and use a flashlight to inspect the linings **(see illustration)**. For a more thorough brake inspection, follow the procedure below.

14 Refer to Chapter 9 and remove the rear brake drums.

15 Note the thickness of the lining material on the rear brake shoes **(see illustration)** and look for signs of contamination by brake fluid and grease. If the lining material is within 1.6 mm of the recessed rivets or metal shoes, renew the brake shoes. The shoes should also be renewed if they are cracked, glazed (shiny lining surfaces) or contaminated with brake fluid or grease. See Chapter 9 for the renewal procedure.

16 Check the shoe return and hold-down springs and the adjusting mechanism to make

sure they're refitted correctly and in good condition. Deteriorated or distorted springs, if not renewed, could allow the linings to drag and wear prematurely.

17 Check the wheel cylinders for leakage by carefully peeling back the rubber boots **(see illustration)**. If brake fluid is noted behind the boots, the wheel cylinders must be renewed (see Chapter 9).

18 Check the drums for cracks, score marks, deep scratches and hard spots, which will appear as small discoloured areas. If imperfections cannot be removed with emery cloth, the drums must be resurfaced by an engine reconditioner (see Chapter 9 for more detailed information).

19 Refit the brake drums.

20 Refit the wheels and nuts.

21 Remove the axle stands and lower the vehicle.

22 Tighten the wheel nuts to the torque listed in this Chapter's Specifications.

Brake vacuum servo check

23 Sit in the driver's seat and perform the following sequence of tests.

24 With the brake fully depressed, start the engine – the pedal should move down a little when the engine starts.

25 With the engine running, depress the brake pedal several times – the travel distance should not change.

14.17 Carefully peel back the wheel cylinder boot and check for leaking fluid indicating that the cylinder must be renewed or rebuilt

16.2 Use a small screwdriver to carefully lever out the old gasket – take care not to damage the cap

26 Depress the brake, stop the engine and hold the pedal in for about 30 seconds – the pedal should neither sink nor rise.

27 Restart the engine, run it for about a minute and turn it off. Then firmly depress the brake several times – the pedal travel should decrease with each application.

28 If your brakes do not operate as described above when the preceding tests are performed, the brake vacuum servo has failed. Refer to Chapter 9 for the renewal procedure.

Handbrake

29 Slowly pull up on the handbrake and count the number of clicks you hear until the handle is up as far as it will go. The adjustment is correct if you hear the specified number of clicks. If you hear more or fewer clicks, it's time to adjust the handbrake (refer to Chapter 9).

30 An alternative method of checking the handbrake is to park the vehicle on a steep hill with the handbrake set and the transmission in Neutral (be sure to stay in the vehicle for this procedure). If the handbrake cannot prevent the vehicle from rolling, it is in need of adjustment (see Chapter 9).

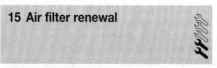

15 Air filter renewal

1 On all diesel models, the air filter is located inside a housing at the left-hand side of the engine compartment.

2 To remove the air filter, release the spring clips that keep the two halves of the air filter housing together, then pull the cover away and, noting how the filter is fitted, remove the air filter element.

3 Inspect the outer surface of the filter element. If it is dirty, renew it. If it is only moderately dusty, it can be re-used by blowing it clean from the back to the front surface with compressed air. Because it is a pleated paper type filter, it cannot be washed or oiled. If it cannot be cleaned satisfactorily with compressed air, discard and renew it. While the cover is off, be careful not to drop anything down into the housing.

Caution: Never drive the vehicle with the

16.5 Inspect the filler hose for cracks and make sure the clamps are tight

air cleaner removed. Excessive engine wear could result.

4 Wipe out the inside of the air filter housing.

5 Place the new filter element into the air cleaner housing, making sure it seats properly.

6 Refitting of the cover is the reverse of removal.

16 Fuel system check

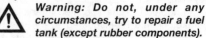

⚠ *Warning: Fuel is extremely flammable, so take extra precautions when you work on any part of the fuel system. Don't smoke or allow open flames or bare light bulbs near the work area, and don't work in a garage where a gas-type appliance (such as a water heater or a clothes dryer) is present. Since fuel is carcinogenic, wear fuel-resistant gloves when there's a possibility of being exposed to fuel, and, if you spill any fuel on your skin, rinse it off immediately with soap and water. Mop-up any spills immediately and do not store fuel-soaked rags where they could ignite. When you perform any kind of work on the fuel system, wear safety glasses and have a fire extinguisher on hand. Diesel fuel is only slightly less dangerous than petrol, so take the same precautions when dealing with diesel fuel.*

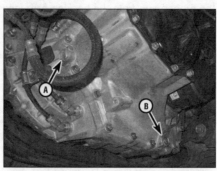

17.1 Remove the check/fill plug and use your finger as a dipstick to check the manual transmission lubricant level

A Check/fill plug   B Drain plug

1 If you smell fuel while driving or after the vehicle has been sitting in the sun, inspect the fuel system immediately.

2 Remove the fuel filler cap and inspect it for damage and corrosion. The gasket should have an unbroken sealing imprint. If the gasket is damaged or corroded, remove it and fit a new one **(see illustration)**.

3 Inspect the fuel feed and return lines for cracks.

4 Since some components of the fuel system – the fuel tank and part of the fuel feed and return lines, for example – are underneath the vehicle, they can be inspected more easily with the vehicle raised on a hoist. If that's not possible, raise the vehicle and support it securely on axle stands.

5 With the vehicle raised and safely supported, inspect the fuel tank and filler neck for punctures, cracks and other damage. The connection between the filler neck and the tank is particularly critical. Sometimes a rubber filler neck will leak because of loose clamps or deteriorated rubber **(see illustration)**. These are problems a home mechanic can usually rectify.

⚠ *Warning: Do not, under any circumstances, try to repair a fuel tank (except rubber components).*

6 Carefully check all rubber hoses and metal lines leading away from the fuel tank. Check for loose connections, deteriorated hoses, crimped lines and other damage. Carefully inspect the lines from the tank to the fuel injection system. Repair or renew damaged sections as necessary (see Chapter 4B).

17 Manual transmission lubricant level check

1 The manual transmission does not have a dipstick. To check the fluid level, raise the vehicle and support it securely on axle stands, then remove the underbody splash shield. On the front side of the transmission housing, you will see a plug **(see illustration)**. Remove it. If the lubricant level is correct, it should be up to the lower edge of the hole.

2 If the transmission needs more lubricant (if the level is not up to the hole), use a syringe or a gear oil pump to add more. Stop filling the transmission when the lubricant begins to run out the hole.

3 Refit the plug and tighten it securely. Drive the vehicle a short distance, then check for leaks.

18 Transfer case lubricant level check (4WD models)

1 Raise the vehicle and support it securely on axle stands.

2 Using the appropriate spanner, unscrew the plug from the transfer case.

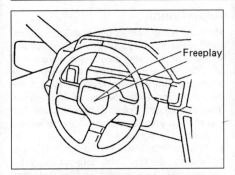

19.1 Steering wheel freeplay is the amount of travel between an initial steering input and the point at which the front wheels begin to turn (indicated by a slight resistance)

19.7 To check a balljoint for wear, try to lever the control arm up and down to make sure there is no play in the balljoint (if there is, renew it)

19.8 Push on the balljoint boot to check for damage

3 Use your little finger to reach inside the housing to feel the lubricant level. The level should be at or near the bottom of the plug hole. If it isn't, add the recommended lubricant through the plug hole with a syringe or squeeze bottle.
4 Refit and tighten the plug. Check for leaks after the first few miles of driving.

19 Steering and suspension check
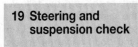

Note: *For detailed illustrations of the steering and suspension components, refer to Chapter 10.*

With the wheels on the ground

1 With the vehicle stopped and the front wheels pointed straight-ahead, rock the steering wheel gently back-and-forth. If freeplay **(see illustration)** is excessive, a front wheel bearing, steering shaft universal joint or lower arm balljoint is worn or the steering gear is out of adjustment or broken. Refer to Chapter 10 for the appropriate repair procedure.
2 Other symptoms, such as excessive vehicle body movement over rough roads, swaying (leaning) around corners and binding as the steering wheel is turned, may indicate faulty steering and/or suspension components.
3 Check the shock absorbers by pushing down and releasing the vehicle several times at each corner. If the vehicle does not come back to a level position within one or two bounces, the shocks/struts are worn and must be renewed. When bouncing the vehicle up-and-down, listen for squeaks and noises from the suspension components. Additional information on suspension components can be found in Chapter 10.

Under the vehicle

4 Raise the vehicle with a jack and support it securely on axle stands. See *Jacking and vehicle support* at the back of this book for the proper jacking points.
5 Check the tyres for irregular wear patterns

and proper inflation. See *Weekly checks* for information regarding tyre wear and Chapter 10 for the wheel bearing renewal procedures.
6 Inspect the universal joint between the steering shaft and the steering gear housing. Check the steering gear housing for grease leakage or oozing. Make sure that the dust seals and boots are not damaged and that the boot clamps are not loose. Check the steering linkage for looseness or damage. Check the tie-rod ends for excessive play. Look for loose bolts, broken or disconnected parts and deteriorated rubber bushings on all suspension and steering components. While an assistant turns the steering wheel from side-to-side, check the steering components for free movement, chafing and binding. If the steering components do not seem to be reacting with the movement of the steering wheel, try to determine where the slack is located.
7 Check the balljoints for wear by trying to move each control arm up-and-down with a lever **(see illustration)** to ensure that its balljoint has no play. If any balljoint does have play, renew it. See Chapter 10 for the balljoint renewal procedure.
8 Inspect the balljoint boots for damage and leaking grease **(see illustration)**. Renew the balljoints if they are damaged (see Chapter 10).
9 At the rear of the vehicle, inspect the suspension arm bushings for deterioration.

20.2 Flex the driveshaft boots by hand to check for cracks and/or leaking grease

20 Driveshaft boot check

1 The driveshaft boots are very important because they prevent dirt, water and foreign material from entering and damaging the constant velocity (CV) joints. Oil and grease can cause the boot material to deteriorate prematurely, so it's a good idea to wash the boots with soap and water. Because it constantly pivots back-and-forth following the steering action of the front hub, the outer CV boot wears out sooner and should be inspected regularly.
2 Inspect the boots for tears and cracks as well as loose clamps **(see illustration)**. If there is any evidence of cracks or leaking lubricant, they must be renewed as described in Chapter 8.

21 Rear differential lubricant level check (4WD models)

1 Raise the vehicle and support it securely on axle stands.
2 Using the appropriate spanner, unscrew the plug from the rear differential **(see illustration)**.
3 Use your little finger to reach inside the housing to feel the lubricant level. The level

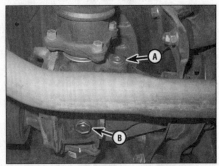

21.2 Location of the rear differential check/fill plug (A) – B is the drain plug (4WD models)

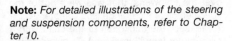

22.2 The pollen filter is retained in the blower case by clips on each side

should be at or near the bottom of the plug hole. If it isn't, add the recommended lubricant through the plug hole with a syringe or squeeze bottle.

4 Refit and tighten the plug. Check for leaks after the first few miles of driving.

22 Pollen filter renewal

1 Open the glovebox door, push in on the sides and allow the door to hang down (see Chapter 11 if necessary).

2 Pull the filter element straight out of the case **(see illustration)**.

3 Refitting is the reverse of removal.

23.5a Install the valve lifter tool as shown and squeeze the handles together to depress the valve follower, then hold the follower down with the smaller tool so the shim can be removed

23.5c ... a pair of tweezers or a magnet as shown here

23 Valve clearance check and adjustment

⚠ **Warning: These models are equipped with airbags. Always disable the airbag system before working in the vicinity of any airbag system component to avoid the possibility of accidental deployment of the airbag(s), which could cause personal injury (see Chapter 12).**
Note: *To carry out the following procedure leaving the camshafts in position requires the use of a special valve lifter tool. The alternative is to remove the camshafts after making the following check.*

Check

1 Disconnect the negative cable from the battery.

2 Remove the valve cover as described in Chapter 2C.

3 Turn the crankshaft so that the inlet camshaft lobes of No 1 cylinder are pointing upwards, then use feeler blades to measure the clearances between the lobes and follower shims. Record the measurements which are out of specification. Turn the crankshaft so that the exhaust camshaft lobes of No 1 cylinder are pointing upwards, and record the clearances. Measure the remaining valve clearances in the same manner.

23.5b Keep pressure on the follower with the smaller tool and remove the shim with a small screwdriver ...

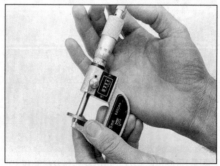

23.7 Measure the shim thickness with a micrometer

Adjustment

Note: *All diesel models use renewable adjustment shims that ride on top of the followers.*

4 If any of the valve clearances were out of specification and you have the special valve lifter tool, turn the crankshaft pulley until the camshaft lobe above the first valve which you intend to adjust is pointing upward, away from the shim. If you do not have the special tool proceed to paragraph 6.

5 Position the notch in the valve follower toward the centre. Then depress the valve follower with the special valve lifter tools **(see illustration)**. Place the special valve lifter tool in position as shown, with the longer jaw of the tool gripping the lower edge of the cast follower boss and the upper, shorter jaw gripping the upper edge of the follower itself. Depress the valve follower by squeezing the handles of the valve lifter tool together, then hold the follower down with the smaller tool and remove the larger one. Remove the adjusting shim with a small screwdriver or a pair of tweezers **(see illustrations)**. Note that the wire hook on the end of some valve lifter tool handles can be used to clamp both handles together to keep the follower depressed while the shim is removed.

6 If any of the valve clearances were out of adjustment and you don't have the special valve lifter tool, remove the camshaft(s) from over the follower(s) that was/were out of the specified clearance range (see Chapter 2C).

7 Measure the thickness of the shim with a micrometer **(see illustration)**. To calculate the correct thickness of a new shim that will place the valve clearance within the specified value, use the following formula:

$$N = T + (A - V)$$

T = Thickness of the old shim.
A = Valve clearance measured.
N = Thickness of the new shim.
V = Desired valve clearance (see this Chapter's Specifications).

8 Select a shim with a thickness as close as possible to the valve clearance calculated. The shims are available in several sizes.
Note: *Through careful analysis of the shim sizes needed to bring the out-of-specification valve clearance within specification, it is often possible to simply move a shim that has to come out anyway to another location requiring a shim of that particular size, thereby reducing the number of new shims that must be purchased.*

9 If you are using the special lifter tool, place it in position, with the longer jaw of the tool gripping the lower edge of the cast follower boss and the upper, shorter jaw gripping the upper edge of the follower itself, press down the valve lifter by squeezing the handles of the valve lifter tool together and fit the new adjusting shim (note that the wire hook on the end of one valve lifter tool handle can be used to clamp the handles together to keep the follower depressed while the shim is inserted. Measure the clearance with a feeler gauge to

make sure that your calculations are correct. If you are not using the special tool, proceed to paragraph 11.

10 Repeat this procedure until all the valves which are out of clearance have been corrected.

11 Fit the proper thickness follower(s) in position, making sure to lubricate them with camshaft installation grease first. **Note:** *Apply the lubricant to the underside of the follower where it contacts the valve stem, the walls of the follower and the face of the follower.*

12 Where removed, refit the camshaft(s) (see Chapter 2C).

13 Refit the valve cover and remaining components using a reversal of the removal procedure.

Every 20 000 miles or 2 years

24 Brake fluid change

⚠ *Warning: Brake fluid can harm your eyes and damage painted surfaces, so use extreme caution when handling or pouring it. Do not use brake fluid that has been standing open or is more than one year old. Brake fluid absorbs moisture from the air. Excess moisture can cause a dangerous loss of braking effectiveness.*

1 At the specified intervals, the brake fluid should be drained and renewed. Since the brake fluid may drip or splash when pouring it, place plenty of rags around the master cylinder to protect any surrounding painted surfaces.

2 Before beginning work, purchase the specified brake fluid (see *Lubricants and fluids*).

3 Remove the cap from the master cylinder reservoir.

4 Using a hand-held suction pump or similar device, withdraw the fluid from the master cylinder reservoir.

5 Add new fluid to the master cylinder until it rises to the line indicated on the reservoir.

6 Bleed the brake system as described in Chapter 9 at all four brakes until new and uncontaminated fluid is expelled from the bleeder screw. Be sure to maintain the fluid level in the master cylinder as you perform the bleeding process. If you allow the master cylinder to run dry, air will enter the system.

7 Refill the master cylinder with fluid and check the operation of the brakes. The pedal should feel solid when depressed, with no sponginess.

⚠ *Warning: Do not operate the vehicle if you are in doubt about the effectiveness of the brake system.*

25 Cooling system servicing (draining, flushing and refilling)

⚠ *Warning: Do not allow engine coolant (antifreeze) to come in contact with your skin or painted surfaces of the vehicle. Rinse off spills immediately with plenty of water. Antifreeze is highly toxic if ingested. Never leave antifreeze lying around in an* open container or in puddles on the floor; children and pets are attracted by its sweet smell and may drink it. Check with local authorities on disposing of used antifreeze. Many communities have collection centres which will see that antifreeze is disposed of safely. Antifreeze is flammable under certain conditions - be sure to read the precautions on the container.

Note: *Coolant renewal at this interval applies to Standard Coolant (Red/Green only) and not to Long Life Coolant (Pink).*

1 Periodically, the cooling system should be drained, flushed and refilled to replenish the antifreeze mixture and prevent formation of rust and corrosion, which can impair the performance of the cooling system and cause engine damage. When the cooling system is serviced, all hoses and the radiator cap should be checked and renewed if necessary.

Draining

2 Apply the handbrake and block the wheels. If the vehicle has just been driven, wait several hours to allow the engine to cool down before beginning this procedure. Where necessary, remove the engine undertray.

3 Once the engine is completely cool, remove the radiator cap.

4 Move a large container under the left-hand side of the radiator to catch the coolant. Attach a 10 mm inner diameter hose to the drain fitting to direct the coolant into the container (some models are already equipped with a hose), then open the drain fitting (a pair of pliers may be required to turn it) **(see illustration)**.

5 After the coolant stops flowing out of the radiator, move the container under the engine block drain plug. Loosen the plug and allow the coolant in the block to drain.

6 While the coolant is draining, check the condition of the radiator hoses, heater hoses and clamps (refer to Section 11 if necessary). Renew any damaged clamps or hoses.

Flushing

7 Once the system is completely drained, remove the thermostat from the engine (see Chapter 3). Then refit the thermostat housing without the thermostat. This will allow the system to be thoroughly flushed.

8 Tighten the radiator drain plug. Turn your heating system controls to Hot, so that the heater core will be flushed at the same time as the rest of the cooling system.

9 Disconnect the upper radiator hose from the radiator, then place a garden hose in the upper radiator inlet and flush the system until the water runs clear at the upper radiator hose **(see illustration)**.

10 In severe cases of contamination or clogging of the radiator, remove the radiator (see Chapter 3) and have a radiator repair facility clean and repair it if necessary.

11 Many deposits can be removed by the chemical action of a cleaner available at car accessory stores. Follow the procedure outlined in the manufacturer's instructions. **Note:** *When the coolant is regularly drained*

25.4 On most models you will have to remove a cover for access to the radiator drain fitting located at the bottom of the radiator – before opening the valve, push a short section of 10 mm ID hose onto the plastic fitting (arrowed) to prevent the coolant from splashing

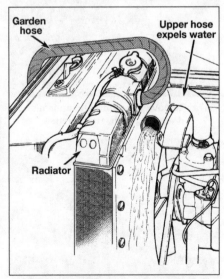

25.9 With the thermostat removed, disconnect the upper radiator hose and flush the radiator and engine block with a garden hose

26.4 Be sure to check each exhaust system rubber mounting for damage

and the system refilled with the correct antifreeze/water mixture, there should be no need to use chemical cleaners or descalers.

12 Remove the overflow hose from the coolant recovery reservoir. Drain the reservoir and flush it with clean water, then reconnect the hose.

Refilling

13 Close and tighten the radiator drain. Refit and/or tighten the block drain plug. Refit the thermostat (see Chapter 3).

14 Place the heater temperature control in the maximum heat position.

15 Slowly add new coolant (a 50/50 mixture of water and antifreeze) to the radiator until it's full. Add coolant to the reservoir up to the lower mark.

16 Leave the radiator cap off and run the engine in a well-ventilated area until the thermostat opens (coolant will begin flowing

27.7a Remove the automatic transmission drain plug with a hex wrench

27.8a After loosening the front bolts, remove the rear transmission sump bolts and . . .

through the radiator and the upper radiator hose will become hot).

17 Turn the engine off and let it cool. Add more coolant mixture to bring the level back up to the lip on the radiator filler neck.

18 Squeeze the upper radiator hose to expel air, then add more coolant mixture if necessary. Renew the radiator cap.

19 Start the engine, allow it to reach normal operating temperature and check for leaks. Where removed, refit the engine undertray.

26 Exhaust system check

1 With the engine cold (at least three hours after the vehicle has been driven), check the complete exhaust system from its starting point at the engine to the end of the tailpipe. This should be done on a hoist where unrestricted access is available.

2 Check the pipes and connections for evidence of leaks, severe corrosion or damage. Make sure that all brackets and hangers are in good condition and tight.

3 At the same time, inspect the underside of the body for holes, corrosion, open seams, etc, which may allow exhaust gases to enter the passenger compartment. Seal all body openings with silicone or body putty.

4 Rattles and other noises can often be traced to the exhaust system, especially the mountings and supports. Try to move the pipes, silencer and catalytic converter. If the components can come in contact with the

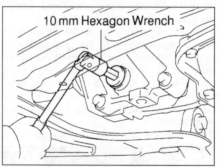

27.7b Later models also have a drain plug on the differential case

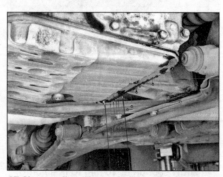

27.8b . . . allow the remaining fluid to drain out

body or suspension parts, secure the exhaust system with new mountings (see illustration).

5 Check the running condition of the engine by inspecting inside the end of the tailpipe. The exhaust deposits here are an indication of engine state-of-tune. If the pipe is black and sooty or coated with white deposits, the engine is in need of a tune-up, including a thorough fuel system inspection.

27 Automatic transmission fluid and filter change

Note: *Some filters are not actually 'filters', but fine-mesh screens which can be cleaned with solvent instead of being renewed.*

1 At the specified time intervals, the automatic transmission fluid should be drained and renewed.

2 Before beginning work, purchase the correct transmission fluid (see *Lubricants and fluids*).

3 Other tools necessary for this job include axle stands to support the vehicle in a raised position, spanners, drain pan, newspapers and clean rags.

4 The fluid should be drained immediately after the vehicle has been driven. Hot fluid is more effective than cold fluid at removing built-up sediment.

⚠️ **Warning: Hot fluid can scald – wear protective gloves.**

5 After the vehicle has been driven to warm-up the fluid, raise it and support it on axle stands for access to the transmission and differential drain plugs.

6 Move the necessary equipment under the vehicle, being careful not to touch any of the hot exhaust components.

7 Place the drain pan under the drain plug in the transmission sump and remove the drain plug with the Allen key (see illustration). Be sure the drain sump is in position, as fluid will come out with some force. Once the fluid is drained, refit the drain plug securely. On 2001 and later 2WD models there's also a drain plug on the transmission's differential housing. Remove the plug and allow the fluid to drain (see illustration). After the fluid has drained, refit the plug (using a new gasket) and tighten it to the torque listed in this Chapter's Specifications.

8 Remove the front transmission sump bolts, then loosen the rear bolts and carefully lever the sump loose with a screwdriver and allow the remaining fluid to drain (see illustrations). Once the fluid had drained, remove the bolts and lower the sump.

9 Remove the filter retaining bolts, disconnect the clip (some models) and lower the filter from the transmission (see illustration). Be careful when lowering the filter as it contains residual fluid.

10 Place the new (or cleaned) filter in position, connect the clip (if equipped) and insert the bolts. Tighten the bolts to the torque listed in the Specifications Section at the beginning of this Chapter.

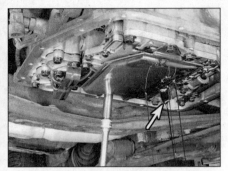

27.9 Remove the filter bolts and lower the filter (be careful, there may be some residual fluid)

27.11 Noting their locations, remove any magnets and wash them and the sump in solvent before refitting them

29.2 Transfer case drain plug

11 Carefully clean the gasket surfaces of the fluid sump, removing all traces of old gasket material. Noting their location, remove the magnets, wash the sump in clean solvent and dry it with compressed air. Be sure to clean and refit any magnets **(see illustration)**.

12 Fit a new gasket, place the fluid sump in position and refit the bolts in their original positions. Tighten the bolts to the torque listed in this Chapter's Specifications.

13 Lower the vehicle.

14 With the engine off, add new fluid to the transmission through the dipstick tube (see *Lubricants and fluids* for the recommended fluid type and capacity). Use a funnel to prevent spills. It is best to add a little fluid at a time, continually checking the level with the dipstick (see *Weekly checks*). Allow the fluid time to drain into the sump.

15 Start the engine and shift the selector into all positions from P to L, then shift into P and apply the handbrake.

16 With the engine idling, check the fluid level. Add fluid up to the Cool level on the dipstick.

28 Manual transmission lubricant change
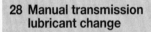

1 Raise the vehicle and support it securely on axle stands, then remove the engine undertray.

2 Remove the drain plug(s) and drain the lubricant **(see illustration 17.1)**.

3 Refit the drain plug(s) and tighten to the torque listed in this Chapter's Specifications.

4 Add new lubricant until it is even with the lower edge of the filler hole (Section 17). See *Lubricants and fluids* for the specified lubricant type.

29 Transfer case lubricant change (4WD models)
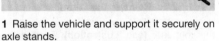

1 Raise the vehicle and support it securely on axle stands.

2 Remove the drain plug and drain the lubricant **(see illustration)**.

3 Refit the drain plug and tighten it to the torque listed in this Chapter's Specifications.

4 Add new lubricant until it is even with the lower edge of the filler hole (see Section 18). See *Lubricants and fluids* for the specified lubricant type.

30 Rear differential lubricant change (4WD models)
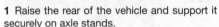

1 Raise the rear of the vehicle and support it securely on axle stands.

2 Remove the drain plug and drain the

lubricant **(see illustration 21.2)**.

3 Refit the drain plug and tighten it to the torque listed in this Chapter's Specifications.

4 Add new lubricant until it is even with the lower edge of the filler hole (see Section 20). See *Lubricants and fluids* for the specified lubricant type.

31 Positive Crankcase Ventilation (PCV) valve and hose check and renewal

1 The PCV valve and hose is located in the valve cover.

2 Disconnect the hose, then unscrew the PCV valve from the cover. Reattach the hose.

3 With the engine idling at normal operating temperature, place your finger over the end of the valve. If there's no vacuum at the valve, check for a plugged hose or valve. Renew any plugged or deteriorated hoses.

4 Turn off the engine. Remove the PCV valve from the hose. Connect a clean piece of hose and blow through the valve from the valve cover (cylinder head) end. If air will not pass through the valve in this direction, renew it with a new one.

5 When purchasing a new PCV valve, make sure it's for your particular vehicle. Compare the old valve with the new one to make sure they're the same.

Every 40 000 miles or 4 years

32 Fuel filter renewal

1 Access to the fuel filter is gained by removing the air cleaner assembly as described in Chapter 4B.

2 Position a container beneath the fuel filter to catch spilt fuel, then disconnect the supply and return hoses **(see illustrations)**.

3 At the connector, disconnect the wiring for the fuel heater on top of the filter assembly **(see illustration)**.

32.2a Fuel filter location

32.2b Disconnecting the supply and return hoses

32.3 Disconnecting the wiring from the fuel filter

32.5 Removing the fuel filter

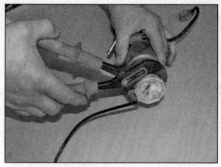

32.6a Use a pair of grips to unscrew the fuel level warning switch ...

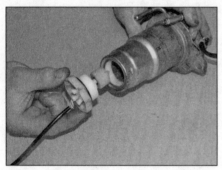

32.6b ... and remove it from the bottom of the filter canister

32.6c Recover the O-ring seal

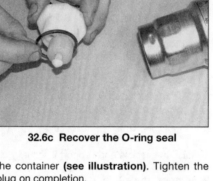

32.7a Use an oil filter removal strap to unscrew the canister ...

4 At the connector, disconnect the wiring for the fuel level warning switch on the bottom of the filter assembly.

5 Unscrew the mounting nuts and lift the filter assembly from the support bracket, then loosen the drain plug and drain the fuel into

the container **(see illustration)**. Tighten the plug on completion.

6 Mount the filter body in a vice and unscrew the fuel level warning switch from the bottom of the filter canister. Recover the O-ring seal **(see illustrations)**.

7 Unscrew the filter canister and discard. Toyota technicians use a special ring spanner which engages the multi-flats on the canister perimeter, however, an oil filter removal strap can be used instead **(see illustrations)**.

8 Clean the contact surfaces of the new filter canister and body, and smear a little fuel oil onto them.

9 Screw on the canister until it contacts the body, then tighten it an additional 3/4-turn by hand only.

10 Apply a little fuel oil to a new O-ring seal, and locate it on the fuel level warning switch. Screw the switch into the filter canister and tighten securely.

11 Fit the filter assembly to the support bracket and tighten the mounting nuts.

12 Reconnect the wiring to the level warning switch and heater.

13 Reconnect the feed and supply hoses.

14 Refit the air cleaner assembly.

15 Operate the hand pump on top of the fuel filter until resistance is felt indicating that the filter is primed.

16 Run the engine and check for leaks.

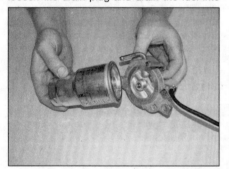

32.7b ... and remove it from the filter body

33.1a Disconnect the wiring from the airflow meter ...

33 Air filter element renewal

1 The air cleaner and housing assembly is located on the left-hand side of the engine compartment. First, disconnect the wiring from the airflow meter which is fitted to the air cleaner top cover, and unclip it from the support **(see illustrations)**.

33.1b ... and unclip it from the support

33.3a Release the spring clips ...

2 Loosen the clip and disconnect the air outlet hose from the top cover.

3 Release the spring clips and remove the top cover from the air cleaner body **(see illustration)**.

4 Remove the element, noting that it is fitted with its larger section facing downwards **(see illustration)**.

5 Clean the air cleaner body and top cover of dust and dirt and any leaves.

6 Fit the element with its larger section downwards, and refit the top cover, securing it with the spring clips.

7 Reconnect the air outlet hose to the top cover and secure by tightening the clip.

8 Reconnect the wiring to the airflow meter.

33.3b . . . and remove the air cleaner top cover

33.4 Removing the air cleaner element

Every 50 000 miles or 5 years

34 In-tank fuel filter renewal	**1** Refer to Chapter 4B and remove the fuel level sending unit. With the unit placed in a suitable container, use a clean brush to clear any sediment from the filter, then refit the unit.	**2** Where fitted, any in-line filters must also be renewed at this time.

Every 60 000 miles

35 Timing belt renewal	**1** Refer to Chapter 2C.

Every 90 000 miles

36 High-pressure fuel pipes renewal	**1** Refer to Chapter 4B.

Every 180 000 miles

37 High-pressure fuel pump renewal	**1** Refer to Chapter 4B.

Notes

Chapter 2 Part A:
Petrol engines – 2000 and earlier

Contents

Section number

Camshaft oil seal – renewal	9
Camshafts and valve lifters – removal, inspection and refitting	10
Crankshaft left-hand oil seal – renewal	15
Crankshaft right-hand oil seal – renewal	8
Cylinder head – removal and refitting	11
Engine mountings – check and renewal	16
Exhaust manifold – removal and refitting	6
Flywheel/driveplate – removal and refitting	14

Section number

General information	1
Intake manifold – removal and refitting	5
Oil pump – removal, inspection and refitting	13
Repair operations possible with the engine in the vehicle	2
Sump – removal and refitting	12
Timing belt and sprockets – removal, inspection and refitting	7
Top Dead Centre (TDC) for number one piston – locating	3
Valve cover – removal and refitting	4

Degrees of difficulty

Easy, suitable for novice with little experience 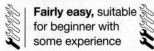	**Fairly easy,** suitable for beginner with some experience	**Fairly difficult,** suitable for competent DIY mechanic	**Difficult,** suitable for experienced DIY mechanic	**Very difficult,** suitable for expert DIY or professional

Specifications

General

Engine designation and capacity:

3S-FE	1998 cc
Cylinder numbers (timing belt end-to-transmission end)	1-2-3-4
Firing order	1-3-4-2

Cylinder head

Warpage limits:

Cylinder head-to-block surface	0.05 mm
Intake and exhaust manifolds	0.08 mm

Camshaft

Journal diameter (all)	26.959 to 26.975 mm
Runout limit	0.04 mm

Bearing oil clearance:

Standard	0.025 to 0.062 mm
Service limit	0.10 mm

Lobe height:

Intake camshaft:

Standard	42.01 to 42.11 mm
Service limit	41.90 mm

Exhaust camshaft:

Standard	40.06 to 40.16 mm
Service limit	39.95 mm

Camshaft thrust clearance (endplay):

Intake camshaft:

Standard	0.045 to 0.100 mm
Service limit	0.12 mm

Exhaust camshaft:

Standard	0.030 to 0.085 mm
Service limit	0.10 mm

Camshaft gear spring end gap	22.5 to 22.9 mm

Camshaft gear backlash:

Standard	0.020 to 0.200 mm
Service limit	0.30 mm

Valve lifter:

Diameter	30.966 to 30.976 mm
Bore diameter	31.000 to 31.016 mm

Lifter oil clearance:

Standard	0.024 to 0.052 mm
Service limit	0.07 mm

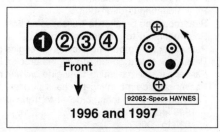

1996 and 1997

Cylinder numbering and distributor rotation

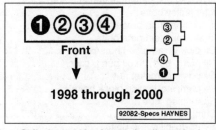

1998 through 2000

Cylinder numbering and coil terminal location

Timing belt

Idler pulley spring free length:
1996 and 1997	46.0 mm
1998 to 2000	42.0 mm

Oil pump

Driven rotor-to-case clearance:
Standard	0.10 to 0.16 mm
Service limit	0.20 mm

Rotor tip clearance:
Standard	0.04 to 0.16 mm
Service limit	0.20 mm

Torque wrench settings

	lbf ft	Nm
Camshaft bearing cap bolts	14	19
Camshaft sprocket bolt	40	54
Crankshaft main oil seal retainer bolts	9	12
Crankshaft pulley-to-crankshaft bolt	80	108
Cylinder head bolts (in sequence – **see illustration 11.23**):		
Step 1	36	49
Step 2	Tighten an additional 90° (1/4 turn)	
Driveplate bolts (automatic transmission)	61	83
Engine balancer assembly mounting bolts	36	49
Engine mountings:		
Front mounting through-bolt	47	64
Front mounting bracket-to-transmission bolts ...	47	64
Front mounting-to-crossmember nuts	59	80
Rear mounting through-bolt	47	64
Rear mounting bracket-to-transmission bolts	47	64
Rear mounting-to-crossmember nuts	82	111
Passenger side mounting bracket-to-engine bolts	38	51
Passenger side mounting-to-engine bracket bolt	27	36
Passenger side mounting-to-engine bracket nuts	38	51
Passenger side mounting-to-chassis bolts	47	64
Left-hand side mounting bracket-to transmission bolts/nuts:		
1996 and 1997	47	64
1998 to 2000	38	51
Left-hand side mounting through bolt	47	64
Exhaust manifold nuts/bolts	36	49
Flywheel bolts (manual transmission)	65	88
Idler pulley bolts	31	42
Intake manifold brace bolts	31	42
Intake manifold nuts/bolts	14	19
Oil pick-up (strainer) nuts/bolts	4	5
Oil pump body to oil pump case	7	9
Oil pump sprocket nut	18	24
Oil pump-to-engine block bolts	7	9
Spark plug tube nuts	33	45
Sump-to-block bolts	4	5
Sump-to-oil pump bolts	4	5

1 General information

This Part of Chapter 2 is devoted to in-vehicle repair procedures for the 2000 and earlier four-cylinder engine. All information concerning engine removal, refitting and overhaul can be found in Part C of this Chapter.

The following repair procedures are based on the assumption that the engine is fitted in the vehicle. If the engine has been removed from the vehicle and mounted on a stand, many of the steps outlined in this Part of Chapter 2 will not apply.

The Specifications included in this Part of Chapter 2 apply only to the in vehicle procedures contained in this Part. Part D of Chapter 2 contains the general Specifications for all the engines covered by this manual.

During the years covered by this manual, the 2000 and earlier four-cylinder engine in the RAV4 is designated the 3S-FE. This engine design includes dual overhead camshafts (DOHC), four valves per cylinder and a timing belt which drives the camshafts.

2 Repair operations possible with the engine in the vehicle

Many major repair operations can be accomplished without removing the engine from the vehicle.

Clean the engine compartment and the exterior of the engine with some type of degreaser before any work is done. It will make the job easier and help keep dirt out of the internal areas of the engine.

Depending on the components involved,

it may be helpful to remove the bonnet to improve access to the engine as repairs are performed (refer to Chapter 11 if necessary). Cover the wings to prevent damage to the paint. Special pads are available, but an old bedspread or blanket will also work.

If vacuum, exhaust, oil or coolant leaks develop, indicating a need for gasket or seal renewal, the repairs can generally be made with the engine in the vehicle. The intake and exhaust manifold gaskets, sump gasket, crankshaft oil seals and cylinder head gasket are all accessible with the engine in place.

Exterior engine components, such as the intake and exhaust manifolds, the sump, the oil pump, the water pump, the starter motor, the alternator and the fuel system components can be removed for repair with the engine in place.

Since the cylinder head can be removed without removing the engine, camshaft and valve component servicing can also be accomplished with the engine in the vehicle. Renewal of the timing belt and pulleys is also possible with the engine in the vehicle.

3 Top Dead Centre (TDC) for number one piston – locating

1 Top Dead Centre (TDC) is the highest point in the cylinder that each piston reaches as it travels up-and-down when the crankshaft turns. Each piston reaches TDC on the compression stroke and again on the exhaust stroke, but TDC generally refers to piston position on the compression stroke. The timing marks on the vibration damper fitted on the end of the crankshaft are referenced to the number one piston at TDC on the compression stroke.

2 Positioning the piston(s) at TDC is an essential part of procedures such as valve adjustment and timing belt and sprocket renewal.

3 In order to bring any piston to TDC, the crankshaft must be turned using one of the methods outlined below. When looking at the timing belt end of the engine, normal crankshaft rotation is clockwise.

⚠ **Warning: Before beginning this procedure, be sure to place the transmission in Neutral and remove the ignition key.**

a) The preferred method is to turn the crankshaft with a large socket and bar attached to the large bolt threaded into the center of the crankshaft pulley.
b) If an assistant is available to turn the ignition switch to the Start position in short bursts, you can get the piston close to TDC. Use a socket and bar as described in Paragraph a) to complete the procedure.

4 Disable the ignition system by disconnecting the primary electrical connectors at the ignition coil pack/modules (see Chapter 5).

5 Remove the spark plugs and fit a compression gauge in the number one cylinder. Turn the crankshaft clockwise with a socket and bar as described above.

6 When the piston approaches TDC, compression will be noted on the compression gauge. Continue turning the crankshaft until the notch in the crankshaft damper is aligned with the TDC mark on the front cover (see illustration). At this point number one cylinder is at TDC on the compression stroke. If the marks aligned but there was no compression, the piston was on the exhaust stroke. Continue rotating the crankshaft 360° (one complete turn).

7 After the number one piston has been positioned at TDC on the compression stroke, TDC for any of the remaining cylinders can be located by turning the crankshaft 180° and following the firing order (refer to the Specifications). Rotating the engine 180° past TDC No 1 will put the engine at TDC compression for cylinder No 3.

4 Valve cover – removal and refitting

Removal

1 Disconnect the negative cable from the battery.

2 Detach the breather hose from the valve cover.

3 Remove the HT leads from the spark plugs, handling them by the boots, not pulling on the leads.

4 Remove the wiring harness bolts at the timing belt cover and move the harness aside. Also remove the accelerator cable bracket from the intake manifold and position it aside to allow access for valve cover removal.

5 Remove the spark plug tube nuts, then detach the cover and gasket from the head. The spark plug tube nuts are used to hold the cover in place (see illustration). If the cover is stuck to the head, bump the end with a block of wood and a hammer to jar it loose. If that doesn't work, try to slip a flexible putty knife between the head and cover to break the seal.

4.5 The valve cover is held in place by the large spark plug tube nuts (arrows)

3.6 Align the crankshaft drivebelt pulley notch (arrow) with the 0 on the timing plate

Caution: Don't lever at the cover-to-head joint or damage to the sealing surfaces may occur, leading to oil leaks after the cover is refitted.

Refitting

6 The mating surfaces of the housing or cylinder head and cover must be clean when the cover is refitted. Use a gasket scraper to remove all traces of sealant and old gasket material, then clean the mating surfaces with lacquer thinner or acetone. If there's residue or oil on the mating surfaces when the cover is refitted, oil leaks may develop.

7 Apply RTV sealant to the gasket/seal joints (see illustration). Fit the spark plug tube grommets in the valve cover with the index marks facing the timing belt end of the engine.

8 Position a new valve cover gasket on the cylinder head, then refit the valve cover and spark plug tube nuts.

9 Tighten the spark plug tube nuts to the torque listed in this Chapter's Specifications in three or four equal steps.

10 Refit the remaining parts, run the engine and check for oil leaks.

5 Intake manifold – removal and refitting

⚠ *Warning: Wait until the engine is completely cool before beginning this procedure.*

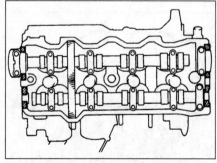

4.7 Apply sealant to the eight points indicated by the shaded areas before installing the valve cover

5.5a The various hoses should be marked to ensure correct reinstallation

5.5b Press in on the clips to release the wiring harness retainers

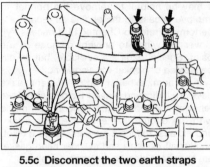

5.5c Disconnect the two earth straps (arrows) from the bulkhead side of the intake manifold, then disconnect the knock sensor

5.6a Remove the bolts (arrows) from the intake manifold-to-block braces (seen from below)

5.6b Disconnect the electrical connectors from the coil pack, then remove the mounting bolts (arrows) and remove the coil pack mount/intake brace

11 Refit the remaining parts in the reverse order of removal.
12 Before starting the engine, check the throttle linkage for smooth operation.
13 Check the coolant and add some, if necessary, to bring it to the appropriate level. Run the engine and check for coolant and vacuum leaks.
14 Road test the vehicle and check for proper operation of all accessories, including the cruise control system.

6 Exhaust manifold – removal and refitting

> ⚠ **Warning: The engine must be completely cool before beginning this procedure.**

Removal

Removal

1 Disconnect the negative cable from the battery.
2 Loosen the air cleaner hose clamp at the throttle body and remove the air cleaner top (four clamps), resonator and hose.
3 Disconnect the coolant hoses from the throttle body and plug them to prevent coolant leakage.
4 Remove the EGR valve and the vacuum modulator valve (see Chapter 6A) from the intake manifold.
5 Label and detach any wire harness and control cables or hoses connected to the intake manifold and the throttle body (see illustrations). Carefully lift the wire harness over the manifold.
6 Unbolt the intake manifold-to-engine braces (see illustrations).

7 Remove the mounting nuts/bolts (see illustration), then detach the manifold from the engine.

Refitting

8 Use a scraper to remove all traces of old gasket material and sealant from the manifold and cylinder head (see illustration), then clean the mating surfaces with lacquer thinner or acetone. If the gasket was leaking, have the manifold checked for warpage at an engine reconditioning specialist and resurfaced if necessary.
9 Fit a new gasket, then position the manifold on the head and insert the nuts/bolts.
10 Tighten the nuts/bolts in three or four equal steps to the torque listed in this Chapter's Specifications. Work from the centre out towards the ends to avoid warping the manifold.

1 Disconnect the negative cable from the battery.
2 Unplug the oxygen sensor wire harness and the clamp over the harness. If you're fitting a new exhaust manifold, remove the sensor (see Chapter 6A).
3 Remove the upper heat insulator from the manifold (see illustration).
4 Apply penetrating oil to the exhaust manifold mounting nuts/bolts.
5 Disconnect the exhaust pipe from the exhaust manifold (see Chapter 4A).
6 Remove the exhaust manifold brace (some models have two braces) and lower heat insulator (see illustration).

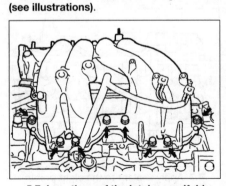

5.7 Locations of the intake manifold bolts/nuts

5.8 Remove all traces of old gasket material and sealant with a scraper – be careful not to gouge the aluminium manifold

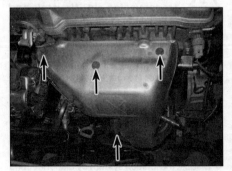

6.3 Remove the exhaust manifold heat insulator bolts (arrows)

7 Remove the nuts and detach the manifold and gasket (see illustration).

Refitting

8 Use a scraper to remove all traces of old gasket material and carbon deposits from the manifold and cylinder head mating surfaces. If the gasket was leaking, have the manifold checked for warpage at an engine reconditioning specialist and resurfaced if necessary.

9 Position a new gasket over the cylinder head studs.

10 Refit the manifold and thread the mounting nuts into place.

11 Working from the centre out, tighten the nuts to the torque listed in this Chapter's Specifications in three or four equal steps.

12 Refit the remaining parts in the reverse order of removal.

13 Run the engine and check for exhaust leaks.

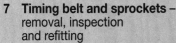

7 Timing belt and sprockets – removal, inspection and refitting

Removal

1 Disconnect the negative cable from the battery.

2 Chock the rear wheels and apply the handbrake.

3 Loosen the nuts on the right front wheel and raise the vehicle. Support the front of the vehicle securely on axle stands.

4 Remove the right front wheel and the lower splash shield.

5 Remove the power steering reservoir tank and bracket (see Chapter 10). If equipped with ABS brakes, remove the ABS actuator and bracket (see Chapter 9).

6 Remove the spark plugs and auxiliary drivebelts (see Chapter 1A).

7 Remove the alternator and bracket (see Chapter 5). Also disconnect the wire harness bracket for the diagnostic socket.

8 Support the engine from underneath with a jack (use a wood block on the jack and place the block under the sump) and remove the right engine mounting and engine support rod (see Section 16)

9 Remove the upper timing belt cover screws, pull up the wiring harness (see Section 4) and remove the upper (No 2) timing belt cover and gaskets (see illustration).

10 Position the number one piston at TDC on the compression stroke (see Section 3). Make sure the small hole in the camshaft pulley is aligned with the TDC mark on the cam bearing cap (see illustration).

11 If you plan to re-use the timing belt, apply match marks on the sprocket and belt and an arrow indicating direction of travel on the belt (see illustration).

12 Loosen the upper (No 1) idler pulley set bolt and unhook the spring (see illustration). Slip the timing belt off the sprocket. If you're

6.6 Unbolt the exhaust manifold flange brace (arrow) near the front engine mount

6.7 Remove the exhaust manifold nuts (arrows) at the cylinder head

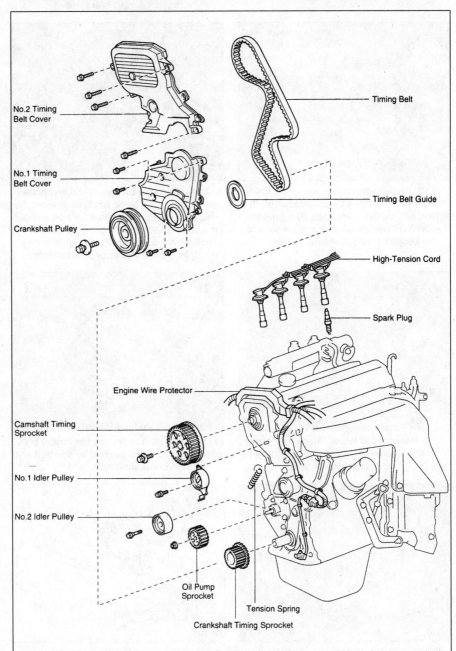

7.9 Timing belt components

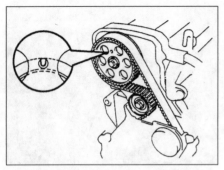

7.10 Align the upper camshaft sprocket timing marks with the number 1 cylinder at TDC

7.11 If you intend to re-use the timing belt, apply match marks on the camshaft sprocket and belt (arrow)

7.12 Loosen the upper idler pulley set bolt (arrow) and unhook the spring

7.13 Remove the valve cover and hold the camshaft with a large spanner on the raised hex as the sprocket bolt is loosened – DO NOT use the timing belt tension to keep the sprocket from turning

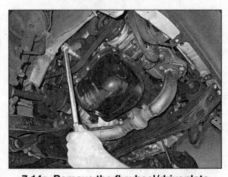

7.14a Remove the flywheel/driveplate cover and use a lever wedged against the ring gear teeth or a converter bolt to hold the crankshaft while loosening the pulley bolt with a socket bar – the bolt is very tight, so use the appropriate tools

7.14b Often the crankshaft pulley can be removed with even applications of a lever – if you use a puller, it must be the type that attaches to the hub only (do not use a jaw-type puller)

7.15 Remove the lower timing belt cover bolts (arrows) and slip the cover and gaskets off the engine

7.16 If you plan to re-use the timing belt, apply match marks (arrow) on the belt and crankshaft sprocket

7.17a The crankshaft sprocket should slide off the crankshaft easily

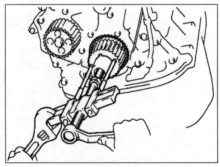

7.17b If the crankshaft sprocket is stuck, remove it with a puller

removing the upper part of the belt only, for camshaft seal renewal or cylinder head removal, it isn't necessary to detach the belt from the crankshaft sprocket.

13 If the camshaft sprocket is worn or damaged, remove the valve cover, hold the rear (intake) camshaft with a large spanner and remove the bolt, then detach the sprocket (see illustration).

14 Remove the crankshaft pulley bolt. With the flywheel inspection cover removed, wedge a large screwdriver into the flywheel/driveplate ring gear teeth or against a converter bolt to keep the engine from turning. Use a bar and socket to loosen the pulley bolt (see illustration). Remove the bolt and detach the pulley with levers or a vibration damper puller (see illustration). Do not use an outside-jaw gear puller. Before the pulley is removed completely, double-check that the crankshaft is still at TDC.

15 Remove the lower (No 1) timing belt cover and gaskets (see illustration) and slip the belt guide off the crankshaft.

16 If you plan to re-use the timing belt, apply match marks on the crankshaft sprocket and belt (see illustration).

17 Slip the timing belt off the sprocket and remove it. If the sprocket is worn or damaged, or if you need to renew the crankshaft oil seal, remove the sprocket from the crankshaft (see illustrations).

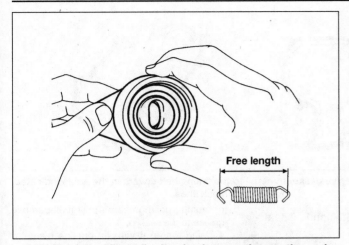

7.18 Check the idler pulley bearing for smooth operation and measure the free length of the tension spring for comparison to this Chapter's Specifications

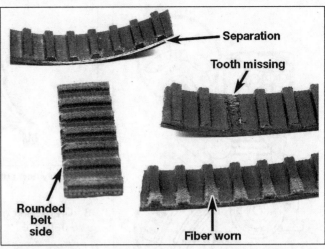

7.20 Check the timing belt for cracked and missing teeth – wear on one side of the belt indicates sprocket misalignment problems

Inspection

Caution: Do not bend, twist or turn the timing belt inside out. Do not allow it to come in contact with oil, coolant or fuel. Do not utilise timing belt tension to keep the camshaft or crankshaft from turning when fitting the sprocket bolt(s). Do not turn the crankshaft or camshaft more than a few degrees (if necessary for tooth alignment) while the timing belt is removed.

18 Remove the idler pulleys and check the bearings for smooth operation and excessive play. Inspect the spring for damage and compare the free length to this Chapter's Specifications **(see illustration)**.

19 If the timing belt broke during engine operation, the belt may have been contaminated or overtightened.

20 If the belt teeth are cracked or missing **(see illustration)**, the water pump, oil pump or camshaft(s) may have seized.

Caution: If the timing belt broke during engine operation, the valves may have come in contact with the pistons, causing damage. Check the valve clearance (see Chapter 1A) – bent valves usually will have excessive clearance, indicating damage that will require head removal to repair.

21 If there is noticeable wear or cracks on the face of the belt, check to see if there are nicks or burrs on the idler pulleys.

22 If there is wear or damage on only one side of the belt, check the belt guide and the alignment of the sprockets.

23 Renew the timing belt if obvious wear or damage is noted or if it is the least bit questionable. Correct any problems which contributed to belt failure prior to belt refitting.

Note: Professionals recommend renewing the belt whenever it is removed, since belt failure can lead to expensive engine damage. The manufacturer recommends changing the belt at 60 000 mile intervals.

Refitting

24 Remove all dirt, oil and grease from the timing belt area at the front of the engine.

25 If they were removed, refit the idler pulleys and tension spring. The upper (No 1) idler should be pulled back against spring tension as far as possible and the bolt temporarily tightened. Also refit the crankshaft and camshaft sprockets if removed. The crankshaft sprocket must be fitted with the crankshaft sensor teeth facing inward toward the oil pump.

26 Recheck the camshaft and crankshaft timing marks to be sure they are properly aligned. The small hole in the camshaft sprocket must be aligned with the mark on the camshaft bearing cap (see Paragraph 10) and the crankshaft sprocket must be aligned with the keyway facing straight up with the No 1 piston at TDC.

27 Fit the timing belt on the crankshaft, oil pump, water pump and idler pulleys. If the original belt is being refitted, align the marks made during removal (see paragraphs 11 and 16).

28 Slip the belt guide onto the crankshaft with the cupped side facing out **(see illustration)**.

29 Refit the lower timing belt cover and

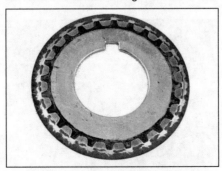

7.28 The belt guide should be installed with the tooth marks in contact with the timing belt and the cupped side facing out

crankshaft pulley and recheck the TDC marks.

30 Slip the timing belt over the camshaft sprocket. Keep tension on the side nearest the front of the vehicle **(see illustration)**. If the original belt is being refitted, align the marks made during removal.

31 Loosen the upper (No 1) idler pulley bolt 1/2-turn, allowing the spring to apply pressure to the idler pulley.

32 Slowly turn the crankshaft clockwise 1-7/8 revolutions until the crank pulley mark lines up with the 45° BTDC (before TDC for number one cylinder) mark on the lower belt cover, then tighten the idler pulley bolt to the torque listed in this Chapter's Specifications.

33 Rotate the crankshaft 2-1/8 revolutions to TDC and recheck the timing marks **(see illustration)**. With the crankshaft at TDC for number one cylinder, the camshaft sprocket hole must line up with the timing mark. If the marks are not aligned exactly as shown, repeat the belt refitting procedure.

Caution: DO NOT start the engine until you're absolutely certain that the timing

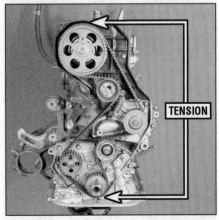

7.30 There should be moderate tension on the side of the belt facing the front of the vehicle

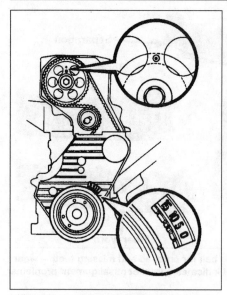

7.33 The marks should align as shown at Top Dead Centre

belt is fitted correctly. Serious and costly engine damage could occur if the belt is fitted wrong.

34 Refit the remaining parts in the reverse order of removal. **Note:** *When refitting the covers, if the sealing material is cut or compressed, clean the covers and apply new self-stick gasket material (see illustration).*

35 Run the engine and check for proper operation.

8.2a Wrap tape around the screwdriver tip and carefully work the crankshaft oil seal out of the bore – DO NOT nick or scratch the crankshaft in the process

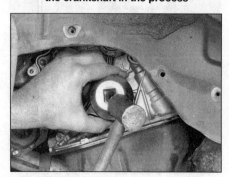

8.4 Gently drive the new seal into place with the spring side facing into the engine

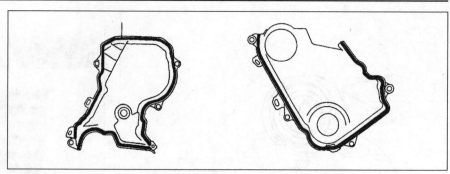

7.34 Apply new adhesive gasket material to the timing belt covers in the areas indicated by the thick black lines

8 Crankshaft right-hand oil seal – renewal

1 Remove the timing belt and crankshaft sprocket (see Section 7).

2 Note how far the seal is recessed in the bore, then carefully lever it out of the oil pump housing with a screwdriver or seal removal tool **(see illustration)**. Don't scratch the housing bore or damage the crankshaft in the process (if the crankshaft is damaged, the new seal will end up leaking). **Note:** *The seal may be easier to remove if the old seal lip is cut with a sharp utility knife first **(see illustration)**.*

3 Clean the bore in the housing and coat the outer edge of the new seal with engine oil

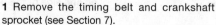

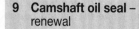

Cut Position

8.2b The seal may be removed more easily by carefully cutting the lip as indicated

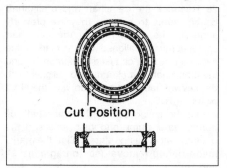

9.3 Carefully lever the camshaft seal out of the bore – DO NOT nick or scratch the camshaft journal

or multipurpose grease. Apply multipurpose grease to the seal lip.

4 Using a socket with an outside diameter slightly smaller than the outside diameter of the seal, carefully drive the new seal into place with a hammer **(see illustration)**. Make sure it's fitted squarely and driven in to the same depth as the original. If a socket isn't available, a short section of large diameter pipe will also work. Check the seal after refitting to make sure the spring didn't pop out of place.

5 Refit the crankshaft sprocket and timing belt (see Section 7).

6 Run the engine and check for oil leaks at the seal.

9 Camshaft oil seal – renewal

1 Remove the timing belt, upper idler pulley, and camshaft sprocket (see Section 7).

2 Remove the rear timing belt cover.

3 Note how far the seal is seated in the bore, then carefully lever it out with a small screwdriver **(see illustration)**. Don't scratch the bore or damage the camshaft in the process (if the camshaft is damaged, the new seal will end up leaking).

4 Clean the bore and coat the outer edge of the new seal with engine oil or multipurpose grease. Apply multipurpose grease to the seal lip.

5 Using a socket with an outside diameter slightly smaller than the outside diameter of the seal, carefully drive the new seal into place with a hammer. Make sure it's fitted squarely and driven in to the same depth as the original. If a socket isn't available, a short section of pipe will also work.

6 Refit the timing belt rear cover, camshaft sprocket, and timing belt (see Section 7).

7 Run the engine and check for oil leaks at the camshaft seal.

10 Camshafts and valve lifters – removal, inspection and refitting

Note: *Before beginning this procedure, obtain two 6 x 1.0 mm bolts, 16 to 20 mm long. They will be referred to as 'service bolts' in the text.*

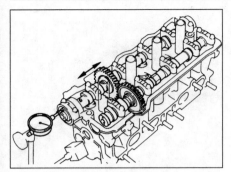

10.4 Mount a dial indicator as shown to measure camshaft endplay

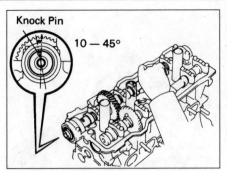

10.5 Turn the intake camshaft until the knock pin is 10° to 45° to the left of 12 o'clock position

10.6 Install a service bolt through the sub-gear, into the main gear (arrow)

Removal

1 Remove the valve cover as described in Section 4.

2 Remove the distributor (see Chapter 5) if equipped.

3 Remove the timing belt, camshaft sprocket and rear timing belt cover (see Sections 7 and 9).

4 Measure the camshaft thrust clearance (endplay) with a dial indicator **(see illustration)**. If the clearance is greater than the service limit, renew the camshaft and/or the cylinder head.

Exhaust camshaft

5 Position the knock pin in the INTAKE camshaft at 10° to 45° left of vertical **(see illustration)**. This will position the exhaust camshaft lobes so the camshaft will be pushed out evenly by the valve spring pressure.

6 Secure the exhaust camshaft sub-gear to the main gear by fitting one of the service bolts into a threaded hole **(see illustration)**.

7 Remove the transmission end exhaust camshaft bearing cap bolts and detach the bearing cap.

8 Loosen the number 1, 2 and 4 exhaust camshaft bearing cap bolts in 1/4-turn increments until the bolts can be removed by hand. Lift off the first, second and fourth bearing caps.

9 Finally, loosen the number 3 bearing cap bolts in 1/4-turn increments until they can be removed by hand, then detach the No 3 cap.

Caution: As the bearing cap bolts are

being loosened, make sure the camshaft is moving up evenly. If one end or the other stops moving and the cam gets cocked, start again by refitting the bearing caps and resetting the knock pin. DO NOT try to lever or force the camshaft out.

10 Lift the camshaft straight up and out of the head.

11 To disassemble the exhaust camshaft gear, mount it in a vice with the jaws gripping the large hex on the shaft.

12 Fit a second service bolt in the unthreaded hole in the camshaft sub-gear. Using a screwdriver positioned against the service bolt just fitted, rotate the sub-gear clockwise and remove the first service bolt from the threaded hole.

13 Remove the sub-gear snap-ring.

14 The wave washer, sub-gear and camshaft gear spring can now be removed from the camshaft.

Intake camshaft

15 Position the knock pin in the intake camshaft at 80° to 115° left of vertical **(see illustration)**.

16 Remove the timing belt end intake camshaft bearing cap bolts and detach the bearing cap and oil seal.

Caution: Do not lever the cap off. If it doesn't come loose easily, leave it in place without bolts.

17 Loosen the number 1, 3 and 4 intake camshaft bearing cap bolts in 1/4-turn increments until the bolts can be removed by

hand. Lift off the first, third and fourth bearing caps.

18 Finally, loosen the number 2 bearing cap bolts in 1/4-turn increments until they can be removed by hand, then detach the No 2 bearing cap.

Caution: As the bearing cap bolts are being loosened, make sure the camshaft is moving up evenly. If one end or the other stops moving and the cam gets cocked, start again by refitting the bearing caps and resetting the knock pin. DO NOT try to lever or force the camshaft out.

19 Lift the camshaft straight up and out of the head.

Inspection

20 Measure the end gap (distance between the ends) of the camshaft gear spring **(see illustration)** and compare it to this Chapter's Specifications. If not as specified, renew the spring.

21 Carefully label, then remove the valve lifters and shims **(see illustration)**.

22 Inspect each lifter for scuffing and score marks **(see illustration)**.

23 Measure the outside diameter of each lifter and the corresponding lifter bore inside diameter. Subtract the lifter diameter from the lifter bore diameter to determine the oil clearance. Compare it to this Chapter's Specifications. If the oil clearance is excessive, a new head and/or new lifters will be required.

24 Store the lifters in a clean box, separated from each other, so they won't be damaged.

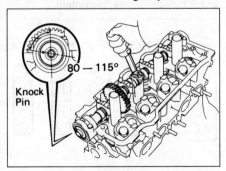

10.15 Turn the intake camshaft until the knock pin is 80° to 115° to the left of the 12 o'clock position

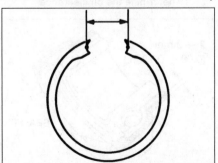

10.20 Measure the distance between the ends of the camshaft gear spring

10.21 Wipe the oil off the valve shims and mark the intakes I and the exhausts E – a magnetic tool works well for removing lifters

10.22 Wipe off the oil and inspect each lifter for wear and scuffing

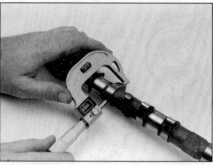

10.26 Measure the lobe heights on each camshaft – if any lobe height is less than the specified allowable minimum, renew that camshaft

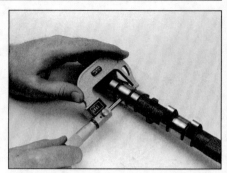

10.27 Measure each journal diameter with a micrometer (if any journal measures less than the specified limit, renew the camshaft)

Make sure the shims stay with the lifters (don't mix them up).

25 Visually examine the cam lobes and bearing journals for score marks, pitting, galling and evidence of overheating (blue, discoloured areas). Look for flaking away of the hardened surface layer of each lobe.

26 Using a micrometer, measure the height of each camshaft lobe **(see illustration)**. Compare your measurements with this Chapter's Specifications. If the height for any one lobe is less than the specified minimum, renew the camshaft.

27 Using a micrometer, measure the diameter of each journal at several points **(see illustration)**. Compare your measurements with this Chapter's Specifications. If the diameter of any one journal is less than specified, renew the camshaft.

28 Check the oil clearance for each camshaft journal as follows:
a) Clean the bearing caps and the camshaft journals with lacquer thinner or acetone.
b) Carefully lay the camshaft(s) in place in the head. Don't fit the lifters and don't use any lubrication.
c) Lay a strip of Plastigauge on each journal **(see illustration)**.
d) Refit the bearing caps with the arrows pointing toward the timing belt end of the engine.
e) Tighten the bolts to the specified torque in 1/4-turn increments. **Note:** Don't turn the camshaft while the Plastigauge is in place.
f) Remove the bolts and detach the caps.
g) Compare the width of the crushed Plastigauge (at its widest point) to the

scale on the Plastigage envelope **(see illustration)**.
h) If the clearance is greater than specified, renew the camshaft and/or cylinder head.
i) Scrape off the Plastigauge with your fingernail or the edge of a credit card – don't scratch or nick the journals or bearing caps.

29 Temporarily refit the camshafts without fitting the lifters or exhaust camshaft sub-gear.

30 Measure the gear backlash (the free play between the gear teeth) with a dial indicator **(see illustration)** and compare it to this Chapter's Specifications.

Refitting

Intake camshaft

31 Apply moly-base grease or engine assembly lubricant to the lifters, then refit them in their original locations. Make sure the valve adjustment shims are in place in the lifters.

32 Apply moly-base grease or engine assembly lubricant to the camshaft lobes and bearing journals.

33 Position the intake camshaft in the cylinder head with the knock pin 80-degrees to the left of vertical **(see illustration 10.15)**.

34 Apply a thin coat of RTV sealant to the outer edge of the front bearing cap-to-cylinder head mating surface **(see illustration)**. **Note:** The cap must be fitted immediately or the sealer will dry prematurely.

35 Refit the bearing caps in numerical order with the arrows pointing toward the timing belt end of the engine **(see illustration)**.

10.28a Lay a strip of Plastigauge on each camshaft journal

10.28b Compare the width of the crushed Plastigauge to the scale on the envelope to determine the oil clearance

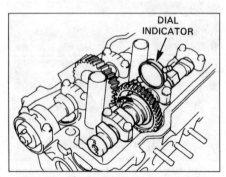

10.30 Position a dial indicator as shown here to measure gear backlash

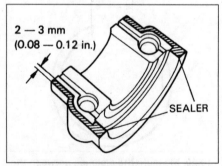

10.34 Apply sealant to the shaded areas of the front intake camshaft bearing cap

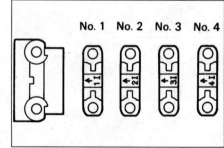

10.35 Intake camshaft bearing cap arrangement – the arrows point toward the timing belt end of the engine

36 Following the recommended tightening sequence **(see illustration)**, tighten the bearing cap bolts in 1/4-turn increments to the torque listed in this Chapter's Specifications.

37 Refer to Section 9 and fit a new camshaft oil seal.

Exhaust camshaft

38 Reassemble the exhaust camshaft gear. Refit the cam gear spring, sub-gear and wave washer in the gear. Secure them with the snap-ring.

39 Fit the service bolt in the unthreaded hole, turn the sub-gear with a screwdriver and fit the second service bolt in the threaded hole. Tighten it to clamp the sub-gear to the camshaft gear, then remove the first bolt.

40 Apply moly-base grease or engine assembly lubricant to the lifters, then refit them in their original locations. Make sure the valve adjustment shims are in place in the lifters.

41 Apply moly-base grease or engine assembly lubricant to the camshaft lobes and bearing journals.

42 Rotate the INTAKE camshaft until the knock pin is positioned 10-degrees to the left of vertical **(see illustration 10.5)**.

43 Align the exhaust camshaft gear with the intake camshaft gear by matching up the timing marks on the gears **(see illustration)**. *Caution: There are also assembly reference marks on each gear, above the timing marks – do not mistake them for the timing marks.*

44 Roll the exhaust camshaft down into position. Turn the intake camshaft back-and-forth a little until the exhaust camshaft sits in the bearings evenly.

45 Refit the bearing caps in numerical order with the arrows pointing toward the timing belt end of the engine **(see illustration)**.

46 Following the recommended sequence **(see illustration)**, tighten the bearing cap bolts in 1/4-turn increments to the torque listed in this Chapter's Specifications.

47 Remove the service bolt from the camshaft gear.

48 Remove and refit the semi-circular plugs into the cylinder head with new packing material. Refit the rear timing belt cover on the cylinder head and the timing belt sprocket on the intake camshaft and tighten the bolt to the torque listed in this Chapter's Specifications. Prevent the camshaft from turning by holding it with a spanner on the large hex **(see illustration 7.13)**.

49 Refit the timing belt (see Section 7).

50 The remainder of refitting is the reverse of the removal procedure.

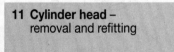

11 Cylinder head –
removal and refitting

Note: *The engine must be completely cool before beginning this procedure.*

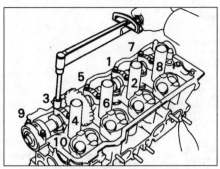

10.36 INLET camshaft bearing cap bolt tightening sequence

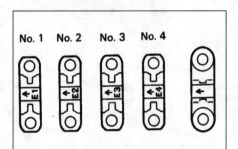

10.45 Exhaust camshaft bearing cap arrangement – the arrows point toward the timing belt end of the engine

Removal

1 Relieve the fuel system pressure (see Chapter 4A) then, disconnect the negative cable from the battery.

2 Drain the coolant from the engine block and radiator (see Chapter 1A).

3 Drain the engine oil and remove the oil filter (see Chapter 1A).

4 Remove the air cleaner housing. Also remove the fuel rail and fuel injectors (see Chapter 4A).

5 Remove the intake manifold (see Section 5).

6 Remove the exhaust manifold (see Section 6).

7 Remove the timing belt, camshaft sprocket and upper idler pulley (see Section 7).

8 Remove the rear timing belt cover. **Note:** *Disconnect the camshaft position sensor at this time (see Chapter 6A).*

9 Remove the camshafts and lifters (see Section 10).

11.12a If the head is stuck, lever only at the overhang, not between the mating surfaces

10.43 Align the camshaft timing gears as shown here

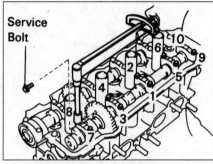

10.46 EXHAUST camshaft bearing cap bolt tightening sequence

10 Label and remove any remaining items, such as coolant fittings, tubes, cables, hoses or wires **(see illustration 5.5a)**. At this point the head should be ready for removal.

11 Using an 8 mm hex head socket bit and a bar, loosen the cylinder head bolts in 1/4-turn increments until they can be removed by hand. Loosen the cylinder head bolts **opposite** of the recommended tightening sequence **(see illustration 11.23)** to avoid warping or cracking the head.

12 Lift the cylinder head off the engine block. If it's stuck, very carefully lever up at the transmission end, beyond the gasket surface **(see illustrations)**.

13 Remove all external components from the head to allow for thorough cleaning.

Refitting

14 The mating surfaces of the cylinder head and block must be perfectly clean when the head is refitted.

15 Use a gasket scraper to remove all traces of carbon and old gasket material **(see illustration)**, then clean the mating surfaces with lacquer thinner or acetone. If there's oil on the mating surfaces when the head is refitted, the gasket may not seal correctly and leaks could develop. When working on the block, stuff the cylinders with clean rags to keep out debris. Use a vacuum cleaner to remove material that falls into the cylinders.

16 Check the block and head mating surfaces for nicks, deep scratches and other damage. If damage is slight, it can be removed with a file; if it's excessive, machining may be the only alternative.

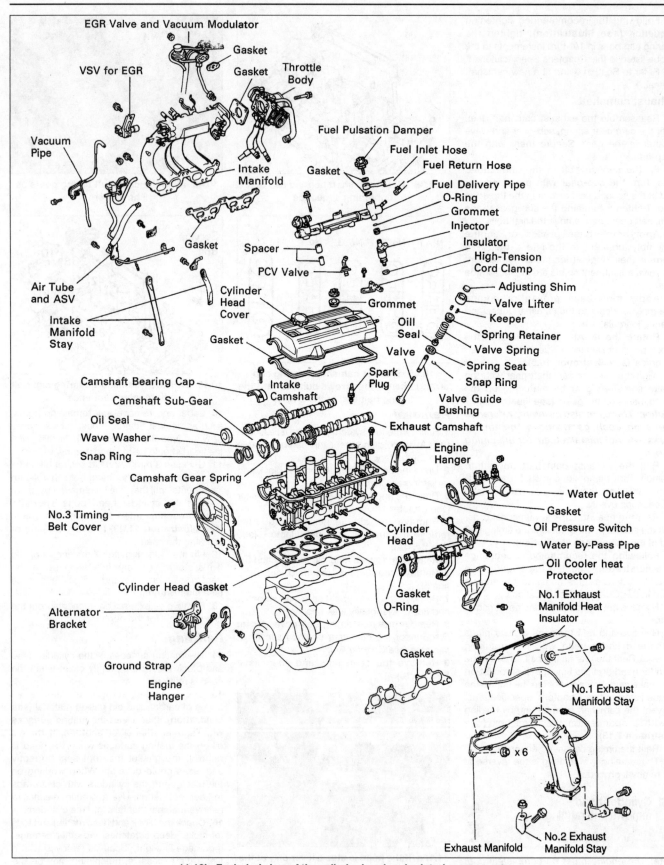

11.12b Exploded view of the cylinder head and related components

11.15 Remove all traces of old gasket material – the cylinder head and block mating surfaces must be perfectly clean to ensure a good gasket seal

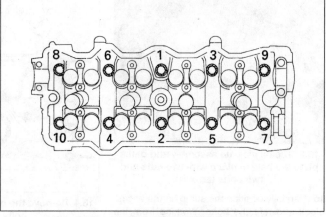

11.23 Cylinder head bolt TIGHTENING sequence

17 Use a tap of the correct size to chase the threads in the cylinder head bolt holes, then clean the holes with compressed air – make sure that nothing remains in the holes.

 Warning: Wear eye protection when using compressed air.

18 Use a wire brush on the bolt threads to remove corrosion and restore the threads. Dirt, corrosion, sealant and damaged threads will affect torque readings.
19 Refit the components that were removed from the head.
20 Position the new gasket over the dowel pins in the block.
21 Carefully set the head on the block without disturbing the gasket.
22 Before fitting the head bolts, apply a small amount of clean engine oil to the threads.
23 Fit the bolts in their original locations and tighten them finger tight. Following the recommended sequence, tighten the bolts to the torque listed in this Chapter's Specifications **(see illustration)**. Note: *The bolts should be lightly oiled on the threads and under the heads, and washers must be used.*
24 The remaining refitting steps are the reverse of removal.
25 Check and adjust the valves as necessary (see Chapter 1A).
26 Refill the cooling system, fit a new oil filter

and add oil to the engine (see Chapter 1A).
27 Run the engine and check for leaks. Set the ignition timing (see Chapter 5) and road test the vehicle.

12 Sump – removal and refitting

Removal

1 Disconnect the negative cable from the battery.
2 Apply the handbrake and chock the rear wheels.
3 Raise the front of the vehicle and support it securely on axle stands.
4 Remove the splash shields under the engine, if equipped.
5 Drain the engine oil and remove the oil filter (see Chapter 1A). Remove the oil dipstick.
6 Disconnect the three nuts holding the front exhaust pipe to the exhaust manifold, then the two bolts/nuts where the converter attaches to the rest of the exhaust system (see Chapter 4A).
7 Unbolt the two bolts and remove the support bracket, then remove the front exhaust pipe. Remove the brace from the exhaust manifold (see Section 6).

8 Remove the front (radiator side) block-to-transmission brace **(see illustration)**.
9 Remove the bolts and detach the sump. If it's stuck, lever it loose very carefully with a small screwdriver or putty knife **(see illustration)**. Don't damage the mating surfaces of the sump and block or oil leaks could develop.

Refitting

10 Use a scraper to remove all traces of old gasket material and sealant from the block and sump. Clean the mating surfaces with lacquer thinner or acetone.
11 Make sure the threaded bolt holes in the block are clean.
12 Check the sump flange for distortion, particularly around the bolt holes. If necessary, place the pan on a block of wood and use a hammer to flatten and restore the gasket surface.
13 Inspect the oil pump pick-up tube assembly for cracks and a blocked strainer. If the pick-up was removed, clean it thoroughly and refit it now, using a new O-ring or gasket. Tighten the nuts/bolts to the torque listed in this Chapter's Specifications.
14 Apply a 5 mm wide bead of RTV sealant to the sump flange **(see illustration)**. Note: *The sump must be fitted within 5 minutes once the sealant has been applied.*

12.8 Remove the bolts (arrows) on the front (radiator side) block-to-transmission brace

12.9 Carefully lever the sump away from the block – if the mating surfaces are damaged, oil leaks could develop

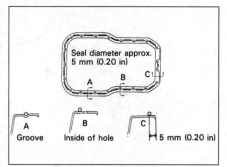

12.14 Apply a bead of RTV sealant to the sump flange

13.2 The oil pick-up assembly and baffle plate are held in place with two nuts and two bolts (arrows)

15 Carefully position the sump on the engine block and refit the bolts. Working from the centre out, tighten them to the torque listed in this Chapter's Specifications in three or four steps.

16 The remainder of refitting is the reverse of removal. Be sure to add oil and fit a new

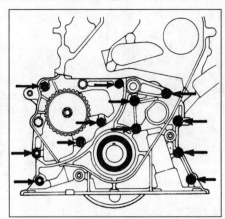

13.4 Remove the oil pump case-to-block bolts (arrows)

oil filter. Use new 'doughnut' gaskets on each end of the front exhaust pipe.

17 Run the engine and check for oil pressure and leaks.

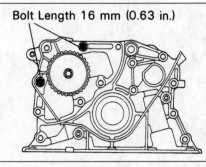

13.5a Remove the oil pump body-to-oil pump case bolts

Bolt Length 16 mm (0.63 in.)

13 Oil pump – removal, inspection and refitting

Removal

1 Remove the sump (see Section 12).

2 Remove the nuts/bolts and detach the oil pick-up tube assembly **(see illustration)**.

3 Support the engine securely from above and remove the lower idler pulley, crankshaft pulley, timing belt, and crankshaft sprocket (see Section 7).

4 Remove the 12 bolts and detach the oil pump housing from the engine **(see illustration)**. You may have to lever carefully between the main bearing cap and the pump housing with a screwdriver.

5 Remove the two remaining bolts **(see illustration)** and separate the pump body from the case. Lift out the driven rotor and remove the O-ring **(see illustration)**.

6 Clamp the pump sprocket in a well-padded vice **(see illustration)** and remove the sprocket nut and sprocket. Remove the drive rotor.

7 Use a scraper to remove all traces of sealant and old gasket material from the pump case and engine block, then clean the mating surfaces with lacquer thinner or acetone.

8 Remove the oil pressure relief valve circlip **(see illustration)**, retainer, spring and piston.

> ⚠️ **Warning: The spring is tightly compressed – be careful and wear eye protection.**

Inspection

9 Clean all components with solvent, then inspect them for wear and damage.

10 Check the oil pressure relief valve piston sliding surface and valve spring. If either the spring or the valve is damaged, they must be renewed as a set.

11 Check the driven rotor-to-case and drive rotor tip clearance with feeler blades **(see illustrations)** and compare the results to this Chapter's Specifications. If the clearance is excessive, renew the rotors as a set. If necessary, renew the oil pump case and body.

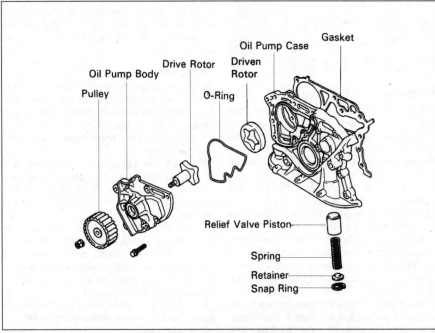

Oil Pump Body
Pulley
Drive Rotor
O-Ring
Driven Rotor
Oil Pump Case
Gasket

Relief Valve Piston
Spring
Retainer
Snap Ring

13.5b Oil pump components

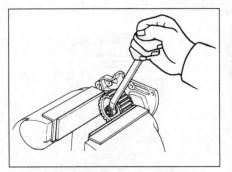

13.6 Hold the oil pump sprocket in a well-padded vice while the retaining nut is removed

13.8 Remove the circlip to disassemble the oil pressure relief valve

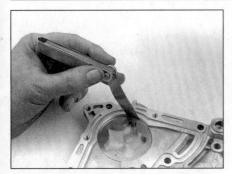

13.11a Measure the driven rotor-to-case clearance . . .

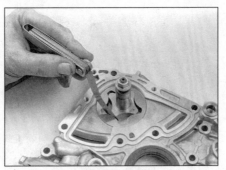

13.11b . . . and the rotor tip clearance with a feeler blade

13.14 Oil pump case ready for pump body installation; note that the seal is in place, the O-ring is in place and the mark on the driven rotor is facing out (arrow)

Refitting

12 Lever the old drive rotor shaft seal out with a screwdriver. Using a deep socket and a hammer, carefully drive a new seal into place. Apply multipurpose grease to the seal lip.

13 Fit a new crankshaft seal using the same procedure as outlined in the previous step. Apply multipurpose grease to the seal lip.

14 Fit a new O-ring, then lubricate the driven rotor with clean engine oil and place it in the pump case with the mark facing out **(see illustration)**.

15 Lubricate the shaft and fit the drive rotor in the pump body, then refit the sprocket and tighten the nut to the torque listed in this Chapter's Specifications.

16 Pack the pump cavity with petroleum jelly and attach the pump body to the case with the 16 mm-long bolts **(see illustration 13.5a)**.

17 Lubricate the oil pressure relief valve piston with clean engine oil and refit the valve components in the pump case.

18 Place a new gasket on the engine block (the dowel pins should hold it in place).

19 Position the pump case against the block and refit the mounting bolts.

20 Tighten the bolts to the torque listed in this Chapter's Specifications in three or four steps. Follow a criss-cross pattern to avoid warping the case.

21 Using a new gasket, refit the oil pick-up tube assembly and baffle plate. Tighten the fasteners to the torque listed in this Chapter's Specifications.

22 Refit the remaining parts in the reverse order of removal.

23 Add oil, start the engine and check for oil pressure and leaks.

24 Recheck the engine oil level.

14 Flywheel/driveplate – removal and refitting

Removal

1 Refer to Chapter 7A or 7B and remove the transmission. If it's leaking, now would be a very good time to renew the pump seal/O-ring (automatic transmission only).

2 Remove the pressure plate and clutch disc (Chapter 8) (manual transmission equipped vehicles). Now is a good time to check/renew the clutch components.

3 Use a centre punch or paint to make alignment marks on the flywheel/driveplate and crankshaft to ensure correct alignment during refitting **(see illustration)**.

4 Remove the bolts that secure the flywheel/driveplate to the crankshaft. If the crankshaft

turns, wedge a screwdriver in the ring gear teeth to jam the flywheel.

5 Remove the flywheel/driveplate from the crankshaft. Since the flywheel is fairly heavy, be sure to support it while removing the last bolt. Automatic transmission equipped vehicles have spacers on both sides of the driveplate **(see illustration)**. Keep them with the driveplate.

Refitting

6 Clean the flywheel to remove grease and oil. Inspect the surface for cracks, rivet grooves, burned areas and score marks. Light scoring can be removed with emery cloth. Check for cracked and broken ring gear teeth. Lay the flywheel on a flat surface and use a straight-edge to check for warpage.

7 Clean and inspect the mating surfaces of the flywheel/driveplate and the crankshaft. If the crankshaft seal is leaking, renew it before refitting the flywheel/driveplate.

8 Position the flywheel/driveplate against the crankshaft. Be sure to align the marks made during removal. Note that some engines have an alignment dowel or staggered bolt holes to ensure correct refitting. Before fitting the bolts, apply thread-locking compound to the threads.

14.3 Mark the flywheel/driveplate and the crankshaft so they can be reassembled in the same relative positions

14.5 On vehicles with an automatic transmission, there is a spacer plate on each side of the driveplate; when refitting, line up the spacers with the locating pin (arrow)

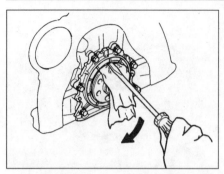

15.2 The quick way to renew the main oil seal is to simply lever the old one out with a screwdriver, lubricate the crankshaft journal and the lip of the new seal with multipurpose grease and push the new seal into place – the seal lip is very stiff and can be easily damaged during installation if you're not careful

9 Wedge a screwdriver in the ring gear teeth to keep the flywheel/driveplate from turning and tighten the bolts to the torque listed in this Chapter's Specifications. Follow a criss-cross pattern and work up to the final torque in three or four steps.

10 The remainder of refitting is the reverse of the removal procedure.

15 Crankshaft left-hand oil seal – renewal
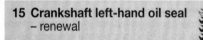

1 The transmission must be removed from the vehicle for this procedure (see Chapter 7A or 7B).

2 The seal can be renewed without removing the sump or removing the seal retainer. However, this method is not recommended because the lip of the seal is quite stiff and it's possible to cock the seal in the retainer bore or damage it during refitting. If you want to take the chance, lever out the old seal with a screwdriver **(see illustration)**. Apply multipurpose grease to the crankshaft seal journal and the lip of the new seal and carefully push the new seal into place. The lip is stiff so carefully work it onto the seal journal of the crankshaft with a smooth object like the end of an extension as you tap the seal into place. Don't rush it or you may damage the seal.

16.8 Working from below, remove the right-hand side engine mounting bracket retaining nut (arrow)

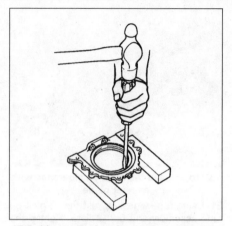

15.5 After removing the retainer assembly from the block, support it between two wood blocks and drive out the old seal with a screwdriver and hammer

3 The following method is recommended but requires removal of the sump (see Section 12) and the seal retainer.

4 After the sump has been removed, remove the bolts, detach the seal retainer and remove all the old gasket material.

5 Position the seal and retainer assembly between two wood blocks on a workbench and drive the old seal out from the back side with a screwdriver **(see illustration)**.

6 Drive the new seal into the retainer with a block of wood **(see illustration)** or a section of pipe slightly smaller in diameter than the outside diameter of the seal.

7 Lubricate the crankshaft seal journal and the lip of the new seal with multi-purpose grease. Position a new gasket on the engine block.

8 Slowly and carefully push the seal onto the crankshaft. The seal lip is stiff, so work it onto the crankshaft with a smooth object such as the end of an extension as you push the retainer against the block.

9 Insert and tighten the retainer bolts to the torque listed in this Chapter's Specifications. The bottom sealing flange of the retainer must not extend below the bottom sealing flange (sump rail) of the block.

10 The remaining steps are the reverse of removal.

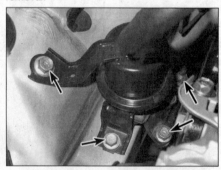

16.9 Working from above, remove the right-hand side engine mounting nuts/bolts (arrows)

15.6 Drive the new seal into the retainer with a block of wood or a section of pipe, if you have one large enough – make sure that you don't cock the seal in the retainer bore

16 Engine mountings – check and renewal

1 The engine mountings seldom require attention, but broken or deteriorated mountings should be renewed immediately or the added strain placed on the transmission components may cause damage or wear.

Check

2 During the check, the engine must be raised slightly to remove the weight from the mountings.

3 Raise the vehicle and support it securely on axle stands, then remove the splash shields under the engine (if equipped) and position a jack under the engine sump. Place a large block of wood between the jack head and the sump, then carefully raise the engine just enough to take the weight off the mountings. Do not position the wood block under the drain plug.

> ⚠ **Warning: DO NOT place any part of your body under the engine when it's supported only by a jack.**

4 Check the mountings to see if the rubber is cracked, hardened or separated from the bushing in the centre of the mounting.

5 Check for relative movement between the mounting plates and the engine or frame (use a large screwdriver or lever to attempt to move the mountings). If movement is noted, lower the engine and tighten the mounting fasteners.

6 Rubber preservative should be applied to the mountings to slow deterioration.

Renewal

7 Disconnect the negative battery cable from the battery, then raise the vehicle and support it securely on axle stands (if not already done). Support the engine as described in Paragraph 3.

Right-hand side engine mounting

8 Working below the vehicle, remove the nut securing the right side mounting to the engine bracket **(see illustration)**.

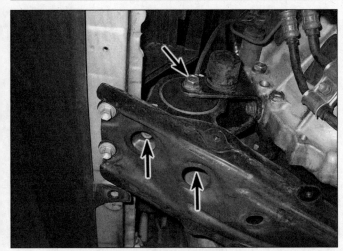

16.12 Transmission mounting bolts (arrows) – front mounting shown, rear mounting similar

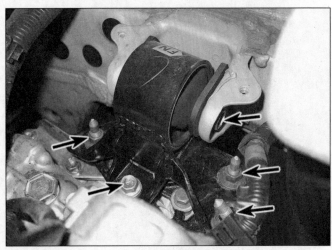

16.16 Left-hand side transmission mounting nuts/bolts (arrows)

9 Working above in the engine compartment, remove the remaining nut and bolts securing the right side mounting to the engine bracket **(see illustration)**. If the vehicle is equipped with ABS brakes it will be necessary to remove the ABS actuator and bracket first to allow access to the mounting (see Chapter 9).

10 Detach the mounting from the vehicle.

11 Refitting is the reverse of removal. Use thread-locking compound on the mounting bolts/nuts and be sure to tighten them securely.

Caution: Be sure to bleed the brakes properly if the vehicle is equipped with an Antilock Brake System (see Chapter 9).

Front and rear transmission mountings

12 Working up through the holes in the centre suspension crossmember detach the mounting-to-crossmember retaining bolts **(see illustration)**.

13 Remove the through-bolt securing the mounting to the transmission bracket and detach the mounting from the vehicle.

14 Refitting is the reverse of removal. Use thread-locking compound on the mounting bolts/nuts and be sure to tighten them securely.

Left-hand side transmission mounting

15 Remove the air filter housing (see Chapter 4A).

16 Remove the nuts and bolts securing the mounting to the transmission **(see illustration)**.

17 Remove the though-bolt securing the mounting to the chassis and remove the mounting from the vehicle.

18 Refitting is the reverse of removal. Use thread-locking compound on the mounting bolts/nuts and be sure to tighten them securely.

Chapter 2 Part B:
Petrol engines – 2001 and later

Contents

Section number

Camshafts and followers – removal, inspection and refitting 7
Crankshaft left-hand oil seal – renewal 16
Crankshaft pulley/vibration damper – removal and refitting 11
Crankshaft right-hand oil seal – renewal 12
Cylinder head – removal and refitting. 10
Engine mountings – check and renewal. 17
Exhaust manifold – removal and refitting. 9
Flywheel/driveplate – removal and refitting 15
General information 1

Section number

Intake manifold – removal and refitting 8
Oil pump – removal and refitting 14
Repair operations possible with the engine in the vehicle. 2
Sump – removal and refitting 13
Timing chain and sprockets – removal, inspection and refitting 6
Top Dead Centre (TDC) for number one piston – locating 3
Valve cover – removal and refitting. 4
Variable Valve Timing (VVT) system – description 5

Degrees of difficulty

Easy, suitable for novice with little experience	Fairly easy, suitable for beginner with some experience	Fairly difficult, suitable for competent DIY mechanic	Difficult, suitable for experienced DIY mechanic	Very difficult, suitable for expert DIY or professional

Specifications

General
Engine designation and capacity
  1ZZ-FE . . . . 1794 cc
  1AZ-FE . . . . 1998 cc
Cylinder numbers (timing chain end-to-transmission end) 1-2-3-4
Firing order 1-3-4-2

Cylinder head
Cylinder head gasket face:
  Warpage limit . . . . 0.05 mm
Inlet and exhaust manifold faces:
  Warpage limit:
    1ZZ-FE . . . . 0.10 mm
    1AZ-FE . . . . 0.08 mm

Timing chain
Timing chain stretch limit (see illustration 6.20a):
  8 links (16 pins). . . . . 122.6 mm
Timing chain sprocket wear limit (see illustration 6.20b):
  Camshaft sprocket(s) (with chain) . . . . 97.3 mm
  Crankshaft sprocket (with chain) . . . . 51.6 mm
Timing chain guide wear limit. . . . . 1.0 mm

Oil pump
Drive chain stretch limit:
  4 links (8 pins). . . . . 52.4 mm
Drive chain sprocket wear limit (with chain). 48.2 mm
Drive chain guide wear limit . . . . 0.5 mm

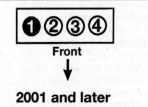

Cylinder numbering and coil terminal
identification diagram

Camshaft and followers

Journal diameter:
    No 1 journal . . . .   35.971 to 35.985 mm
    All others. . . . .   22.959 to 22.975 mm
Bearing oil clearance:
    No 1 journal:
        Intake . . . .   0.007 to 0.038 mm
        Exhaust . . . .   0.015 to 0.054 mm
    All others. . . . .   0.025 to 0.062 mm
Runout limit . . . .   0.03 mm
Thrust clearance (endplay):
    Intake . . . .   0.040 to 0.095 mm
    Exhaust. . . . .   0.080 to 0.135 mm
Lobe height:
    Intake camshaft:
        Standard . . . .   46.495 to 46.595 mm
        Service limit (minimum). . . . .   46.385 mm
    Exhaust camshaft:
        Standard. . . . .   45.983 to 46.083 mm
        Service limit (minimum). 45.873
Valve follower:
    Diameter . . . .   30.966 to 30.976 mm
    Bore diameter. . . . .   31.009 to 31.025 mm
Follower oil clearance:
    Standard. . . . .   0.033 to 0.059 mm
    Service limit . . . .   0.079 mm

Torque wrench settings

	lbf ft	Nm
Auxiliary drivebelt tensioner	44	60
Camshaft bearing cap bolts:		
Journal No 1 (intake and exhaust)	22	30
All others.	7	9
Camshaft sprocket bolts	40	54
Crankshaft pulley/vibration damper bolt	125	170
Cylinder head bolts (in sequence – **see illustration 10.24**):		
Step 1	58	79
Step 2	Tighten an additional 90º	
Driveplate bolts (automatic transmission)	72	98
Engine mountings:		
Passenger's side mounting:		
Mounting-to-frame bolts.	38	52
Mounting-to engine mounting bracket nuts/bolts	38	52
Driver's side mounting:		
Mounting-to-frame bolts.	41	56
Mounting through-bolt	41	56
Front mounting:		
Mounting-to-frame bolts.	41	56
Mounting through-bolt	41	56
Rear mounting:		
Mounting-to-frame bolts.	41	56
Mounting through-bolt	65	88
Exhaust manifold brace bolts.	33	45
Exhaust manifold heat shield bolts	9	12
Exhaust manifold nuts/bolts.	25	34
Exhaust pipe-to-exhaust manifold bolts	32	43
Flywheel bolts (manual transmission).	96	130
Intake manifold nuts/bolts	22	30
Lower crankcase-to-engine block bolts.	25	34
Oil pump bolts	15	20
Oil pump drive chain tensioner.	9	12
Oil pump sprocket bolt	20	27
Sump bolts.	7	9
Timing chain cover bolts (**see illustrations 7.14a and 7.14b**):		
Timing chain cover nuts	7	9
Timing chain guide bolts (stationary)	7	9
Timing chain tensioner nuts	7	9
Timing chain tensioner pivot arm bolt	14	19
10 mm head	7	9
12 mm head	15	21
14 mm head	32	43
Valve cover	8	11

1 General information

This Part of Chapter 2 is devoted to in-vehicle repair procedures for the 2001 and later four-cylinder engine. All information concerning engine removal, refitting and overhaul can be found in Part D of this Chapter.

The following repair procedures are based on the assumption that the engine is installed in the vehicle. If the engine has been removed from the vehicle and mounted on a stand, many of the steps outlined in this Part of Chapter 2 will not apply.

The Specifications included in this Part of Chapter 2 apply only to the in-vehicle procedures contained in this Part. Part D of Chapter 2 contains the general Specifications for all the engines covered by this manual.

2001-on four-cylinder engines in the RAV4 are designated 1ZZ-FE (1.8L) and 1AZ-FE (2.0L). These engines incorporate an aluminium cylinder block with a lower crankcase to strengthen the lower half of the block. Although the cylinder head utilises the usual dual overhead camshafts (DOHC) with four valves per cylinder as in previous model years, it is of new design. The camshafts are driven from a single timing chain off the crankshaft, and a Variable Valve Timing (VVT) system is incorporated on the intake camshaft to increase horsepower and decrease emissions.

2 Repair operations possible with the engine in the vehicle

Many major repair operations can be accomplished without removing the engine from the vehicle.

Clean the engine compartment and the exterior of the engine with some type of degreaser before any work is done. It will make the job easier and help keep dirt out of the internal areas of the engine.

Depending on the components involved, it may be helpful to remove the bonnet to improve access to the engine as repairs are performed (refer to Chapter 11 if necessary). Cover the wings to prevent damage to the paint. Special pads are available, but an old bedspread or blanket will also work.

If vacuum, exhaust, oil or coolant leaks develop, indicating a need for gasket or seal renewal, the repairs can generally be made with the engine in the vehicle. The intake and exhaust manifold gaskets, sump gasket, crankshaft oil seals and cylinder head gasket are all accessible with the engine in place.

Exterior engine components, such as the intake and exhaust manifolds, the sump, the oil pump, the water pump, the starter motor, the alternator and the fuel system components can be removed for repair with the engine in place.

Since the cylinder head can be removed without removing the engine, camshaft and valve component servicing can also be accomplished with the engine in the vehicle. Renewal of the timing chain and sprockets is also possible with the engine in the vehicle.

3 Top Dead Centre (TDC) for number one piston – locating

1 Top Dead Centre (TDC) is the highest point in the cylinder that each piston reaches as it travels up the cylinder bore. Each piston reaches TDC on the compression stroke and again on the exhaust stroke, but TDC generally refers to piston position on the compression stroke.

2 Positioning the piston(s) at TDC is an essential part of many procedures such as valve adjustment, and camshaft and timing chain/sprocket removal.

3 Before beginning this procedure, be sure to place the transmission in Neutral and apply the handbrake or chock the rear wheels. Disable the ignition system by disconnecting the primary electrical connectors at the ignition coils (see Chapter 5). Also disable the fuel system (see Chapter 4A, Section 2).

4 In order to bring any piston to TDC, the crankshaft must be turned using one of the methods outlined below. When looking at the right-hand end of the engine, normal crankshaft rotation is clockwise.

 a) The preferred method is to turn the crankshaft with a socket and ratchet bar attached to the bolt threaded into the front of the crankshaft. Turn the bolt in a clockwise direction only.

 b) If an assistant is available to turn the ignition switch to the Start position in short bursts, you can get the piston close to TDC. Make sure your assistant is out of the vehicle, away from the ignition switch, then use a socket and ratchet as described in paragraph (a) to complete the procedure.

5 Remove the spark plugs (see Chapter 1A) and fit a compression gauge in the number one spark plug hole **(see illustration)**. It should be a gauge with a screw-in fitting and a hose at least 15 cm long.

6 Rotate the crankshaft using one of the methods described above while observing for pressure on the compression gauge. The moment the gauge shows pressure indicates that the number one cylinder has begun the compression stroke.

7 Once the compression stroke has begun, TDC for the compression stroke is reached by bringing the piston to the top of the cylinder.

8 Continue turning the crankshaft until the notch in the crankshaft damper is aligned with the TDC or the 0 mark on the timing chain cover **(see illustration)**. At this point, the number one cylinder is at TDC on the compression stroke. If the marks are aligned

3.5 A compression gauge can be used in the number one plug hole to assist in finding TDC

but there was no compression, the piston was on the exhaust stroke; continue rotating the crankshaft 360° (1-turn). **Note:** *If a compression gauge is not available, you can simply place a blunt object over the spark plug hole and listen for compression as the engine is rotated. Once compression at the No 1 spark plug hole is noted the remainder of the procedure is the same.*

9 After the number one piston has been positioned at TDC on the compression stroke, TDC for any of the remaining cylinders can be located by turning the crankshaft 180° and following the firing order (refer to the Specifications). Rotating the engine 180° past TDC on No 1 will put the engine at TDC compression for cylinder No 3.

4 Valve cover – removal and refitting

Removal

1 Disconnect the cable from the negative terminal of the battery.

2 Disconnect the electrical connectors from the ignition coils, remove the nuts securing the wiring harness to the valve cover and position the ignition coil wiring harness aside. Then remove the ignition coil pack from each of the spark plugs (see Chapter 5).

3 Detach the PCV hoses from the valve cover.

4 Remove the valve cover mounting nuts,

3.8 Align the groove in the damper with the 0 mark on the timing chain cover

4.4 Valve cover bolt locations

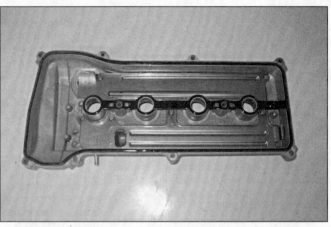

4.5 The valve cover gasket and the spark plug tube seals are incorporated into a single rubber O-ring-like seal – press the gasket evenly into the grooves around the underside of the valve cover and the spark plug openings

4.6 Apply sealant at the timing chain cover-to-cylinder head joint before refitting the valve cover

then detach the valve cover and gasket from the cylinder head **(see illustration)**. If the valve cover is stuck to the cylinder head, bump the end with a wood block and a hammer to jar it loose. If that doesn't work, try to slip a flexible putty knife between the cylinder head and valve cover to break the seal.

Caution: Don't lever at the valve cover-to-cylinder head joint or damage to the sealing surfaces may occur, leading to oil leaks after the valve cover is refitted.

Refitting

5 Remove the valve cover gasket from the

valve cover and clean the mating surfaces with lacquer thinner or acetone. Fit a new rubber gasket, pressing it evenly into the grooves around the underside of the valve cover. **Note:** *Make sure the spark plug tube seals are in place on the underside of the valve cover before refitting it (see illustration).* The mating surfaces of the timing chain cover, the cylinder head and valve cover must be perfectly clean when the valve cover is refitted. If there's residue or oil on the mating surfaces when the valve cover is refitted, oil leaks may develop.

6 Apply RTV sealant at the timing chain cover-to-cylinder head joint, then refit the valve cover and bolts **(see illustration)**.

7 Tighten the nuts/bolts to the torque listed in this Chapter's Specifications in three or four equal steps.

8 Refit the remaining parts, run the engine and check for oil leaks.

5 Variable Valve Timing (VVT) system – description

1 The VVT system varies intake camshaft timing by directing oil pressure to advance or retard the intake camshaft sprocket/actuator assembly. Changing the intake camshaft

timing during certain engine conditions increases engine power output, fuel economy and reduces emissions.

2 System components include the Engine Control Module (ECM), the VVT oil control valve (OCV) and the intake camshaft sprocket/actuator assembly **(see illustrations)**.

3 The ECM uses inputs from the following sensors to turn the oil control valve on or off:

  a) *Vehicle Speed Sensor (VSS).*
  b) *Throttle Position Sensor (TPS).*
  c) *Mass Airflow (MAF) sensor.*
  d) *Engine Coolant Temperature (ECT) sensor.*

4 Once the VVT oil control valve is actuated by the ECM it directs the specified amount of oil pressure from the engine to advance or retard the intake camshaft sprocket/actuator assembly.

5 The intake camshaft sprocket/actuator assembly is equipped with an inner hub that is attached to the camshaft. The inner hub consists of a series of fixed vanes that use oil pressure as a wedge against the vanes to rotate the camshaft. The higher the oil pressure (or flow) the more the actuator assembly will rotate, thereby advancing or retarding the camshaft.

6 When oil is applied to the advance side of the vanes, the actuator can advance the camshaft up to 21° in a clockwise direction. When oil is applied to the retard side of the vanes, the actuator will start to rotate the camshaft anti-clockwise back to 0° which is the normal position of the actuator during engine operation under no load or at idle. The ECM can also send a signal to the oil control valve to stop oil flow to both (advance and retard) passages to hold camshaft advance in its current position.

7 Under light engine loads, the VVT system will retard the camshaft timing to decrease valve overlap and stabilise engine output. Under medium engine loads, the VVT system will advance the camshaft timing to increase valve overlap, thereby increasing fuel

5.2a The Variable Valve Timing (VVT) oil control valve is located at the rear of the cylinder head

5.2b The intake camshaft actuator assembly (arrowed) is only visible with the valve cover removed

6.7 Verify the engine is at TDC by observing the position of the camshaft sprocket marks (lower arrows) – they must be aligned with the marks on the camshaft bearing caps (upper arrows)

6.9 If an engine support fixture is not available, the engine can be supported from below using a hydraulic jack and a block of wood

economy and decreasing exhaust emissions. Under heavy engine loads at low RPM, the VVT system will advance the camshaft timing to help close the intake valve faster, which improves low to midrange torque. Under heavy engine loads at high RPM, the VVT system will retard the camshaft timing to slow the closing of the intake valve to improve engine horsepower.

6 Timing chain and sprockets – removal, inspection and refitting

 Warning: Wait until the engine is completely cool before beginning this procedure.

Note: *Special tools are required for this procedure. Read through the entire procedure and acquire the necessary tools and equipment before beginning work.*

Removal

1 Detach the cable from the negative terminal of the battery.
2 Remove the auxiliary drivebelt (see Chapter 1A) and the alternator (see Chapter 5).
3 Remove and the valve cover (see Section 4) and the ABS actuator if equipped (see Chapter 9).
4 With the handbrake applied and the rear wheels chocked, loosen the right front wheel nuts, then raise the front of the vehicle and support it securely on axle stands. Remove the right front wheel and the right splash shield from the wheel arch.
5 Drain the cooling system (see Chapter 1A).
6 While the coolant is draining, refer to Chapter 10 and remove the power steering pump from the engine without disconnecting the fluid lines. Tie the power steering pump to the body with a piece of wire and position it out of the way.
7 Position the number one piston at TDC on the compression stroke (see Section 3).

Visually confirm the engine is at TDC on the compression stroke by verifying that the timing mark on the crankshaft pulley/vibration damper is aligned with the 0 mark on the timing chain cover and the camshaft sprocket marks are aligned and parallel with the top of the timing chain cover **(see illustration)**. **Note:** *There are two sets of marks on the camshaft sprockets. The marks that align at TDC are for TDC reference only; the other two marks are used to align the sprockets with the timing chain during refitting.*

8 Remove the crankshaft pulley/vibration damper, being careful not to rotate the engine from TDC (see Section 11). If the engine rotates off TDC during this step, reposition the engine back to TDC before proceeding. The engine should be left at TDC for the No 1 piston during this entire procedure.
9 Support the engine from above, using an engine support fixture, or from below using a hydraulic jack. Use a wood block between the hydraulic jack and the engine to prevent damage **(see illustration)**.
10 Remove the passenger side engine mounting (see Section 17).
11 Remove the auxiliary drivebelt tensioner and the crankshaft position sensor from the timing chain cover **(see illustration)**. Also

6.11 Drivebelt tensioner mounting bolts

remove the bolt securing the crankshaft position sensor wiring harness to the timing chain cover.
12 Remove the sump (see Section 13).
13 Detach the main wiring harness junction and remove the timing chain tensioner from the rear side of the timing chain cover **(see illustrations)**.
14 Remove the timing chain cover bolts and lever the cover off the engine **(see illustrations)**.
15 Slide the crankshaft position sensor reluctor ring off the crankshaft **(see illustration)**.
16 Remove the timing chain tensioner pivot

6.13a Remove the two bolts securing the main harness to the timing chain cover and position the harness aside

6.13b Timing chain tensioner mounting nuts (arrowed)

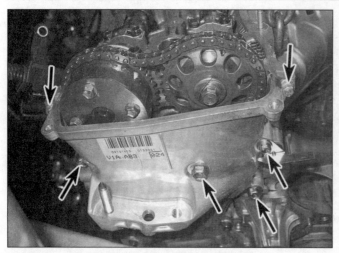

6.14a Timing chain cover upper bolts

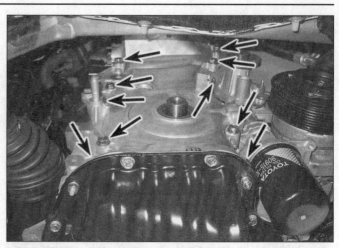

6.14b Timing chain cover lower bolts – make a note of the bolt
sizes, locations and lengths as your removing them as they must
be refitted back in the original position

6.14c It will be necessary to remove the
timing chain cover studs . . .

6.14d . . . before levering the timing chain
cover off the engine

arm/chain guide and the lower chain guide
(see illustration).
17 Lift the timing chain off the camshaft
sprockets and remove the timing chain and the
crankshaft sprocket as an assembly from the
engine. The crankshaft sprocket should slip

off the crankshaft by hand. If not, use several
flat-bladed screwdrivers to evenly lever the
sprocket off the crankshaft. **Note:** *If you intend
to re-use the timing chain, use white paint or
chalk to make a mark indicating the front of the
chain. If a used timing chain is refitted with the*

*wear pattern in the opposite direction, noise
and increased wear may occur.*
18 Remove the stationary timing chain guide
(see illustration 6.16).
19 To remove the camshaft sprockets,
loosen the bolts while holding the camshaft
with a spanner **(see illustration)**. Note
the identification marks on the camshaft
sprockets before removal, then remove the
bolts. Pull on the sprockets by hand until they
slip off the dowels. If necessary, use a small
puller, with the legs inserted in the relief holes,
to pull the sprockets off. **Note:** *These models
are equipped with variable valve timing, which
consists of an actuator assembly attached to
the intake camshaft sprocket. When removing
the intake camshaft sprocket on these models
only loosen and remove the centre bolt, which
fastens the sprocket to the camshaft. Do not
loosen the outer four bolts that secure the
actuator to the sprocket.*

6.15 Slide the crankshaft position sensor reluctor ring off the
crankshaft – note the F mark (arrowed) on the front (it must be
facing outward upon refitting)

6.16 Timing chain guide mounting details

A Pivot bolt
B Tensioner pivot arm/chain
 guide
C Stationary chain guide
 mounting bolts
D Stationary chain guide
E Lower timing chain guide

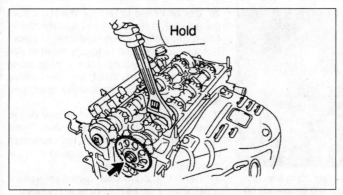

6.19 Hold the camshaft with a spanner to keep it from rotating as the sprocket bolts are loosened – when loosening the intake camshaft sprocket, loosen the centre bolt only which secures the sprocket to the camshaft

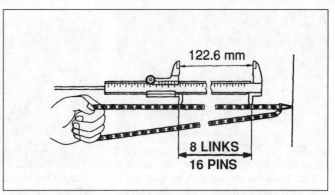

6.20a Timing chain stretch is measured by checking the length of the chain between 8 links (16 pins) at 3 or more places (selected randomly) around the chain – if chain stretch exceeds the specifications between any 8 links, the chain must be renewed

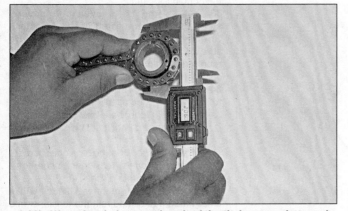

6.20b Wrap the chain around each of the timing sprockets and measure the diameter of the sprockets across the chain rollers – if the measurement is less than the minimum sprocket diameter, the chain and the timing sprockets must be renewed

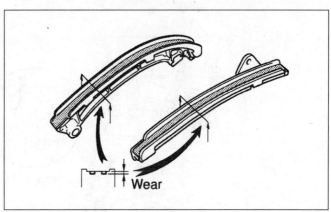

6.21 Timing chain guide wear is measured from the top of the chain contact surface to the bottom of the wear grooves

Inspection

20 Visually inspect all parts for wear and damage. Check the timing chain for loose pins, cracks, worn rollers and side plates. Check the sprockets for hook-shaped, chipped and broken teeth. Also check the timing chain for stretching and the diameter of the timing sprockets for wear with the chain assembled on the sprockets **(see illustrations)**. Be sure to measure across the chain rollers when checking the sprocket diameter and to measure chain stretch at three or more places around the chain. Maximum chain elongation and minimum sprocket diameter (with chain) should not exceed the amount listed in this Chapter's Specifications. Renew the timing chain and sprockets as a set if the engine has high mileage or fails inspection.

21 Check the chain guides for excessive wear **(see illustration)**. Renew the chain guides if scoring or wear exceeds the amount listed in this Chapter's Specifications. Note that some scoring of the timing chain guide shoes is normal. If excessive wear is indicated, it will also be necessary to inspect the chain guide oil hole on the front of the block for clogging **(see illustration 14.5d)**.

Refitting

22 Remove all traces of old sealant from the timing chain cover and the mating surfaces of the engine block and cylinder head.

23 Make sure the camshafts are positioned with the dowel pins at the top in the 12 o'clock position, then refit both camshaft sprockets in their original locations by aligning the dowel pin hole on the rear of the sprockets with dowel pin on the camshaft. Apply medium strength thread locking compound to the camshaft sprocket bolt threads and make sure the washers are in place. Hold the camshaft from turning as described in paragraph 19 and tighten the bolts to the torque listed in this Chapter's Specifications.

24 Rotate the camshafts as necessary to align the TDC marks on the camshaft sprockets **(see illustration 6.7)**.

25 If the crankshaft has been rotated off TDC during this procedure, it will be necessary to rotate the crankshaft until the keyway is pointing straight up in the 12 o'clock position with the centreline of the cylinder bores.

26 Refit the stationary timing chain guide **(see illustration 6.16)**.

27 Loop the timing chain around the crankshaft sprocket and align the No 1 coloured link with the mark on the crankshaft sprocket. Refit the chain and crankshaft sprocket as an assembly on the engine, then refit the lower timing chain guide **(see illustration)**. **Note:** *There are three coloured links on the timing chain. The No 1 coloured link is the link furthest from the two coloured links that are closest together.*

6.27 Loop the timing chain around the crankshaft sprocket and align the No 1 coloured link with the mark on the crankshaft sprocket, then fit the chain and crankshaft sprocket as an assembly on the engine and install the lower chain guide

6.28 Loop the timing chain up over the exhaust camshaft and around the intake camshaft, while aligning the remaining two coloured links with the marks on the camshaft sprockets

6.29 After the tensioner pivot arm is refitted, make sure the tab (arrowed) on the pivot arm can't move past the stopper on the cylinder head

29 Use one hand to remove the slack from the left side of the chain and refit the timing chain tensioner pivot arm/chain guide. Tighten the pivot bolt to torque listed in this Chapter's Specifications. After refitting, make sure the tab on the pivot arm can't move past the stopper on the cylinder head **(see illustration)**.

30 Reconfirm that the number one piston is still at TDC on the compression stroke and that the timing marks on the crankshaft and camshaft sprockets are aligned with the coloured links on the chain.

31 Refit the crankshaft position sensor reluctor ring with the F mark facing outward.

32 Apply a bead of RTV sealant to the timing chain cover sealing surfaces **(see illustrations)**. Place the timing chain cover in position on the engine and refit the bolts in their original locations.

33 Tighten the bolts evenly in several steps to the torque listed in this Chapter's Specifications **(see illustration)**. Be sure to follow the sealant manufacturer's recommendations for assembly and sealant curing times.

34 Reload and lock the timing chain tensioner to its 'zero' position as follows:
 a) Raise the ratchet pawl and push the plunger inward until it bottoms out **(see illustration)**.
 b) Engage the hook on the tensioner body with the pin on the tensioner plunger to lock the plunger in place.

35 Lubricate the tensioner O-ring with a small amount of oil and refit the tensioner into the timing chain cover with the hook facing up **(see illustration)**.

36 Refit the crankshaft pulley/vibration damper (see Section 11).

37 Rotate the engine anti-clockwise slightly to set the chain tension **(see illustration)**. As the engine is rotated, the hook on the tensioner body should release itself from the pin on the plunger and allow the plunger to spring out and apply tension to the timing chain. If the plunger does not spring outward and apply tension to the timing chain, press downward on the pivot arm and release the hook with a screwdriver.

38 Rotate the engine clockwise several turns

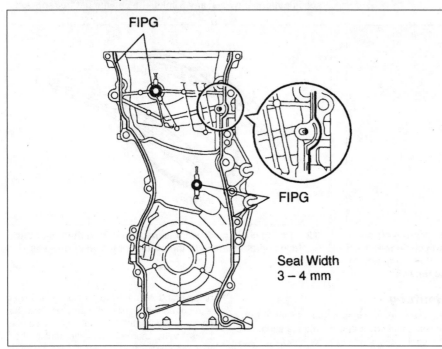

FIPG

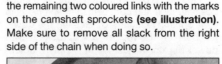

FIPG

Seal Width
3 – 4 mm

6.32a Timing chain cover sealant details

28 Slip the timing chain into the lip of the stationary timing chain guide and over the exhaust camshaft sprocket, then around the intake camshaft sprocket making sure to align the remaining two coloured links with the marks on the camshaft sprockets **(see illustration)**. Make sure to remove all slack from the right side of the chain when doing so.

6.32b Also apply a bead of sealant on each side of the parting line between the cylinder head and the engine block

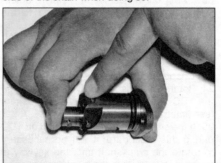

6.34 Raise the ratchet pawl and push the plunger inward until the hook on the tensioner body can be engaged with pin on the plunger to lock the plunger in place

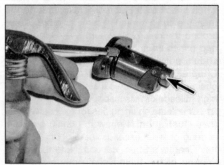

6.35 Apply a small amount of oil to the tensioner O-ring and insert the tensioner into the timing chain cover with the hook facing upward

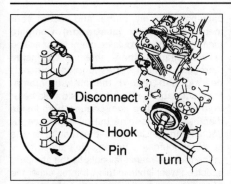

6.37 Rotate the engine anti-clockwise to disengage the hook from the plunger pin on the tensioner, then rotate it clockwise and confirm that the plunger has extended outward against the pivot arm/chain guide

and reposition the number one piston at TDC on the compression stroke (see Section 3). Visually confirm that the timing mark on the crankshaft pulley/vibration damper is aligned with the 0 mark on the timing chain cover and the camshaft sprocket marks are aligned and parallel with the top of the timing chain cover **(see illustration 6.7).**

39 The remainder of the refitting is the reverse of removal.

7 Camshafts and followers – removal, inspection and refitting

Note: *The camshafts should always be thoroughly inspected before refitting and camshaft endplay should always be checked prior to camshaft removal (see paragraph 13).*

Removal

1 Disconnect the cable from the negative terminal of the battery.

2 Remove the valve cover (see Section 4).

3 Refer to Section 3 and place the engine on TDC for number 1 cylinder. Visually confirm the engine is at TDC on the compression stroke by verifying that the timing mark on the crankshaft pulley/vibration damper is aligned with the 0 mark on the timing chain cover and the camshaft sprocket TDC marks are aligned and parallel with the top of the

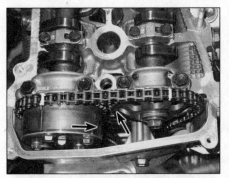

7.4 With the TDC marks aligned, apply a dab of paint to the timing chain links where they meet the upper timing marks on the camshaft sprockets

timing chain cover **(see illustrations 3.8 and 6.7).**

4 With the TDC marks aligned, apply a dab of paint to the timing chain links where they meet the upper timing marks on the camshaft sprockets **(see illustration). Note:** *There are two sets of marks on the camshaft sprockets. The marks that align at TDC are for TDC reference only, the other two marks are used to align the sprockets with the timing chain during refitting.*

5 Using a spanner to hold the camshaft sprockets from turning, loosen the camshaft sprocket bolts several turns **(see illustration 6.19).** If the camshaft sprockets have rotated during the bolt loosening process, rotate the engine clockwise until the TDC marks on the cam sprockets are realigned.

6 Remove the timing chain tensioner from the timing cover **(see illustrations 6.13a and 6.13b)** and the camshaft position sensor from the cylinder head (see Chapter 6A).

7 Remove the camshaft sprocket retaining bolts. Disengage the timing chain from the sprockets and remove the camshaft sprockets from the engine. Make sure to note that the Variable Valve Timing (VVT) actuator is refitted on the intake (rear) camshaft. After removing the sprockets, hang the timing chain up with a piece of wire and attach it to an object on the bulkhead **(see illustration).** This will prevent the timing chain from falling into the engine as the remaining steps in this procedure are

7.7 With the camshaft sprockets removed, hang the timing chain out of the way with a piece of wire and place a rag in the timing chain cover opening to prevent foreign objects from falling into the engine

performed. Also place a rag into the opening of the timing chain cover to prevent any foreign objects from falling into the engine.

8 Verify the markings on the camshaft bearing caps. The caps should be marked from 1 to 5 with an I or an E mark on the cap indicating whether they're for the intake or exhaust camshaft **(see illustration).**

9 Loosen the camshaft bearing caps in two or three steps, in the **reverse** order of the tightening sequence **(see illustration 7.22).** *Caution: Keep the caps in order. They must go back in the same location they were removed from.*

10 Detach the bearing caps, then remove the camshaft(s) from the cylinder head. Mark the camshaft(s) 'Intake' or 'Exhaust' to avoid mixing them up. **Note:** *When looking at the engine from the front of the vehicle, the forward facing cam is the exhaust camshaft and the cam nearest the bulkhead is the intake camshaft. It is very important that the camshafts are returned to their original locations during refitting.*

11 Remove the followers from the cylinder head, keeping them in order with their respective valve and cylinder **(see illustrations).** *Caution: Keep the followers in order. They must go back in the position from which they were removed.*

12 Inspect the camshafts, camshaft bearings and followers as described below. Also inspect the camshaft sprockets for wear on the teeth.

7.8 The camshaft bearing caps are numbered and have an arrow that should face the timing chain end of the engine

7.11a Mark the followers (I for intake, E for exhaust, and number their location) and remove them with a magnetic retrieval tool

7.11b Mark up a cardboard box to store the followers and bearing caps in order

7.13 Mount a dial indicator as shown to measure camshaft endplay – lever the camshaft forward and back and read the endplay on the dial

7.14a Inspect the No 2 to No 5 cam bearing surfaces in the cylinder head for pits, score marks and abnormal wear – if wear or damage is noted, the cylinder head must be renewed

Inspect the chains for cracks or excessive wear of the rollers, and for stretching (see Section 6). If any of the components show signs of excessive wear they must be renewed.

Inspection

13 Before the camshafts are removed from the engine, check the camshaft endplay by placing a dial indicator with the stem in line with the camshaft and touching the snout **(see illustration)**. Push the camshaft all the way to the rear and zero the dial indicator. Next, lever the camshaft to the front as far as possible and check the reading on the dial indicator. The distance it moves is the endplay. If the endplay for the intake camshaft

is greater than the Specifications listed in this Chapter, check the thrust surfaces of the No 1 journal bearing for wear. If the thrust surface is worn, the bearings must be renewed. If the endplay for the exhaust camshaft is greater than the Specifications listed in this Chapter, the camshaft or the cylinder head (or both) may need to be renewed.

14 With the camshafts removed, visually check the camshaft bearing surfaces in the cylinder head for pitting, score marks, galling and abnormal wear. If the bearing surfaces are damaged, the cylinder head or the No 1 journal bearings of the intake camshaft may have to be renewed **(see illustration)**.

15 Measure the outside diameter of each

camshaft bearing journal and record your measurements **(see illustration)**. Compare them to the journal outside diameter specified in this Chapter, then measure the inside diameter of each corresponding camshaft bearing and record the measurements. Subtract each cam journal outside diameter from its respective cam bearing bore inside diameter to determine the oil clearance for each bearing. Compare the results to the specified journal-to-bearing clearance. If any of the measurements fall outside the standard specified wear limits in this Chapter, either the camshaft or the cylinder head, or both, must be renewed.

16 Using a micrometer, measure the height of each camshaft lobe **(see illustration)**. Compare your measurements with this Chapter's Specifications. If the height for any one lobe is less than the specified minimum, renew the camshaft.

17 Check the camshaft runout by placing the camshaft back into the cylinder head and set up a dial indicator on the centre journal. Zero the dial indicator. Turn the camshaft slowly and note the dial indicator readings. If the measured runout exceeds the specified runout, renew the camshaft.

18 Inspect each follower for scuffing and score marks **(see illustration)**.

19 Measure the outside diameter of each follower **(see illustration)** and the corresponding follower bore inside diameter. Subtract the follower diameter from the

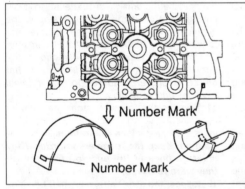

Cylinder head journal bore diameter:

Mark 1	40.000 – 40.008 mm (1.5748 – 1.5751 in.)
Mark 2	40.009 – 40.017 mm (1.5752 – 1.5755 in.)
Mark 3	40.018 – 40.025 mm (1.5755 – 1.5758 in.)

7.14b If the No 1 journal bearings are worn or damaged – it will be necessary to renew

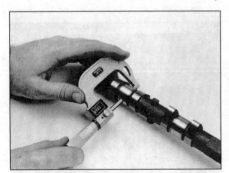

7.15 Measure each journal diameter with a micrometer – if any journal measures less than the specified limit, renew the camshaft

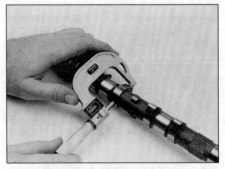

7.16 Measure the lobe heights on each camshaft – if any lobe height is less than the specified allowable minimum, renew that camshaft

7.18 Wipe off the oil and inspect each follower for wear and scuffing

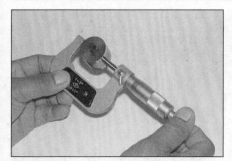

7.19 Measure the outside diameter of each follower and the inside diameter of each follower bore to determine the oil clearance measurement

7.20a Place the thrust bearing for the intake camshaft in the No 1 journal on the cylinder head . . .

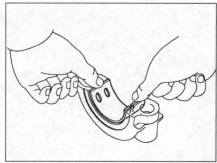

7.20b . . . and the upper bearing in the intake camshaft No 1 journal bearing cap

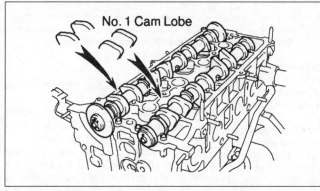

7.20c Place the camshafts in the cylinder head with the No 1 cylinder lobes pointing outward at approximately a 30° angle

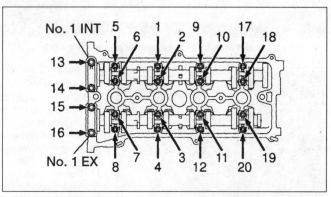

7.22 Camshaft bearing cap bolt TIGHTENING sequence

follower bore diameter to determine the oil clearance. Compare it to this Chapter's Specifications. If the oil clearance is excessive, a new cylinder head and/or new followers will be required.

Refitting

20 If the No 1 journal bearings for intake camshaft were removed or renewed, refit them into the cylinder head and the bearing cap now **(see illustrations)**. Apply moly-based engine assembly lubricant to the camshaft lobes and journals and refit the camshaft into the cylinder head with the No 1 cylinder camshaft lobes pointing outward away from each other, and the dowel pins facing upward **(see illustration)**. If the old camshafts are being used, make sure they're refitted in the exact location from which they came.

21 Refit the bearing caps and bolts and tighten them hand tight.

22 Tighten the bearing cap bolts in several equal steps, to the torque listed in this Chapter's Specifications, using the proper tightening sequence **(see illustration)**.

23 Engage the camshaft sprocket teeth with the timing chain links so that the match marks made during removal align with the upper timing marks on the sprockets, then position the sprockets over the dowels on the camshaft hubs and refit the camshaft sprocket bolts finger tight. At this point the mark on the crankshaft pulley should be aligned with the 0 mark on the timing chain cover, the camshaft

sprocket TDC marks should be aligned and parallel with the top of the timing chain cover and the timing chain match marks should be aligned with the upper timing sprocket marks with all of the slack in the chain positioned towards the tensioner side of the engine **(see illustration 7.4)**.

24 Double check that the timing sprockets are returned to the proper camshaft and tighten the camshaft sprocket bolts to the torque listed in this Chapter's Specifications.

25 Refit the timing chain tensioner as described in Section 6, paragraphs 34 and 35.

26 The remainder of refitting is the reverse of removal.

8 Intake manifold – removal and refitting

⚠ **Warning: Wait until the engine is completely cool before beginning this procedure.**

Removal

1 Relieve the fuel system pressure (see Chapter 4A), then disconnect the negative cable from the battery.

2 Remove the air intake duct and resonator (see Chapter 4A). Then remove the cowl cover and vent tray (see Chapter 11).

3 Remove the fuel rail and injectors as an assembly. Also remove the throttle linkage

and the throttle body from the intake manifold (see Chapter 4A).

4 Label and detach the PCV and vacuum hoses connected to the rear of the intake manifold **(see illustration)**.

5 Raise the vehicle and support it securely on axle stands. Working below the vehicle, remove the manifold lower mounting bolts **(see illustration)**.

6 Working from above, remove the intake manifold upper mounting nuts and bolts. Remove the manifold, the gasket and the manifold insulator from the engine **(see illustration)**.

Refitting

7 Clean the mating surfaces of the intake

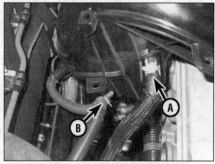

8.4 Label and disconnect the vacuum hoses (A) and the wire harness retainers (B) from the intake manifold

8.5 Intake manifold lower bolt locations (arrowed)

8.6 Intake manifold upper bolt locations (arrowed)

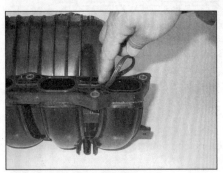

8.8 Press the gasket into the groove on the intake manifold

manifold and the cylinder head mounting surface with lacquer thinner or acetone. If the gasket shows signs of leaking, check the manifold for warpage with a straight-edge. If the manifold is warped it must be renewed.

8 Press a new gasket into the grooves on the intake manifold **(see illustration)**. Refit the manifold and gasket over the studs on the cylinder head.

9 Tighten the manifold-to-cylinder head nuts/ bolts in three or four equal steps to the torque listed in this Chapter's Specifications. Work from the centre out towards the ends to avoid warping the manifold.

10 Refit the remaining parts in the reverse order of removal. Check the coolant level, adding as necessary (see *Weekly checks*).

11 Before starting the engine, check the throttle linkage for smooth operation.

12 Run the engine and check for coolant and vacuum leaks.

13 Road test the vehicle and check for proper operation of all accessories, including the cruise control system, if equipped.

9 Exhaust manifold – removal and refitting

⚠️ *Warning: The engine must be completely cool before beginning this procedure.*

Removal

1 Disconnect the negative cable from the battery.

2 Raise the front of the vehicle and support it securely on axle stands. Working below the vehicle, remove the lower splash shields.

3 Apply penetrating oil to the bolts and springs retaining the exhaust pipe to the manifold. After the bolts have soaked, remove the bolts retaining the exhaust pipe to the manifold. Separate the front exhaust pipe from the manifold, being careful not to damage the oxygen sensor **(see illustration)**.

4 Unbolt the lower exhaust manifold supports and remove them from the engine. Also disconnect the oxygen sensor connectors.

5 Working in the engine compartment, remove the upper heat shield from the manifold **(see illustration)**. **Note:** *There is also a lower heat shield, but it is attached to the manifold from underneath and does not need to be removed.*

6 Remove the nuts/bolts and detach the manifold and gasket **(see illustration)**.

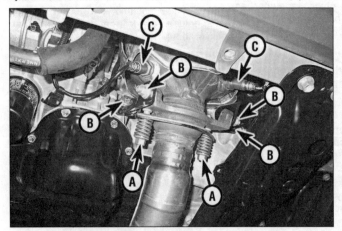

9.3 Working below the vehicle, remove the exhaust pipe-to-manifold mounting bolts (A) and lower the front exhaust pipe. Be careful not to damage the oxygen sensor (C)

B Indicates the mounting bolts for the exhaust manifold lower support

9.5 Working from the engine compartment, remove the upper heat shield mounting bolts (arrowed) . . .

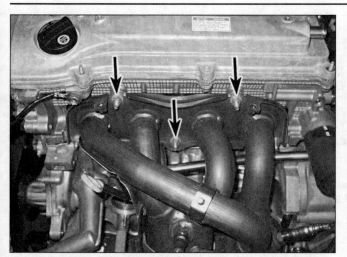

9.6 . . . and the exhaust manifold retaining nuts, then slide the manifold from the studs on the cylinder head and remove from above

10.11 Disconnect the following components from the driver's side of the cylinder head and position the electrical wiring harness aside

A Earth strap	E Coolant temperature
B Camshaft position sensor	sensor
C Coolant hoses	F Radio noise suppressor
D Oil pressure sending unit	G Oxygen sensor connector

Refitting

7 Use a scraper to remove all traces of old gasket material and carbon deposits from the manifold and cylinder head mating surfaces. If the gasket shows signs of leaking, check the manifold for warpage with a straight-edge. If the manifold is warped it must be renewed. **Note:** *If the manifold is being renewed it will be necessary to remove the lower heat shield and fasten it to the new manifold.*

8 Position a new gasket over the cylinder head studs, noting any directional marks or arrows on the gasket which may be present.

9 Refit the manifold and screw on the mounting nuts.

10 Working from the centre out, tighten the nuts/bolts to the torque listed in this Chapter's Specifications in three or four equal steps.

11 Refit the remaining parts in the reverse order of removal.

12 Run the engine and check for exhaust leaks.

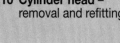

10 Cylinder head –
removal and refitting

> ⚠ **Warning: The engine must be completely cool before beginning this procedure.**

Removal

1 Relieve the fuel system pressure (see Chapter 4A), then disconnect the cable from the negative terminal of the battery.

2 Drain the engine coolant (see Chapter 1A).

3 Remove the auxiliary drivebelt and the alternator (see Chapter 5).

4 Remove the valve cover (see Section 4).

5 Remove the throttle body, fuel injectors and fuel rail (see Chapter 4A).

6 Remove the intake manifold (see Section 8).

7 Remove the exhaust manifold (see Section 9).

8 Remove the timing chain and camshaft sprockets (see Section 6).

9 Remove the camshafts and followers (see Section 7).

10 Remove the variable valve timing control valve **(see illustration 5.2a)**.

11 Label and remove the coolant hoses and electrical connections from the cylinder head **(see illustration)**.

12 Using a 10 mm hex-head socket bit and a long socket bar, loosen the cylinder head bolts in 1/4-turn increments until they can be removed by hand. Loosen the cylinder head bolts in the **reverse** order of the recommended tightening sequence **(see illustration 10.24)** to avoid warping or cracking the cylinder head.

13 Lift the cylinder head off the engine block. If it's stuck, very carefully lever up at the transmission end, beyond the gasket surface **(see illustration)**.

14 Remove any remaining external components

from the cylinder head to allow for thorough cleaning and inspection.

Refitting

15 The mating surfaces of the cylinder head and block must be perfectly clean when the cylinder head is refitted.

16 Use a gasket scraper to remove all traces of carbon and old gasket material **(see illustration)**, then clean the mating surfaces with lacquer thinner or acetone. If there's oil on the mating surfaces when the cylinder head is refitted, the gasket may not seal correctly and leaks could develop. When working on the block, stuff the cylinders with clean rags to keep out debris. Use a vacuum cleaner to remove material that falls into the cylinders.

17 Check the block and cylinder head mating surfaces for nicks, deep scratches and other damage. If damage is slight, it can be removed with a file; if it's excessive, machining may be the only alternative.

18 Use a tap of the correct size to chase the threads in the cylinder head bolt holes, then

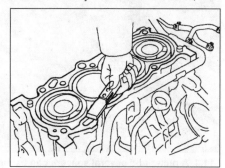

10.13 Lever the cylinder head off the engine block at the casting protrusion – be careful not to damage the mating surfaces

10.16 Remove all traces of old gasket material – the cylinder head and block mating surfaces must be perfectly clean to ensure a good gasket seal

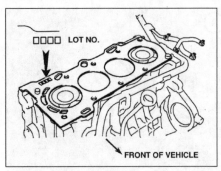

10.21a Place the head gasket over the dowels in the block with the marks facing UP

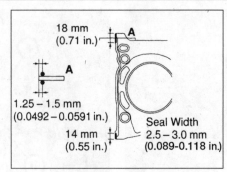

10.21b Apply RTV sealant to the areas on the cylinder head gasket as shown

18 mm (0.71 in.)

1.25 – 1.5 mm (0.0492 – 0.0591 in.)

14 mm (0.55 in.)

Seal Width 2.5 – 3.0 mm (0.089-0.118 in.)

the recommended sequence, tighten the bolts to the torque listed in this Chapter's Specifications (see illustration). Step 2 of the tightening sequence requires each bolt to be tightened an additional 90°. If you don't have an angle-torque attachment for your torque wrench, simply apply a paint mark at one edge of each cylinder head bolt and tighten the bolt until that mark is 90° (1/4-turn) from where you started.

25 The remaining refitting is a reverse of removal.

26 Check and adjust the valves as necessary (see Chapter 1A).

27 Change the engine oil and filter (see Chapter 1A.

28 Refill the cooling system (see Chapter 1A), run the engine and check for leaks.

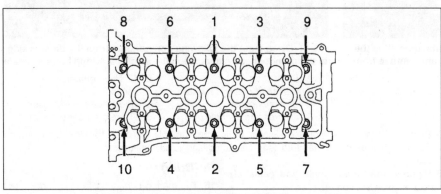

10.24 Cylinder head bolt TIGHTENING sequence

11 Crankshaft pulley/ vibration damper – removal and refitting

1 Detach the cable from the negative terminal of the battery.

2 Remove the auxiliary drivebelt (see Chapter 1A).

3 With the handbrake applied and the selector in Park (automatic) or 4th gear (manual), loosen the nuts from the right front wheel, then raise the front of the vehicle and support it securely on axle stands. Remove the right front wheel and the right splash shield from the wheel arch.

4 Remove the bolt from the front of the crankshaft. A long socket bar will probably be necessary, since the bolt is very tight (see illustration).

5 Using a puller that bolts to the crankshaft hub, remove the crankshaft pulley from the crankshaft (see illustration). Note: *Depending on the type of puller you have it may be*

clean the holes with compressed air – make sure that nothing remains in the holes.

 Warning: Wear eye protection when using compressed air.

19 Using a wire brush, clean the threads on each bolt to remove corrosion and restore the threads. Dirt, corrosion, sealant and damaged threads will affect torque readings.

20 Refit the components that were removed from the cylinder head.

21 Position the new gasket over the dowel pins in the block (see illustration). Then apply RTV sealant to the end of the cylinder head gasket as shown (see illustration).

22 Carefully set the cylinder head on the block without disturbing the gasket.

23 Before refitting the cylinder head bolts, apply a small amount of clean engine oil to the threads and under the bolt heads.

24 Refit the bolts in their original locations and tighten them finger tight. Following

11.4 A puller and several spacers can be mounted to the centre hub of the pulley to keep the crankshaft from turning as the pulley retaining bolt is loosened – fit the socket over the crankshaft bolt head before fitting the puller, then insert the extension through the centre hole of the puller

11.5 Refit the puller back onto the crankshaft pulley with the centre bolt attached and remove the crankshaft pulley

11.6 Align the keyway in the crankshaft pulley hub with the Woodruff key in the crankshaft (arrowed)

12.2 Carefully lever the old seal out of the timing chain cover – don't damage the crankshaft in the process

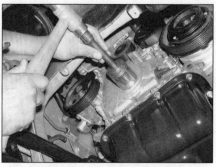

12.3 Drive the new seal into place with a large socket and hammer

necessary to support the engine from above, remove the right side engine mounting and lower to engine to gain sufficient clearance to use the puller.

Caution: Do not use a jaw-type puller – it will damage the pulley/damper assembly.

6 To refit the crankshaft pulley, slide the pulley onto the crankshaft as far as it will go, then use a socket or metal tube to press the pulley onto the crankshaft. Note that the slot (keyway) in the hub must be aligned with the Woodruff key in the end of the crankshaft **(see illustration)** and that the crankshaft bolt can also be used to press the crankshaft pulley into position.

7 Tighten the crankshaft bolt to the torque and angle of rotation listed in this Chapter's Specifications.

8 The remaining refitting steps are the reverse of removal.

12 Crankshaft right-hand oil seal – renewal

1 Remove the crankshaft pulley (see Section 11).

2 Note how the seal is fitted – the new one must be fitted to the same depth and facing the same way. Carefully lever the oil seal out of the cover with a seal puller or a large screwdriver **(see illustration)**. Be very careful not to distort the cover or scratch the crankshaft. Wrap electrician's tape around the tip of the screwdriver to avoid damage to the crankshaft.

3 Apply clean engine oil or multipurpose grease to the outer edge of the new seal, then refit it in the cover with the lip (spring side) facing in. Drive the seal into place with a seal driver or a large socket and a hammer **(see illustration)**. Make sure the seal enters the bore squarely and stop when the front face is at the proper depth.

4 Check the surface on the pulley hub that the oil seal rides on. If the surface has been grooved from long-time contact with the seal, a press-on sleeve may be available to renew the sealing surface **(see illustration)**. This sleeve is pressed into place with a hammer and a block of wood and is commonly available at car accessory shops for various applications.

5 Lubricate the pulley hub with clean engine oil and refit the crankshaft pulley (see Section 11).

6 Refit the crankshaft pulley retaining bolt and tighten it to the torque listed in this Chapter's Specifications.

7 The remainder of refitting is the reverse of the removal.

13 Sump – removal and refitting

Removal

1 Disconnect the cable from the negative terminal of the battery.

2 Apply the handbrake and chock the rear wheels.

3 Raise the front of the vehicle and support it securely on axle stands.

4 Remove the two plastic splash shields under the engine, if equipped.

5 Drain the engine oil and remove the oil filter (see Chapter 1A). Remove the oil dipstick.

6 Remove the bolts and detach the sump. If it's stuck, lever it loose very carefully with a small screwdriver or putty knife **(see illustrations)**. Don't damage the mating surfaces of the pan and block or oil leaks could develop.

Refitting

7 Use a scraper to remove all traces of old sealant from the block and sump. Clean the mating surfaces with lacquer thinner or acetone.

8 Make sure the threaded bolt holes in the block are clean.

9 Check the sump flange for distortion,

12.4 If the sealing surface of the pulley hub has a wear groove from contact with the seal, it may be possible to obtain a sleeve from a motor factor

13.6a Sump mounting bolts

13.6b Lever the sump loose with a screwdriver or putty knife – be careful not to damage the mating surfaces of the sump and block or oil leaks may develop

13.11 Sump sealant application details

Seal Width
4.0 – 4.5 mm
(0.157-0.0177 in.)

14.2a Rotate the engine 90° anti-clockwise (from TDC) and set the crankshaft key to the left horizontal position (A), then remove the oil pump drive chain tensioner and bolt (B)

14.2b Using a screwdriver to lock the lower gear in place, loosen the retaining bolt and remove the drive chain and lower gear from the engine

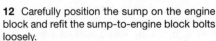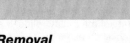

14.3 Oil pump mounting bolts (arrowed)

14 Oil pump – removal and refitting

Removal

1 Refer to Section 6, paragraphs 1 to 17, and remove the timing chain and the crankshaft sprocket.
2 Remove the oil pump drive chain and sprockets **(see illustrations)**.
3 Remove the three bolts and detach the oil pump body from the engine **(see illustration)**. You may have to lever carefully between the front of the block and the pump body with a screwdriver to remove it.
4 Use a scraper to remove all traces of sealant and old gasket material from the pump body and engine block, then clean the mating surfaces with lacquer thinner or acetone.
5 Inspect the oil pump and chain for wear and damage. If the oil pump shows signs of wear or you're in doubt about its condition it is simply best to renew it. The oil pump drive chain and tensioner, however, can be inspected as follows **(see illustrations)**. Also check the oil jet for blockage **(see illustration)**.

particularly around the bolt holes. Remove any nicks or burrs as necessary.
10 Inspect the oil pump pick-up tube assembly for cracks and a blocked strainer. If the pick-up was removed, clean it thoroughly and refit it now, using a new gasket. Tighten the nuts/bolts to the torque listed in this Chapter's Specifications.
11 Apply a 5 mm wide bead of RTV sealant to the mating surface of the sump **(see illustration)**. Note: *Be sure to follow the sealant manufacturer's recommendations for assembly and sealant curing times.*

12 Carefully position the sump on the engine block and refit the sump-to-engine block bolts loosely.
13 Working from the centre out, tighten the sump-to-engine block bolts to the torque listed in this Chapter's Specifications in three or four steps.
14 The remainder of refitting is the reverse of removal. Be sure to wait at least one hour before adding oil to allow the sealant to properly cure.
15 Run the engine and check for oil pressure and leaks.

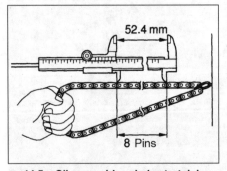

14.5a Oil pump drive chain stretch is measured by checking the length of the chain between 4 links (8 pins) at 3 or more places (selected randomly) around the chain – if chain stretch exceeds the specifications between any 4 links, the chain must be renewed

52.4 mm

8 Pins

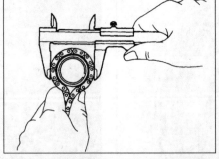

14.5b Wrap the chain around each of the oil pump drive sprockets and measure the diameter of the sprockets across the chain rollers – if the measurement is less than the minimum sprocket diameter, the chain and the sprockets must be renewed

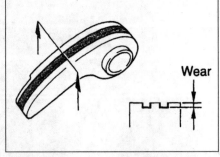

14.5c Oil pump chain guide wear is measured from the top of the chain contact surface to the bottom of the wear grooves

Wear

Refitting

6 Lubricate the pump cavity by pouring a small amount of clean engine oil into the inlet side of the oil pump and turning the drive gearshaft.

7 Position the oil pump and a new gasket against the block and refit the mounting bolts.

8 Tighten the bolts to the torque listed in this Chapter's Specifications in several steps. Follow a criss-cross pattern to avoid warping the body.

9 With the crankshaft key still set in the left horizontal position and the flat on the oil pump drive shaft facing upward, refit the drive chain and sprockets so that the coloured links on the chain align with the alignment marks on the drive gears **(see illustration)**.

10 Tighten the lower drive sprocket retaining bolt to the torque listed in this Chapter's Specifications.

11 Refit the remaining parts in the reverse order of removal.

12 Add oil to the proper level, start the engine and check for oil pressure and leaks.

15 Flywheel/driveplate –
removal and refitting

The flywheel/driveplate removal and refitting for 2001 and later engines is identical to that for the flywheel/driveplate procedure for the 2000 and earlier engines. Refer to Chapter 2 Part A for the procedure and use the torque figures in this Chapter's Specifications.

16 Crankshaft left-hand oil seal
– renewal

1 Remove the transmission (see Chapter 7A or 7B).

2 Remove the flywheel/driveplate (see Section 15).

3 Lever the oil seal from the rear of the engine with a screwdriver **(see illustration)**. Be careful not to nick or scratch the crankshaft

14.5d Check that the oil jet is free of debris – a blockage here will lead to an excessively worn timing chain, oil pump drive chain and guides

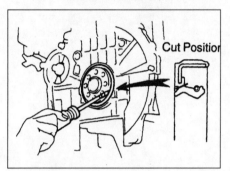

16.3 Carefully lever out the old seal with a screwdriver – it may be helpful to cut the seal lip with a razor blade first to make removal of the seal easier

or the seal bore. Be sure to note how far it's recessed into the bore before removal so the new seal can be fitted to the same depth. Thoroughly clean the seal bore in the block with a clean rag. Remove all traces of oil and dirt.

4 Lubricate the outside diameter of the seal and fit the seal over the end of the crankshaft. Make sure the lip of the seal points toward the engine. Preferably, a seal installation tool (available at most car accessory shops) is needed to press the new seal back into place. If the proper seal installation tool is unavailable, use a large socket, section of pipe or a blunt tool and carefully drive the new seal squarely

14.9 Fit the oil pump drive chain with the coloured links aligned with the marks on the sprockets

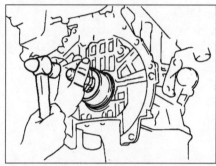

16.4 The oil seal can be pressed into place with a seal installation tool – be sure the seal is refitted squarely into the seal bore and flush with the engine

into the seal bore and flush with the edge of the engine block **(see illustration)**.

5 Refit the flywheel/driveplate (see Section 15).

6 Refit the transmission (see Chapter 7A or 7B).

17 Engine mountings –
check and renewal

The engine mounting renewal procedure for 2001 and later engines is identical to that for the 2000 and earlier engines. Refer to Chapter 2 Part A for the procedure and use the torque figures in this Chapter's Specifications.

Chapter 2 Part C:
Diesel engines

Contents

Section number

Camshaft oil seal (timing belt end) – renewal. 9
Camshafts and followers – removal and refitting. 10
Crankshaft oil seal (timing belt end) – renewal. 8
Crankshaft oil seal (transmission end) – renewal 15
Cylinder head – removal and refitting. 11
Engine mountings – removal and refitting 16
Exhaust manifold – removal and refitting 6
Flywheel/driveplate – removal and refitting 14
General information 1

Section number

Intake manifold – removal and refitting 5
Oil pump and sump upper housing – removal, inspection and
    refitting 13
Repair operations possible with the engine in the vehicle 2
Sump – removal and refitting 12
Timing belt and sprockets – removal, inspection and refitting. 7
Top Dead Centre (TDC) for number one piston – locating 3
Valve cover – removal and refitting. 4

Degrees of difficulty

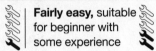

Easy, suitable for novice with little experience	Fairly easy, suitable for beginner with some experience	Fairly difficult, suitable for competent DIY mechanic	Difficult, suitable for experienced DIY mechanic	Very difficult, suitable for expert DIY or professional

Specifications

General

Engine code	1CD-FTV (D-4D)
Capacity.	1995 cc
Bore and stroke	82.2 x 94.0 mm
Compression ratio	18.6 : 1
Cylinder numbers	1-2-3-4 (timing belt end-to-transmission end)
Firing order.	1-3-4-2

Oil pump

Driven rotor-to-case clearance:	
Standard.	0.10 to 0.17 mm
Service limit	0.20 mm
Rotor tip clearance:	
Standard.	0.08 to 0.16 mm
Service limit	0.20 mm

Cylinder head

Warpage limits:	
Cylinder head-to-block surface	0.08 mm
Intake and exhaust manifolds.	0.20 mm

Manifolds

Warpage limits:	
Intake	0.1 mm
Exhaust.	0.4 mm

Camshafts

Endfloat	0.035 to 0.110 mm
Journal oil clearance:	
Standard.	0.025 to 0.062 mm
Maximum	0.08 mm
Journal diameter	26.969 to 26.985 mm
Runout (max)	0.06 mm
Lobe height:	
Standard:	
Intake	46.57 to 46.67 mm
Exhaust.	47.52 to 47.62 mm
Minimum:	
Intake	46.10 mm
Exhaust.	47.05 mm

Torque wrench settings

	lbf ft	Nm
Alternator bracket	27	37
Auxiliary drivebelt tensioner pulley (for alternator)	30	40
Auxiliary heater	9	12
Camshaft bearing caps	15	20
Camshaft oil seal housing	7	9
Camshaft sprocket	65	88
Common rail bolts	32	43
Coolant outlet elbow	15	21
Crankshaft oil seal housing	5	7
Crankshaft position sensor	7	9
Crankshaft pulley centre bolt	130	176
Cylinder head bolts:		
Stage 1	33	45
Stage 2	Angle-tighten a further 90°	
Stage 3	Angle-tighten a further 90°	
Stage 4	Angle-tighten a further 90°	
EGR valve to cylinder head	13	18
Engine mounting bracket to block	27	37
Engine mounting bracket to water pump	47	64
Exhaust manifold	34	46
Flywheel	65	88
Glow plug	9	12
High-pressure fuel pump sprocket	76	103
Idler pulley to cylinder head	25	34
Injector leak-off pipe to cylinder head	15	21
Intake manifold	15	21
Oil dipstick tube	13	18
Oil filter bracket/adapter	25	34
Oil level sensor	5	7
Oil pump	23	31
Oil pump sprocket	27	37
Oil pick-up tube to upper housing:		
Bolt	15	21
Nut	10	13
Relief valve plug to oil pump	36	49
Strainer to oil pump	10	13
Sump drain plug	25	34
Sump to upper housing	9	12
Sump upper housing:		
10 mm bolt	6	8
12 mm bolt	15	21
Throttle body to intake manifold	15	21
Timing belt cover	5	7
Timing belt plate to oil seal housing	7	9
Timing belt tensioner to water pump	15	21
Vacuum pump to cylinder head	20	27
Valve cover	10	13

1 General information

This Part of Chapter 2 is devoted to in-vehicle repair procedures for the 2.0 litre D-4D turbodiesel in-line four cylinder engine. This engine utilises a cast-iron engine block with an aluminium cylinder head. The aluminium cylinder head is equipped with pressed-in valve guides, hardened valve seats and houses the double overhead camshafts, which are driven from the crankshaft by a timing belt. Standard, adjustable followers with shims are used to actuate the valves. The

oil pump is mounted at the timing belt end of the engine and is driven by the timing belt.

All information concerning engine removal and refitting and engine block and cylinder head overhaul can be found in Part D of this Chapter.

The following repair procedures are based on the assumption that the engine is fitted in the vehicle. If the engine has been removed from the vehicle and mounted on a stand, many of the steps outlined in this Part of Chapter 2 will not apply.

The Specifications included in this Part of Chapter 2 apply only to the procedures contained in this Part. Part D of Chapter 2 contains the Specifications necessary for cylinder head and engine block overhauling.

2 Repair operations possible with the engine in the vehicle

Many major repair operations can be accomplished without removing the engine from the vehicle.

Clean the engine compartment and the exterior of the engine with some type of degreaser before any work is done. It will make the job easier and help keep dirt out of the internal areas of the engine.

Depending on the components involved, it may be helpful to remove the bonnet to improve access to the engine as repairs are

3.6a The TDC mark on the exhaust camshaft must be aligned with the upper surface of the cylinder head

3.6b TDC marks on the crankshaft sprocket and oil pump housing

performed (refer to Chapter 11 if necessary). Cover the wings to prevent damage to the paint. Special pads are available, but an old bedspread or blanket will also work.

If intake, exhaust, oil or coolant leaks develop, indicating a need for gasket or seal renewal, the repairs can generally be made with the engine in the vehicle. The intake and exhaust manifold gaskets, sump gasket, crankshaft oil seals and cylinder head gasket are all accessible with the engine in place.

Exterior engine components, such as the intake and exhaust manifolds, the sump, the oil pump, the water pump, the starter motor, the alternator and the fuel system components can be removed for repair with the engine in place.

Since the cylinder head can be removed without removing the engine, camshaft and valve component servicing can also be accomplished with the engine in the vehicle. Renewal of the timing belt and sprockets is also possible with the engine in the vehicle.

In extreme cases caused by a lack of necessary equipment, repair or renewal of piston rings, pistons, connecting rods and big-end bearings is possible with the engine in the vehicle. However, this practice is not recommended because of the cleaning and preparation work that must be done to the components involved.

3 Top Dead Centre (TDC) for number one piston – locating

1 Top Dead Centre (TDC) is the highest point in the cylinder that each piston reaches as it travels up-and-down when the crankshaft turns. Each piston reaches TDC on the compression stroke and again on the exhaust stroke, but TDC generally refers to piston position on the compression stroke. The timing marks on the flywheel (manual transmission) or the torque converter (automatic transmission)

are referenced to the number one piston at TDC.

2 Positioning the piston(s) at TDC is an essential part of procedures such as timing belt and sprocket renewal.

⚠ **Warning: Before beginning this procedure, be sure to place the transmission in Neutral, apply the handbrake and remove the ignition key.**

3 In order to bring any piston to TDC, the crankshaft must be turned with a large socket and bar attached to the large bolt threaded into the centre of the crankshaft pulley. When looking at the timing belt end of the engine, normal crankshaft rotation is clockwise.

4 Disable the fuel injection system by disconnecting the wiring to the fuel injectors on the top of the engine.

5 Remove the timing belt upper cover and the glow plugs (see Chapter 5) and fit a compression gauge in the number one cylinder glow plug hole. **Note:** *Be sure to use a diesel compression gauge that can handle at least 35 bar. Turn the crankshaft clockwise with a socket and bar as described above.*

6 When the piston approaches TDC, compression will be noted on the compression gauge. Continue turning the crankshaft until the timing mark on the exhaust camshaft sprocket is at the 3 o'clock position and aligned with the upper surface of the cylinder head. At this point, the number one cylinder is at TDC on the compression stroke. To make a further check that the crankshaft is accurately positioned, it will be necessary to remove the crankshaft pulley and lower timing belt cover in order to check that the TDC mark on the crankshaft sprocket is aligned with the corresponding mark on the oil pump. At the same time, the TDC mark on the fuel pump sprocket will be in alignment with the mark on the water pump housing **(see illustrations)**. **Note:** *If a diesel compression gauge is not available, you can simply place your finger over the glow plug hole and feel for compression as the engine is rotated. Once compression at*

3.6c TDC marks on the fuel pump sprocket and water pump housing

the No 1 glow plug hole is noted the remainder of the procedure is the same.

7 After the number one piston has been positioned at TDC on the compression stroke, TDC for any of the remaining cylinders can be located by turning the crankshaft 180 degrees and following the firing order (refer to the Specifications). Rotating the engine 180 degrees past TDC for No 1 will put the engine at TDC compression for cylinder No 3.

4 Valve cover – removal and refitting

Removal

1 Remove the intercooler (see Chapter 4B) and engine top covers. Also, unscrew the bolts securing the upper timing belt cover to the valve cover, and remove the intercooler outlet hose **(see illustration)**.

2 Refer to Chapter 4B and remove the high-pressure injector pipes from the injectors and common rail. Tape over the open fuel apertures to prevent entry of dust and dirt.

3 Disconnect the wiring from the injectors and unclip it from the supports, then disconnect the crankcase ventilation hose from the valve cover **(see illustrations)**.

4.1 Removing the intercooler outlet hose

4.3a Unclip the injector wiring from the supports . . .

4.3b . . . then disconnect it from the injectors . . .

4.3c . . . and position to one side

4.3d Disconnecting the crankcase ventilation hose

4 Prise out the glow plug seals (see illustrations).

5 Progressively unscrew the bolts and detach the valve cover from the cylinder head (see

illustration). Remove the gasket and renew if necessary.

6 If the cover is stuck to the head, tap the end with a block of wood and a hammer to jar it

loose. If that doesn't work, try to slip a flexible putty knife between the head and cover to break the seal. Be careful not to damage the gasket.

Caution: Don't prise at the cover-to-head joint or damage to the sealing surfaces may occur, leading to oil leaks after the cover is reinstalled.

7 Remove the semi-circular rubber grommet from the cylinder head and clean away any traces of sealant (see illustration). If necessary, also remove the injector seals from the valve cover.

Refitting

8 The mating surfaces of the cylinder head and cover must be clean when the cover is fitted. If necessary, use a gasket scraper to remove all traces of old gasket material from the cylinder head, then clean the mating surfaces with lacquer thinner or acetone. If there's residue or oil on the mating surfaces when the cover is fitted, oil leaks may develop.

9 Apply sealant to the semi-circular grommet and locate it on the cylinder head.

10 Fit the valve cover gasket to the groove in the valve cover (see illustration). Ensure that the gasket is correctly seated, and take care to avoid displacing it as the valve cover is lowered into position.

11 Apply sealant to the joints where the camshaft end housings contact the cylinder head, then lower the valve cover into position (see illustration).

12 Insert the bolts and tighten them progressively to the specified torque.

4.4a Prise out the glow plug seals . . .

4.4b . . . and remove them from the valve cover

4.5 Removing the valve cover

4.7 Semi-circular rubber grommet located in the cylinder head

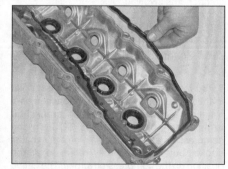

4.10 Fit the new gasket to the groove in the valve cover

13 Refit the glow plug seals **(see illustration)**.

14 Fit the high-pressure pipes to the injectors and common rail with reference to Chapter 4B.

15 Refit the injector seals and wiring.

16 Refit the upper timing belt cover, engine top covers and intercooler (see Chapter 4B).

5 Intake manifold – removal and refitting

Removal

1 The intake manifold is located on the front of the cylinder head. First, remove the intercooler (see Chapter 4B) and engine top covers.

2 Refer to Chapter 4B and remove the high-pressure injector pipes from the injectors, common rail and high-pressure pump. Tape over the open fuel apertures to prevent entry of dust and dirt. **Note:** *Toyota recommend renewal of the injector pipes whenever the injectors and/or the common rail are removed. They also recommend renewal of the fuel inlet pipe whenever the common rail or supply pump are removed.*

3 Unbolt the cover from over the high-pressure fuel pump, and remove the insulator.

4 Unscrew the bolts and remove the inlet air duct and throttle body together with the gasket.

5 Loosen the common rail mounting bolts.

6 Unscrew the bolts and nuts, and remove the intake manifold together with the gasket.

Refitting

7 Use a scraper to remove all traces of old gasket material and sealant from the manifold and cylinder head, then clean the mating surfaces with lacquer thinner or acetone. Keep in mind that the intake manifold and the cylinder head are made of aluminium, so aggressive scraping is not suggested. If the gasket was leaking, have the manifold checked for warpage and resurfaced if necessary.

8 Refit the intake manifold together with a new gasket and tighten the bolts and nuts to the specified torque.

9 Fully tighten the common rail bolts to the specified torque.

10 Refit the inlet air duct and throttle body

4.11 Refitting the valve cover onto the cylinder head

together with a new gasket, and tighten the bolts to the specified torque.

11 Refit the insulator and cover over the high-pressure pump, and tighten the bolts.

12 Refit the high-pressure injector pipes with reference to Chapter 4B.

13 Refit the engine top covers and intercooler (see Chapter 4B).

6 Exhaust manifold – removal and refitting

⚠️ *Warning: Wait until the engine is completely cool before beginning this procedure.*

Removal

1 The exhaust manifold is located on the rear of the cylinder head. First, remove the turbocharger as described in Chapter 4B.

6.2a Unbolt and remove the EGR tube . . .

6.2c . . . and cylinder head

4.13 Refit the glow plug seals

2 Unbolt the EGR cooler tube from the exhaust manifold and cylinder head, and recover the gaskets **(see illustrations)**.

3 Apply penetrating oil to the exhaust manifold mounting nuts, then unscrew them and remove the exhaust manifold from the cylinder head. Recover the collars and gasket **(see illustrations)**.

Refitting

4 Use a scraper to remove all traces of old gasket material and carbon deposits from the manifold and cylinder head mating surfaces. If the gasket was leaking, have the manifold checked for warpage.

5 Locate the new gasket on the cylinder head studs, then refit the exhaust manifold followed by the collars and nuts **(see illustrations)**. Progressively tighten the nuts to the specified torque.

6.2b . . . and remove the gaskets from the exhaust manifold . . .

6.3a Unscrew the nuts and recover the collars . . .

6.3b . . . then remove the exhaust manifold

6.5a Locate a new gasket on the cylinder head studs . . .

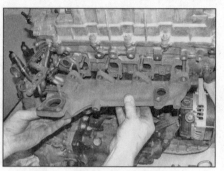

6.5b . . . then refit the exhaust manifold . . .

6.5c . . . making sure that the collars are located beneath the nuts

6 Refit the EGR cooler tube together with new gaskets, and tighten the mounting nuts/bolts.
7 Refit the turbocharger as described in Chapter 4B.
8 Run the engine and check for exhaust leaks.

7.3a Unscrew the nuts . . .

7 Timing belt and sprockets – removal, inspection and refitting

1 The primary function of the timing belt is to drive the camshafts, but it is also used to drive the high-pressure fuel pump and the water pump. Should the belt slip or break in service, the valve timing will be disturbed and piston-to-valve contact may occur, resulting in serious engine damage.
2 For this reason, it is important that the timing belt is tensioned correctly, and inspected regularly for signs of wear or deterioration.

Removal

3 Remove the intercooler (see Chapter 4B) and engine top covers. At the same time, release the vacuum hose from the support clip **(see illustrations)**.

4 Remove the glow plugs as described in Chapter 5, in order to facilitate turning the engine later.
5 Remove the auxiliary drivebelt(s) as described in Chapter 1B. Access is very limited, and it is recommended that the right-hand side headlight is removed (see Chapter 12) – this procedure also includes removal of the front bumper.
6 Remove the crankshaft pulley **(see illustrations)**.
7 Unscrew the bolts and remove the upper timing belt cover from the cylinder head/valve cover **(see illustration)**.
8 Unbolt and remove the alternator drivebelt tensioner pulley, then unscrew the bolts and remove the lower timing belt cover from the cylinder block **(see illustration)**. Also, where fitted, remove the oil pump insulator strip.
9 Remove the timing belt guide/washer from the end of the crankshaft **(see illustration)**.

7.3b . . . release the vacuum hose . . .

7.3c . . . and remove the engine top cover

7.6a Hold the crankshaft pulley stationary with a suitable tool while loosening the bolt

7.6b Unscrew the bolt . . .

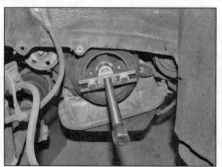

7.6c . . . then use a puller to release the pulley from the nose of the crankshaft . . .

7.6d . . . and withdraw the crankshaft pulley

7.7 Removing the upper timing belt cover

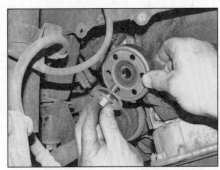

7.8a Unbolt and remove the alternator drivebelt tensioner pulley . . .

7.8b . . . then unbolt the lower timing belt cover from the cylinder block

10 Unbolt the power steering pump together with the tensioner and position it to one side without disconnecting the hydraulic fluid lines **(see illustration)**.

11 Support the engine with a hydraulic jack and block of wood, then remove the right-hand side engine mounting (see Section 16), then unscrew the bolts and remove the engine mounting bracket from the engine. For improved access through the headlight aperture, also unbolt and remove the support bracket **(see illustrations)**.

12 Set the engine to TDC on No 1 cylinder as described in Section 3.

13 If the timing belt is to be re-used, mark its normal direction of rotation to ensure it is refitted correctly.

14 Unscrew the bolt and remove the timing belt spacer/guide located beneath the camshaft sprocket **(see illustration)**.

15 Progressively unscrew the two bolts and

7.9 Removing the timing belt guide/washer from the end of the crankshaft

remove the tensioner **(see illustrations)**. Also if necessary, unbolt the tensioner roller and arm.

16 Release the timing belt from the camshaft, high-pressure pump, water pump, crankshaft

7.10 Unbolt the power steering pump and tensioner and position to one side

and oil pump sprockets, and withdraw from the engine **(see illustration)**.

17 To remove the camshaft sprocket, hold it stationary with a suitable lever inserted in the holes, then unscrew and remove the centre bolt.

7.11a For improved access, unbolt and remove the support bracket

7.11b Removing the right-hand upper engine mounting from the inner body

7.11c Removing the right-hand lower engine mounting from the engine

7.14 Removing the timing belt spacer/guide from beneath the camshaft sprocket

7.15a Unscrew the two bolts . . .

7.15b . . . and remove the tensioner

7.16 Removing the timing belt

7.17a Unscrew the centre bolt while holding the sprocket stationary . . .

7.17b . . . then pull off the sprocket . . .

7.17c . . . and recover the Woodruff key

7.18a Remove the crankshaft sprocket . . .

7.18b . . . and recover the Woodruff keys from the nose of the crankshaft

Using a puller, draw the sprocket from the end of the exhaust camshaft, and recover the Woodruff key (see illustrations). Due to the minimal clearance between the sprocket and inner body, it may not be possible to use a puller with the engine *in situ*, however, careful use of two levers may be sufficient to release it.

18 To remove the crankshaft sprocket, slide it from the end of the crankshaft. If it is tight, use a suitable puller attached to the bolt holes provided. Remove the Woodruff keys (see illustrations).

19 Removal of the high-pressure supply pump sprocket is covered in Chapter 4B. It is removed by holding it stationary and

unscrewing the nut, then withdrawing using a suitable puller.

20 Unscrew the bolt and remove the tensioner idler pulley from the cylinder block. Also, if necessary unbolt and remove the front idler.

Inspection

Caution: Do not bend, twist or turn the timing belt inside out. Do not allow it to come in contact with oil, coolant or fuel. Do not turn the crankshaft or camshaft more than a few degrees (if necessary for tooth alignment) while the timing belt is removed.

21 Check the sprockets and idlers for

excessive wear and renew them if necessary. Check the tensioner as follows. First check the integrity of the internal oil seal – if there is more that the faintest trace of oil on the seal, renew the tensioner. With the tensioner pushrod on the side of the workbench, press on the body to check that the pushrod does not move. Measure the protrusion of the pushrod – if it is more than 10.6 mm, renew the tensioner (see illustration).

22 Examine the belt for evidence of contamination by coolant or lubricant. If this is the case, find the source of the contamination before progressing any further. Check the belt for signs of wear or damage, particularly

7.21 Measuring the protrusion of the timing belt tensioner pushrod

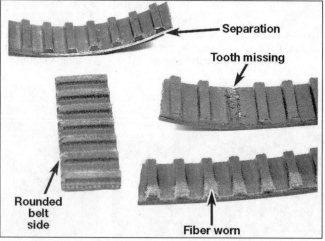

7.22 Check the timing belt for cracked and missing teeth – wear on one side of the belt indicates sprocket misalignment problems

7.28a Refit the camshaft sprocket . . .

7.28b . . . and secure with the centre bolt

7.29a Using a G-clamp to compress tensioner pushrod

7.29b Using an Allen key to set the tensioner

7.30a Refit the tensioner roller and arm . . .

7.30b . . . then refit the tensioner . . .

around the leading edges of the belt teeth (see illustration).

Caution: If the belt appears to be in good condition and can be re-used, it is essential that it is reinstalled the same way around, otherwise accelerated wear will result, leading to premature failure.

23 Renew the belt if its condition is in doubt; the cost of belt renewal is negligible compared with potential cost of the engine repairs, should the belt fail in service. Similarly, if the belt is known to have covered more than 36 000 miles, it is prudent to renew it regardless of condition, as a precautionary measure.

Refitting

24 Ensure that the crankshaft is still set to TDC on No 1 cylinder, as described in Section 3.
25 Refit the idler pulley and idlers, and tighten the bolts to the specified torque.

26 If removed, refit the high-pressure pump sprocket with reference to Chapter 4B.
27 Fit the Woodruff key, then refit the crankshaft sprocket, using a metal tube if necessary to drive it into position.
28 Fit the Woodruff key, then refit the camshaft sprocket on the camshaft. Hold the sprocket stationary, then refit the centre bolt and tighten to the specified torque (see illustrations).
29 Before refitting the tensioner, it must be set as follows. Using a press or suitable alternative, press the pushrod into the tensioner body until the holes are aligned, then insert a 1.3 mm diameter pin or alternative through the holes and release the press (see illustrations).
30 Where removed, refit the tensioner roller and arm and tighten the bolt, then refit the tensioner to the cylinder block and tighten the bolts to the specified torque (see illustrations).

31 Check that the crankshaft and camshaft are both still set to TDC on No 1 cylinder, then fit the timing belt onto the camshaft sprocket, high-pressure pump sprocket, water pump sprocket, crankshaft sprocket, rear idler pulley, water pump and tensioner pulley, in that order (see illustration).

Caution: If refitting a used belt, observe the direction of rotation markings on the belt.

32 Check the position of the timing belt, then pull out the pin to release the pushrod against the tensioner pulley and tension the belt (see illustration).
33 Temporarily refit the crankshaft pulley bolt, then turn the engine through two complete revolutions and set it to TDC again. Do not turn the engine anti-clockwise during this procedure. Check that the timing marks on the crankshaft and camshaft sprockets align correctly, then remove the crankshaft pulley bolt.

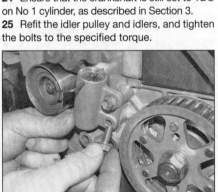

7.30c . . . and insert and tighten the mounting bolts

7.31 Refitting the timing belt

7.32 Pull out the pin to set the tensioner

7.35 Refit the right-hand side engine mounting bracket to the engine

7.38 Refit the timing belt guide/washer to the end of the crankshaft

7.40 Refitting the lower timing belt cover . . .

7.42 . . . and upper timing belt cover

7.43 Refitting the crankshaft pulley

34 Refit the timing belt spacer/guide beneath the camshaft sprocket and tighten the bolt.
35 Refit the right-hand side engine mounting bracket then refit the mounting to the inner body (see Section 16) and tighten the bolts to the specified torque **(see illustration)**.

Remove the hydraulic jack.
36 Where removed, refit the support bracket behind the headlight aperture and tighten the bolts.
37 Refit the power steering pump together with the tensioner and tighten the bolts.

38 Refit the timing belt guide/washer to the end of the crankshaft **(see illustration)**.
39 Clean the mating surfaces of the lower timing belt cover, and check the condition of the gasket. If it requires renewal, remove the old gasket then remove the backing paper and fit the new gasket to the cover, making sure it is fully in the groove. If there is a gap between the ends of the gasket, apply sealant with the same profile as the gasket.
40 Fit the oil pump insulator (where fitted) then refit the lower timing belt cover and tighten the bolts **(see illustration)**.
41 Clean the mating surfaces of the upper timing belt cover, and check the condition of the gasket. If necessary, renew the gasket as described in paragraph 39.
42 Refit the upper timing belt cover and tighten the bolts **(see illustration)**.
43 Refit the crankshaft pulley **(see illustration)**.
44 Refit the auxiliary drivebelt(s) as described in Chapter 1B. If removed, refit the headlight (see Chapter 12).
45 Refit the glow plugs as described in Chapter 5.
46 Refit the intercooler (see Chapter 4B) and engine top covers.

8 Crankshaft oil seal (timing belt end) – renewal

1 Remove the timing belt and crankshaft sprocket (see Section 7).
2 Note how far the seal is recessed in the bore, then carefully lever it out of the oil pump housing with a screwdriver or seal removal tool. The seal may be easier to remove if the old seal lip is cut with a sharp utility knife first **(see illustrations)**. Don't scratch the housing bore or damage the crankshaft in the process (if the crankshaft is damaged, the new seal will end up leaking).
3 Clean the bore in the housing and coat the outer edge of the new seal with engine oil or multipurpose grease. Apply multipurpose grease to the seal lip.
4 Put the new seal over the crankshaft and then use the crankshaft sprocket and centre bolt to press the seal into place **(see illustrations)**. Make sure it's fitted squarely

8.2a If necessary, cut away the oil seal lip before . . .

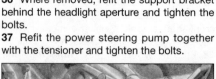

8.2b . . . using a screwdriver to lever out the old seal

8.4a Locate the new oil seal over the crankshaft . . .

8.4b . . . and use the crankshaft sprocket and centre bolt to press the seal into position . . .

8.4c ... using a block of wood to ensure it is flush with the surface of the oil pump

10.4 Removing the camshaft position sensor

10.5a Remove the brake vacuum pump from the rear of the cylinder head ...

10.5b ... and recover the large O-ring seal ...

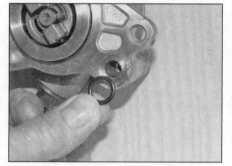

10.5c ... and small O-ring seal

10.7 Removing the camshaft oil seal retainer from the cylinder head

and driven in to the same depth as the original using a block of wood (see illustration). Check the seal after refitting to make sure the spring didn't pop out of place.

5 Refit the crankshaft sprocket and timing belt (see Section 7).

6 Run the engine and check for oil leaks at the seal.

9 Camshaft oil seal (timing belt end) – renewal

1 Remove the timing belt and camshaft sprocket as described in Section 7.

2 Note how far the seal is recessed in the bore, then carefully prise it out of the housing with a

screwdriver or seal removal tool. Don't scratch the housing bore or damage the camshaft in the process otherwise the seal will leak. **Note:** *The seal may be easier to remove if the old seal lip is cut with a sharp utility knife first.*

3 Clean the bore in the housing and coat the outer edge of the new seal with engine oil or multipurpose grease. Apply multipurpose grease to the seal lip.

4 Using a socket with an outside diameter slightly smaller than the outside diameter of the seal, carefully drive the new seal into place with a hammer. Make sure it's fitted squarely and driven in to the same depth as the original. If a socket isn't available, a short section of large diameter pipe will also work. Check the seal after fitting to make sure the spring didn't pop out of place.

5 Refit the timing belt and camshaft sprocket as described in Section 7.

6 Run the engine and check for leaks at the front seal.

10 Camshafts and followers – removal and refitting

Removal

1 Drain the engine coolant (see Chapter 1B).

2 Remove the valve cover as described in Section 4.

3 Remove the timing belt and camshaft sprocket as described in Section 7.

4 Unscrew the bolt and remove the camshaft position sensor from the rear of the cylinder head (see illustration).

5 Unscrew the two mounting bolts and remove the brake vacuum pump from the cylinder head. Recover the two O-ring seals (see illustrations).

6 Unbolt and remove the injector leak-off pipe.

7 Unscrew the bolts and lever the camshaft oil seal retainer away from the front of the cylinder head (see illustration). Prise out the oil seal as a new one must be fitted on reassembly.

8 Identify the position of each of the camshaft bearing caps on the cylinder head.

9 Progressively loosen the camshaft bearing cap bolts using the sequence shown, then remove the bearing caps followed by the camshafts and camshaft carrier (see illustrations).

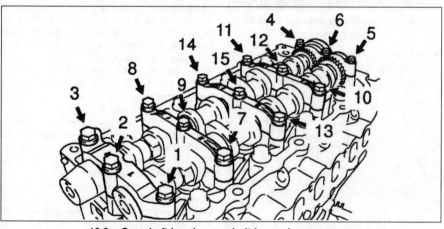

10.9a Camshaft bearing cap bolt loosening sequence

10.9b Remove the camshaft bearing
caps . . .

10.9c . . . followed by the camshafts . . .

10.9d . . . and camshaft carrier

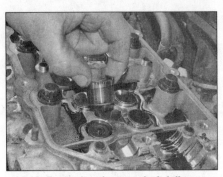

10.10 Removing the camshaft followers

10.12 Insert the camshaft followers and
shims to their correct bores

10.13 Locate the camshaft carrier on the
cylinder head

*Caution: Failure to unscrew the bolts in
sequence may result in damage to the
cylinder head.*

10 Using a magnet or suction pad,
withdraw the camshaft followers and shims

from their bores, keeping them identified
for position to ensure correct refitting **(see
illustration)**.

11 Inspect the camshaft and followers as
described in Chapter 2A.

Refitting

12 Insert the camshaft followers and shims
to their correct bores, having lightly oiled
the bores; check that the followers can be
rotated smoothly in the bores by hand **(see
illustration)**.

13 Locate the camshaft carrier on the cylinder
head **(see illustration)**.

14 Oil the bearing surfaces of the carrier
and intake camshaft, then lower the intake
camshaft onto the cylinder head, in its
position nearest the front of the head **(see
illustrations)**. Position the camshaft so that
the lobes of cylinders 3 and 4 are facing
downwards.

15 Oil the bearing surfaces of the carrier and
exhaust camshaft, then lower the exhaust
camshaft onto the cylinder head, in its position
at the rear of the head, at the same time
aligning the TDC marks on the gear of each
camshaft. The marks are on the inner face of
each gear **(see illustration)**.

16 Clean the mating surface of camshaft
bearing cap 5 and apply sealant as shown
(see illustration).

17 Refit all the camshaft bearing caps in their
correct position, then progressively tighten
them to the specified torque in sequence **(see
illustrations)**

18 Check and adjust the valve clearances as
described in Chapter 1B.

19 Clean the mating surface of the camshaft
oil seal retainer, and apply a 2 to 4 mm wide
bead of sealant as shown **(see illustration)**.
Refit the retainer and tighten the bolts to the
specified torque.

10.14a Oil the bearing surfaces . . .

10.14b . . . then lower the inlet camshaft
onto the cylinder head

10.15 Align the TDC marks on the camshaft
gears before fitting the bearing caps

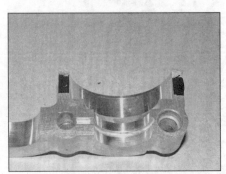

10.16 Apply sealant to the camshaft
bearing cap 5 as shown

10.17a Refitting the camshaft bearing caps

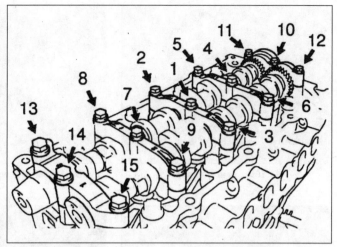

10.17b Camshaft bearing cap bolt tightening sequence

20 Fit a new oil seal to the retainer as follows. Locate the new oil seal over the end of the camshaft, then use a metal tube to drive it in the retainer until flush with the outer edge.

21 Clean the semi-circular grommet and apply sealant to its grooves, then locate it on the end of the cylinder head.

22 Refit the injector leak-off pipe and tighten the union bolts to the specified torque.

23 Fit new O-ring seals to the vacuum pump, then align the drive lugs with the slot in the camshaft and refit the pump. Insert the bolts and tighten to the specified torque.

24 Refit the timing belt and camshaft sprocket as described in Section 7.

25 Refit the valve cover as described in Section 4.

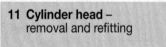

11 Cylinder head –
  removal and refitting

 Warning: Wait until engine is completely cool before beginning this procedure.

Removal

1 Drain the engine coolant (see Chapter 1B).

2 Remove the intercooler (see Chapter 4B) and engine top covers.

3 Refer to Section 7 and remove the timing belt and the camshaft sprocket. Also, unbolt and remove the timing belt triangular inner cover **(see illustration)**.

4 Remove the turbocharger as described in Chapter 4B.

5 Unscrew the nuts and remove the exhaust manifold from the cylinder head. Recover the collars and gasket.

6 Unscrew the bolt and remove the camshaft position sensor from the rear of the cylinder head.

7 Where fitted, unbolt the cover from over the high-pressure fuel pump, and remove the insulator.

8 Disconnect the wiring and vacuum hose, then unscrew the bolts and remove the inlet air duct and throttle body together with the gasket **(see illustrations)**.

9 Loosen the common rail mounting bolts. This is necessary to allow room for the intake manifold to be removed.

10 Unscrew the bolts and nuts, and remove the intake manifold together with the gasket **(see illustration)**.

11 Unbolt the timing belt cover bracket.

12 Remove the crankcase ventilation hose.

13 Unbolt the water outlet elbow and recover the gasket **(see illustrations)**.

14 Remove the bolts and withdraw the common rail **(see illustration)**.

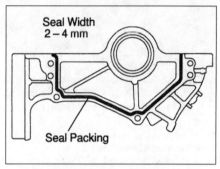

10.19 Apply sealant to the camshaft oil seal retainer as shown

11.3 Removing the timing belt triangular inner cover

11.8a Unscrew the bolts ...

11.8b ... and remove the air inlet duct together with throttle body and gasket

11.10a Removing the inlet manifold ...

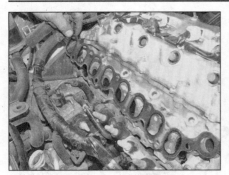

11.10b . . . and gasket

11.13a Unbolt the water outlet elbow . . .

11.13b . . . and recover the gasket

11.14 Removing the common rail

11.16a EGR valve location

11.16b Removing the EGR valve

15 If necessary, unscrew and remove the water temperature sensor.

16 Unscrew the single bolt and two nuts and remove the EGR valve and gasket **(see illustrations)**.

17 Unscrew the two mounting bolts and remove the vacuum pump from the end of the cylinder head **(see illustration)**. Recover the two O-ring seals.

18 Where fitted on the end of the cylinder

head, remove the caps and unscrew the three nuts from the auxiliary heater plug supply terminals. Unscrew and remove the heater plugs. **Note:** *An auxiliary heater is only fitted to models in cold climates.*

19 Loosen the clips and disconnect the fuel hose and oil cooler hose.

20 Unscrew and remove the injector leak-off valve, pipe and gasket.

21 Unbolt and remove the injector leak-off pipe **(see illustrations)**.

22 Remove the injectors as described in Chapter 4B. This procedure includes removal of the valve cover.

23 Unscrew the bolts and lever the camshaft oil seal retainer away from the cylinder head **(see illustration)**. Prise out the oil seal as a new one must be fitted on reassembly.

24 Identify the position of each of the camshaft bearing caps on the cylinder head.

25 Progressively loosen the camshaft bearing cap bolts using the sequence shown **(see illustration 10.9a)**, then remove the bearing caps followed by the camshafts and camshaft carrier.

Caution: Failure to unscrew the bolts in sequence may result in damage to the cylinder head.

26 Progressively loosen the cylinder head bolts using the sequence shown **(see illustration)** then remove the bolts together with their washers.

Caution: Failure to unscrew the bolts in sequence may result in cylinder head warpage or cracking.

27 Check that all wiring has been disconnected, then carefully lift the cylinder

11.17 Removing the vacuum pump

11.21a Unscrew the union bolts . . .

11.21b . . . and remove the injector leak-off pipe

11.23 Removing the camshaft oil seal retainer

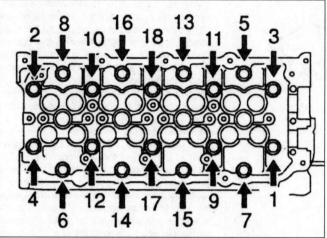

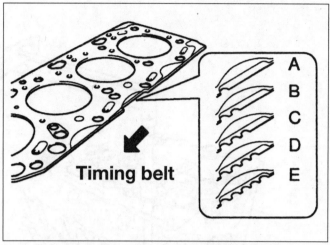

11.26 Cylinder head bolt loosening sequence

11.34 Cylinder head gasket identification cut-outs

head from the dowels on the cylinder block, and place it on the workbench.

28 Remove the gasket from the top of the block. Do not discard the gasket – it will be needed for identification purposes.

Refitting

29 The mating faces of the cylinder head and cylinder block must be perfectly clean before refitting the head. Use a hard plastic or wood scraper to remove all traces of gasket and carbon; also clean the piston crowns. Take particular care during the cleaning operations, as aluminium alloy is easily damaged. Also, make sure that the carbon is not allowed to enter the oil and water passages – this is particularly important for the lubrication system, as carbon could block the oil supply to the engine's components. Using adhesive tape and paper, seal the water, oil and bolt holes in the cylinder block.

30 Check the mating surfaces of the cylinder block and the cylinder head for nicks, deep scratches and other damage. If slight, they may be removed carefully with abrasive paper.

31 If warpage of the cylinder head gasket surface is suspected, use a straight-edge to check it for distortion (see Specifications), but note that head machining may not be possible.

32 Clean out the cylinder head bolt holes

using a suitable tap. Be sure they are clean and dry before refitting of the head bolts.

33 On diesel engines it is possible for the piston crowns to strike and damage the valve heads if the camshaft is rotated with the timing belt removed and the crankshaft set to TDC. For this reason, the crankshaft must be set to a position other than TDC on No 1 cylinder before the cylinder head is reinstalled. Use a spanner and socket on the crankshaft pulley centre bolt to turn the crankshaft anti-clockwise until all four pistons are positioned halfway down their bores (approximately 90-degrees before TDC).

34 Examine the old cylinder head gasket for manufacturer's identification markings. These will be in the form of punched cut-outs on the front edge of the gasket **(see illustration)**. Unless new pistons have been fitted, the new cylinder head gasket must be the same type as the old one.

35 If new pistons have been fitted as part of an engine overhaul, before purchasing the new cylinder head gasket, measure the piston projection as follows to determine the thickness of head gasket to be used. Rotate the engine so that the No 1 piston is located at TDC. Using a dial indicator or a depth micrometer measure the distance that the piston protrudes past the gasket surface of the block **(see illustration)**. Repeat the measuring process on the remaining three cylinders and

record the highest reading. Five different-thickness head gaskets are available for diesel engines depending on the amount the piston protrudes above the gasket surface. Compare the highest reading to the gasket selection chart below to select the proper head gasket thickness. Purchase a new gasket according to the results of the measurement (see table below).

36 Cut off the heads from two of the old cylinder head bolts to use as alignment dowels during cylinder head refitting. Also cut a slot in the end of the each bolt, big enough for a screwdriver blade so that the alignment dowels can be removed after the cylinder head is fitted. A simple hand-held hacksaw can be used to fabricate the alignment dowels.

37 Refit the alignment dowels in the outer rear holes of the cylinder block and position the new head gasket on the cylinder block, engaging it with the locating dowels. Ensure that the manufacturer's TOP and part number markings face up.

38 With the help of an assistant, place the cylinder head centrally on the cylinder block, ensuring that the locating dowels engage with the recesses in the cylinder head. Check that the head gasket is correctly seated before allowing the full weight of the cylinder head to rest upon it.

39 Oil the threads and the underside of the bolt heads and washers, then carefully

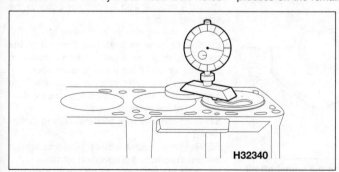

11.35 Measuring the piston projection with a dial indicator (DTI)

Piston projection table

Piston projection	Gasket cut-outs	Gasket thickness
0.165 to 0.220 mm	1 (A)	0.85 to 0.95 mm
0.220 to 0.270 mm	2 (B)	0.90 to 1.00 mm
0.270 to 0.320 mm	3 (C)	0.95 to 1.05 mm
0.320 to 0.370 mm	4 (D)	1.00 to 1.10 mm
0.370 to 0.425 mm	5 (E)	1.05 to 1.15 mm

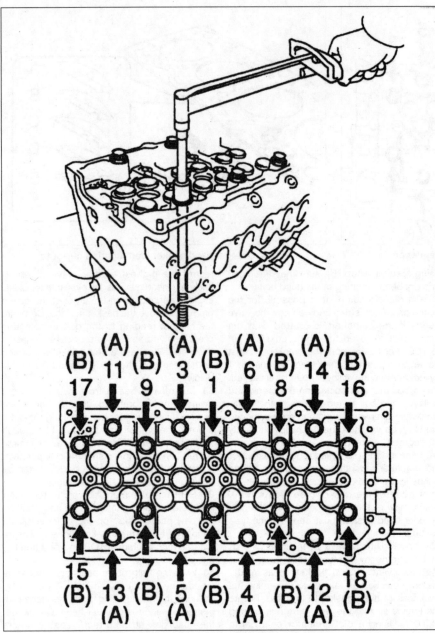

11.41 Cylinder head bolt tightening sequence

A = 160 mm   B = 104 mm

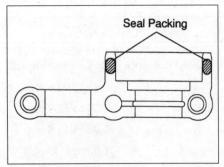

11.48 Apply sealant to the shaded area of bearing cap 5

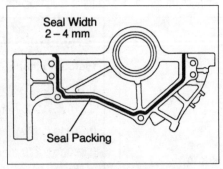

11.51 Apply sealant to the camshaft oil seal retainer as shown

guide each bolt into its relevant hole and screw them in hand tight. Be sure to use NEW cylinder head bolts, as the old bolts are stretch-type that will not obtain the correct torque readings if re-used. Note that the bolts for the outer rows are longer than those for the inner rows.

40 Unscrew the home-made alignment dowels using a flat-bladed screwdriver and refit the remaining two bolts hand-tight.

41 Working progressively and in sequence **(see illustration)**, tighten the cylinder head bolts to the Stage 1 torque wrench setting.

42 Angle-tighten the bolts in the same sequence by the Stage 2 angle. **Note:** *It is recommended that an angle measuring gauge be used to ensure accuracy. If a gauge is not available, use white paint to make alignment marks between the bolt head and cylinder head prior to tightening; the marks can then be used to check the bolt has been rotated through the correct angle during tightening.*

43 Angle-tighten the bolts in the same sequence by the Stage 3 angle.

44 Angle-tighten the bolts in the same sequence by the Stage 4 angle.

45 Locate the camshaft carrier on the cylinder head.

46 Oil the bearing surfaces of the carrier and intake camshaft, then lower the intake camshaft onto the cylinder head, in its position nearest the front of the head. Position the camshaft so that the lobes of cylinders 3 and 4 are facing downwards.

47 Oil the bearing surfaces of the carrier and exhaust camshaft, then lower the exhaust camshaft onto the cylinder head, in its position at the rear of the head, at the same time aligning the marks on the gear of each camshaft. The marks are on the inner face of each gear.

48 Clean the mating surface of camshaft bearing cap 5 and apply sealant as shown **(see illustration)**.

49 Refit all the camshaft bearing caps in their correct position, then progressively tighten them to the specified torque in sequence **(see illustration 10.17b)**.

50 Check and adjust the valve clearances as described in Chapter 1B.

51 Clean the mating surface of the camshaft oil seal retainer, and apply a 2 to 4 mm wide bead of sealant as shown **(see illustration)**. Refit the retainer and tighten the bolts to the specified torque.

52 Fit a new oil seal to the retainer as follows. Locate the new oil seal over the end of the camshaft, then use a metal tube to drive it in the retainer until flush with the outer edge.

53 Clean the semi-circular grommet and apply sealant to its grooves, then locate it on the end of the cylinder head.

54 Refit the injectors as described in Chapter 4B.

55 Refit the injector leak-off pipe and tighten the union bolts to the specified torque.

56 Refit the injector leak-off valve, pipe and gasket.

57 Refit the fuel hose and oil cooler hose.
58 Where fitted, refit the auxiliary heater plugs and caps.
59 Fit new O-ring seals to the vacuum pump, then align the drive lugs with the slot in the camshaft and refit the pump. Insert the bolts and tighten to the specified torque.
60 Refit the EGR valve together with a new gasket, and tighten the bolts to the specified torque.
61 Refit the water temperature sensor.
62 Refit the common rail but do not tighten the bolts at this stage.
63 Refit the collant outlet elbow together with a new gasket, and tighten the bolts to the specified torque.
64 Refit the crankcase ventilation hose.
65 Refit the timing belt cover bracket and tighten the bolts to the specified torque.
66 Refit the intake manifold together with a new gasket and tighten the bolts and nuts to the specified torque **(see illustration)**.
67 Fully tighten the common rail bolts to the specified torque.
68 Refit the inlet air duct and throttle body together with a new gasket, and tighten the bolts to the specified torque. Reconnect the wiring and vacuum hose.
69 Where applicable, refit the insulator and cover over the high-pressure pump, and tighten the bolts.
70 Refit the camshaft position sensor.
71 Refit the exhaust manifold together with a new gasket. Refit the collars and bolts and tighten to the specified torque.
72 Refit the turbocharger as described in Chapter 4B.
73 Refit the timing belt and camshaft sprocket as described in Section 7. Also refit the triangular timing belt inner cover.
74 Refit the engine top covers and intercooler as described in Chapter 4B.
75 Refill the engine with coolant as described in Chapter 1B. Run the engine and check for leaks.

12 Sump –
removal and refitting
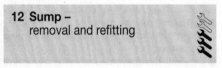

Removal

1 Apply the handbrake, then jack up the front of the vehicle and support on axle stands. Remove the undertray.
2 Drain the engine oil and remove the oil filter (see Chapter 1B). Remove the oil dipstick.
3 Disconnect the wiring from the oil level sensor **(see illustration)**.
4 Unscrew the bolts and remove the sump. If it's stuck, prise it loose very carefully with a screwdriver or putty knife. Don't damage the mating surfaces of the sump and housing or oil leaks could develop.
5 If required, unbolt the oil level sensor from the sump and recover the gasket **(see illustration)**.

11.66 Refitting the inlet manifold

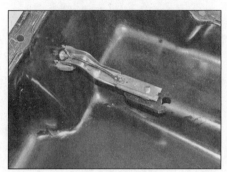
12.5 View of the oil level sensor inside the sump

Refitting
6 Clean all sealant from the sump and block mating surfaces.
7 If removed, refit the oil level sensor together with a new gasket and tighten the bolts.
8 Apply a 4 to 7 mm wide bead of sealant on the sump flange, making sure that it is around the inner side of the bolt holes **(see illustrations)**.

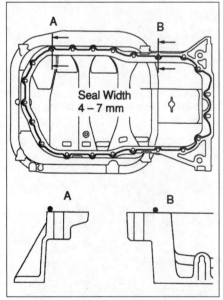
12.8b . . . as shown in the diagram

12.3 Oil level sensor on the sump

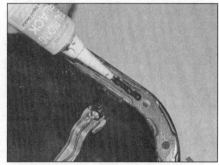
12.8a Apply sealant to the sump . . .

9 Carefully position the sump on the engine block and insert the bolts **(see illustration)**. Progressively tighten them to the specified torque wrench setting.
10 The remainder of refitting is a reversal of removal. Add oil and a new filter, then run the engine and check for leaks.

13 Oil pump and sump upper housing – removal, inspection and refitting

Removal
1 Remove the sump as described in Section 12.
2 Remove the timing belt as described in Section 7. Also remove the crankshaft sprocket and front idler **(see illustration)**.

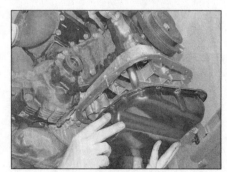
12.9 Refitting the sump

13.2 Removing the timing belt front idler

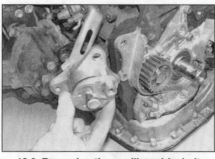

13.3 Removing the auxiliary drivebelt tensioner bracket from below the alternator

13.4 Removing the O-ring from the dipstick tube

13.5 Removing the oil pressure relief valve from the the upper housing

13.6 Removing the oil pick-up tube and gasket

13.7 Removing the sump insulator

3 Unbolt and remove the auxiliary drivebelt tensioner bracket from below the alternator **(see illustration)**.

4 Unscrew the support bolt, then remove the

13.8a Remove the oil filter housing . . .

13.8b . . . and recover the O-ring seal

13.9 Crankshaft position sensor on the oil pump housing

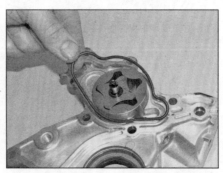

13.10 Removing the oil pump O-ring seal

dipstick tube from the sump upper housing. Remove the O-ring from the tube **(see illustration)**.

5 If required, unbolt and remove the oil level

sensor. Also, if required, the oil pressure relief valve may be unbolted from the sump upper housing **(see illustration)**.

6 Unscrew the flange and support nuts and bolts, and remove the oil pick-up tube and gasket **(see illustration)**.

7 Unscrew the bolt and remove the sump insulator **(see illustration)**.

8 Unscrew the bolts and withdraw the sump upper housing from the bottom of the engine block, then recover the two O-ring seals. If it's stuck, prise it loose very carefully with a screwdriver or putty knife. Don't damage the mating surfaces of the sump and block or oil leaks could develop. If necessary, the oil filter housing may be removed from the upper housing and the O-ring seal recovered **(see illustration)**.

9 Unscrew the bolt and remove the crankshaft position sensor from the oil pump housing **(see illustration)**.

10 Unscrew the bolts and remove the oil pump over the front of the crankshaft and from the cylinder block. If it's stuck, carefully lever it away by inserting a screwdriver from below. Remove the O-ring seal **(see illustration)**.

Inspection

11 Refer to Part A of this Chapter. Fit a new crankshaft oil seal to the oil pump housing with reference to Section 8 **(see illustrations)**.

Refitting

12 If fitting a new oil pump, remove the stud from the old one and transfer to the new one.

13 Clean the mating surfaces of the oil pump

13.11a Checking the driven rotor-to-case clearance . . .

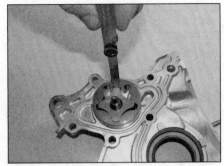

13.11b . . . and the rotor tip clearance with a feeler gauge

13.11c Drive out the old oil seal from the inside of the housing . . .

13.11d . . . then use a drift to drive in the new oil seal until flush with the outside surface of the housing

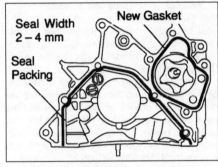

13.13a Apply sealant to the oil pump as shown

13.13b Cut the sealant tube to provide a 2 to 4 mm wide bead of sealant

and cylinder block, then apply a 2 to 4 mm wide bead of sealant to the oil pump housing making sure that it is around the inner side of the bolt holes **(see illustrations)**. Locate a new gasket around the oil pump rotor area.

14 Inject oil into the oil pump cavity in the block, then refit the oil pump onto the location dowels and tighten the bolts to the specified torque **(see illustrations)**. Check that the pump sprocket turns freely.

15 Refit the crankshaft position sensor and tighten the bolts to the specified torque.
16 Clean the mating surfaces of the sump upper housing and block, then apply a 4 to 7 mm wide bead of sealant to the housing as shown **(see illustration 12.8a and 12.8b)**. Note how the bead runs on the inner and outer sides of the bolt holes **(see illustration)**.
17 Fit two new O-ring seals, then refit the upper housing and progressively tighten the bolts to the specified torque **(see illustrations)**.
18 If removed, refit the oil filter housing together with a new O-ring seal, and tighten the mounting nuts/bolt.
19 Refit the sump insulator and tighten the bolt to the specified torque.
20 Refit the oil pick-up tube together with a new gasket, and tighten the nuts and bolts to the specified torque.
21 Refit the oil level sensor and tighten to the specified torque.

13.14a Inject oil into the oil pump cavity . . .

13.14b . . . then refit the oil pump . . .

13.14c . . . onto the location dowels

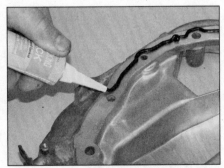

13.16 Apply a 4 to 7 mm wide bead of sealant to the upper sump housing

13.17a Fit two new O-ring seals in the grooves provided . . .

13.17b . . . then refit the upper housing

22 Refit the dipstick tube together with a new O-ring and tighten the support bolt.
23 Refit the auxiliary drivebelt adjustment bracket and tighten the bolts to the specified torque.
24 Refit the timing belt, crankshaft sprocket and front idler as described in Section 7.
25 Refit the sump as described in Section 12.

14 Flywheel/driveplate – removal and refitting

Removal

1 A dual mass flywheel is fitted on diesel models. The flywheel/driveplate removal and refitting procedure is identical to that described in Chapter 2A, however, use the torque settings given in the Specifications at the beginning of this Chapter.

2 If necessary, for example to renew the crankshaft oil seal, unbolt and remove the engine rear plate.

Refitting

3 Refitting is a reversal of removal.

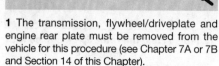

15 Crankshaft oil seal (transmission end) – renewal

1 The transmission, flywheel/driveplate and engine rear plate must be removed from the vehicle for this procedure (see Chapter 7A or 7B and Section 14 of this Chapter).
2 The seal can be renewed without removing the sump, sump upper housing or the seal housing. However, this method is not recommended because the lip of the seal is quite stiff and it's possible to cock the seal in the retainer bore or damage it during fitting. If you want to take the chance, prise out the old seal with a screwdriver. Apply multipurpose grease to the crankshaft seal journal and the lip of the new seal and carefully push the new seal into place. The lip is stiff so carefully work it onto the journal of the crankshaft with a smooth object like the end of an extension as you tap the seal into place. Don't rush it or you may damage the seal.
3 The following method is recommended but requires removal of the sump, sump upper housing and the seal housing. Refer to Sections 12 and 13 for the removal of the sump and upper housing, but do not remove the oil pump.

4 Unscrew the bolts and remove the seal housing, then clean away all traces of sealant from the housing and block.
5 Position the seal and housing assembly between two wood blocks on a workbench and drive the old seal out from the back side with a screwdriver.
6 Drive the new seal into the housing with a block of wood or a section of pipe slightly smaller in diameter than the outside diameter of the seal.
7 Apply a 2 mm to 3 mm wide bead of sealant to the flange of the housing, so that it is on the inner sides of the bolt holes.
8 Lubricate the crankshaft seal journal and the lip of the new seal with multipurpose grease.
9 Slowly and carefully push the seal and housing onto the crankshaft. The seal lip is stiff, so work it onto the crankshaft with a smooth object such as the end of an extension as you push the housing against the block.
10 Insert and tighten the housing bolts to the specified torque.
11 Refit the sump upper housing and the sump as described in Sections 12 and 13.
12 Refit the engine rear plate, flywheel/driveplate transmission and engine rear plate as described in Chapter 7A or 7B.

16 Engine mountings – removal and refitting

Refer to Chapter 2A.

Chapter 2 Part D:
Engine removal and overhaul procedures

Contents

Section number

Crankshaft – inspection 16
Crankshaft – refitting 19
Crankshaft – removal 13
Cylinder block – cleaning and inspection. 14
Cylinder compression check 3
Cylinder head – dismantling 9
Cylinder head – reassembly 11
Cylinder head and valves – cleaning and inspection 10
Engine – removal and refitting 7
Engine overhaul – dismantling sequence. 8
Engine overhaul – reassembly sequence 18

Section number

Engine overhauling alternatives 5
Engine removal – methods and precautions 6
General information – engine overhaul. 1
Initial start-up after reassembly 22
Main and big-end bearings – inspection 17
Oil pressure check 2
Piston rings – refitting. 20
Pistons/connecting rods – inspection 15
Pistons/connecting rods – refitting. 21
Pistons/connecting rods – removal 12
Vacuum gauge diagnostic checks 4

Degrees of difficulty

Easy, suitable for novice with little experience	**Fairly easy,** suitable for beginner with some experience	**Fairly difficult,** suitable for competent DIY mechanic	**Difficult,** suitable for experienced DIY mechanic	**Very difficult,** suitable for expert DIY or professional

Specifications

General
Engine designation:
  Petrol:
    2000 and earlier 3S-FE
    2001-on . . . .   1ZZ-FE and 1AZ-FE
  Diesel 1CD-FTV (D-4D)
Capacity:
  3S-FE . . . .   2.0 litres (1998 cc)
  1ZZ-FE . . . .   1.8 litres (1794 cc)
  1AZ-FE . . . .   2.0 litres (1998 cc)
  1CD-FTV (D-4D) . . . .   2.0 litres (1995 cc)

General (continued)

Bore and stroke:
3S-FE . . . . 86.0 x 86.0 mm
1AZ-FE . . . . 86.0 x 86.0 mm
1CD-FTV (D-4D) . . . . 82.2 x 94.0 mm

Cylinder compression pressure @ 250 rpm:	Standard	Minimum	Difference between cylinders
1996 and 1997	12.8 bar or more	9.3 bar	1.0 bar or less
1998 to 2000	12.3 bar or more	8.8 bar	1.0 bar or less
2001 and later – petrol	12.7 bar or more	10.0 bar	1.0 bar or less
2001 and later – diesel	27.5 bar or more	22.6 bar	4.9 bar or less

Oil pressure (engine warm):
2000 and earlier
At idle . . . . 0.3 bar minimum
At 3000 rpm . . . . 2.5 to 4.9 bar
2001 and later – petrol
At idle . . . . 0.3 bar minimum
At 3000 rpm . . . . 2.5 to 5.4 bar
2001 and later – diesel
At idle . . . . 0.3 bar minimum
At 4500 rpm . . . . 2.5 to 5.9 bar

Cylinder head

Valve seat angle . . . . 45°
Valve seat width:
Petrol engines . . . . 1.0 to 1.4 mm
Diesel engines:
Intake . . . . 1.2 to 1.6 mm
Exhaust . . . . 1.6 to 2.0 mm

Pistons and piston rings

Piston diameter:
2000 and earlier models:
2.0 litre petrol engines . . . . 85.837 to 85.867 mm
2001 and later models:
1.8 litre petrol engines . . . . 78.955 to 78.965 mm
2.0 litre petrol engines . . . . 85.925 to 85.935 mm
2.0 litre diesel engines . . . . 82.148 to 82.182 mm

Piston ring end gap:	Standard	Maximum
2000 and earlier 2.0 litre petrol engines:		
Top compression ring	0.27 to 0.47 mm	1.07 mm
Second compression ring	0.45 to 0.65 mm	1.25 mm
Oil control ring	0.10 to 0.45 mm	1.05 mm
2001 and later models:		
1.8 litre petrol engines:		
Top compression ring	0.25 to 0.35 mm	1.05 mm
Second compression ring	0.35 to 0.50 mm	1.20 mm
Oil control ring	0.15 to 0.40 mm	1.05 mm
2.0 litre petrol engines:		
Top compression ring	0.27 to 0.37 mm	0.90 mm
Second compression ring	0.37 to 0.47 mm	1.00 mm
Oil control ring	0.10 to 0.40 mm	0.80 mm
2.0 litre diesel engines:		
Top compression ring	0.27 to 0.43 mm	0.82 mm
Second compression ring	0.39 to 0.58 mm	1.00 mm
Oil control ring	0.20 to 0.44 mm	0.90 mm

Cylinder block

Maximum gasket face warpage . . . . 0.05 mm
Cylinder bore diameter (nominal):
2000 and earlier 2.0 litre petrol engines . . . . 86.00 to 86.03 mm
2001 and later models:
1.8 litre petrol engines . . . . 79.00 to 79.013 mm
2.0 litre petrol engines . . . . 86.00 to 86.013 mm
2.0 litre diesel engines . . . . 82.200 to 82.213 mm

Crankshaft

Crankshaft endfloat:
  2000 and earlier models:
    2.0 litre petrol engines:
      Standard .... 0.02 to 0.22 mm
      Maximum .... 0.30 mm
      Thrustwasher thickness .... 2.440 to 2.490 mm
  2001 and later models:
    1.8 litre engines:
      Standard .... 0.04 to 0.24 mm
      Maximum .... 0.30 mm
      Thrustwasher thickness .... 1.93 to 1.98 mm
    2.0 litre petrol engines:
      Standard .... 0.04 to 0.24 mm
      Maximum .... 0.30 mm
      Thrustwasher thickness .... 2.430 to 2.480 mm
    2.0 litre diesel engines:
      Standard .... 0.04 to 0.24 mm
      Maximum .... 0.30 mm
      Thrustwasher thickness .... 2.680 to 2.730 mm

Valves and related components

Valve stem diameter:
  2000 and earlier models:
    2.0 litre petrol engines:
      Intake .... 5.970 to 5.985 mm
      Exhaust .... 5.965 to 5.980 mm
  2001 and later models:
    1.8 and 2.0 litre petrol engines:
      Intake .... 5.470 to 5.485 mm
      Exhaust .... 5.465 to 5.480 mm
    2.0 litre diesel engines:
      Intake .... 5.970 to 5.985 mm
      Exhaust .... 5.960 to 5.975 mm
Valve spring free length:
  2000 and earlier models:
    2.0 litre engines .... 40.95 to 42.80 mm
  2001 and later models:
    1.8 litre petrol engines .... 43.4 mm
    2.0 litre petrol engines .... 45.7 mm
    2.0 litre diesel engines .... 40.45 mm

Torque wrench settings

	lbf ft	Nm
Petrol engines		
Connecting rod bearing cap nuts:		
Stage 1	18	25
Stage 2	Angle tighten a further 90°	
Lower crankcase-to-cylinder block bolts	25	34
Main bearing cap bolts:		
2000 and earlier models	43	58
2001 and later 2.0 litre models:		
Stage 1	15	20
Stage 2	30	40
Stage 3	Angle tighten a further 90°	
2001 and later 1.8 litre models:		
12-point head bolts:		
Stage 1	16	22
Stage 2	32	44
Stage 3	Angle tighten a further 45°	
Stage 4	Angle tighten a further 45°	
6-point head bolts	14	19
Diesel engines		
Connecting rod bearing cap nuts:		
Stage 1	22	30
Stage 2	Angle tighten a further 90°	
Main bearing cap bolts	85	115

2.2 On petrol engines, the oil pressure sending unit (arrowed) is located on the left-hand end of the cylinder head – 2001 and later shown, 2000 and earlier similar

1 General information – engine overhaul

Included in this portion of Chapter 2 are general information and diagnostic testing procedures for determining the overall mechanical condition of your engine.

The information ranges from advice concerning preparation for an overhaul and the purchase of parts and/or components to detailed, step-by-step procedures covering removal and refitting.

The following Sections have been written to help you determine whether your engine needs to be overhauled and how to remove and install it. For information concerning in-vehicle engine repair, see Chapter 2A, 2B or 2C.

The Specifications included in this Part are general in nature and include only those necessary for testing the oil pressure and checking the engine compression. Refer to Chapter 2A, 2B or 2C for additional engine Specifications.

It's not always easy to determine when, or if, an engine should be completely overhauled, as a number of factors must be considered.

High mileage is not necessarily an indication that an overhaul is needed, while low mileage doesn't preclude the need for an overhaul. Frequency of servicing is probably the most important consideration. An engine that's had

2.3 The oil pressure can be checked by removing the sending unit and installing a pressure gauge in its place

regular and frequent oil and filter changes, as well as other required maintenance, will most likely give many thousands of miles of reliable service. Conversely, a neglected engine may require an overhaul very early in its life.

Excessive oil consumption is an indication that piston rings, valve seals and/or valve guides are in need of attention. Make sure that oil leaks aren't responsible before deciding that the rings and/or guides are bad. Perform a cylinder compression check to determine the extent of the work required (see Section 3). Also check the vacuum readings under various conditions (see Section 4).

Check the oil pressure with a gauge installed in place of the oil pressure sending unit and compare it to this Chapter's Specifications (see Section 2). If it's extremely low, the bearings and/or oil pump are probably worn out.

Loss of power, rough running, knocking or metallic engine noises, excessive valve train noise and high fuel consumption rates may also point to the need for an overhaul, especially if they're all present at the same time. If a complete tune-up doesn't remedy the situation, major mechanical work is the only solution.

An engine overhaul involves restoring the internal parts to the specifications of a new engine. During an overhaul, the piston rings are renewed and the cylinder walls are reconditioned (rebored and/or honed). If a rebore is done by an automotive machine shop, new oversize pistons will also be installed. The main bearings, connecting rod bearings and camshaft bearings are generally renewed and, if necessary, the crankshaft may be reground to restore the journals. Generally, the valves are serviced as well, since they're usually in less-than-perfect condition at this point. While the engine is being overhauled, other components, such as the distributor, starter and alternator, can be overhauled as well. The end result should be a like-new engine that will give many trouble free miles. **Note:** *Critical cooling system components such as the hoses, auxiliary drivebelts, thermostat and water pump should be renewed when an engine is overhauled. The radiator should be checked carefully to ensure that it isn't clogged or leaking (see Chapter 3). If you purchase an overhauled engine or short block, some reconditioners will not guarantee their engines unless the radiator has been professionally flushed. Also, we don't recommend overhauling the oil pump – always install a new one when an engine is overhauled.*

Overhauling the internal components on today's engines is a difficult and time-consuming task which requires a significant amount of special tools and is best left to a professional engine reconditioner. A competent engine reconditioner will handle the inspection of your old parts and offer advice concerning the reconditioning or renewal of the original engine. Never purchase parts or have machine work done on other components until the block has been thoroughly inspected

by a professional reconditioner. As a general rule, time is the primary cost of an overhaul, especially since the vehicle may be tied up for two weeks or more. Be aware that some engine reconditioners only have the capability to overhaul the engine you bring them, while other reconditioners have a large inventory of overhauled exchange engines in stock. Also be aware that many reconditioners could take as much time as two weeks to completely overhaul your engine depending on workload. Sometimes it makes more sense to simply exchange your engine for another engine that's already overhauled to save time.

2 Oil pressure check
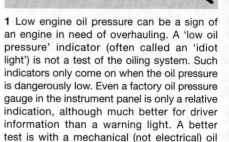

1 Low engine oil pressure can be a sign of an engine in need of overhauling. A 'low oil pressure' indicator (often called an 'idiot light') is not a test of the oiling system. Such indicators only come on when the oil pressure is dangerously low. Even a factory oil pressure gauge in the instrument panel is only a relative indication, although much better for driver information than a warning light. A better test is with a mechanical (not electrical) oil pressure gauge.

2 Find the oil pressure indicator sending unit. On petrol engines it is located on the left-hand end of the cylinder head **(see illustration)**, whereas on diesel engines it is located on the rear of the cylinder block, near the oil filter.

3 Remove the oil pressure sending unit and install a fitting which will allow you to directly connect your hand-held, mechanical oil pressure gauge **(see illustration)**. Use Teflon tape (PTFE) or sealant on the threads of the adapter and the fitting on the end of your gauge's hose.

4 Connect an accurate tachometer to the engine, according to the tachometer manufacturer's instructions.

5 Check the oil pressure with the engine running (normal operating temperature) at the specified engine speed, and compare it to this Chapter's Specifications. If it's extremely low, the bearings and/or oil pump are probably worn out.

3 Cylinder compression check

1 A compression check will tell you what mechanical condition the upper end of your engine (pistons, rings, valves, head gaskets) is in. Specifically, it can tell you if the compression is down due to leakage caused by worn piston rings, defective valves and seats or a blown head gasket. **Note:** *The engine must be at normal operating temperature and the battery must be fully-charged for this check.*

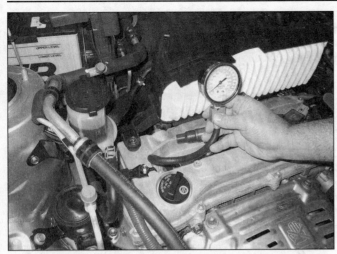

3.5 A compression gauge with a threaded fitting for the spark plug/glow plug hole is preferred over the type that requires hand pressure to maintain the seal – on petrol models, be sure to block open the throttle valve as far as possible during the compression check

4.4 On petrol engines, a simple vacuum gauge can be handy in diagnosing engine condition and performance

2 Begin by cleaning the area around the spark plugs (Chapter 1A) or glow plugs (Chapter 5) before you remove them. Compressed air should be used, if available, otherwise a small brush will work. The idea is to prevent dirt from getting into the cylinders as the compression check is being done.

3 Remove all of the spark plugs (Chapter 1A) or glow plugs (Chapter 5) from the engine.

4 On petrol engines, disable the ignition system by disconnecting the wiring from the ignition coils or modules (see Chapter 5). On diesel engines, disconnect the wiring from the fuel injectors (Chapter 4B). **Note:** *As a result of the wiring being disconnected, faults will be stored in the ECU memory. These must be erased after the compression test.*

5 Install the compression gauge in the No 1 spark plug/glow plug hole **(see illustration)**.

 Warning: If you are checking the compression on a diesel engine, make sure the gauge is capable of reading pressures up to 34 bars.

6 On petrol engines, have an assistant hold the throttle wide open.

7 Crank the engine over at least seven compression strokes and watch the gauge. The compression should build-up quickly in a healthy engine. Low compression on the first stroke, followed by gradually increasing pressure on successive strokes, indicates worn piston rings. A low compression reading on the first stroke, which doesn't build-up during successive strokes, indicates leaking valves or a blown head gasket (a cracked head could also be the cause). Deposits on the undersides of the valve heads can also cause low compression. Record the highest gauge reading obtained.

8 Repeat the procedure for the remaining cylinders and compare the results to this Chapter's Specifications.

Petrol engines only

 Warning: DO NOT perform this procedure on a diesel engine. Checking compression on a diesel engine with oil in the cylinder could cause it to fire, which would damage the gauge and possibly the engine, and could cause injury.

9 If the readings are below normal, add some engine oil (about three squirts from a plunger-type oil can) to each cylinder, through the spark plug hole, and repeat the test.

10 If the compression increases after the oil is added, the piston rings are definitely worn. If the compression doesn't increase significantly, the leakage is occurring at the valves or head gasket. Leakage past the valves may be caused by burned valve seats and/or faces or warped, cracked or bent valves.

All engines

11 If two adjacent cylinders have equally low compression, there's a strong possibility that the head gasket between them is blown. The appearance of coolant in the combustion chambers or the crankcase would verify this condition.

12 If one cylinder is slightly lower than the others, and the engine has a slightly rough idle, a worn lobe on the camshaft could be the cause.

13 If the compression is unusually high, the combustion chambers are probably coated with carbon deposits. If that's the case, the cylinder head should be removed and decarbonised.

14 If compression is way down or varies greatly between cylinders, it would be a good idea to have a leak-down test performed by an automotive repair shop. This test will pinpoint exactly where the leakage is occurring and how severe it is.

15 After all of the cylinders have been checked, release the throttle and reconnect the wiring.

4 Vacuum gauge diagnostic checks

Note: *This procedure does not apply to diesel engines.*

A vacuum gauge provides valuable information about what is going on in the engine at a low cost. You can check for worn rings or cylinder walls, leaking head or intake manifold gaskets, incorrect fuel system adjustments, restricted exhaust, stuck or burned valves, weak valve springs, improper ignition or valve timing and ignition problems.

Unfortunately, vacuum gauge readings are easy to misinterpret, so they should be used in conjunction with other tests to confirm the diagnosis.

Both the absolute readings and the rate of needle movement are important for accurate interpretation. Most gauges measure vacuum in inches of mercury (in-Hg). The following references to vacuum assume the diagnosis is being performed at sea level. As elevation increases (or atmospheric pressure decreases), the reading will decrease. For every 1000 foot increase in elevation above approximately 2000 feet, the gauge readings will decrease about one inch of mercury.

Connect the vacuum gauge directly to intake manifold vacuum, not to ported (throttle body) vacuum **(see illustration)**. Be sure no hoses are left disconnected during the test or false readings will result.

Before you begin the test, allow the engine to warm-up completely. Block the wheels and set the handbrake. With the transmission in

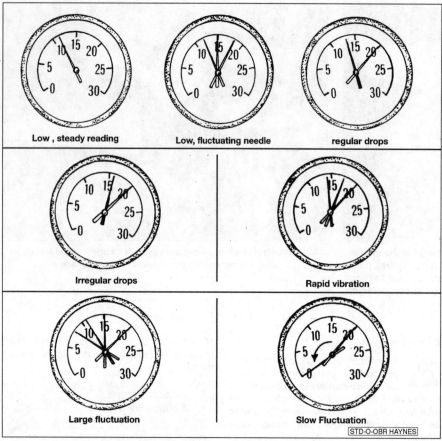

4.6 Typical vacuum gauge diagnostics readings

Park or Neutral, start the engine and allow it to run at normal idle speed.

 Warning: Keep your hands and the vacuum gauge clear of the fans.

Read the vacuum gauge; an average, healthy engine should normally produce about 17 to 22 in-Hg with a fairly steady needle **(see illustration)**. Refer to the following vacuum gauge readings and what they indicate about the engine's condition:

a) *A low steady reading usually indicates a leaking gasket between the intake manifold and cylinder head(s) or throttle body, a leaky vacuum hose, late ignition timing or incorrect camshaft timing.*

b) *If the reading is three to eight inches below normal and it fluctuates at that low reading, suspect an intake manifold gasket leak at an intake port, or a faulty fuel injector.*

c) *If the needle has regular drops of about two to four inches at a steady rate, the valves are probably leaking. Perform a compression check to confirm this.*

d) *An irregular drop or down-flick of the needle can be caused by a sticking valve or an ignition misfire. Perform a compression check and inspect the spark plugs.*

e) *A rapid vibration of about four in-Hg vibration at idle combined with exhaust smoke indicates worn valve guides. If the rapid vibration occurs with an increase in engine speed, check for a leaking intake manifold gasket or head gasket, weak valve springs, burned valves or ignition misfire.*

f) *A slight fluctuation, say one inch up and down, may mean ignition problems. Check all the usual tune-up items and, if necessary, run the engine on an ignition analyser.*

g) *If there is a large fluctuation, perform a compression check to look for a weak or dead cylinder or a blown head gasket.*

h) *If the needle moves slowly through a wide range, check for a clogged PCV system, incorrect idle fuel mixture, throttle body or intake manifold gasket leaks.*

i) *Check for a slow return after revving the engine by quickly snapping the throttle open until the engine reaches about 2,500 rpm and let it shut. Normally the reading should drop to near zero, rise above normal idle reading (about 5 in-Hg over) and then return to the previous idle reading. If the vacuum returns slowly and doesn't peak when the throttle is snapped shut, the rings may be worn. If there is a long delay, look for a restricted exhaust* system (often the silencer or catalytic converter). An easy way to check this is to temporarily disconnect the exhaust ahead of the suspected part and redo the test.

5 Engine overhauling alternatives

The do-it-yourselfer is faced with a number of options when purchasing an overhauled engine. The major considerations are cost, warranty, parts availability and the time required for the reconditioner to complete the project. The decision to renew the engine block, piston/connecting rod assemblies and crankshaft depends on the final inspection results of your engine. Only then can you make a cost-effective decision whether to have your engine overhauled or simply purchase an exchange engine for your vehicle.

Some of the overhauling alternatives include:

Individual parts – If the inspection procedures reveal that the engine block and most engine components are in reusable condition, purchasing individual parts and having a reconditioner rebuild your engine may be the most economical alternative. The block, crankshaft and piston/connecting rod assemblies should all be inspected carefully by a machine shop first.

Short block – A short block consists of an engine block with a crankshaft and piston/connecting rod assemblies already installed. All new bearings are incorporated and all clearances will be correct. The existing camshafts, valve train components, cylinder head and external parts can be bolted to the short block with little or no machine shop work necessary.

Long block – A long block consists of a short block plus an oil pump, sump, cylinder head, valve cover, camshaft and valve train components, timing sprockets and chain/belt or gears and timing cover. All components are installed with new bearings, seals and gaskets incorporated throughout. The refitting of manifolds and external parts is all that's necessary.

Low mileage used engines – Some companies now offer low-mileage used engines which is a very cost effective way to get your vehicle up and running again. These engines often come from vehicles which have been written off in accidents or come from other countries which have a higher vehicle turnover rate. A low-mileage used engine also usually has a similar warranty like the newly remanufactured engines.

Give careful thought to which alternative is best for you and discuss the situation with local automotive machine shops, auto parts dealers and experienced reconditioners before ordering or purchasing parts.

6 Engine removal – methods and precautions

If you've decided that an engine must be removed for overhaul or major repair work, several preliminary steps should be taken.

Locating a suitable place to work is extremely important. Adequate work space, along with storage space for the vehicle, will be needed. If a shop or garage isn't available, at the very least a flat, level, clean work surface made of concrete or asphalt is required.

Cleaning the engine compartment and engine before beginning the removal procedure will help keep tools clean and organised.

An engine hoist or A-frame will also be necessary. Make sure the equipment is rated in excess of the combined weight of the engine and transmission. Safety is of primary importance, considering the potential hazards involved in lifting the engine out of the vehicle.

If the engine is being removed by a novice, a helper should be available. Advice and aid from someone more experienced would also be helpful. There are many instances when one person cannot simultaneously perform all of the operations required when lifting the engine out of the vehicle.

Plan the operation ahead of time. Arrange for or obtain all of the tools and equipment you'll need prior to beginning the job. Some of the equipment necessary to perform engine removal and refitting safely and with relative ease are (in addition to an engine hoist) a heavy duty floor jack, complete sets of spanners and sockets as described in the rear of this manual, wooden blocks and plenty of rags and cleaning solvent for mopping-up spilled oil, coolant and fuel. If the hoist must be rented, make sure that you arrange for it in advance and perform all of the operations possible without it beforehand. This will save you money and time.

Plan for the vehicle to be out of use for quite a while. A machine shop will be required to perform all of the work which is beyond the scope of the home mechanic. These shops often have a busy schedule, so it would be a good idea to consult them before removing the engine in order to accurately estimate the amount of time required to rebuild or repair components that may need work.

Always be extremely careful when removing and installing the engine. Serious injury can result from careless actions. Plan ahead, take your time and a job of this nature, although major, can be accomplished successfully.

7 Engine – removal and refitting

⚠️ **Warning 1: The models covered by this manual are equipped with airbags. Always disable the airbag system before working in the vicinity of airbag system components to avoid the possibility of accidental deployment of the airbag, which could cause personal injury (see Chapter 12).**

⚠️ **Warning 2: Petrol is extremely flammable (and diesel fuel only slightly less volatile), so take extra precautions when you work on any part of the fuel system. Don't smoke or allow open flames or bare light bulbs near the work area, and don't work in a garage where a gas-type appliance (such as a water heater or a clothes dryer) is present. Since petrol is carcinogenic, wear latex gloves when there's a possibility of being exposed to fuel, and, if you spill any fuel on your skin, rinse it off immediately with soap and water. Mop-up any spills immediately and do not store fuel-soaked rags where they could ignite. On petrol models, the fuel system is under constant pressure, so, if any fuel lines are to be disconnected, the fuel pressure in the system must be relieved first (see Chapter 4A for more information). When you perform any kind of work on the fuel system, wear safety glasses and have a fire extinguisher on hand.**

Note: *Engine removal on these models is a difficult job, especially for the do-it-yourself mechanic working at home. Because of the vehicle's design, the manufacturer states that the engine and transmission have to be removed as a unit from the bottom of the vehicle, not the top. With a jack and axle stands the vehicle can't be raised high enough and supported safely enough for the engine/ transmission assembly to slide out from underneath. The manufacturer recommends that removal of the engine/transmission assembly only be performed on a vehicle hoist.*

Removal

1 Park the vehicle on a frame-contact type vehicle hoist. The pads of the hoist arms must contact the body along each side of the vehicle (see *Jacking and vehicle support* at the rear of this manual).

2 If you're removing a petrol engine, relieve the fuel system pressure (see Chapter 4A).

3 Disconnect the negative cable from the battery, then place protective covers on the wings and cowl and remove the bonnet (see Chapter 11).

4 Remove the air cleaner assembly (see Chapter 4A or 4B). Also, where applicable, disconnect the accelerator cable and bracket from the engine and position them aside.

5 Remove the cowl cover and the vent tray (see Chapter 11).

6 Remove the battery. On 2001 and later models also remove the battery tray (see Chapter 5).

7 On 2000 and earlier petrol models, remove the charcoal canister (see Chapter 6A or 6B). On 2001 and later models, remove the coolant reservoir (see Chapter 3).

8 Loosen the front wheel nuts and the driveshaft/hub nuts, then raise the vehicle on the hoist. Drain the cooling system and engine oil and remove the auxiliary drivebelts (see Chapter 1A or 1B).

9 Clearly label, then disconnect all vacuum lines, coolant and emissions hoses, wiring harness connectors, earth straps and fuel lines. Masking tape and/or a touch up paint applicator work well for marking items **(see illustration)**. Take instant photos or sketch the locations of components and brackets.

10 Remove the engine wiring harness connectors from the engine compartment junction box. Also detach the wiring harness connectors from the ECM in the passenger compartment (see Chapter 6A or 6B) and pull the wiring harness from the passenger compartment into the engine compartment.

11 Remove the alternator and the starter motor (see Chapter 5) **(see illustrations)**.

7.9 Label both ends of each wire and hose before disconnecting it

7.11a Removing the alternator ...

7.11b ... and starter motor

7.14 Removing the radiator

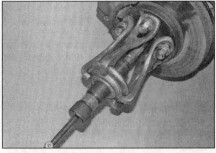

7.18 Using a puller to press the driveshaft out of the steering knuckle during driveshaft removal

7.19a Detaching the anti-roll bar from the front crossmember

7.19b Remove the mounting bolts . . .

7.19c . . . and lower the front crossmember from the engine

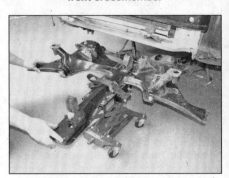

7.19d Removing the front crossmember from under the vehicle

12 Remove the power steering pump (see Chapter 10).

13 Remove the cooling fan(s), shroud(s) and radiator (see Chapter 3). **Note:** *This step is not absolutely necessary, but it will help avoid damage to the cooling fans and radiator as the engine is lowered out of the vehicle. If the radiator is not taken out it will still be necessary to detach the transmission oil cooler lines from the bottom of the radiator on automatic transmission equipped vehicles.*

14 On air conditioned models, unbolt the air conditioning compressor and set it aside. Do not disconnect the refrigerant hoses. On these models, to provide additional room to move the compressor to one side when the engine is being removed, it is recommended that the radiator is removed, and the condenser protected with a suitable piece of card **(see illustration).**

15 Detach the front exhaust pipe from the exhaust manifold (see Chapter 4A or 4B).

16 Disconnect the shift linkage from the transmission, then detach the cables from the front crossmember (see Chapter 7A or 7B). Also disconnect any wiring harness connectors from the transmission.

17 If equipped with a manual transmission disconnect the clutch release cylinder from the transmission (see Chapter 8).

18 Remove the front driveshafts (see Chapter 8). On 4WD vehicles, drain the transfer case oil, and remove the rear propeller shaft **(see illustration).**

19 On 2001 and later models, detach the anti-roll bar from the crossmember (see Chapter 10). Also remove the two bolts securing the steering gear to the front crossmember and the bolts securing the lower balljoints to the lower control arms referring

the Chapter 10. Tie the steering gear to the bulkhead. If preferred, the front crossmember may be unbolted from the engine at this stage and removed from under the vehicle – it is quite heavy and a trolley will be helpful **(see illustrations).**

20 Attach a lifting sling or chain to the engine **(see illustration).** Position an engine hoist and connect the sling to it. Take up the slack until there is slight tension on the sling or chain. Remember that the transmission end of the engine will be heavier, so position the chain on the hoist so it balances the engine and transmission level with the vehicle.

21 Recheck to be sure nothing except the mountings are still connecting the engine to the vehicle or to the transmission. Disconnect and label anything still remaining.

22 Remove the through-bolt on the left-hand side transmission mount and the passenger side engine mounting.

23 If still in position, remove the front crossmember and the centre crossmember mounting bolts **(see illustration).**

24 Slowly lower the engine/transmission from the vehicle. **Note:** *Placing a sheet of hardboard or panelling between the engine and the floor makes moving the engine easier.*

25 Once the engine is on the floor, disconnect the engine lifting hoist and raise the vehicle hoist until the engine can be slid out from underneath. **Note:** *A helper will be needed to move the engine.*

26 Reconnect the chain or sling and raise the engine with the hoist several inches off the ground. Where necessary, remove the through-bolts on the front and rear mountings

7.20 With the chain or sling attached securely to the engine, take up the slack until there is slight tension on the chain

7.23 Front (and centre) crossmember-to-chassis bolts – petrol engine shown

and slide the front crossmember out from under the engine. Lower the engine back to the ground and separate the engine from the transmission (see Chapter 7A or 7B). Disregard the steps that do not apply since the transmission is already removed from the vehicle.

27 Remove the driveplate/flywheel and mount the engine on a stand.

Refitting

28 Check the engine/transmission mountings. If they're worn or damaged, renew them.

29 On manual transmission equipped models, inspect the clutch components (see Chapter 8) and on automatic models inspect the converter seal and bushing.

30 On manual transmission equipped vehicles, apply a dab of high temperature grease to the splines of the input shaft. On automatic transmission equipped models, apply a dab of grease to the nose of the torque converter.

31 Carefully guide the transmission into place, following the procedure outlined in Chapter 7A or 7B.

Caution: Do not use the bolts to force the engine and transmission into alignment. It may crack or damage major components.

32 Install the engine-to-transmission bolts and tighten them securely.

33 Slide the engine/transmission over a sheet of hardboard or panelling until it is in the appropriate position under the vehicle, then lower the vehicle over the engine.

34 Roll the engine hoist into position, attach the chain or sling in a position that will allow a good balance and slowly raise the engine until the mounting at the transmission end can be attached.

35 Support the transmission with a floor jack for extra security, then refit the front crossmember and attach the right-hand side engine mounting.

36 Refit the remaining components in the reverse order of removal.

37 Add coolant, oil, power steering and transmission fluids as needed (see Chapter 1A or 1B).

38 Run the engine and check for proper operation and leaks. Shut off the engine and recheck the fluid levels.

8 Engine overhaul – dismantling sequence

1 It is much easier to dismantle and work on the engine if it is mounted on a portable engine stand. These stands can often be hired from a tool hire shop. Before the engine is mounted on a stand, the flywheel/driveplate should be removed, so that the stand bolts can be tightened into the end of the cylinder block/crankcase.

2 If a stand is not available, it is possible to dismantle the engine with it blocked up on a

sturdy workbench, or on the floor. Be extra careful not to tip or drop the engine when working without a stand.

3 If you are going to obtain a reconditioned engine, all the external components must be removed first, to be transferred to the new engine (just as they will if you are doing a complete engine overhaul yourself). These components include the following:

Emissions control components.
Distributor (1997 and earlier petrol engines).
Spark plug leads and spark plugs (petrol engines).
Ignition coils (1998 and later petrol engines).
Glow plug/preheating system components (diesel engines).
Thermostat and housing cover.
Water pump (2001 and later petrol engines).
Water bypass tube where applicable.
EFI components (petrol engines).
Intake/exhaust manifolds.
Oil filter.
Engine mounting brackets.
Clutch and flywheel/driveplate.
Engine rear plate (2000 and earlier).

Note: *When removing the external components from the engine, pay close attention to details that may be helpful or important during refitting. Note the installed position of gaskets, seals, spacers, pins, brackets, washers, bolts and other small items.*

4 If you are obtaining a short engine (which consists of the engine cylinder block/crankcase, crankshaft, pistons and connecting rods all assembled), then the cylinder head, sump, oil pump and lower crankcase (2001 and later petrol engines), water pump (2000 and earlier petrol engines) and timing belt/chain components will have to be removed also.

5 If you are planning a complete overhaul, the engine can be dismantled, and the internal components removed, in the order given.

Timing belt covers, timing belt, sprockets, tensioner and idler pulleys (Part A or C of this Chapter).
Timing chain cover, chain, sprockets and associated components (Part B of this Chapter).

Intake and exhaust manifolds (Part A, B or C of this Chapter).
Cylinder head (Part A, B or C of this Chapter).
Sump (Part A, B or C of this Chapter).
Piston/connecting rod assemblies (Section 12).
Flywheel/driveplate (Part A, B or C of this Chapter).
Oil pump (Part A, B or C of this Chapter).
Crankshaft (Section 13).

6 Before beginning the dismantling and overhaul procedures, make sure that you have all of the correct tools necessary. Refer to *Tools and working facilities* for further information.

9 Cylinder head – dismantling

Note: *New and reconditioned cylinder heads can be obtained from the manufacturer and engine overhaul specialists. Be aware that some specialist tools are required for the dismantling and inspection procedures, and new components may not be readily available. It may therefore be more practical and economical for the home mechanic to purchase a reconditioned head, rather than dismantle, inspect and recondition the original head.*

1 Remove the cylinder head as described in Part A, B or C of this Chapter. This procedure includes removal of the camshafts, followers, and the intake and exhaust manifolds. As applicable, unbolt and remove the coolant outlet and thermostat housing, the alternator upper mounting bracket, and any additional brackets, sensors or related components.

2 Using a valve spring compressor, compress each valve spring in turn until the split collets can be removed. Release the compressor, and lift off the spring retainer, spring and spring seat. Withdraw the valve through the combustion chamber **(see illustrations)**.

3 If, when the valve spring compressor is screwed down, the spring retainer refuses to free and expose the split collets, gently tap the top of the tool, directly over the retainer, with a light hammer. This will free the retainer.

9.2a Using a compressor tool to compress the valve springs

9.2b Remove the spring retainer ...

9.2c . . . spring . . .

9.2d . . . and spring seat . . .

9.2e . . . then remove the valve from the combustion chamber

9.4 Using pliers or special removal tool, extract the valve stem seal from the top of the guide

4 Using a pair of pliers or special removal tool, carefully extract the valve stem seal from the top of the guide **(see illustration)**.

5 It is essential that each valve is stored together with its collets, retainer, spring, and spring seat. The valves should also be kept in their correct sequence, unless they are so badly worn that they are to be renewed. If they are going to be kept and used again, place each valve assembly in a labelled polythene bag or similar small container. Note that the valves of No 1 cylinder are nearest to the timing belt/chain end of the engine.

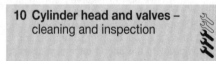

10 Cylinder head and valves –
cleaning and inspection

1 Thorough cleaning of the cylinder head and valve components, followed by a detailed

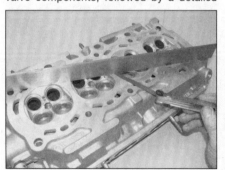

10.6 Checking the cylinder head surface for distortion

inspection, will enable you to decide how much valve service work must be carried out during the engine overhaul. **Note:** *If the engine has been severely overheated, it is best to assume that the cylinder head is warped – check carefully for signs of this.*

Cleaning

2 Scrape away all traces of old gasket material from the cylinder head.
3 Scrape away the carbon from the combustion chambers and ports, then wash the cylinder head thoroughly with paraffin or a suitable solvent.
4 Scrape off any heavy carbon deposits that may have formed on the valves, then use a power-operated wire brush to remove deposits from the valve heads and stems.

Inspection

Note: *Be sure to perform all the following*

10.13 Grinding-in the valves

inspection procedures before concluding that the services of an engine overhaul specialist are required. Make a list of all items that require attention.

Cylinder head

5 Inspect the head very carefully for cracks, evidence of coolant leakage, and other damage. If cracks are found, a new cylinder head should be obtained.
6 Use a straight-edge and feeler blade to check that the cylinder head surface is not distorted **(see illustration)**. If it is, it may be possible to have it machined by an engine overhaul specialist.
7 Examine the valve seats in each of the combustion chambers. If they are severely pitted, cracked, or burned, they will need to be renewed or recut by an engine overhaul specialist. If they are only slightly pitted, this can be removed by grinding-in the valve heads and seats with fine valve-grinding compound, as described below.
8 Check the valve guides for wear by inserting the relevant valve, and checking for side-to-side movement of the valve. A very small amount of movement is acceptable, however, if excessive, seek the advice of an engine overhaul specialist.
9 If in any further doubt as to the condition of the cylinder head, have it inspected by an engine overhaul specialist.

Valves

10 Examine the head of each valve for pitting, burning, cracks, and general wear. Check the valve stem for scoring and wear ridges. Rotate the valve, and check for any obvious indication that it is bent. Look for pits and excessive wear on the tip of each valve stem. Renew any valve that shows any signs of wear or damage.
11 If the valves are in satisfactory condition, they should be ground (lapped) into their respective seats, to ensure a smooth, gas-tight seal. If the seat is only lightly pitted, or if it has been recut, fine grinding compound only should be used to produce the required finish. Coarse valve-grinding compound should not be used, unless a seat is badly burned or deeply pitted. If this is the case, the cylinder head and valves should be inspected by an expert, to decide whether seat recutting, or even the renewal of the valve or seat insert is required.
12 Valve grinding is carried out as follows. Place the cylinder head upside-down on a bench.
13 Smear a trace of the appropriate grade of valve-grinding compound on the seat face, and press a suction grinding tool onto the valve head. With a semi-rotary action, grind the valve head to its seat, lifting the valve occasionally to redistribute the grinding compound **(see illustration)**. A light spring placed under the valve head will greatly ease this operation.
14 If coarse grinding compound is being used, work only until a dull, matt even surface

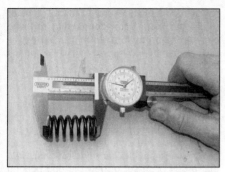

10.16 Measuring the free length of the valve springs

10.17 Checking the valve springs for squareness

11.1 The exhaust valve stem seals are marked EX and the inlet seals are marked IN

is produced on both the valve seat and the valve, then wipe off the used compound, and repeat the process with fine compound. When a smooth unbroken ring of light grey matt finish is produced on both the valve and seat, the grinding operation is complete. Do not grind-in the valves any further than absolutely necessary.

15 When all the valves have been ground-in, carefully wash off *all* traces of grinding compound using paraffin or a suitable solvent, before reassembling the cylinder head.

Valve components

16 Examine the valve springs for signs of damage and discoloration. The Toyota procedure for checking the condition of valve springs involves measuring the force necessary to compress each spring to a specified height. This is not possible without the use of the Toyota special test equipment, and therefore spring checking must be entrusted to a Toyota dealer. A rough idea of the condition of the spring can be gained by measuring the spring free length, and comparing it to the length given in this Chapter's Specifications **(see illustration)**.

17 Stand each spring on a flat surface, and position a square alongside the edge of the spring **(see illustration)**. Measure the gap between the upper and lower edges of the spring and the square.

18 If any of the springs are damaged, distorted or have lost their tension, obtain a complete new set of springs. It is normal to renew the valve springs as a matter of course if a major overhaul is being carried out.

19 Renew the valve stem oil seals regardless of their apparent condition. They are normally supplied in the engine gasket set.

11 Cylinder head – reassembly

1 Working on the first valve, dip the new valve stem seal in clean engine oil and ease it over the valve stem onto the guide. Use a suitable socket or metal tube to press the seal firmly onto the guide. Note that although the seals are theoretically colour-coded for identification purposes, in practice, the colour of the

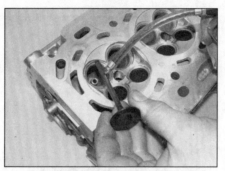

11.2 Lubricate the stems of the valves before inserting them in their guides

seals does not always agree with the Toyota documentation. On 2000 and earlier engines, the intake seals should be brown or grey, and the exhaust seals should be black. On 2001 and later engines, it is possible to discern an identification mark on the top of the seal face (you will probably need a magnifying glass to see this). With careful observation it will be seen that the exhaust valve stem seals are marked EX, and the intake seals are marked IN **(see illustration)**. **Note:** *The intake and exhaust valves require different seals – DO NOT mix them up.*

2 Lubricate the stems of the valves, and insert the valves into their original locations in the cylinder head. If new valves are being fitted, insert them into the locations to which they have been ground **(see illustration)**.

3 Refit the spring seat, then locate the valve

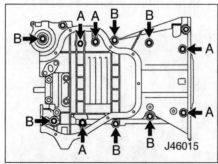

12.2a Lower crankcase retaining bolt locations – 2001 and later 2.0 litre petrol engines

A Long bolts   B Short bolts

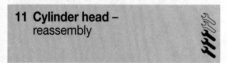

Use a dab of grease to retain the collets on the valve stems.

spring on top of its seat and refit the spring retainer.

4 Compress the valve spring with the valve spring compressor tool, and locate the split collets in the recess in the valve stem. Release the compressor, then repeat this procedure on the remaining valves **(see Haynes hint)**.

5 With all the valves installed, place the cylinder head on blocks on the bench and, using a hammer and interposed block of wood, tap the end of each valve stem to settle the components.

6 The cylinder head and associated components may now be refitted as described in Part A, B or C of this Chapter.

12 Pistons/connecting rods – removal

1 Remove the timing belt/chain, cylinder head, sump (and sump upper housing on diesel engines), oil pump pick-up tube, or oil pump and, where applicable, the oil cooler and water by-pass pipe, as described in Part A, B or C of this Chapter.

2 On 2001 and later 2.0 litre petrol engines, gradually and evenly slacken and remove the eleven bolts securing the lower crankcase to the cylinder block, noting the different bolt lengths. Use a flat-bladed screwdriver to gently prise the lower crankcase from the cylinder block, at the cast-in leverage points **(see illustrations)**. Collect the O-ring from the joint face on the oil filter side, and remove the oil seal from the end of the crankshaft.

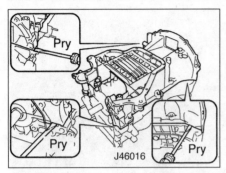

12.2b Removing the lower crankcase from the cylinder block – 2001 and later 2.0 litre petrol engines

12.6a Unscrewing the nuts/bolts from No 1 piston big-end bearing cap

use a hammer and centre-punch, paint or similar, to mark each connecting rod and big-end bearing cap with its respective cylinder number on the flat machined surface provided.

5 Turn the crankshaft to bring pistons 1 and 4 to BDC (bottom dead centre).

6 Unscrew the nuts/bolts from No 1 piston big-end bearing cap. Take off the cap, and recover the bottom half bearing shell. If the bearing shells are to be re-used, tape the cap and the shell together **(see illustrations)**. Note that a complete set of new big-end bearing cap bolts/nuts will be required for reassembly.

7 Where necessary, to prevent the possibility of damage to the crankshaft bearing journals, tape over the connecting rod bolt threads or fit a length of plastic hose to them.

8 Using a hammer handle, push the piston up through the bore, and remove it from the top of the cylinder block. Recover the bearing shell, and tape it to the connecting rod for safe-keeping **(see illustration)**.

9 Loosely refit the big-end cap to the connecting rod, and secure with the nuts/bolts – this will help to keep the components in their correct order.

10 Remove No 4 piston assembly in the same way.

11 Turn the crankshaft through 180° to bring pistons 2 and 3 to BDC (bottom dead centre), and remove them in the same way.

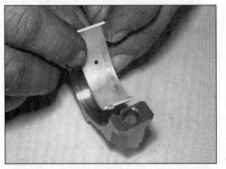

12.6b Recovering the bottom half bearing shell from the big-end bearing cap

12.8 Recovering the upper half bearing shell from the connecting rod

3 If there is a pronounced wear ridge at the top of any bore, it may be necessary to remove it with a scraper or ridge reamer, to avoid piston damage during removal. Such a ridge indicates excessive wear of the cylinder bore.

4 Each connecting rod and bearing cap should be identified for its respective cylinder, however the markings do not include the cylinder number. Make a note of the markings and the respective cylinders, or alternatively

13 Crankshaft – removal

1 Remove the timing belt/chain, sump (and sump upper housing on diesel engines), oil pump and pick-up tube and flywheel/driveplate with reference to Part A, B or C of this Chapter (the engine must be removed from the vehicle) then, where applicable, unbolt the rear engine plate and oil seal housing and recover the gasket **(see illustrations)**.

2 Remove the pistons and connecting rods, as described in Section 12. **Note:** *If no work is to be done on the pistons and connecting rods, there is no need to remove the cylinder head, or to push the pistons out of the cylinder bores. The pistons should just be pushed far*

13.1a Remove the rear engine plate (where fitted) . . .

13.1b . . . then unscrew the bolts . . .

13.1c . . . remove the oil seal housing . . .

13.1d . . . and recover the gasket – 2000 and earlier engines

13.3 Checking the crankshaft endfloat with a dial gauge

13.5 Checking the crankshaft endfloat with feeler blades on the centre (No 3) main bearing

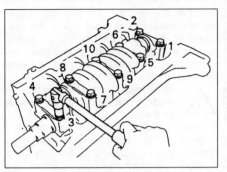

13.6a Main bearing cap bolt slackening sequence

13.6b Main bearing caps are numbered and marked with an arrow towards the timing end of the engine

enough up the bores to position them clear of the crankshaft journals.

3 Before the crankshaft is removed, check the endfloat. Mount a dial indicator with the probe in line with the crankshaft **(see illustration)**.

4 Push the crankshaft fully one way and zero the dial indicator. Next, lever the crankshaft the other way as far as possible and check the reading on the dial indicator. The distance that it moves is the endfloat. If it's greater than specified, check the crankshaft thrust surfaces for wear. If no wear is evident, new thrustwashers should correct the endfloat.

5 If a dial indicator isn't available, feeler gauges can be used. Gently lever or push the crankshaft fully one way. Slip feeler gauges between the crankshaft and the face of the number 3 (thrust) main bearing to determine the clearance **(see illustration)**.

All except 1.8 litre petrol

6 Working in sequence, slacken the main bearing cap retaining bolts by a turn at a time **(see illustration)**. Once all bolts are loose, unscrew and remove them from the cylinder block. Note that the caps are normally numbered from the timing belt/chain end of the engine, and in addition an arrow points to the timing end **(see illustration)**. If identification markings are not evident, suitably mark them to indicate cap location and fitted direction. Note that on 2001 and later engines, a complete set of new main bearing cap bolts will be required for reassembly.

7 Remove the main bearing caps and recover the lower main bearing shells. Tape each shell to its relevant cap for safe-keeping. Also recover the thrustwashers either side of the centre main bearing cap keeping them identified for position.

8 Carefully lift out the crankshaft, taking care not to displace the upper main bearing shells.

9 Recover the upper bearing shells from the cylinder block, and tape them to their respective positions on the main bearing caps. Remove the thrustwasher halves from the side of centre main bearing, and store them with the main bearing cap.

1.8 litre petrol engines

10 Working in a diagonal sequence, gradually and evenly slacken and remove the ten

13.10 Removing the hexagon head bolts securing the main bearing ladder to the cylinder block – 1.8 litre petrol engines

hexagon-head bolts securing the main bearing ladder to the cylinder block **(see illustration)**. Note that it will be necessary to remove the oil filter union to access one of the bolts beneath.

11 Working in the **reverse** of the tightening sequence **(see illustration 19.19)**, gradually and evenly slacken and remove the ten central 12-point head bolts securing the main bearing ladder to the cylinder block **(see illustration)**. Note that a complete set of new 12-point head bolts will be required for reassembly.

12 Use a flat-bladed screwdriver to gently prise the main bearing ladder from the cylinder block, at the cast-in leverage points. Ensure the lower bearing shells stay in their original positions in the bearing ladder.

13 Carefully lift out the crankshaft, taking care not to displace the upper main bearing shells. Remove the oil seal from the end of the

13.11 Removing the 12-point head bolts securing the main bearing ladder to the cylinder block – 1.8 litre petrol engines

crankshaft.

14 Recover the upper bearing shells from the cylinder block, and tape them to their respective positions on the main bearing ladder. Remove the thrustwasher halves from the side of centre main bearing, and store them with the main bearing ladder.

14 Cylinder block – cleaning and inspection

Cleaning

1 Remove all external components and electrical switches/sensors from the block, and unbolt the alternator and power steering pump brackets as applicable **(see illustrations)**.

2 For complete cleaning, the core plugs

14.1a Removing the oil pressure sensor from the cylinder block

14.1b Power steering pump lower mounting bracket

14.1c Alternator adjustment bracket on the right-hand end of the cylinder block

should ideally be removed. Drill a small hole in the plugs, then insert a self-tapping screw into the hole. Pull out the plugs by pulling on the screw with a pair of grips, or by using a slide hammer.

3 Scrape all traces of sealant from the cylinder block/crankcase, taking care not to damage the gasket/sealing surfaces.

4 Remove all oil gallery plugs (where fitted). The plugs are usually very tight – they may have to be drilled out, and the holes retapped. Use new plugs when the engine is reassembled.

5 If any of the castings are extremely dirty, all should be steam-cleaned.

6 After the castings are returned, clean all oil holes and oil galleries one more time. Flush all internal passages with warm water until the water runs clear. Dry thoroughly, and apply a light film of oil to all mating surfaces and the cylinder bores, to prevent rusting. If you have access to compressed air, use it to speed up the drying process, and to blow out all the oil holes and galleries.

 Warning: Wear eye protection when using compressed air.

7 If the castings are not very dirty, you can do an adequate cleaning job with hot, soapy water and a stiff brush. Take plenty of time, and do a thorough job. Regardless of the cleaning method used, be sure to clean all oil holes and galleries very thoroughly, and to dry all components well. Protect the cylinder bores as described above, to prevent rusting.

8 All threaded holes must be clean, to ensure accurate torque readings during reassembly.

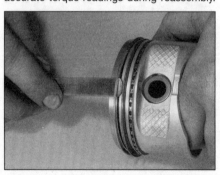

15.2 Carefully expand the rings from the top of the piston

To clean the threads, run the correct-size tap into each of the holes to remove rust, corrosion, thread sealant or sludge, and to restore damaged threads. If possible, use compressed air to clear the holes of debris produced by this operation.

 Warning: Wear eye protection when cleaning out these holes in this way.

9 Apply suitable sealant to the new oil gallery plugs, and insert them into the holes in the block. Tighten them securely. Similarly use a suitable sealant on new core plugs and tap them into place using a close-fitting tube or socket.

10 If the engine is not going to be reassembled right away, cover it with a large plastic bag to keep it clean; protect all mating surfaces and the cylinder bores as described above, to prevent rusting.

Inspection

11 Visually check the block for cracks, rust and corrosion. Look for stripped threads in the threaded holes. It's also a good idea to have the block checked for hidden cracks by an engine reconditioning specialist who has the equipment to do this type of work, especially if the vehicle had a history of overheating or using coolant. If defects are found, have the block repaired, if possible, or renewed.

12 If in any doubt as to the condition of the cylinder block, have it inspected and measured by an engine reconditioning specialist. If the bores are worn or damaged, they will be able to carry out any necessary reboring (where possible), and supply appropriate oversized pistons, etc.

15 Pistons/connecting rods – inspection

1 Before the inspection process can begin, the piston/connecting rod assemblies must be cleaned, and the original piston rings removed from the pistons. **Note:** *Always use new piston rings when the engine is reassembled.*

2 Carefully expand the old rings over the tops of the pistons – note that the oil control ring assembly normally incorporates two rails and an expander. The use of two or three

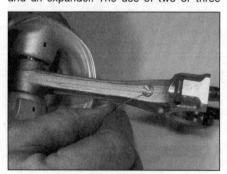

15.5 Checking the connecting rod oil jet hole for blockage

old feeler blades will be helpful in preventing the rings dropping into empty grooves **(see illustration)**. Be careful not to scratch the piston with the ends of the ring. The rings are brittle, and will snap if they are spread too far. They're also very sharp – protect your hands and fingers. Always remove the rings from the top of the piston.

3 Scrape away all traces of carbon from the top of the piston. A hand-held wire brush (or a piece of fine emery cloth) can be used, once the majority of the deposits have been scraped away.

4 Remove the carbon from the ring grooves in the piston, using an old ring. Break the ring in half to do this (be careful not to cut your fingers – piston rings are sharp). Be careful to remove only the carbon deposits – do not remove any metal, and do not nick or scratch the sides of the ring grooves.

5 Once the deposits have been removed, clean the piston/connecting rod assembly with paraffin or a suitable solvent, and dry thoroughly. Make sure that the oil return holes in the ring grooves are clear, and check that the oil jet holes are also clear **(see illustration)**.

6 If the pistons and cylinder walls aren't damaged or worn excessively, and if the cylinder block is not rebored, new pistons won't be necessary. Normal piston wear appears as even vertical wear on the piston thrust surfaces and slight looseness of the top ring in its groove. New piston rings, however, should always be used when an engine is rebuilt.

7 Carefully inspect each piston for cracks around the skirt, around the gudgeon pin holes, and at the piston ring lands (between the ring grooves).

8 Look for scoring and scuffing on the thrust faces of the skirt, holes in the piston crown and burned areas at the edge of the crown. If the skirt is scored or scuffed, the engine may have been suffering from overheating and/or abnormal combustion, which caused excessively high operating temperatures. The cooling and lubrication systems should be checked thoroughly. A hole in the piston crown is an indication that abnormal combustion (pre-ignition) was occurring. Burned areas at the edge of the piston crown are usually evidence of spark knock (detonation). If any of the above problems exist, the causes must be corrected or the damage will occur again. The causes may include inlet air leaks, incorrect air/fuel mixture, incorrect ignition timing and EGR system malfunctions.

9 Corrosion of the piston, in the form of small pits, indicates that coolant is leaking into the combustion chamber and/or the crankcase. Again, the cause must be corrected or the problem may persist in the rebuilt engine.

10 If in any doubt as to the condition of the pistons and connecting rods, have them inspected and measured by an engine reconditioning specialist. If new parts are required, they will be able to supply appropriate-sized pistons/rings, and rebore (where possible) or hone the cylinder block.

16 Crankshaft – inspection

1 Clean the crankshaft using paraffin or a suitable solvent, and dry it, preferably with compressed air if available. Be sure to clean the oil holes with a pipe cleaner or similar probe, to ensure that they are not obstructed.

 Warning: Wear eye protection when using compressed air.

2 Check the main and big-end bearing journals for uneven wear, scoring, pitting and cracking.
3 Big-end bearing wear is accompanied by distinct metallic knocking when the engine is running (particularly noticeable when the engine is pulling from low speed) and some loss of oil pressure.
4 Main bearing wear is accompanied by severe engine vibration and rumble – getting progressively worse as engine speed increases – and again by loss of oil pressure.
5 Check the bearing journal for roughness by running a finger lightly over the bearing surface. Any roughness (which will be accompanied by obvious bearing wear) indicates that the crankshaft requires regrinding (where possible) or renewal.
6 If the crankshaft has been reground, check for burrs around the crankshaft oil holes (the holes are usually chamfered, so burrs should not be a problem unless regrinding has been carried out carelessly). Remove any burrs with a fine file or scraper, and thoroughly clean the oil holes as described previously.
7 Have the crankshaft journals measured by an engine reconditioning specialist. If the crankshaft is worn or damaged, they may be able to regrind the journals and supply suitable undersize bearing shells. If no undersize shells are available and the crankshaft has worn beyond the specified limits, it will have to be renewed. Consult your Toyota dealer or engine specialist for further information on parts availability.

17 Main and big-end bearings – inspection

1 Even though the main and big-end bearings should be renewed during the engine overhaul, the old bearings should be retained for close examination, as they may reveal valuable information about the condition of the engine.
2 Bearing failure can occur due to lack of lubrication, the presence of dirt or other foreign particles, overloading the engine, or corrosion. Regardless of the cause of bearing failure, the cause must be corrected (where applicable) before the engine is reassembled, to prevent it from happening again **(see illustration)**.
3 When examining the bearing shells, remove them from the cylinder block, the main

bearing caps/ladder, the connecting rods and the connecting rod big-end bearing caps. Lay them out on a clean surface in the same general position as their location in the engine. This will enable you to match any bearing problems with the corresponding crankshaft journal. *Do not* touch any shell's bearing surface with your fingers while checking it, or the delicate surface may be scratched.
4 Dirt and other foreign matter gets into the engine in a variety of ways. It may be left in the engine during assembly, or it may pass through filters or the crankcase ventilation system. It may get into the oil, and from there into the bearings. Metal chips from machining operations and normal engine wear are often present. Abrasives are sometimes left in engine components after reconditioning, especially when parts are not thoroughly cleaned using the proper cleaning methods. Whatever the source, these foreign objects often end up embedded in the soft bearing material, and are easily recognised. Large particles will not embed in the bearing, and will score or gouge the bearing and journal. The best prevention for this cause of bearing failure is to clean all parts thoroughly, and keep everything spotlessly-clean during engine assembly. Frequent and regular engine oil and filter changes are also recommended.
5 Lack of lubrication (or lubrication breakdown) has a number of interrelated causes. Excessive heat (which thins the oil), overloading (which squeezes the oil from the bearing face) and oil leakage (from excessive bearing clearances, worn oil pump or high engine speeds) all contribute to lubrication breakdown. Blocked oil passages, which usually are the result of misaligned oil holes in a bearing shell, will also oil-starve a bearing, and destroy it. When lack of lubrication is the cause of bearing failure, the bearing material is wiped or extruded from the steel backing of the bearing. Temperatures may increase to the point where the steel backing turns blue from overheating.
6 Driving habits can have a definite effect on bearing life. Full-throttle, low-speed operation (labouring the engine) puts very high loads on bearings, tending to squeeze out the oil film. These loads cause the bearings to flex, which produces fine cracks in the bearing face (fatigue failure). Eventually, the bearing material will loosen in pieces, and tear away from the steel backing.
7 Short-distance driving leads to corrosion of bearings, because insufficient engine heat is produced to drive off the condensed water and corrosive gases. These products collect in the engine oil, forming acid and sludge. As the oil is carried to the engine bearings, the acid attacks and corrodes the bearing material.
8 Incorrect bearing installation during engine assembly will lead to bearing failure as well. Tight-fitting bearings leave insufficient bearing running clearance, and will result in oil starvation. Dirt or foreign particles trapped behind a bearing shell result in high spots on the bearing, which lead to failure.

9 *Do not* touch any shell's bearing surface with your fingers during reassembly; there is a risk of scratching the delicate surface, or of depositing particles of dirt on it.
10 As mentioned at the beginning of this Section, the bearing shells should be renewed as a matter of course during engine overhaul; to do otherwise is false economy.

18 Engine overhaul – reassembly sequence

1 Before reassembly begins, ensure that all new parts have been obtained, and that all necessary tools are available. Read through the entire procedure, to familiarise yourself with the work involved, and to ensure that all items necessary for reassembly of the engine are at hand. In addition to all normal tools and materials, thread-locking compound will be needed. A suitable tube of liquid sealant will also be required for the joint faces that are fitted without gaskets; it is recommended that Toyota sealant (available from your Toyota dealer) is used.
2 In order to save time and avoid problems, engine reassembly can be carried out in the following order:
 a) Crankshaft (Section 19).
 b) Piston/connecting rod assemblies (Sections 20 and 21).
 c) Oil pump, oil pump pick-up tube and oil sea/housing (Part A, B or C of this Chapter).
 d) Sump (Part A, B or C of this Chapter).
 e) Flywheel/driveplate (Part A, B or C of this Chapter).
 f) Cylinder head (Part A, B or C of this Chapter).

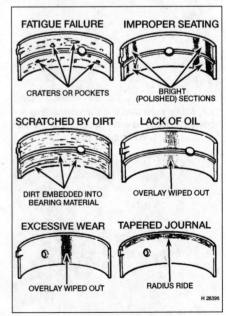

17.2 Typical bearing failures

19.5a Press the bearing shells into their correct locations in the cylinder block . . .

g) *Timing belt/chain, tensioner, sprockets and idler pulleys (Part A, B or C of this Chapter).*
h) *Intake and exhaust manifolds (Part A, B or C of this Chapter).*
i) *Engine external components.*

3 At this stage, all engine components should be absolutely clean and dry, with all faults repaired. The components should be laid out (or in individual containers) on a completely clean work surface.

19 Crankshaft – refitting

1 Crankshaft installation is the first major step in engine reassembly. It's assumed at this point that the engine block and crankshaft have been cleaned, inspected and repaired or reconditioned.

19.8 Make sure that the thrustwashers are correctly located each side of the centre main bearing cap

19.14a Fit the bearing shells with the oil grooves to the cylinder block . . .

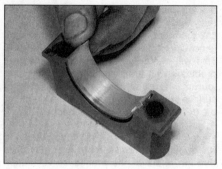

19.5b . . . and caps

2 Position the engine with the bottom facing up.

All except 1.8 litre petrol

3 Remove the main bearing cap bolts and lift out the caps. Lay the caps out in the proper order.
4 If they're still in place, remove the old bearing shells from the block and the main bearing caps. Wipe the main bearing surfaces of the block and caps with a clean, lint-free cloth. They must be kept spotlessly clean.
5 Clean the back sides of the new main bearing shells and lay the bearing half with the oil groove in each main bearing saddle in the block **(see illustration)**. Note that on 2000 and earlier 2.0 litre engines, the centre (No 3) upper and lower main bearing shells are 22.9 mm wide and all the others are 19.2 mm wide – ensure the shells are fitted accordingly. Lay the other bearing half from each bearing

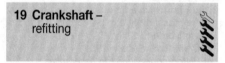

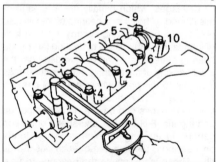

19.9 Main bearing cap tightening sequence

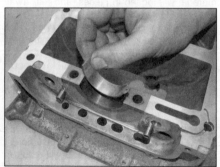

19.14b . . . and fit the plain shells to the main bearing ladder – 1.8 litre petrol engines

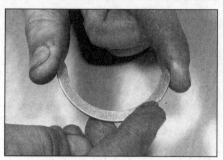

19.6 Use a dab of grease to hold the thrustwashers in position each side of the centre main bearing

set in the corresponding main bearing cap **(see illustration)**. Make sure the tab on each bearing insert fits into the recess in the block or cap. Also, the oil holes in the block must line up with the oil holes in the bearing shell.
6 Position the thrustwashers on either side of the No 3 bearing position with the oil grooves facing outwards. If necessary, they can be held in position with a smear of grease **(see illustration)**.
7 Wipe clean the thrustwashers and bearing faces in the block and lubricate them thoroughly with clean engine oil.
8 Make sure the crankshaft journals are clean, then lay the crankshaft in place in the block. Clean the faces of the bearings in the caps, then lubricate them with clean engine oil. Install the caps in their respective positions with the arrows pointing toward the front of the engine. The tanged lower thrustwashers should be placed on the caps with their oil grooves facing outward and the tangs fitting into the cap slots **(see illustration)**.
9 Apply a light coat of oil to the bolt threads and the undersides of the bolt heads, then install them. Tighten all the main bearing cap bolts to the specified torque, in sequence **(see illustration)**.
10 Rotate the crankshaft a number of times by hand to check for any obvious binding.
11 Check the crankshaft endfloat with a feeler gauge or a dial indicator as described in Section 13. The endfloat should be correct if the crankshaft thrust faces aren't worn or damaged and new thrustwashers have been installed.
12 On all except 2001 and later engines, install a new crankshaft oil seal, then refit the seal housing to the block – see Part A or C of this Chapter.

1.8 litre petrol engines

13 If they're still in place, remove the old bearing shells from the block and the main bearing ladder. Wipe the main bearing surfaces of the block and ladder with a clean, lint-free cloth. They must be kept spotlessly clean.
14 Clean the back sides of the new main bearing shells and lay the bearing half with the oil groove in each main bearing saddle in the block. Lay the other bearing half from each bearing set in the corresponding main bearing ladder **(see illustrations)**. Make sure the tab

on each bearing shell fits into the recess in the block or ladder. Also, the oil holes in the block must line up with the oil holes in the bearing shell.

15 Position the thrustwashers on either side of the No 3 bearing position with the oil grooves facing outwards. If necessary, they can be held in position with a smear of grease.

16 Wipe clean the thrustwashers and bearing faces in the block and lubricate them thoroughly with clean engine oil.

17 Make sure the crankshaft journals are clean, then lay the crankshaft in place in the block. Clean the faces of the bearings in the main bearing ladder, then lubricate them with clean engine oil.

18 Apply a 2 mm wide bead of sealant (Toyota No 08826-00080 or equivalent) to the main bearing ladder **(see illustration)**. Install the main bearing ladder within 3 minutes or the sealant will harden.

19 Refit the 12-point head main bearing ladder bolts (the inner row of 10), and tighten them in sequence to the Stage 1 torque setting, then to the Stage 2 setting **(see illustration)**. Again, working in sequence, tighten the bolts to the Stage 3 angle setting, followed by the Stage 4 angle setting, using an angle-tightening gauge.

20 Refit the remaining hexagon-head bolts to the main bearing ladder and progressively tighten them in a diagonal sequence to the specified torque.

21 Rotate the crankshaft a number of times by hand to check for any obvious binding.

22 Check the crankshaft endfloat with a feeler gauge or a dial indicator as described in Section 13. The endfloat should be correct if the crankshaft thrust faces aren't worn or damaged and new thrustwashers have been installed.

23 Install a new crankshaft oil seal with reference to Part B of this Chapter.

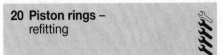

20 Piston rings – refitting

1 Before fitting the new piston rings, the ring end gaps must be checked.

2 Lay out the piston/connecting rod assemblies and the new ring sets so the ring sets will be matched with the same piston and cylinder during the end gap measurement and engine assembly.

3 Insert the top (number one) ring into the first cylinder and square it up with the cylinder walls by pushing it in with the top of the piston. The ring should be near the bottom of the cylinder, at the lower limit of ring travel.

4 To measure the end gap, slip feeler gauges between the ends of the ring until a gauge equal to the gap width is found **(see illustration)**. The feeler gauge should slide between the ring ends with a slight amount of drag. Compare the measurement to that given in the Specifications. If the gap is larger or smaller than specified, double-check to make sure you have the correct rings before proceeding.

5 If the gap is too small (unlikely if genuine Toyota parts are used), it must be enlarged, or the ring ends may contact each other during engine operation, causing serious damage. Ideally, new piston rings providing the correct end gap should be fitted. As a last resort, the end gap can be increased by filing the ring ends very carefully with a fine file. Mount the file in a vice with soft jaws, slip the ring over the file with the ends contacting the file face, and slowly move the ring to remove material from the ends. Take care, as piston rings are sharp, and are easily broken.

6 With new piston rings, it is unlikely that the end gap will be too large. If the gaps are too

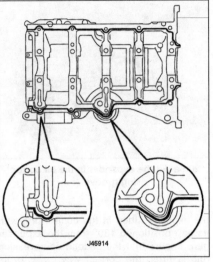

19.18 Apply a 2 mm wide bead of sealant to the main bearing ladder – 1.8 litre petrol engines

large, check that you have the correct rings for your engine and for the particular cylinder bore size.

7 Repeat the checking procedure for each ring in the first cylinder, and then for the rings in the remaining cylinders. Remember to keep rings, pistons and cylinders matched up.

8 Once the ring end gaps have been checked and if necessary corrected, the rings can be fitted to the pistons.

9 Fit the piston rings using the same technique as for removal. Fit the bottom (oil control) ring first, and work up. When fitting a three-piece oil control ring, first insert the expander, then fit the lower rail with its gap positioned 120° from the expander gap, then fit the upper rail with its gap positioned 120° from the lower rail **(see illustrations)**. When fitting a two-piece oil control ring, first insert

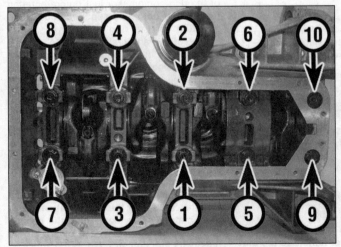

19.19 Main bearing ladder bolt tightening sequence – 1.8 litre petrol engines

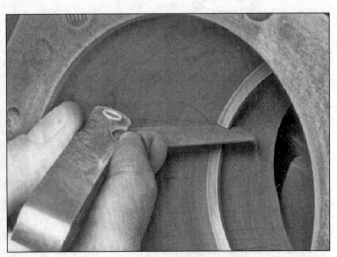

20.4 With the piston ring square in the bore, measure the end gap with a feeler gauge

20.9a Fit the expander in the oil control ring groove . . .

20.9b . . . followed by the lower and upper rails

the expander, then fit the control ring with its gap positioned 180° from the expander gap. Ensure that the second compression ring is fitted the correct way up, with its identification mark (either a dot of paint or the word TOP stamped on the ring surface) at the top, and the stepped surface at the bottom. Arrange the gaps of the top and second compression rings 120° either side of the oil control ring gap, but make sure that none of the ring gaps are positioned over the gudgeon pin hole. **Note:** *Always follow any instructions supplied with the new piston ring sets – different manufacturers may specify different procedures. Do not mix up the top and second compression rings, as they have different cross-sections.*

21 Pistons/connecting rods – refitting

1 Before installing the piston/connecting rod assemblies, the cylinder walls must be perfectly clean, the top edge of each cylinder must be chamfered, and the crankshaft must be in place.
2 Remove the cap from the end of the number one connecting rod (refer to the marks made during removal). Remove the original bearing shells and wipe the bearing surfaces of the connecting rod and cap with a clean, lint-free cloth. They must be kept spotlessly clean.
3 Clean the back side of the new upper

bearing shell, then lay it in place in the connecting rod. Make sure the tab on the bearing fits into the recess in the rod so the oil holes line up. Don't hammer the bearing insert into place and be very careful not to nick or gouge the bearing face.
4 Clean the back side of the other bearing shell and install it in the rod cap. Again, make sure the tab on the bearing fits into the recess in the cap, and don't apply any lubricant. It's critically important that the mating surfaces of the bearing and connecting rod are perfectly clean and oil-free when they're assembled.
5 Position the piston ring gaps at staggered intervals around the piston **(see illustrations)**.
6 Where applicable, slip a section of plastic or rubber hose over each connecting rod cap bolt to protect the cylinder bore.
7 Lubricate the piston and rings with clean engine oil and attach a piston ring compressor to the piston. Leave the skirt protruding about 8.0 mm to guide the piston into the cylinder. The rings must be compressed until they're flush with the piston.
8 Rotate the crankshaft until the number one connecting rod journal is at BDC (bottom dead centre) and apply a coat of engine oil to the cylinder wall.
9 Gently insert the piston/connecting rod assembly into the number one cylinder bore and rest the bottom edge of the ring compressor on the cylinder block. Ensure that the piston front marking (in the form of one or two indentations or a single protrusion) on the piston crown is toward the timing belt/chain end of the engine.
10 Tap the top edge of the ring compressor to ensure it's contacting the block around its entire circumference.
11 Gently tap on the top of the piston with the end of a wooden hammer handle **(see illustration)** while guiding the end of the connecting rod into place on the crankshaft journal. The piston rings may try to pop out of the ring compressor just before entering the cylinder bore, so keep some downward pressure on the ring compressor. Work slowly, and if any resistance is felt as the piston enters the cylinder, stop immediately. Find out what's binding and fix it before proceeding.
Caution: Do not, for any reason, force the piston into the cylinder – you might break a ring and/or the piston.
12 Make sure the bearing faces are perfectly clean, then lubricate them with clean engine oil.
13 Slide the connecting rod into place on the journal, remove the protective hoses from the rod cap bolts, and fit the bearing cap. Note that the faces with the identification marks must match (which means that the bearing shell locating tabs abut each other). Fit the nuts/bolts and tighten them to the specified torque.
14 Tighten the bearing cap retaining nuts/

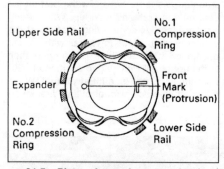

21.5a Piston ring end gap spacing – 2000 and earlier 2.0 litre petrol engines

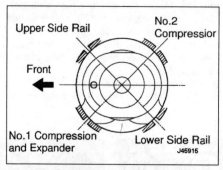

21.5b Piston ring end gap spacing – 1.8 litre petrol engines

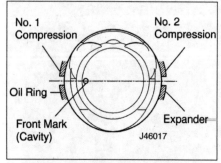

21.5c Piston ring end gap spacing – 2001 and later 2.0 litre petrol and diesel engines

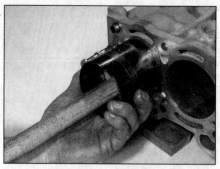

21.11 Using a hammer handle to tap the piston into its bore

bolts to their Stage 1 torque setting, using a torque wrench and socket, then tighten them to the specified Stage 2 angle setting.

15 Rotate the crankshaft and check that it turns freely; some stiffness is to be expected if new components have been fitted, but there should be no signs of binding or tight spots.

16 Refit the remaining three piston/connecting rod assemblies in the same way.

2001-on 2.0 litre petrol engines

17 Ensure that the joint faces of the cylinder block and lower crankcase are thoroughly clean and dry, then place a new O-ring in the oil gallery groove on the cylinder block joint face.

18 Apply a 2.5 to 3.0 mm wide bead of sealant (Toyota No 08826-00080 or equivalent) to the lower crankcase **(see illustration)**. Install the lower crankcase within 3 minutes or the sealant will harden.

19 Refit the six short bolts and five long bolts in their correct positions, and tighten them all hand-tight **(see illustration 12.2a)**. Working in a diagonal sequence, progressively tighten the bolts to the specified torque.

20 Install a new crankshaft oil seal with reference to Part B of this Chapter.

All engines

21 Refit the oil pump, oil pump pick-up tube, sump (and sump upper housing on diesel engines), rear engine plate, cylinder head, timing belt/chain, flywheel/driveplate and the remainder of the external components with reference to Part A, B or C and earlier Sections of this Chapter.

22 Initial start-up after reassembly

Warning: Have a fire extinguisher handy when starting the engine for the first time.

1 Once the engine has been fitted in the vehicle, double-check the engine oil and coolant levels. Remove all of the spark plugs (see Chapter 1A) or glow plugs (see Chapter 5) from the engine.

2 On petrol engines, disable the fuel and ignition systems by disconnecting the wiring from the ignition coil pack/modules (see Chapter 5). On diesel engines, disconnect the wiring from the injectors (see Chapter 4B).

3 Turn over the engine using the starter motor until the oil light goes out.

4 Refit the spark plugs or glow plugs, and reconnect all wiring.

5 Start the engine. It may take a few moments for the fuel system to build-up pressure, but the engine should start without a great deal of effort.

6 After the engine starts, it should be allowed to warm-up to normal operating temperature. While the engine is warming-up, make a thorough check for fuel, oil and coolant leaks.

7 Switch off the engine and recheck the engine oil and coolant levels.

8 Drive the vehicle to an area with minimum traffic, accelerate from 30 to 50 mph, then allow the vehicle to slow to 30 mph with the throttle closed. Repeat the procedure 10 or 12 times. This will load the piston rings and cause them to seat properly against the cylinder walls. Check again for oil and coolant leaks.

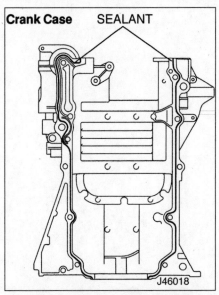

21.18 Apply a 2.5 to 3.0 mm wide bead of sealant to the lower crankcase – 2001 and later 2.0 litre petrol engines

9 Drive the vehicle gently for the first 500 miles (no sustained high speeds) and keep a constant check on the oil level. It is not unusual for an engine to use oil during the running-in period.

10 At approximately 500 to 600 miles, change the oil and filter.

11 For the next few hundred miles, drive the vehicle normally. Do not pamper it or abuse it.

12 After 2000 miles, change the oil and filter again and consider the engine run-in.

Notes

Chapter 3
Cooling, heating and air conditioning systems

Contents

Section number

Air conditioning and heating system – check and maintenance 11
Air conditioning compressor – removal and refitting 13
Air conditioning condenser – removal and refitting 14
Air conditioning receiver/drier – removal and refitting 12
Antifreeze – general information 2
Auxiliary drivebelt check, adjustment and
    renewal . . . . See Chapter 1A or 1B
Blower motor – removal and refitting 8
Coolant level check . . . . See Weekly checks
Coolant temperature sending unit and radiator fan switch – renewal 7
Cooling system check . . . . See Chapter 1A or 1B

Section number

Cooling system servicing (draining, flushing and
    refilling) . . . . See Chapter 1A or 1B
Engine cooling fans – removal and refitting 4
General information 1
Heater/air conditioning control assembly – removal and refitting, and
    cable adjustment 9
Heater matrix – removal and refitting 10
Radiator – removal and refitting 5
Thermostat – check and renewal 3
Underbonnet hose check and renewal . . . . See Chapter 1A or 1B
Water pump – check and renewal 6

Degrees of difficulty

Easy, suitable for novice with little experience 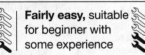	**Fairly easy,** suitable for beginner with some experience	**Fairly difficult,** suitable for competent DIY mechanic	**Difficult,** suitable for experienced DIY mechanic	**Very difficult,** suitable for expert DIY or professional

Specifications

General

Radiator cap pressure rating:
   1996 and 1997 . . . . 0.7 to 1.0 bar
   1998 and later. . . . . 0.9 to 1.2 bar
Thermostat rating:
   Opens . . . . 80° to 84°C
   Fully open. . . . . 95°C
Refrigerant type R-134a
Refrigerant capacity:
   2000 and earlier models. . . . . 700 +/- 50 grams
   2001 and later models . . . . 500 +/- 50 grams

Torque wrench settings

	lbf ft	Nm
Receiver/drier end plug (2001 and later models)	9	12
Thermostat housing bolts.	7	9
Water pump-to-block bolts:		
Petrol engines.	7	9
Diesel engines	23	31

**1.1 Typical petrol engine cooling system component locations –
2000 and earlier shown, 2001 and later similar**

1	Condenser	3	Water pump
2	Thermostat	4	Cooling fans

5	Radiator
6	Coolant reservoir

1 General information

Engine cooling system

All vehicles covered by this manual employ a pressurised engine cooling system with thermostatically controlled coolant circulation

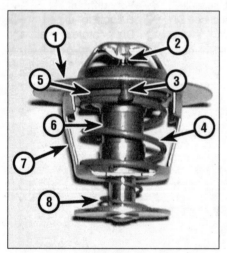

1.2 A typical thermostat

1	Flange	5	Valve seat
2	Piston	6	Valve
3	Jiggle valve	7	Frame
4	Main coil spring	8	Secondary coil spring

(see illustration). An impeller type water pump mounted on the front of the block pumps coolant through the engine. The coolant flows around each cylinder and toward the rear of the engine. Cast-in coolant passages direct coolant around the intake and exhaust ports, and in proximity to the exhaust valve guides.

A wax pellet-type thermostat is located in the thermostat housing on the front of the engine **(see illustration)**. During warm-up, the closed thermostat prevents coolant from circulating through the radiator. When the engine reaches normal operating temperature, the thermostat opens and allows hot coolant to travel through the radiator, where it is cooled before returning to the engine.

The cooling system is sealed by a pressure-type radiator cap located on the top of the radiator (petrol models) or on the top of the expansion tank (diesel models). This raises the boiling point of the coolant, and the higher boiling point of the coolant increases the cooling efficiency of the radiator. On petrol models, if the system pressure exceeds the cap pressure relief value, the excess pressure in the system forces the spring-loaded valve inside the cap off its seat and allows the coolant to escape through the overflow tube into a coolant reservoir. When the system cools, the excess coolant is automatically drawn from the reservoir back into the radiator.

On petrol models, the coolant reservoir serves as both the point at which fresh coolant is added to the cooling system to maintain the proper fluid level and as a holding tank for overheated coolant. This type of cooling system is known as a closed design because coolant that escapes past the pressure cap is saved and re-used.

Heating system

The heating system consists of a blower fan and heater matrix located within the heater box, the inlet and outlet hoses connecting the heater matrix to the engine cooling system and the heater/air conditioning control head on the dashboard. Hot engine coolant is circulated through the heater matrix. When the heater mode is activated, a flap door opens to expose the heater box to the passenger compartment. A fan switch on the control head activates the blower motor, which forces air through the matrix, heating the air.

Air conditioning system

The air conditioning system consists of a condenser mounted in front of the radiator, an evaporator mounted adjacent to the heater matrix under the dashboard, a compressor mounted on the engine, a filter/drier (accumulator) which contains a high-pressure relief valve and the plumbing connecting all of the above.

A blower fan forces the warmer air of the passenger compartment through the evaporator matrix (sort of a radiator-in-reverse), transferring the heat from the air to the refrigerant. The liquid refrigerant boils off into low pressure vapour, taking the heat with it when it leaves the evaporator. The compressor keeps refrigerant circulating through the system, pumping the warmed refrigerant through the condenser where it is cooled and then circulated back to the evaporator.

2 Antifreeze – general information

⚠ *Warning: Do not allow antifreeze to come in contact with your skin or painted surfaces of the vehicle. Rinse off spills immediately with plenty of water. Antifreeze is highly toxic if ingested. Never leave antifreeze lying around in an open container or in puddles on the floor; children and pets are attracted by its sweet smell and may drink it. Check with local authorities about disposing of used antifreeze. Many communities have collection centres which will see that antifreeze is disposed of safely. Never dump used antifreeze on the ground or into drains.*

The cooling system should be filled with a water/ethylene-glycol based antifreeze solution, which will prevent freezing. It also provides protection against corrosion and increases the coolant boiling point.

The cooling system should be drained, flushed and refilled regularly (see Chapter 1A or 1B). The use of antifreeze solutions for periods of longer than two years is likely to cause damage and encourage the formation of rust and scale in the system. If your tap water is 'hard', ie, contains a lot of dissolved minerals, use distilled water with the antifreeze.

Before adding antifreeze to the system, check all hose connections, because antifreeze tends to leak through very minute openings. Engines do not normally consume coolant. Therefore, if the level goes down find the cause and correct it.

The exact mixture of antifreeze-to-water which you should use depends on the relative weather conditions. The mixture should contain at least 50% antifreeze, but should never contain more than 70% antifreeze. Consult the mixture ratio chart on the antifreeze container before adding coolant. Hydrometers are available at most car accessory shops to test the ratio of antifreeze to water (**see illustration**). Use antifreeze which meets the vehicle manufacturer's specifications.

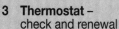
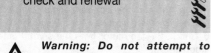

3 Thermostat – check and renewal

> ⚠ **Warning: Do not attempt to remove the radiator cap, coolant or thermostat until the engine has cooled completely.**

General check

1 Before assuming the thermostat is responsible for a cooling system problem, check the coolant level (*Weekly checks*), auxiliary drivebelt tension where applicable (Chapter 1A or 1B) and temperature gauge (or light) operation.

2 If the engine takes a long time to warm-up (as indicated by the temperature gauge or heater operation), the thermostat is probably stuck open. Renew the thermostat.

3 If the engine runs hot, use your hand to check the temperature of the lower radiator hose. If the hose is not hot, but the engine is, the thermostat is probably stuck in the closed position, preventing the coolant inside the radiator from being drawn into the engine. Renew the thermostat.

Caution: Do not drive the vehicle without a thermostat. The computer may stay in open loop and emissions and fuel economy will suffer.

4 If the lower radiator hose is hot, it means that the coolant is flowing and the thermostat is open. Consult the Troubleshooting Section at the rear of this manual for further diagnosis.

Thermostat test

Note: *Frankly, if there is any question about the operation of the thermostat, it's best to renew it – they are not usually expensive items. Testing involves heating in, or over, an open pan of boiling water, which carries with it the risk of scalding. A thermostat which has seen more than five years' service may well be past its best already.*

2.4 An inexpensive hydrometer can be used to test the condition of your coolant

5 A more thorough test of the thermostat can only be made when it is removed from the vehicle (see below). If the thermostat remains in the open position at room temperature, it is faulty and must be renewed.

6 To test it fully, suspend the (closed) thermostat on a length of string or wire in a container of cold water, with a suitable thermometer.

7 Heat the water on a stove while observing the temperature and the thermostat. Neither should contact the sides of the container (**see illustration**).

8 Note the temperature when the thermostat begins to open and when it is fully open. Compare the temperatures to the Specifications in this Chapter. The number

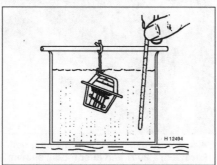

3.7 A thermostat can be accurately checked by heating it in a container of water with a thermometer and observing the opening and fully-open temperature

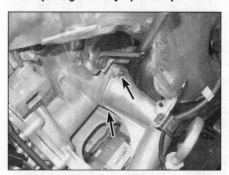

3.13 With the alternator removed, remove the nuts (arrowed) securing the thermostat housing to the side of the engine block – 2001 and later petrol models

stamped into the thermostat is generally the fully-open temperature. Some manufacturers provide Specifications for the beginning-to-open temperature, the fully-open temperature, and sometimes the amount the valve should open.

9 If the thermostat doesn't open and close as specified, or sticks in any position, renew it.

Renewal

10 Disconnect the negative cable from the battery.

11 Drain the coolant from the radiator (see Chapter 1A or 1B). Disconnect the radiator hose from the thermostat housing or water inlet pipe.

12 On 2000 and earlier models, remove the thermostat housing from the back of the water pump housing (**see illustration**). **Note:** *For easier access to the lower bolt, remove the oil filter.*

13 On 2001 and later petrol models, remove the alternator (see Chapter 5) then unbolt the thermostat housing from the engine block (**see illustration**).

14 On diesel models, unbolt the water inlet pipe from the engine block (**see illustration**).

15 Remove the thermostat, noting the direction in which it was installed in the housing, and thoroughly clean the sealing surfaces.

16 Fit a new rubber gasket onto the thermostat (**see illustration**). Make sure it is evenly fitted all the way around.

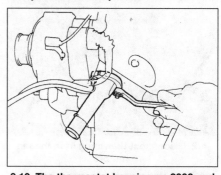

3.12 The thermostat housing on 2000 and earlier models is located behind the water pump – access to the nuts is easier with the oil filter removed

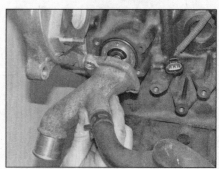

3.14 On diesel models, unbolt the water inlet pipe from the engine block

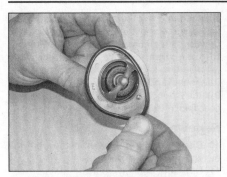

3.16 The thermostat gasket fits around the edge of the thermostat like a grooved sealing ring

17 On 2000 and earlier models, install the thermostat into the thermostat housing, then install the housing and thermostat into the back of the water pump housing. Be sure to position the jiggle pin upward at the highest point.

18 On 2001 and later models, install the thermostat into the engine block, then install the thermostat housing/inlet pipe. Be sure to position the jiggle valve upward at the highest point (see illustration).

19 Tighten the housing bolts to the torque listed in this Chapter's Specifications and reinstall the remaining components in the reverse order of removal.

20 Refill the cooling system (see Chapter 1A or 1B). Run the engine and check for leaks and proper operation.

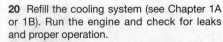

4 Engine cooling fans – removal and refitting

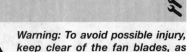

Warning: To avoid possible injury, keep clear of the fan blades, as they may start turning at any time.

1 Disconnect the negative battery cable.
2 Disconnect the wiring connector at the fan motors (see illustration).
3 On 2000 and earlier models, The condenser fan has one bolt on the top and two on the bottom securing the fan to the radiator and the main cooling fan has two bolts at the top and two at the bottom securing the fan to the radiator. On 2001 and later models, the condenser fan has two bolts at the top and one bolt at the bottom, while the main cooling fan has two bolts at the top and two retaining tabs at the bottom.
4 Jack up the front of the vehicle and support it securely on axle stands. Remove the splash shields from below the engine and the lower bolt from the condenser fan (see illustration). Working above in the engine

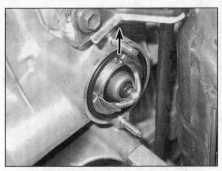

3.18 Position the jiggle valve straight up – 2001 petrol models shown, 2000 and earlier petrol models are similar but the thermostat is installed in the thermostat housing and not in the engine block

compartment unbolt the fan/shrouds from the radiator and lift them from the vehicle (see illustrations).
5 Hold the fan blades and remove the fan retaining screws or nut (see illustration). Note: *The main cooling fan blade is attached with a nut and the condenser fan blade is retained by three screws.*
6 Unbolt the fan motor from the shroud (see illustration).
7 Refitting is the reverse of removal.

4.2 Disconnect the wiring from the fan motors

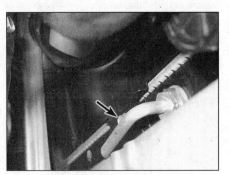

4.4a Condenser fan lower retaining bolt (arrowed) – 2001 and later model shown, 2000 and earlier models have two lower retaining bolts

4.4b Upper retaining bolts for the main cooling fan – on 2001 and later models simply pull the fan upward from the retaining tabs at the bottom. On 2000 and earlier models there are two bolts securing the bottom of the fan to the radiator

4.4c Upper retaining bolts for the condenser fan – 2001 and later model shown, 2000 and earlier models only have one bolt securing the top of the condenser fan

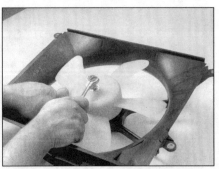

4.5 Remove the fan from the motor – main cooling fan shown, condenser fan has three screws securing it to the fan motor

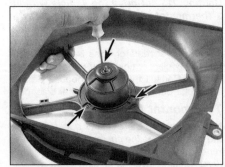

4.6 Remove the screws (arrowed) and separate the motor from the shroud

5.4a Unscrew the bolts . . .

5.4b . . . remove the bracket . . .

5.4c . . . bonnet lock . . .

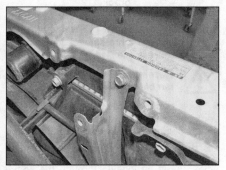

5.4d . . . then unscrew the bolts . . .

5.4e . . . and remove the centre strut

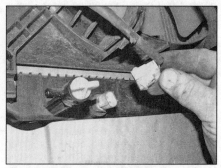

5.7 Disconnect the wiring from the radiator cooling fan switch

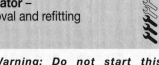

5 Radiator – removal and refitting

⚠️ **Warning: Do not start this procedure until the engine is completely cool. Do not allow antifreeze to come in contact with your skin or painted surfaces of the vehicle. Rinse off spills immediately with plenty of water. Antifreeze is highly toxic if ingested. Never leave antifreeze lying around in an open container or in puddles on the floor; children and pets are attracted by its sweet smell and may drink it. Check with local authorities about disposing of used antifreeze. Many communities have collection centres which will see that antifreeze is disposed of safely. Never dump used antifreeze on the ground or into drains.**

Radiator

1 Disconnect the negative battery cable.
2 Drain the coolant into a container (see Chapter 1A or 1B).
3 On 2000 and earlier models, unbolt the air conditioning condenser from the radiator and position it to one side.
4 On 2001 and later models, remove the radiator grille, the headlight filler panel, and the bonnet lock, then unbolt the engine compartment front strut and crossmember (see Chapter 11) **(see illustrations)**.
5 Remove both the upper and lower radiator hoses.
6 Disconnect the reservoir/expansion tank hose from the radiator filler neck.
7 Remove the cooling fans (see Section 4). Also disconnect the connector from the radiator cooling fan switch **(see illustration)**.

8 If equipped with an automatic transmission, disconnect the cooler lines from the radiator **(see illustration)**. Place a drip pan to catch the fluid and cap the fittings.
9 On 2000 and earlier models, remove the bolts that attach the radiator to its support **(see illustrations)**.
10 Lift out the radiator. Be aware of dripping fluids and the sharp fins. On 2001 and later models, the radiator locates in two lower mountings and two side mountings, in addition to the two upper mountings in the crossmember **(see illustrations)**.
11 With the radiator removed, it can be inspected for leaks, damage and internal blockage. If in need of repairs, have a professional radiator repairer or dealer service department perform the work, as special techniques are required.
12 Bugs and dirt can be cleaned from the radiator with compressed air and a soft

5.8 Remove the automatic transmission cooler lines (arrowed)

5.9a Remove the hold-down clamps from each end of the radiator – 2000 and earlier models

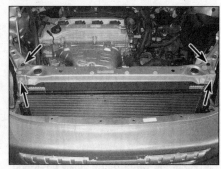

5.9b Radiator support panel retaining bolts (arrowed) – 2001 and later models

5.10a On 2001 and later models, the radiator has two lower mountings ...

5.10b ... and two side mountings in addition to the upper mountings in the crossmember

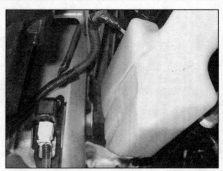

5.17 Typical coolant reservoir removal on petrol models – pull the reservoir off the bracket

brush. Don't bend the cooling fins as this is done.

 Warning: Wear eye protection.

13 Refitting is the reverse of the removal procedure. Be sure the rubber mountings are in place.
14 After refitting, fill the cooling system with the proper mixture of antifreeze and water. Refer to Chapter 1A or 1B if necessary.
15 Start the engine and check for leaks. Allow the engine to reach normal operating temperature, indicated by the upper radiator hose becoming hot. Recheck the coolant level and add more if required.
16 On automatic transmission equipped models, check and add transmission fluid as needed (see Chapter 1A or 1B).

Coolant reservoir/expansion tank

17 On petrol models, the coolant reservoir

6.3 Water pump weep hole location – 2001 and later petrol engine shown

6.4 Rock the water pump pulley back-and-forth – any noticeable movement indicates the need for renewal

simply pulls up and out of the bracket on the inner wing **(see illustration)**. On diesel models, the expansion tank is located on the engine compartment front crossmember.
18 Pour the coolant into a container. Wash out and inspect the reservoir/tank for cracks and chafing. Renew it if damaged.
19 Refitting is the reverse of removal.

6 Water pump – check and renewal

 Warning: Do not start this procedure until the engine is completely cool. Do not allow antifreeze to come in contact with your skin or painted surfaces of the vehicle. Rinse off spills immediately with plenty of water. Antifreeze is highly toxic if ingested. Never leave antifreeze lying around in an open container or in puddles on the floor; children and pets are attracted by its sweet smell and may drink it. Check with local authorities about disposing of used antifreeze. Many communities have collection centres which will see that antifreeze is disposed of safely. Never dump used antifreeze on the ground or into drains.

Check

1 A failure in the water pump can cause serious engine damage due to overheating.
2 With the engine running and warmed to

6.7 Remove the alternator adjusting bar (arrowed)

normal operating temperature, squeeze the upper radiator hose. If the water pump is working properly, a pressure surge should be felt as the hose is released.

 **Warning: Keep hands away from fan blades.**

3 Water pumps are equipped with weep or vent holes. If a failure occurs in the pump seal, coolant will leak from this hole **(see illustration)**. In most cases it will be necessary to use an electric torch to find the hole on the water pump by looking through the space behind the pulley just below the water pump shaft. A slight grey discoloration around the weep hole is normal, while dark brown stains indicate a problem.
4 If the water pump shaft bearings fail there may be a howling sound at the front of the engine while it is running. Bearing wear can be felt if the water pump pulley is rocked up-and-down **(see illustration)**. Do not mistake auxiliary drivebelt slippage, which causes a squealing sound, for water pump failure. Spray automotive auxiliary drivebelt dressing on the belts to eliminate the belt as a possible cause of the noise (2001 and later petrol models only; the water pump on 2000 and earlier petrol models and all diesel models is turned by the timing belt).

Renewal

5 Disconnect the negative battery cable and drain the cooling system.

2000 and earlier petrol models

6 Remove the timing belt and the number 1 and number 2 idler pulleys (see Chapter 2A).
7 Remove the alternator adjusting bar **(see illustration)**. On models with an engine oil cooler, unbolt the air conditioning compressor and set it aside without disconnecting the refrigerant lines (see Section 13). Disconnect the lower radiator hose.
8 Remove the bolts from the water pump **(see illustration)**, noting the locations of the different length bolts and the sequence of removal. Remove the pump and gasket. If necessary, tap the pump loose with a soft-face hammer.
9 It isn't necessary to remove the pump cover (housing), but a thorough job would include removing it to renew the gaskets and O-rings.

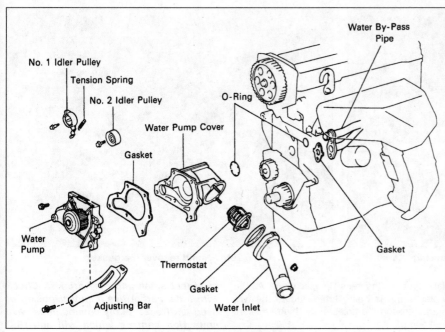

6.8 Water pump components –
2000 and earlier petrol models

Labels: No. 1 Idler Pulley, Tension Spring, No. 2 Idler Pulley, Water Pump Cover, Gasket, Water Pump, Thermostat, Gasket, Adjusting Bar, Water Inlet, O-Ring, Water By-Pass Pipe, Gasket

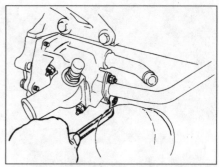

6.10 Disconnect the coolant bypass hose from the water neck – the heater pipe is attached with two nuts

10 Disconnect the coolant bypass hose from the water neck, then remove the two nuts and heater pipe **(see illustration)** and lift out the pump cover (housing).

11 Thoroughly clean all sealing surfaces, removing all traces of old gaskets, sealer and O-rings.

12 Be sure to use new O-rings between the pump cover and engine block and also a new gasket between the heater pipe and cover.

13 Using a new gasket, install the pump and bolts **(see illustrations)** and tighten them to the torque listed in this Chapter's Specifications.

14 Install the remaining parts in the reverse order of removal.

15 Refill the cooling system (see Chapter 1A), run the engine and check for leaks and proper operation.

2001 and later petrol models

16 Loosen the water pump pulley bolts **(see illustration)**, then remove the engine auxiliary drivebelt (see Chapter 1A or 1B).

17 Remove the wiring harness from the clamp on the water pump.

18 Remove the water pump retaining bolts and lever the water pump from the housing on the engine block **(see illustrations)**.

19 Thoroughly clean all sealing surfaces, removing all traces of old gasket sealer.

20 Apply a 1/8 inch bead of RTV sealant to the outside of the groove on the water pump **(see illustration)**.

21 Install the water pump and tighten the bolts and nuts to the torque listed in this Chapter's Specifications.

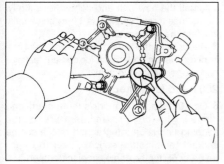

6.13a Install these bolts first . . .

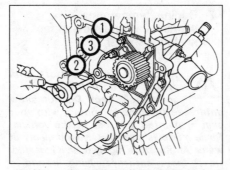

6.13b . . . then tighten these bolts in the order shown

6.16 Loosen the water pump pulley bolts while applying pressure to the engine drivebelt tensioner

6.18a Water pump retaining bolts – 2001 and later petrol models

6.18b Lever the water pump from the housing by the casting protrusion at the top

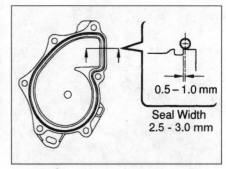

6.20 Water pump sealant application details – 2001 and later petrol models

0.5 – 1.0 mm
Seal Width
2.5 - 3.0 mm

6.29a Remove the water pump and housing ...

6.29b ... and recover the gasket

22 Install the remaining parts in the reverse order of removal.

23 Refill the cooling system (see Chapter 1A), run the engine and check for leaks and proper operation.

Diesel models

Note: *Toyota recommend renewal of the fuel inlet pipe whenever a new water pump is fitted.*

24 Remove the timing belt, crankshaft sprocket, and the number 1 idler pulley and high-pressure fuel pump pulley (see Chapter 2C).

25 Unbolt the cover from over the high-pressure fuel pump, and remove the insulation.

26 Remove the fuel inlet pipe and injector pipes (see Chapter 4B).

27 Remove the inlet manifold (see Chapter 2C).

28 Unscrew the mounting nuts securing the high-pressure fuel pump to the water pump housing studs.

29 Progressively unscrew the water pump mounting bolts and remove the pump from the cylinder block. Remove the gasket and discard **(see illustrations)**.

30 Thoroughly clean all sealing surfaces, removing all traces of old gaskets.

31 Using a new gasket, fit the water pump, insert the bolts and tighten them to the torque listed in this Chapter's Specifications. As the water pump is being fitted, locate the two studs through the holes in the high-pressure fuel pump.

32 Refit the high-pressure fuel pump mounting nuts and tighten them to the specified torque (see Chapter 4B).

33 Refit the inlet manifold (Chapter 2C) and fuel pipes (Chapter 4B), then fit the insulation and cover over the high-pressure pump and tighten the bolts.

34 Refit the pulleys and timing belt (Chapter 2C).

35 Refill the cooling system (see Chapter 1B), run the engine and check for leaks.

7 Coolant temperature sending unit and radiator fan switch – renewal

⚠️ *Warning: Do not start this procedure until the engine is completely cool. Do not allow antifreeze to come in contact with your skin or painted surfaces of the vehicle. Rinse off spills immediately with plenty of water. Antifreeze is highly toxic if ingested. Never leave antifreeze lying around in an open container or in puddles on the floor; children and pets are attracted by its sweet smell and may drink it. Check with local authorities about disposing of used antifreeze. Many communities have collection centres which will see that anti-freeze is disposed of safely. Never dump used antifreeze on the ground or into drains.*

Temperature gauge sending unit

2000 and earlier models

1 Drain the coolant (see Chapter 1A).

2 Disconnect the wiring connector from the sending unit **(see illustration)**.

3 Using a deep socket or spanner, remove the sending unit.

4 Install the new unit and tighten it securely. Do not use thread sealant as it may electrically insulate the sending unit.

5 Reconnect the wiring connector, refill the cooling system and check for coolant leakage and proper gauge function.

2001 and later models

6 On 2001 and later models (both petrol and diesel), the coolant temperature gauge sending unit is an integral part of the engine coolant temperature sensor. Refer to Chapter 6A or 6B for the engine coolant temperature sensor renewal procedure.

Radiator fan switch

7 Raise the front of the vehicle and support it securely on axle stands.

8 Remove the lower splash shields from the vehicle. Drain the coolant (see Chapter 1A or 1B)

9 Disconnect the wiring connector from the radiator fan switch **(see illustration)**.

10 Using a deep socket or spanner, remove the switch.

11 Install the new switch and tighten it securely. Do not use thread sealer as it may electrically insulate the sending unit.

12 Reconnect the wiring connector, refill the cooling system and check for coolant leakage and proper operation of the cooling fans.

7.2 Coolant temperature gauge sending unit location – 2000 and earlier petrol models

7.9 Radiator fan switch location

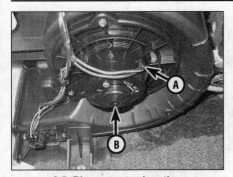

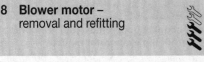

8.5 Blower motor location

A *Blower motor connector*
B *Blower motor*

8 Blower motor – removal and refitting

⚠️ **Warning: The models covered by this manual are equipped with Supplemental Restraint systems (SRS), more commonly known as airbags. Always disconnect the negative battery cable, then the positive battery cable and wait two minutes before working in the vicinity of the impact sensors, steering column or instrument panel to avoid the possibility of accidental deployment of the airbag, which could cause personal injury (see Chapter 12).**

1 Disconnect the negative cable from the battery.
2 The blower unit is located in the passenger compartment above the passenger footwell.
3 On 2000 and earlier models, remove the glove compartment (see Chapter 11).
4 Disconnect the electrical connector from the blower motor.
5 To remove the blower, remove the blower unit retaining screws and lower the unit from the housing **(see illustration)**.
6 If the motor is being renewed, transfer the

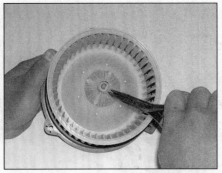

8.6 Use pliers to release and remove the clip, then lift the blower fan off the motor shaft

fan to the new motor prior to refitting **(see illustration)**.
7 Refitting is the reverse of removal. Check for proper operation.

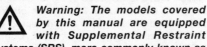

9 Heater/air conditioning control assembly – removal and refitting, and cable adjustment

⚠️ **Warning: The models covered by this manual are equipped with Supplemental Restraint systems (SRS), more commonly known as airbags. Always disable the airbag system before working in the vicinity of any airbag system components to avoid the possibility of accidental deployment of the airbag, which could cause personal injury (see Chapter 12).**

Removal and refitting

1 Disconnect the negative cable from the battery.
2 Remove the centre instrument trim panel (see Chapter 11).
3 On 2000 and earlier models, remove the glovebox and the lower centre trim panel also referring to Chapter 11. Then pull off the

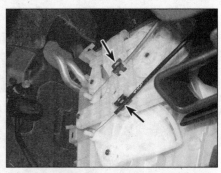

9.5 Disconnect the control cables from the clamps (arrowed) on the heater/air conditioning unit then remove the ends of the cable from the levers – 2001 and later models shown, 2000 and earlier models have three cables to disconnect

control knobs and remove the heater control assembly trim panel.
4 On 2001 and later models, remove the radio (see Chapter 12). Then remove the lower left finish panel from the front of the floor console.
5 Disconnect the heater control cables from the levers on the heater/air conditioning unit **(see illustration)**.
6 Remove the mounting screws located on the front of the control assembly **(see illustrations)**.
7 Pull the control assembly out of the instrument panel with the control cables attached.
8 Refitting is the reverse of the removal procedure.
9 Run the engine and check for proper functioning of the heater (and air conditioning, if equipped).

Cable adjustment

2000 and earlier models

10 To adjust the air inlet control cable set the control lever to RECIRC, install the cable and clamp it in place.
11 To adjust the air mix control cable, set the

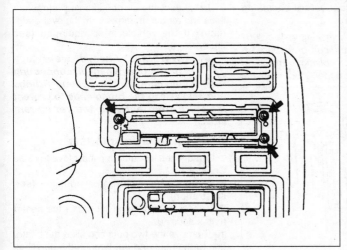

9.6a Heater/air conditioning control assembly mounting screws – 2000 and earlier models

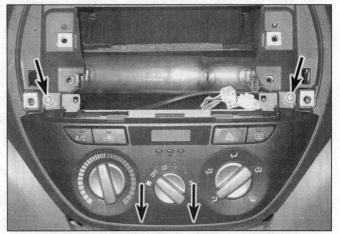

9.6b Heater/air conditioning control assembly mounting screws – 2001 and later models (lower arrows indicate the area of two plastic retaining clips – be careful not to break them)

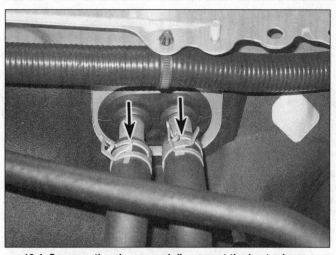

10.4 Squeeze the clamps and disconnect the heater hoses (arrowed) at the bulkhead

10.6 Using a spring-lock coupling tool remove the refrigerant lines (arrowed) from the evaporator matrix

air mix to COOL, install the cable and lock the clamp while applying slight pressure (away from the bulkhead) on the outer cable.

12 To adjust the mode control cable, set the mode damper to the DEF position, install the cable and clamp it in place.

2001 and later models

13 To adjust the air mix control cable, set the air mix to MAX COOL, install the cable and clamp it in place.

14 To adjust the mode control cable, position the mode control lever so it faces the rear of the vehicle. Install the cable and lock the clamp while applying slight pressure (away from the bulkhead) on the outer cable outer cable.

10 Heater matrix –
removal and refitting

⚠️ *Warning 1: The models covered by this manual are equipped with Supplemental Restraint systems (SRS), more commonly known as airbags. Always disable the airbag system before working in the vicinity of any airbag system components to avoid the possibility of accidental deployment of the airbag, which could cause personal injury (see Chapter 12).*

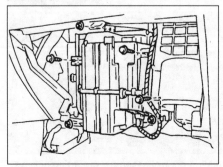

10.8 Evaporator housing mounting screws and nuts – 2000 and earlier models

⚠️ *Warning 2: Do not allow antifreeze to come in contact with your skin or painted surfaces of the vehicle. Rinse off spills immediately with plenty of water. Antifreeze is highly toxic if ingested. Never leave antifreeze lying around in an open container or in puddles on the floor; children and pets are attracted by its sweet smell and may drink it. Check with local authorities about disposing of used antifreeze. Many communities have collection centres which will see that antifreeze is disposed of safely. Never dump used antifreeze on the ground or into drains.*

⚠️ *Warning 3: The air conditioning system is under high pressure. DO NOT loosen any fittings or remove any components until after the system has been discharged. Air conditioning refrigerant should be properly discharged by an air condition specialist. Always wear eye protection when disconnecting air conditioning system fittings.*

⚠️ *Warning 4: Wait until the engine is completely cool before beginning this procedure.*

Note: *Removal of the heater matrix on 2001 and later models is a difficult procedure for the home mechanic, involving removal of the entire instrument panel, floor console*

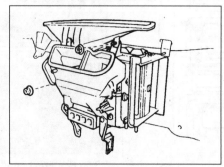

10.10 Heater matrix housing mounting nuts – 2000 and earlier models

and many wiring connectors. If you attempt this procedure at home, keep track of the assemblies by taking notes and keeping screws and other hardware in small, marked plastic bags for reassembly.

1 If the vehicle is equipped with air conditioning, have the air conditioning system discharged at a dealer service department or air conditioning specialist.

2 Turn the heater control setting to HOT. Drain the cooling system (see Chapter 1A or 1B). If the coolant is relatively new, or tests in good condition (see Section 2), save it and re-use it.

3 Disconnect the cable from the negative terminal of the battery.

4 Working in the engine compartment, disconnect the heater hoses where they enter the bulkhead **(see illustration)**.

Caution: If the heater hoses are stuck, it is better to cut off the hoses than to twist them with pliers and risk breaking the heater matrix tubes.

5 Remove the rubber grommets where the heater matrix tubes go through the bulkhead.

6 Disconnect the air conditioning refrigerant lines and rubber grommet from the evaporator matrix if the vehicle is so equipped **(see illustration)**.

⚠️ *Warning: Always wear eye protection when disconnecting air conditioning system fittings and always cap the fitting ends to prevent moisture from entering the refrigerant lines.*

2000 and earlier models

7 Remove the instrument panel glovebox (see Chapter 11).

8 Remove the evaporator housing **(see illustration)**.

9 Detach the rear floor duct from the heater matrix housing.

10 Remove the two nuts and slide the heater unit to the right and out through the glovebox opening **(see illustration)**.

11 Remove the screws securing the defroster

duct to the top of the heater unit, then remove the heater matrix retaining clamp and remove it from the heater matrix housing.

12 Refitting is the reverse of removal.

2001 and later models

13 Remove the entire instrument panel and the reinforcement beam (see Chapter 11).

14 Disconnect the electrical connectors from the blower motor and the blower resistor, then remove the blower unit (see illustration).

15 Remove the rear floor duct.

16 Remove the two nuts and the air conditioning unit.

17 Lever open the claws and remove the thermistor and the wiring harness from the air conditioning unit.

18 Remove the evaporator from the air conditioning unit (see illustration).

19 Detach the retaining screws and remove the heater matrix from the A/C housing (see illustration).

20 Reinstall the remaining parts in the reverse order of removal. Be sure to install the thermistor in the bracket plate with the correct amount protruding as shown (see illustration).

21 Refill the cooling system (see Chapter 1A or 1B), reconnect the battery and run the engine. Check for leaks and proper operation of the system. Have the air conditioning system recharged if equipped.

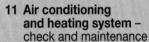

11 Air conditioning and heating system – check and maintenance

Air conditioning system

⚠️ Warning: The air conditioning system is under high pressure. Do not loosen any hose fittings or remove any components until after the system has been discharged. Air conditioning refrigerant should be properly discharged by an air conditioning specialist. Always wear eye protection when disconnecting air conditioning system fittings.

Caution: All models covered by this manual use environmentally-friendly R-134a. This refrigerant (and its appropriate refrigerant

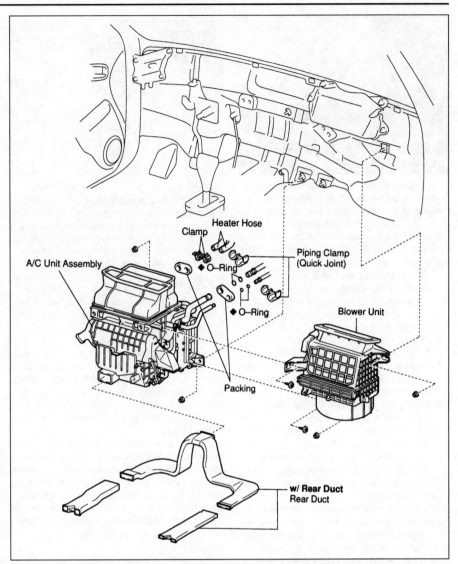

10.14 Heating and air conditioning unit installation details

oils) is not compatible R-12 refrigerant system components and must never be mixed or the components will be damaged.

1 The following maintenance checks should be performed on a regular basis to ensure that

the air conditioning continues to operate at peak efficiency.

a) Inspect the condition of the compressor auxiliary drivebelt. If it is worn or deteriorated, renew it (see Chapter 1A or 1B).

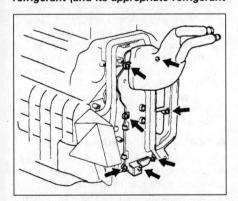

10.18 Evaporator matrix mounting screws – 2001 and later models

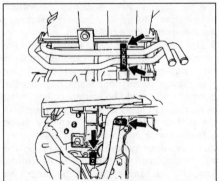

10.19 Heater matrix retaining screws – 2001 and later models

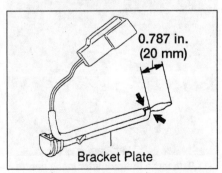

10.20 Install the thermistor in the bracket plate with the end of the thermistor protruding out of the bracket the specified amount

11.1 Check that the evaporator housing drain tube (arrowed) at the bulkhead is clear of any blockage – the view here is from below the engine

b) *Check the auxiliary drivebelt tension and, if necessary, adjust it (see Chapter 1A or 1B).*

c) *Inspect the system hoses. Look for cracks, bubbles, hardening and deterioration. Inspect the hoses and all fittings for oil bubbles or seepage. If there is any evidence of wear, damage or leakage, renew the hose(s).*

d) *Inspect the condenser fins for leaves, bugs and any other foreign material that may have embedded itself in the fins. Use a 'fin comb' or compressed air to remove debris from the condenser.*

e) *Make sure the system has the correct refrigerant charge.*

f) *If you hear water sloshing around in the dash area or have water dripping on the carpet, check the evaporator housing drain tube (see illustration) and insert a piece of wire into the opening to check for blockage.*

2 It's a good idea to operate the system for about ten minutes at least once a month. This is particularly important during the winter months because long-term non-use can cause hardening, and subsequent failure, of the seals. Note that using the Defrost function operates the compressor.

3 If the air conditioning system is not working properly, proceed to Step 6.

4 Because of the complexity of the air conditioning system and the special

11.9 Insert a thermometer in the centre duct while operating the air conditioning system – the output air should be less than the ambient temperature, depending on humidity

Many car accessory shops sell one-shot air conditioning recharge aerosols. These generally contain refrigerant, compressor oil, leak sealer and system conditioner. Some also have a dye to help pinpoint leaks.

⚠️ *Warning: These products must only be used as directed by the manufacturer, and do not remove the need for regular maintenance.*

equipment necessary to service it, in-depth troubleshooting and repairs beyond checking the refrigerant charge and the compressor clutch operation are not included in this manual. However, simple checks and component removal procedures are provided in this Chapter.

5 The most common cause of poor cooling is simply a low system refrigerant charge **(see Tool tip)**. If a noticeable drop in system cooling ability occurs, one of the following quick checks will help you determine whether the refrigerant level is low. Should the system lose its cooling ability, the following procedure will help you pinpoint the cause.

Check

6 Warm the engine up to normal operating temperature.

7 Place the air conditioning temperature selector at the coldest setting and put the blower at the highest setting. Open the doors (to make sure the air conditioning system doesn't cycle off as soon as it cools the passenger compartment).

8 After the system reaches operating temperature, feel the two pipes connected to the evaporator at the bulkhead.

9 The pipe (thinner tubing) leading from the condenser outlet to the evaporator should be cold, and the evaporator outlet line (the thicker tubing that leads back to the compressor) should be slightly colder. If the evaporator outlet is considerably warmer than the inlet, the system needs a charge. Insert a thermometer in the centre air distribution duct **(see illustration)** while operating the air conditioning system at its maximum setting – the temperature of the output air should be noticeably less than the ambient air temperature.

10 If the air isn't as cold as it used to be, the

system probably needs a charge.

11 If the air is warm and the system doesn't seem to be operating properly check the operation of the compressor clutch.

12 Have an assistant switch the air conditioning on while you observe the front of the compressor. The clutch will make an audible click and the centre of the clutch should rotate.

13 If the clutch didn't operate, check the appropriate fuses. Inspect the fuses in the interior fuse panel.

14 If the fuses are OK, refer to the wiring diagrams at the end of Chapter 12 and check the compressor clutch circuit and pressure switch for proper operation.

15 If the compressor clutch circuit and pressure switch are OK, the compressor clutch is probably faulty.

16 If the compressor clutch, relay and related circuits are known to be in good working order and the system is fully-charged with refrigerant and the compressor does not operate under normal conditions, have the ECM and related circuits checked by a dealer service department or other properly-equipped repair facility.

17 Further inspection or testing of the system is beyond the scope of the home mechanic and should be left to a professional.

Heating systems

18 If the carpet under the heater matrix is damp, or if antifreeze vapour or steam is coming through the vents, the heater matrix is leaking. Remove it (see Section 10) and install a new unit (most radiator repair specialists will not repair a leaking heater matrix).

19 If the air coming out of the heater vents isn't hot, the problem could stem from any of the following causes:

a) *The thermostat is stuck open, preventing the engine coolant from warming-up enough to carry heat to the heater matrix. Renew the thermostat (see Section 3).*

b) *There is a blockage in the system, preventing the flow of coolant through the heater matrix. Feel both heater hoses at the bulkhead. They should be hot. If one of them is cold, there is an obstruction in one of the hoses or in the heater matrix, or the heater control valve is shut. Detach the hoses and back flush the heater matrix with a water hose. If the heater matrix is clear but circulation is impeded, remove the two hoses and flush them out with a water hose.*

c) *If flushing fails to remove the blockage from the heater matrix, the matrix must be renewed (see Section 10).*

Air conditioning odours

20 Unpleasant odours that often develop in air conditioning systems are caused by the growth of a fungus, usually on the surface of the evaporator matrix. The warm, humid environment there is a perfect breeding ground for mildew to develop.

11.23 With the glovebox removed, spray the disinfectant through the interior air filter opening

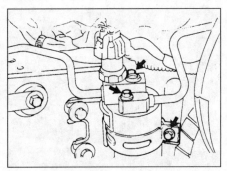

12.3 Receiver/drier mounting details – 2000 and earlier models

12.4 The receiver/drier on 2001 and later models is located in a tube on the side of the condenser – arrow shows location of the end plug

21 The evaporator matrix on most vehicles is difficult to access, and factory dealerships have a lengthy, expensive process for eliminating the fungus by opening up the evaporator case and using a powerful disinfectant and rinse on the matrix until the fungus is gone. You can service your own system at home, but it takes something much stronger than basic household germ-killers or deodorisers.

22 Aerosol disinfectants for automotive air conditioning systems are available in most car accessory shops, but remember when shopping for them that the most effective treatments are also the most expensive. The basic procedure for using these sprays is to start by running the system in the RECIRC mode for ten minutes with the blower on its highest speed. Use the highest heat mode to dry out the system and keep the compressor from engaging by disconnecting the wiring connector at the compressor (see Section 13).

23 The disinfectant can usually comes with a long spray hose. Remove the pollen filter (see Chapter 1A or 1B), point the nozzle inside the hole and to the left towards the evaporator matrix, and spray according to the manufacturer's recommendations **(see illustration)**. Try to cover the whole surface of the evaporator matrix, by aiming the spray up, down and sideways. Follow the manufacturer's recommendations for the length of spray and waiting time between applications.

24 Once the evaporator has been cleaned, the best way to prevent the mildew from coming back again is to make sure your evaporator housing drain tube is clear **(see illustration 11.1)**.

12 Air conditioning receiver/drier – removal and refitting

⚠ *Warning: The air conditioning system is under high pressure. Do not loosen any hose fittings or remove any components until the system has been discharged. Air conditioning*

refrigerant should be properly discharged by an air conditioning repair specialist. Always wear eye protection when disconnecting air conditioning system fittings.

1 Have the refrigerant discharged by an air conditioning repair specialist.
2 Disconnect the negative battery cable.
3 On 2000 and earlier models, disconnect the refrigerant lines **(see illustration)** from the receiver/drier and cap the open fittings to prevent entry of moisture. Loosen the clamp bolt and slip the receiver/drier out of the bracket.
4 On 2001 and later models, remove the condenser (see Section 14). Using an Allen key, detach the end plug **(see illustration)** and remove the dryer from the condenser.
5 Refitting is the reverse of removal. Be sure to tighten the end plug on 2001 and later models to the torque listed in this Chapter's Specifications.
6 Have the system evacuated, charged and leak tested by the specialist who discharged it.

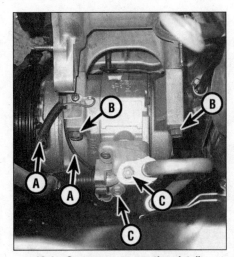

13.4a Compressor mounting details (alternator and thermostat housing removed for clarity) – 2001 and later models shown

   A *Electrical connector*
   B *Upper mounting bolts*
   C *Refrigerant lines*

13 Air conditioning compressor – removal and refitting

⚠ *Warning: The air conditioning system is under high pressure. Do not loosen any hose fittings or remove any components until the system has been discharged. Air conditioning refrigerant should be properly discharged by an air conditioning repair specialist. Always wear eye protection when disconnecting air conditioning system fittings.*

1 Have the refrigerant discharged by an automotive air conditioning specialist.
2 Disconnect the negative cable from the battery. Raise the front of the vehicle and support it securely on axle stands, then remove the lower splash shield from the right side of the vehicle.
3 Remove the auxiliary drivebelt from the compressor (see Chapter 1A or 1B).
4 Detach the wiring connector and the refrigerant lines **(see illustrations)**.
5 Unbolt the compressor and lower it from the vehicle. **Note:** *On diesel models, the compressor is mounted with two bolts and one stud.*
6 If a new or rebuilt compressor is being installed, follow the directions which come with it regarding the proper level of oil prior to refitting.

13.4b Air conditioning compressor lower mounting bolts (arrowed)

14.3 Disconnect the refrigerant lines (arrowed) from the condenser – 2001 and later model shown

14.4 Condenser mounting bolts – 2001 and later model shown

remove any components until the system has been discharged. Air conditioning refrigerant should be properly discharged by an air conditioning specialist. Always wear eye protection when disconnecting air conditioning system fittings.

1 Have the refrigerant discharged by an air conditioning specialist.

2 On 2001 and later models, remove the front bumper (see Chapter 11).

3 Disconnect the inlet and outlet fittings **(see illustration)**. Cap the open fittings immediately to keep moisture and dirt out of the system.

4 Remove the mounting bolts and pull the condenser up and out of the vehicle **(see illustration)**.

5 Install the condenser, brackets and bolts, making sure the rubber cushions fit on the mounting points properly.

6 Reconnect the refrigerant lines, using new O-rings where needed.

7 Refit the remaining parts in the reverse order of removal. Have the system evacuated, charged and leak-tested by the specialist who discharged it.

7 Refitting is the reverse of removal. Replace any O-rings with new ones specifically made for the purpose and lubricate them with refrigerant oil. **Note:** *On diesel models, the mounting spacers must be positioned with the seals toward the cylinder block.*

8 Have the system evacuated, recharged and leak tested by the specialist who discharged it.

14 Air conditioning condenser – removal and refitting

⚠ *Warning: The air conditioning system is under high pressure. Do not loosen any hose fittings or*

Chapter 4 Part A:
Fuel and exhaust systems – petrol engines

Contents

Section number (left column):

Accelerator cable – removal, refitting and adjustment. 11
Air filter housing – removal and refitting. 10
Air filter renewal . . . . See Chapter 1A
Electronic fuel injection system – check 13
Electronic fuel injection system – general information. 12
Exhaust system check . . . . See Chapter 1A
Exhaust system servicing – general information 17
Fuel level sending unit – removal and refitting. 7
Fuel lines and fittings – general information. 4
Fuel pressure regulator – removal and refitting 6
Fuel pressure relief. 2

Section number (right column):

Fuel pulsation damper (2001 and later models) – removal and
   refitting 15
Fuel pump – removal and refitting 5
Fuel pump/fuel pressure – check. 3
Fuel rail and injectors – removal and refitting. 16
Fuel system check . . . . See Chapter 1A
Fuel tank – removal and refitting 8
Fuel tank cleaning and repair – general information 9
General information 1
Throttle body – check, removal and refitting 14
Underbonnet hose check and renewal . . . . See Chapter 1A

Degrees of difficulty

Easy, suitable for novice with little experience	Fairly easy, suitable for beginner with some experience	Fairly difficult, suitable for competent DIY mechanic	Difficult, suitable for experienced DIY mechanic	Very difficult, suitable for expert DIY or professional

Specifications

Fuel system

Fuel system pressure.	3.0 to 3.5 bar
Fuel system hold pressure (after five minutes).	1.4 bar minimum
Injector resistance (approximate).	13.4 to 14.2 ohms

Torque wrench settings

	lbf ft	Nm
Fuel pulsation damper bolts.	7	9
Fuel rail mounting bolts:		
2000 and earlier models.	9	12
2001 and later models	15	20
Fuel tank strap bolts.	29	39
Throttle body mounting bolts:		
2000 and earlier models.	14	19
2001 and later models	22	30

**1.1a Fuel system components –
2000 and earlier models**

1 Fusible link box
2 Intake manifold
3 Throttle body
4 Air filter housing
5 Fuel rail (mounted on top
  of intake manifold)

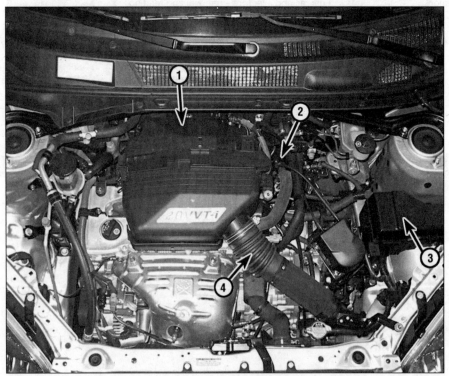

**1.1b Fuel system components –
2001 and later models**

1 Air filter housing
2 Throttle body (under air filter housing)
3 Relay and fusebox
4 Air intake duct

1 General information

The fuel system consists of a fuel tank, an electric fuel pump (located in the fuel tank), a fuel pressure regulator located next to the fuel pump in the tank, an EFI main relay, a fuel pump relay (circuit opening relay), the fuel rail and fuel injectors, an air filter housing and a throttle body unit. All models are equipped with a Sequential Electronic Fuel Injection system (see illustrations).

Sequential Electronic Fuel Injection system

Sequential Electronic Fuel Injection uses timed impulses to inject the fuel directly into the intake port of each cylinder according to its firing order. The injectors are controlled by the Engine Control Module (ECM). The ECM monitors various engine parameters and delivers the exact amount of fuel required into the intake ports. The throttle body serves only to control the amount of air passing into the system. Because each cylinder is equipped with its own injector, much better control of the fuel/air mixture ratio is possible.

Fuel pump and lines

Fuel is circulated from the fuel tank to the fuel injection system through a metal line running along the underside of the vehicle. An electric fuel pump and fuel level sending unit is located inside the fuel tank.

The fuel pump relay is equipped with a primary and secondary circuit. The primary circuit is controlled by the ECM and the secondary circuit is linked directly to the EFI main relay from the ignition switch. With the ignition switch on (engine not running), the ECM will earth the relay for two seconds. During cranking, the ECM earths the fuel pump relay as long as the camshaft position sensor sends its position signal (see Chapter 6A). If there are no reference pulses, the fuel pump will shut off after two seconds.

Exhaust system

The exhaust system consists of an exhaust manifold, exhaust pipes, a catalytic converter, a silencer and a tail pipe.

The catalytic converter is an emission control device added to the exhaust system to reduce pollutants. Refer to Chapter 6A for more information regarding the catalytic converter.

2 Fuel pressure relief

Warning: Petrol is extremely flammable, so take extra precautions when you work on any part of the fuel system. Don't

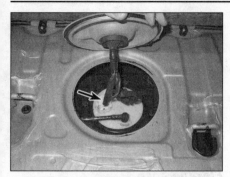

2.2 Disconnect the fuel pump directly at the fuel pump harness connector (arrowed)

smoke or allow open flames or bare light bulbs near the work area, and don't work in a garage where a gas-type appliance (such as a water heater or a clothes dryer) is present. Since petrol is carcinogenic, wear latex gloves when there's a possibility of being exposed to fuel, and, if you spill any fuel on your skin, rinse it off immediately with soap and water. Mop-up any spills immediately and do not store fuel-soaked rags where they could ignite. The fuel system is under constant pressure, so, if any fuel lines are to be disconnected, the fuel pressure in the system must be relieved first. When you perform any kind of work on the fuel system, wear safety glasses and have a fire extinguisher on hand.

1 Remove the fuel filler cap – this will relieve any pressure built-up in the tank.

2 Remove the rear seat and liner to access the fuel pump/sending unit access cover (see Section 5). Disconnect the harness connector **(see illustration)**.

3 Start the engine and allow it to run until it stops. Turn the ignition switch off and disconnect the cable from the negative terminal of the battery before working on the fuel system.

4 The fuel system pressure is now relieved. Place a rag around any fitting to be disconnected to catch the residual fuel as it bleeds off. Dispose of the fuel-soaked rag in an approved safety container.

3.3a This aftermarket fuel pressure testing kit contains all the necessary fittings and adapters, along with the fuel pressure gauge, to test most fuel systems

5 When you're finished working on the fuel system, reconnect the fuel pump/sending unit harness connector and connect the negative cable to the battery.

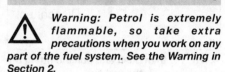

3 Fuel pump/fuel pressure – check

⚠️ **Warning: Petrol is extremely flammable, so take extra precautions when you work on any part of the fuel system. See the Warning in Section 2.**

General checks

1 If you suspect insufficient fuel delivery check the following items first:
 a) Check the battery and make sure it's fully-charged (see Chapter 5).
 b) Check the fuel pump fuse.
 c) Inspect all fuel lines to ensure that the problem is not simply a leak in a line.

2 Verify the fuel pump actually runs. Have an assistant turn the ignition switch to ON – you should hear a brief whirring noise (for approximately two seconds) as the pump comes on and pressurises the system. **Note:** The fuel pump is easily heard through the fuel tank filler neck. If there is no response from the fuel pump (makes no sound), check the fuel pump electrical circuit. If the fuel pump runs, but a fuel system problem is suspected, continue with the fuel pump pressure check.

Pump pressure check

Note 1: In order to perform the fuel pressure test, you will need to obtain a fuel pressure gauge capable of measuring high fuel pressure and the proper adapter set for the specific fuel injection system.

Note 2: 2000 and earlier models are equipped with a bolt-and-washer type fuel line connection at the fuel filter, while 2001 and later models are equipped with an in-line quick-connect fuel fitting. Each type will require a different kind of adapter to enable you to connect a fuel pressure gauge.

Note 3: 2000 and earlier models are equipped with a fuel filter mounted on the left strut

3.3b On 2000 and earlier models attach the fuel pressure gauge to the fuel filter (arrowed) and fuel line; turn the ignition key on and check the fuel pressure

tower in the engine compartment, with an additional fuel strainer mounted integral with the fuel pump assembly in the tank. 2001 and later models are equipped with one fuel filter mounted in the fuel pump assembly.

3 Relieve the fuel system pressure (see Section 2). Connect the fuel pressure gauge.
 a) On 2000 and earlier models, remove the fuse/relay box from the left strut tower, disconnect the fuel filter outlet line and connect an adapter and fuel pressure gauge to the fuel filter and fuel line **(see illustrations)**.
 b) On 2001 and later models, disconnect the fuel tube connector near the fuel rail **(see illustration)** and connect the fuel pressure gauge using the proper adapters.

4 Turn all the accessories off and switch the ignition key on. The fuel pump should run for about two seconds; note the reading on the gauge. If the fuel pressure is higher than specified, renew the fuel pressure regulator. If the pressure is too low, the fuel filter (or in-tank strainer) could be clogged, the lines could be restricted or leaking, a fuel injector could be leaking, or the fuel pressure regulator and/or the fuel pump could be defective.

5 Start the engine and let it idle at normal operating temperature. The pressure should fall within the range listed in this Chapter's Specifications. If the pressure is lower than specified, check the items listed in paragraph 4. **Note:** If no obvious problems are found, most likely the fuel pressure regulator and/or the fuel pump is defective. In this situation, it is recommended that both the fuel pressure regulator and fuel pump are renewed to prevent any future fuel pressure problems.

6 Turn the engine off and check the gauge – the pressure should hold steady. After five minutes it should not drop below the minimum listed in this Chapter's Specifications. If it does drop, the fuel pump or pressure regulator could be defective, or a fuel injector could be leaking.

7 After the testing is done, relieve the fuel pressure (see Section 2) and remove the fuel pressure gauge.

Pump electrical circuit check

8 If the pump does not turn on (makes no

3.3c Location of the fuel tube connector (arrowed) on 2001 and later models

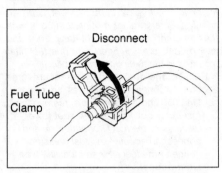

4.12a On quick-connect fuel line fittings, pinch the tabs . . .

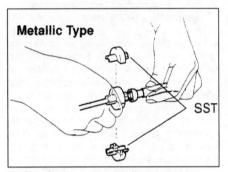

4.12c On metal tube type fuel line fittings, fit the upper and lower sections of the special fuel line disconnection tool . . .

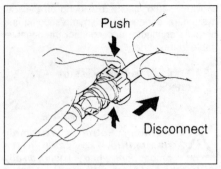

4.12b . . . then push and pull the fitting off the fuel line

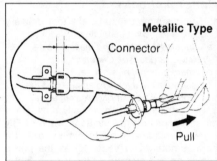

4.12d . . . then insert the tool into the coupler to release the connection

sound) with the ignition switch in the ON position, check the IGN fuse and the EFI fuse located in the engine compartment fuse centre. Also, check the EFI main relay and circuit opening relay. **Note:** *These models are equipped with an EFI main relay and a fuel pump relay (circuit opening relay). On 2000 and earlier models, the EFI main relay is located in the engine compartment fuse/ relay box and the fuel pump relay (circuit opening relay) is located behind the left-hand side kick panel under the dash. On 2001 and later models, the EFI main relay and fuel pump relay (circuit opening relay) are located in the engine compartment fuse/relay box.*

9 If the relays are good and the fuel pump does not operate, check the fuel pump circuit. Refer to the wiring diagrams at the end of Chapter 12.

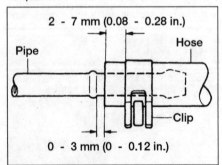

4.13 When attaching a section of rubber hose to a metal fuel line, be sure to overlap the hose as shown, secure it to the line with a new hose clamp of the proper type

4 Fuel lines and fittings – general information

⚠ *Warning: Petrol is extremely flammable, so take extra precautions when you work on any part of the fuel system. See the Warning in Section 2.*

1 Always relieve the fuel pressure before servicing fuel lines or fittings (see Section 2).

2 The fuel line extends from the fuel tank to the engine compartment. The line is secured to the underbody with clip and screw assemblies. This line must be occasionally inspected for leaks, kinks and dents.

3 If evidence of dirt is found in the system or fuel filter during disassembly, the line should be disconnected and blown out. Check the fuel strainer on the fuel gauge sending unit (see Section 5) for damage and deterioration.

Steel tubing

4 If renewal of a fuel line or emission line is called for, use welded steel tubing meeting the manufacturer's specifications or its equivalent.

5 Don't use copper or aluminium tubing; these materials cannot withstand normal vehicle vibration.

6 Because fuel lines used on fuel-injected vehicles are under high pressure, they require special consideration.

7 Some fuel lines have threaded fittings with

O-rings. Any time the fittings are loosened to service or renew components:

a) *Use a flare-nut spanner while loosening and tightening fittings, and hold the stationary portion of the line (or component) with another spanner.*

b) *Check all O-rings for cuts, cracks and deterioration. Renew any that appear hardened, worn or damaged.*

c) *If the lines are renewed, always use original equipment parts, or parts that meet the original equipment standards.*

Flexible hose

⚠ *Warning: Use only original equipment hoses or their equivalent. Others may fail from the high pressures of this system.*

8 Don't route a fuel hose within 100 mm of any part of the exhaust system or within 200 mm of the catalytic converter. Metal lines and rubber hoses must never be allowed to chafe against the frame. A minimum of 5 mm clearance must be maintained around a line or hose to prevent contact with the frame.

9 Some models may be equipped with nylon fuel line and quick-connect fittings at the fuel filter and/or fuel pump. The quick-connect fittings cannot be serviced separately. Do not attempt to service these types of fuel lines in the event the retainer tabs or the line becomes damaged. Renew the entire fuel line as an assembly.

Removal and refitting

10 In the event of any fuel line damage (metal or flexible lines) it is necessary to renew the damaged lines with factory parts. Others may fail from the high pressures of this system.

11 Relieve the fuel pressure.

12 Remove all fasteners attaching the lines to the vehicle body. On fuel lines so equipped, detach the clamp(s) that attach the fuel hoses to the metal lines, then pull the hose off the fitting. Twisting the hoses back-and-forth will allow them to separate more easily. If equipped with quick-connect fittings, hold the connector with one hand and depress the retaining tabs with the other hand, then separate the connector from the pipe **(see illustrations)**.

13 Refitting is the reverse of removal. Be sure to use new O-rings at the threaded fittings (if equipped). On quick-connect fittings, align the retainer locking pawls with the connector grooves. Push the connector onto the pipe until both retaining pawls lock with a clicking sound. When connecting rubber hose to a metal line, make sure it's completely pushed onto the metal line and secured with a hose clamp **(see illustration)**.

5 Fuel pump – removal and refitting

⚠ *Warning: Petrol is extremely flammable, so take extra precautions when you work on any*

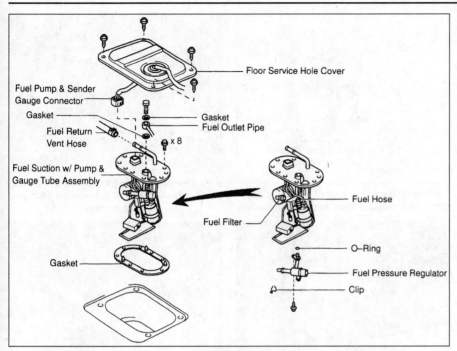

5.4a Exploded view of the fuel pump assembly on 2000 and earlier models

Floor Service Hole Cover

Fuel Pump & Sender Gauge Connector

Gasket

Gasket
Fuel Outlet Pipe

Fuel Return Vent Hose

Fuel Suction w/ Pump & Gauge Tube Assembly

x 8

Fuel Hose

Fuel Filter

Gasket

O–Ring

Fuel Pressure Regulator

Clip

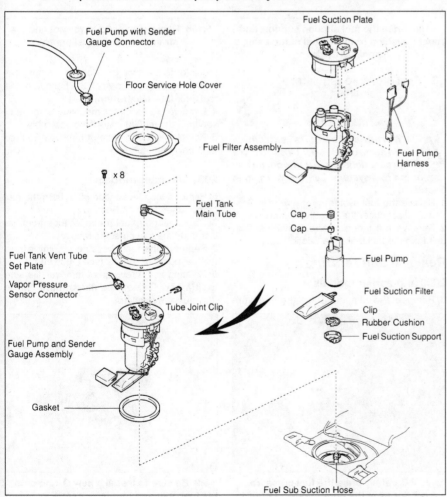

5.4b Exploded view of the fuel pump assembly on 2001 and later models

Fuel Pump with Sender Gauge Connector

Floor Service Hole Cover

Fuel Suction Plate

x 8

Fuel Filter Assembly

Fuel Pump Harness

Fuel Tank Main Tube

Cap

Cap

Fuel Tank Vent Tube Set Plate

Vapor Pressure Sensor Connector

Tube Joint Clip

Fuel Pump

Fuel Suction Filter

Clip

Rubber Cushion

Fuel Suction Support

Fuel Pump and Sender Gauge Assembly

Gasket

Fuel Sub Suction Hose

part of the fuel system. See the Warning in Section 2.

Removal

1 Relieve the fuel system pressure (see Section 2) and remove the fuel tank cap.

2 Disconnect the cable from the negative terminal of the battery.

3 Remove the left rear seat from inside the passenger compartment (see Chapter 11).

4 Remove the fuel pump/sending unit floor service hole cover **(see illustrations)**.

5 Disconnect the electrical connector. Disconnect the fuel line **(see illustration)** and the vapour pressure sensor, if equipped (see Chapter 6A).

6 Remove the fuel pump/sending unit retaining bolts.

7 Carefully withdraw the fuel pump/fuel level sending unit assembly from the fuel tank. **Note:** *On 2001 and later models, disconnect the fuel sub-suction hose once the assembly has been pulled out far enough* **(see illustration)**.

8 Disconnect the electrical connector from the fuel pump *(see illustration)*.

9 Remove the fuel pump from the assembly.

a) *On 2000 and earlier models, slide the hose clamp up the hose, loosen the fuel pump clamp and pull the lower end of the fuel pump loose from the bracket* **(see illustration)**. *Withdraw the pump from the hose.*

b) *On 2001 and later models, disconnect the fuel level sending unit from the fuel suction plate. Remove the fuel filter. Remove the fuel suction plate by levering up on the housing retainers.*

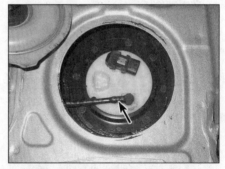

5.5 First remove the floor service hole cover to gain access to the fuel line

5.7 On 2001 and later models, disconnect the fuel sub-suction hose (arrowed)

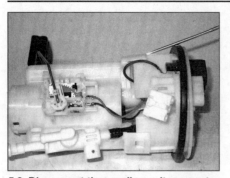

5.8 Disconnect the sending unit connector and the fuel pump connector from the main body

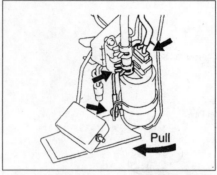

5.9a Pull the lower end of the fuel pump from the bracket – 2000 and earlier models

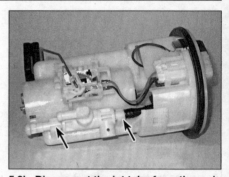

5.9b Disconnect the jet tube from the main body of the fuel pump (arrowed) – 2001 and later models

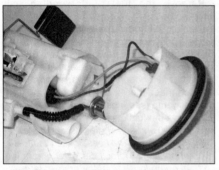

5.9c Disconnect the pump harness from the fuel suction plate and separate the two assemblies – 2001 and later models

5.10a Prise the fuel suction support and rubber cushion from the fuel pump using a small screwdriver

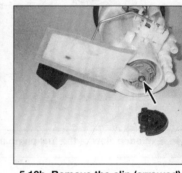

5.10b Remove the clip (arrowed) and the strainer from the fuel pump

Disconnect the fuel pump electrical connector. Remove the upper bracket by levering on the retainers and separating the fuel pump from the housing (see illustrations).

10 Remove the clip securing the inlet strainer to the pump **(see illustrations)**.

11 Remove the strainer and inspect it for contamination. If it is dirty, renew it.

Refitting

12 Reassemble the fuel pump/sending unit in the reverse order of disassembly.

13 Refit the fuel pump/sending unit assembly in the fuel tank. Connect the fuel line and electrical connector. If equipped with a quick-connect fitting, see Section 4.

14 The remainder of refitting is the reverse of removal.

---

6 Fuel pressure regulator – removal and refitting

> ⚠️ **Warning: Petrol is extremely flammable, so take extra precautions when you work on any part of the fuel system. See the Warning in Section 2.**

1 Relieve the fuel system pressure (see Section 2). Disconnect the negative battery cable.

2 Remove the fuel pump/fuel level sending unit from the fuel tank (see Section 5).

Removal and refitting

2000 and earlier models

3 Remove the clip securing the pressure

regulator to the filter, then loosen the hose-to-regulator clamp and detach the hose from the regulator **(see illustration)**.

4 Remove the regulator mounting screw and separate the regulator from the assembly.

5 Refitting is the reverse of removal. Be sure to fit new O-rings.

2001 and later models

6 Remove the fuel suction plate from the fuel pump assembly (see Section 5).

7 Disconnect the fuel return jet tube from the clamp on the fuel pressure regulator.

8 Separate the fuel pressure regulator from the fuel pump assembly **(see illustration)**.

9 Refitting is the reverse of removal. Be sure to fit a new O-ring **(see illustration)** on the fuel pressure regulator.

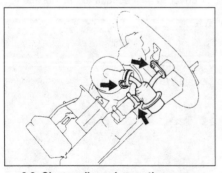

6.3 Clamp, clip and mounting screw locations (arrowed) on 2000 and earlier models

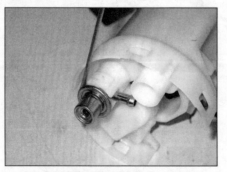

6.8 Carefully prise the fuel pressure regulator from the pump housing – 2001 and later models

6.9 Be sure to install a new O-ring onto the fuel pressure regulator before installing it back into the fuel pump assembly

7.1 An additional fuel level sending unit mounted on the opposite side of the tank monitors the fuel level within the other section of the fuel tank

7.4 Location of the fuel level sending unit (arrowed)

7 Fuel level sending unit – removal and refitting

> **Warning: Petrol is extremely flammable, so take extra precautions when you work on any part of the fuel system. See the Warning in Section 2.**

Note: *These models are equipped with an additional fuel level sending unit located in the right side of the tank, and can be accessed by removing the right-rear seat.*

Removal

1 Remove the fuel pump/fuel level sending unit assembly **(see illustration)** from the fuel tank (see Section 5).
2 Carefully angle the sending unit out of the opening without damaging the fuel level float located at the bottom of the assembly.
3 Disconnect the electrical connectors from the sending unit.

4 Remove the mounting screws or clips **(see illustration)** and separate the sending unit from the assembly.

Refitting

5 Refitting is the reverse of removal.

8 Fuel tank – removal and refitting

> **Warning: Petrol is extremely flammable, so take extra precautions when you work on any part of the fuel system. See the Warning in Section 2.**

Removal

1 Relieve the fuel system pressure (see Section 2).
2 Remove the fuel filler cap to relieve fuel tank pressure.
3 Detach the cable from the negative terminal of the battery.

4 If the tank is full or nearly full, syphon the fuel into an approved container using a syphoning kit (available at most auto parts stores).

> **Warning: Do not start the syphoning action by mouth.**

5 Raise the vehicle and place it securely on axle stands.
6 Remove the exhaust system from the centre exhaust pipe, completely to the rear of the vehicle.
7 On 4WD models, remove the propeller shaft (see Chapter 8).
8 Disconnect the fuel lines, the vapour return line and the fuel inlet pipe from the fuel tank fittings **(see illustration). Note:** *Be sure to plug the hoses to prevent leakage and contamination of the fuel system.*
9 Support the fuel tank with a jack. Place a sturdy plank between the jack head and the fuel tank to protect the tank.
10 Remove the bolts from the fuel tank retaining straps **(see illustrations)**.

8.8 Locations of the fuel vapour and fuel return lines (arrowed) – be sure to remove the inner wheel arch liners to access the fuel tank components

8.10a Remove the fuel tank strap mounting bolts (arrowed) from the body

11 Lower the tank enough to disconnect the electrical connector from the fuel pump/fuel gauge sending unit.

12 Remove the tank from the vehicle.

⚠ *Warning: If the fuel tank is removed from the vehicle, it should not be placed in an area where sparks or open flames could ignite the fumes coming out of the tank. Be especially careful inside garages where a gas-type appliance is located, because it could cause an explosion.*

Refitting

13 Refitting is the reverse of removal.

9 Fuel tank cleaning and repair – general information

Note: *Later models are equipped with plastic tanks which cannot be repaired.*

Any repairs to the fuel tank or filler neck should be carried out by a professional who has experience in this critical and potentially dangerous work. Even after cleaning and flushing of the fuel system, explosive fumes can remain and ignite during repair of the tank.

10 Air filter housing – removal and refitting

Removal

1 Detach the clips, lift up the air cleaner cover and remove the filter element (see Chapter 1A). On 2000 and earlier models, disconnect the harness connector from the Skid Control relays on the side of the air filter housing.

2 On 2000 and earlier models, disconnect the air intake hose from the cover **(see illustrations)**.

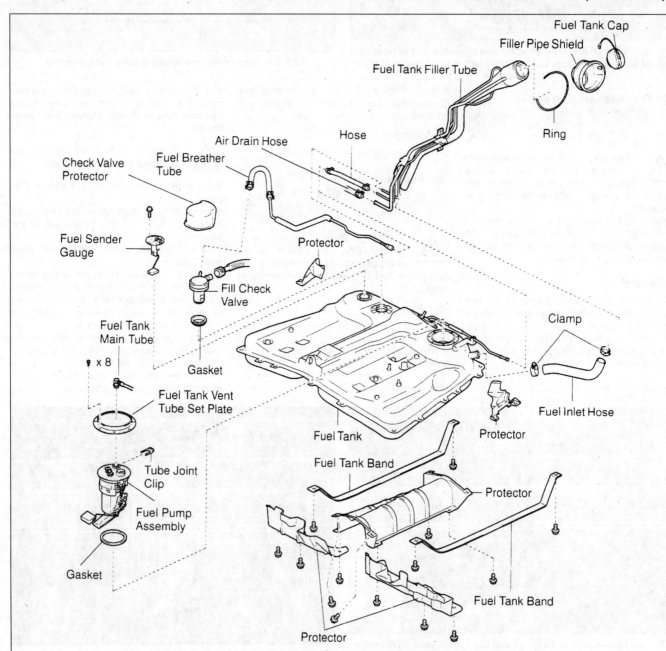

8.10b Exploded view of a typical fuel tank assembly – 2001 and later models shown

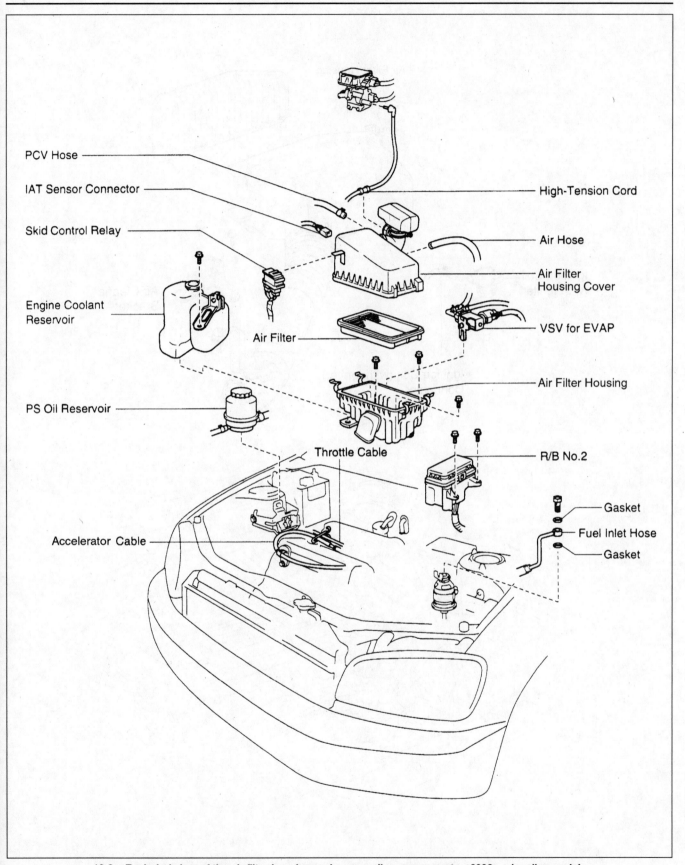

PCV Hose

IAT Sensor Connector

Skid Control Relay

Engine Coolant
Reservoir

Air Filter

PS Oil Reservoir

Throttle Cable

Accelerator Cable

High-Tension Cord

Air Hose

Air Filter
Housing Cover

VSV for EVAP

Air Filter Housing

R/B No.2

Gasket

Fuel Inlet Hose

Gasket

10.2a Exploded view of the air filter housing and surrounding components – 2000 and earlier models

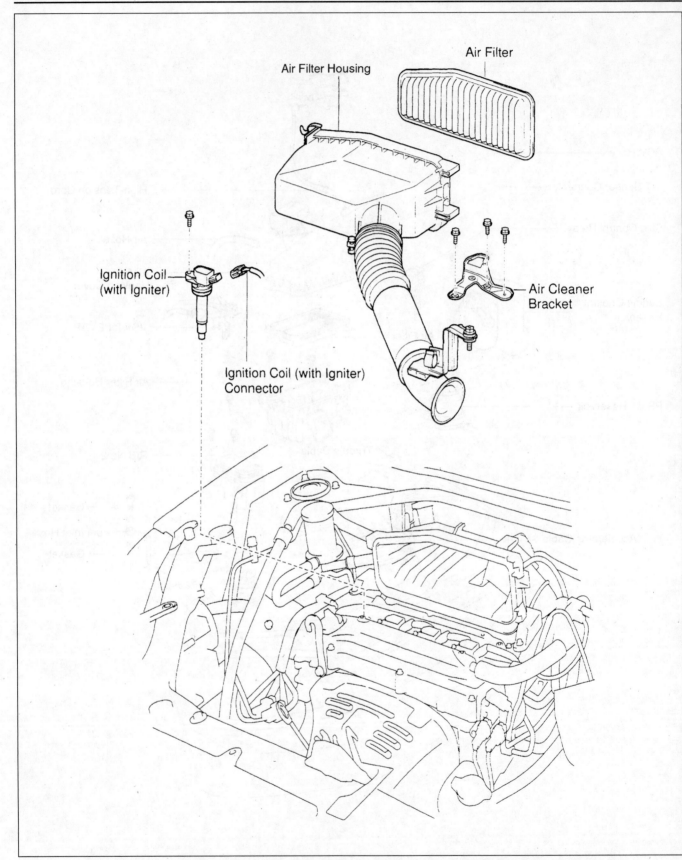

10.2b Exploded view of the air filter housing and surrounding components – 2001 and later models

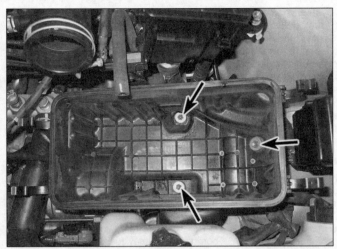

10.3 Remove the three bolts (arrowed) and lift the air filter housing from the engine compartment – 2000 and earlier model shown

10.4 Air intake duct mounting bracket-to-body bolt (A) and air filter cover clips (B)

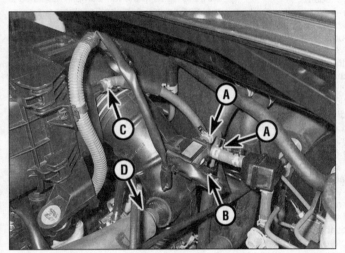

10.5 VSV hoses (A), VSV connector (B), CCV hose (C) and PCV hose (D)

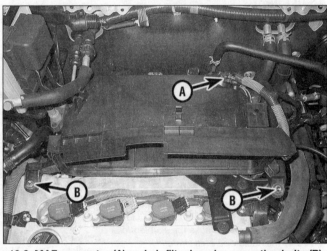

10.6 MAF connector (A) and air filter housing mounting bolts (B)

3 Remove the three bolts and remove the air cleaner assembly from the engine compartment **(see illustration)**.
4 On 2001 and later models, release the two clips and remove the body-to-intake duct mounting bracket bolt **(see illustration)**. Remove the air filter cover and duct as an assembly.

11.2 Loosen the locknuts on the accelerator cable using two spanners

5 Disconnect the EVAP hoses from the VSV **(see illustration)**, unplug the VSV connector, detach the CCV hose from the air filter housing and the PCV hose from the valve cover (see Chapter 6A). Loosen the air intake duct clamp from the throttle body.
6 Disconnect the MAF sensor connector, remove the two bolts, then remove the air filter housing from the engine compartment **(see illustration)**.

Refitting

7 Refitting is the reverse of removal.

11 Accelerator cable – removal, refitting and adjustment

Removal and refitting

1 Detach the cable from the negative terminal of the battery.

2 Loosen the locknut on the threaded portion of the accelerator cable at the throttle body **(see illustration)**.
3 Rotate the throttle lever, then slip the accelerator cable end out of the slot in the lever **(see illustration)**.
4 Detach the accelerator cable from the accelerator pedal **(see illustration)**.

11.3 Rotate the throttle lever and remove the cable end from the slot using long-nose pliers

11.4 Pull the cable end (arrowed) away from the accelerator pedal arm, then pass the cable through the slot in the arm

5 Pull the cable and casing out of the bulkhead into the engine compartment.

6 Refitting is the reverse of removal. Make sure the cable grommet seats completely in the bulkhead.

Adjustment

7 To adjust the cable:
 a) *Lift up on the cable to remove any slack.*
 b) *Turn the adjusting nut until it is 3 mm away from the cable bracket.*
 c) *Tighten the locknut and check cable deflection between the throttle lever and the cable casing. Deflection should be 10 mm to 12 mm. If deflection is not within specifications, loosen the locknut and turn the adjusting nut until the deflection is as specified.*
 d) *After you have adjusted the accelerator cable, have an assistant help you verify that the throttle valve opens all the way when you depress the accelerator pedal to the floor and that it returns to the idle position when you release the accelerator. Verify the cable operates smoothly; it must not bind or stick.*

12 Electronic fuel injection system –
general information

13.7 Use a stethoscope or a screwdriver to determine if the injectors are working properly – they should make a steady clicking sound that rises and falls with engine speed changes

The Electronic Fuel Injection (EFI) system consists of three sub-systems: air intake, electronic control and fuel delivery. The system uses an Engine Control Module (ECM) along with several sensors to determine the proper air/fuel ratio under all operating conditions. Refer to illustrations 1.1a and 1.1b for component locations.

The fuel injection system and the emissions control system are closely linked in function and design. For additional information, refer to Chapter 6A.

Air intake system

The air intake system consists of the air cleaner, the air intake ducts, the throttle body, the idle control system and the intake manifold. 2000 and earlier models are equipped with an intake manifold and plenum as one component. 2001 and later models are equipped with a specially-designed intake manifold with intake manifold tuning. Refer to Chapters 2A or 2B for the manifold renewal procedures.

The throttle body is a single barrel, side-draft design. The lower portion of the throttle body is heated by engine coolant to prevent icing in cold weather. The idle adjusting screw is located on top of the throttle body. A throttle position sensor is attached to the throttle shaft to monitor changes in the throttle opening.

When the engine is idling, the air/fuel ratio is controlled by the idle air control system, which consists of the Engine Control Module (ECM), the Idle Air Control (IAC) valve and the various other sensors (ECT, IAT, TPS, MAP, MAF, etc) working in conjunction with the EFI system. The IAC valve is activated by the ECM depending upon the running conditions of the engine (air conditioning on, power steering demand, cold or warm temperature, etc). This valve regulates the amount of airflow bypassing the throttle plate and into the intake manifold. The ECM receives information from the sensors and adjusts the idle according to the demands of the engine and driver. Finally, to prevent rough running after the engine starts, the starting valve is opened during cranking and immediately after starting to provide additional air into the intake manifold.

Electronic control system

The electronic control system, Engine Control Module and sensors are described in Chapter 6A.

Fuel delivery system

The fuel delivery system consists of these components: The fuel pump, fuel pressure regulator, fuel filter, fuel lines, fuel rail and the fuel injectors. 2000 and earlier models are equipped with a fuel filter mounted on the left strut tower in the engine compartment, with an additional fuel filter mounted in the fuel pump assembly in the tank. 2001 and later models are equipped with one fuel filter mounted in the fuel pump assembly.

The fuel pump is an electric in-line type. Fuel is drawn through an inlet strainer into the pump, flows through the fuel pressure regulator, passes through the fuel filter and is delivered to the injectors. The fuel pressure regulator maintains a constant fuel pressure to the injectors.

The injectors are solenoid-actuated, constant stroke, pintle types consisting of a solenoid, plunger, needle valve and housing. When current is applied to the solenoid coil, the needle valve raises and pressurised fuel fills the injector housing and squirts out the nozzle. The injection quantity is determined by the length of time the valve is open (the length of time during which current is supplied to the solenoid coils). Because it determines opening and closing intervals – which in turn determines the air-fuel mixture ratio – injector timing must be quite accurate.

The EFI main relay, located in the engine compartment relay/fusebox, supplies power to the fuel pump relay (circuit opening relay) from the ignition key. The ECM controls the earthing signal to the fuel pump in response to the starting and camshaft position signals at start-up.

13 Electronic fuel injection system –
check

⚠ **Warning: Petrol is extremely flammable, so take extra precautions when you work on any part of the fuel system. See the Warning in Section 2.**

1 Check all electrical connectors, especially earth connections, for the system. Loose connectors and poor earths can cause many engine control system problems.

2 Verify that the battery is fully-charged because the Engine Control Module (ECM) and sensors cannot operate properly without adequate supply voltage.

3 Refer to Chapter 1A and check the air filter element. A dirty or partially-blocked filter will reduce performance and economy.

4 Check fuel pump operation (Section 3). If the fuel pump fuse is blown, renew it and see if it blows again. If it does, refer to Chapter 12 and the wiring diagrams and look for a short in the wiring harness to the fuel pump.

5 Inspect the vacuum hoses connected to the intake manifold for damage, deterioration and leakage.

6 Remove the air intake duct from the throttle body and check for dirt, carbon, varnish, or other residue in the throttle body, particularly around the throttle plate. If it's dirty, refer to Chapter 6A and troubleshoot the PCV and EGR systems for the cause of excessive varnish/carbon build-up.

7 With the engine running, place an automotive stethoscope against each injector, one at a time, and listen for a clicking sound, indicating operation **(see illustration)**. If you don't have a stethoscope, place the tip of a screwdriver against the injector and listen through the handle. If you hear the injectors operating

but there is a misfire condition present, the electrical circuits are functioning, but the injectors may be dirty or fouled from carbon deposits – commercial cleaning products may help, or the injectors may require renewal.

8 If you can't hear an injector operating, disconnect the injector electrical connector and measure the resistance of the injector **(see illustration)**. Compare the measurement with the resistance value listed in this Chapter's Specifications. Renew any injector whose resistance value does not fall within specifications.

9 If the injector wasn't operating but the resistance reading was within specifications, the ECM or the circuit to the injector may be faulty.

---

14 Throttle body –
check, removal and refitting

> ⚠ **Warning: Petrol is extremely flammable, so take extra precautions when you work on any part of the fuel system. See the Warning in Section 2.**

13.8 Using an ohmmeter, measure the resistance across both terminals of the injector

Check

1 Verify that the throttle linkage operates smoothly.

2 Remove the air intake duct from the throttle body and check for carbon and residue build-up. If it is dirty, clean it with aerosol carburettor cleaner and a tooth brush. Make sure the can specifically states that it is safe with oxygen sensor systems and catalytic converters **(see illustrations)**.

Caution: Do not clean the throttle position

sensor (TPS) or Idle Air Control (IAC) valve with the solvent.

Removal and refitting

> ⚠ **Warning: Wait until the engine is completely cool before beginning this procedure.**

2003 and earlier models

3 Detach the cable from the negative terminal of the battery.

4 Loosen the hose clamps and remove the air intake duct.

5 Detach the accelerator cable from the throttle lever (see Section 11).

6 If you are working on a 2000 or earlier model with an automatic transmission, detach the throttle valve (TV) cable from the throttle lever (see Chapter 7B).

7 Clearly label, then detach, all vacuum and coolant hoses from the throttle body **(see illustration)**. Plug the coolant hoses to prevent coolant leakage.

8 Disconnect the electrical connector from the Throttle Position Sensor (TPS).

9 Remove the throttle body mounting nuts/bolts **(see illustrations)**.

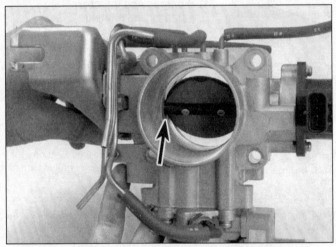

14.2a The area inside the throttle body near the throttle plate (arrowed) suffers from sludge build-up because the PCV hose vents vapour from the crankcase here

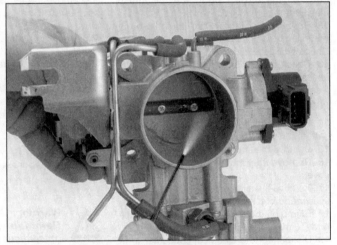

14.2b With the engine off, use aerosol carburettor cleaner (make sure it is safe for use with catalytic converters and oxygen sensors), a toothbrush and a rag to clean the throttle body – open the throttle plate so you can clean behind it

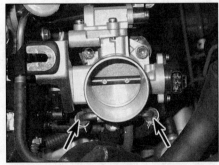

14.7 Remove the coolant hoses from the base of the throttle body (arrowed)

14.9a Location of the throttle body mounting bolts (arrowed) on 2000 and earlier models (4th bolt hidden from view)

14.9b Location of the throttle body mounting bolts (arrowed) on 2001 to 2003 models

14.19 Before detaching the throttle body, disconnect the electrical connector (A), disconnect the electrical harness from this clip (B), disengage the fuel hose (C) from the clip on the fuel pipe bracket and detach both coolant hoses (D)

14.21 To detach the throttle body from the intake manifold, remove these mounting bolts

10 Detach the throttle body and gasket from the intake manifold.

11 Refitting of the throttle body is the reverse of removal. Be sure to use a new gasket between the throttle body and the intake manifold.

12 Be sure to tighten the throttle body mounting nuts/bolts to the torque listed in this Chapter's Specifications.

13 Check the coolant level and add some, if necessary, to bring it to the appropriate level (see *Weekly checks*).

2004 and later models

14 Disconnect the cable from the negative battery terminal (see Chapter 5, Section 1).

15 Remove the strut brace (see Chapter 10).

16 Remove the intake duct and air filter cover.

17 Remove the air filter housing with the MAF sensor and bracket (see Section 10).

18 Clamp off the coolant hoses to the throttle body to minimize coolant loss.

19 Disconnect the electrical connecter from the throttle body and disengage the electrical harness from the clip on the fuel pipe bracket (see illustration).

20 Disengage the fuel hose from the fuel pipe

15.6 Location of the fuel pulsation damper mounting bolts (arrowed – other bolt hidden from view)

bracket, then clearly label and disconnect the vacuum and coolant hoses from the throttle body. Plug the coolant hoses to prevent coolant leakage.

21 Remove the throttle body mounting bolts (see illustration) and remove the throttle body.

22 Remove and discard the old throttle body gasket.

23 Refitting is the reverse of removal. Be sure to use a new gasket and tighten the throttle body mounting bolts to the torque listed in this Chapter's Specifications. Check the coolant level, adding as necessary (see *Weekly checks*).

15 Fuel pulsation damper (2001 and later models) – removal and refitting

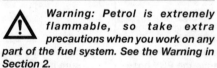

Warning: Petrol is extremely flammable, so take extra precautions when you work on any part of the fuel system. See the Warning in Section 2.

Removal

1 Relieve the fuel system pressure (see Section 2).

2 Disconnect the negative battery cable.

3 Remove the air filter housing (see Section 10).

4 Remove the accelerator cable from the throttle valve (see Section 11).

5 Remove the fuel tube clamp from the fuel line and disconnect the line using a special tool (see Section 4).

6 Remove the mounting bolts from the fuel pulsation damper (see illustration).

7 Separate the fuel pulsation damper from the fuel rail.

Refitting

8 Refitting is the reverse of removal. Be sure

to fit a new O-ring onto the fuel pulsation damper. Tighten the bolts to the torque listed in this Chapter's Specifications.

16 Fuel rail and injectors – removal and refitting

Warning: Petrol is extremely flammable, so take extra precautions when you work on any part of the fuel system. See the Warning in Section 2.

Removal

1 Relieve the fuel pressure (see Section 2).

2 Detach the cable from the negative terminal of the battery.

2000 and earlier models

3 Remove the valve cover (see Chapter 2A).

4 Remove the throttle body (see Section 14).

5 Remove the two clamps and disconnect the wiring harness from the intake manifold (see illustration). Disconnect the four injector connectors from the injectors.

6 Remove the engine wire protector from the right side of the intake manifold.

7 Remove the EGR valve and the EGR pipe (see Chapter 6A).

8 Remove the top fitting on the fuel filter (see Chapter 1A) and separate the fuel line from the fuel filter.

9 Disconnect the brake booster vacuum hose at the intake manifold.

10 Disconnect the fuel lines from the fuel rail (see illustration).

11 Remove the fuel rail bolts (see illustration) and separate the fuel rail from the fuel injectors.

12 Remove the fuel injector(s) from the fuel rail (see illustration) and place them aside in a clearly-labelled storage container.

13 If you intend to re-use the same injectors,

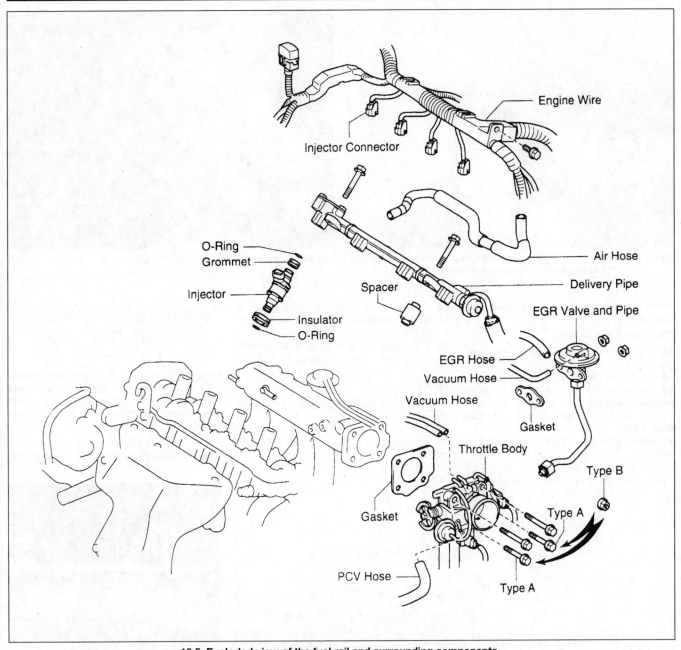

Engine Wire

Injector Connector

O-Ring
Grommet

Injector

Insulator
O-Ring

Spacer

Air Hose

Delivery Pipe

EGR Valve and Pipe

EGR Hose
Vacuum Hose

Gasket

Vacuum Hose

Throttle Body

Gasket

Type B

Type A

PCV Hose

Type A

**16.5 Exploded view of the fuel rail and surrounding components –
2000 and earlier models**

**16.10 Disconnect the fuel lines from the
fuel rail**

**16.11 Remove the fuel rail mounting bolts
(arrowed)**

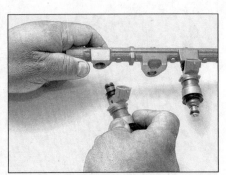

**16.12 Simultaneously twist and pull the
injector to remove it from the fuel rail**

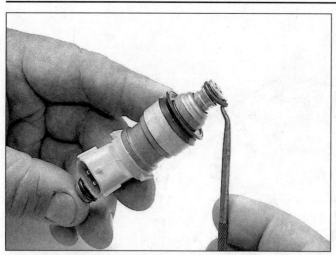

16.13 If you plan to refit the original injectors, remove and discard the O-rings and grommets and renew them

16.16a Disconnect the harness clamps from the intake manifold

renew the grommets and O-rings (see illustration).

2001 and later models

14 Remove the air filter housing (see Section 10).
15 Disconnect the PCV hose (see Chapter 6A).
16 Disconnect the fuel lines from the fuel rail (see illustrations).
17 Remove the fuel rail mounting bolts (see illustration).
18 Remove the fuel rail with the fuel injectors attached.

19 Remove the fuel injector(s) from the fuel rail (see illustration) and place them aside in a clearly-labelled storage container.
20 If you intend to re-use the same injectors, renew the grommets and O-rings.

Refitting

21 Refitting of the fuel injectors is the reverse of removal.
22 Tighten the fuel rail mounting bolts to the torque listed in this Chapter's Specifications.

17 Exhaust system servicing – general information

⚠ Warning: Inspection and repair of exhaust system components should be done only after the system components have cooled completely.

1 The exhaust system consists of the exhaust manifold, catalytic converter, the silencer, the

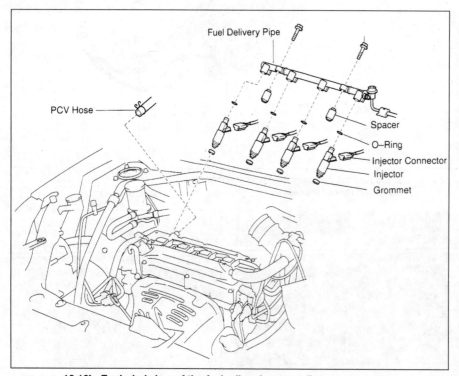

16.16b Exploded view of the fuel rail and surrounding components – 2001 and later models

Fuel Delivery Pipe

PCV Hose

Spacer
O–Ring
Injector Connector
Injector
Grommet

16.17 Remove the fuel rail mounting bolts (arrowed)

16.19 Be sure to fit new O-rings on the injectors and the fuel pressure regulator

17.1a The exhaust pipe and the catalytic converter are fastened to the underbody using rubber hangers (arrowed)

17.1b Inspect the exhaust system hangers (arrowed) for cracks

17.4 Lubricate the exhaust system nuts and bolts with penetrating oil before attempting to loosen them

tailpipe and all connecting pipes, brackets, hangers and clamps. The exhaust system is attached to the body with mounting brackets and rubber hangers **(see illustrations)**. If any of these parts are damaged or deteriorated, excessive noise and vibration will be transmitted to the body.

2 Conducting regular inspections of the exhaust system will keep it safe and quiet. Look for any damaged or bent parts, open seams, holes, loose connections, excessive corrosion or other defects which could allow exhaust fumes to enter the vehicle. Deteriorated exhaust system components should not be repaired – they should be renewed.

3 If the exhaust system components are extremely corroded or rusted together, they will probably have to be cut from the exhaust system. The convenient way to accomplish

this is to have an exhaust repair specialist remove the corroded sections with a cutting torch. If, however, you want to save money by doing it yourself and you don't have an oxy/acetylene welding outfit with a cutting torch, simply cut off the old components with a hacksaw. If you have compressed air, special pneumatic cutting chisels can also be used. If you do decide to tackle the job at home, be sure to wear eye protection to protect your eyes from metal chips and work gloves to protect your hands.

4 Here are some simple guidelines to apply when repairing the exhaust system:
a) Work from the back to the front when removing exhaust system components.
b) Apply penetrating oil to the exhaust system component nuts/bolts to make them easier to remove **(see illustration)**.

c) Use new gaskets, rubber hangers and clamps when fitting exhaust system components.
d) Apply anti-seize compound to the threads of all exhaust system fasteners during reassembly. Be sure to allow sufficient clearance between newly fitted parts and all points on the underbody to avoid overheating the floorpan and possibly damaging the interior carpet and insulation. Pay particularly close attention to the catalytic converter and its heat shield.

⚠ **Warning: The catalytic converter operates at very high temperatures and takes a long time to cool. Wait until it's completely cool before attempting to remove the converter. Failure to do so could result in serious burns.**

Chapter 4 Part B:
Fuel and exhaust systems – diesel engines

Contents

Section number

Air cleaner and inlet system – removal and refitting. 6
Exhaust system – general information. 15
Exhaust system inspection. See Chapter 1B
Fuel filter and heater – removal, renewal and refitting 7
Fuel level sending unit – removal and refitting 3
Fuel lines and fittings – general information. 2
Fuel tank – removal and refitting 4
Fuel tank cleaning and repair. 5

General information 1
High-pressure common rail – removal and refitting. 9
High-pressure fuel lines – removal and refitting. 10
High-pressure fuel pump – checking, removal and refitting. 8
Injectors – testing, removal and refitting 11
Intercooler – removal and refitting 14
Throttle body/module – testing, removal and refitting 12
Turbocharger – testing, removal and refitting. 13

Degrees of difficulty

Easy, suitable for novice with little experience 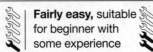	Fairly easy, suitable for beginner with some experience	Fairly difficult, suitable for competent DIY mechanic	Difficult, suitable for experienced DIY mechanic	Very difficult, suitable for expert DIY or professional

Specifications

Fuel injection system
Type . . . . Denso Turbocharged Direct Injection Common Rail

High-pressure fuel pump
Resistance between terminals of rear wiring sockets . . . . 1.5 to 1.7 ohms at 20°C
Resistance between terminals of fuel temperature sensor . . . . 0.5 to 3.0 ohms at 40°C

Fuel injectors
Resistance at 20°C. . . . . 2.5 to 3.1 ohms

Throttle body
Resistance between terminals 1 or 3 and 2, and 4 or 6 and 5 at 20°C . 18 to 22 ohms

Turbocharger
Type . . . . Variable nozzle vane

Torque wrench settings	lbf ft	Nm
Common rail bolts	32	43
Fuel injectors	19	26
High-pressure fuel pump:		
Mounting nuts.	15	21
Support bracket bolts.	15	21
Drive sprocket	76	103
High-pressure injector pipe union nuts:		
To injectors	25	34
To common rail.	30	41
High-pressure pump fuel inlet pipe:		
To common rail.	27	37
To pump	23	31
Support bolt	6	8
Inlet manifold nuts and bolts	15	21
Leak-off check valve	15	21
Leak-off check valve plug	7	10
Leak-off pipe hollow bolts	12	16
Leak-off pipe union bolt	9	12
Oil dipstick tube support	13	18
Throttle body/module inlet elbow to inlet manifold	15	21
Throttle body/module to inlet elbow	15	21
Turbocharger:		
To exhaust manifold	39	53
To catalytic converter	18	25
Turbocharger EGR cooler tube.	18	25

1 General information

⚠️ **Warning 1: Diesel fuel isn't as volatile as petrol, but it is flammable, so take extra precautions when you work on any part of the fuel system. Don't smoke or allow naked flames or bare light bulbs near the work area. Don't work in a garage or other enclosed space where there is a gas-type appliance (such as a water heater or clothes dryer). Avoid direct skin contact with diesel fuel – wear protective clothing, safety glasses and gloves when handling fuel system components and have a fire extinguisher on hand. Ensure that the work area is well-ventilated.**

⚠️ **Warning 2: Fuel injectors operate at extremely high pressures and the jet of fuel produced at the nozzle is capable of piercing skin, with potentially fatal results. When working with pressurised injectors, take great to avoid exposing any part of the body to the fuel spray. It is recommended that any pressure testing of the fuel system components should be carried out by a diesel fuel systems specialist.**

Caution: Under no circumstances should diesel fuel be allowed to come into contact with coolant hoses, wiring or rubber components – wipe off accidental spillage immediately. Hoses that have been contaminated with fuel for an extended period should be renewed. Diesel fuel systems are particularly sensitive to contamination from dirt, air and water. Pay particular attention to cleanliness when working on any part of the fuel system, to prevent the entry of dirt. Thoroughly clean the area around fuel unions before disconnecting them. Store dismantled components in sealed containers to prevent contamination and the formation of condensation. Only use lint-free cloths and clean fuel for component cleaning. Avoid using compressed air when cleaning components in place.

Diesel models covered by this manual are equipped with a Denso Turbocharged Direct Injection Common Rail fuel injection system (**see illustration**). The fuel lift pump is immersed in the fuel inside the tank, and delivers a constant supply of fuel to the fuel filter in the engine compartment. Fuel from the fuel filter is delivered to the high-pressure fuel pump, then by the common rail and pipes to the electronic fuel injectors, where it is sequentially injected directly into the combustion chamber of each cylinder. A fuel pressure regulator on the common rail maintains a constant fuel pressure to the fuel injectors, and returns excess fuel to the tank through the return line. This constant flow system also helps to reduce fuel temperature.

The electronic fuel injectors are located beneath the engine valve cover in the cylinder head, directly above the combustion chambers, and are controlled by the Engine Control Module (ECM). The ECM monitors various engine parameters and delivers the exact amount of fuel, in the correct sequence, to each cylinder. This Chapter's information pertains to the air and fuel delivery components of the system only. Refer to Chapter 6B for information regarding the electronic engine control system.

The exhaust system consists of an exhaust manifold and catalytic converter, turbocharger, front exhaust pipe and catalytic converter, centre pipe and silencer, and tailpipe and silencer. Each of these components is renewable. For further information regarding the catalytic converters, refer to Chapter 6B.

All diesel models are equipped with a variable-nozzle-vane turbocharger and intercooler. The turbocharger increases power by using an exhaust gas-driven turbine to pressurise the intake charge before it enters the combustion chambers. The amount of intake manifold pressure (boost) is regulated by an exhaust by-pass valve (wastegate). The wastegate regulator valve is controlled by the ECM. The heated compressed air is routed through an air-to-air radiator (intercooler). The intercooler removes excess heat from the compressed air, increasing its density and allowing for more boost pressure.

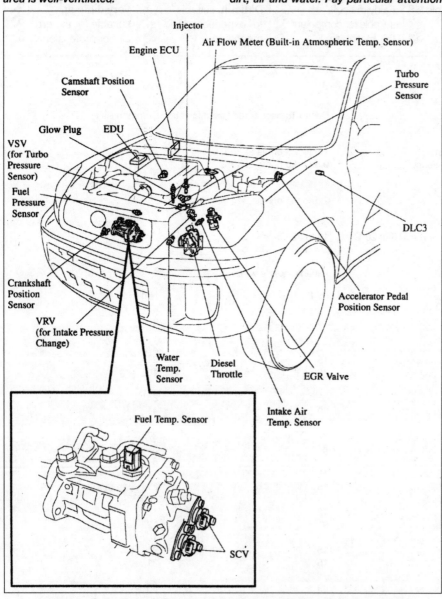

1.1 Denso Turbocharged Direct Injection Common Rail fuel injection system

2 Fuel lines and fittings – general information

1 The main fuel supply line extends from the fuel tank to the fuel filter on the left-hand side of the engine compartment, and is secured to the underbody with clips. This line should be inspected occasionally for leaks, kinks and dents.

2 Fuel enters the fuel filter through a flexible hose, and is taken from the filter to the high-pressure fuel pump also by flexible hose. To remove a hose, loosen the clips at each end and disconnect it. Make sure the clips are fully-tightened when refitting.

3 From the high-pressure fuel pump, the fuel is taken to the common rail by a single high-pressure fuel inlet pipe, then by individual high-pressure pipes to the four electronic injectors. These high-pressure pipes must be renewed if the components at either end of them are renewed, however, they may be re-used if the components are original. To remove them, unscrew the union nuts and release the pipes from any support clips. Refitting is a reversal of removal, but tighten the union nuts to the specified torque.

4 A leak-off pipe returns excess fuel from the injectors to the fuel tank. Access to the leak-off pipe and injectors is by removal of the valve cover, and details are given in Section 11 for the removal of the injectors. Also in Section 11 are details of pressure-checking the leak-off pipe.

3 Fuel level sending unit – removal and refitting

The procedure is similar to that for removing the fuel level sending unit on petrol engine models. Refer to Chapter 4A.

4 Fuel tank – removal and refitting

The procedure is similar to that for removing the fuel tank on petrol engine models. Refer to Chapter 4A.

5 Fuel tank cleaning and repair

Refer to Section 9 in Chapter 4A.

6.4 Removing the air cleaner element

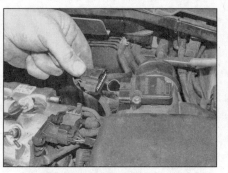

6.1a Disconnect the wiring from the airflow meter . . .

6 Air cleaner and inlet system – removal and refitting

Removal

1 The air cleaner and housing assembly is located on the left-hand side of the engine compartment. First, disconnect the wiring from the airflow meter which is fitted to the air cleaner top cover, and unclip it from the support **(see illustrations)**.

2 Loosen the clip and disconnect the air outlet hose from the top cover.

3 Release the spring clips and remove the top cover from the air cleaner body **(see illustration)**.

4 Remove the element, noting that it is fitted

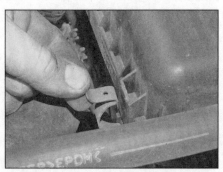

6.3a Release the spring clips . . .

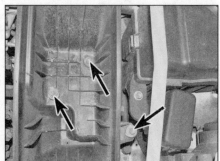

6.5a Unscrew the mounting bolts . . .

6.1b . . . and unclip it from the support

with its larger section facing downwards **(see illustration)**.

5 Unscrew the mounting bolt securing the air cleaner body to the inner body, then release the inlet elbow from the front crossmember and remove it from the engine compartment **(see illustrations)**.

Refitting

6 Clean the air cleaner body and top cover of dust and dirt and any leaves, then locate the body in position making sure that the inlet elbow is engaged with the front crossmember. Insert the mounting bolt and tighten securely.

7 Fit the element with its larger section downwards, and refit the top cover, securing it with the spring clips.

8 Reconnect the air outlet hose to the top cover and secure by tightening the clip.

9 Reconnect the wiring to the airflow meter.

6.3b . . . and remove the air cleaner top cover

6.5b . . . and remove the air cleaner body while releasing the inlet elbow from the engine compartment front crossmember

7.2a Fuel filter location

7.2b Disconnecting the supply and return hoses

7.3 Disconnecting the wiring from the fuel filter

7 Fuel filter and heater –
removal, renewal and refitting

Fuel filter

Removal

1 Access to the fuel filter is gained by removing the air cleaner assembly as described in Section 6.

2 Position a container beneath the fuel filter to catch spilt fuel, then disconnect the supply and return hoses **(see illustrations)**.

3 At the connector, disconnect the wiring for the fuel heater on top of the filter assembly **(see illustration)**.

4 At the connector, disconnect the wiring for the fuel level warning switch on the bottom of the filter assembly.

5 Unscrew the mounting nuts and lift the filter assembly from the support bracket, then loosen the drain plug and drain the fuel into the container **(see illustration)**. Tighten the plug on completion.

6 Mount the filter body in a vice and unscrew the fuel level warning switch from the bottom of the filter canister. Recover the O-ring seal **(see illustrations)**.

7 Unscrew the filter canister and discard. Toyota technicians use a special ring spanner which engages the multi-flats on the canister perimeter, however, an oil filter removal strap can be used instead **(see illustrations)**.

Refitting

8 Clean the contact surfaces of the new filter canister and body, and smear a little fuel oil onto them.

9 Screw on the canister until it contacts the body, then tighten it an additional 3/4 turn by hand only.

10 Apply a little fuel oil to a new O-ring seal, and locate it on the fuel level warning switch. Screw the switch into the filter canister and tighten securely.

11 Fit the filter assembly to the support bracket and tighten the mounting nuts.

12 Reconnect the wiring to the level warning switch and heater.

13 Reconnect the feed and supply hoses.

14 Refit the air cleaner assembly.

15 Operate the hand pump on top of the fuel filter until resistance is felt indicating that the filter is primed.

16 Run the engine and check for leaks.

Fuel heater

Removal

17 The fuel heater is located on the top of the fuel filter **(see illustration)**. For improved access, remove the air cleaner assembly as described in Section 6.

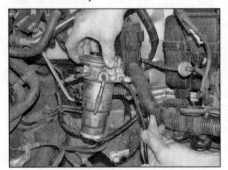

7.5 Removing the fuel filter

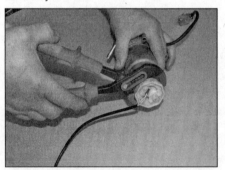

7.6a Use a pair of grips to unscrew the fuel level warning switch . . .

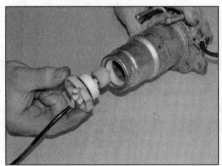

7.6b . . . and remove it from the bottom of the filter canister

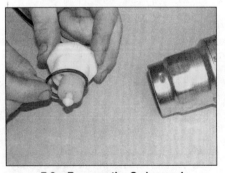

7.6c Recover the O-ring seal

7.7a Use an oil filter removal strap to unscrew the canister . . .

7.7b . . . and remove it from the filter body

18 Disconnect the wiring.

19 Undo the mounting screws noting that the earth cable is located on one of them, and lift the heater from the filter body.

Testing

20 Connect a vacuum pump to the vacuum port on the heater, and apply vacuum of 0.35 bar. Now use an ohmmeter to measure the resistance between the wiring plug terminal 1 and the heater body. At 20°C ambient temperature, the resistance should be between 0.5 and 2.0 ohms.

21 With no vacuum applied to the port, there should be no continuity between the wiring plug terminal 1 and the heater body.

22 If the resistance is not as given, renew the heater.

Refitting

23 Refitting is a reversal of removal, but tighten the screws securely.

---

8 High-pressure fuel pump – checking, removal and refitting

Checking

1 The only check that can be made by the home mechanic is the resistance across the terminals in the two wiring sockets. First, disconnect the wiring plugs.

2 Connect an ohmmeter across the terminals in each of the wiring sockets, and check that the resistance is within the limits given in the Specifications.

3 Now use the ohmmeter to check that there is no continuity between the upper terminal and earth.

4 If either of the checks gives an incorrect result, renew the high-pressure fuel pump.

Removal

5 Unbolt the power steering pump and position it to one side (see Chapter 10). For better access, remove the right-hand front headlight with reference to Chapter 12.

6 Clean the area around the high-pressure fuel pump, in particular the fuel pipes and union nuts, to prevent entry of dust and dirt into the fuel system.

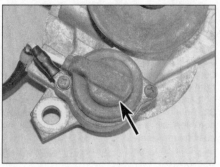

7.17 The fuel heater is located on the top of the fuel filter

7 Remove the crankshaft pulley as described in Chapter 2C.

8 Remove the timing belt as described in Chapter 2C.

9 Unscrew the union nuts and remove the injector pipes from the injectors and common rail. Tape over or plug the open apertures of the pipes, injectors and common rail. **Note:** *Toyota recommend renewal of the injector pipes whenever the injectors and/or the common rail are renewed.*

10 Unscrew the bolt securing the fuel inlet pipe to the inlet manifold, then unscrew the union nuts and remove the pipe from the high-pressure fuel pump and common rail. **Note:** *Toyota recommend renewal of the fuel inlet pipe whenever the common rail or supply pump are renewed.*

11 Unbolt the cover from the high-pressure fuel pump. Also, remove the insulator.

12 Loosen only the common rail mounting bolts. Also, disconnect the wiring from the fuel pressure sensor fly-lead.

13 Disconnect the wiring from the throttle body/module, then unscrew the bolts securing the air inlet elbow to the inlet manifold, and withdraw the elbow together with the throttle body/module.

14 Unscrew the nuts and bolts and remove the inlet manifold and common rail. Recover the gasket.

15 Disconnect the two wiring plugs from the rear of the high-pressure pump. Also, disconnect the fuel temperature sensor wiring from the top of the pump.

16 Remove the high-pressure fuel pump drive sprocket as follows. Hold the sprocket stationary with a suitable lever engaged in the holes, then unscrew the retaining nut. Using a suitable puller, draw the sprocket from the pump driveshaft **(see illustrations)**.

17 Unbolt the engine oil dipstick tube from the high-pressure pump bracket, then pull the tube from the sump upper housing and recover the O-ring seal **(see illustration)**.

18 Unscrew the bolts and remove the pump support bracket **(see illustration)**.

19 Release the clips and disconnect the two fuel hoses from the pump. Tape over the apertures to prevent entry of dust and dirt.

20 Unscrew the mounting nuts and remove the high-pressure fuel pump from the studs **(see illustration)**. **Note:** *The pump may be difficult to release from the water pump housing due to corrosion.*

8.16a Hold the sprocket stationary and unscrew the sprocket retaining nut . . .

8.16b . . . then use a puller to release the sprocket from the fuel pump driveshaft . . .

8.16c . . . and withdraw the sprocket

8.17 Removing the engine oil dipstick tube from the sump upper housing

8.18 Removing the high-pressure fuel pump support bracket

8.20 Removing the high-pressure fuel pump from the mounting studs

Refitting

21 Locate the high-pressure fuel pump on the mounting studs, then fit the nuts and tighten them to the specified torque.

22 Reconnect the fuel hoses and secure with the clips.

23 Refit the pump support bracket and initially hand-tighten all the bolts. Now fully-tighten the bolts on the cylinder block to the specified torque, followed by the bolts on the pump.

23 Refit the oil dipstick tube together with a new O-ring seal and tighten the support bolts to the specified torque.

24 Align the high-pressure fuel pump drive sprocket with the groove in the driveshaft, and fully press on. Screw on the retaining nut, then hold the sprocket with a suitable lever while the nut is tightened to the specified torque.

25 Reconnect the two wiring plugs to the rear of the high-pressure pump, and the wiring plug to the fuel temperature sensor on the top of the pump.

26 Refit the inlet manifold and common rail together with a new gasket, then progressively tighten the inlet manifold mounting nuts and bolts to the specified torque.

27 Tighten the common rail mounting bolts to the specified torque.

28 Reconnect the wiring to the fuel pressure sensor fly-lead.

29 Refit the throttle body/module and inlet elbow to the inlet manifold together with a new gasket, and tighten the bolts to the specified torque. Reconnect the wiring.

30 Refit the insulator over the high-pressure pump (see illustration) making sure it is correctly aligned with the inlet manifold. The

insulator must not touch the union bolt of the pump.

31 Refit the pump cover and tighten the bolts.

32 Refit the fuel inlet pipe to the high-pressure pump and common rail and tighten the union nuts to the specified torque. Fit the support bolt and tighten to the specified torque.

33 Refit the injector pipes to the injectors and common rail, and tighten the union nuts to the specified torque.

34 Refit the injector pipes as described in Section 10.

35 Refit the timing belt and crankshaft pulley as described in Chapter 2C.

36 Refit the power steering pump, and where removed, the headlight.

37 Start the engine and check for fuel leaks.

9 High-pressure common rail – removal and refitting

Removal

1 Clean the area around the high-pressure fuel pipes and union nuts, to prevent entry of dust and dirt into the fuel system.

2 Drain the cooling system as described in Chapter 1B.

3 Remove the intercooler (see Section 14) and engine top covers.

4 Unscrew the union nuts and remove the injector pipes from the injectors and common rail. Tape over or plug the open apertures of the pipes, injectors and common rail. **Note:** *Toyota recommend renewal of the injector pipes whenever the injectors and/or the common rail are renewed.*

5 Unscrew the bolt securing the fuel inlet pipe to the inlet manifold, then unscrew the union nuts and remove the pipe from the high-pressure fuel pump and common rail. Tape over the open apertures. **Note:** *Toyota recommend renewal of the fuel inlet pipe whenever the common rail or supply pump are renewed.*

6 Unscrew the bolts and remove the water outlet elbow from the left-hand end of the cylinder head. Recover the gasket.

7 Where applicable on early models, disconnect the fuel pressure sensor wiring

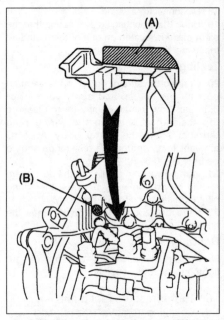

8.30 Align the shaded areas of the insulator (A) and inlet manifold (B) with each other

connector from the fly-lead support bracket.

8 Release the clip and disconnect the fuel return hose from the common rail.

9 Unscrew the mounting bolts and remove the common rail from the inlet manifold. Where applicable on later models, disconnect the fuel pressure sensor wiring **(see illustration)**.

Refitting

10 Refitting is a reversal of removal, but fit new gaskets and tighten all mounting bolts and nuts to the specified torque. Finally, refill the cooling system as described in Chapter 1B.

10 High-pressure fuel lines – removal and refitting

Removal

1 Remove the intercooler (see Section 14) and engine top covers.

2 Unscrew the support clamp nuts to release the injector pipes, then unscrew the union nuts and remove the injector pipes from the injectors and common rail. Tape over or plug the open apertures of the pipes, injectors and common rail **(see illustrations)**. **Note:** *Toyota recommend renewal of the injector pipes whenever the injectors and/or the common rail are renewed.*

3 Unscrew the bolt securing the fuel inlet pipe to the inlet manifold, then unscrew the union nuts and remove the pipe from the high-pressure fuel pump and common rail **(see illustration)**. Tape over the open apertures. **Note:** *Toyota recommend renewal of the fuel inlet pipe whenever the common rail or supply pump are renewed.*

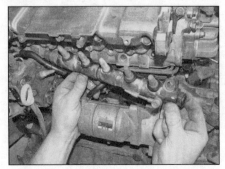

9.9a Remove the common rail from the inlet manifold ...

9.9b ... and disconnect the fuel pressure sensor wiring – later model shown

10.2a Unscrew the support clamp nuts . . .

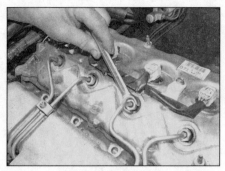

10.2b . . . then unscrew the union nuts . . .

10.2c . . . and remove the injector pipes

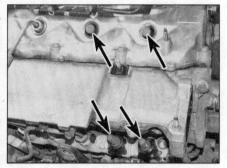

10.2d Cover the open apertures to prevent entry of dust and dirt

10.3 Removing the fuel inlet pipe from the high-pressure fuel pump and common rail

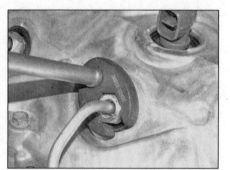

10.4 Using a crow's foot adapter to tighten the union nuts to the correct torque

Refitting

4 Refitting is a reversal of removal, but tighten the union nuts to the specified torque. As a socket cannot be used, a 'crow's foot' adapter will be required (see illustration).

11 Injectors –
testing, removal and refitting

Testing

1 The resistance of the injectors may be checked before removing them from the engine. First, remove the intercooler and engine top covers.
2 Disconnect the wiring from the injectors.
3 Connect an ohmmeter between the terminals of each of the injectors in turn, and check that the resistance is within the limits given in the Specifications.

4 Now use the ohmmeter to check that there is no continuity between the terminals and earth.
5 If the resistance is not correct, renew the injectors.

Removal

6 Unbolt the coolant expansion tank from the front of the engine compartment, and position to one side.
7 Release the engine wiring harness from its location near the common rail.
8 Remove the high-pressure fuel lines as described in the previous Section. Tape over the open apertures to prevent entry of dust and dirt. **Note:** *Toyota recommend renewal of the injector pipes whenever the injectors and/or the common rail are renewed. Toyota recommend renewal of the fuel inlet pipe whenever the common rail or supply pump are renewed.*

9 Remove the lower injection pipe support clamps from the inlet manifold.
10 Remove the valve cover as described in Chapter 2C.
11 Place cloth rags beneath the fuel leak-off pipe, to collect spilt fuel.
12 At the timing belt end of the fuel leak-off pipe, unscrew and remove the union bolt and recover the double sealing washer.
13 Unscrew the four hollow bolts securing the leak-off pipe to the cylinder head, remove the leak-off pipe, and recover the double sealing washers (see illustrations).
14 Identify the fuel injectors for position to ensure correct refitting, as the engine control module (ECM) uses this information when injecting fuel.
15 Unscrew and remove the injector mounting bolts and recover the washers and clamps. Note the convex side of the washer abuts the top of the clamp (see illustrations).

11.13a Unscrew the four hollow bolts . . .

11.13b . . . remove the leak-off pipe, and recover the double sealing washers

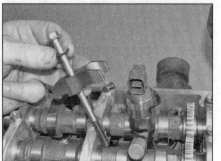

11.15a Unscrew the mounting bolt, and remove it together with the clamp

11.15b The convex side of the washer abuts the top of the clamp

11.16a Use a lever to release the injector ...

11.16b ... and remove from the cylinder head

11.16c Injector removed from the cylinder head

11.16d Keep the injectors in separate plastic bags

11.20 Use a narrow screwdriver to guide the new nozzle seats into the cylinder head

16 Using a lever or screwdriver, withdraw the injectors from the cylinder head, keeping them identified for position. It is a good idea to place each injector in a plastic bag (see illustrations).
17 Remove the O-ring and back-up ring seals from the injectors.
18 Remove the nozzle seats from the cylinder head.

Refitting

19 Before refitting the injectors, thoroughly clean the cylinder head, injectors, leak-off pipe, and fuel lines.
20 Locate four new nozzle seats in the cylinder head. To ensure they locate correctly, use a narrow screwdriver to guide them into position (see illustration).

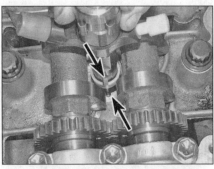

11.22 Insert the injector in the cylinder head so that the tag locates in the slot. Note also that the spring opening is aligned with the tag

21 Position the spring on each injector so that its opening is over the injector locating tag. Fit new O-ring and back-up ring seals to the injectors, and smear some fresh engine oil on the O-rings.
22 Align the injector tag with the slot in the cylinder head, and press the injector into position (see illustration). If the injector moves up due to the reaction of the O-ring seal, remove it completely and insert again.
Caution: Make sure the injector is located in the correct cylinder as noted previously.
23 Insert the remaining injectors in the same manner, then lightly oil under the heads of the clamp bolts and fit them together with the clamps and washers. The washers must be located on the clamps with the tapered side facing downwards.
24 Hand-tighten the bolts initially, then fully tighten them to the specified torque.
25 Refit the fuel leak-off pipe together with new double sealing washers, making sure that the washer ties are facing forward. Oil under the heads of the four hollow bolts, then insert them and tighten to the specified torque. Note: If the bolts are overtightened, the leak-off pipe must be renewed.
26 Refit the timing belt end of the leak-off pipe to the cylinder head together with a new double sealing washer. Oil under the head of the union bolt, then insert it and tighten to the specified torque. Note: If the bolt is overtightened, the leak-off pipe must be renewed.
27 At this stage, Toyota recommend making a

pressure check of the leak-off pipe, however, if the following check is made, it will be necessary to obtain a new check valve.
a) First, disconnect the flexible leak-off hose from the fuel outlet check valve pipe on the timing belt end of the cylinder head, then use an Allen key to unscrew the plug from the check valve. Remove the spring and ball, and tighten the plug back into the check valve, then connect a pump and gauge to the check valve pipe, and apply 1.0 bar for 10 minutes.
b) Use soapy water to check for any air bubbles from the leak-off pipe connections. If evident, remove the leak-off pipe and renew the double washers, then refit it and make the check again.
c) After confirming the connections are good, unscrew the check valve and remove the union pipe, then fit a new check valve with new double washers to the pipe, and tighten to the specified torque. Reconnect the hose to the check valve pipe.
28 Refit the valve cover as described in Chapter 2C.
29 Refit the lower injection pipe support clamps to the inlet manifold.
30 Refit the high-pressure fuel lines as described in the previous Section.
31 Refit the engine wiring harness, and connect the wiring to the injectors.
32 Refit the coolant expansion tank and tighten the mounting bolt.
33 Start the engine and check for fuel leaks.

12.4 Disconnecting the wiring

12 Throttle body/module – testing, removal and refitting

Testing

1 The throttle body is located on an air inlet elbow on the left-hand end of the inlet manifold. The internal windings may be checked for resistance without removing the unit. First, disconnect the wiring plug.
2 Using an ohmmeter, check that the resistance between terminals 1 or 3 and 2, and 4 or 6 and 5 are as given in the Specifications. If not, renew the throttle body.

Removal

3 Loosen the clip and disconnect the air inlet hose from the throttle body.
4 Disconnect the wiring and the vacuum hose **(see illustration)**.
5 Unscrew the mounting bolts and remove the throttle body complete with air inlet elbow from the inlet manifold. Recover the gasket **(see illustrations)**.
6 Unscrew the mounting nuts and remove the throttle body from the air inlet elbow. Recover the gasket.

Refitting

7 Refitting is a reversal of removal, but fit new gaskets and tighten the mounting nuts to the specified torque.

13 Turbocharger – testing, removal and refitting

Testing

1 The turbocharger is a precision component which can be severely damaged by a lack of lubrication or from foreign material entering the air intake duct. Turbocharger failure may be indicated by poor engine performance, blue/grey exhaust smoke or unusual noises from the turbocharger. If a turbocharger failure is suspected, check the following areas:
a) Check the intake air duct for looseness or damage. Make sure there are no

12.5a Unscrew the mounting bolts and remove the throttle body and air inlet elbow from the inlet manifold ...

restrictions in the air intake system, dirty air filter element or damaged intercooler.
b) Check the system vacuum hoses for restrictions or damage.
c) Check the system wiring for damage and electrical connectors for looseness or corrosion.
d) Make sure the wastegate actuator linkage is not binding.
e) Check the exhaust system for damage or restrictions.
f) Check the lubricating oil supply and return pipes for damage or restrictions.
g) If the turbocharger requires renewal due to failure, be sure to change the engine oil and filter (see Chapter 1B).
2 Complete diagnosis of the turbocharger and control system require special techniques and equipment. If the previous checks fail to identify the problem, take the vehicle to a dealership service department or other properly-equipped repair facility for diagnosis.

13.6a Turbocharger heat shields

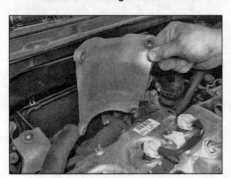

13.7 ... and lower heat shield

12.5b ... then recover the gasket

Removal

⚠ *Warning: Wait until the engine is completely cool before beginning this procedure.*

3 Drain the cooling system as described in Chapter 1B.
4 Loosen the clips and disconnect the air inlet and outlet hoses from the intercooler.
5 Unscrew the mounting nuts and lift the intercooler from the top of the engine.
6 Unbolt and remove the upper heat shield from the turbocharger **(see illustrations)**.
7 Unbolt the lower heat shields from the rear of the exhaust manifold catalytic converter **(see illustration)**. Access to the lower bolt is best from below. Note that due to the restricted access, the large vented heat shield cannot be removed from behind the engine until after the turbocharger is removed.
8 Loosen the clips and disconnect the intercooler and air outlet hoses from the turbocharger **(see illustrations)**.

13.6b Unbolt the upper heat shield ...

13.8a Removing the intercooler hose ...

13.8b . . . and air outlet hose

13.9 Disconnect the vacuum hose from the turbocharger wastegate

13.10a Unbolt the intercooler stay . . .

13.10b . . . and turbocharger stay

13.11 Removing the catalytic converter stay

Recover the gasket **(see illustrations)**.

13 Loosen the clips and disconnect the coolant hoses from the turbocharger.

14 Unscrew the bolt from the oil inlet and outlet pipe support bracket.

15 Loosen the clip and disconnect the turbo oil outlet hose.

16 Unbolt the turbo oil inlet/return pipe flange from the turbocharger – if necessary also unscrew the union nut and remove the pipe from the cylinder block. Recover the gasket and sealing washers **(see illustration)**.

17 Unbolt the remaining stay, then unscrew the mounting nuts and remove the turbocharger from the exhaust manifold **(see illustrations)**. Recover the gasket. Take care not to damage the actuator pushrod.

18 If required, unbolt and remove the EGR cooler tube **(see illustration)**.

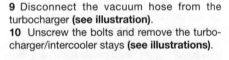

9 Disconnect the vacuum hose from the turbocharger **(see illustration)**.

10 Unscrew the bolts and remove the turbocharger/intercooler stays **(see illustrations)**.

11 Unscrew the bolts and remove the catalytic converter stay **(see illustration)**.

12 Unscrew the nuts and separate the catalytic converter from the turbocharger.

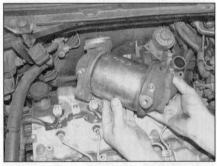

13.12a Removing the catalytic converter

13.12b The catalytic converter is attached to the turbocharger with studs and nuts

13.12c Removing the gasket from the turbocharger

13.16 Turbocharger oil inlet/return pipe flange and gasket (shown with turbocharger removed)

13.17a Unbolt the remaining stay . . .

13.17b . . . then unscrew the mounting nuts and remove the turbocharger from the exhaust manifold

13.18 Removing the EGR tube

13.19 Recover the remaining heat shield

cooler, loosen the clip and disconnect the air hose from the turbocharger.

4 Unscrew the mounting nuts/bolts and lift the intercooler from the top of the engine. If necessary, the grille may be unbolted from the top of the intercooler **(see illustrations)**.

Refitting

5 Refitting is a reversal of removal.

19 Recover the remaining heat shield from the rear of the engine **(see illustration)**.

Refitting

20 Refitting is the reverse of removal with the following additions:

a) *Renew all gaskets, seals, union bolt washers and self-locking nuts.*
b) *Tighten the nuts and bolts to the torques listed in this Chapter's Specifications.*
c) *Change the engine oil and filter (see Chapter 1B).*
d) *Refill the cooling system (see Chapter 1B).*
e) *Before starting the engine, disconnect the injector feed wiring and crank the engine over until oil pressure builds.*

14 Intercooler –
removal and refitting

Removal

1 The intercooler is located on top of the engine, with support legs securing it clear of the engine top covers **(see illustration)**.

2 At the front of the intercooler, loosen the clip and disconnect the air hose leading to the throttle body module on the inlet manifold **(see illustration)**.

3 At the left-hand rear corner of the inter-

15 Exhaust system –
general information

⚠️ **Warning: Inspection and repair of exhaust system components should be done only after the system components have cooled completely.**

1 The exhaust system consists of the exhaust manifold and catalytic converter, turbocharger, front exhaust pipe and catalytic converter, centre pipe and silencer, and tailpipe and silencer. The front exhaust pipe is attached to the catalytic converter by spring-tensioned bolts and a circular exhaust gasket **(see illustration)**. The exhaust system is attached to the body with mounting brackets and rubber hangers. If any of these parts are damaged or deteriorated, excessive noise and vibration will be transmitted to the body.

14.1 The intercooler is located on top of the engine

14.2 Disconnecting the hose leading to the throttle body module

14.4a Unscrew the mounting nuts/bolts . . .

14.4b . . . and lift the intercooler from the top of the engine

15.1 The front exhaust pipe is sealed to the catalytic converter with a circular gasket

2 Conducting regular inspections of the exhaust system will keep it safe and quiet. Look for any damaged or bent parts, open seams, holes, loose connections, excessive corrosion or other defects which could allow exhaust fumes to enter the vehicle. Deteriorated exhaust system components should not be repaired – they should be renewed.

3 If the exhaust system components are extremely corroded or rusted together, they will probably have to be cut from the exhaust system.

4 Here are some simple guidelines to apply when repairing the exhaust system:
   a) Work from the back to the front when removing exhaust system components.
   b) Apply penetrating oil to the exhaust system component fasteners to make them easier to remove.
   c) Use new gaskets, hangers and clamps when installing exhaust system components.
   d) Apply anti-seize compound to the threads of all exhaust system nuts and bolts during reassembly. Be sure to allow

sufficient clearance between newly fitted parts and all points on the underbody to avoid overheating the floorpan and possibly damaging the interior carpet and insulation. Pay particularly close attention to the catalytic converters and heat shields.

⚠ **Warning: The catalytic converters operate at very high temperatures and take a long time to cool. Wait until completely cool before attempting to remove the converters. Failure to do so could result in serious burns.**

Chapter 5
Engine electrical systems

Contents

Section number

Alternator – removal and refitting............................ 12
Auxiliary drivebelt check, adjustment and
  renewal.................................... See Chapter 1A or 1B
Battery – emergency jump starting 2
Battery – testing, removal and refitting 3
Battery cables – renewal 4
Battery check, maintenance and charging..... See Chapter 1A or 1B
Charging system – general information and precautions.......... 10
Charging system – testing 11
Distributor (1996 and 1997 petrol models) – removal and refitting .. 9
General information, precautions and battery disconnection 1
Glow plug system (diesel models) – general information.......... 16

Section number

Glow plugs (diesel models) – testing and renewal.............. 17
Ignition coil(s) (petrol models) – testing and renewal 7
Ignition module (1996 and 1997 petrol models) – removal and
  refitting 8
Ignition system (petrol models) – general information and
  precautions... 5
Ignition system (petrol models) – testing 6
Spark plug renewal............................. See Chapter 1A
Starter motor – removal and refitting 15
Starter motor and circuit – testing 14
Starting system – general information and precautions........... 13

Degrees of difficulty

Easy, suitable for novice with little experience	Fairly easy, suitable for beginner with some experience	Fairly difficult, suitable for competent DIY mechanic	Difficult, suitable for experienced DIY mechanic	Very difficult, suitable for expert DIY or professional

Specifications

Ignition coil (petrol models)
1996 and 1997 models:
  Primary resistance .... 0.35 to 0.55 ohms
  Secondary resistance:
    Cold .... 9.0 to 15.4 kohms
    Hot .... 11.4 to 18.1 kohms
1998 to 2000 models:
  Primary resistance .... Not available
  Secondary resistance:
    Cold .... 9.7 to 16.7 kohms
    Hot .... 12.4 to 19.6 kohms
2001 and later .... Not available

Charging system
Charging voltage .... 13.5 to 15.0 volts
Standard amperage:
  No load.. 10 amps or less
  With load.. 30 amps or more

Torque wrench setting	lbf ft	Nm
Glow plugs (diesel engines)	10	13

**1.1a Charging and ignition system components –
1996 and 1997 LHD models**

1 Battery	3 Ignition coil	5 Spark plug leads
2 Ignition module	4 Distributor	6 Alternator

**1.1b Charging and ignition system components –
2001 and later LHD petrol models**

1 Battery (under cowl cover)	3 Relay and fusebox	5 Alternator
2 Ignition module/spark plug assembly	4 Starter	

1 General information, precautions and battery disconnection

The engine electrical systems include all ignition, charging and starting components **(see Illustrations)**. Because of their engine-related functions, these components are discussed separately from body electrical devices such as the lights, the instruments, etc (which are included in Chapter 12).

Precautions

Always observe the following precautions when working on the electrical system:

a) *Be extremely careful when servicing engine electrical components. They are easily damaged if tested, connected or handled improperly.*

b) *Never leave the ignition switched on for long periods of time when the engine is not running.*

c) *Never disconnect the battery cables while the engine is running.*

d) *Maintain correct polarity when connecting battery cables from another vehicle during jump starting – see the 'Jump starting' section at the front of this manual.*

e) *Always disconnect the negative battery cable from the battery before working on the electrical system, but read the following battery disconnection procedure first.*

It's also a good idea to review the safety-related information regarding the engine electrical systems located in the *Safety first!* section at the front of this manual, before beginning any operation included in this Chapter.

Battery disconnection

Several systems on the vehicle require battery power to be available at all times, either to ensure their continued operation (such as the radio, alarm system, power door locks, windows, etc) or to maintain control unit memories such as that in the engine management system's Engine Control Module (ECM) which would be lost if the battery were to be disconnected. Therefore, whenever the battery is to be disconnected, first note the following to ensure that there are no unforeseen consequences of this action:

a) *The engine management system's ECM will lose the information stored in its memory when the battery is disconnected. This includes idling and operating values, any fault codes detected and system monitors required for emissions testing. Whenever the battery is disconnected, the computer will require a certain period of time to 'relearn' the operating values (see Chapter 6A or 6B).*

b) *On any vehicle with power door locks, it is a wise precaution to remove the key from the ignition and to keep it with you, so that it does not get locked* inside if the power door locks should engage accidentally when the battery is reconnected.

Devices known as 'memory-savers' can be used to avoid some of the above problems. Precise details vary according to the device used. Typically, it is plugged into the cigarette lighter and is connected by its own wires to a spare battery; the vehicle's own battery is then disconnected from the electrical system, leaving the 'memory-saver' to pass sufficient current to maintain audio unit security codes and ECM memory values, and also to run permanently live circuits such as the clock and radio memory, all the while isolating the battery in the event of a short-circuit occurring while work is carried out.

⚠️ **Warning 1: Some of these devices allow a considerable amount of current to pass, which can mean that many of the vehicle's systems are still operational when the main battery is disconnected. If a 'memory-saver' is used, ensure that the circuit concerned is actually 'dead' before carrying out any work on it.**

⚠️ **Warning 2: If work is to be performed around any of the airbag system components, the battery must be disconnected. If a memory-saver device is used, power will be supplied to the airbag and personal injury may result if the airbag is accidentally deployed.**

The battery on these vehicles is located in the corner of the engine compartment (see Section 3). If you're working on a 2001 or later model, remove the cowl cover for access (see Chapter 11). To disconnect the battery for service procedures requiring power to be cut from the vehicle, peel back the insulator (if equipped), loosen the negative cable clamp nut and detach the negative cable from the negative battery post (see Section 3). Isolate the cable end to prevent it from accidentally coming into contact with the battery post.

2 Battery – emergency jump starting

Refer to the *Jump starting* procedure at the front of this manual.

3 Battery – testing, removal and refitting

⚠️ **Warning: Hydrogen gas is produced by the battery, so keep open flames and lighted cigarettes away from it at all times. Always wear eye protection when working around a battery. Rinse off spilled electrolyte immediately with large amounts of water.**

Testing

1 A battery cannot be accurately tested until it is at or near a fully-charged state. Disconnect the negative battery cable from the battery and perform the following tests:

a) *Battery state of charge test* – Visually inspect the indicator eye (if equipped) on the top of the battery. If the indicator eye is dark in colour, charge the battery as described in Chapter 1A or 1B. If the battery is equipped with removable caps, check the battery electrolyte. The electrolyte level should be above the upper edge of the plates. If the level is low, add distilled water. DO NOT OVERFILL. The excess electrolyte may spill over during periods of heavy charging. Test the specific gravity of the electrolyte using a hydrometer **(see illustration)**. Remove the caps and extract a sample of the electrolyte and observe the float inside the barrel of the hydrometer. Follow the instructions from the tool manufacturer and determine the

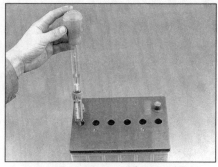

3.1a Use a battery hydrometer to draw electrolyte from the battery cell – this hydrometer is equipped with a thermometer to make temperature corrections

specific gravity of the electrolyte for each cell. A fully-charged battery will indicate approximately 1.270 (green zone) at 20-degrees C. If the specific gravity of the electrolyte is low (red zone), charge the battery as described in Chapter 1A or 1B.

b) *Open circuit voltage test* – Using a digital voltmeter, perform an open circuit voltage test **(see illustration)**. Connect the negative probe of the voltmeter to the negative battery post and the positive probe to the positive battery post. The battery voltage should be greater than 12.5 volts. If the battery is less than the specified voltage, charge the battery before proceeding to the next test. Do not proceed with the battery load test until the battery is fully charged.

c) *Battery load test* – An accurate check of the battery condition can only be performed with a load tester (available at most car accessory shops). This test evaluates the ability of the battery to operate the starter and other accessories during periods of heavy amperage draw (load). Connect a battery load testing tool to the battery terminals **(see illustration)**.

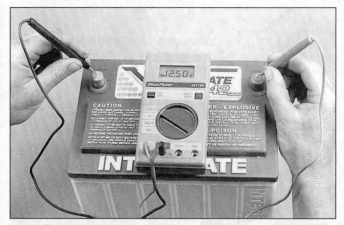

3.1b To test the open circuit voltage of the battery, connect the black probe of the voltmeter to the negative terminal and the red probe to the positive terminal of the battery – a fully-charged battery should indicate approximately 12.5 volts depending on the outside air temperature

3.1c Some battery load testers are equipped with an ammeter which enables the battery load to be precisely dialed in, as shown – less expensive testers have a load switch and a voltmeter only

3.4 Remove the two nuts (arrowed) and detach the hold-down clamps

Load test the battery according to the tool manufacturer's instructions. Maintain the load on the battery for 15 seconds and observe that the battery voltage does not drop below 9.6 volts. If the battery condition is weak or defective, the tool will indicate this condition immediately. **Note:** *Cold temperatures will cause the voltage reading to drop slightly.*

d) **Battery drain test** – *This test will indicate whether there's a constant drain on the vehicle's electrical system that can cause the battery to discharge. Make sure all accessories are turned off. If the vehicle has an underbonnet light, verify it's working properly, then disconnect it. Connect one lead of a digital ammeter to the disconnected negative battery cable clamp and the other lead to the negative battery post. A drain of approximately 100 milliamps or less is considered normal (due to the engine control computer clocks, digital radios and other components which normally cause an ignition-off battery drain). An excessive drain (approximately 500 milliamps or more) will cause the battery to discharge. The problem circuit or component can be located by removing the fuses, one at a time, until the excessive drain stops and normal drain is indicated on the meter.*

Removal and refitting

Caution: Always disconnect the negative cable first and connect it up last or the battery may be shorted by the tool being used to loosen the cable clamps.

4.4a The negative battery cable is attached to the chassis (arrowed) as well as the engine to ensure a proper earth

Note 1: *On RHD models, the battery is located in the left-hand rear corner of the engine compartment. On LHD models, it is located in the right-hand rear corner.*
Note 2: *If you're working on a 2001 or later model, remove the cowl cover for access (see Chapter 11).*

2 Loosen the cable clamp nut and remove the negative battery cable from the negative battery post. Isolate the cable end to prevent it from accidentally coming into contact with the battery post.
3 Loosen the cable clamp nut and remove the positive battery cable from the positive battery post.
4 Remove the battery hold-down clamp **(see illustration)**.
5 Lift out the battery. Be careful – it's heavy.
Note: *Battery straps and handlers are available at most car accessory shops for a reasonable price. They make it easier to remove and carry the battery.*
6 While the battery is out, inspect the battery tray for corrosion. If corrosion exists, clean the deposits with a mixture of baking soda and water to prevent further corrosion. Flush the area with plenty of clean water and dry thoroughly.
7 If you are renewing the battery, make sure you renew it with a battery with the identical dimensions, amperage rating, cold cranking rating, etc.
8 When fitting the battery, make sure the centre notch in the battery foot is aligned with the hold-down clamp hole in the battery tray. Fit the hold-down clamp and tighten the bolt securely. Do not overtighten the bolt.
9 The remainder of refitting is the reverse of removal.

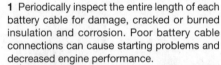

4   Battery cables –
renewal

1 Periodically inspect the entire length of each battery cable for damage, cracked or burned insulation and corrosion. Poor battery cable connections can cause starting problems and decreased engine performance.
2 Check the cable-to-terminal connections at the ends of the cables for cracks, loose wire

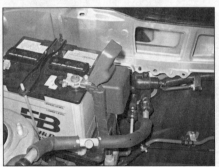

4.4b Note the routing of the positive cable

strands and corrosion. The presence of white, fluffy deposits under the insulation at the cable terminal connection is a sign that the cable is corroded and should be renewed. Check the terminals for distortion, missing mounting bolts and corrosion.
3 When removing the cables, always disconnect the negative cable from the negative battery post first and connect it up last or the battery may be shorted by the tool used to loosen the cable clamps. Even if only the positive cable is being renewed, be sure to disconnect the negative cable from the negative battery post first (see Chapter 1A or 1B for further information regarding battery cable maintenance).
4 Disconnect the old cables from the battery, then disconnect them from the opposite end. Detach the cables from the starter solenoid, under-bonnet fusebox and earth terminals, as necessary **(see illustrations)**. Note the routing of each cable to ensure correct refitting.
5 If you are renewing either or both of the battery cables, take them with you when buying new cables. It is vitally important that you renew the cables with identical parts. Cables have characteristics that make them easy to identify: Positive cables are usually red and larger in cross-section; earth cables are usually black and smaller in cross-section.
6 Clean the threads of the starter solenoid or earth connection with a wire brush to remove rust and corrosion. Apply a light coat of battery terminal corrosion inhibitor or petroleum jelly to the threads to prevent future corrosion.
7 Attach the cable to the terminal and tighten the mounting nut/bolt securely.
8 Before connecting a new cable to the battery, make sure that it reaches the battery post without having to be stretched.
9 After fitting the cables, connect the negative cable to the negative battery post.

5   Ignition system (petrol models) – general information and precautions

Conventional electronic ignition (1996 and 1997 models)

1 1996 and 1997 models are equipped with a conventional electronic ignition system. This

4.4c Disconnect the positive battery cable from the starter (petrol model shown)

6.1a On 2001 and later models, first remove the front half of the air filter housing for access to the coil/ignition module assemblies, then remove a mounting bolt and lift one of the units from the cylinder head

6.1b Next, install a calibrated ignition tester – simply connect it to the coil/ignition module assembly, clip the tester to a convenient earth and operate the starter with the ignition on – if there is enough power to fire the plug, sparks will be visible between the electrode tip and the tester body

system includes the ignition switch, the battery, the pick-up coil (distributor), the ignition coil, the ignition module, the crankshaft position sensor, the spark plugs and the primary (low voltage) and secondary (high voltage) wiring circuits.

2 The Electronic Control Module (ECM) controls the ignition timing using the data provided by the information sensors which monitors various engine functions (such as rpm, intake air volume, engine temperature, etc). The ECM ensures perfect spark timing under all operating conditions. The ignition module is a separate component from the distributor and is mounted on the right side of the engine compartment.

3 This electronic ignition system incorporates the pick-up coil inside the distributor, the external coil mounted near the distributor on the intake manifold and the ignition module mounted in the engine compartment for cooling purposes.

Distributorless Ignition System (1998 and later models)

4 1998 and later models are equipped with a Distributorless Ignition System (DIS). There are two different versions of the DIS on these models. 1998 to 2000 models incorporate a single ignition/coil module mounted on the intake manifold on a large bracket. 2001 and later models use a separate ignition/coil module for each cylinder, mounted directly over each spark plug. There are no secondary ignition HT leads with this system.

Single ignition/coil module (1998 to 2000 models)

5 1998 to 2000 models are equipped with an early version of DIS. The DIS system includes the camshaft position sensor, the crankshaft position sensor, ignition/coil module (one coil for a pair of cylinders) and the ECM (computer). The single ignition/coil module is mounted

near the front of the engine. The camshaft and crankshaft sensors send cylinder identification signals to the ECM, which causes the ignition module to trigger the correct coil. The ignition module distributes the signal to the proper coil driver circuit and determines dwell period based on coil primary current flow. This DIS system uses a 'wasted spark' method of spark distribution. Each cylinder is paired with its companion cylinder in the firing order: 1 & 4, 3 & 2; the cylinder under compression fires simultaneously with its companion cylinder, which is on the exhaust stroke. Since the cylinder on the exhaust stroke requires very little of the available voltage to fire its spark plug, most of the voltage is used to fire the plug of the cylinder on the compression stroke.

6 The ignition module is mounted on a bracket on the intake manifold. HT leads run to each spark plug from the module.

Ignition module/spark plug assemblies (2001 and later models)

7 2001 and later models are equipped with the latest version of DIS. This DIS system includes the camshaft position sensor, the crankshaft position sensor, an ignition module/spark plug assembly for each cylinder and the ECM (computer). The coil and ignition module are built into one unit and mounted over each cylinder's spark plug. The camshaft and crankshaft sensors generate cylinder identification signals which allow the ECM to trigger the correct HT coil assembly. The ignition module distributes the signal to the coil driver circuit and determines dwell period based on coil primary current flow. The spark is direct (cylinder specific) and sequenced to the engine's firing order. There is no 'wasted spark' effect with this system.

All models

8 When working on the ignition system, take the following precautions:

a) *Do not keep the ignition switch on for more than 10 seconds if the engine will not start.*

b) *Always connect a tachometer in accordance with the manufacturer's instructions. Some tachometers may be incompatible with this ignition system. Consult a dealer before buying a tachometer for use with this vehicle.*

c) *Never allow the ignition coil terminals to touch earth. Earthing the coil could result in damage to the ignition module and/or the ignition coil.*

d) *Do not disconnect the battery when the engine is running.*

---

6 Ignition system (petrol models) – testing

⚠ *Warning: Because of the high voltage generated by the ignition system, extreme care should be taken whenever an operation is performed involving ignition components. This not only includes the ignition module, coil and HT leads, but related components such as plug connectors, tachometer and other test equipment as well.*

1 If the engine turns over but won't start, disconnect the HT lead from any spark plug and attach it to a calibrated ignition tester (available at most car accessory shops) **(see illustrations)**.

2 Connect the clip on the tester to a bolt or metal bracket on the engine.

3 Relieve the fuel pressure (see Chapter 4A). Keep the fuel system disabled while performing the ignition system checks.

4 Crank the engine and watch the end of the tester to see if bright blue, well-defined sparks occur.

5 If sparks occur, sufficient voltage is reaching

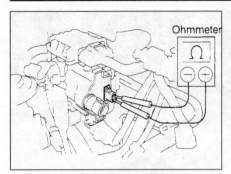

7.1 Checking the primary resistance on a 1996 and 1997 model

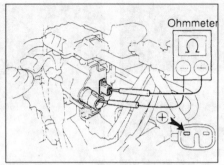

7.2a Checking the secondary resistance on a 1996 and 1997 model

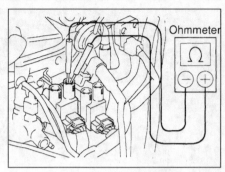

7.2b Checking the secondary resistance on a 1998 to 2000 model

7.5 The ignition coil on 1996 and 1997 models is mounted on a bracket on the engine compartment bulkhead

the spark plug to fire it (repeat the check at the remaining HT leads to verify that all the ignition coils are functioning). However, the plugs themselves may be fouled, so remove and check them as described in Chapter 1A or fit new ones.

6 If no sparks or intermittent sparks occur, check for battery voltage to the ignition coils. Refer to the wiring diagrams at the end of Chapter 12. If battery voltage is present, check the coil resistance (see Section 7).

7 Also, if no sparks or intermittent sparks occur, check the HT leads to each spark plug (see Chapter 1A).

8 If the checks are all correct, there may be a defective pick-up coil (1996 and 1997 models), camshaft position sensor (1998 and later models) and/or crankshaft position sensor.

7 Ignition coil(s) (petrol models) – testing removal and refitting

Testing

Note 1: There are no specifications available for the primary resistance check on 1998 to 2000 models, or checks for the coil/ignition modules on 2001 and later ignition systems.
Note 2: The following checks should be made with the engine cold. If the engine is hot, the resistance will be greater.

1 Check the primary resistance of the ignition coil. With the ignition key off, disconnect the

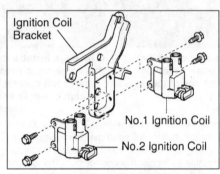

7.11 The ignition coil on 1998 to 2000 models is mounted on a bracket at the left end of the cylinder head

electrical harness connector(s) from each coil. Connect an ohmmeter across the coil primary terminals **(see illustration)**. The resistance should be as listed in this Chapter's Specifications. If not, renew the coil.
2 Check the secondary resistance of each ignition coil. With the ignition key off, label and detach the HT leads from each coil. Connect an ohmmeter across the two secondary terminals of each coil **(see illustrations)**. The resistance should be as listed in this Chapter's Specifications. If not, renew the coil.

Removal and refitting

3 Disconnect the negative cable from the battery.

1996 and 1997 models

4 Disconnect the ignition coil electrical connector. Detach the coil wire.

8.3 The ignition module on 1996 and 1997 models is located on the engine compartment bulkhead

5 Remove the bolts from the mounting bracket and separate the bracket/coil assembly from the engine **(see illustration)**.
6 Remove the bolts securing the ignition coil to the mounting bracket and remove the coil.
7 Refitting is the reverse of the removal procedure.

1998 to 2000 models

8 Remove the throttle body from the intake manifold (see Chapter 4A).
9 Remove the air filter housing cover (see Chapter 1A).
10 Disconnect the ignition coil electrical connector(s) from each individual coil pack. Label each connector so they don't get mixed up. Label and detach the HT leads.
11 Remove the bolts securing the ignition coil bracket to the engine **(see illustration)** and remove the bracket coil.
12 Separate the coil from the bracket.
13 Refitting is the reverse of the removal procedure.

2001 and later models

14 Remove the front half of the air filter housing (see Chapter 1A).
15 Each ignition coil/ignition module assembly is secured by one bolt. Unscrew the bolt, disconnect the electrical connector and pull the coil/ignition module assembly straight up, using a twisting motion.
16 Refitting is the reverse of removal.

8 Ignition module (1996 and 1997 petrol models) – removal and refitting

Note: On 1998 and later models the ignition modules are integral with the ignition coils.

Removal

1 Disconnect the negative cable from the battery.
2 Disconnect the electrical connector from the ignition module.
3 Remove the ignition module mounting screws **(see illustration)**.
4 Remove the ignition module from the engine compartment.

Refitting

5 Refitting is the reverse of removal.

9 Distributor (1996 and 1997 petrol models) – removal and refitting

Removal

1 Detach the cable from the negative battery terminal.

2 Disconnect the electrical connectors from the distributor.

3 Look for a raised 1 on the distributor cap. This marks the location for the number one cylinder HT lead terminal. If the cap does not have a mark for the number one terminal, locate the number one spark plug and trace the wire back to the terminal on the cap. Refer to the firing order schematics in the Specifications in Chapter 1A.

4 Remove the distributor cap (see Chapter 1A) and turn the engine over until the rotor is pointing toward the number one spark plug terminal (see locating TDC procedure in Chapter 2A).

5 Mark the distributor base and the engine block to ensure that the distributor is refitted correctly **(see illustration)**. Also, remove the distributor cap and make a mark on the edge of the distributor housing directly below the rotor tip and in line with it.

6 Remove the distributor hold-down bolt, then pull the distributor straight out to remove it.

Caution: DO NOT turn the crankshaft while the distributor is out of the engine, or the alignment marks will be useless.

Refitting

Note: *If the crankshaft has been moved while the distributor is out, locate Top Dead Centre (TDC) for the number one piston (see Chapter 2A) and position the distributor and the rotor accordingly.*

7 Fit a new distributor O-ring.

8 Align the cut-out portion of the coupling with the groove in the housing **(see illustration)**.

9 Insert the distributor into the engine in exactly the same relationship to the block that it was in when removed.

10 If the distributor does not seat completely, recheck the alignment marks between the distributor base and the block to verify that the distributor is in the same position it was in before removal. Also, check the rotor to see if it's aligned with the mark you made on the edge of the distributor.

11 The remainder of refitting is the reverse of removal.

12 Tighten the distributor hold-down bolt securely.

10 Charging system – general information and precautions

The charging system includes the alternator, an internal voltage regulator, a charge indicator, the battery, a fusible link and the wiring between all the components. The charging

9.5 Make an alignment mark on the base of the distributor and the cylinder head (arrowed)

system supplies electrical power for the ignition system, the lights, the radio, etc. The alternator is driven by an auxiliary drivebelt.

The purpose of the voltage regulator is to limit the alternator's voltage to a preset value. This prevents power surges, circuit overloads, etc, during peak voltage output.

The charging system doesn't ordinarily require periodic maintenance. However, the auxiliary drivebelt, battery and wires and connections should be inspected at the intervals outlined in Chapter 1A or 1B.

The instrument panel warning light should come on when the ignition key is turned to Start, then should go off immediately. If it remains on, there is a malfunction in the charging system. Some vehicles are also equipped with a voltmeter. If the voltmeter indicates abnormally high or low voltage, check the charging system (see Section 11).

Be very careful when making electrical circuit connections and note the following:

a) *When reconnecting wires to the alternator from the battery, be sure to note the polarity.*

b) *Before using arc welding equipment to repair any part of the vehicle, disconnect the wires from the alternator and the battery terminals.*

c) *Never start the engine with a battery charger connected.*

d) *Always disconnect both battery leads before using a battery charger.*

e) *The alternator is driven by an engine auxiliary drivebelt which could cause*

11.2 Connect a voltmeter to the battery terminals and check the battery voltage with the engine off and again with the engine running

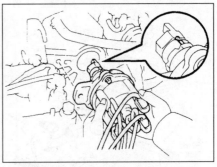

9.8 Align the cut-out portion of the coupling with the groove in the housing

serious injury if your hand, hair or clothes become entangled in it with the engine running.

f) *Because the alternator is connected directly to the battery, it could arc or cause a fire if overloaded or shorted out.*

11 Charging system – testing

1 If a malfunction occurs in the charging circuit, do not immediately assume that the alternator is causing the problem. First, check the following items:

a) *Make sure the battery cable clamps, where they connect to the battery, are clean and tight.*

b) *Test the condition of the battery (see Section 3). If it does not pass all the tests, renew it.*

c) *Check the external alternator wiring and connections.*

d) *Check the auxiliary drivebelt condition and tension (see Chapter 1A or 1B).*

e) *Check the alternator mounting bolts for tightness.*

f) *Run the engine and check the alternator for abnormal noise.*

g) *Check the fusible links (if equipped) in the engine compartment fusebox (see Chapter 12). If they're blown, determine the cause and repair the circuit.*

h) *Check the charge light on the instrument panel. It should illuminate when the ignition key is turned on (engine not running). If it does not, check the circuit from the alternator to the charge light on the instrument panel.*

i) *Check all the fuses that are in series with the charging system circuit. The location of these fuses and fusible links may vary from year and model but the designations are generally the same. Refer to the wiring schematics at the end of Chapter 12 for additional information.*

2 With the ignition key off, check the battery voltage with no accessories operating **(see illustration)**. It should be approximately 12.5 volts. It may be slightly higher if the engine had been operating within the last hour.

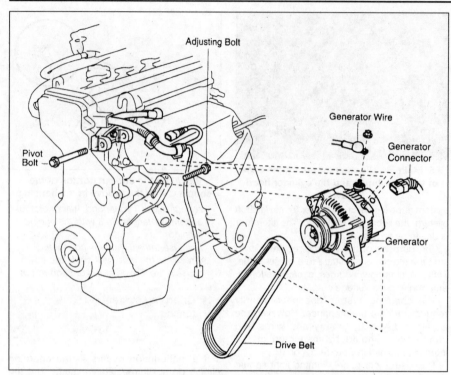

12.3a Alternator installation details on 2000 and earlier petrol models

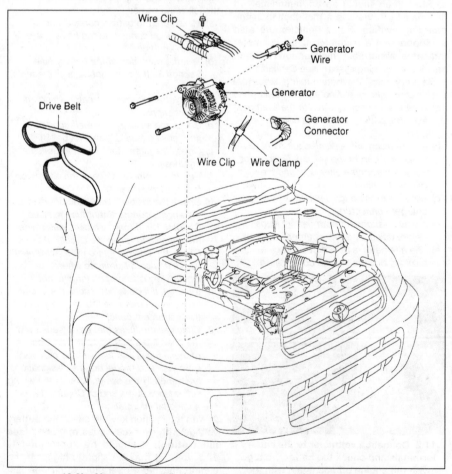

12.3b Alternator installation details on 2001 and later petrol models

3 Start the engine and check the battery voltage again. It should now be greater than the voltage recorded in paragraph 2, but not more than 14.5 volts. Turn on all the vehicle accessories (air conditioning, rear window demister, blower motor, etc) and increase the engine speed to 2000 rpm – the voltage should not drop below the voltage recorded in paragraph 2.

4 If the indicated voltage is greater than the specified charging voltage, renew the voltage regulator. **Note:** *It is recommended to renew the alternator/voltage regulator as a complete unit, using either a reconditioned or new alternator.*

5 If the indicated voltage reading is less than the specified charging voltage, the alternator is probably defective. Have the charging system checked at a dealer service department or other properly-equipped repair facility. **Note:** *Many parts stores will bench-test an alternator off the vehicle. Refer to your local parts store regarding their policy (many will perform this service free of charge).*

12 Alternator – removal and refitting

Removal

1 Detach the cable from the negative terminal of the battery.

2 Remove the auxiliary drivebelt(s) (see Chapter 1A or 1B).

3 Detach the electrical connectors from the alternator **(see illustrations)**.

4 On 2000 and earlier petrol models and all diesel models, remove the alternator adjustment and pivot bolts.

5 On 2001 and later petrol models, remove the alternator mounting bolts **(see illustration)**.

6 Remove the alternator from the mounting bracket.

7 If you are renewing the alternator, take the old alternator with you. Make sure that the new/reconditioned unit is identical to the old alternator. Look at the terminals – they should be the same in number, size and locations as the terminals on the old alternator. Finally,

12.5 Location of the alternator mounting bolts – 2001 and later petrol models (arrowed)

look at the identification markings – they will be stamped in the housing or printed on a tag or plaque affixed to the housing. Make sure that these numbers are the same on both alternators.

8 Many new/reconditioned alternators do not have a pulley fitted, so you may have to transfer the pulley from the old unit to the new/reconditioned one. When buying an alternator, find out the dealer's policy regarding the pulleys – some dealers will perform this service free of charge.

Refitting

9 Refitting is the reverse of removal.
10 Check the charging voltage to verify proper operation of the alternator (see Section 11).

13 Starting system – general information and precautions

The starting system consists of the battery, the starter motor, the starter solenoid and the electrical circuit connecting the components. The solenoid is mounted directly on the starter motor. The starter circuit consists of the ignition switch, the starter relay, the fuses, the harness wiring to the solenoid and the heavy gauge wiring to the starter. The manual transmission starting systems include the clutch start switch mounted at the clutch pedal while automatic transmission systems include the Park/Neutral Position (PNP) switch mounted on the transmission.

The solenoid/starter motor assembly is fitted on the upper part of the transmission bellhousing.

When the ignition key is turned to the Start position, the starter solenoid is actuated through the starter control circuit. The starter solenoid then connects the battery to the starter. The battery supplies the electrical energy to the starter motor, which does the actual work of cranking the engine.

The starter motor on some vehicles equipped with a manual transmission can be operated only when the clutch pedal is depressed; the starter on a vehicle equipped with an automatic transmission can be operated only when the transmission selector lever is in Park or Neutral.

Always observe the following precautions when working on the starting system:

a) *Excessive cranking of the starter motor can overheat it and cause serious damage. Never operate the starter motor for more than 15 seconds at a time without pausing to allow it to cool for at least two minutes.*

b) *The starter is connected directly to the battery and could arc or cause a fire if mishandled, overloaded or short circuited.*

c) *Always detach the cable from the negative terminal of the battery before working on the starting system.*

14 Starter motor and circuit – testing

1 If a malfunction occurs in the starting circuit, do not immediately assume that the starter is causing the problem. First, check the following items:

a) *Make sure the battery cable clamps, where they connect to the battery, are clean and tight.*

b) *Check the condition of the battery cables (see Section 4). Renew any defective battery cables.*

c) *Test the condition of the battery (see Section 3). If it does not pass all the tests, renew it.*

d) *Check the starter solenoid wiring and connections. Refer to the wiring diagrams at the end of Chapter 12.*

e) *Check the starter mounting bolts for tightness.*

f) *Check the fusible links (if equipped) in the engine compartment fusebox (see Chapter 12). If they're blown, determine the cause and repair the circuit. Also, check the ignition switch circuit for correct operation (see Chapter 12).*

g) *Check the operation of the Park/Neutral Position switch (automatic transmission) or clutch start switch (manual transmission). Make sure the shift lever is in Park or Neutral (automatic transmission) or the clutch pedal is pressed (manual transmission). Refer to Chapter 7B for the Park/Neutral Position switch check and adjustment procedure. Refer to the Chapter 12 wiring diagrams, if necessary, when performing circuit checks. These systems must operate correctly to provide battery voltage to the ignition solenoid.*

h) *Check the operation of the starter relay. The starter relay is located in the fuse/relay box inside the engine compartment. Refer to Chapter 12 for the testing procedure.*

2 If the starter does not actuate when the ignition switch is turned to the Start position, check for battery voltage to the solenoid. This will determine if the solenoid is receiving the correct voltage signal from the ignition switch. Connect a test light or voltmeter to the starter solenoid S terminal (the small-diameter wire) while an assistant turns the ignition switch to the Start position. If voltage is not available, refer to the wiring diagrams in Chapter 12 and check all the fuses and relays in series with the starting system. If voltage is available but the starter motor does not operate, remove the starter from the engine compartment (see Section 15) and bench-test the starter (see paragraph 5).

3 If the starter turns over slowly, check the starter cranking voltage and the current draw from the battery. This test must be performed with the starter assembly on the engine.

14.3 To use an inductive ammeter, simply hold the ammeter over the positive or negative cable (whichever cable has better clearance)

Crank the engine over (for 10 seconds or less) and observe the battery voltage. It should not drop below 8.0 volts on manual transmission models or 8.5 volts on automatic transmission models. Also, observe the current draw using an ammeter **(see illustration)**. It should not exceed 400 amps or drop below 250 amps.
Caution: The battery cables may be excessively heated because of the large amount of amperage being drawn from the battery. Discontinue the testing until the starting system has cooled down.

4 If the starter motor cranking amp values are not within the correct range, renew it. There are several conditions that may affect the starter cranking potential. The battery must be in good condition and the battery cold-cranking rating must not be under-rated for the particular application. Be sure to check the battery specifications carefully. The battery terminals and cables must be clean and not corroded. Also, in cases of extreme cold temperatures, make sure the battery and/or engine block is warmed before performing the tests.

5 If the starter is receiving voltage but does not activate, remove and check the starter/solenoid assembly on the bench. Most likely the solenoid is defective. In some rare cases, the engine may be seized so be sure to try and rotate the crankshaft pulley (see Chapter 2A, 2B or 2C) before proceeding. With the starter/solenoid assembly mounted in a vice on the bench, fit one jumper cable from the negative battery terminal to the body of the starter. Fit the other jumper cable from the positive battery terminal to the B+ terminal on the starter. Fit a starter switch and apply battery voltage to the solenoid S terminal (for 10 seconds or less) and see if the solenoid plunger, shift lever and overrunning clutch extends and rotates the pinion drive. If the pinion drive extends but does not rotate, the solenoid is operating but the starter motor is defective. If there is no movement but the solenoid clicks, the solenoid and/or the starter motor is defective. If the solenoid plunger extends and rotates the pinion drive, the starter/solenoid assembly is working properly.

15.6 The starter motor mounting bolts are accessible from the front and from the back (bolt not visible) of the starter motor assembly – 2001 petrol model shown

15 Starter motor –
removal and refitting

Removal

1 Detach the cable from the negative terminal of the battery.
2 Remove the air filter housing (see Chapter 4A or 4B). On diesel models, also remove the intercooler air ducting.
3 Where necessary, remove the cruise control actuator from the engine compartment and position the assembly off to the side without disconnecting the cables.
4 Remove the coolant reservoir/expansion tank from the engine compartment (see Chapter 3).

16.8a Remove the caps and unscrew the nuts from the tops of the glow plugs . . .

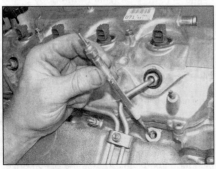

16.9 Unscrew and remove the glow plugs from the cylinder head

5 Detach the electrical connectors from the starter/solenoid assembly. **Note:** *Access is difficult and if necessary the wiring may be disconnected after unbolting the starter motor.*
6 Remove the starter motor mounting bolts **(see illustration)**. Remove the starter motor assembly from the engine compartment.

Refitting

7 Refitting is the reverse of removal.

16 Glow plug system (diesel models) –
general information

To assist cold starting, diesel engine models are equipped with a preheating system, which comprises four glow plugs, a glow plug relay, a dash-mounted warning lamp, the Engine Control Module (ECM) and the associated electrical wiring.

The glow plugs are miniature electric heating elements, encapsulated in a metal case with a probe at one end and electrical connection at the other. Each combustion chamber has a glow plug threaded into it. When the glow plug is energised, the air in the combustion chamber is heated, allowing optimum combustion temperature to be achieved more readily before fuel is injected into the cylinder.

The duration of the preheating period is governed by the Engine Control Module, which monitors the temperature of the engine via the coolant temperature sensor and alters the preheating time to suit the conditions.

A dash-mounted warning lamp informs the

16.8b . . . then remove the electrical supply strip

16.10 Tighten the glow plugs with a torque wrench

driver that preheating is taking place. The lamp extinguishes when sufficient preheating has taken place to allow the engine to be started, but power will still be supplied to the glow plugs for a further period until the engine is started. If no attempt is made to start the engine, the power supply to the glow plugs is switched off to prevent battery drain and glow plug burn-out.

After the engine has been started, the glow plugs continue to operate for a further period of time. This helps to improve fuel combustion while the engine is warming-up, resulting in quieter, smoother running and reduced exhaust emissions.

The Check Engine warning lamp will illuminate during normal driving if a preheating system malfunction occurs and a diagnostic trouble code will be stored in the ECM memory. Refer to Chapter 6B for additional information on the On-Board Diagnostic system.

17 Glow plugs (diesel engine) –
testing and renewal

Testing

1 Remove the intercooler (Chapter 4B) followed by the engine top covers.
2 Disconnect the electrical connector from the engine coolant temperature sensor (see Chapter 6B). **Note:** *This will allow the glow plugs to be energised, regardless of engine temperature.*
3 Remove the grommets from the tops of the glow plug terminals, then connect a 12 volt test light or voltmeter to one of the terminals and switch on the ignition. Battery voltage should be indicated on the meter for approximately 20 seconds. If no voltage is indicated, check the glow plug fuses and glow plug relay (see Chapter 12).
4 With the ignition switched off, remove the caps then unscrew the nuts and remove the electrical supply strip from the tops of the glow plugs. Position the strip to one side.
5 Connect the clip of a 12 volt test light to the *positive* battery terminal. Touch the electrical terminal on each glow plug with the test light tip. If the glow plug is good, the test light will illuminate.
6 Renew any defective glow plugs. Refit the electrical supply strip and tighten the nuts, then reconnect the wiring to the coolant temperature sensor.

Renewal

7 If not already done, remove the intercooler (Chapter 4B) and engine top covers.
8 With the ignition switched off, remove the caps and unscrew the nuts from the glow plugs terminals, then remove the electrical supply strip and position to one side.
9 Using a deep socket, remove the glow plugs from the cylinder head.
10 Refitting is the reverse of removal. Tighten the glow plugs to the torque listed in this Chapter's Specifications.

Chapter 6 Part A:
Emissions and engine control systems – petrol engines

Contents

Section number

Accelerator Pedal Position (APP) sensor – removal and refitting. . . . 19
Camshaft Position (CMP) sensor (1998 and later models) – removal
  and refitting. 10
Catalytic converter 18
Crankshaft Position (CKP) sensor – removal and refitting 9
Engine Control Module (ECM) – removal and refitting 3
Engine Coolant Temperature (ECT) sensor – removal and refitting . . 8
Evaporative emissions control (EVAP) system 17
Exhaust Gas Recirculation (2000 and earlier) – component description
  and renewal 16
General information 1
Idle Air Control (IAC) valve – removal and refitting 14

Section number

Intake Air Temperature (IAT) sensor (2000 and earlier models) –
  removal and refitting 7
Knock sensor – removal and refitting 12
Manifold Absolute Pressure sensor (2000 and earlier models) –
  removal and refitting 5
Mass Airflow (MAF) sensor (2001 and later models) – removal and
  refitting 6
On-Board Diagnostic (OBD) system and trouble codes 2
Oxygen sensor and air/fuel sensor – general information, and
  removal and refitting 11
Positive Crankcase Ventilation (PCV) system 15
Throttle Position Sensor (TPS) – removal and refitting 4
Vehicle Speed Sensor (VSS) – removal and refitting 13

Degrees of difficulty

Easy, suitable for novice with little experience 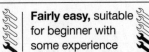	**Fairly easy,** suitable for beginner with some experience	**Fairly difficult,** suitable for competent DIY mechanic	**Difficult,** suitable for experienced DIY mechanic	**Very difficult,** suitable for expert DIY or professional

1 General information

To prevent pollution of the atmosphere from incompletely burned and evaporating gases, and to maintain good driveability and fuel economy, a number of emission control systems are incorporated (see illustrations). They include the:

On-Board Diagnostic (OBD) II system.
Electronic Fuel Injection (EFI) system.
Exhaust Gas Recirculation (EGR) system (2000 and earlier models).

Evaporative Emissions Control (EVAP) system.
Positive Crankcase Ventilation (PCV) system.
Catalytic converter.

All of these systems are linked, directly or indirectly, to the emission control system.

The Sections in this Chapter include general descriptions, checking procedures within the scope of the home mechanic (when possible) and component renewal procedures for each of the systems listed above.

Before assuming that an emissions control system is malfunctioning, check the fuel and ignition systems carefully. The diagnosis of some emission control devices requires specialised tools, equipment and training. If checking and servicing become too difficult or if a procedure is beyond your ability, consult a dealer service department or other properly-equipped repair facility. Remember, the most frequent cause of emissions problems is simply a loose or broken vacuum hose or wire, so always check the hose and wiring connections first.

This doesn't mean, however, that emission control systems are particularly difficult to maintain and repair. You can quickly and easily perform many checks and service procedures at home with common test equipment and hand tools.

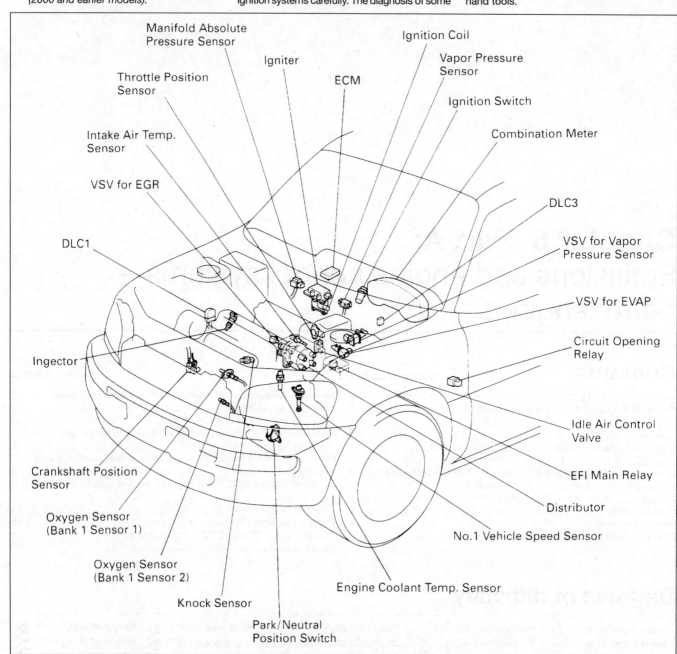

1.1a Typical emission and engine control system components – 1996 and 1997 models (1998 to 2000 similar)

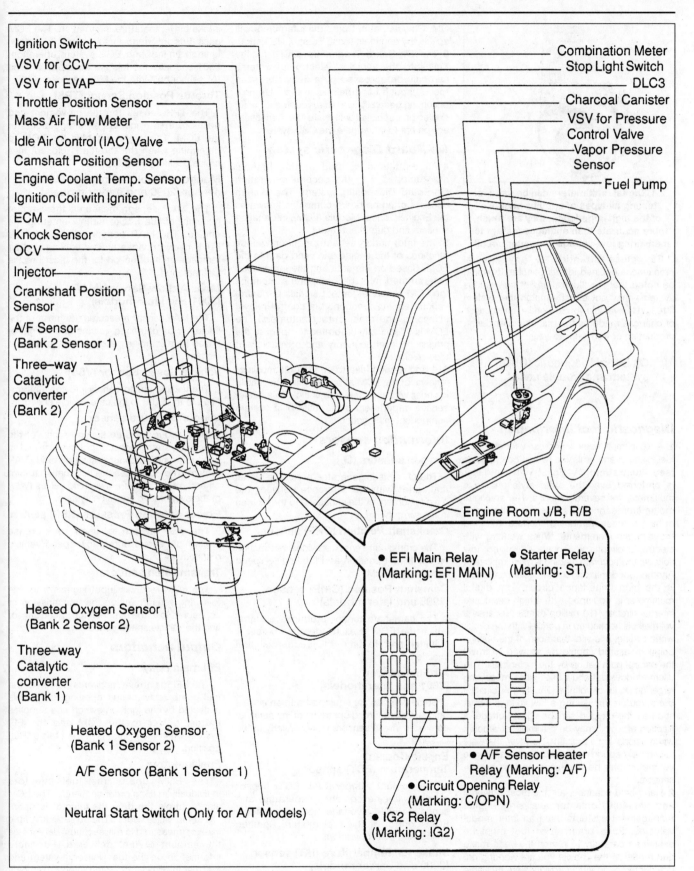

Ignition Switch
VSV for CCV
VSV for EVAP
Throttle Position Sensor
Mass Air Flow Meter
Idle Air Control (IAC) Valve
Camshaft Position Sensor
Engine Coolant Temp. Sensor
Ignition Coil with Igniter
ECM
Knock Sensor
OCV
Injector
Crankshaft Position Sensor
A/F Sensor (Bank 2 Sensor 1)
Three–way Catalytic converter (Bank 2)

Combination Meter
Stop Light Switch
DLC3
Charcoal Canister
VSV for Pressure Control Valve
Vapor Pressure Sensor
Fuel Pump

Heated Oxygen Sensor (Bank 2 Sensor 2)
Three–way Catalytic converter (Bank 1)
Heated Oxygen Sensor (Bank 1 Sensor 2)
A/F Sensor (Bank 1 Sensor 1)
Neutral Start Switch (Only for A/T Models)

Engine Room J/B, R/B

• EFI Main Relay (Marking: EFI MAIN)
• Starter Relay (Marking: ST)
• A/F Sensor Heater Relay (Marking: A/F)
• Circuit Opening Relay (Marking: C/OPN)
• IG2 Relay (Marking: IG2)

1.1b Typical emission and engine control system components – 2001 and later models

2.1 Digital multimeters can be used for testing all types of circuits; because of the high impedance, they are much more accurate than analogue meters for measuring low-voltage computer circuits

Pay close attention to any special precautions outlined in this Chapter. It should be noted that the illustrations of the various systems may not exactly match the system fitted on the vehicle you're working on because of changes made by the manufacturer during production or from year-to-year.

2 On Board Diagnostic (OBD) system and trouble codes

Diagnostic tool information

1 A digital multimeter is necessary for checking fuel injection and emission related components **(see illustration)**. A digital volt-ohmmeter is preferred over the older style analogue multimeter for several reasons. The analogue multimeter cannot display the volts-ohms or amps measurement in hundredths and thousandths increments. When working with electronic circuits which are often very low voltage, this accurate reading is most important. Another good reason for the digital multimeter is the high impedance circuit. The digital multimeter is equipped with a high resistance internal circuitry (10 million ohms). Because a voltmeter is hooked up in parallel with the circuit when testing, it is vital that none of the voltage being measured should be allowed to travel the parallel path set up by the meter itself. This dilemma does not show itself when measuring larger amounts of voltage (9 to 12 volt circuits) but if you are measuring a low voltage circuit such as the oxygen sensor signal voltage, a fraction of a volt may be a significant amount when diagnosing a problem. However, there are several exceptions where using an analogue voltmeter may be necessary to test certain sensors.

2 Hand-held scanners are the most powerful and versatile tools for analysing engine management systems used on later model vehicles. Each brand scan tool must be examined carefully to match the year, make and model of the vehicle you are working on. Often interchangeable cartridges are available to access the particular manufacturer (Ford, GM, Chrysler, etc). Some manufacturers will specify by continent (Asia, Europe, USA, etc).

3 The On-Board Diagnostic (OBD) facility built into the vehicles' electronic systems can only be accessed by a dedicated scan tool. Although hand-held scan tools are now becoming generally available, your local Toyota dealer or specialist will have the necessary equipment to interrogate the OBD system.

On-Board Diagnostic system

4 All models described in this manual are equipped with the second generation On-Board Diagnostic system. The system consists of an on-board computer, known as the Engine Control Module (ECM), information sensors and output actuators.

5 The information sensors monitor various functions of the engine and send data to the ECM. Based on the data and the information programmed into the computer's memory, the ECM generates output signals to control various engine functions via control relays, solenoids and other output actuators. The ECM is specifically calibrated to optimise the emissions, fuel economy and driveability of the vehicle.

6 It isn't a good idea to attempt diagnosis or renewal of the ECM at home while the vehicle is under warranty. Take the vehicle to a dealer service department if the ECM or a system component malfunctions.

Information sensors

Oxygen sensors (O$_2$)

The O$_2$ sensor generates a voltage signal that varies with the difference between the oxygen content of the exhaust and the oxygen in the surrounding air.

Crankshaft Position (CKP) sensor

The crankshaft sensor provides information on crankshaft position and the engine speed signal to the ECM.

Camshaft Position (CMP) sensor (1998 and later models)

The camshaft sensor produces a signal which the ECM uses to identify number 1 cylinder and to time the sequential fuel injection.

Air/Fuel sensor (2001 and later models)

Some vehicles are equipped with an air/fuel ratio sensor mounted upstream of the catalytic converter. These sensors work similarly to the O$_2$ sensors.

Engine Coolant Temperature (ECT) sensor

The coolant temperature (ECT) sensor monitors engine coolant temperature and sends the ECM a voltage signal that affects ECM control of the fuel mixture, ignition timing, and EGR operation.

Intake Air Temperature (IAT) sensor (2000 and earlier models)

The IAT sensor provides the ECM with intake air temperature information. The ECM uses this information to control fuel flow, ignition timing, and EGR system operation. 2001 and later models are equipped with an IAT sensor built into the MAF sensor.

Throttle Position Sensor (TPS)

The TPS senses throttle movement and position, then transmits a voltage signal to the ECM. This signal enables the ECM to determine when the throttle is closed, in a cruise position, or wide open.

Manifold Absolute Pressure (MAP) sensor (2000 and earlier models)

The MAP sensor measures the amount (volume) of the intake airflow entering the engine. The MAP sensor (along with the IAT sensor) provides airflow volume and air temperature information for the most precise fuel metering.

Mass Airflow Sensor (MAF) (2001 and later models)

The MAF sensor measures the mass of the intake air by detecting volume and weight of the air from samples passing over the hot wire element.

Vehicle Speed Sensor (VSS)

The vehicle speed sensor provides information to the ECM to indicate vehicle speed.

Vapour pressure sensor

The vapour pressure sensor is part of the evaporative emission control system and is used to monitor vapour pressure in the EVAP system. The ECM uses this information to turn on and off the vacuum switching valves (VSV) of the evaporative emission system.

Power Steering Pressure (PSP) switch

The PSP switch is used to increase engine idle speed during low-speed vehicle manoeuvres.

Transmission sensors

The ECM receives input signals from the following sensors inside the transmission or connected to it: the direct clutch speed sensor and the vehicle speed sensor.

Output actuators

EFI main relay

The EFI main relay activates power to the fuel pump relay (circuit opening relay). It is activated by the ignition switch and supplies battery power to the ECM and the EFI system when the switch is in the Start or Run position.

Fuel injectors

The ECM opens the fuel injectors individually in firing order sequence. The ECM also controls the time the injector is open, called the 'pulse width'. The pulse width of the injector (measured in milliseconds) determines the amount of fuel delivered. For more information on the fuel delivery system and the fuel injectors, including injector removal and refitting, refer to Chapter 4A.

2.8 16-pin Data Link Connector (DLC)/ diagnostic socket (arrowed)

Ignition module (1996 and 1997 models)

The ignition module triggers the ignition coil and determines proper spark advance based on inputs from the ECM. The module is mounted on the inner wing near the corner of the engine compartment. Refer to Chapter 5 for more information.

Idle Air Control (IAC) valve

The IAC valve controls the amount of air to bypass the throttle plate when the throttle valve is closed or at idle position. The IAC valve opening and the resulting airflow is controlled by the ECM. Refer to Chapter 4A for more information on the IAC valve.

EVAP Vacuum Switching Valve (VSV)

The EVAP vacuum switching valve is a solenoid valve, operated by the ECM to purge the fuel vapour canister and route fuel vapour to the intake manifold for combustion. This valve is also called the purge control valve.

Obtaining trouble codes

7 The ECM will illuminate the CHECK ENGINE light (also called the Malfunction Indicator Light) on the dash if it recognises a component fault for two consecutive drive cycles. It will continue to set the light until the ECM does not detect any malfunction for three or more consecutive drive cycles.

8 The diagnostic codes for the OBD-II system can be extracted from the ECM by plugging a generic OBD-II scan tool **(see illustration 2.1)** into the ECM's data link connector/diagnostic socket **(see illustration)**, which is located under the driver's end of the dash.

9 Plug the scan tool into the 16-pin data link connector (DLC), and then follow the instructions included with the scan tool to extract any stored diagnostic codes.

Diagnostic Trouble Codes

Code	Code identification
P0100	Mass airflow sensor or circuit fault
P0101	Mass airflow sensor range or performance problem
P0105	Manifold absolute pressure sensor or circuit fault
P0106	Manifold absolute pressure range or performance problem

P0110	Intake air temperature sensor or circuit fault
P0115	Engine coolant temperature sensor or circuit fault
P0116	Engine coolant temperature sensor range or performance problem
P0120	Throttle position sensor or circuit fault
P0121	Throttle Position sensor range or performance problem
P0125	Insufficient coolant temperature for closed loop; oxygen sensor heater malfunction
P0128	Thermostat malfunction
P0130	Preconverter oxygen sensor or circuit fault
P0133	Preconverter oxygen sensor circuit slow response fault
P0135	Preconverter oxygen sensor heater fault
P0136	Post-converter oxygen sensor or circuit fault
P0141	Post-converter oxygen sensor heater or circuit fault
P0158	Post-converter oxygen sensor heater or circuit fault
P0161	Post-converter oxygen sensor heater or circuit fault
P0171	Fuel injection system lean
P0172	Fuel injection system rich
P0174	Fuel injection system lean
P0175	Fuel injection system rich
P0300	Multiple cylinder misfire detected
P0301	Cylinder No 1 misfire detected
P0302	Cylinder No 2 misfire detected
P0303	Cylinder No 3 misfire detected
P0304	Cylinder No 4 misfire detected
P0325	Knock sensor or circuit fault
P0335	Crankshaft position sensor or circuit fault
P0336	Camshaft position sensor or range performance fault
P0340	Camshaft position sensor or circuit fault
P0401	EGR insufficient flow detected
P0402	EGR excessive flow detected
P0420	Catalytic converter system fault
P0430	Catalytic converter system fault
P0440	EVAP system malfunction
P0441	EVAP system incorrect purge flow detected
P0442	EVAP system leak detected
P0446	EVAP canister vent control valve circuit fault
P0450	EVAP system pressure sensor or circuit fault
P0451	EVAP system pressure sensor range or performance problem
P0500	Vehicle speed sensor or circuit fault
P0505	Idle air control valve or circuit fault

P0710	Automatic transmission fluid temperature sensor or circuit fault
P0711	Automatic transmission fluid temperature sensor range performance or circuit fault
P0750	Automatic transmission shift solenoid A stuck open or closed
P0753	Automatic transmission shift solenoid A circuit fault
P0755	Automatic transmission shift solenoid B stuck open or closed
P0758	Automatic transmission shift solenoid B circuit fault
P0765	Automatic transmission shift solenoid D stuck open or closed
P0768	Automatic transmission shift solenoid D circuit fault
P0770	Automatic transmission shift solenoid E stuck open or closed
P0773	Automatic transmission shift solenoid E circuit fault
P1130	Air/fuel ratio sensor or range performance fault
P1133	Air/fuel ratio sensor or circuit fault
P1135	Air/fuel ratio sensor heater or circuit fault
P1153	Air/fuel ratio sensor or circuit fault
P1155	Air/fuel ratio sensor heater or circuit fault
P1300 (2000 and earlier)	Ignition system malfunction (No 1 ignition module circuit fault)
P1300 (2001 and later)	Ignition system malfunction (No 1 coil/ignition module circuit fault)
P1305 (2001 and later)	Ignition system malfunction (No 2 coil/ignition module circuit fault)
P1310 (2000 and earlier)	Ignition system malfunction (No 2 ignition module circuit fault)
P1310 (2001 and later)	Ignition system malfunction (No 3 coil/ignition module circuit fault)
P1315 (2001 and later)	Ignition system malfunction (No 4 coil/ignition module circuit fault)
P1335	Crankshaft position sensor or circuit fault
P1346	VVT (variable valve timing) sensor circuit fault
P1349	VVT (variable valve timing) system malfunction
P1500	Starter signal circuit malfunction
P1520	Brake light signal malfunction
P1600	ECM battery supply malfunction
P1656	OCV (oil control valve) circuit malfunction
P1725	Automatic transmission input turbine speed sensor circuit fault
P1730	Automatic transmission counter gear speed sensor circuit fault
P1780	Park/Neutral position switch or circuit fault

3 Engine Control Module (ECM) – removal and refitting

⚠️ **Warning: The models covered by this manual are equipped with Supplemental Restraint systems (SRS), more commonly known as airbags. Always disable the airbag system before working in the vicinity of any airbag system components to avoid the possibility of accidental deployment of the airbag, which could cause personal injury (see Chapter 12).**

Caution: To avoid electrostatic discharge damage to the ECM, handle the ECM only by its case. Do not touch the electrical terminals during removal and refitting. If available, ground yourself to the vehicle with an antistatic ground strap, available at computer supply stores.

Removal

1 On LHD models, the Engine Control Module (ECM) is located under the dash near the centre console on the left-hand side of the vehicle on 2000 and earlier models **(see illustration)**. On 2001 and later LHD models, the ECM is located inside the passenger compartment to the right of the glovebox, behind the cowl side trim panel **(see illustration)**. **Note:** *On RHD models, the ECM is located on opposite sides.*

2 Disconnect the cable from the negative battery terminal.

2000 and earlier models

3 Working inside the left-hand compartment, remove the carpet and the underdash trim (see Chapter 11).

4 Unplug the electrical connectors from the ECM.

Caution: The ignition switch must be turned

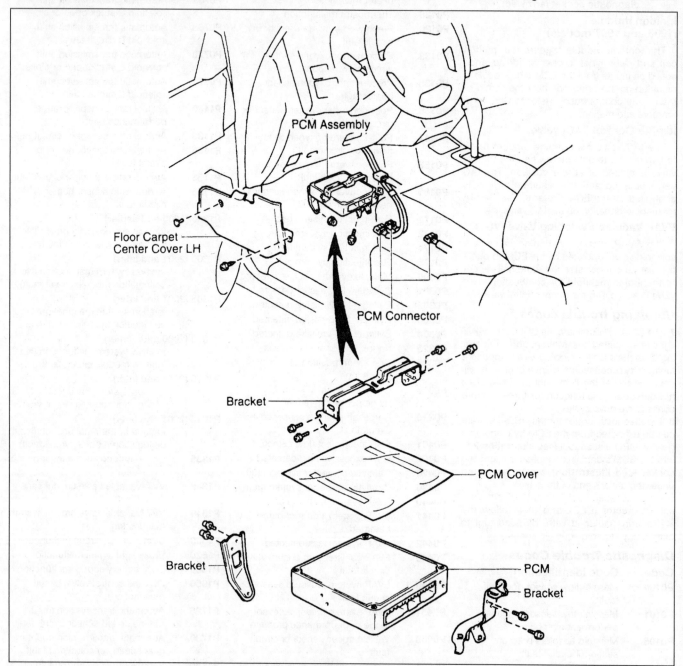

Floor Carpet Center Cover LH

PCM Assembly

PCM Connector

Bracket

PCM Cover

Bracket

PCM

Bracket

3.1a Typical ECM mounting details – 2000 and earlier LHD models

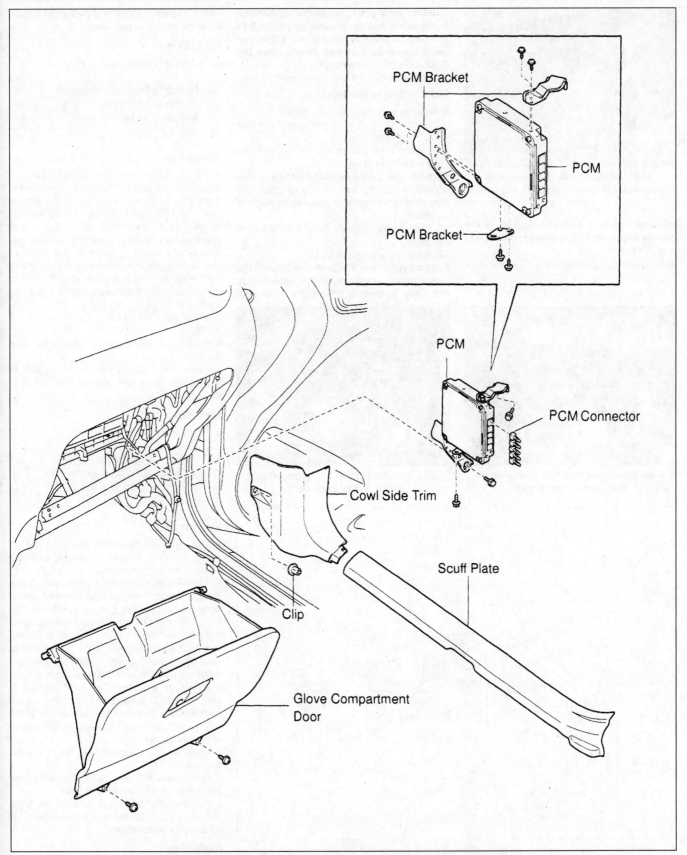

3.1b Typical ECM mounting details – 2001 and later LHD models

3.10 Location of the ECM harness connector (arrowed) on 2001 and later models

off when pulling out or plugging in the electrical connectors to prevent damage to the ECM.

5 Remove the retaining bolts from the ECM bracket.

6 Carefully remove the ECM.

4.4a Location of the TPS (arrowed) on 2000 and earlier models

Caution: Avoid any static electricity damage to the computer by grounding yourself to the body before touching the ECM and using a special antistatic pad to store the ECM on once it is removed.

7 Refitting is the reverse of removal.

2001 and later models

8 Remove the glovebox (see Chapter 11).

9 Remove the right scuff plate and cowl side trim (see Chapter 11).

10 Unplug the electrical connectors from the ECM **(see illustration)**.

Caution: The ignition switch must be turned off when pulling out or plugging in the electrical connectors to prevent damage to the ECM.

11 Remove the retaining bolts from the ECM bracket.

12 Carefully remove the ECM.

Caution: Avoid any static electricity damage to the computer by grounding yourself to the body before touching the ECM and

4.4b Location of the TPS (arrowed) on 2001 and later models

using a special anti-static pad to store the ECM on once it is removed.

Refitting

13 Refitting is the reverse of removal.

4 Throttle Position Sensor (TPS) – removal and refitting

Removal

1 The Throttle Position Sensor (TPS) is located on the end of the throttle shaft on the throttle body. By monitoring the output voltage from the TPS, the ECM can determine fuel delivery based on throttle valve angle (driver demand). A broken or loose TPS can cause intermittent bursts of fuel from the injectors and an unstable idle because the ECM thinks the throttle is moving. A problem with the TPS circuits will set a diagnostic trouble code (see Section 2).

2 Make sure the ignition key is in the off position.

3 Disconnect the electrical connector from the TPS.

4 Remove the screws that retain the TPS to the throttle body and remove the TPS **(see illustrations)**.

Refitting

5 Refitting is the reverse of removal.

5 Manifold Absolute Pressure sensor (2000 and earlier models) – removal and refitting

Removal

1 The Manifold Absolute Pressure (MAP) sensor monitors the intake manifold pressure changes resulting from changes in engine load and speed and converts the information into a voltage output. The ECM uses the MAP sensor to control fuel delivery and ignition timing. The ECM will receive information as a voltage signal that will vary from 1.9 to 2.1 volts at closed throttle (high vacuum) and 0.3 to 0.5 volt at wide open throttle (low vacuum). The voltage range values will vary slightly according to changes in altitude. The MAP sensor is attached to a bracket mounted on the engine compartment firewall. A problem in any of the MAP sensor circuits will set a diagnostic trouble code (see Section 2).

2 Make sure the ignition key is in the off position.

3 Disconnect the electrical connector and vacuum hose from the MAP sensor.

4 Remove the bolt that retains the MAP sensor to the bulkhead and remove the MAP sensor **(see illustration)**.

Refitting

5 Refitting is the reverse of removal.

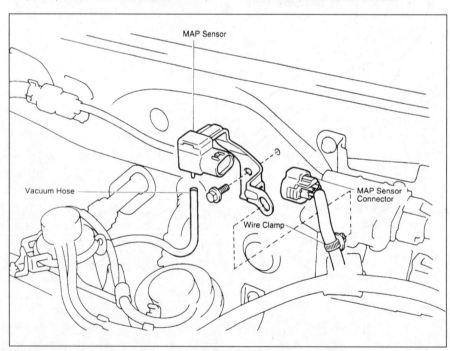

5.4 The MAP sensor is located on the bulkhead at the rear of the engine compartment on 2000 and earlier models

6.3 Location of the MAF sensor (arrowed)

6.5 Location of the MAF sensor mounting bolts (arrowed)

6 Mass Airflow (MAF) sensor (2001 and later models) – removal and refitting

Removal

1 The Mass Airflow (MAF) sensor is located on the air intake duct. The MAF system circuit consists of a platinum hot wire, a thermistor and a control circuit inside a plastic housing. The sensor uses a hot wire sensing element to measure the molecular mass (weight) of air entering the engine. As the throttle opens, increasing volume of air passes over the hot wire, which cools the wire. The MAF sensor circuit is designed to maintain the hot wire at a constant preset temperature by controlling the current flow through the hot wire. So, as the wire cools, the ECM increases the flow of current through the hot wire in order to maintain the wire at a constant temperature. The output voltage signal of the MAF sensor

Temperature (degrees - F)	Resistance (ohms)
212	125
194	250
176	300
158	400
140	500
122	625
112	750
104	875
95	1000
86	1500
76	2000
68	2500
58	3000
50	3500
40	4000
32	4500

7.1 Coolant temperature and intake air temperature sensors approximate temperature vs resistance values

varies in accordance with this current flow. This voltage signal is measured by the ECM, which converts this signal into a digital wave form, calculates the fuel injector pulse width (duration) and turns the injectors on and off accordingly. A problem in the MAF sensor circuit will set a diagnostic trouble code (see Section 2).

2 Make sure the ignition key is in the off position.

3 Disconnect the electrical connector from the MAF sensor (see illustration).

4 Remove the air filter assembly (see Chapter 4A).

5 Remove the two sensor retaining bolts and remove the MAF sensor and O-ring (see illustration).

Refitting

6 Refitting is the reverse of removal. Be sure to fit a new O-ring between the MAF sensor and the intake duct.

7 Intake Air Temperature (IAT) sensor (2000 and earlier models) – removal and refitting

Note: 2001 and later models are equipped with an IAT sensor that is built into the MAF sensor (see Section 6).

Removal

1 The Intake Air Temperature (IAT) sensor is a thermistor (a resistor which varies the value of its resistance in accordance with temperature changes). The change in the resistance values will directly affect the voltage signal from the sensor to the ECM. As the sensor temperature DECREASES, the resistance values will INCREASE. As the sensor temperature INCREASES, the resistance values will DECREASE (see illustration). A problem in any of the IAT sensor circuits will set a diagnostic trouble code.

2 Make sure the ignition key is in the off position.

3 Disconnect the electrical connector from the IAT sensor (see illustration).

4 Remove the IAT sensor from the air filter housing.

Refitting

5 Refitting is the reverse of removal.

8 Engine Coolant Temperature (ECT) sensor – removal and refitting

⚠ **Warning: Wait until the engine has cooled completely before beginning this procedure.**
Caution: Handle the coolant sensor with care. Damage to this sensor will affect the operation of the entire fuel injection system.

Removal

1 The Engine Coolant Temperature (ECT) sensor is a thermistor (a resistor which varies the value of its resistance in accordance with temperature changes). The change in the resistance values will directly affect the voltage signal from the sensor to the ECM. As the sensor temperature DECREASES, the resistance values will INCREASE. As the sensor temperature INCREASES, the

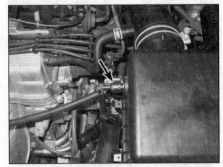

7.3 Location of the Intake Air Temperature sensor (arrowed) on a 1996 model

8.4a Location of the ECT sensor (arrowed) on 2000 and earlier models

8.4b Location of the ECT sensor (arrowed) on 2001 and later models

9.4a The crankshaft sensor harness location (arrowed) on a 1996 model

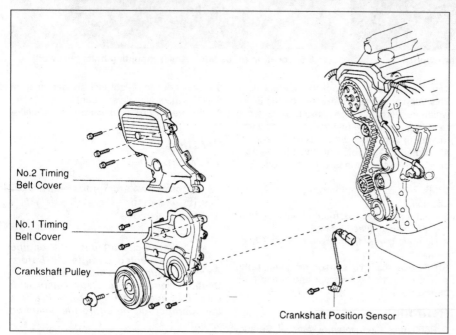

No.2 Timing Belt Cover

No.1 Timing Belt Cover

Crankshaft Pulley

Crankshaft Position Sensor

9.4b Crankshaft position sensor mounting details on 2000 and earlier models

resistance values will DECREASE. A problem in any of the ECT sensor circuits will set a diagnostic trouble code.

2 Make sure the ignition key is in the off position.

3 Drain the cooling system sufficiently to bring the coolant level below the ECT.

4 Disconnect the electrical connector and carefully unscrew the sensor **(see illustrations)**.

5 Wrap the threads of the new sensor with Teflon sealing tape (PTFE) to prevent leakage and thread corrosion.

Refitting

6 Refitting is the reverse of removal.

9.5 Location of the crankshaft position sensor harness connector (arrowed) on 2001 and later models

9.6 Location of the crankshaft position sensor (arrowed) on 2001 and later models

9 Crankshaft Position (CKP) sensor – removal and refitting

Removal

1 The Crankshaft Position sensor (CKP) determines the timing for the fuel injection and ignition on each cylinder. On 2000 and earlier models, the crankshaft position sensor is mounted under the timing belt cover, next to the crankshaft gear. On 2001 and later models, the sensor is mounted on the timing chain cover next to the crankshaft pulley. A problem in the crankshaft position sensor circuit will set a diagnostic trouble code (see Section 2).

2 Disconnect the cable from the negative battery terminal.

3 Working under the vehicle, remove the inner wheel arch liner (see Chapter 11).

4 The timing belt cover must be removed to access the sensor on 2000 and earlier models **(see illustrations)**. Refer to Chapter 2A for the timing belt cover removal procedure.

5 Disconnect the crankshaft position sensor electrical connector **(see illustration)**.

6 Remove the bolt and detach the sensor **(see illustration)**.

Refitting

7 Refitting is the reverse of removal.

10 Camshaft Position (CMP) sensor (1998 and later models) – removal and refitting

Removal

1 The Camshaft Position sensor determines the position of the No 1 piston in its cylinder for sequential fuel injection signals to each cylinder. The sensor is mounted on the cylinder head near the camshaft sprocket **(see illustrations)**. A problem in the camshaft position sensor circuit will set a diagnostic trouble code (see Section 2).

2 Make sure the ignition key is in the off position.

3 Remove the air filter housing (see Chapter 4A).

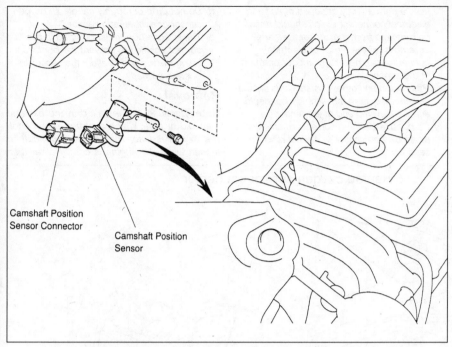

10.1a Camshaft position sensor mounting details on 2000 and earlier models

Camshaft Position
Sensor Connector

Camshaft Position
Sensor

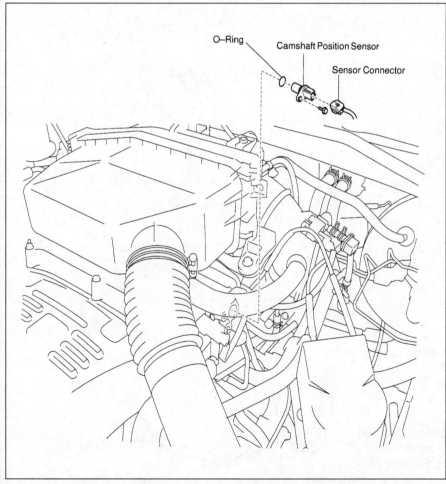

O–Ring

Camshaft Position Sensor

Sensor Connector

10.1b Camshaft position sensor mounting details on 2001 and later models

4 Disconnect the harness connector, remove the mounting screws and remove the camshaft sensor from the cylinder head **(see illustration)**.

Refitting

5 Refitting is a reversal of removal.

11 Oxygen sensor and air/fuel sensor – general information, and removal and refitting

General information

1 All vehicles covered by this manual have On-Board Diagnostics II (OBD-II) engine management systems, which means that they have the ability to verify the accuracy of the basic feedback loop between the oxygen sensor and the ECM. They accomplish this by using an oxygen sensor or air/fuel sensor ahead of the catalytic converter and an oxygen sensor behind the catalytic converter. By sampling the exhaust gas before and after the catalytic converter, the ECM can determine the efficiency of the converter and can even predict when it will fail.
2 The primary (upstream) oxygen sensor is located in the exhaust manifold and the secondary (downstream) oxygen sensor is located behind the catalytic converter. The downstream sensor on all models is a heated oxygen sensor **(see illustration overleaf)**. Some models are equipped with a heated upstream oxygen sensor. On 2001 and later models, the upstream sensor is an air/fuel sensor.
3 Don't confuse oxygen sensors and air/fuel sensors. They're similar in appearance, but they operate differently and have different operating characteristics. Like an oxygen sensor, the air/fuel sensor provides a variable voltage output to the ECM that's proportional to the air/fuel mixture ratio in the exhaust stream. The air/fuel sensor doesn't 'switch' back-and-forth like an oxygen sensor at the 14.7 to 1 stoichiometric threshold. Instead, it alters a ECM-controlled voltage between 3.3 volts (at the positive ECM terminal for the air/fuel sensor) and 3.0 volts (at the negative ECM terminal for the air/fuel sensor) in direct proportion to the amount of

10.4 Location of the camshaft sensor (arrowed) on 2001 and later models

oxygen in the exhaust. As the air/fuel mixture in the exhaust becomes leaner, the air/fuel sensor voltage increases (within its operating range of 3.0 to 3.3 volts). Like an oxygen sensor, the air/fuel sensor doesn't operate correctly until it's warmed up. Also, like an oxygen sensor, the air/fuel sensor has a heating element which enables it to warm-up quickly.

4 Special care must be taken whenever a sensor is serviced.

a) *Oxygen sensors and air/fuel sensors have a permanently attached pigtail and electrical connector which should not be removed from the sensor. Damage or removal of the pigtail or electrical connector can adversely affect operation of the sensor.*

b) *Grease, dirt and other contaminants should be kept away from the electrical connector and the louvered end of the sensor.*

c) *Do not use cleaning solvents of any kind on an oxygen sensor or air/fuel ratio sensor.*

d) *Do not drop or roughly handle an oxygen sensor or air/fuel ratio sensor.*

e) *The silicone boot must be fitted in the correct position to prevent the boot from being melted and to allow the sensor to operate properly.*

Removal

Note: *Because it is installed in the exhaust manifold or pipe, which contracts when cool, the oxygen sensor may be very difficult to loosen when the engine is cold. Rather than*

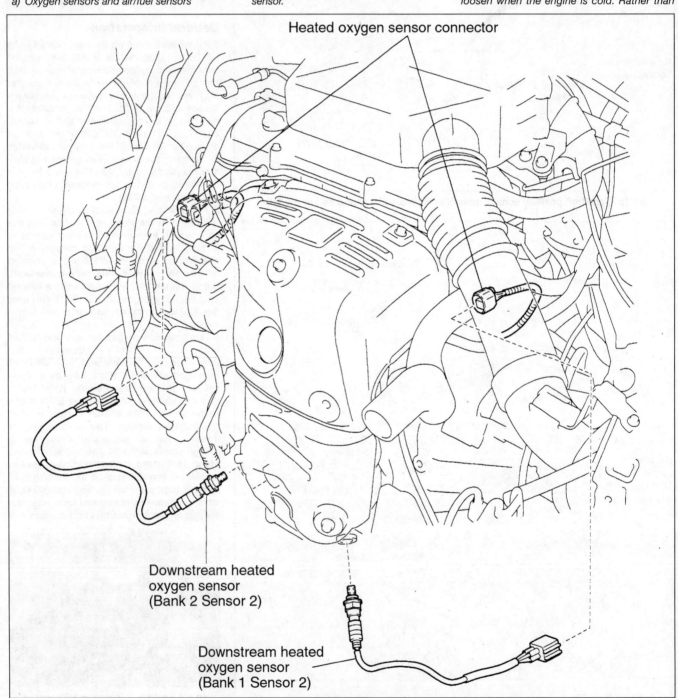

Heated oxygen sensor connector

Downstream heated oxygen sensor (Bank 2 Sensor 2)

Downstream heated oxygen sensor (Bank 1 Sensor 2)

11.2 Location of the downstream oxygen sensors on 2001 and later models

11.7 Location of the upstream oxygen sensor (arrowed) on bank number 2 on 2001 and later models

11.8a Location of the downstream oxygen sensor (arrowed) on bank number 1 on 2001 and later models

risk damage to the sensor (assuming you are planning to re-use it in another manifold or pipe), start and run the engine for a minute or two, then shut it off. Be careful not to burn yourself during the following procedure.

5 Disconnect the cable from the negative terminal of the battery.

6 If you're renewing the downstream sensor, raise the vehicle and secure it on axle stands. Access the oxygen sensor harness and then unplug the electrical connector.

7 The upstream sensor can be renewed without raising the vehicle **(see illustration)**. Unplug the sensor electrical connector.

8 Unscrew the sensor from the exhaust manifold or exhaust pipe **(see illustrations)**. **Note:** *The best tool for removing an oxygen sensor is a special slotted socket, especially if you're planning to re-use a sensor. If you don't have this tool, and you plan to re-use the sensor, be extremely careful when unscrewing the sensor.*

Refitting

9 Apply anti-seize compound to the threads of the sensor to facilitate future removal. The threads of new sensors should already be coated with this compound, but if you're planning to re-use an old sensor, recoat the threads. Fit the sensor and tighten it securely.

11.8b Use a slotted socket to remove the oxygen sensor from the exhaust manifold

10 Reconnect the electrical connector of the pigtail lead to the main wiring harness.

11 Lower the vehicle (if it was raised), test drive the car and verify that no trouble codes have been set.

12 Knock sensor – removal and refitting

Warning: Wait for the engine to cool completely before performing this procedure.

Removal

1 The knock control system is designed to reduce spark knock during periods of heavy detonation. This allows the engine to use optimal spark advance to improve driveability.

The knock sensor detects abnormal vibration in the engine and produces a voltage output which increases with the severity of the knock. The voltage signal is monitored by the ECM, which retards ignition timing until the detonation ceases. The knock sensor is located on the backside of the engine block, directly below the cylinder head (facing toward the rear of the engine compartment).

2 Disconnect the cable from the negative terminal of the battery.

3 Drain the cooling system (see Chapter 1A).

4 If you're working on a 2000 or earlier 4WD model, or any 2001 or later model, remove the intake manifold (see Chapter 2A or 2B). If you're working on a 2000 or earlier 2WD model, raise the front of the vehicle and support it securely on axle stands.

5 Disconnect the electrical connector and remove the knock sensor **(see illustrations)**.

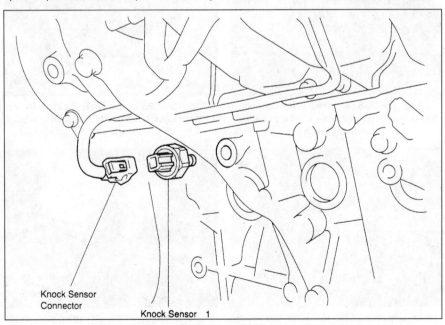

Knock Sensor Connector

Knock Sensor 1

12.5a Knock sensor details on 2000 and earlier models

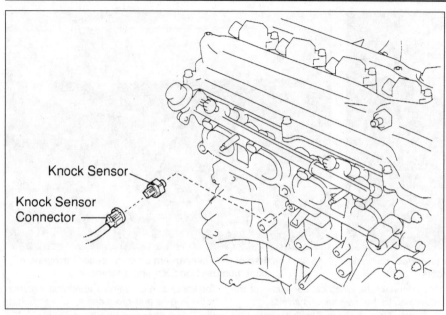

12.5b Knock sensor details on 2001 and later models

Refitting

6 If you're going to re-use the old sensor, coat the threads with thread sealant. New sensors are precoated with thread sealant, do not apply any additional sealant or the operation of the sensor may be affected.

7 Fit the knock sensor and tighten it securely (approximately 30 lbf ft/41 Nm). Don't overtighten the sensor or damage may occur. The remainder of refitting is the reverse of removal. Refill the cooling system and check for leaks.

13 Vehicle Speed Sensor (VSS) – removal and refitting

Removal

1 The Vehicle Speed Sensor (VSS) **(see illustrations)** is located on top of the transmission. This sensor is an electronic component that produces a pulsing voltage

signal whenever the sensor shaft is rotated. These voltage pulses are monitored by the ECM, which uses this information to help control the fuel and ignition systems and transmission shifting.

2 Disconnect the electrical connector from the VSS.

3 Unscrew the VSS from the transmission. Recover the O-ring and discard.

Refitting

4 Refitting is the reverse of removal, but fit a new O-ring.

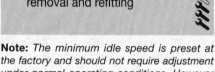

14 Idle Air Control (IAC) valve – removal and refitting

Note: *The minimum idle speed is preset at the factory and should not require adjustment under normal operating conditions. However if the throttle body has been renewed or you suspect the minimum idle speed has been tampered with (for example, if the idle speed screw was removed from the throttle body), have the vehicle checked by a dealer service department or other qualified repair garage.*

Removal

1 The engine idle speed is controlled by the Idle Air Control (IAC) valve **(see illustrations)**. The IAC valve controls the amount of air that bypasses the throttle plate into the intake manifold. The IAC valve is controlled by the ECM in accordance with the demands on the engine (air conditioning, power steering) and the operating conditions (cold or warmed-up).

2 Remove the throttle body (see Chapter 4A).

3 Remove the mounting screws and detach the IAC valve and gasket.

Refitting

4 Refitting is the reverse of removal. Be sure to use a new gasket when fitting the IAC valve.

15 Positive Crankcase Ventilation (PCV) system

1 The Positive Crankcase Ventilation (PCV) system **(see illustration)** reduces hydrocarbon emissions by scavenging crankcase vapours. It does this by circulating fresh air from the air cleaner through the crankcase, where it mixes with blow-by gases and is then rerouted through a PCV valve to the intake manifold.

2 The main components of the PCV system are the PCV valve, a blow-by filter and the vacuum hoses connecting these two components with the engine. Refer to illustrations 17.1a and 17.1b for locations of the PCV valve.

3 To maintain idle quality, the PCV valve restricts the flow when the intake manifold vacuum is high. If abnormal operating conditions (such as piston ring problems)

13.1a The VSS (arrowed) is located on top of the transmission – 2000 and earlier model shown

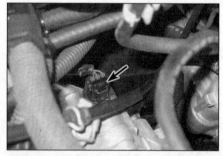

13.1b The VSS (arrowed) is located on top of the transmission – 2001 and later model shown

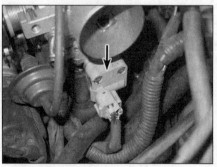

14.1a Location of the IAC valve (arrowed) on 2000 and earlier models

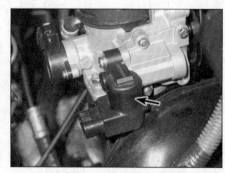

14.1b Location of the IAC valve (arrowed) on 2001 and later models

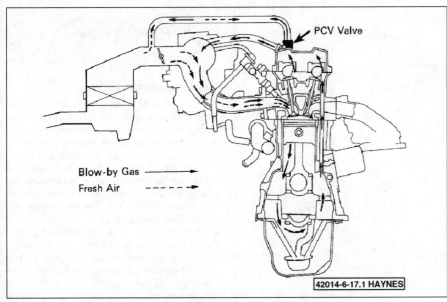

15.1 Vapour flow diagram of a typical PCV system

16.4 Location of the EGR valve (arrowed)

arise, the system is designed to allow excessive amounts of blow-by gases to flow back through the crankcase vent tube into the air cleaner to be consumed by normal combustion.

4 Checking and renewal of the PCV valve is covered in Chapter 1A.

16 Exhaust Gas Recirculation (2000 and earlier) – component description and renewal

General description

1 To reduce oxides of nitrogen (NOx) emissions, some of the exhaust gases are recirculated through the EGR valve to the intake manifold to lower combustion temperatures.

2 The EGR system consists of an EGR valve, an EGR modulator, a Vacuum Switching Valve (VSV) and the vacuum lines to the throttle body. The position of the EGR valve is controlled by vacuum which is controlled by the Engine Control Module (ECM). Refer to illustration 17.1a for the EGR component locations.

Removal and refitting

EGR valve

3 Remove the throttle body (see Chapter 4A).
4 Detach the vacuum hose from the EGR valve. Disconnect the EGR pipe, remove the EGR valve mounting bolts and remove the EGR valve from the intake manifold (see illustration). Check the valve for sticking and heavy carbon deposits. If the valve is sticking or clogged with deposits, clean or renew it.

Caution: Don't immerse the valve in solvent.
5 Refitting is the reverse of removal. Be sure to use new gaskets.

EGR vacuum modulator and modulator filter

6 Clearly label and disconnect the vacuum hoses to the EGR vacuum modulator. Remove the EGR vacuum modulator from its bracket.
7 If you're planning to re-use the old modulator, pull the cover off and check the filters (see illustrations). Clean them with compressed air and then refit the cover. If the filters cannot be cleaned, renew them or renew the modulator.
8 Refitting is the reverse of removal.

Vacuum Switching Valve (VSV)

9 Locate the VSV near the exhaust manifold (see illustration 17.1a). Unplug the electrical connector from the VSV. Clearly label and disconnect the vacuum hoses attached to the VSV.
10 Remove the VSV from its mounting bracket. If you have difficulty removing the VSV from the bracket, remove the bracket bolt, remove the entire assembly and separate the VSV from the bracket off the vehicle.
11 Refitting is the reverse of removal.

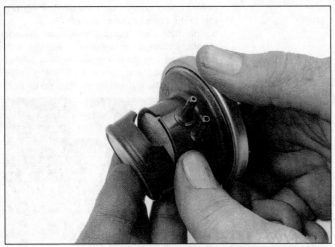

16.7a To remove the EGR vacuum modulator filters for cleaning, remove the cap . . .

16.7b . . . pull out the two filters and blow them out with compressed air; make sure the coarse side of the outer filter faces out when refitting the filters

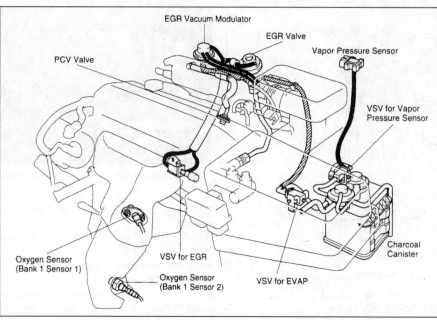

17.1a EVAP system component locations – 2000 and earlier models

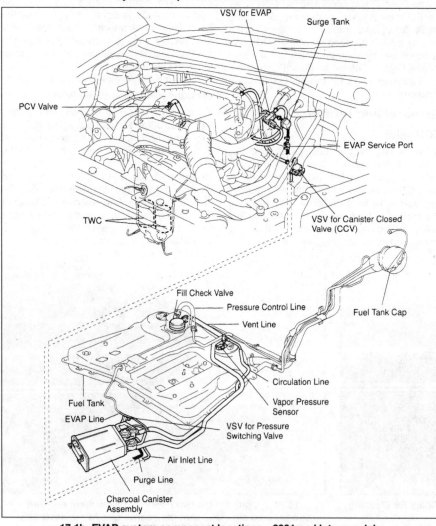

17.1b EVAP system component locations – 2001 and later models

17 Evaporative emissions control (EVAP) system

General description

1 The fuel evaporative emissions control (EVAP) system absorbs fuel vapours and, during engine operation, releases them into the engine intake where they mix with the incoming air-fuel mixture. On 2000 and earlier models, the charcoal canister is mounted in the engine compartment (see illustration). On 2001 and later models, the charcoal canister is mounted behind the fuel tank under the vehicle (see illustration).

2 When the engine is not operating, fuel vapours are transferred from the fuel tank, throttle body and intake manifold to the charcoal canister where they are stored. When the engine is running, the fuel vapours are purged from the canister by the purge control valve. The gases are consumed in the normal combustion process. The electronic purge control valve is directly controlled by the ECM.

3 The fuel filler cap is fitted with a two-way valve as a safety device. The valve vents fuel vapours to the atmosphere if the EVAP system fails.

4 The EVAP system also incorporates a vapour pressure sensor. This sensor detects abnormal vapour pressure in the system. On 2000 and earlier models, the vapour pressure sensor is mounted on the engine compartment firewall. On 2001 and later models, the vapour pressure sensor is mounted in the fuel pump/ sending unit assembly on top of the fuel tank.

5 After the engine has been running and warmed up to a preset temperature, the Vacuum Switching Valve (VSV) opens. The vacuum switching valve (purge control valve) allows intake manifold vacuum to draw the fuel vapours from the canister to the intake manifold, where they are mixed with intake air before being burned with the air/fuel mixture inside the combustion chambers.

6 The fuel tank vapour pressure sensor monitors changes in pressure inside the tank and, when the pressure exceeds a preset threshold, opens a vacuum switching valve (see illustrations), which allows a purge port

17.6a Location of the EVAP Vacuum Switching Valve (VSV) on 2000 and earlier models (arrowed)

in the canister to admit fuel tank vapours into the canister.

Removal and refitting

Charcoal canister

7 Disconnect the cable from the negative battery terminal.

8 On 2001 and later models, raise the rear of the vehicle and support it securely on axle stands.

9 Unplug all electrical connectors and clearly label and disconnect the vent hoses to the charcoal canister, remove the bolts and separate the canister from the engine compartment or the underside of the vehicle. Refer to the illustrations at the beginning of this section if necessary.

10 Refitting is the reverse of removal.

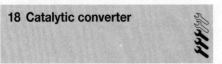

18 Catalytic converter

Note: *On 2001 and later models, the front catalytic converter is incorporated into the exhaust manifold. Refer to Chapter 2B for the exhaust manifold removal and refitting procedure.*

General description

1 The catalytic converter is an emission control device added to the exhaust system to reduce pollutants from the exhaust gas stream. There are two types of converters. The conventional oxidation catalyst reduces the levels of hydrocarbon (HC) and carbon monoxide (CO). The three-way catalyst lowers the levels of oxides of nitrogen (NOx) as well as hydrocarbons (HC) and carbon monoxide (CO). These models are equipped only with three-way catalytic converters.

Check

2 The test equipment for a catalytic converter is expensive and highly sophisticated. If you suspect that the converter on your vehicle is malfunctioning, take it to a dealer or authorised emissions inspection facility for diagnosis and repair.

3 Whenever the vehicle is raised for servicing of underbody components, check the converter for leaks, corrosion, dents and other damage. Check the welds/flange bolts that attach the front and rear ends of the converter to the exhaust system. If damage is discovered, the converter should be renewed.

4 Although catalytic converters don't break too often, they can become plugged. The easiest way to check for a restricted converter is to use a vacuum gauge to diagnose the effect of a blocked exhaust on intake vacuum.

a) *Connect a vacuum gauge to an intake manifold vacuum source (see Chapter 2D).*

b) *Warm the engine to operating temperature, place the transmission in Park (automatic) or Neutral (manual) and apply the handbrake.*

17.6b Location of the EVAP Vacuum Switching Valve (VSV) on 2001 and later models (arrowed)

c) *Note and record the vacuum reading at idle.*

d) *Quickly open the throttle to near full throttle and release it shut. Note and record the vacuum reading.*

e) *Perform the test three more times, recording the reading after each test.*

f) *If the reading after the fourth test is more than one in-Hg lower than the reading recorded at idle, the exhaust system may be restricted (the catalytic converter could be plugged or an exhaust pipe or silencer could be restricted).*

Removal and refitting

5 Be sure to spray the nuts on the exhaust flange studs before removing them from the catalytic converter.

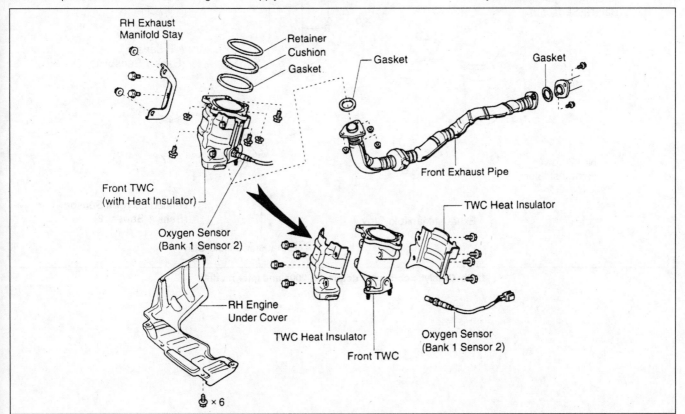

18.6a Catalytic converter details on 2000 and earlier models

6 Remove the nuts and separate the catalytic converter from the exhaust system **(see illustrations)**.

7 Refitting is the reverse of removal.

19 Accelerator Pedal Position (APP) sensor –
removal and refitting

Note: *The APP sensor is located at the upper end of the accelerator pedal assembly. The APP sensor and the accelerator pedal are removed as a single assembly.*

Removal

1 Disconnect the cable from the negative battery terminal (see Chapter 5, Section 1).
2 Disconnect the APP sensor electrical connector.
3 Remove the accelerator pedal/APP sensor assembly.

Refitting

4 Refitting is the reverse of removal. Be sure to tighten the accelerator pedal assembly mounting bolts securely.

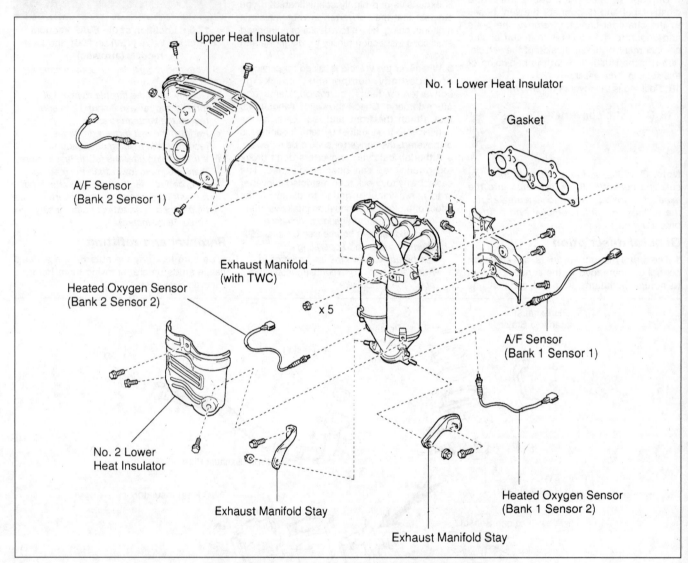

Upper Heat Insulator

No. 1 Lower Heat Insulator

Gasket

A/F Sensor
(Bank 2 Sensor 1)

Exhaust Manifold
(with TWC)

Heated Oxygen Sensor
(Bank 2 Sensor 2)

x 5

A/F Sensor
(Bank 1 Sensor 1)

No. 2 Lower
Heat Insulator

Exhaust Manifold Stay

Exhaust Manifold Stay

Heated Oxygen Sensor
(Bank 1 Sensor 2)

18.6b Catalytic converter details on 2001 and later models

Chapter 6 Part B:
Emissions and engine control systems – diesel engine

Contents

Section number

Accelerator pedal and position sensor – testing, removal and
   refitting 11
Airflow meter – removal, testing and refitting 3
Camshaft position sensor – testing, removal and refitting 9
Coolant temperature sensor – testing, removal and refitting 4
Crankcase ventilation system – general information 15
Crankshaft position sensor – testing, removal and refitting 10
Electronic Driving Unit – testing, removal and refitting 12
Engine Control Module – removal and refitting 13

Section number

Exhaust Gas Recirculation (EGR) system components – testing,
   removal and refitting 16
Fuel pressure limiter – general information 14
Fuel pressure sensor – testing 7
Fuel temperature sensor – testing and renewal 5
General information 1
Intake air temperature sensor – testing, removal and refitting 6
On-Board Diagnostic (OBD) system and trouble codes 2
Turbo pressure sensor – testing 8

Degrees of difficulty

Easy, suitable for novice with little experience	Fairly easy, suitable for beginner with some experience	Fairly difficult, suitable for competent DIY mechanic	Difficult, suitable for experienced DIY mechanic	Very difficult, suitable for expert DIY or professional

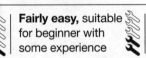

Specifications

Airflow meter

Resistance at 20°C	2.19 to 2.67 kohms
Resistance at 60°C	0.5 to 0.68 kohms

Fuel temperature sensor

Resistance at 40°C	0.5 to 3.0 ohms

Coolant and air temperature sensors

Resistance at 20°C	2000 to 3000 ohms
Resistance at 60°C	400 to 700 ohms

Electronic vacuum regulating valve

Resistance at 20°C	11 to 13 ohms

Camshaft and crankshaft position sensors

Resistance – cold (< 50°C)	1630 to 2740 ohms
Resistance – hot (>50°C)	2065 to 3225 ohms

Torque wrench settings	lbf ft	Nm
Air temperature sensor	25	34
Camshaft position sensor	7	9
Coolant temperature sensor	15	21
Crankshaft position sensor	7	9

1 General information

To prevent pollution of the atmosphere from incompletely burned fuel and to maintain good driveability and fuel economy, a number of emission control systems are incorporated **(see illustration)**. They include the:

Electronic engine control system.
Crankcase ventilation system.
Exhaust Gas Recirculation system.
Catalytic converters.

All of these systems are linked, directly or indirectly, to the emission control system.

The Sections in this Chapter include general descriptions, checking procedures within the scope of the home mechanic (when possible) and component renewal procedures for each of the systems listed above.

Before assuming that an emissions control system is malfunctioning, check the fuel system carefully. The diagnosis of some emission control devices requires specialised tools, equipment and training. If checking and servicing become too difficult or if a procedure is beyond your ability, consult a dealer service department or other properly-equipped repair facility. Remember, the most frequent cause of emissions problems is simply a loose or broken vacuum hose or

lead, so always check the hose and wiring connections first.

This doesn't mean, however, that emission control systems are particularly difficult to maintain and repair. You can quickly and easily perform many checks and do most of the regular maintenance at home with common hand tools. Pay close attention to any special precautions outlined in this Chapter. It should be noted that the illustrations of the various systems may not exactly match the system fitted on the vehicle you're working on because of changes made by the manufacturer during production or from year-to-year.

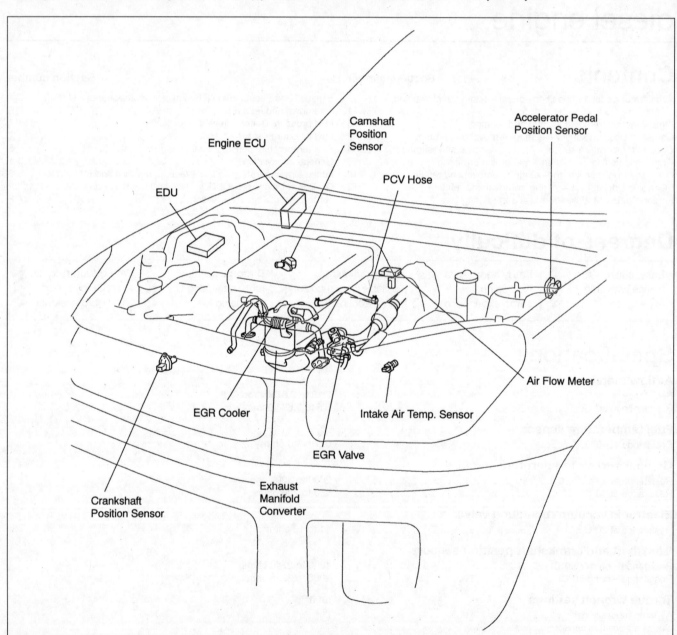

1.1 Emission and engine control system components – LHD shown

2 On-Board Diagnostic (OBD) system and trouble codes

Diagnostic tool information

1 A digital multimeter is necessary for checking fuel injection and emission related components. A digital volt-ohmmeter is preferred over the older style analogue multimeter for several reasons. The analogue multimeter cannot display the volts-ohms or amps measurement in hundredths and thousandths increments. When working with electronic circuits which are often very low voltage, this accurate reading is most important. Another good reason for the digital multimeter is the high impedance circuit. The digital multimeter is equipped with a high resistance internal circuitry (10 million ohms). Because a voltmeter is hooked up in parallel with the circuit when testing, it is vital that none of the voltage being measured should be allowed to travel the parallel path set up by the meter itself. This dilemma does not show itself when measuring larger amounts of voltage (9 to 12 volt circuits) but if you are measuring a low voltage circuit such as sensor signal voltage, a fraction of a volt may be a significant amount when diagnosing a problem. However, there are several exceptions where using an analogue voltmeter may be necessary to test certain sensors.

2 Hand-held scanners are the most powerful and versatile tools for analysing engine management systems used on later model vehicles. Each brand scan tool must be examined carefully to match the year, make and model of the vehicle you are working on. Often interchangeable cartridges are available to access the particular manufacturer (Ford, GM, Chrysler, etc). Some manufacturers will specify by continent (Asia, Europe, USA, etc).

3 The On-Board Diagnostic (OBD) facility built into the vehicles' electronic systems, can only be accessed by a dedicated scan tool. Although hand-held scan tools are now becoming generally available, your local dealer or specialist will have the necessary equipment to interrogate the OBD system.

On-Board Diagnostic system

4 All models described in this manual are equipped with the second generation On-Board Diagnostic system. The system consists of an on-board computer, known as the Engine Control Module (ECM), information sensors and output actuators.

5 The information sensors monitor various functions of the engine and send data to the ECM. Based on the data and the information programmed into the computer's memory, the ECM generates output signals to control various engine functions via control relays, solenoids and other output actuators. The ECM is specifically calibrated to optimise the emissions, fuel economy and driveability of the vehicle. It isn't a good idea to attempt diagnosis or renewal of the ECM at home while the vehicle is under warranty. Take the vehicle to a dealer service department if the ECM or a system component malfunctions.

Information sensors

Airflow meter

The airflow meter measures the amount of air passing through the sensor body and ultimately entering the engine. The ECM uses this information to control fuel injection quantity and turbocharger boost pressure.

Coolant temperature sensor

The engine coolant temperature sensor monitors engine coolant temperature. The ECM uses this information to control fuel injection quantity and timing.

Fuel temperature sensor

The fuel temperature sensor monitors the temperature of the fuel being delivered to the fuel injectors. The ECM uses this information to control fuel injection quantity and timing.

Intake air temperature sensor

The intake air temperature sensor monitors the temperature of the air entering the intake manifold. The ECM uses this information to control fuel injection quantity and timing.

Fuel pressure sensor

The fuel pressure sensor monitors the fuel pressure in the common rail. The ECM uses this information to control fuel injection quantity and timing.

Turbo pressure sensor

The turbo pressure sensor monitors the air pressure in the intake manifold. The ECM uses this information to control the turbocharger wastegate. The ECM calculates the engine torque needed depending on driver demand and engine operating conditions, and then adjusts the boost pressure to meet the demands.

Camshaft position sensor

The camshaft position sensor produces a signal which the ECM uses to identify number 1 cylinder and to time the sequential fuel injection.

Crankshaft position sensor

The crankshaft position sensor monitors crankshaft position (TDC) and speed during each engine revolution. The ECM uses this information to control fuel injection quantity and timing.

Accelerator pedal and position sensor

The throttle position sensor forms part of the accelerator pedal module, and senses throttle movement and position. The ECM uses this information to control fuel delivery and engine speed according to driver demand.

Vehicle speed sensor

The vehicle speed sensor provides information to the ECM to indicate vehicle speed.

Miscellaneous ECM inputs

In addition to the various sensors, the ECM monitors various switches and circuits to determine vehicle operating conditions. The switches and circuits include:
a) Air conditioning system.
b) Antilock brake system.
c) Barometric pressure sensor (inside ECM).
d) Battery voltage.
e) Brake switch.
f) Clutch pedal switch.
g) Cruise control system.
h) Park/neutral position switch.
i) Power steering pressure switch.

Output actuators

Check Engine light

The ECM will illuminate the CHECK ENGINE light if a malfunction in the electronic engine control system occurs.

Glow plugs

The ECM controls the operation of the glow plug system. The glow plugs allow the engine to start easily in cold conditions.

Turbocharger wastegate regulator valve

The ECM monitors intake manifold pressure and controls the turbocharger wastegate with the wastegate regulator valve. The engine control system calculates the engine torque needed depending on driver demand and engine operating conditions, the ECM will then adjust the boost pressure to meet the demands.

Obtaining trouble codes

Note: The diagnostic trouble codes on all models can only be extracted from the Engine Control Module (ECM) using a specialised diagnostic tool. Have the vehicle diagnosed by a dealer service department or other qualified repair facility if the proper tool is not available.

6 The ECM will illuminate the CHECK ENGINE light on the dash if it recognises a fault in the system. The light will remain illuminated until the problem is repaired and the code is cleared or the ECM does not detect any malfunction for several consecutive drive cycles.

7 The diagnostic codes for the On-Board Diagnostic (OBD) system can only be extracted from the ECM using a diagnostic tool. The tool is programmed to interface with the OBD system by plugging into the diagnostic connector (see Chapter 6A, Section 2). When used, the diagnostic tool has the ability to diagnose in-depth driveability problems. If the tool is not available and intermittent driveability problems exist, have the vehicle checked at a dealer service department or other qualified garage.

Clearing trouble codes

8 After the system has been repaired, the codes must be cleared from the ECM memory using a scan tool. Do not attempt to clear the codes by disconnecting battery power. If battery power is disconnected from the ECM, the ECM will lose the current engine operating parameters and driveability will suffer until the ECM is programmed with a scan tool.

9 Always clear the codes from the ECM before starting the engine after a new electronic emission control component is fitted onto the engine. The ECM stores the operating parameters of each sensor. The ECM may set a trouble code if a new sensor is allowed to operate before the parameters from the old sensor have been erased.

Diagnostic trouble codes

10 The accompanying list of diagnostic trouble codes is a compilation of all the codes that may be encountered using a generic scan tool. Additional trouble codes may be available with the use of the manufacturer-specific scan tool. Not all codes pertain to all models and not all codes will illuminate the CHECK ENGINE light when set. All models require a scan tool to access the diagnostic trouble codes.

Code	Code identification	Trouble area	Code	Code identification	Trouble area
12	Engine speed sensor circuit	Open or short in sensor circuit Camshaft position sensor Camshaft sprocket Engine ECM	35	Turbo pressure sensor circuit	Open or short in circuit Turbo pressure sensor Vacuum hose disconnected or blocked Engine ECM
13	Engine speed sensor circuit	Open or short in sensor circuit Crankshaft position sensor Crankshaft sprocket Engine ECM	39	Fuel temperature sensor circuit	Open or short in sensor circuit Fuel pressure sensor Engine ECM
15	Throttle control motor circuit	Open or short in throttle control motor circuit Throttle control motor Throttle valve Engine ECM	42	Vehicle speed sensor signal circuit	Open or short in sensor circuit Vehicle speed sensor Instrument cluster Engine ECM
19 (1 or 2)	Accelerator pedal position sensor circuit	Open or short in sensor circuit Accelerator pedal position sensor Engine ECM	49	Fuel pressure sensor circuit	Open or short in sensor circuit Fuel pressure sensor Engine ECM
22	Coolant temperature sensor circuit	Open or short in sensor circuit Coolant temperature sensor Engine ECM	51	Stop-light switch signal	Short Stop-light switch Engine ECM
24 (1)	Intake air temperature sensor circuit	Open or short in sensor circuit Intake air temperature sensor Engine ECM	71	EGR control circuit	Step motor Wire harness Engine ECM
24 (2)	Atmospheric temperature sensor circuit	Open or short in sensor circuit Atmospheric temperature sensor (in airflow meter) Engine ECM	78 (3)	Fuel pump circuit	Short in engine ECM SCV Engine ECM
31	Airflow meter circuit	Open or short in airflow meter circuit Airflow meter Engine ECM	78 (7)	Fuel line circuit	Fuel line Supply pump Common rail Injector Pressure limiter EDU Engine ECM
32	Injector correction resistance circuit	Open or short in circuit Injector correction resistance Engine ECM	78 (8)	Fuel pump circuit	Wire harness SCV Engine ECM
34 (2)	Turbocharger system malfunction	Turbocharger EGR valve Airflow meter Engine ECM	89	Interior IC malfunction	Engine ECM
			97	EDU circuit malfunction	Open or short in EDU circuit EDU Open or short in SCV circuit SCV Injector Engine ECM
34 (3)	Turbocharger sticking detected (closed)	Turbocharger EGR valve Airflow meter Engine ECM	99	Engine immobiliser system	Open or short in system circuit Transponder key amplifier Transponder key computer Transponder key coil Engine ECM
34 (4)	Turbocharger sticking detected (open)	Turbocharger EGR valve Airflow meter Engine ECM			

3 Airflow meter – removal, testing and refitting

Removal

1 The airflow meter is located in the outlet of the air cleaner top cover. First, disconnect the wiring **(see illustration)**.
2 Undo the screws and remove the airflow meter.

Testing

3 Using an ohmmeter as shown **(see illustration)**, check that the resistance of the airflow meter is as given in the Specifications.
4 Now reconnect the wiring and use a voltmeter to back-probe the terminals as shown **(see illustration)**. With the ignition switched on, blow air through the airflow meter and check that the voltage fluctuates.
5 If the airflow meter is faulty, renew it.

Refitting

6 Refitting is a reversal of removal.

4 Coolant temperature sensor – testing, removal and refitting

1 The coolant temperature sensor is located in the cylinder head, beneath the left-hand end of the intake manifold. The sensor is a thermistor (a resistor which varies the value of its resistance in accordance with temperature changes). The change in the resistance values will directly affect the voltage signal from the sensor to the ECM. As the sensor temperature INCREASES, the resistance values will DECREASE. As the sensor temperature DECREASES, the resistance values will INCREASE.

Testing

2 Check the terminals in the connector and

3.1 Disconnecting the wiring from the airflow meter

the wires leading to the sensor for looseness and breaks. Repair as required.
3 With the ignition switch off, disconnect the wiring plug from the intake air temperature sensor. Using an ohmmeter, measure the resistance between the terminals. With the engine cool (20°C), the resistance should be 2.0 to 3.0 kohms. Reconnect the wiring plug to the sensor, start the engine and warm it up until it reaches operating temperature. Disconnect the connector and check the resistance again. At 60°C the resistance should be 400 to 700 ohms. If the sensor resistance test results are incorrect, renew the engine coolant temperature sensor.

Removal

⚠️ **Warning: Wait until the engine is completely cool before beginning this procedure.**

4 Partially drain the cooling system (see Chapter 1B).
5 Disconnect the wiring plug from the sensor and use a 19 mm socket to unscrew the sensor from the cylinder head. Recover the seal.

Refitting

6 Refitting is a reversal of removal, but refill the cooling system (see Chapter 1B).

5 Fuel temperature sensor – testing and renewal

1 The fuel temperature sensor is a thermistor (a resistor which varies the value of its resistance in accordance with temperature changes). The change in the resistance values will directly affect the voltage signal from the sensor to the ECM. As the sensor temperature INCREASES, the resistance values will DECREASE. As the sensor temperature DECREASES, the resistance values will INCREASE.

Testing

2 The fuel temperature sensor is located in the high-pressure fuel pump body. It cannot be renewed separately. Check the terminals in the connector and the wires leading to the high-pressure pump for looseness and breaks. Repair as required.
3 With the ignition off, disconnect the wiring from the sensor.
4 Connect an ohmmeter between the terminals, and check that the resistance is 0.5 to 3.0 ohms.

Renewal

5 If the resistance is not as specified, the complete high-pressure fuel pump must be renewed as described in Chapter 4B. Note also that the fuel inlet pipe must also be renewed at the same time.

6 Intake air temperature sensor – testing, removal and refitting

1 The intake air temperature sensor is located in the air intake elbow on the left-hand end of the intake manifold. The sensor is a thermistor (a resistor which varies the value of its resistance in accordance with temperature

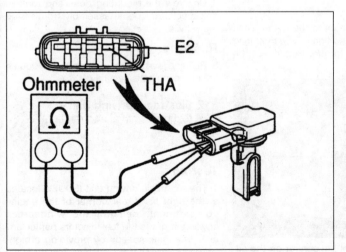

3.3 Checking the resistance of the airflow meter

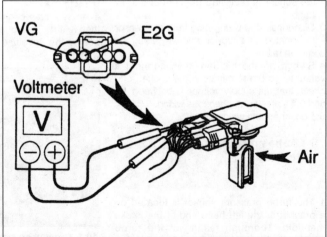

3.4 Using a voltmeter to check the operation of the airflow meter

changes). The change in the resistance values will directly affect the voltage signal from the sensor to the ECM. As the sensor temperature INCREASES, the resistance values will DECREASE. As the sensor temperature DECREASES, the resistance values will INCREASE.

Testing

2 Check the terminals in the connector and the wires leading to the sensor for looseness and breaks. Repair as required.
3 With the ignition switch off, disconnect the wiring plug from the intake air temperature sensor. Using an ohmmeter, measure the resistance between the terminals. With the engine cool (20°C), the resistance should be 2.0 to 3.0 kohms. Reconnect the wiring plug to the sensor, start the engine and warm it up until it reaches operating temperature. Disconnect the connector and check the resistance again. At 60°C the resistance should be 400 to 700 ohms. If the sensor resistance test results are incorrect, renew the temperature sensor.

Removal

4 Disconnect the wiring plug from the sensor and use a 22 mm socket to unscrew the sensor from the air intake elbow.

Refitting

5 Refitting is a reversal of removal, but tighten the sensor to the specified torque.

7 Fuel pressure sensor – testing

1 The fuel pressure sensor is located on the right-hand end of the common rail. It cannot be renewed separately, and if faulty, the complete common rail must be renewed.
2 Thorough testing of the fuel pressure sensor is best left to a Toyota dealer who will have the equipment necessary to make the check, however, the following check will determine if the sensor is receiving the correct supply voltage.
3 Disconnect the wiring plug from the sensor – it is located on a support mid-way along the common rail.
4 Switch on the ignition, then connect a voltmeter to the terminals in the socket, and check that the supply voltage is between 4.5 and 5.5 volts. If not, check the wiring.
5 Reconnect the wiring plug.

8 Turbo pressure sensor – testing

1 The turbo pressure sensor is located on a bracket at the left-hand end of the intake manifold. Thorough testing of the turbo pressure sensor is best left to a Toyota dealer who will have the equipment necessary to

9.3 Removing the camshaft position sensor

make the check, however, the following check will determine if the sensor is receiving the correct supply voltage.
2 Disconnect the wiring plug from the sensor.
3 Switch on the ignition, then connect a voltmeter to the terminals in the socket, and check that the supply voltage is between 4.5 and 5.5 volts. If not, check the wiring.
4 Reconnect the wiring plug.

9 Camshaft position sensor – testing, removal and refitting

Testing

1 The camshaft position sensor is located on a support bracket at the right-hand rear of the cylinder head.
2 Disconnect the wiring plug from the sensor, then connect an ohmmeter between the terminals on the sensor and check that the resistance is as given in the Specifications. If not, renew the sensor.

Removal

3 With the wiring plug disconnected, unscrew the mounting bolt and remove the sensor from the support bracket (see illustration).

Refitting

4 Apply a little engine oil to the O-ring seal, then refit the sensor and tighten the mounting bolt to the specified torque. Reconnect the wiring.

10.1 Crankshaft position sensor on the oil pump housing

10 Crankshaft position sensor – testing, removal and refitting

Testing

1 The crankshaft position sensor is located on the oil pump housing at the right-hand front of the engine (see illustration). Access is limited and is best gained by raising the front of the vehicle and supporting on axle stands.
2 Disconnect the wiring plug from the sensor, then connect an ohmmeter between the terminals on the sensor and check that the resistance is as given in the Specifications. If not, renew the sensor.

Removal

3 With the wiring plug disconnected, unscrew the mounting bolt and remove the sensor from the oil pump housing.

Refitting

4 Apply a little engine oil to the O-ring seal, then refit the sensor and tighten the mounting bolt to the specified torque. Reconnect the wiring.

11 Accelerator pedal and position sensor – testing, removal and refitting

Testing

1 The accelerator pedal and position sensor are integral as a single module. The sensor detects the opening angle of the accelerator pedal, and outputs a corresponding voltage to the engine ECM.
2 For reasons of safety, testing of the sensor is best left to a Toyota dealer.

Removal

3 Pull back the carpet as necessary for access, then disconnect the two wiring plugs.
4 Unscrew the mounting bolts and remove the accelerator pedal assembly from inside the vehicle.

Refitting

5 Refitting is a reversal of removal, but tighten the mounting bolts securely.

12 Electronic Driving Unit – testing, removal and refitting

Testing

1 The electronic driving unit (EDU) is located at the right-hand rear corner of the engine compartment, beneath the windscreen cowling. It drives the fuel injectors particularly at high engine speeds by providing a high-voltage, quick-charging system. Testing of the EDU system is best left to a Toyota dealer.

Removal

2 Remove the windscreen cowling with reference to Chapter 11.
3 Disconnect the two wiring plugs.
4 Unscrew the mounting bolts and remove the EDU.

Refitting

5 Refitting is a reversal of removal, but tighten the mounting bolts securely.

13 Engine Control Module – removal and refitting

Refer to Chapter 6A.

14 Fuel pressure limiter – general information

1 The fuel pressure limiter is located on the left-hand end of the high pressure common rail, where the fuel return hose is connected. To check the limiter, position a container beneath it then disconnect the hose.
2 Disconnect the wiring from the injectors, then crank the engine. No more than 10 cc/minute leakage of fuel is permitted, otherwise the complete common rail must be renewed.

15 Crankcase ventilation system – general information

1 When the engine is running, a certain amount of the gases produced during combustion escapes past the piston rings into the crankcase as blow-by gases. The crankcase ventilation system is designed to reduce the resulting hydrocarbon emissions (HC) by routing the gases and vapours from the crankcase into the intake manifold and combustion chambers, where they are consumed during engine operation.
2 Crankcase vapours pass through a hose connected from the valve cover to the air intake duct. The oil/air separator at the valve cover separates the oil suspended in the blow-by gases and allows the oil to drain back into the crankcase. The crankcase vapours are drawn from the oil/air separator through a hose connected to the air intake duct where they mix with the incoming air and are burned during the normal combustion process.
3 A blocked breather, valve or hose will cause excessive crankcase pressures resulting in oil

16.16a Withdraw the EGR valve from the studs ...

leaks and sludge build-up in the crankcase. Check the components for restrictions and clean or renew the components as necessary. Be sure to check the basic mechanical condition of the engine before condemning the crankcase ventilation system.

16 Exhaust Gas Recirculation (EGR) system components – testing, removal and refitting

1 The Exhaust Gas Recirculation (EGR) system is used to lower NOx (oxides of nitrogen) emission levels caused by high combustion temperatures. The EGR valve recirculates a small amount of exhaust gases into the intake manifold. The additional mixture lowers the temperature of combustion thereby reducing the formation of NOx compounds.
2 The EGR system consists of the EGR valve, EGR cooler tube (engine coolant-cooled), vacuum damper, electronic vacuum regulating valve, and the connecting vacuum hoses. The EGR valve is bolted to the left-hand end of the cylinder head. Vacuum for the system is supplied by the brake vacuum pump mounted on the left-hand end of the cylinder head.
3 The ECM controls the EGR flow rate by energising the EGR vacuum regulating valve. When the valve is energised vacuum is applied to the EGR valve, opening the EGR passage. The vacuum is cut by the ECM de-energising the EGR vacuum regulating valve.

Testing

Electronic vacuum regulating valve

4 The vacuum regulating valve may be checked in situ. First, disconnect the wiring plug.
5 Connect an ohmmeter between the two terminals on the valve, and check that the resistance is as given in the Specifications.
6 Using the ohmmeter, check that there is no

16.16b ... and remove the gasket

continuity between either of the terminals and the valve body.
7 Apply 6 volts DC to the terminals, then apply vacuum to the outlet (outer) port, and check that there is no interruption of the supply voltage.

EGR valve

8 Remove the EGR valve as described later in this Section.
9 Check the ports for heavy carbon deposits which can cause the internal shaft to stick. Clean as necessary.
10 Apply a vacuum of 7.9 in-Hg to the diaphragm chamber, and check that the internal shaft rises to open the upper intake port. Blow through the port and check that the passage is clear to the lower outlet port. Maintain the vacuum to check that the diaphragm holds the shaft open.
11 Refit the EGR valve as described later in this Section.

Removal

Electronic vacuum regulating valve

12 Disconnect the vacuum hoses and wiring plug.
13 Unscrew the mounting bolts and remove the valve from the EGR valve.

EGR valve

14 Remove the electronic vacuum regulating valve as described earlier.
15 Disconnect the vacuum hose from the diaphragm unit.
16 Unscrew the mounting bolt and nuts, and withdraw the EGR valve from the studs on the cylinder head. Remove the gasket and discard as a new one must be used on refitting **(see illustrations)**.

Refitting

17 Refitting is a reversal of removal. When refitting the EGR valve, renew the gasket and tighten the mounting nuts and bolt securely.

Chapter 7 Part A:
Manual transmission

Contents

	Section number		Section number
Gearchange cables – removal and refitting	2	Manual transmission overhaul – general information	6
Gearchange lever – removal and refitting	3	Oil seal renewal	See Chapter 7B
General information	1	Reversing light switch – check, removal and refitting	4
Lubricant change	See Chapter 1A or 1B	Transmission mountings – check, removal and	
Lubricant level check	See Chapter 1A or 1B	refitting	See Chapter 2A, 2B or 2C
Manual transmission – removal and refitting	5	Transmission oil cooler – removal and refitting	7

Degrees of difficulty

Easy, suitable for novice with little experience	Fairly easy, suitable for beginner with some experience	Fairly difficult, suitable for competent DIY mechanic	Difficult, suitable for experienced DIY mechanic	Very difficult, suitable for expert DIY or professional

Specifications

Torque wrench settings	lbf ft	Nm
Transmission-to-engine bolts:		
2000 and earlier (see illustrations 5.11a, 5.22a and 5.45a):		
Bolts A	47	64
Bolt B	26	35
Bolts C	22	30
Bolt D	34	46
Bolt E	18	25
Bolts F	7	9
Bolts G (where fitted)	27	37
2001 and later (see illustrations 5.11b, 5.22b and 5.45b):		
Bolts A	47	64
Bolts B	34	46
Bolts C (where fitted)	32	44

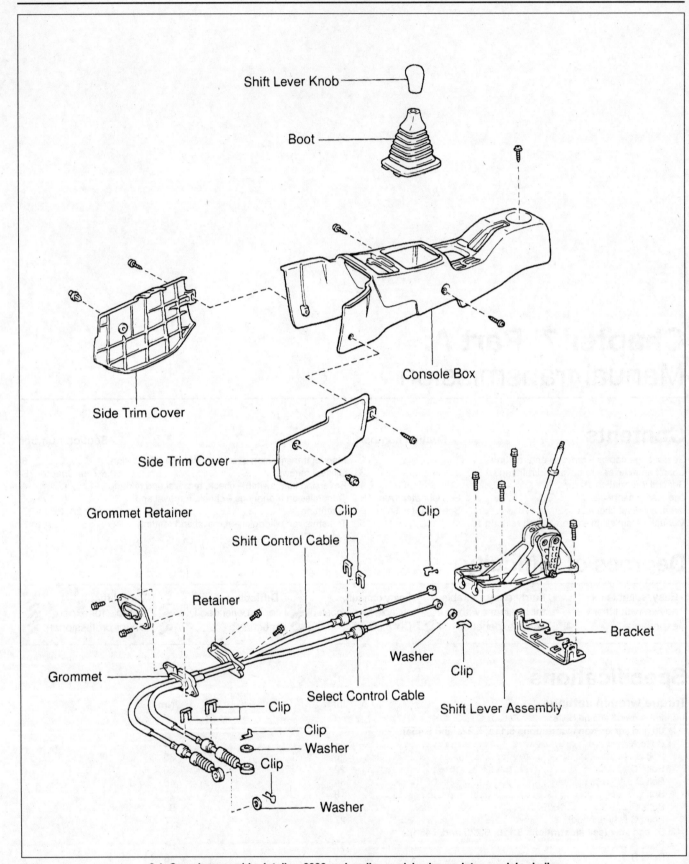

Shift Lever Knob

Boot

Console Box

Side Trim Cover

Side Trim Cover

Grommet Retainer

Shift Control Cable

Clip

Clip

Retainer

Grommet

Washer

Clip

Select Control Cable

Shift Lever Assembly

Bracket

Clip

Clip

Washer

Clip

Washer

2.1 Gearchange cable details – 2000 and earlier models shown, later models similar

1 General information

The vehicles covered by this manual are equipped with a 5-speed manual transmission or a 4-speed automatic transmission. Information on the manual transmission is included in this Part of Chapter 7. Service procedures for the automatic transmission are contained in Chapter 7B.

The manual transmission is a compact, two-piece, lightweight aluminium alloy housing containing both the transmission and differential assemblies.

Because of the complexity, unavailability of parts and special tools necessary, internal repair procedures for the manual transmission are beyond the scope of this manual. The bulk of information in this Chapter is devoted to removal and refitting procedures.

2 Gearchange cables – removal and refitting

Note: *The gearchange cables are not adjustable. If they become stretched or worn, causing gearchanging problems, they must be renewed.*

1 In the engine compartment, remove the retaining clips and washers and disconnect the gearchange cables from the selecting bellcrank **(see illustration)**.
2 Remove the cable retainers from the cable bracket. Also, on 2000 and earlier models, follow the cables to the bulkhead and unbolt the cable grommet retainer.
3 Remove the centre console (see Chapter 11).
4 Remove the cable housing clips from the gearchange lever base.
5 Remove the retaining clips and washers from the cable ends and disconnect the cables from the gearchange lever assembly.
6 Trace the cables to the bulkhead and unbolt the interior grommet retainer. Pull the cable assembly through the bulkhead.
7 Refitting is the reverse of removal.

3 Gearchange lever – removal and refitting

1 Remove the centre console (see Chapter 11).
2 Remove the gearchange cable retainers and disconnect both cables from the gearchange lever (see Section 2).
3 Remove the retaining bolts from the gearchange lever base **(see illustration 2.1)** and detach the gearchange lever from the vehicle.
4 Refitting is the reverse of removal.

4.1 The reversing light switch is threaded into the top of the transmission case

4 Reversing light switch – check, removal and refitting

Check

1 The reversing light switch is located on top of the transmission **(see illustration)**.
2 Turn the ignition key to the On position and move the gearchange lever to the Reverse position. The switch should close the reversing light circuit and turn on the reversing lights.
3 If it doesn't, check the reversing light fuse (see Chapter 12).
4 If the fuse is good, unplug the electrical connector from the switch and, using an ohmmeter, check continuity of the switch with the gearchange lever in Neutral and then in Reverse. The meter should indicate continuity when the gearchange lever is in Reverse only. If it doesn't, renew the switch.
5 If the switch is working properly, check the wire between the fuse and the switch; if there is voltage, note whether one or both reversing lights have failed.
6 If neither bulb lights up, the bulbs could be the problem, but it's more likely that the wire between the switch and the bulbs has an open circuit somewhere.

Removal and refitting

7 Disconnect the electrical connector from the reversing light switch.
8 Unscrew the switch from the case.
9 To test the new switch before refitting, simply check continuity across the switch

terminals: with the plunger depressed, there should be continuity; with the plunger free, there should be no continuity.
10 Screw in the new switch and tighten it securely.
11 Connect the electrical connector.
12 Check the operation of the reversing lights.

5 Manual transmission – removal and refitting

2WD models

Removal

1 Disconnect the negative cable from the battery.
2 Remove the air filter housing (see Chapter 4A or 4B). Remove the coolant reservoir (see Chapter 3).
3 Loosen the driveshaft/hub nuts (see Chapter 8) and the wheel nuts.
4 Remove the clutch release cylinder and the clutch hydraulic line (see Chapter 8).
Caution: Do not depress the clutch pedal while the release cylinder is detached from the transmission.
5 Unplug the electrical connector from the reversing light switch (see Section 4) and the speed sensor.
6 Remove the earth cable retaining bolt and detach the earth cable from the transmission.
7 Disconnect the gearchange cables from the transmission (see Section 2).
8 Detach any wire harness clamps from the engine and/or transmission and set the harnesses aside.
9 Remove the starter (see Chapter 5).
10 Attach a hoist to the lifting hook at the transmission end of the engine. If no hook is provided, use a bolt of the proper size and thread pitch to attach the hoist to a hole at the end of the cylinder head. The engine must be supported at all times while the transmission is out of the vehicle.
11 Remove the upper transmission-to-engine mounting bolts **(see illustrations)**. Note the location of any earth connectors or brackets, so that they may be refitted in their original location.

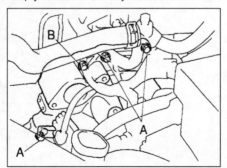

5.11a Upper transmission-to-engine bolts – 2000 and earlier 2WD models

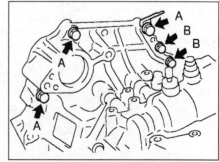

5.11b Upper transmission-to-engine bolts – 2001 and later 2WD models

12 Unbolt the left engine mounting from the transmission (see the appropriate part of Chapter 2).

13 Raise the vehicle and support it securely on axle stands. Remove the wheels and the under-vehicle splash shields.

14 Drain the transmission fluid (see Chapter 1A or 1B). Remove the driveshafts (see Chapter 8).

15 Remove the front exhaust pipe (see Chapter 4A or 4B).

16 Disconnect the lubricant cooler hoses from the transmission, if equipped. Be prepared for spillage, and plug the hoses and the lines on the transmission.

17 Unbolt the steering gear from the suspension crossmember. Support the steering gear from above with a length of rope or wire. **Note:** *You can tie the rope or wire to the hoist* **(see illustration).**

18 Remove the front suspension crossmember (see Chapter 10) and the longitudinal crossmember.

19 On 2000 and earlier models, remove the stiffener plate and the engine end plate.

20 Support the transmission with a jack (preferably a special jack made for this purpose; these jacks are available at most equipment rental yards). Safety chains will help steady the transmission on the jack.

21 Remove the left power train mounting and the mounting bracket.

22 Remove the rest of the bolts securing the transmission to the engine **(see illustrations)**.

23 Make a final check that all wires and hoses have been disconnected from the transmission.

24 Lower the left-hand end of the engine while simultaneously lowering the transmission, then roll the transmission and jack toward the side of the vehicle. Once the input shaft is clear of the splines in the clutch hub, lower the transmission and remove it from under the vehicle. Try to keep the transmission as level as possible.

25 The clutch components can now be inspected (see Chapter 8). In most cases, new clutch components should be routinely fitted whenever the transmission is removed.

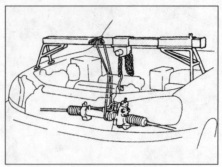

5.17 After unbolting the steering gear from the crossmember, support it with a length of wire or rope from the hoist

Refitting

26 Refitting of the transmission is a reversal of the removal procedure, but note the following points:

a) *Apply a little high-temperature grease to the splines on the transmission input shaft.*

b) *Tighten the transmission mounting bolts to the torque values listed in this Chapter's Specifications.*

c) *Tighten the suspension crossmember mounting bolts and the steering gear fasteners to the torque values listed in the Chapter 10 Specifications.*

d) *Tighten the driveshaft/hub nuts to the torque value listed in the Chapter 8 Specifications.*

e) *Tighten the wheel nuts to the torque listed in the Chapter 1A or 1B Specifications.*

f) *Fill the transmission with the correct type and amount of lubricant as described in Chapter 1A or 1B.*

4WD models

⚠ **Warning 1: Petrol is extremely flammable (as is diesel fuel to a lesser degree) so take extra precautions when you work on any part of the fuel system. Don't smoke or allow open flames or bare light bulbs near the work area, and don't work in a garage where a gas-type appliance (such as a**

water heater or a clothes dryer) is present. Since petrol is carcinogenic, wear latex gloves when there's a possibility of being exposed to fuel, and, if you spill any fuel on your skin, rinse it off immediately with soap and water. Mop-up any spills immediately and do not store fuel-soaked rags where they could ignite. The fuel system is under constant pressure, so, if any fuel lines are to be disconnected, the fuel pressure in the system must be relieved first. When you perform any kind of work on the fuel system, wear safety glasses and have a Class B type fire extinguisher on hand.**

⚠ **Warning 2: The air conditioning system is under high pressure – have an air conditioning specialist evacuate the system and recover the refrigerant before disconnecting any of the hoses or fittings.**

Note: *Transmission removal on 4WD models is a difficult job, especially for the do-it-yourself mechanic working at home. Because of the vehicle's design, the manufacturer states that the engine and transmission have to be removed as a unit from the bottom of the vehicle, not the top. With a jack and axle stands the vehicle can't be raised high enough and supported safely enough for the engine/transmission assembly to slide out from underneath. The manufacturer recommends that removal of the engine/transmission assembly only be performed on a vehicle hoist.*

27 Disconnect the cable from the negative terminal of the battery. Remove the bonnet (see Chapter 11).

28 Refer to Chapter 2D, *Engine – removal and refitting*, for information on the preliminary engine removal procedure, such as disconnecting electrical connectors, control cables and hoses. Make sure no hoses or wires are attached to the engine or transmission from above.

29 Loosen the driveshaft/hub nuts and the wheel nuts. Remove the wheels.

30 Detach the gearchange cables from the transmission (see Section 2).

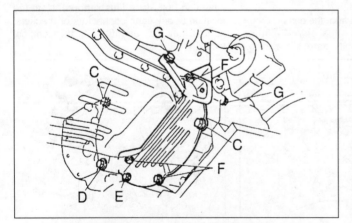

5.22a Lower transmission-to-engine bolts – 2000 and earlier 2WD models

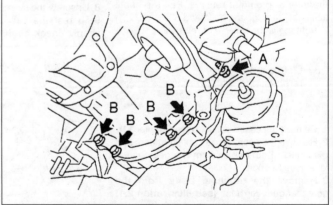

5.22b Lower transmission-to-engine bolts – 2001 and later 2WD models

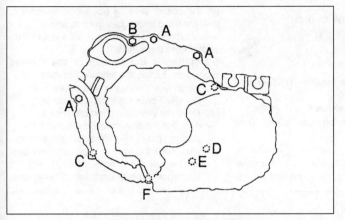

**5.45a Transmission-to-engine bolts –
2000 and earlier 4WD models**

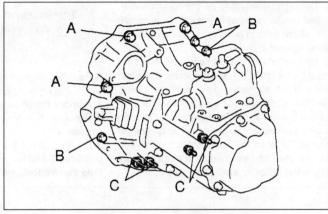

**5.45b Transmission-to-engine bolts –
2001 and later 4WD models**

31 Raise the vehicle on the hoist.

32 Remove the under-vehicle splash shield(s).

33 Remove the driveshaft and driveshafts (see Chapter 8).

34 If you're working on a 2000 or earlier model, remove the power steering pump and suspend it out of the way (see Chapter 10).

35 Remove the front section of the exhaust system (see Chapter 4A or 4B).

36 Remove the suspension crossmember and longitudinal crossmember.

37 Lower the vehicle and attach an engine hoist to the engine/transmission assembly. Make sure the hoist chain or sling is long enough to allow the engine/transmission assembly to be lowered to the ground.

38 Unbolt the right and left engine mountings from the engine/transmission assembly (see the appropriate part of Chapter 2).

39 Lower the engine/transmission assembly to the ground, then disconnect the hoist.

40 Raise the vehicle on the hoist and remove the engine/transmission assembly out from underneath.

41 Remove the starter.

42 Label and disconnect all electrical connectors from the transmission.

43 Label and disconnect the vacuum hoses from the transfer vacuum actuator, then unbolt and remove the actuator.

44 On 2000 and earlier models, unbolt all three stiffener plates from the transmission and transfer case. On 2001 and later models, remove the single stiffener plate.

45 Remove the transmission-to-engine bolts **(see illustrations)**. **Note:** *Note the locations of the bolts so they can be returned to their original positions when the transmission is refitted.*

46 Separate the transmission from the engine. On 2000 and earlier models, pull the transmission approximately two to three inches away from the engine, swing the left end of the transmission back, then continue to pull the transmission away from the engine **(see illustrations)**.

47 Refitting is the reverse of the removal procedure, noting the points listed in paragraph 26.

6   Manual transmission overhaul – general information

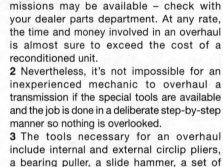

1 Overhauling a manual transmission is a difficult job for the do-it-yourselfer. It involves the disassembly and reassembly of many small parts. Numerous clearances must be precisely measured and, if necessary, changed with select-fit spacers and snap-rings. As a result, if transmission problems arise, it can be removed and refitted by a competent do-it-yourselfer, but overhaul should be left to a transmission repair specialist. Reconditioned transmissions may be available – check with your dealer parts department. At any rate, the time and money involved in an overhaul is almost sure to exceed the cost of a reconditioned unit.

2 Nevertheless, it's not impossible for an inexperienced mechanic to overhaul a transmission if the special tools are available and the job is done in a deliberate step-by-step manner so nothing is overlooked.

3 The tools necessary for an overhaul include internal and external circlip pliers, a bearing puller, a slide hammer, a set of pin punches, a dial indicator and possibly a hydraulic press. In addition, a large, sturdy workbench and a vice or transmission stand will be required.

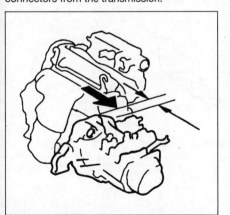

5.46a When removing the transmission from the engine on 2000 and earlier 4WD models, pull it away from the engine approximately two or three inches . . .

5.46b . . . move the end of the transmission in the direction of the arrow . . .

5.46c . . . then continue to separate the transmission from the engine

4 During disassembly of the transmission, make careful notes of how each piece comes off, where it fits in relation to other pieces and what holds it in place.

5 Before taking the transmission apart for repair, it will help if you have some idea what area of the transmission is malfunctioning. Certain problems can be closely tied to specific areas in the transmission, which can make component examination and renewal easier. Refer to the *Troubleshooting* section at the rear of this manual for information regarding possible sources of trouble.

7 Transmission oil cooler – removal and refitting

Note: *This procedure applies to 2000 and earlier 4WD models only.*

1 Remove the under-vehicle splash shields.

2 Remove the front bumper cover (see Chapter 11).

3 Using a flare nut spanner if available, unscrew the union nuts from the oil cooler **(see illustration)**. Hold the stationary fittings

on the cooler with an open-end spanner to prevent the cooler tubes from twisting.

4 Unbolt the cooler clamps and detach the cooler from the vehicle.

5 Refitting is the reverse of the removal procedure, noting the following points:

a) *Install new O-rings on the cooler line fittings. Tighten the fittings securely.*

b) *Drive the vehicle a short distance to circulate the transmission lubricant through the cooler, then park the vehicle and check the transmission lubricant level as described in Chapter 1A or 1B. Add the proper type of lubricant as necessary.*

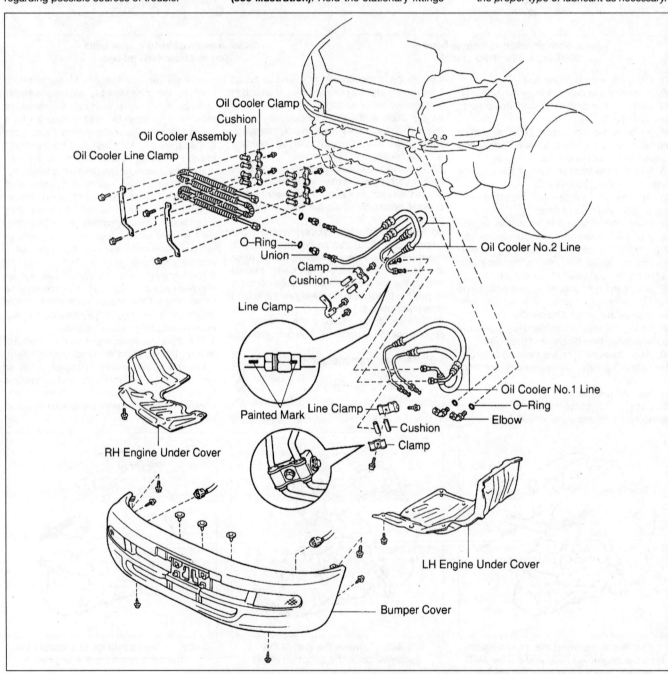

7.3 Transmission oil cooler details – 2000 and earlier 4WD models

Chapter 7 Part B:
Automatic transmission

Contents

Section number

Automatic transmission – removal and refitting. 8
Automatic transmission fluid and filter change . See Chapter 1A or 1B
Automatic transmission fluid level check. . . . . . See Chapter 1A or 1B
Automatic transmission overhaul – general information 9
Automatic transmission/differential lubricant level
　 check/change. . . . . See Chapter 1A or 1B
Diagnosis – general 2

Section number

General information 1
Oil seal renewal 3
Park/Neutral Position (PNP) switch – adjustment, removal and
　 refitting 6
Shift cable – removal, refitting and adjustment 5
Shift lock system – description and check. 7
Throttle Valve (TV) cable – check, adjustment, removal and refitting 4

Degrees of difficulty

Easy, suitable for novice with little experience 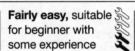	Fairly easy, suitable for beginner with some experience 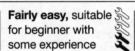	Fairly difficult, suitable for competent DIY mechanic 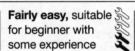	Difficult, suitable for experienced DIY mechanic 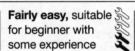	Very difficult, suitable for expert DIY or professional

Specifications

Shift lock system

Shift lock solenoid resistance.	26 to 33 ohms
Key interlock solenoid resistance.	12.5 to 16.5 ohms

Torque wrench settings

	lbf ft	Nm
Manual valve retaining bolts (4WD models)	8	11
Park/Neutral Position switch	4	6
Torque converter-to-driveplate bolts:		
1996 to 2000.	20	27
2001 and later:		
2WD models	32	43
4WD models	30	40
Transmission-to-engine bolts (1996 to 2000):		
2WD:		
Three upper bolts	47	64
Lower rear bolts		
Small	18	25
Large	34	46
4WD:		
14 mm head bolts.	47	64
12 mm head bolts.	34	46
Transfer case-to-transmission bolts	27	37
Transmission-to-engine bolts (2001 and later):		
Three upper bolts	47	64
Four lower bolts	32	44
Two rear-side bolts	34	46
Valve body bolts.	8	11

1 General information

All information on the automatic transmission is included in this Part of Chapter 7. Information for the manual transmission can be found in Part A of this Chapter.

Because of the complexity of the automatic transmissions and the specialised equipment necessary to perform most service operations, this Chapter contains only those procedures related to general diagnosis, routine maintenance, adjustment, and removal and refitting.

If the transmission requires major repair work, it should be left to a dealer service department or an automatic transmission repair specialist. Once properly diagnosed you can, however, remove and refit the transmission yourself and save the expense, even if the repair work is done by a transmission specialist.

2 Diagnosis – general

Note: *Automatic transmission malfunctions may be caused by five general conditions: poor engine performance, improper adjustments, hydraulic malfunctions, mechanical malfunctions or malfunctions in the computer or its signal network. Diagnosis of these problems should always begin with a check of the easily repaired items: fluid level and condition (see Chapter 1A or 1B), shift linkage adjustment and, on 2000 and earlier models, throttle valve linkage adjustment. Next, perform a road test to determine if the problem has been corrected or if more diagnosis is necessary. Because the transmission relies on many sensors in the engine control system, and since the transmission shift points are controlled by the Engine Control Module (2001 and later models), you'll also want to check to see if any trouble codes have been stored on the ECM (see Chapter 6A or 6B for a list of trouble codes and how to extract them). If the problem persists after the preliminary tests and corrections are completed, additional diagnosis should be done by a dealer service department or automatic transmission repair specialist. Refer to the 'Troubleshooting' section at the rear of this manual for information on symptoms of transmission problems.*

Preliminary checks

1 Drive the vehicle to warm the transmission to normal operating temperature.
2 Check the fluid level as described in Chapter 1A or 1B:
   a) *If the fluid level is unusually low, add enough fluid to bring the level within the designated area of the dipstick, then check for external leaks (see below).*
   b) *If the fluid level is abnormally high, drain off the excess, then check the drained fluid for*

contamination by coolant. The presence of engine coolant in the automatic transmission fluid indicates that a failure has occurred in the internal radiator walls that separate the coolant from the transmission fluid (see Chapter 3).
   c) *If the fluid is foaming, drain it and refill the transmission, then check for coolant in the fluid, or a high fluid level.*
3 Check the engine idle speed. **Note:** *If the engine is malfunctioning, do not proceed with the preliminary checks until it has been repaired and runs normally.*
4 Check the throttle valve cable for freedom of movement (2000 and earlier models only). Adjust it if necessary (see Section 4). **Note:** *The throttle valve cable may function properly when the engine is shut off and cold, but it may malfunction once the engine is hot. Check it cold and at normal engine operating temperature.*
5 Inspect the shift cable (see Section 5). Make sure that it's properly adjusted and that the cable operates smoothly.

Fluid leak diagnosis

6 Most fluid leaks are easy to locate visually. Repair usually consists of renewing a seal or gasket. If a leak is difficult to find, the following procedure may help.
7 Identify the fluid. Make sure it's transmission fluid and not engine oil or brake fluid (automatic transmission fluid is a deep red colour).
8 Try to pinpoint the source of the leak. Drive the vehicle several miles, then park it over a large sheet of cardboard. After a minute or two, you should be able to locate the leak by determining the source of the fluid dripping onto the cardboard.
9 Make a careful visual inspection of the suspected component and the area immediately around it. Pay particular attention to gasket mating surfaces. A mirror is often helpful for finding leaks in areas that are hard to see.
10 If the leak still cannot be found, clean the suspected area thoroughly with a degreaser or solvent, then dry it.
11 Drive the vehicle for several miles at normal operating temperature and varying speeds. After driving the vehicle, visually inspect the suspected component again.
12 Once the leak has been located, the cause must be determined before it can be properly repaired. If a gasket is renewed but the sealing flange is bent, the new gasket will not stop the leak. The bent flange must be straightened.
13 Before attempting to repair a leak, check to make sure that the following conditions are corrected or they may cause another leak. **Note:** *Some of the following conditions cannot be fixed without highly specialised tools and expertise. Such problems must be referred to a transmission specialist or a dealer service department.*

Gasket leaks

14 Check the sump periodically. Make sure

the bolts are tight, no bolts are missing, the gasket is in good condition and the sump is flat (dents in the sump may indicate damage to the valve body inside).
15 If the sump gasket is leaking, the fluid level or the fluid pressure may be too high, the vent may be plugged, the sump bolts may be too tight, the sump sealing flange may be warped, the sealing surface of the transmission housing may be damaged, the gasket may be damaged or the transmission casting may be cracked or porous. If sealant instead of gasket material has been used to form a seal between the sump and the transmission housing, it may be the wrong sealant.

Seal leaks

16 If a transmission seal is leaking, the fluid level or pressure may be too high, the vent may be plugged, the seal bore may be damaged, the seal itself may be damaged or improperly fitted, the surface of the shaft protruding through the seal may be damaged or a loose bearing may be causing excessive shaft movement.
17 Make sure the dipstick tube seal is in good condition and the tube is properly seated. Periodically check the area around the speedometer gear or sensor for leakage. If transmission fluid is evident, check the O-ring for damage.

Case leaks

18 If the case itself appears to be leaking, the casting is porous and will have to be repaired or renewed.
19 Make sure the oil cooler hose fittings are tight and in good condition.

Fluid comes out vent pipe or fill tube

20 If this condition occurs, the transmission is overfilled, there is coolant in the fluid, the case is porous, the dipstick is incorrect, the vent is plugged or the drain-back holes are plugged.

3 Oil seal renewal

1 Oil leaks frequently occur due to wear of the driveshaft oil seals and/or the speedometer drive gear oil seal and O-rings. Renewal of these seals is relatively easy, since the repairs can be performed without removing the transmission from the vehicle.

Driveshaft oil seals

2 The driveshaft oil seals are located on the sides of the transmission, where the inner ends of the driveshafts are splined into the differential side gears. If you suspect that a driveshaft oil seal is leaking, raise the vehicle and support it securely on axle stands. If the seal is leaking, you'll see lubricant on the side of the transmission, below the seal.

3 Remove the driveshaft (see Chapter 8).
4 Using a screwdriver or lever, carefully prise the oil seal out of the transmission bore **(see illustration)**.
5 If the oil seal cannot be removed with a screwdriver or lever, a special oil seal removal tool (available at car accessory shops) will be required.
6 Using a seal installation tool, a large section of pipe or a large deep socket as a drift, fit the new oil seal. Drive it into the bore squarely to the proper depth **(see illustration)**:

1996 to 2000 2WD models

Right side: 0 (flush with the case) +/- 0.5 mm
Left side: 5.2 +/- 0.5 mm

1996 to 2000 4WD models

Either side: 0 (flush with the case) +/- 0.5 mm

2001 and later 2WD models

Either side: 0 (flush with the case) +/- 0.5 mm

2001 and later 4WD models

Right side: 1.0 +/- 0.5 mm
Left side: 0 (flush with the case) +/- 0.5 mm

7 Lubricate the lip of the new seal with multipurpose grease, then refit the driveshaft (see Chapter 8). Be careful not to damage the lip of the new seal.

Speed sensor O-ring

8 There are two speed sensors mounted on the transmission; one is an input turbine speed sensor which monitors the rotational speed of the input shaft, the other monitors the rotational speed of the output shaft (driveshaft). They are both mounted in a similar fashion, using a hold-down bolt and sealed by an O-ring. Look for lubricant around the sensor housing to determine if the O-ring is leaking.
9 Unplug the electrical connector and unbolt the vehicle speed sensor from the transmission **(see illustration)**.
10 Using a scribe or a small screwdriver, remove the O-ring from the sensor **(see illustration)** and fit a new O-ring. Lubricate the new O-ring with automatic transmission fluid to protect it during refitting of the sensor.
11 Refitting is the reverse of removal.

Extension housing oil seal (4WD models only)

12 Remove the propeller shaft (see Chapter 8).
13 Using a seal removal tool or a large screwdriver, carefully prise the oil seal out of the extension housing. Do not damage the splines on the transfer output shaft.
14 Using a seal driver, a large section of pipe or a very large deep socket as a drift, fit the new oil seal. Drive it into the bore squarely to a depth of 1.5 +/- 0.4 mm.
15 Lubricate the splines of the transfer output shaft and the outside of the propeller shaft yoke with lightweight grease, then refit the propeller shaft (see Chapter 8). Be careful not to damage the lip of the new seal.

3.4 Carefully prise out the driveshaft oil seal with a seal removal tool or a large screwdriver; make sure you don't damage the seal bore or the new seal may leak

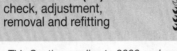
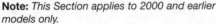

4 Throttle Valve (TV) cable – check, adjustment, removal and refitting

Note: *This Section applies to 2000 and earlier models only.*

Check

1 Remove the air filter housing and the air intake duct (see Chapter 4A or 4B).
2 Have an assistant press the accelerator pedal all the way to the floor and hold it while you measure the distance between the end of the cable casing and the stop on the cable.
3 If the measurement taken is as shown **(see illustration)**, the cable is properly adjusted. If it's out of range, adjust it as follows.

Adjustment

4 Have your assistant continue to hold the pedal down while you loosen the adjusting nuts and adjust the cable housing so that the distance between the end of the boot and the stopper on the cable is within the range shown.
5 Tighten the adjusting nuts securely, recheck the clearance and make sure the throttle valve opens all the way when the throttle is depressed.

Removal and refitting

6 Loosen the cable locknut and detach the cable from the bracket at the throttle body.

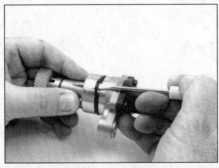

3.10 Remove the oil seal O-ring from the speed sensor with a small screwdriver; make sure you don't scratch the surface of the sensor or gouge the O-ring groove

3.6 Use a seal installer, a large socket or a piece of pipe to install the new seal

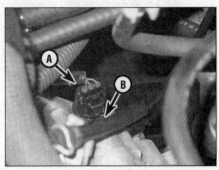

3.9 Unplug the speed sensor electrical connector (A), remove the bolt (B) and pull the speed sensor unit straight out of the transmission – Vehicle Speed Sensor shown, input turbine speed sensor similar

7 Disconnect the cable from the throttle linkage.
8 Detach the cable from the bracket on the transmission.
9 Follow the cable down to where it enters the transmission housing. Remove the cable hold-down bolt.
10 Drain the transmission fluid, remove the sump and the filter (see Chapter 1A or 1B).
11 If you're working on a 1996 or 1997 2WD model, remove the two bolts and bracket that secure the oil tubes. Carefully prise the oil tubes out with a large screwdriver.
12 Remove the manual detent spring **(see illustration)**. **Note:** *On 2WD models the spring is secured by one bolt; on 4WD models it's secured by two.*

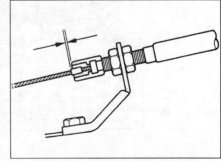

4.3 The distance between the stop and the cable casing should be 0 to 1 mm when the accelerator pedal is depressed to the floor

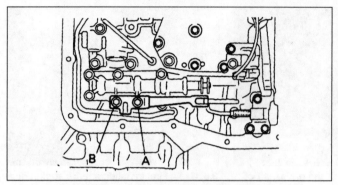

**4.12 Remove the manual detent spring –
4WD model shown; 2WD models have only one bolt**

A 14 mm bolt   B 37 mm bolt

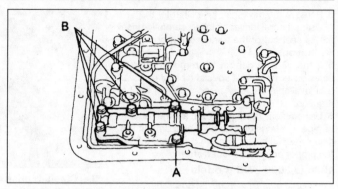

**4.13 On 4WD models, remove these bolts and detach the
manual valve**

A 22 mm bolt   B 37 mm bolt

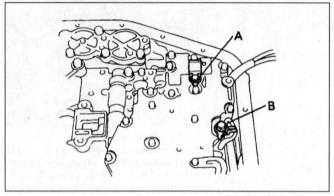

**4.16 On 4WD models, remove these two bolts, then prise out the
small oil tube, being careful not to damage it**

A 39 mm bolt   B 43 mm bolt

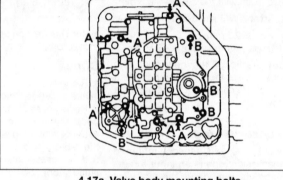

**4.17a Valve body mounting bolts –
1996 and 1997 2WD models**

A 20 mm bolt   B 30 mm bolt   C 55 mm bolt

13 If you're working on a 4WD model, remove the five bolts and detach the manual valve **(see illustration)**.

14 If you're working on a 1996 or 1997 2WD model, or a 4WD model, unplug the electrical connectors from the solenoids.

15 On 4WD models, remove the bolt and clamp, then carefully prise out all eight oil tubes with a large screwdriver.

16 On 4WD models, remove the bolts securing the electrical connector clamp and the retaining clamp over the small oil tube, then carefully prise out the tube **(see illustration)**.

17 Remove the valve body bolts **(see illustrations)**. Separate the valve body from the transmission and detach the throttle valve cable from the cam on the valve body **(see illustration)**.

18 Refitting is the reverse of removal. Be sure to tighten the valve body and related

fasteners to the torque listed in this Chapter's Specifications. Refer to Chapter 1A or 1B for the torque specifications for the sump bolts and the type and quantity of transmission fluid required to refill the transmission.

19 If you are fitting a new cable, the stop on the cable must be crimped to the cable as follows:
a) *With the upper end of the cable detached from the throttle body, bend the cable to a radius of approximately 20 cm.*

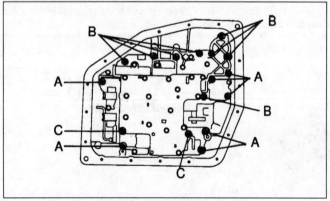

**4.17b Valve body mounting bolts –
1998 to 2000 2WD models**

A 20 mm bolt   B 28 mm bolt   C 50 mm bolt

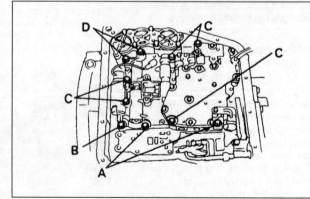

**4.17c Valve body mounting bolts –
1996 to 2000 4WD models**

A 22 mm bolt   B 32 mm bolt   C 43 mm bolt   D 55 mm bolt

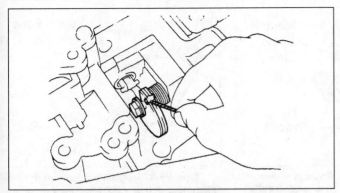

4.17d Once the valve body has been lowered from the transmission, the throttle valve cable can be detached from the cam

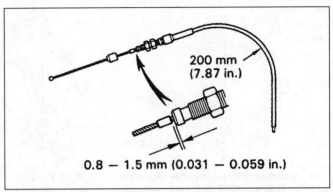

200 mm (7.87 in.)

0.8 – 1.5 mm (0.031 – 0.059 in.)

4.19 Cable stop positioning details

5.2 Remove the nut securing the shift cable to the manual lever (A), then remove the clip (B) and detach the shift cable from the bracket

5.4a Lever the end of the shift cable off the pin on the shifter assembly . . .

5.4b . . . then squeeze the tabs on the cable casing and detach the cable from the shifter housing

b) *Pull the inner cable out of the cable casing until you feel a slight resistance, position the cable stop 0.8 to 1.5 mm from the end of the cable casing, then crimp the stop to the cable (see illustration).*
20 Connect the cable to the throttle body and bracket, then adjust the cable as described in Paragraphs 4 and 5.

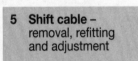
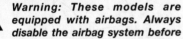

5 Shift cable – removal, refitting and adjustment

Warning: These models are equipped with airbags. Always disable the airbag system before

working in the vicinity of any airbag system component to avoid the possibility of accidental deployment of the airbag(s), which could cause personal injury (see Chapter 12).

Removal and refitting

1 Remove the under-vehicle splash shield. If helpful for access, raise the front of the vehicle and support it securely on axle stands.
2 Disconnect the shift cable from the manual shift lever at the transmission and detach it from the bracket on the front of the transmission **(see illustration)**. Also detach the cable from the clip on the top of the transmission, if equipped.
3 Remove the centre console (see Chapter 11).

4 Lever the cable end off the pin on the shifter assembly, then squeeze the tabs on the cable casing and detach the cable from the shifter housing **(see illustrations)**.
5 Pull the cable through the grommet in the bulkhead.
6 Refitting is the reverse of removal.
7 When you're done, adjust the shift cable.

Adjustment

8 Loosen the nut on the manual shift lever at the transmission **(see illustration 5.2)**.
9 At the transmission, place the manual shift lever in the Neutral position **(see illustrations)**.
10 Move the shift lever inside the vehicle to the Neutral position.
11 Have an assistant hold the shift lever

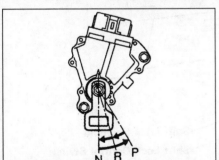

5.9a Manual shift lever Park, Reverse and Neutral positions – 1996 and 1997 2WD models and 1996 to 2000 4WD models

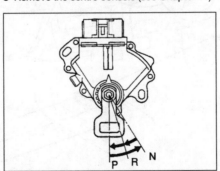

5.9b Manual shift lever Park, Reverse and Neutral positions – 1998 to 2000 2WD models

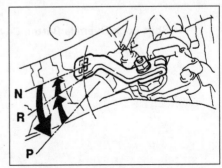

5.9c Manual shift lever Park, Reverse and Neutral positions – 2001 and later models

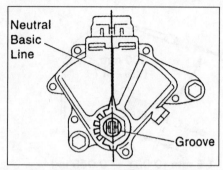

6.5a Park/Neutral Position switch alignment details – 1996 and 1997 2WD models shown, 1998 to 2000 2WD models similar

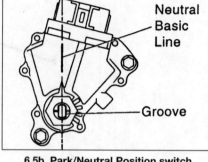

6.5b Park/Neutral Position switch alignment details – 1996 to 2000 4WD models

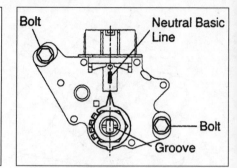

6.5c Park/Neutral Position switch alignment details – 2001 and later models

(inside the vehicle) with a slight pressure toward the Reverse position while you tighten the nut at the manual shift lever securely.

12 Check the operation of the transmission in each shift lever position (try to start the engine in each gear – the starter should operate in the Park and Neutral positions only).

6 Park/Neutral Position (PNP) switch – adjustment, removal and refitting

Adjustment

1 If the engine will start with the shift lever in any position other than Park or Neutral, adjust the Park/Neutral Position switch.

2 Apply the handbrake and chock the rear wheels. Raise the front of the vehicle and support it securely on axle stands. Remove the under-vehicle splash shield and shift the transmission into Neutral.

3 Loosen the switch retaining bolts.

4 Shift the transmission into Neutral.

5 Align the line on the PNP switch with

the groove in the manual lever shaft **(see illustrations)**.

6 Tighten the switch retaining bolts securely and check the operation of the switch. If the vehicle still starts in any position other than Park or Neutral, renew the switch.

Removal and refitting

7 Disconnect the negative cable from the battery.

8 Apply the handbrake and chock the rear wheels. Raise the front of the vehicle and support it securely on axle stands. Remove the under-vehicle splash shield and shift the transmission into Neutral.

9 Remove the nut and lift off the manual shift lever.

10 Unplug the electrical connector.

11 Remove the retaining bolts and lift the switch off the shift shaft.

12 To refit, line up the flats on the shift shaft with the flats in the switch and push the switch onto the shaft.

13 Rotate the switch until the neutral basic line aligns with the groove **(see illustrations 6.5a, 6.5b and 6.5c)**. Tighten the

bolts securely and plug in the electrical connector.

14 Refit the shift lever, connect the negative battery cable and verify the engine will not start with the shift lever in any position other than Park or Neutral.

7 Shift lock system – description and check

⚠️ **Warning: These models are equipped with airbags. Always disable the airbag system before working in the vicinity of any airbag system component to avoid the possibility of accidental deployment of the airbag(s), which could cause personal injury (see Chapter 12).**

Description

1 The shift lock system **(see illustrations)** prevents the shift lever from being shifted out of Park or Neutral until the brake pedal is applied. It also prevents the key from being

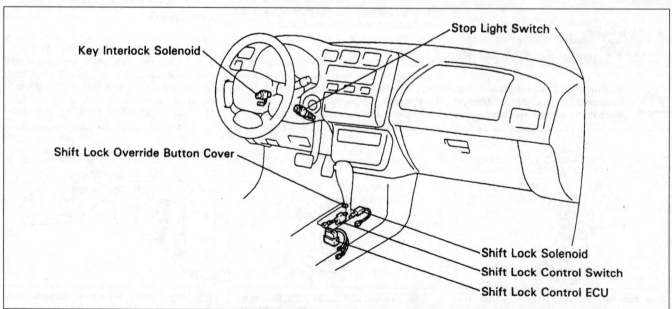

7.1a Shift lock system components – 1996 and 1997 models

removed from the ignition lock cylinder until the shift lever is placed in the Park position.

Check

Key interlock solenoid

2 Remove the steering column covers (see Chapter 11).

3 Unplug the electrical connector for the key interlock solenoid.

4 Using an ohmmeter, measure the resistance between the two terminals on the solenoid side of the connector and compare your measurements with the resistance listed in this Chapter's Specifications.

5 Using jumper wires, momentarily apply battery voltage between the same two terminals. Verify that the solenoid makes an audible 'click' when energised.

Caution: Don't apply battery voltage any longer than necessary for this check, as the solenoid could be damaged.

6 If the key interlock solenoid fails either of these tests, renew it.

Shift lock solenoid
(1996 and 1997 models only)

7 Remove the centre console (see Chapter 11).

8 Unplug the shift lock solenoid connector.

9 Using an ohmmeter, measure the resistance between the two terminals of the connector (on the solenoid side of the connector), and compare your measurement with the resistance listed in this Chapter's Specifications.

10 Using jumper wires, momentarily apply battery voltage to the same two terminals and verify that there's an audible 'click' from the solenoid.

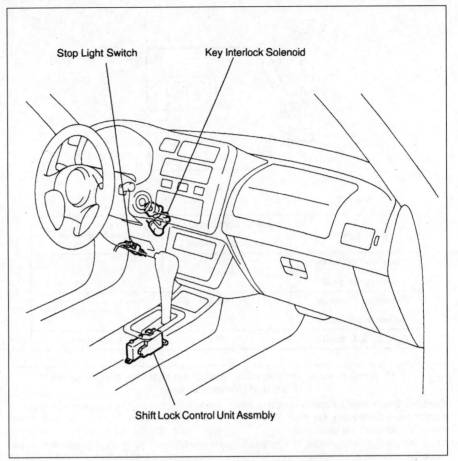

7.1b Shift lock system components – 1998 to 2000 models

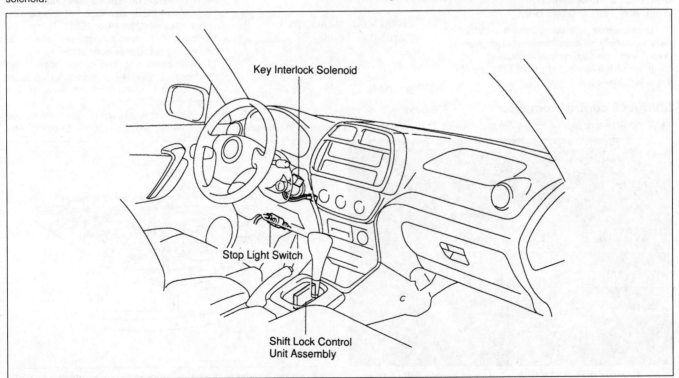

7.1c Shift lock system components – 2001 and later models

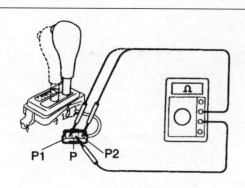

Shift position	Tester condition to terminal number	Specified value
P position (Release button is not pushed)	P — P 1	Continuity
P position (Release button is pushed)	P — P 1 P — P 2	Continuity
R, N, D, 2, L position	P — P 2	Continuity

7.12 Terminal guide and continuity table for the shift lock control switch (1996 and 1997 models only)

Caution: Don't apply battery voltage any longer than necessary for this check, as the solenoid could be damaged.

11 If the shift lock solenoid fails either of these tests, renew it.

Shift lock control switch (1996 and 1997 models only)

12 Unplug the electrical connector and verify that there's continuity between the indicated terminals in each shift lever position **(see illustration)**.

13 If the shift lock control switch fails any of these tests, renew it.

Shift lock control computer

14 If the above components are functioning properly but the shift lock system still does not, by process of elimination the shift lock control unit is probably defective. Before renewing it, however, check the wiring harnesses between the related components for open or short circuit conditions.

8 Automatic transmission – removal and refitting

2WD models

Removal

1 Disconnect the cable from the negative terminal of the battery. Remove the bonnet (see Chapter 11).

2 Remove the air filter housing (see Chapter 4A or 4B).

3 Remove the coolant reservoir (see Chapter 3).

4 If you're working on a 2000 or earlier model, disconnect the throttle valve cable from the throttle body and bracket.

5 Remove the starter (see Chapter 5).

6 Label and disconnect all electrical connectors from the transmission. Also remove the bolt and detach the earth cable.

7 Remove the transmission-to-engine bolts that are accessible from above **(see illustration)**.

8 Attach a hoist to the lifting hook at the transmission end of the engine **(see illustration)**. If no hook is provided, use a bolt of the proper size and thread pitch to attach the support fixture chain to a hole at the end of the cylinder head.

9 Unbolt the left-side engine mounting from the transmission (see the appropriate part of Chapter 2).

10 Loosen the driveshaft/hub nuts and the wheel nuts, raise the front of the vehicle and support it securely on axle stands. Remove the wheels.

11 Remove the under-vehicle splash shield(s).

12 Disconnect the shift cable from the manual lever on the transmission, then detach the cable from its bracket and any other securing clips (see Section 5).

13 Drain the transmission lubricant (see Chapter 1A or 1B).

14 Remove the driveshafts (see Chapter 8).

15 Remove the front section of the exhaust system (see Chapter 4A or 4B).

16 Mark and disconnect any electrical connectors accessible from below.

17 Disconnect the fluid cooler hoses from the transmission. Be prepared for spillage, and plug the hoses and the lines on the transmission.

18 Unbolt the steering gear from the suspension crossmember. Support the

8.7 Remove these three transmission-to-engine bolts before raising the vehicle

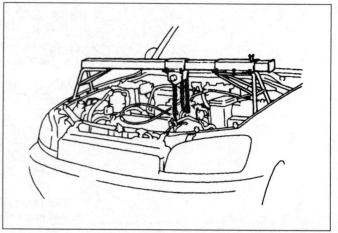

8.8 Attach a hoist to the lifting hook at the transmission end of the engine

steering gear from above with a length of rope or wire. **Note:** *You can tie the rope or wire to the hoist.*

19 On 2001 and later models, remove the torque converter access plug, then mark the relationship of the torque converter to the driveplate **(see illustrations)**.

20 Detach the shift cable from the cross-member (1996 and 1997 models).

21 On 2001 and later models, detach the anti-roll bar links from the anti-roll bar (see Chapter 10).

22 Remove the front suspension crossmember and the longitudinal crossmember.

23 On 2000 and earlier models, remove the stiffener plate, followed by the torque converter access cover **(see illustration)**.

24 If you're working on a 2000 or earlier model, mark the relationship of the torque converter to the driveplate **(see illustration 8.19b)**.

25 Remove the driveplate-to-torque converter bolts. Turn the crankshaft for access to each bolt. Turn the crankshaft in a clockwise direction only (as viewed from the front).

26 Support the transmission with a jack – preferably a jack made for this purpose. Safety chains will help steady the transmission on the jack.

27 Remove the remaining bolts securing the transmission to the engine. A long extension and a U-joint socket will greatly simplify this. **Note:** *Different length bolts are used – be sure to note the location of each bolt so they can be returned to their original positions when the transmission is refitted.*

28 Move the transmission to the rear to disengage it from the engine block dowel pins and make sure the torque converter is detached from the driveplate. Lower the transmission with the jack. Clamp a pair of locking pliers on the bellhousing case. The pliers will prevent the torque converter from falling out while you're removing the transmission.

Refitting

29 Refitting of the transmission is a reversal of the removal procedure, but note the following points:

a) *As the torque converter is refitted, ensure that the drive tangs at the centre of the torque converter hub engage with the recesses in the automatic transmission fluid pump inner gear. This can be confirmed by turning the torque converter while pushing it towards the transmission. If it isn't fully engaged, it will 'clunk' into place.*

b) *When refitting the transmission, make sure the alignment marks you made on the torque converter and driveplate line up.*

c) *Fit all of the torque converter-to-driveplate bolts before tightening any of them.*

d) *Tighten the torque converter-to-driveplate bolts to the specified torque.*

e) *Tighten the transmission mounting bolts to the correct torque.*

8.19a Prise out this access plug . . .

f) *Tighten the suspension crossmember mounting bolts and the steering gear bolts to the torque values listed in the Chapter 10 Specifications.*

g) *Tighten the driveshaft/hub nuts to the torque value listed in the Chapter 8 Specifications.*

h) *Tighten the wheel nuts to the torque listed in the Chapter 1A or 1B Specifications.*

i) *Fill the transmission with the correct type and amount of automatic transmission fluid as described in Chapter 1A or 1B.*

j) *On completion, adjust the shift cable and, on 2000 and earlier models, the throttle valve cable.*

4WD models

⚠️ *Warning 1: Petrol is extremely flammable (and diesel to a lesser degree) so take extra precautions when you work on any part of the fuel system. Don't smoke or allow open flames or bare light bulbs near the work area, and don't work in a garage where a gas-type appliance (such as a water heater or a clothes dryer) is present. Since petrol is carcinogenic, wear latex gloves when there's a possibility of being exposed to fuel, and, if you spill any fuel on your skin, rinse it off immediately with soap and water. Mop-up any spills immediately and do not store fuel-soaked rags where they could ignite. The fuel system is under constant pressure, so, if any fuel lines are to be disconnected, the fuel pressure in the system must be relieved first. When you perform any kind of work on the fuel system, wear safety glasses and have a fire extinguisher on hand.*

⚠️ *Warning 2: The air conditioning system is under high pressure – have an air conditioning specialist evacuate the system and recover the refrigerant before disconnecting any of the hoses or fittings.*

Note: *Transmission removal on 4WD models is a difficult job, especially for the do-it-yourself mechanic working at home. Because of the vehicle's design, the manufacturer states that the engine and transmission have to be removed as a unit from the bottom of the vehicle, not the top. With a floor jack and*

8.19b . . . then mark the relationship of the torque converter to the driveplate

axle stands the vehicle can't be raised high enough and supported safely enough for the engine/transmission assembly to slide out from underneath. The manufacturer recommends that removal of the engine/transmission assembly only be performed on a vehicle hoist.

30 Disconnect the cable from the negative terminal of the battery. Remove the bonnet (see Chapter 11).

31 Refer to Chapter 2D, *Engine – removal and refitting*, for information on the preliminary engine removal procedure, such as disconnecting electrical connectors, control cables and hoses. Make sure no hoses or wires are attached to the engine or transmission from above.

32 Loosen the driveshaft/hub nuts and the wheel nuts. Remove the wheels.

33 Raise the vehicle on the hoist.

34 Remove the under-vehicle splash shield(s).

35 Detach the shift cable from the transmission (see Section 5).

36 Remove the driveshaft and driveshafts (see Chapter 8).

37 If you're working on a 2000 or earlier model, remove the power steering pump and suspend it out of the way (see Chapter 10).

38 Remove the front section of the exhaust system (see Chapter 4A or 4B).

39 Remove the suspension crossmember and longitudinal crossmember.

40 Lower the vehicle and attach an engine hoist to the engine/transmission assembly. Make sure the hoist chain or sling is long enough to allow the engine/transmission assembly to be lowered to the ground.

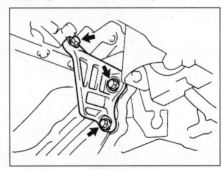

8.23 Unbolt the stiffener plate from the engine and transmission – 2000 and earlier models only

41 Unbolt the right and left engine mountings from the engine/transmission assembly (see the appropriate part of Chapter 2).

42 Lower the engine/transmission assembly to the ground, then disconnect the hoist.

43 Raise the vehicle on the hoist and remove the engine/transmission assembly out from underneath.

44 Remove the starter.

45 Remove the stiffener plate (upper and lower) and, on 2000 and earlier models, the torque converter access cover. On 2001 and later models, remove the torque converter access plug.

46 Mark the relationship of the torque converter to the driveplate, then remove the driveplate-to-torque converter bolts as described earlier in this Section.

47 Remove the transmission/transfer case mounting bolts, then separate the transmission from the engine. **Note:** *Different length bolts are used – be sure to note the location of each bolt so they can be returned to their original positions when the transmission is refitted.*

48 Refitting is the reverse of the removal procedure, noting the points listed in Paragraph 29.

9 Automatic transmission overhaul – general information

In the event of a problem occurring, it will be necessary to establish whether the fault is electrical, mechanical or hydraulic in nature, before repair work can be contemplated. Diagnosis requires detailed knowledge of the transmission's operation and construction, as well as access to specialised test equipment, and so is deemed to be beyond the scope of this manual. It is therefore essential that problems with the automatic transmission are referred to a dealer service department or automatic transmission repair specialist for assessment.

Note that a faulty transmission should not be removed before the vehicle has been diagnosed by a knowledgeable technician equipped with the proper tools, as troubleshooting must be performed with the transmission fitted in the vehicle.

Chapter 8
Clutch and driveshafts

Contents

Section number

Centre support bearing (4WD models) – removal and refitting 12
Clutch – description and check 2
Clutch components – removal, inspection and refitting.......... 6
Clutch hydraulic system – bleeding 5
Clutch master cylinder – removal and refitting................ 3
Clutch release bearing and lever – removal, inspection and refitting 7
Clutch slave cylinder – removal and refitting 4

Section number

Clutch start switch – removal and refitting.................... 8
Differential (4WD models) – removal and refitting 14
Differential oil seals (4WD models) – renewal.................. 13
Driveshaft boot – renewal.................................. 10
Driveshafts – removal and refitting.......................... 9
General information 1
Propeller shaft (4WD models) – check, removal and refitting 11

Degrees of difficulty

Easy, suitable for novice with little experience	Fairly easy, suitable for beginner with some experience	Fairly difficult, suitable for competent DIY mechanic	Difficult, suitable for experienced DIY mechanic	Very difficult, suitable for expert DIY or professional

Specifications

Driveshaft standard length

Front (2000 and earlier):
  Right:
    2WD
      M/T .... 842.9 mm
      A/T .... 844.6 mm
    4WD .... 511.2 mm
  Left:
    2WD
      M/T .... 542.6 mm
      A/T .... 548.5 mm
    4WD .... 508.0 mm
Front (2001 and later):
  Right:
    2WD .... 858.5 mm
    4WD .... 920.5 mm
  Left:
    2WD .... 585.4 mm
    4WD .... 520.5 mm
Rear (2000 and earlier):
  Right.. 599.4 mm
  Left... 553.4 mm
Rear (2001 and later):
  Right.. 611.9 mm
  Left... 564.9 mm

Differential pinion shaft bearing preload

Rear, 4WD models, with used bearing.......................... 0.6 to 0.8 Nm

Torque wrench settings

	lbf ft	Nm
Clutch pressure plate bolt	14	19
Differential cover mounting bolts (4WD models)	34	46
Differential front mounting bracket bolts (4WD models)	86	117
Differential pinion flange nut (4WD models) (see Section 13):		
Initial	80	108
Maximum	173	235
Differential rear mounting bracket-to-body bolts.................	48	65
Differential rear mounting bracket-to-differential bolts (4WD models)..	101	137
Driveshaft/hub nut	159	216
Driveshaft universal joint flange-to-cross groove joint.............	20	27
Propeller shaft centre support bearing bolts (4WD models)	27	37
Propeller shaft flange-to-rear differential bolts (4WD models)........	54	73
Rear drive axle-to-side gear shaft flange.......................	41	56

1 General information

The information in this Chapter deals with the components from the rear of the engine to the front wheels, except for the transmission, which is dealt with in the previous Chapter. For the purposes of this Chapter, these components are grouped into two categories – clutch and driveshafts. Separate Sections within this Chapter offer general descriptions and checking procedures for components in each of the two groups.

Since nearly all the procedures covered in this Chapter involve working under the vehicle, make sure it's securely supported on sturdy axle stands or on a hoist where the vehicle can be easily raised and lowered.

2 Clutch – description and check

1 All vehicles with a manual transmission use a single dry plate, diaphragm spring type clutch **(see illustration)**. The clutch disc has a splined hub which allows it to slide along the splines of the transmission input shaft. The clutch and pressure plate are held in contact by spring pressure exerted by the diaphragm in the pressure plate.

2 The clutch release system is operated by hydraulic pressure. The hydraulic release system consists of the clutch pedal, a master cylinder, the hydraulic line, a slave cylinder which actuates the clutch release lever and the clutch release (or throw-out) bearing.

3 When pressure is applied to the clutch pedal to release the clutch, hydraulic pressure is exerted against the outer end of the clutch release lever. As the lever pivots, the shaft fingers push against the release bearing. The bearing pushes against the fingers of the diaphragm spring of the pressure plate assembly, which in turn releases the clutch plate.

4 Terminology can be a problem regarding the clutch components because common names have in some cases changed from that used by the manufacturer. For example, the driven plate is also called the clutch plate or disc, the pressure plate assembly is sometimes referred to as the clutch cover, the clutch release bearing is sometimes called a throw-out bearing, and the release cylinder is sometimes called the operating or slave cylinder.

5 Other than renewing components that have obvious damage, some preliminary checks should be performed to diagnose a clutch system failure.

a) The first check should be of the fluid level in the brake master cylinder since it also serves as the reservoir for the clutch release system (see 'Weekly checks'). If the fluid level is low, add fluid as necessary and inspect the hydraulic clutch system for leaks. If the master cylinder reservoir has run dry, bleed the system (see Section 5) and retest the clutch operation.

b) To check 'clutch spin down time'. run the engine at normal idle speed with the transmission in Neutral (clutch pedal up – engaged). Disengage the clutch (pedal down), wait several seconds and shift the transmission into Reverse. No grinding noise should be heard. A grinding noise would most likely indicate a problem in the pressure plate or the clutch disc.

c) To check for complete clutch release, run the engine (with the handbrake applied to prevent movement) and hold the clutch pedal approximately 12 mm from the floor. Shift the transmission between 1st gear and Reverse several times. If the shift is not smooth, component failure is indicated. Check the slave cylinder pushrod travel. With the clutch pedal depressed completely the slave cylinder pushrod should extend substantially. If it doesn't, check the fluid level in the clutch master cylinder.

d) Visually inspect the clutch pedal bushing at the top of the clutch pedal to make sure there is no sticking or excessive wear.

e) Under the vehicle, check that the clutch release lever is solidly mounted on the ball-stud.

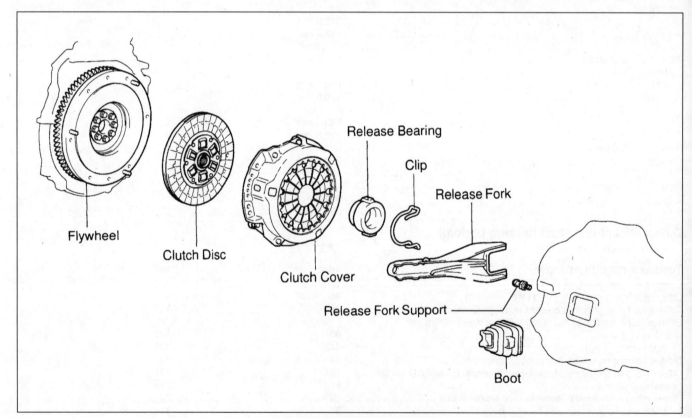

2.1 Typical clutch assembly details

Flywheel

Clutch Disc

Clutch Cover

Release Bearing

Clip

Release Fork

Release Fork Support

Boot

3 Clutch master cylinder – removal and refitting

Removal

1 Disconnect the negative cable from the battery.

2 Under the dashboard, disconnect the pushrod from the top of the clutch pedal. It's held in place with a clevis pin. To remove the clevis pin, remove the clip.

3 If the vehicle is equipped with cruise control, remove the cruise control actuator cover and the three bolts securing the actuator and place it aside.

4 Clamp a pair of locking pliers onto the fluid feed hose, a couple of inches downstream of the reservoir. The pliers should be just tight enough to prevent fluid flow when the hose is disconnected.

5 Disconnect the hydraulic line at the clutch master cylinder **(see illustration)**. If available, use a flare-nut spanner on the union nut, to protect it from being rounded off. Have rags handy, as some fluid will be lost as the line is removed. Loosen the fluid feed hose clamp and detach the hose from the cylinder.

Caution: Don't allow brake fluid to come into contact with paint, as it will damage the finish.

6 Working under the facia on the driver's side, unscrew the two clutch master cylinder retaining nuts and remove the cylinder.

Refitting

7 Position the master cylinder on the bulkhead, fitting the mounting nuts finger-tight.

8 Connect the hydraulic line to the master cylinder, moving the cylinder slightly as necessary to thread the union nut properly into the bore. Don't cross-thread the nut as it's fitted. Attach the fluid feed hose to the cylinder.

9 Tighten the mounting nuts and the hydraulic

line union nut securely and connect the fluid feed hose.

10 Connect the pushrod to the clutch pedal.

11 Remove the locking pliers from fluid feed hose. Fill the master cylinder reservoir with brake fluid conforming to DOT 4 specifications and bleed the clutch system (see Section 5).

4 Clutch slave cylinder – removal and refitting

Removal

1 Disconnect the negative cable from the battery.

2 Disconnect the hydraulic line at the slave cylinder **(see illustrations)**. If available, use a flare-nut spanner on the union nut, which will prevent the nut from being rounded off. Have a small can and rags handy, as some fluid will be spilled as the line is removed.

3 Remove the slave cylinder mounting bolts.

4 Remove the slave cylinder.

Refitting

5 Refit the slave cylinder on the clutch housing, but don't completely tighten the bolts yet. Make sure the pushrod is seated in the release fork pocket.

6 Connect the hydraulic line to the slave cylinder, and then tighten the slave cylinder mounting bolts securely. Using a flare-nut spanner, tighten the union nut securely.

7 Fill the master cylinder reservoir with brake fluid conforming to DOT 4 specifications and bleed the clutch system as described in Section 5.

5 Clutch hydraulic system – bleeding

1 The hydraulic system should be bled of all air whenever any part of the system has been

3.5 Use a flare-nut spanner when disconnecting the hydraulic line union nut to prevent rounding off the corners of the nut

removed or if the fluid level has been allowed to fall so low that air has been drawn into the master cylinder. The procedure is similar to bleeding a brake system.

2 Fill the master cylinder with new brake fluid conforming to DOT 4 specifications.

Caution: Do not re-use any of the fluid coming from the system during the bleeding operation or use fluid which has been inside an open container for an extended period of time.

3 Locate the bleed valve on the clutch slave cylinder. Remove the dust cap, which fits over the bleed valve, and push a length of clear tubing over the valve. Place the other end of the hose into a clear container with about two inches of brake fluid in it. The hose end must be submerged in the fluid.

4 Have an assistant depress the clutch pedal and hold it. Open the bleed valve on the slave cylinder, allowing fluid to flow through the hose. Close the bleed valve when fluid stops flowing from the hose. Once closed, have your assistant release the pedal.

5 Continue this process until all air is evacuated from the system, indicated by a full, solid stream of fluid being ejected from the bleed valve each time and no air bubbles in the hose or container. Keep a close watch on the fluid level inside the master cylinder

4.2a Use a flare-nut spanner when disconnecting the hydraulic line union nut, then remove the mounting bolts – petrol engine

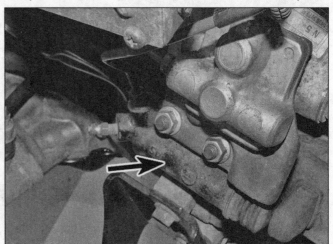

4.2b Clutch slave cylinder – diesel engine

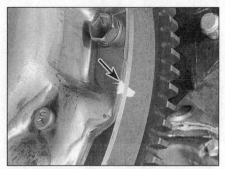

6.6 Mark the relationship of the pressure plate to the flywheel (just in case you're going to re-use the old pressure plate)

reservoir; if the level drops too low, air will be sucked back into the system and the process will have to be started all over again.

7 Refit the dust cap. Check carefully for proper operation before placing the vehicle in normal service.

6 Clutch components – removal, inspection and refitting

⚠ **Warning: Dust produced by clutch wear and deposited on clutch components is hazardous to your health. DO NOT blow it out with compressed air and DO NOT inhale it. DO NOT use petrol or petroleum based solvents to remove the dust. Brake system cleaner should be used to flush**

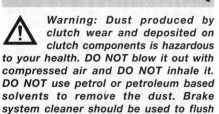

6.12a Inspect the pressure plate friction surface for score marks, cracks and signs of overheating

the dust into a drain pan. After the clutch components are wiped clean with a rag, dispose of the contaminated rags and cleaner in a labelled, covered container.

Removal

1 Access to the clutch components is normally accomplished by removing the transmission, leaving the engine in the vehicle. If, of course, the engine is being removed for major overhaul, then the opportunity should always be taken to check the clutch for wear and renew worn components as necessary. However, the relatively low cost of the clutch components compared to the time and labour involved in gaining access to them warrants their renewal any time the engine or transmission is removed, unless they are new or in near-perfect condition. The following procedures assume that the engine will stay in place.

2 Remove the slave cylinder (see Section 4). Hang it out of the way with a piece of wire – it isn't necessary to disconnect the hose.

3 Remove the transmission from the vehicle (see Chapter 7A).

4 The release fork and release bearing can remain attached to the transmission for the time being.

5 To support the clutch disc during removal, insert a clutch alignment tool through the clutch disc hub.

6 Carefully inspect the flywheel and pressure plate for indexing marks. The marks are usually an X, an O or a white letter. If they cannot be found, scribe marks yourself so the pressure plate and the flywheel will be in the same alignment during refitting **(see illustration)**.

7 Slowly loosen the pressure plate-to-flywheel bolts. Work in a diagonal pattern and loosen each bolt a little at a time until all spring pressure is relieved. Then hold the pressure plate securely and completely remove the bolts, followed by the pressure plate and clutch disc.

Inspection

8 Ordinarily, when a problem occurs in the clutch, it can be attributed to wear of the clutch disc. However, all components should be inspected at this time.

9 Inspect the flywheel for cracks, heat checking, score marks and other damage. If

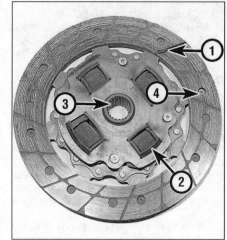

6.10 The clutch disc

1 **Lining** – *this will wear down in use*
2 **Springs or dampers** – *check for cracking and deformation*
3 **Splined hub** – *the splines must not be worn and should slide smoothly on the transmission input shaft splines*
4 **Rivets** – *these secure the lining and will damage the flywheel or pressure plate if allowed to contact the surfaces*

the imperfections are slight, a machine shop can resurface it to make it flat and smooth. Refer to the appropriate part of Chapter 2 for the flywheel removal procedure.

10 Inspect the lining on the clutch disc. There should be at least 1 mm of lining above the rivet heads. Check for loose rivets, distortion, cracks, broken springs and other obvious damage **(see illustration)**. As mentioned above, ordinarily the clutch disc is renewed as a matter of course, so if in doubt about the condition, renew it.

11 The release bearing should be renewed along with the clutch disc (see Section 7).

12 Check the machined surface and the diaphragm spring fingers of the pressure plate **(see illustrations)**. If the surface is grooved or otherwise damaged, renew the pressure plate assembly. Also check for obvious damage, distortion, cracking, etc. Light glazing can be removed with emery cloth or sandpaper. If a new pressure plate is indicated, new or factory rebuilt units are available.

NORMAL FINGER WEAR

EXCESSIVE WEAR

EXCESSIVE FINGER WEAR

BROKEN OR BENT FINGERS

6.12b Renew the pressure plate if excessive wear is noted

6.14 Centre the clutch disc in the pressure plate with a clutch alignment tool

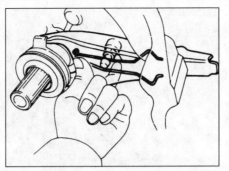

7.3 Reach behind the release lever and disengage the lever from the ball-stud by pulling on the retention spring, then remove the lever and bearing

7.4 To check the operation of the bearing, hold it by the outer race and rotate the inner race while applying pressure – the bearing should turn smoothly – if it doesn't, renew it

Refitting

13 Before refitting, carefully wipe the flywheel and pressure plate machined surfaces clean. It's important that no oil or grease is on these surfaces or the lining of the clutch disc. Handle these parts only with clean hands.

14 Position the clutch disc and pressure plate with the clutch held in place with an alignment tool **(see illustration)**. Make sure it's fitted properly (most clutch discs will be marked 'flywheel side' or something similar – if not marked, fit the clutch disc with the damper springs or cushion toward the transmission).

15 Tighten the pressure plate-to-flywheel bolts only finger-tight, working around the pressure plate.

16 Centre the clutch disc by ensuring the alignment tool is through the splined hub and into the recess in the crankshaft. Wiggle the tool up, down or side-to-side as needed to bottom the tool. Tighten the pressure plate-to-flywheel bolts a little at a time, working in a criss-cross pattern to prevent distortion of the cover. After all of the bolts are snug, tighten them to the torque listed in this Chapter's Specifications. Remove the alignment tool.

17 Using high-temperature grease, lubricate the inner groove of the release bearing (see Section 7). Also place a light film of grease

on the release lever contact areas and the transmission input shaft bearing retainer.

18 Refit the clutch release bearing (see Section 7).

19 Refit the transmission, slave cylinder and all components removed previously, tightening all bolts securely.

7 Clutch release bearing and lever – removal, inspection and refitting

⚠ **Warning: Dust produced by clutch wear and deposited on clutch components is hazardous to your health. DO NOT blow it out with compressed air and DO NOT inhale it. DO NOT use petrol or petroleum based solvents to remove the dust. Brake system cleaner should be used to flush the dust into a drain pan. After the clutch components are wiped clean with a rag, dispose of the contaminated rags and cleaner in a labelled, covered container.**

Removal

1 Disconnect the negative cable from the battery.

2 Remove the transmission (see Chapter 7A).

3 Remove the clutch release lever from the

ball-stud, and then remove the bearing from the lever **(see illustration)**.

Inspection

4 Hold the bearing by the outer race and rotate the inner race while applying pressure **(see illustration)**. If the bearing doesn't turn smoothly or if it's noisy, renew the bearing/hub assembly. Wipe the bearing with a clean rag and inspect it for damage, wear and cracks. Don't immerse the bearing in solvent – it's sealed for life and to do so would ruin it. Also check the release lever for cracks and bends.

Refitting

5 Fill the inner groove of the release bearing with high-temperature grease. Also apply a light coat of the same grease to the transmission input shaft splines and the front bearing retainer **(see illustration)**.

6 Lubricate the release lever ball socket, lever ends and slave cylinder pushrod socket with high-temperature grease **(see illustration)**.

7 Attach the release bearing to the release lever. On models that use a retaining clip, make sure it engages properly with the lever.

8 Slide the release bearing onto the transmission input shaft front bearing retainer while

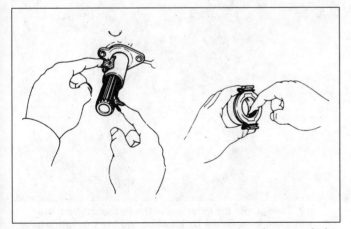

7.5 Apply a thin coat of high-temperature grease to the transmission bearing retainer and also fill the release bearing groove

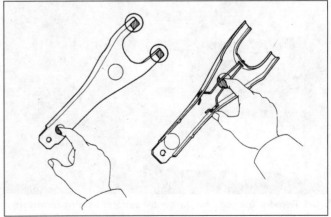

7.6 Apply high-temperature grease to the release lever in the areas indicated

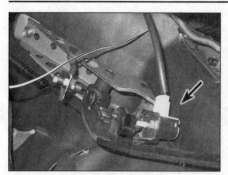

8.1 The clutch start switch is located under the facia on a bracket in front of the clutch pedal

9.1 If the driveshaft nut is 'staked', use a centre punch to unstake it (wheel removed for clarity)

9.2 Loosen the driveshaft/hub nut with a long bar

passing the end of the release lever through the opening in the clutch housing. Push the clutch release lever onto the ball-stud until it's firmly seated.

9 Apply a light coat of high-temperature grease to the face of the release bearing where it contacts the pressure plate diaphragm fingers.

10 The remainder of refitting is the reverse of the removal procedure.

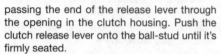

8 Clutch start switch –
removal and refitting

Removal

1 The clutch start switch is located near the top of the clutch pedal, facing the opposite direction of the cruise control switch (or pedal stopper) **(see illustration)**.

2 Unplug the electrical connector. Loosen the nut near the body of the switch, and then unscrew the switch.

Refitting

3 Refitting is the reverse of removal.

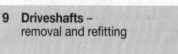

9 Driveshafts –
removal and refitting

Front

Removal

1 Remove the wheel cover or hub cap. Remove the split pin and nut lock (2000 and earlier models). On 2001 and later models, unstake the nut with a punch or chisel **(see illustration)**.

2 Unlock the hub nut with a socket and long bar **(see illustration)**.

3 Loosen the wheel nuts, raise the vehicle and support it securely on axle stands. Remove the wheel. Drain the transmission lubricant (see Chapter 1A or 1B).

4 Remove the nuts and bolt securing the ball-joint to the control arm, then lever the control arm down and separate the lower control arm from the balljoint (see Chapter 10). Now remove the driveshaft/hub nut.

5 Swing the knuckle/hub assembly out (away from the vehicle) until the end of the driveshaft is free of the hub. **Note:** *If the driveshaft*

splines stick in the hub, tap on the end of the driveshaft with a plastic hammer. Support the outer end of the driveshaft with a piece of wire to avoid unnecessary strain on the inner CV joint.

6 If you're working on the right-side axle on a 2WD automatic transmission remove the bolts from the centre bearing bracket **(see illustration)**. If you're working on a 2WD manual transmission remove the circlip from the centre bearing using a hammer and screwdriver.

7 Carefully lever the inner end of the drive-shaft from the transmission – or, on models so equipped, the intermediate shaft – using a large screwdriver or lever positioned between the transmission or bearing support and the CV joint housing **(see illustration)**. Support the CV joints and carefully remove the driveshaft from the vehicle.

Refitting

8 Extract the old spring clip from the inner end of the driveshaft and fit a new one **(see illustrations)**. Lubricate the differential or intermediate shaft seal with multi-purpose grease and raise the driveshaft into position while supporting the CV joints.

9.6 Remove the bolts for the centre support bearing (arrowed)

9.7 To separate the inner end of the driveshaft from the transmission, lever on the CV joint housing like this with a large screwdriver or lever – you may need to give the lever a sharp rap with a brass hammer

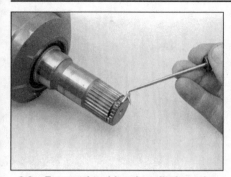

9.8a Extract the old spring clip from the inner end of the driveshaft with a small screwdriver or awl

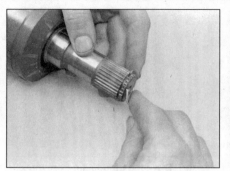

9.8b To fit the new spring clip, start one end in the groove and work the clip over the shaft end, into the groove

9 Insert the splined end of the inner CV joint or the intermediate shaft into the differential side gear and make sure the spring clip locks in its groove. If you're fitting a driveshaft/intermediate shaft assembly, fit the centre support bearing bolts or circlip, as applicable.
10 Apply a light coat of multi-purpose grease to the outer CV joint splines, pull out on the strut/steering knuckle assembly and fit the stub axle into the hub.
11 Reconnect the balljoint to the lower control arm and tighten the nuts (see the torque specifications in Chapter 10).
12 If you're working on a 2001 or later model, fit a new driveshaft/hub nut. Tighten the hub nut securely, but don't try to tighten it to the actual torque specification until you've lowered the vehicle to the ground.
13 Grasp the inner CV joint housing (not the driveshaft) and pull out to make sure the driveshaft has seated securely in the transmission.
14 Fit the wheel and nuts, then lower the vehicle.
15 Tighten the wheel nuts to the torque listed in the Chapter 1A or 1B Specifications. Tighten the hub nut to the torque listed in this Chapter's Specifications. On 2000 and earlier models, fit the nut lock and new split pin. On 2001 and later models, stake the nut to the groove in the driveshaft, using a hammer and punch.
16 Refill the transmission with the recommended type and amount of lubricant (see Chapter 1A or 1B).

Rear (4WD models)

Removal

17 Remove the wheel cover or hub cap. Remove the split pin and nut lock from the driveshaft/hub nut. Unlock the hub nut loose with a socket and long bar.
18 Chock the front wheels to prevent the vehicle from rolling. Loosen the wheel nuts, raise the rear of the vehicle and support it securely on axle stands. Remove the wheel.
19 On vehicles with ABS, remove the ABS speed sensor (see Chapter 9).
20 Remove the driveshaft/hub nut and cage.
21 Make reference marks on the driveshaft flange and the differential side gear flange **(see illustration)**.

22 Remove the four nuts and washers **(see illustration)** and detach the axle from the differential side gear flange, then remove the outer end of the driveshaft from the hub.

Refitting

23 Refitting is the reverse of removal. Fit a new driveshaft/hub nut. Tighten the hub nut securely, but don't try to tighten it to the actual torque specification until you've lowered the vehicle. Fit the wheel and nuts, then lower the vehicle. Tighten the wheel nuts to the torque listed in the Chapter 1A or 1B Specifications. Tighten the driveshaft/hub nut to the torque listed in this Chapter's Specifications, then fit the nut cage and a new split pin.

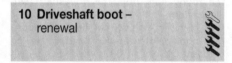

10 Driveshaft boot – renewal

Note 1: *If the CV joint boots must be renewed, explore all options before beginning the job. Complete rebuilt driveshafts are available on an exchange basis, which eliminates much time and work. Whichever route you choose to take, check on the cost and availability of parts before disassembling the vehicle.*
Note 2: *Some dealer stores carry 'split' type repair boots, which can be fitted without removing the driveshaft from the vehicle. This is a convenient alternative; however, the driveshaft should be removed and the CV joint disassembled and cleaned to ensure the joint is free from contaminants such as moisture*

10.3 Lift the tabs on the boot clamps with a small screwdriver, then open the clamps

9.21 Mark the relationship of the driveshaft flange to the differential side gear flange

9.22 Remove the four nuts and washers (fourth nut hidden from view)

and dirt which will accelerate CV joint wear. Do NOT disassemble the outboard CV joint.

Disassembly

1 Remove the driveshaft (see Section 9).
2 Mount the driveshaft in a vice with wood lined jaws to prevent any damage. Check the CV joint for excessive play in the radial direction, which indicates worn parts. Check for smooth operation throughout the full range of motion for each CV joint. If a boot is torn, disassemble the joint, clean the components and inspect for damage due to loss of lubrication and possible contamination by foreign matter.
3 Using a small screwdriver, lever the retaining tabs of the clamps up to loosen them and slide them off **(see illustration)**.
4 Using a screwdriver, carefully lever up on the edge of the outer boot and push it away from the CV joint. Old and worn boots can

10.4 Remove the boot from the inner CV joint and slide the joint housing from the tripod

10.6 Remove the circlip with a pair of circlip pliers

10.7 Drive the tripod joint from the driveshaft with a brass punch and hammer; be careful not to damage the bearing surfaces or the splines on the shaft

10.10a Wrap the splined area of the shaft with tape to prevent damage to the boots when removing or installing them

10.10b Install the tripod with the recessed portion of the splines facing the axle shaft

10.10c Place grease at the bottom of the CV joint housing

10.10d Install the boot clamps onto the shaft, then insert the tripod into the housing, followed by the rest of the grease

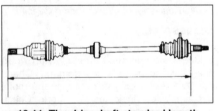

10.11 The driveshaft standard length should be set to the dimension listed in this Chapter's Specifications before the boot clamps are tightened

be cut off. Pull the inner CV joint boot back from the housing and slide the housing off the tripod **(see illustration)**.

5 Mark the tripod and driveshaft to ensure that they are reassembled properly.

6 Remove the tripod joint circlip with a pair of circlip pliers **(see illustration)**.

7 Use a hammer and a brass punch to drive

the tripod joint from the driveshaft **(see illustration)**.

8 If you haven't already cut them off, remove both boots. **Note:** *Do NOT disassemble the outboard CV joint. If you're working on a right side driveshaft, you'll also have to cut off the clamp for the dynamic damper and slide the damper off.* **Note:** *The damper may have to be pressed off with a hydraulic press. Also, before removing the damper, measure its position from the end of the driveshaft – when reassembling, it must be returned to the same spot.*

Check

9 Thoroughly clean all components, including the outer CV joint assembly, with solvent until the old CV joint grease is completely removed. Inspect the bearing surfaces of the inner tripods and housings for cracks, pitting, scoring and other signs of wear. It's not possible to inspect

the bearing surfaces of the inner and outer races of the outer CV joint, but you can at least check the surfaces of the ball bearings themselves. If they're in good shape, so are the races; if they're not, neither are the races. If the inner CV joint is worn, you can buy a new inner CV joint and fit it on the old driveshaft; if the outer CV joint is worn, you'll have to purchase a new outer CV joint and driveshaft (they're sold pre-assembled).

Reassembly

10 Wrap the splines on the inner end of the driveshaft with electrical or duct tape to protect the boots from the sharp edges of the splines. Slide the clamps and boot(s) onto the driveshaft, then place the tripod on the shaft. Apply grease to the tripod assembly and inside the housing. Insert the tripod into the housing and pack the remainder of the grease around the tripod **(see illustrations)**.

10.12a Equalise the pressure inside the boot by inserting a small, dull screwdriver between the boot and the outer race

10.12b To install the new clamps, bend the tang down . . .

10.12c . . . then tap the tabs over to hold it in place

11 Slide the boot into place, making sure both ends seat in their grooves. Adjust the length of the driveshaft to the dimension listed in this Chapter's Specifications **(see illustration)**.
12 Equalise the pressure in the boot, then tighten and secure the boot clamps **(see illustrations)**.
13 Refit the driveshaft assembly (see Section 9).

11 Propeller shaft (4WD models) – check, removal and refitting

Check

1 Raise the rear of the vehicle and support it securely on axle stands. Chock the front wheels to keep the vehicle from rolling off the stands. Release the handbrake and place the transmission in Neutral.
2 Crawl under the vehicle and visually inspect the propeller shaft. Look for any dents or cracks in the tubing. If any are found, the propeller shaft must be renewed.
3 Check for oil leakage at the front and rear of the propeller shaft. Leakage where the propeller shaft connects to the transfer case indicates a defective transfer case seal. Leakage where the propeller shaft connects to the differential indicates a defective pinion seal.
4 While under the vehicle, have an assistant rotate a rear wheel so the propeller shaft will rotate. As it does, make sure the universal joints are operating properly without binding, noise or looseness. Listen for any noise from the centre bearing, indicating it's worn or damaged. Also check the rubber portion of the centre bearing for cracking or separation.
5 The universal joints can also be checked with the propeller shaft motionless, by gripping your hands on either side of the joint and attempting to twist the joint. Any movement at all in the joint is a sign of considerable wear. Lifting up on the shaft will also indicate movement in the universal joints. If the joints are worn, front or rear portion of the propeller shaft must be renewed as an assembly.
6 Finally, check the propeller shaft mounting bolts at the ends to make sure they're tight.

Removal

8 Raise the rear of the vehicle and support it securely on axle stands. Chock the front wheels to prevent the vehicle from rolling. Place the transmission in Neutral with the handbrake off.
9 Make reference marks on the propeller shaft flange and the differential pinion flange in line with each other **(see illustration)**. This is to make sure the propeller shaft is refitted in the same position to preserve the balance.
10 Remove the rear universal joint bolts. Turn the propeller shaft (or wheels) as necessary to bring the bolts into the most accessible position. Remove the four bolts, nuts and washers **(see illustration)**.

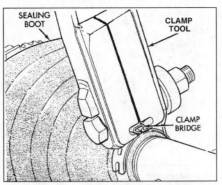

10.12d If your new boot came with crimp-type clamps, a special tool such as this one (available at most auto parts stores) will be required to tighten them properly

11 Unbolt the centre support bearing from the floor **(see illustration)**.
12 Pull out the front of the propeller shaft from the transmission and remove the propeller shaft assembly.

Refitting

13 Lubricate the lips of the transfer case seal with multipurpose grease. Carefully guide the intermediate shaft yoke into the transfer case and then fit the mounting bolts through the centre support bearing, but don't tighten them yet.
14 Reconnect the propeller shaft to the pinion flange. Be sure to align the marks and tighten

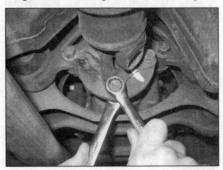

11.10 Using a second spanner to hold each nut, loosen all four bolts

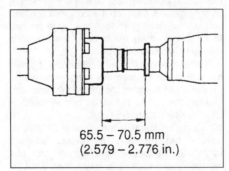

11.15a Adjust the gap between the CV joint cover and the raised part of the rear propeller shaft to the dimension shown . . .

65.5 – 70.5 mm
(2.579 – 2.776 in.)

11.9 Mark the relationship of the propeller shaft to the differential pinion flange

the bolts to the torque listed in this Chapter's Specifications.
15 Adjust the position of the centre support bearing **(see illustrations)**, then tighten the bolts to the torque listed in this Chapter's Specifications.

12 Centre support bearing (4WD models) – removal and refitting

Removal

1 Remove the propeller shaft (see Section 11).
2 Mark the relationship of the universal joint flange to the cross groove joint flange on the propeller shaft **(see illustration)**.

11.11 The propeller shaft centre support bearing is retained by two bolts

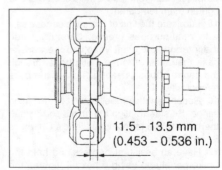

11.15b . . . then adjust the distance between the rear of the centre support bearing and the rear of the rubber insulator to the dimension shown

11.5 – 13.5 mm
(0.453 – 0.536 in.)

12.2 Mark the relationship of the universal joint flange to the cross-groove joint flange

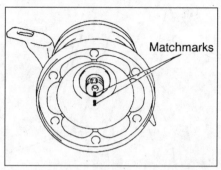

Matchmarks

12.6 Mark the relationship of the flange to the shaft

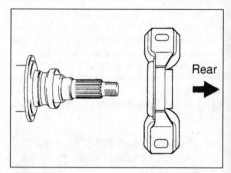

Rear

12.10 Install the centre support bearing in the direction shown

3 Using a hex bit, remove the six bolts and separate the two halves of the propeller shaft.
4 Using a hammer and punch unstake the nut from the universal joint flange.
5 Place the intermediate shaft in a vice lined with wood to hold the front flange and remove the nut and washer.
Caution: Don't tighten the vice excessively, as the shaft could be damaged.
6 Apply alignment marks onto the flange and shaft **(see illustration)**.
7 Using a two-jaw puller, remove the joint flange.
8 Remove the washer and centre support bearing.
9 Place the propeller shaft in the vice and check that the cross groove joint moves smoothly. If there is damage to the joint or grease leakage from the boot, the rear shaft should be renewed.

Refitting

10 Place the centre bearing and washer on the intermediate shaft **(see illustration)**.
11 Place the flange on the shaft with the marks aligned, followed by a new washer and nut.
12 Use the vice to hold the flange while tightening down the nut. Tighten the nut to the torque value listed in this Chapter's Specifications.
13 Using a hammer and punch, stake the nut into the groove on the shaft.
14 Align the marks on the two halves of the propeller shaft, refit the washers and bolts and tighten them temporarily.
15 Lubricate the lips of the transfer case seal with multipurpose grease. Carefully guide the intermediate shaft yoke into the transfer case then insert the mounting bolts through the centre support bearing. Tighten the bolts temporarily.
16 Reconnect the propeller shaft to the pinion flange. Be sure to align the marks and tighten the bolts to the torque listed in this Chapter's Specifications.
17 Have an assistant depress and hold the brake pedal and using a hex bit, tighten the bolts securing the two halves of the propeller shaft securely.
18 Adjust the position of the centre support bearing as described in Section 11.

13 Differential oil seals (4WD models) – renewal

Pinion oil seal

Removal

1 Raise the rear of the vehicle and support it securely on axle stands. Chock the front wheels to prevent the vehicle from rolling. Place the transmission in Neutral with the handbrake off.
2 Mark the relationship of the propeller shaft to the pinion flange, then unbolt it from the flange (see Section 11). Suspend the propeller shaft with a piece of wire (don't let it hang by the centre support bearing).
3 Using a hammer and a punch, unstake the pinion flange nut.
4 A flange holding tool will be required to keep the companion flange from moving while the self-locking pinion nut is loosened. An oil filter removal tool will also work.
5 Remove the pinion nut.
6 Withdraw the flange. It may be necessary to use a two-jaw puller engaged behind the flange to draw it off. Do not attempt to lever or hammer behind the flange or hammer on the end of the pinion shaft.
7 Lever out the old seal and discard it.

Refitting

8 Lubricate the lips of the new seal and fill the space between the seal lips with wheel bearing grease, then tap it evenly into position with a seal installation tool or a large socket. Make sure it enters the housing squarely and is tapped in to its full depth.
9 Refit the pinion flange; if necessary, tighten the pinion nut to draw the flange into place. Do not try to hammer the flange into position. Tighten the nut to the initial torque listed in this Chapter's Specifications.
10 Using an suitable torque wrench (dial or beam-type), measure the torque required to rotate the pinion and tighten the nut in small increments (no more than 9 lbf ft/ 12 Nm) until it matches the pinion shaft bearing preload listed in this Chapter's Specifications. If the maximum torque listed in this Chapter's Specifications is reached

before the specified preload is obtained, the bearing spacer in the differential must be renewed.
11 Once the proper preload is reached, stake the collar of the nut into the slot in the pinion shaft.
12 Reconnect the propeller shaft to the pinion flange (see Section 11). Check the differential lubricant level and add some, if necessary, to bring it to the appropriate level (see Chapter 1A or 1B).

Driveshaft oil seals

Torque-sensing limited slip differential

13 Raise the rear of the vehicle and support it securely on axle stands. Chock the front wheels to prevent the vehicle from rolling. Place the transmission in Neutral with the handbrake off.
14 Remove the side gear shaft with a slide hammer or carefully lever between the inner side of the shaft's flange and differential case using levers positioned on each side. Remove the shaft.
15 Carefully lever out the side gear shaft oil seal with a seal removal tool or a large screwdriver; make sure you don't scratch the seal bore.
16 Using a seal installer or a large deep socket as a drift, fit the new oil seal. Drive it into the bore squarely and make sure it's completely seated.
17 Lubricate the lip of the new seal with multi-purpose grease, then fit the side gearshaft. Be careful not to damage the lip of the new seal.
18 Check the differential lubricant level and add some, if necessary, to bring it to the appropriate level (see Chapter 1A or 1B).

2-pinion differential

19 If the vehicle is equipped with a 2-pinion differential, remove the differential from the vehicle (see Section 14).
20 Working on a bench, remove the bolts from the differential cover and separate the cover from the differential.
21 Using long-nose pliers, remove the circlip from the side gearshaft **(see illustration)**, and remove the shaft.
22 Carefully lever out the side gear shaft oil seal with a seal removal tool or a large

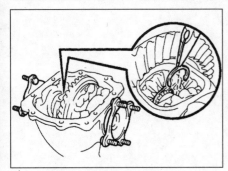

13.21 Use long-nose pliers to remove the circlips (2-pinion differential)

14.5 Differential rear mounting bolts

14.6 Differential front mounting bolts

screwdriver; make sure you don't scratch the seal bore.

23 Using a seal installer or a large deep socket as a drift, fit the new oil seal. Drive it into the bore squarely and make sure it's completely seated.

24 Lubricate the lip of the new seal with multi-purpose grease, then fit the side gearshaft. Be careful not to damage the lip of the new seal.

25 Using the long-nose pliers, fit a new circlip to the side gear shaft.

26 Remove all traces of old sealant from the cover and mating surface.

27 Apply a small bead of RTV sealant to the differential and carefully fit the cover and bolts. Tighten the bolts to the torque values listed in this Chapter's Specifications.

28 The remainder of refitting is the reverse of removal.

14 Differential (4WD models) – removal and refitting

Removal

1 Raise the rear of the vehicle and support it securely on axle stands. Chock the front wheels to prevent the vehicle from rolling. Place the transmission in Neutral with the handbrake off.

2 Drain the differential lubricant (see Chapter 1A or 1B).

3 Detach the driveshafts from the differential side gears (see Section 9). Support the driveshafts with wire or rope – don't let them hang by the other CV joints.

4 Mark the relationship of the propeller shaft to the pinion flange, then unbolt from the flange (see Section 11). Suspend the propeller shaft with a piece of wire (don't let it hang by the centre support bearing).

5 Support the differential with a jack. Remove the two mounting bracket bolts at the rear of the differential **(see illustration)**.

6 Remove the two differential front mounting bolts **(see illustration)**. Slowly lower the jack and remove the differential out from under the vehicle.

Refitting

7 Refitting is the reverse of the removal procedure. Tighten all bolts to the torque values listed in this Chapter's Specifications. Fill the differential with the proper lubricant (see Chapter 1A or 1B).

Chapter 9
Brakes

Contents

Section number

Anti-lock Brake System (ABS) – general information, component
   removal and refitting.................................... 2
Brake disc – inspection, removal and refitting................. 5
Brake hoses and lines – inspection and renewal................ 9
Brake hydraulic system – bleeding 10
Brake light switch – check, removal and refitting............. 15
Brake pedal – check and adjustment........................ 14
Disc brake caliper – removal and refitting 4
Disc brake pads – removal and refitting...................... 3
Drum brake shoes – removal and refitting.................... 6

Section number

General information 1
Handbrake – adjustment 12
Handbrake cables – removal and refitting 13
Handbrake shoes (models with rear disc brakes) inspection, removal
   and refitting.. 16
Master cylinder – removal, refitting and reservoir/grommet renewal 8
Servo – check, removal and refitting 11
Vacuum pump – testing, removal and refitting................. 17
Wheel cylinder – removal and refitting....................... 7

Degrees of difficulty

Easy, suitable for novice with little experience	Fairly easy, suitable for beginner with some experience	Fairly difficult, suitable for competent DIY mechanic	Difficult, suitable for experienced DIY mechanic	Very difficult, suitable for expert DIY or professional

Specifications

General

Brake fluid type	See *Weekly checks*
Brake pedal height (from floor covering):	
2000 and earlier models..................................	157 to 167 mm
2001 and later models	170 to 180 mm
Brake pedal free play	1.2 to 6.35 mm
Brake pedal reserve distance (minimum):	
2000 and earlier models..................................	75 mm
2001 and later models	118 mm
Brake light switch-to-pedal clearance	0.5 to 2.4 mm
Servo pushrod-to-master cylinder piston clearance	0.0 mm

Disc brakes

Minimum brake pad thickness.............................	See Chapter 1A or 1B
Disc minimum thickness	Cast or stamped into disc
Disc runout limit	0.05 mm

Drum brakes

Shoe friction material minimum thickness.....................	See Chapter 1A or 1B
Drum maximum diameter.................................	Cast or stamped into drum

Handbrake

Handbrake lever travel	6 to 8 clicks

Torque wrench settings

	lbf ft	Nm
Brake hose-to-caliper banjo bolts	22	30
Brake vacuum pump to cylinder head	20	27
Caliper backplate-to-steering knuckle bolts	78	106
Caliper mounting bolts...................................	20	27
Deceleration sensor mounting nuts	41	56
Master cylinder-to-brake servo nuts	9	12
Servo mounting nuts	9	12
Wheel cylinder mounting bolts.............................	7	10
Wheel nuts	See Chapter 1A or 1B	
Wheel speed sensor bolt (front or rear)	6	8

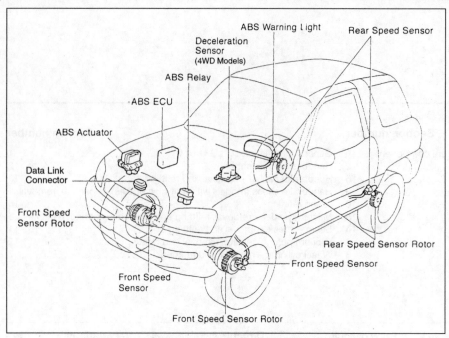

**2.1a Anti-Lock Brake System (ABS) component locations –
2000 and earlier LHD models**

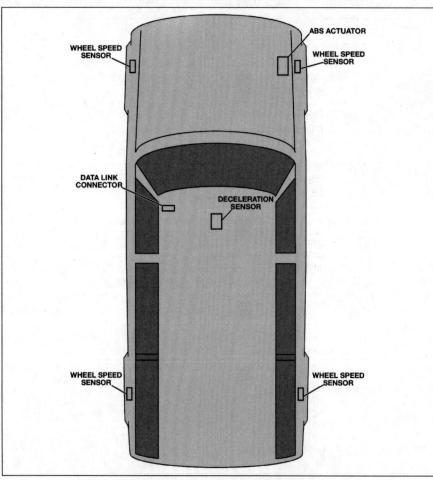

**2.1b Anti-Lock Brake System (ABS) component locations –
2001 and later LHD models**

1 General information

The vehicles covered by this manual are equipped with hydraulically-operated front and rear brake systems. The front brakes are disc type and the rear brakes are disc or drum type. Both the front and rear brakes are self-adjusting. The disc brakes automatically compensate for pad wear, while the drum brakes incorporate an adjustment mechanism which is activated as the handbrake is applied.

Hydraulic system

The hydraulic system consists of two separate circuits. The master cylinder has separate reservoirs for the two circuits, and, in the event of a leak or failure in one hydraulic circuit, the other circuit will remain operative. A dual proportioning valve on the bulkhead provides brake balance between the front and rear brakes.

Servo

The servo, utilising engine manifold vacuum and atmospheric pressure to provide assistance to the hydraulically-operated brakes, is mounted on the bulkhead in the engine compartment.

Handbrake

The handbrake operates the rear brakes only, through cable actuation. It's activated by a lever mounted in the centre console.

Service

After completing any operation involving disassembly of any part of the brake system, always test drive the vehicle to check for proper braking performance before resuming normal driving. When testing the brakes, perform the tests on a clean, dry, flat surface. Conditions other than these can lead to inaccurate test results.

Test the brakes at various speeds with both light and heavy pedal pressure. The vehicle should stop evenly without pulling to one side or the other. Avoid locking the brakes, because this wears the tyres and diminishes braking efficiency and control of the vehicle.

Tyres, vehicle load and wheel alignment are factors which also affect braking performance.

2 Anti-lock Brake System (ABS) – general information, component removal and refitting

1 The Anti-lock Brake System (ABS) **(see illustrations)** is designed to maintain vehicle steerability, directional stability and optimum deceleration under severe braking conditions and on most road surfaces. It does so by monitoring the rotational speed of each wheel and controlling the brake line pressure to each wheel during braking. This prevents the wheel from locking up.

Components

Actuator assembly

2 The actuator assembly consists of an electric hydraulic pump and four solenoid valves. The electric pump provides hydraulic pressure to charge the reservoirs in the actuator, which supplies pressure to the braking system. The pump and reservoirs are housed in the actuator assembly. The solenoid valves modulate brake line pressure during ABS operation.

Speed sensors

3 The speed sensors, which are located at each wheel, generate small electrical pulsations when the toothed sensor rotors are turning, sending a variable voltage signal to the ABS electronic control module (ECM) indicating wheel rotational speed.
4 The front speed sensors **(see illustration)** are mounted on the steering knuckles in close relationship to the toothed sensor rotors, which are integral with the outer constant velocity (CV) joints.
5 On all 2000 and earlier models, and 2001 and later 4WD models, the rear wheel sensors are bolted to the trailing arms **(see illustration)**. On 2001 and later 2WD models the sensors are pressed into the centre of the rear hub assemblies **(see illustration)**.

Deceleration sensor

6 2000 and earlier 4WD models, and all 2001 and later models, are equipped with a deceleration sensor mounted under the centre console. This sensor relays negative acceleration data to the ABS computer, which uses this information to determine the forward pitch of the vehicle during panic stops.

ABS computer

7 The ABS electronic control module (ECM), which is mounted behind the passenger's side kick panel on 2000 and earlier models, or integral with the ABS actuator on 2001 and later models, is the 'brain' of the ABS system. The function of the ECM is to accept and process information received from the wheel speed sensors to control the hydraulic line pressure, avoiding wheel lock-up. The ECM also constantly monitors the system, even under normal driving conditions, to find faults within the system. If a problem develops within the system, an ABS light will glow on the dashboard. A diagnostic code will also be stored in the ECM, which will indicate the problem area or component.

Diagnosis and repair

8 If a fault does develop in the ABS system, the vehicle must be taken to a Toyota dealer service department or other qualified garage for fault diagnosis and repair. However, first carry out the following simple checks:

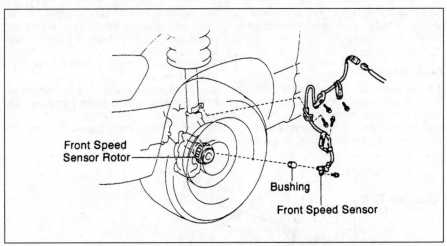

2.4 ABS front wheel speed sensor and sensor rotor

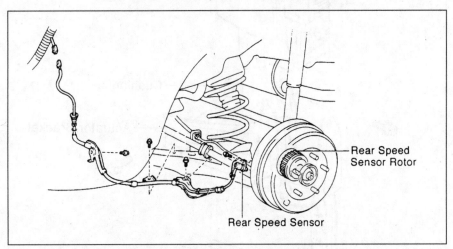

2.5a ABS rear wheel speed sensor and sensor rotor – all 2000 and earlier models, and 2001 and later 4WD models

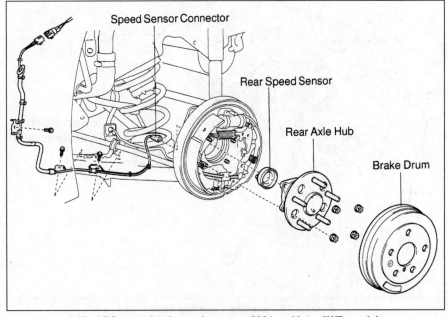

2.5b ABS rear wheel speed sensor – 2001 and later 2WD models

a) Check the brake fluid level in the reservoir.
b) Check that all electrical connectors are securely connected.
c) Check the fuses.

ABS actuator

9 Place some rags under the ABS actuator to catch any brake fluid that spills. Using a flare-nut wrench, unscrew the brake line fittings from the ABS actuator **(see illustrations)**.
10 Remove the power steering fluid reservoir and position it aside (see Chapter 10). On 2000 and earlier models, also unbolt the power steering hose bracket from the ABS actuator bracket.
11 Unplug the electrical connector(s) from the ABS actuator.
12 Unbolt the ABS actuator bracket from the body and remove the actuator from the engine compartment.
13 If necessary, unbolt the actuator from the bracket.

14 Refitting is the reverse of removal. Bleed the brake system as described in Section 10.

Front wheel speed sensor

15 Loosen the wheel nuts, raise the front of the vehicle and support it securely on axle stands. Block the wheels at the opposite end.
16 Remove the inner wing liner (see Chapter 11).
17 Follow the sensor wiring harness up to the electrical connector, then unplug the connector.
18 Unbolt the wiring harness securing brackets.
19 Remove the sensor mounting bolt and detach the sensor and bushing from the steering knuckle **(see illustration 2.4)**.
20 Refitting is the reverse of removal. Be sure to tighten the sensor mounting bolt to the torque listed in this Chapter's Specifications. Tighten the wheel nuts to the torque listed in the Chapter 1A or 1B Specifications.

Rear wheel speed sensor

All except 2001 and later 2WD models

21 Remove the rear seat cushion and the rear side trim panel (see Chapter 11).
22 Unplug the electrical connector, then push the grommet and wiring harness through the floor.
23 Loosen the wheel nuts, raise the rear of the vehicle and support it securely on axle stands. Block the wheels at the opposite end.
24 Unbolt the handbrake cable from the suspension arm.
25 Unbolt the wiring harness securing brackets.
26 Remove the sensor mounting bolt and detach the sensor and bushing from the rear axle carrier **(see illustration 2.5a)**.
27 Refitting is the reverse of removal. Be sure to tighten the sensor mounting bolt to the torque listed in this Chapter's Specifications. Tighten the wheel nuts to the torque listed in the Chapter 1A or 1B Specifications.

2001 and later 2WD models

28 Loosen the wheel nuts, raise the rear of the vehicle and support it securely on axle stands. Block the wheels at the opposite end.
29 Unplug the electrical connector from the wheel speed sensor **(see illustration 2.5b)**.
30 Remove the rear hub and bearing assembly (see Chapter 10).
31 The speed sensor can be removed from the back of the hub and bearing assembly with a slide hammer and bearing puller attachment. To fit the new sensor, it is recommended that a press be used, along with an adapter that bears only on the outer flange of the sensor. Do not tap on the sensor or adapter to fit it, as the sensor may be damaged.
32 Refitting is the reverse of the removal procedure. Tighten the hub and bearing assembly bolts to the torque listed in the Chapter 10 Specifications. Tighten the wheel nuts to the torque listed in the Chapter 1A or 1B Specifications.

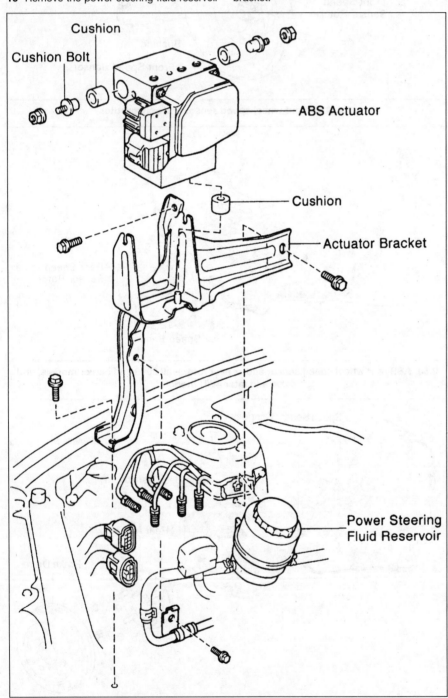

2.9a ABS actuator mounting details – 2000 and earlier models; 1996 4WD models are slightly different

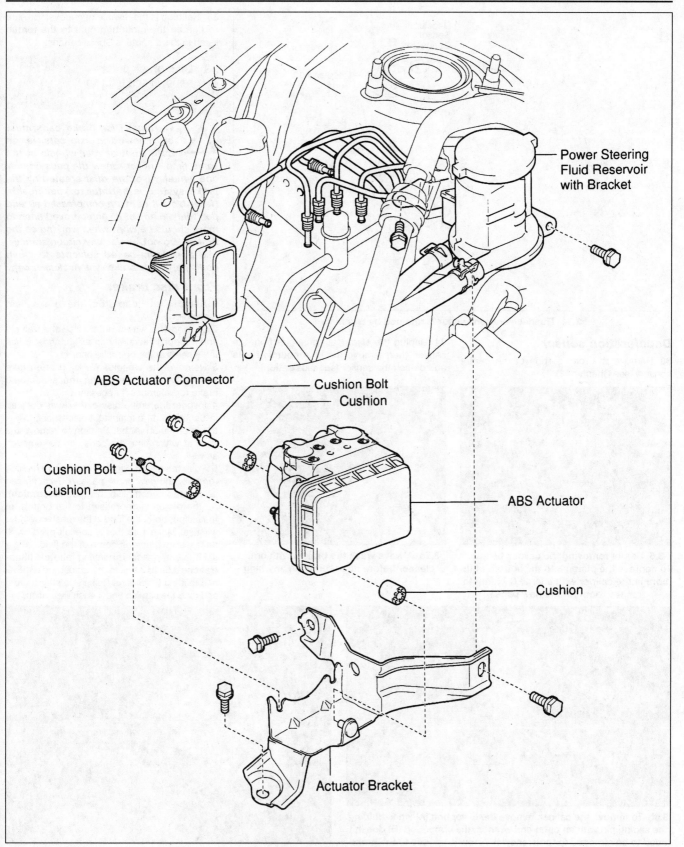

Power Steering
Fluid Reservoir
with Bracket

ABS Actuator Connector

Cushion Bolt

Cushion

Cushion Bolt

Cushion

ABS Actuator

Cushion

Actuator Bracket

2.9b ABS actuator mounting details –
2001 and later models

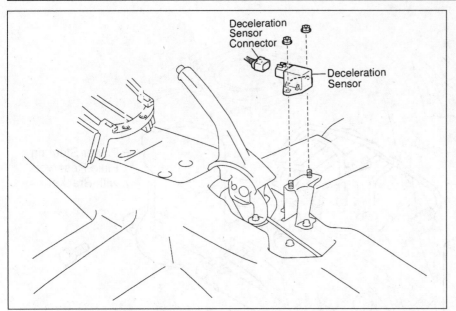

2.34 The deceleration sensor is retained by two nuts

Deceleration sensor

33 Remove the rear portion of the centre console (see Chapter 11).

34 Unplug the electrical connector from the sensor, then remove the two mounting nuts and detach the sensor **(see illustration)**.

35 Refitting is the reverse of removal. Be sure to tighten the mounting nuts to the torque listed in this Chapter's Specifications.

3 Disc brake pads – removal and refitting

⚠️ **Warning: Disc brake pads must be renewed in axle sets, ie, on both front or rear wheels at the same time – never renew the pads on only one wheel. Also, the dust created by the brake system is harmful to your health. Never blow it out with compressed air and don't inhale any of it. An approved filtering mask should be worn when working on the brakes. Do not, under any circumstances, use petroleum-based solvents to clean brake parts. Use brake system cleaner only.**

Front disc brakes

1 Remove the cap from the brake fluid reservoir.

2 Loosen the wheel nuts, raise the vehicle and support it securely on axle stands. Block the wheels at the opposite end.

3 Remove the wheels. Work on one brake assembly at a time, using the assembled brake for reference if necessary.

4 Inspect the brake disc carefully as outlined in Section 5. If machining is necessary, follow the information in that Section to remove the disc, at which time the pads can be removed as well.

5 Push the piston back into its bore to provide room for the new brake pads. A C-clamp can be used to accomplish this **(see illustration)**. As the piston is depressed to the bottom of the caliper bore, the fluid in the master cylinder will rise. Make sure that it doesn't overflow. If necessary, siphon off some of the fluid.

6 Follow the accompanying photos **(illustrations 3.6a to 3.6q)**, for the actual pad removal and refitting procedure. Be sure to stay in order and read the caption under each illustration.

3.5 Before removing the caliper, be sure to depress the piston into the bottom of its bore in the caliper with a large C-clamp to make room for the new pads

3.6a Always wash the brakes with brake cleaner before disassembling anything

3.6b To remove the caliper, remove the lower bolt (A) while holding the sliding pin with an open-end wrench; the upper bolt (B) doesn't need to be removed for pad renewal. Arrow (C) points to the brake hose banjo bolt, which shouldn't be unscrewed unless the caliper is being removed for renewal, or for hose renewal

3.6c Pivot the caliper up and support it in this position for access to the brake pads

3.6d Remove the outer shim . . .

3.6e . . . and the inner shim from the outer brake pad

3.6f Remove the outer brake pad

3.6g Remove the outer shim . . .

3.6h . . . and the inner shim from the inner brake pad

3.6i Remove the inner brake pad

3.6j Remove the pad support plates; inspect the plates for damage and renew as necessary (they should fit snugly)

3.6k If equipped, remove the wear indicator from the old inner brake pad and transfer it to the new inner pad (if the wear indicator is worn or bent, renew it)

3.6l Install the pad support plates, the new inner brake pad and the shims; make sure the ears on the pad are properly engaged with the pad support plates as shown

3.6m Install the outer pad and the shims

3.6n Pull out the lower sliding pin and clean it off (if either boot is damaged, remove it by levering the flange of the metal bushing that retains the boot) . . .

3.6o . . . and apply a coat of high-temperature grease to the pin

3.6p The upper pin can be slid out of its bushing with the caliper attached

3.6q If you have difficulty installing the caliper over the new pads, use a C-clamp to bottom the piston in its bore, then try again – it should now slip over the pads. Install the caliper and tighten the caliper mounting bolt to the specified torque

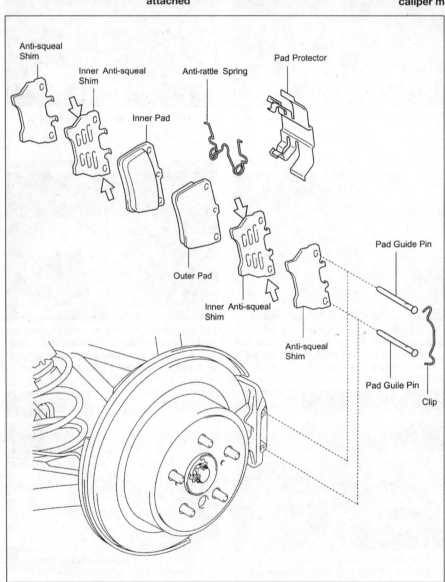

3.9 Rear disc brake details

7 When refitting the caliper, be sure to tighten the mounting bolts to the torque listed in this Chapter's Specifications. After the job has been completed, firmly depress the brake pedal a few times to bring the pads into contact with the disc. Check the level of the brake fluid, adding some if necessary. Check the operation of the brakes carefully before placing the vehicle into normal service.

Rear disc brakes

Note: *On models equipped with rear disc brakes it is not necessary to remove the caliper for brake pad removal and refitting.*

8 Wash the brake with brake system cleaner.
9 Carefully lever the brake pad protector from the pad guide pins **(see illustration)**.

⚠️ *Warning: Be careful not to disfigure any components while removing them – some of these components can be re-used.*

10 Remove the guide pin retainer clip, then pull out the pins using a pair of pliers. While pulling out the guide pins, cover the anti-rattle spring with your hand so it doesn't pop out and get lost.
11 Using a large pair of pliers, squeeze the pad against the caliper housing to compress the piston into its bore, making room for the new brake pads. **Note:** *Apply force on the brake pad centre of the piston; this will keep the piston from binding in its bore, allowing the piston to be more easily compressed.*
12 Slide the two pads with the anti-squeal shims out from the caliper.
13 Inspect the brake disc as described in Section 5.
14 Apply a thin coat of disc brake grease to both sides of the inner anti-squeal shims, then attach the inner and outer anti-squeal shims to both inner and outer brake pads.
15 Making sure the guide pin holes on the anti-squeal shims are properly aligned with the guide pin holes on the brake pads and the wear indicator tab on the inner pad is facing downward, fit the brake pads into the caliper.
16 Fit the anti-rattle spring, guide pins, guide

pin retaining clip and the brake pad protector.
17 Pump the brakes several times to bring the brake pads in contact with the brake disc.
18 Check the level of the brake fluid, adding some if necessary. Check the operation of the brakes carefully before placing the vehicle into normal service.

4 Disc brake caliper – removal and refitting

⚠️ **Warning: Dust created by the brake system is harmful to your health. Never blow it out with compressed air and don't inhale any of it. An approved filtering mask should be worn when working on the brakes. Do not, under any circumstances, use petroleum-based solvents to clean brake parts. Use brake system cleaner only.**
Note: *If renewal is indicated (usually because of fluid leakage), it is recommended that the calipers be renewed, not overhauled. New and factory rebuilt units are available on an exchange basis, which makes this job quite easy. Always renew the calipers in pairs – never renew just one of them.*

Removal

1 Loosen the front wheel nuts, raise the front of the vehicle and place it securely on axle stands. Remove the wheel.
2 Remove the bolt and disconnect the brake hose from the caliper **(see illustration 3.6b)**.

5.2 To remove the torque plate, remove these two bolts (arrowed); be careful not to lose the pad support plates

5.4a To check disc runout, mount a dial indicator as shown and rotate the disc

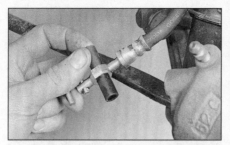

4.2 Using a piece of rubber hose of the appropriate size, plug the brake line; this will prevent brake fluid from leaking out and dirt and moisture from contaminating the system

Plug the brake hose to keep contaminants out of the brake system and to prevent losing any more brake fluid than is necessary **(see illustration)**. Discard the sealing washers – new ones should be used during refitting. **Note:** *If the caliper is being removed for access to another component, don't disconnect the hose.*
3 Refer to Section 3 for the caliper removal procedure (it's part of the brake pad removal and refitting procedure). If the caliper is being removed for access to another component, hang it from the coil spring with a piece of wire **(see illustration)**.

Refitting

4 Refit the caliper by reversing the removal procedure. Remember to renew the sealing washers (gaskets) at the brake hose-to-caliper connection.
5 Bleed the brake circuit according to the

5.3 The brake pads on this vehicle were obviously neglected, as they wore down to the rivets and cut deep grooves into the disc – wear this severe means the disc must be renewed

5.4b Using a swirling motion, remove the glaze from the disc surface with sandpaper or emery cloth

4.3 Never let the caliper hang by the brake hose – use a piece of wire to tie it to the coil spring

procedure in Section 10. Make sure there are no leaks from the hose connections. Test the brakes carefully before returning the vehicle to normal service.

5 Brake disc – inspection, removal and refitting

Inspection

1 Loosen the wheel nuts, raise the vehicle and support it securely on axle stands. Remove the wheel and refit the nuts to hold the disc in place against the hub flange. **Note:** *If the nuts don't contact the disc when screwed on all the way, refit washers under them.*
2 Remove the brake caliper as outlined in Section 4. It isn't necessary to disconnect the brake hose. After removing the caliper bolts, suspend the caliper out of the way with a piece of wire **(see illustration 4.3)**. Remove the two backplate-to-steering knuckle bolts **(see illustration)** and detach the backplate.
3 Visually inspect the disc surface for score marks and other damage. Light scratches and shallow grooves are normal after use and may not always be detrimental to brake operation, but deep scoring requires disc removal and refinishing by a specialist. Be sure to check both sides of the disc **(see illustration)**. If pulsating has been noticed during application of the brakes, suspect disc runout (note that this is a side-effect of ABS operation during heavy braking).
4 To check disc runout, place a dial indicator at a point about 15 mm from the outer edge of the disc **(see illustration)**. Set the indicator to zero and turn the disc. The indicator reading should not exceed the specified allowable runout limit. If it does, the disc should be refinished by a specialist. **Note:** *The discs should be resurfaced regardless of the dial indicator reading, as this will impart a smooth finish and ensure a perfectly flat surface, eliminating any brake pedal pulsation or other undesirable symptoms related to questionable discs. At the very least, if you elect not to have the discs resurfaced, remove the glaze from the surface with emery cloth or sandpaper, using a swirling motion (see illustration).*

5.5a The minimum thickness dimension is cast into the rear of the disc (typical)

5.5b Use a micrometer to measure disc thickness

5.6a If the rear disc is difficult to remove, remove this plug . . .

5.6b . . . insert a screwdriver through the hole (the hole must be at the 6 o'clock position, because that's where the adjuster is located) and rotate the adjuster to back the handbrake shoe away from the drum surface in the disc

5 It's absolutely critical that the disc not be machined to a thickness under the specified minimum thickness. The minimum thickness is cast or stamped into the inside of the disc **(see illustration)**. The disc thickness can be checked with a micrometer **(see illustration)**.

Removal

6 Remove the nuts that were put on to hold the disc in place and slide the disc off the hub. If you're removing a rear disc and it won't come off, it may be interfering with the handbrake shoes; remove the plug **(see illustration)** and rotate the adjuster to back the handbrake shoes away from the drum surface within the disc **(see illustration)**.

Refitting

7 Place the disc in position over the threaded studs.

8 Refit the backplate and caliper, tightening the bolts to the torque values listed in this Chapter's Specifications.

9 Refit the wheel, then lower the vehicle to the ground. Tighten the nuts to the torque listed in the Chapter 1A or 1B Specifications. Depress the brake pedal a few times to bring the brake pads into contact with the disc. Bleeding won't be necessary unless the brake hose was disconnected from the caliper. Check the operation of the brakes carefully before driving the vehicle.

6 Drum brake shoes – removal and refitting

⚠️ *Warning: Drum brake shoes must be renewed on both wheels at the same time – never renew the shoes on only one wheel. Also, the dust created by the brake system is harmful to your health. Never blow it out with compressed air and don't inhale any of it. An approved filtering mask should be worn when working on the brakes. Do not, under any circumstances, use petroleum-based solvents to clean brake parts. Use brake system cleaner only.*

Caution: Whenever the brake shoes are renewed, the return and hold-down springs should also be renewed. Due to the continuous heating/cooling cycle the springs are subjected to, they can lose tension over a period of time and may allow the shoes to drag on the drum and wear at a much faster rate than normal.

1 Loosen the wheel nuts, raise the rear of the vehicle and support it securely on axle stands. Block the front wheels to keep the vehicle from rolling.

2 Release the handbrake.

3 Remove the wheel. **Note:** *All four rear brake shoes must be renewed at the same time, but to avoid mixing up parts, work on only one brake assembly at a time.*

4 Follow the accompanying illustrations for the brake shoe removal and refitting procedure **(see illustrations 6.4a to 6.4dd)**. Be sure to stay in order and read the caption under each illustration. **Note:** *If the brake drum cannot be easily pulled off the axle and shoe assembly, make sure the handbrake is completely released. If the drum still cannot be pulled off, the brake shoes will have to be retracted. This is done by first removing the plug from the brake drum. With the plug removed, pull the lever off the adjuster star wheel with a hooked tool while turning the adjuster wheel with another screwdriver, moving the shoes away from the drum **(see illustration 6.4b)**. The drum should now come off.*

6.4a Mark the relationship of the drum to the hub, so the drum will retain its dynamic balance after reassembly

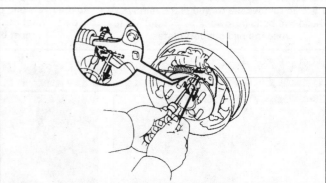

6.4b If the brake drum is hanging up on the shoes because of excessive wear, remove the plug from the drum, pull the adjuster lever away from the star wheel with a hooked tool and turn the star wheel with a screwdriver to retract the brake shoes

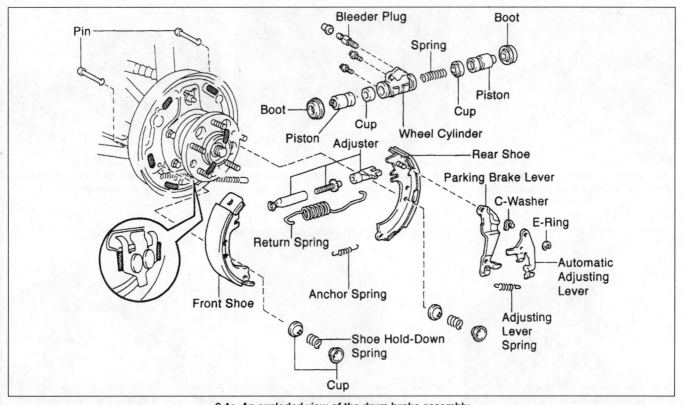

6.4c An exploded view of the drum brake assembly

6.4d Before removing anything, clean the brake assembly with brake cleaner and allow it to dry; DO NOT USE COMPRESSED AIR TO BLOW OFF BRAKE DUST (hub removed for clarity)

6.4e Unhook the return spring from its hole in the front shoe

6.4f Using a hold-down spring tool, remove the hold-down spring by pushing in and rotating it 1/4-turn

6.4g Remove the front shoe and unhook the anchor spring from the rear shoe

6.4h Remove the rear shoe hold-down spring

6.4i Force the spring back from the handbrake lever and disengage the cable from the lever, then remove the rear shoe assembly

6.4j Unhook the return spring from rear shoe, then remove the spring and adjuster assembly

6.4k Unhook the adjusting lever spring from the shoe

6.4l Remove the adjuster end from the rear shoe assembly

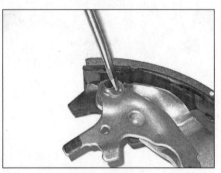

6.4m Lever open the C-clip and detach the adjuster lever from the rear shoe

6.4n Lever off the clip . . .

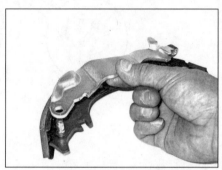

6.4o . . . and detach the handbrake lever from the rear shoe

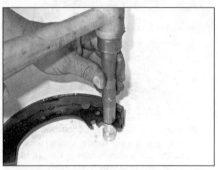

6.4p Drive the pin out of the old rear shoe . . .

6.4q . . . and install it into the new rear shoe

6.4r Place the handbrake lever on the pin and secure it with a new clip . . .

6.4s . . . then install the adjuster lever on the pin and secure it with a new clip

6.4t Attach the adjuster end to the rear shoe

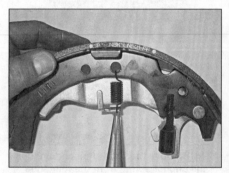

6.4u Connect the adjuster lever spring

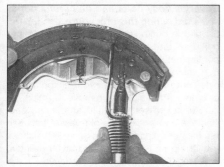

6.4v Insert the adjuster screw into the adjuster end, then connect the return spring to the hole in the shoe

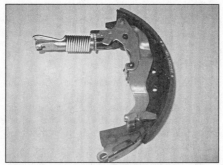

6.4w Front view of the assembled rear shoe/adjuster assembly

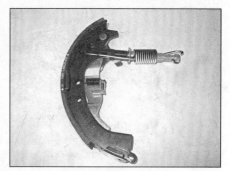

6.4x Rear view of the assembled rear shoe/adjuster assembly

6.4y Apply high-temperature grease to the friction points of the backing plate

6.4z Attach the handbrake cable to the handbrake lever . . .

6.4aa . . . then position the rear shoe on the backing plate and install the hold-down spring and retainer

6.4bb Hook both ends of the return spring into their holes in the front and rear shoes

6.4cc Position the front shoe on the backing plate and install the hold-down spring and retainer

6.4dd Connect the return spring to the hole in the front shoe

6.5 The maximum drum diameter is cast into the drum (typical)

5 Before refitting the drum, it should be checked for cracks, score marks, deep scratches and hard spots, which will appear as small discoloured areas. If the hard spots cannot be removed with fine emery cloth or if any of the other conditions listed above exist, the drum must be taken to a specialist to have it resurfaced. **Note:** *Professionals recommend resurfacing the drums each time a brake job is done. Resurfacing will eliminate the possibility of out-of-round drums. If the drums are worn so much that they can't be resurfaced without exceeding the maximum allowable diameter (stamped or cast into the drum), then new ones will be required (see illustration). At the*

very least, if you elect not to have the drums resurfaced, remove the glaze from the surface with emery cloth using a swirling motion.

6 Refit the brake drum on the axle flange. Using a screwdriver inserted through the adjusting hole in the brake drum **(see illustration 6.4b)**, turn the adjuster star wheel until the brake shoes drag on the drum as the drum is rotated, then back off the star wheel until the shoes don't drag. Refit the plug in the drum.

7 Refit the wheel and nuts. Lower the vehicle and tighten the nuts to the torque listed in the Chapter 1A or 1B Specifications.

8 Make a number of forward and reverse

7.4 Disconnect the brake line fitting (1), then remove the two wheel cylinder bolts (2)

stops and operate the handbrake to adjust the brakes until satisfactory pedal action is obtained.

9 Check the operation of the brakes carefully before driving the vehicle.

7 Wheel cylinder – removal and refitting

Note: *If renewal is indicated (usually because of fluid leakage or sticky operation), it is recommended that the wheel cylinders be renewed, not overhauled. Always renew the wheel cylinders in pairs – never renew just one of them.*

Removal

1 Raise the rear of the vehicle and support it securely on axle stands. Block the front wheels to keep the vehicle from rolling.

2 Remove the brake shoe assembly (see Section 6).

3 Remove all dirt and foreign material from around the wheel cylinder.

4 Disconnect the brake line **(see illustration)** with a flare-nut wrench, if available. Don't pull the brake line away from the wheel cylinder.

5 Remove the wheel cylinder mounting bolts.

6 Detach the wheel cylinder from the brake backing plate. Immediately plug the brake line to prevent fluid loss and contamination.

Refitting

7 Place the wheel cylinder in position and fit the bolts finger-tight. Connect the brake line to the cylinder, being careful not to cross-thread the fitting. Tighten the wheel cylinder bolts to the torque listed in this Chapter's Specifications.

8 Tighten the brake line securely and fit the brake shoe assembly (see Section 6).

9 Bleed the brakes (see Section 10).

10 Check the operation of the brakes carefully before driving the vehicle.

8 Master cylinder – removal, refitting and reservoir/grommet renewal

Removal

1 If you're working on a 2000 or earlier model, remove the air filter housing cover (See Chapter 4A or 4B) and the fuse/relay box from the left strut tower.

2 Unplug the electrical connector for the fluid level warning switch **(see illustration)**.

3 Remove as much fluid as possible from the reservoir with a large syringe or a poultry baster.

⚠️ **Warning: If a poultry baster is used, never again use it for the preparation of food.**

4 Place rags under the fittings and prepare caps or plastic bags to cover the ends of the lines once they're disconnected. Loosen the fittings at the ends of the brake lines where they enter the master cylinder. To prevent rounding off the flats, use a flare-nut wrench, which wraps around the fitting hex.

Caution: Brake fluid will damage paint.

Cover all body parts and be careful not to spill fluid during this procedure.

5 Pull the brake lines away from the master cylinder and plug the ends to prevent contamination.

6 Remove the two nuts attaching the master cylinder to the vacuum servo. Pull the master cylinder off the studs to remove it. Again, be careful not to spill the fluid as this is done. Remove and discard the old gasket between the master cylinder and the servo. Also check the O-ring on the end of the master cylinder, renewing it if it is cracked or hardened.

Refitting

Note: *Before fitting a new or reconditioned master cylinder, check the clearance between the servo pushrod and the pocket in the master cylinder piston. If necessary, adjust the length of the servo pushrod (see Section 11).*

7 Bench bleed the master cylinder before fitting it. Because it will be necessary to apply pressure to the master cylinder piston and, at the same time, control flow from the brake line outlets, it is recommended that the mater cylinder be mounted in a vice, with the jaws of the vice clamping on the mounting flange.

8 Attach a pair of bleeder tubes (available at most accessory shops) to the outlet ports of the master cylinder **(see illustration)**.

9 Fill the reservoir with brake fluid of the recommended type (see *Weekly checks*).

10 Slowly push the pistons into the master cylinder (a large cross-head screwdriver can be used for this) – air will be expelled from the pressure chambers and into the reservoir. Because the tubes are submerged in fluid, air can't be drawn back into the master cylinder when you release the pistons.

11 Repeat the procedure until no more air bubbles are present.

12 Remove the bleed tubes, one at a time, and fit plugs in the open ports to prevent fluid leakage and air from entering. Fit the reservoir cap.

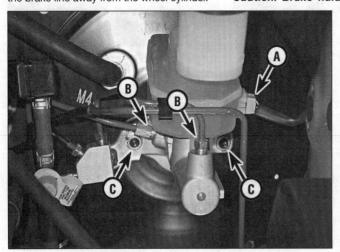

8.2 Master cylinder mounting details

A	Electrical connector	C	Mounting nuts
B	Brake line fittings		

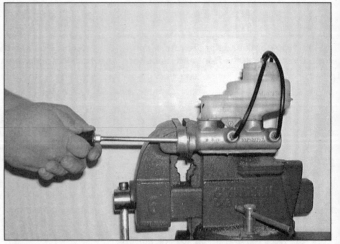

8.8 The best way to bleed air from the master cylinder before installing it on the vehicle is with a pair of bleeder tubes that direct brake fluid into the reservoir during bleeding

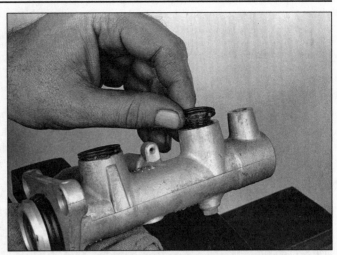

8.17 Have an assistant depress the brake pedal and hold it down, then loosen the fitting nut, allowing the air and fluid to escape; repeat this procedure on both fittings until the fluid is clear of air bubbles

8.22 After the reservoir has been removed, pull the grommets from the master cylinder body; if they're hard, cracked or damaged, or have been leaking, renew them

13 Fit the master cylinder over the studs on the servo and tighten the nuts only finger-tight at this time. Don't forget to use a new gasket.

14 Thread the brake line fittings into the master cylinder. Since the master cylinder is still a bit loose, it can be moved slightly so the fittings thread in easily. Don't strip the threads as the fittings are tightened.

15 Tighten the mounting nuts to the torque listed in this Chapter's Specifications. Tighten the brake line fittings securely.

16 Plug in the electrical connector to the fluid level warning switch.

17 Fill the master cylinder reservoir with fluid, then bleed the master cylinder and the brake system (see Section 10). To bleed the master cylinder on the vehicle, have an assistant depress the brake pedal and hold it down. Loosen the fitting to allow air and fluid to escape (see illustration). Tighten the fitting, then allow your assistant to return the pedal to its rest position. Repeat this procedure on both fittings until the fluid is free of air bubbles. Check the operation of the brake system carefully before driving the vehicle.

Reservoir/grommet renewal

Note: *The brake fluid reservoir can be renewed separately from the master cylinder body if it becomes damaged. If there is leakage between the reservoir and the master cylinder body, the grommets on the reservoir can be renewed.*

18 Remove as much fluid as possible from the reservoir with a large syringe or a poultry baster.

 Warning: If a poultry baster is used, never again use it for the preparation of food.

19 Place rags under the master cylinder to absorb any fluid that may spill out once the reservoir is detached from the master cylinder.

Caution: Brake fluid will damage paint. Cover all body parts and be careful not to spill fluid during this procedure.

20 Remove the screw that retains the reservoir to the master cylinder.

21 Pull the reservoir out of the master cylinder body.

22 Pull the grommets out of the master cylinder (see illustration).

23 Lubricate the new grommets with clean brake fluid, then press them into place.

24 Push the reservoir into the grommets and secure it with the screw.

25 Refill the reservoir with the recommended brake fluid (see *Weekly checks*) and check for leaks.

26 Bleed the master cylinder (see illustration 8.17), followed by the remainder of the system (see Section 10).

9 Brake hoses and lines – inspection and renewal

Inspection

1 About every six months, with the vehicle raised and supported securely on axle stands, the rubber hoses which connect the steel brake lines with the front and rear brake assemblies should be inspected for cracks, chafing of the

9.3 Unscrew the brake line threaded fitting with a flare-nut wrench to protect the fitting corners from being rounded off

outer cover, leaks, blisters and other damage. These are important and vulnerable parts of the brake system and inspection should be complete. A light and mirror will be helpful for a thorough check. If a hose exhibits any of the above conditions, renew it.

Renewal

Front brake hose

2 Loosen the wheel nuts, raise the vehicle and support it securely on axle stands. Remove the wheel.

3 At the body bracket, unscrew the brake line fitting from the hose (see illustration). Use a flare-nut wrench to prevent rounding off the corners. If the bracket begins to bend, hold the hose fitting with an open-ended spanner.

4 Remove the U-clip from the female fitting at the bracket with a pair of pliers (see illustration), then pass the hose through the bracket.

5 At the caliper end of the hose, remove the banjo fitting bolt, then separate the hose from the caliper. Note that there are two copper sealing washers on either side of the fitting – they should be renewed during refitting.

6 Unbolt the hose from the bracket on the strut.

9.4 Pull off the U-clip with a pair of pliers

7 Refitting is the reverse of removal. Make sure the hose isn't twisted between the caliper and the strut bracket. Tighten the banjo bolt to the torque listed in this Chapter's Specifications, and tighten the brake hose-to-brake line fitting securely.

8 Bleed the caliper (see Section 10).

9 Fit the wheel and nuts, lower the vehicle and tighten the nuts to the torque listed in the Chapter 1A or 1B Specifications.

Rear brake hose

10 The rear brake hose serves as the flexible connection between two rigid metal lines, one on the body and the other on the trailing arm. Both ends of the hose are attached to these metal lines with threaded fittings and U-clips. Refer to Paragraphs 2, 3 and 4. Be sure to bleed the wheel cylinder when you're done (see Section 10).

Metal brake lines

11 When renewing brake lines, be sure to use the correct parts. Don't use copper tubing for any brake system components. Purchase steel brake lines from a dealer or accessory shop.

12 Prefabricated brake line, with the tube ends already flared and fittings fitted, is available at accessory shops and dealer parts departments. These lines can bent to the proper shape with a tubing bender.

13 When fitting the new line, make sure it's securely supported in the brackets and has plenty of clearance between moving or hot components.

14 After refitting, check the master cylinder fluid level and add fluid as necessary. Bleed the brake system (see Section 10) and test the brakes carefully before driving the vehicle in traffic.

10 Brake hydraulic system – bleeding

⚠️ **Warning: Wear eye protection when bleeding the brake system. If the fluid comes in contact with your eyes, immediately rinse them with water and seek medical attention.**

Note: *Bleeding the hydraulic system is necessary to remove any air that manages to find its way into the system when it's been opened during removal and refitting of a hose, line, caliper or master cylinder.*

1 You'll probably have to bleed the system at all four brakes if air has entered it due to low fluid level, or if the brake lines have been disconnected at the master cylinder or ABS hydraulic actuator.

2 If a brake line was disconnected only at a wheel, then only that caliper or wheel cylinder needs to be bled.

3 If a brake line is disconnected at a fitting located between the master cylinder and any of the brakes, the entire system must be bled. And, if the master cylinder has run dry or has

been renewed, bleed the master cylinder as described in Section 8, Paragraph 17, followed by the remainder of the system.

4 Remove any residual vacuum from the brake vacuum servo by applying the brake several times with the engine off.

5 Remove the master cylinder reservoir cap and fill the reservoir with brake fluid. Refit the cap. **Note:** *Check the fluid level often during the bleeding operation and add fluid as necessary to prevent the fluid level from falling low enough to allow air bubbles into the master cylinder.*

6 Have an assistant on hand, as well as a supply of new brake fluid, a clear plastic container partially filled with clean brake fluid, a length of clear tubing to fit over the bleeder valve and a spanner to open and close the bleeder valve.

7 Beginning at the right rear wheel, loosen the bleeder valve slightly, then tighten it to a point where it's snug but can still be loosened quickly and easily.

8 Place one end of the tubing over the bleeder valve and submerge the other end in brake fluid in the container **(see illustration)**.

9 Have the assistant depress the brake pedal slowly and hold the pedal down firmly.

10 While the pedal is held down, open the bleeder valve just enough to allow a flow of fluid to leave the valve. Watch for air bubbles to exit the submerged end of the tube. When the fluid flow slows after a couple of seconds, close the valve and have your assistant release the pedal.

11 Repeat paragraphs 9 and 10 until no more air is seen leaving the tube, then tighten the bleeder valve and proceed to the left rear wheel, the right front wheel and the left front wheel, in that order, and perform the same procedure. Be sure to check the fluid in the master cylinder reservoir frequently.

12 Never use old brake fluid. It contains moisture which can boil, rendering the brakes inoperative.

13 Refill the master cylinder with fluid at the end of the operation.

10.8 When bleeding the brakes, a hose is connected to the bleed screw at the caliper or wheel cylinder and then submerged in brake fluid – air will be seen as bubbles in the tube and container (all air must be expelled before moving to the next wheel)

14 Check the operation of the brakes. The pedal should feel solid when depressed, with no sponginess. If necessary, repeat the entire process.

⚠️ **Warning: Do not operate the vehicle if the ABS light or BRAKE light fails to go out, if the brakes feel low or spongy, or if you have any doubts as to the effectiveness of the brake system.**

11 Servo – check, removal and refitting

Operating check

1 Depress the brake pedal several times with the engine off and make sure there's no change in the pedal reserve distance.

2 Depress the pedal and start the engine. If the pedal goes down slightly, operation is normal.

Air-tightness check

3 Start the engine and turn it off after one or two minutes. Depress the brake pedal slowly several times. If the pedal depresses less each time, the servo is airtight.

4 Depress the brake pedal while the engine is running, then stop the engine with the pedal depressed. If there's no change in the pedal reserve travel after holding the pedal for 30 seconds, the servo is airtight.

Removal

5 Brake servo units shouldn't be disassembled. They require special tools not normally found in most garages. Because of its critical relationship to brake performance, the servo should be only replaced with a new or rebuilt one.

6 Disconnect the hose leading from the engine to the servo. Be careful not to damage the hose when removing it from the servo fitting.

7 Remove the brake master cylinder (see Section 8). If you're working on a 2000 or earlier model, also remove the air intake duct and the fuse/relay block.

8 Remove the left side lower finish panel from the instrument panel (see Chapter 11).

9 Remove the pedal return spring.

10 Locate the pushrod clevis connecting the servo to the brake pedal **(see illustration)**. Remove the clevis pin retaining clip with pliers and pull out the pin.

11 Remove the four nuts holding the brake servo to the bulkhead **(see illustration 11.10)**; you may need a light to see them.

12 Slide the servo straight out from the bulkhead until the studs clear the holes.

Refitting

13 Refitting procedures are basically the reverse of removal. Tighten the clevis locknut securely and the servo mounting nuts to the torque listed in this Chapter's Specifications.

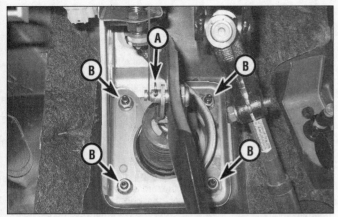

11.10 To disconnect the brake vacuum servo pushrod from the brake pedal, remove the retaining clip (A); to detach the servo from the bulkhead, remove the four mounting nuts (B)

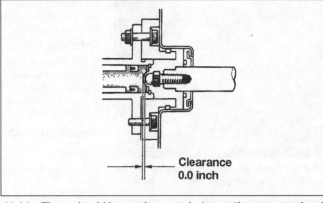

Clearance 0.0 inch

11.14a There should be no clearance between the servo pushrod and the master cylinder pushrod, but no interference either; if there is interference between the two, the brakes may drag; if there is clearance, there will be excessive brake pedal travel

14 If a new brake servo unit is being fitted, check the pushrod clearance **(see illustration)** as follows:

a) *Measure the distance that the pushrod protrudes from the master cylinder mounting surface on the front of the brake servo, including the gasket. Write this down **(see illustration)**. This is dimension A.*

b) *Measure the distance from the mounting flange to the end of the master cylinder **(see illustration)**. Write this down. This is dimension B.*

c) *Measure the distance from the end of the master cylinder to the bottom of the pocket in the piston **(see illustration)**. Write this down. This is dimension C.*

d) *Subtract measurement B from measurement C, then subtract measurement A from the difference between B and C. This the pushrod clearance.*

e) *Compare your calculated pushrod clearance to the pushrod clearance listed in this Chapter's Specifications. If necessary, adjust the pushrod length to achieve the correct clearance **(see illustration)**.*

15 After the final refitting of the master cylinder and brake hoses and lines, the brake pedal height and free play must be adjusted and the system must be bled. See the appropriate Sections of this Chapter for the procedures.

12 Handbrake – adjustment

1 The handbrake lever, when properly adjusted, should travel six to eight clicks, when a moderate pulling force is applied. If it travels less than the specified minimum number of clicks, there's a chance the handbrake might not be releasing completely and might be dragging on the drum. If the lever can be pulled up more than the specified maximum number of clicks, the handbrake may not hold adequately on an incline, allowing the car to roll.
2 To gain access to the handbrake cable adjuster, remove the centre console (see Chapter 11).
3 Loosen the locknut (the upper nut) while holding the adjusting nut (lower nut) with a spanner **(see illustration)**. Turn the adjusting nut until the desired travel is attained. Tighten the locknut.
4 Refit the centre console.

11.14b Measure the distance that the pushrod protrudes from the brake servo at the master cylinder mounting surface (including the gasket)

11.14c Measure the distance from the mounting flange to the end of the master cylinder

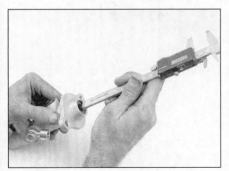

11.14d Measure the distance from the piston pocket to the end of the master cylinder

11.14e To adjust the length of the servo pushrod, hold the serrated portion of the rod with a pair of pliers and turn the adjusting screw in or out, as necessary, to achieve the desired setting

12.3 Loosen the locknut, then turn the adjusting nut until the desired handle travel is obtained

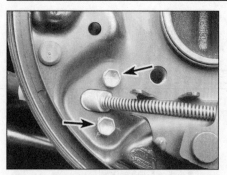

13.4 Unscrew the bolts (arrowed) from the backing plate and pass the cable through

13 Handbrake cables –
removal and refitting

Equaliser-to-handbrake cable

Removal

1 Relieve the fuel system pressure, then disconnect the cable from the negative terminal of the battery.

2 Loosen the rear wheel nuts, raise the rear of the vehicle and support it securely on axle stands. Block the front wheels. Remove the wheel. Make sure the handbrake is completely released, then remove the brake drum.

3 Remove the brake shoes and disconnect the cable from the handbrake lever (see Section 6).

4 Remove the two cable retaining bolts from the backing plate (**see illustration**) and pull the cable through the backing plate.

5 Remove the fuel tank (see Chapter 4A or 4B). Also remove the heat shields from above the exhaust system.

6 Unbolt the cable clamps from the trailing arm and floorpan, then disconnect the cable from the equaliser.

Refitting

7 Refitting is the reverse of removal. Apply a light coat of grease to the portion of the cable end that engages with the equaliser.

8 Adjust the handbrake when you're done (see Section 12).

Equaliser-to-brake lever cable

Removal

9 Remove the centre console (see Chapter 11).

10 With the lever in the down (off) position, remove the locknut and the adjusting nut (see Section 12) and detach the cable from the lever.

11 Raise the rear of the vehicle and support it securely on axle stands.

12 Remove the heat shields from above the exhaust system, if necessary, for access to the handbrake equaliser.

13 Turn the cable end 90-degrees and disconnect it from the equaliser.

14 Lever out the rubber grommet from the floor and pull the cable through the hole in the pan.

Refitting

15 Refitting is the reverse of removal. Apply a light coat of grease to the portion of the cable end that engages with the equaliser. Also, coat the sealing edge of the rubber grommet with silicone sealant to ensure that it remains watertight.

16 Adjust the handbrake lever when you're done (see Section 12).

14 Brake pedal –
check and adjustment

Pedal height

1 Measure the pedal height (**see illustration**) and compare your measurement to the pedal height listed in this Chapter's Specifications. If the pedal height is incorrect, adjust it as follows:

2 Remove the steering column lower finish panel and air duct.

3 Unplug the electrical connector from the brake light switch.

4 Loosen the brake light switch locknut and remove the brake light switch.

5 Loosen the pushrod locknut.

6 Adjust the pedal height by turning the pedal pushrod.

7 Tighten the pushrod locknut.

8 Refit the brake light switch and turn it until it lightly contacts the pedal stopper.

9 Back off the brake light switch one turn.

10 Measure the distance (clearance A) between the threaded portion of the brake light switch and the pedal (**see illustration**) and compare your measurement to the clearance listed in this Chapter's Specifications. If the clearance is not as specified, repeat the previous two paragraphs and try again.

11 Tighten the brake light switch locknut.

12 Plug in the brake light switch electrical connector.

13 Verify that brake lights come on when the brake pedal is depressed, and go off when the brake pedal is released.

14 Check the pedal free play (see below).

Pedal free play

15 Stop the engine, if it's running, and depress the brake pedal several times until there's no more vacuum left in the servo.

16 Push in the pedal until you feel some resistance, then measure the distance between the released pedal and this point at which you can feel resistance (**see illustration**). Compare your measurement with the pedal free play listed in this Chapter's Specifications.

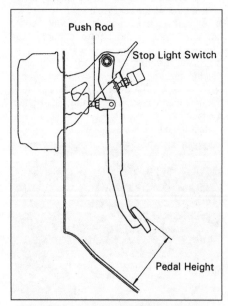

14.1 Brake pedal height is the distance between the pedal and the bulkhead when the pedal is released

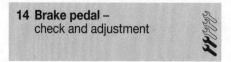

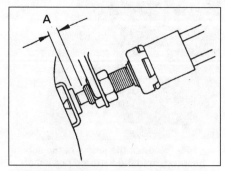

14.10 Clearance A is the distance between the brake light switch body and the pedal arm

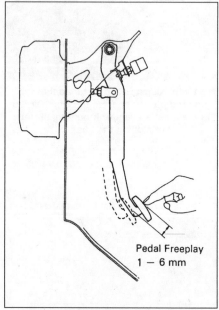

Pedal Freeplay
1 – 6 mm

14.16 Brake pedal freeplay is the distance between the pedal when it's released and the point at which some resistance is first felt when the pedal is depressed

17 Check the brake light switch clearance. If the brake light switch clearance is okay, troubleshoot the brake system.

Pedal reserve

18 Start the engine, depress the brake pedal a few times, then press down hard and hold it.
19 Pedal reserve travel is measured from the floor to the top of the pedal while it's being depressed. Compare your measurement to the pedal reserve listed in this Chapter's Specifications.
20 If the pedal reserve is less than specified, check the adjustment of the rear brake shoes and/or the brake servo pushrod-to-master cylinder piston clearance. If the brake pedal feels spongy, bleed the brake system (see Section 10).

15 Brake light switch – check, removal and refitting

Check

1 The brake light switch is located on a bracket at the top of the brake pedal **(see illustration 14.1)**. The switch activates the brake lights at the rear of the vehicle when the pedal is depressed.
2 To check the brake light switch, simply note whether the brake lights come on when the pedal is depressed and go off when the pedal is released. If they don't, check the fuse first (see Chapter 12). If the fuse is good, adjust the switch as described in Section 14 (adjusting the switch is part of brake pedal adjustment).
3 If the lights still don't come on, either the switch is not getting voltage, the switch itself is defective, or the circuit between the switch and the lights is defective. There is always the remote possibility that all of the brake light bulbs are burned out, but this is not very likely.
4 Use a voltmeter or test light to verify that there's voltage present at one side of the switch connector. If no voltage is present, troubleshoot the circuit from the switch to the fusebox. If there is voltage present, check for voltage on the other terminal when the brake pedal is depressed. If no voltage is present, renew the switch. If there is voltage present, troubleshoot the circuit from the switch to the brake lights (see the *Wiring diagrams* at the end of Chapter 12).

Removal

5 Unplug the electrical connector for the brake light switch.
6 Loosen the locknut and unscrew the switch from the pedal bracket.

Refitting

7 Refitting is the reverse of removal.
8 Adjust the brake pedal and brake light switch (see Section 14).

16 Handbrake shoes (models with rear disc brakes) – inspection, removal and refitting

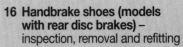

⚠ *Warning 1: Dust created by the brake system is hazardous to your health. Never blow it out with compressed air and don't inhale any of it. An approved filtering mask should be worn when working on the brakes. Do not, under any circumstances, use petroleum-based solvents to clean brake parts. Use brake system cleaner only.*

⚠ *Warning 2: Handbrake shoes must be renewed on both wheels at the same time – never renew the shoes on only one wheel.*

1 Remove the brake disc (see Section 5).
2 Inspect the thickness of the lining material on the shoes. If the lining has worn down to 2 mm or less, the shoes must be renewed.
3 Remove the hub and bearing assembly (see Chapter 10). **Note:** *It is possible to perform the shoe removal and refitting procedure without removing the hub and bearing assembly, although working room is limited.*
4 Wash off the brake parts with brake system cleaner **(see illustration)**.
5 Follow the accompanying illustrations for the brake shoe removal and refitting procedure **(see illustrations 16.5a to 16.5u)**. Be sure to stay in order and read the caption under each illustration.

16.4 Before disassembling it, be sure to wash the handbrake assembly with brake cleaner

16.5a Remove the rear handbrake shoe return spring from the anchor pin . . .

16.5b . . . and unhook it from the rear shoe

16.5c Remove the front handbrake shoe return spring from the anchor pin . . .

16.5d . . . and unhook it from the front shoe

16.5e Remove the rear shoe hold-down spring and pull out the pin

16.5f Remove the shoe strut from between the shoes

16.5g Remove the front shoe hold-down spring and pull out the pin

16.5h Remove the adjuster and the tension spring (the tension spring, which is not visible in this photo, is behind the adjuster and is attached to both shoes)

16.5i Pop the C-washer off the pivot pin on the back of the rear shoe . . .

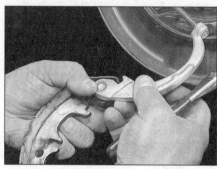

16.5j . . . and pull the handbrake lever off the pivot pin

16.5k Apply a thin coat of high-temperature grease to the contact surfaces of the backing plate

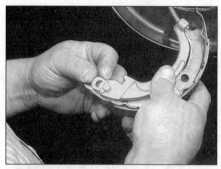

16.5l Slide the handbrake lever onto the pivot pin and install a new C-washer

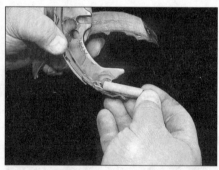

16.5m Attach the tension spring to the rear of the rear shoe . . .

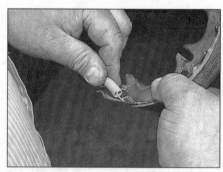

16.5n . . . and to the rear of the front shoe

16.5o Flip the shoes around and install the adjuster; make sure both ends of the adjuster are properly engaged with the shoes as shown

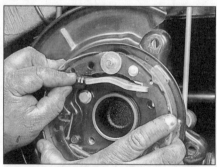

16.5p Place the shoes in position and install the strut and spring as shown; make sure the ends of the strut are properly engaged with the shoes as shown

16.5q Install the front shoe return spring . . .

16.5r . . . and the rear shoe return spring

16.5s Install the rear shoe hold-down spring . . .

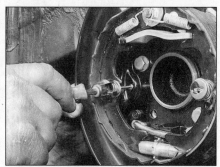

16.5t . . . and the front shoe hold-down spring

16.5u This is how the handbrake assembly should look when you're done

6 Refit the brake disc. Temporarily thread three of the wheel nuts onto the studs to hold the disc in place.

7 Remove the hole plug from the brake disc. Adjust the handbrake shoe clearance by turning the adjuster star wheel with a brake adjusting tool or screwdriver until the shoes contact the disc and the disc can't be turned (see illustrations 5.6a and 5.6b). Back off the adjuster eight notches, then refit the hole plug.

8 Refit the caliper bracket and brake caliper (see Section 4). Be sure to tighten the bolts to the torque listed in this Chapter's Specifications.

9 Refit the wheel and tighten the nuts to the torque specified in Chapter 1A or 1B.

10 Set the handbrake and count the number of clicks that it travels. It should be between about five to seven clicks – if it's not, adjust the handbrake as described in Section 12.

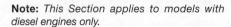

17 Vacuum pump – testing, removal and refitting

Note: *This Section applies to models with diesel engines only.*

Testing

1 The most common symptom of a failed vacuum pump is a hard brake pedal. Check the operation of the brake servo as described in Section 11.

2 If the servo doesn't operate properly, remove the vacuum hose from the brake servo and connect a vacuum gauge to it.

3 Start the engine and watch the gauge. Vacuum should register on the gauge almost immediately.

4 If vacuum does not register on the gauge, renew the vacuum pump.

Removal

5 Loosen the clamp and disconnect the vacuum hose from the pump.

6 Unscrew the mounting bolts and withdraw the vacuum pump from the left-hand end of the cylinder head. Recover the two O-ring seals and discard them, as new ones must be used on refitting. Be prepared for a little loss of engine oil from the cylinder head.

Refitting

7 Wipe clean the mating surfaces of the vacuum pump and cylinder head, then fit two new O-ring seals, align the pump driveshaft with the camshaft, and refit it. Insert the mounting bolts and tighten to the specified torque.

8 Reconnect the vacuum hose and tighten the clamp.

Chapter 10
Suspension and steering systems

Contents

Section number

Balljoint – removal and refitting 6
Coil spring (rear) – removal and refitting. 12
Control arm – removal, inspection and refitting 5
General information 1
Hub and bearing assembly (front) – removal and refitting 8
Hub and bearing assembly (rear) – removal and refitting. 13
Power steering pump – removal and refitting 19
Power steering system – bleeding 20
Shock absorber (rear) – removal, inspection and refitting 10
Stabiliser bar and bushings (front) – removal and refitting. 4
Stabiliser bar and bushings (rear) – removal and refitting 9
Steering column – removal and refitting. 15

Section number

Steering gear – removal and refitting. 18
Steering gear boots – renewal 17
Steering knuckle and hub – removal and refitting 7
Steering wheel – removal and refitting. 14
Strut assembly (front) – removal, inspection and refitting 2
Strut/spring assembly – removal and refitting 3
Suspension arms (rear) – removal and refitting 11
Tie-rod ends – removal and refitting. 16
Wheel alignment – general information 23
Wheel studs – removal and refitting. 21
Wheels and tyres – general information 22

Degrees of difficulty

Easy, suitable for novice with little experience	**Fairly easy,** suitable for beginner with some experience	**Fairly difficult,** suitable for competent DIY mechanic	**Difficult,** suitable for experienced DIY mechanic	**Very difficult,** suitable for expert DIY or professional

Specifications

Torque wrench settings	lbf ft	Nm
Front suspension		
Balljoints:		
Balljoint-to-control arm bolt/nuts	94	128
Balljoint-to-steering knuckle nut:		
2000 and earlier models	94	128
2001 and later models	98	133
Control arm:		
Front pivot bolt:		
2000 and earlier models	126	171
2001 and later models	101	137
Rear pivot stud nut (2000 and earlier models)	101	137
Rear bushing bolt (2001 and later models).	101	137
Rear bushing bracket bolts (2000 and earlier models).	101	137
Rear bushing bracket nut (2000 and earlier models)	21	28
Stabiliser bar:		
Bracket bolts	22	30
Link nuts:		
2000 and earlier models:		
2-door models	47	64
4-door models	83	113
2001 and later models	32	44
Struts:		
Strut-to-steering knuckle bolts/nuts:		
2000 and earlier models	117	158
2001 and later models	105	142
Strut upper mounting nuts	59	80
Shock absorber shaft nut	34	46
Suspension crossmember bolts:		
2000 and earlier:		
Front bolts.	152	206
Rear bolts	101	137
2001 and later:		
Front bolts.	82	111
Rear bolts	115	156

Torque wrench settings (continued)

	lbf ft	Nm
Rear suspension		
Hub and bearing assembly to trailing arm:		
1996 and 1997 models	59	80
1998 to 2000 models:		
2WD	38	51
4WD	59	80
2001 and later models	37	50
Shock absorber:		
Upper mounting nut:		
2000 and earlier models	18	25
2001 and later models	11	15
Lower mounting bolt	27	37
Stabiliser bar:		
Link nuts	32	44
Bracket bolts	14	19
Suspension arms:		
Trailing arm-to-body bolt	98	133
Upper suspension arm-to-body bolt/nut	83	113
Upper suspension arm to trailing arm:		
2000 and earlier models	76	103
2001 and later models	83	113
Lower suspension arm-to-body bolt	83	113
Lower suspension arm to trailing arm:		
2000 and earlier models	76	103
2001 and later models	83	113
Steering		
Airbag module Torx screws	7	9
Power steering pressure line-to-pump union bolt	38	52
Power steering pump bolts:		
Pump mounting bracket to engine (2000 and earlier)	32	43
Pump to mounting bracket (2000 and earlier)	32	43
Pump mounting bolts (2001 and later)	32	43
Power steering pulley nut (2000 and earlier models only)	32	43
Steering gear mounting bolts:		
2000 and earlier models	83	113
2001 and later models	101	137
Steering wheel nut:		
2000 and earlier models	25	34
2001 and later models	35	47
Tie-rod end-to-steering knuckle nut	36	49
U-joint-to-pinion shaft pinch-bolt	26	35
Wheels		
Wheel nuts	76	103

1 General information

The front suspension (see illustration) is a MacPherson strut design. The upper end of each strut/coil spring assembly is attached to the vehicle's body strut support. The lower end of the strut assembly is connected to the upper end of the steering knuckle. The steering knuckle is attached to a balljoint mounted on the outer end of the suspension control arm. A stabiliser bar (anti-roll bar) reduces body roll.

The rear suspension (see illustration) employs a trailing arm, two lateral suspension arms, a coil spring and shock absorber per side, and, on 2001 and later models, a stabiliser bar (anti-roll bar).

The rack-and-pinion steering gear is located behind the engine/transmission assembly on the front suspension crossmember and actuates the tie-rods, which are attached to the steering knuckles. The inner ends of the tie-rods are protected by rubber boots which should be inspected periodically for secure attachment, tears and leaking lubricant (which would indicate a failed rack seal).

The power assist system consists of a belt-driven pump and associated lines and hoses. The fluid level in the power steering pump reservoir should be checked periodically (see *Weekly checks*).

The steering wheel operates the steering shaft, which actuates the steering gear through universal joints. Looseness in the steering can be caused by wear in the steering shaft universal joints, the steering gear, the tie-rod ends and loose retaining bolts.

Precautions

Frequently, when working on the suspension or steering system components, you may come across nuts and bolts which seem impossible to loosen. Those on the underside of the vehicle are continually subjected to water, road grime, mud, etc, and can become rusted or 'frozen', making them extremely difficult to remove. In order to unscrew these stubborn nuts and bolts without damaging them (or other components), be sure to use lots of penetrating oil and allow it to soak in for a while. Using a wire brush to clean exposed threads will also ease removal of the nut or bolt and prevent damage to the threads. Sometimes a sharp blow with a hammer and punch will break the bond between a nut and bolt threads, but care must be taken to prevent the punch from slipping off the nut/bolt and ruining the threads. Heating the stuck nut/bolt and surrounding area sometimes helps too. A long socket bar extension will increase leverage, but never use an extension

**1.1 Front suspension and steering components –
2001 and later models shown, earlier models similar**

1 Strut/coil spring assembly
2 Steering knuckle
3 Balljoint
4 Control arm
5 Steering gear
6 Suspension crossmember

1.2 Typical rear suspension components

1 Shock absorber
2 Coil spring
3 Upper suspension arm
4 Lower suspension arm
5 Trailing arm

2.4a Mark the relationship of the strut to the steering knuckle (to preserve the camber setting when reassembling)

2.4b To detach the strut from the steering knuckle, remove the two nuts, then knock out the bolts with a hammer and punch

2.6 To detach the upper end of the strut from the body, remove the upper mounting nuts (arrowed)

on a ratchet – the ratchet mechanism could be damaged. Sometimes tightening the nut or bolt first will help to break it loose. Nut/bolts that require drastic measures to remove should always be renewed.

Since most of the procedures dealt with in this Chapter involve jacking up the vehicle and working underneath it, a good pair of axle stands will be needed. A hydraulic jack is the preferred type of jack to lift the vehicle, and it can also be used to support certain components during various operations.

⚠ *Warning: Never, under any circumstances, rely on a jack to support the vehicle while working on it. Whenever any of the suspension or steering nut/bolts are loosened or removed they must be inspected and, if necessary, renewed with ones of the same part number or of original equipment quality and design. Torque specifications must be followed for proper reassembly and component retention. Never attempt to heat or straighten any suspension or steering components. Instead, renew any bent or damaged part with a new one.*

2 Strut assembly (front) – removal, inspection and refitting

Removal

1 Loosen the wheel nuts, raise the vehicle and support it securely on axle stands. Remove the wheel.
2 Unbolt the brake hose bracket from the strut. If the vehicle is equipped with ABS, detach the speed sensor wiring harness from the strut by removing the clamp bracket bolt.
3 If you're working on a 2001 or later model, detach the stabiliser bar link from the bracket on the strut (see Section 4).
4 Mark the relationship of the strut to the steering knuckle **(see illustration)**. Note: *Also mark the positions of the bolt heads, as special camber adjusting bolts may have been fitted at some point.* Remove the strut-to-knuckle nuts **(see illustration)** and knock the bolts out with a hammer and punch.
5 Separate the strut from the steering knuckle.

Be careful not to overextend the inner CV joint. Also, don't let the steering knuckle fall outward and strain the brake hose.
6 Support the strut and spring assembly with one hand and remove the three strut-to-body nuts **(see illustration)**. Remove the assembly out from the wheel arch.

Inspection

7 Check the strut body for leaking fluid, dents, cracks and other obvious damage which would warrant repair or renewal.
8 Check the coil spring for chips or cracks in the spring coating (this will cause premature spring failure due to corrosion). Inspect the spring seat for cuts, hardness and general deterioration.
9 If any problems exist, proceed to the strut disassembly procedure (see Section 3).

Refitting

10 Guide the strut assembly up into the wheel arch and insert the upper mounting studs through the holes in the body. Once the studs protrude, fit the nuts so the strut won't fall back through. This is most easily accomplished with the help of an assistant, as the strut is quite heavy and awkward.
11 Slide the steering knuckle into the strut flange and insert the two bolts. Fit the nuts, align the previously-made alignment marks and tighten them to the torque listed in this Chapter's Specifications.
12 Connect the brake hose bracket to the strut and tighten the bolt securely. If the

3.3 Install the spring compressor according to the tool manufacturer's instructions and compress the spring until all pressure is relieved from the upper spring seat

vehicle is equipped with ABS, fit the speed sensor wiring harness bracket.
13 If you're working on a 2001 or later model, connect the stabiliser bar link to the strut bracket. Tighten the nut to the torque listed in this Chapter's Specifications.
14 Fit the wheel and nuts, then lower the vehicle and tighten the nuts to the torque listed in the Specifications.
15 Tighten the upper mounting nuts to the torque listed in this Chapter's Specifications.
16 Drive the vehicle to an alignment specialist to have the front end alignment checked, and if necessary, adjusted.

3 Strut/spring assembly – removal and refitting

1 If the struts or coil springs exhibit the telltale signs of wear (leaking fluid, loss of damping capability, chipped, sagging or cracked coil springs) explore all options before beginning any work. The strut/shock absorber assemblies are not serviceable and must be renewed if a problem develops. However, strut assemblies complete with springs may be available on an exchange basis, which eliminates much time and work. Whichever route you choose to take, check on the cost and availability of parts before disassembling your vehicle.

⚠ *Warning: Disassembling a strut is potentially dangerous and utmost attention must be directed to the job, or serious injury may result. Use only a high-quality spring compressor and carefully follow the manufacturer's instructions furnished with the tool. After removing the coil spring from the strut assembly, set it aside in a safe, isolated area.*

Disassembly

2 Remove the strut assembly following the procedure described in the previous Section. Mount the strut assembly in a vice. Line the vice jaws with wood or rags to prevent damage to the unit and don't tighten the vice excessively.
3 Following the tool manufacturer's instructions, fit the spring compressor (which can be obtained at most car accessory shops) on the spring and compress it sufficiently to

3.4 Remove the shock absorber shaft nut – if the upper spring seat turns while loosening the nut, immobilise it with a chain wrench or strap wrench

3.5 Lift the suspension support off the shock absorber shaft

3.6 Remove the spring seat from the shock absorber shaft

relieve all pressure from the upper spring seat **(see illustration)**. This can be verified by wiggling the spring.

3.7 Remove the compressed spring assembly – keep the ends of the spring pointed away from your body

4 Loosen the shock absorber shaft nut with a socket **(see illustration)**.
5 Remove the nut and suspension support

(see illustration). Inspect the bearing in the suspension support for smooth operation. If it doesn't turn smoothly, renew the suspension support. Check the rubber portion of the suspension support for cracking and general deterioration. If there is any separation of the rubber, renew it.
6 Lift the spring seat and upper insulator from the shock absorber shaft **(see illustration)**. Check the rubber spring seat for cracking and hardness, renewing it if necessary.
7 Carefully lift the compressed spring from the assembly **(see illustration)** and set it in a safe place.

⚠️ *Warning: Never place your head near the end of the spring.*

8 Slide the rubber bumper off the shock absorber shaft.
9 Check the lower insulator (if equipped) for wear, cracking and hardness and renew it if necessary.

Reassembly

10 If the lower insulator is being renewed, set it into position with the dropped portion seated in the lowest part of the seat. Extend the shock absorber rod to its full length and fit the rubber bumper **(see illustration)**.
11 Carefully place the coil spring onto the lower insulator, with the end of the spring resting in the lowest part of the insulator **(see illustration)**.
12 Fit the upper insulator and spring seat, making sure that the flats in the hole in the seat match up with the flats on the shock absorber shaft **(see illustration)**.

3.11 When installing the spring, make sure the end fits into the recessed portion of the lower seat (arrowed)

3.12 The flats on the shock absorber shaft (arrowed) must match up with the flats in the spring seat

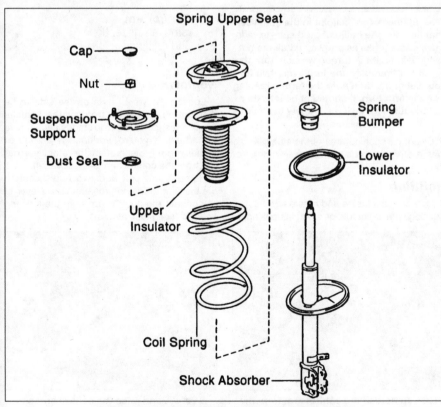

Cap

Nut

Suspension Support

Dust Seal

Spring Upper Seat

Upper Insulator

Spring Bumper

Lower Insulator

Coil Spring

Shock Absorber

3.10 Typical strut and coil spring assembly details – 2000 and earlier models shown, later models similar

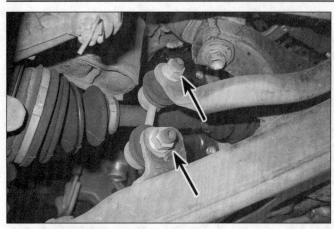

4.2a 2000 and earlier models – if you're removing the stabiliser bar, detach the bar from the link by removing the upper nut; if you're removing the control arm, remove the lower nut and detach the link from the arm

4.2b 2001 and later models – the stabiliser bar link is connected to a bracket on the strut instead of the control arm (if you're just removing the stabiliser bar, simply disconnect the links from the bar, not the strut)

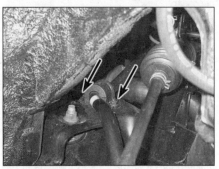

4.3 Stabiliser bar bracket bolts

13 Fit the dust seal and suspension support to the shock absorber shaft.
14 Fit the nut and tighten it to the torque listed in this Chapter's Specifications.
15 Fit the strut assembly following the procedure outlined previously (see Section 2).

4 Stabiliser bar and bushings (front) – removal and refitting

Removal

1 Loosen the front wheel nuts. Raise the front of the vehicle and support it securely on axle stands. Apply the handbrake and block the rear wheels to keep the vehicle from rolling off the stands. Remove the front wheels.
2 Detach the stabiliser bar link from the bar **(see illustrations)**. If the ball-stud turns with the nut, use an Allen key to hold the stud.
3 Unbolt the stabiliser bar bushing clamps **(see illustration)**. Guide the stabiliser bar out from between the crossmember and the body.
4 While the stabiliser bar is off the vehicle, slide off the retainer bushings and inspect them. If they're cracked, worn or deteriorated, renew them. It's also a good idea to inspect the stabiliser bar link. To check it, flip the balljoint stud side-to-side five or six times as shown **(see illustration)**, then fit the nut.

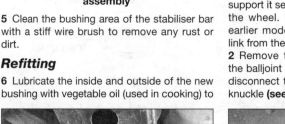

4.4 To check the balljoint in the stabiliser bar link, flip the balljoint stud side-to-side five or six times as shown, install the nut and, using a lbf in torque wrench, turn the nut continuously one turn every two to four seconds, then note the torque reading on the fifth turn. It shouldn't be less than about 0.4 lbf in; if it is, renew the link assembly

5 Clean the bushing area of the stabiliser bar with a stiff wire brush to remove any rust or dirt.

Refitting

6 Lubricate the inside and outside of the new bushing with vegetable oil (used in cooking) to

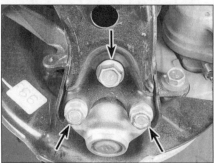

5.2a To detach the control arm from the steering knuckle balljoint, remove this bolt and these two nuts (arrowed) . . .

simplify reassembly. The slits of the bushings must face the rear of the vehicle. Also, the bushings must be positioned to the outside of the paint line (2000 and earlier models) or to the outside of the bushing stop (2001 and later models).
Caution: Don't use petroleum or mineral-based lubricants or brake fluid – they will lead to deterioration of the bushings.
7 Refitting is the reverse of removal. Tighten the nut/bolts to the torque values listed in this Chapter's Specifications.

5 Control arm – removal, inspection and refitting

Removal

1 Loosen the wheel nuts on the side to be dismantled, raise the front of the vehicle, support it securely on axle stands and remove the wheel. If you're working on a 2000 or earlier model, disconnect the stabiliser bar link from the control arm (see Section 4).
2 Remove the bolt and two nuts securing the balljoint to the control arm. Use a lever to disconnect the control arm from the steering knuckle **(see illustrations)**.

5.2b . . . and prise the control arm and balljoint apart with a large lever or screwdriver

5.3 To detach the front of the control arm from the crossmember, remove this pivot bolt (arrowed)

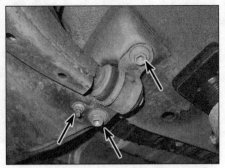

5.4a To detach the rear end of the control arm on a 2000 or earlier model, remove the nut and two bolts

5.4b To detach the rear end of the control arm on a 2001 or later model, remove this bolt (arrowed)

3 Remove the control arm front pivot bolt **(see illustration)**. **Note:** *If you're working on a 2000 or earlier model with an automatic transmission, and you're removing the left side control arm, the suspension crossmember must be supported, unbolted and then lowered to allow bolt removal.*
4 Remove the rear pivot bushing bracket (2000 and earlier models) **(see illustration)** or the rear bushing bolt (2001 and later models) **(see illustration)**.
5 Remove the control arm.

Inspection

6 Check the control arm for distortion and the bushings for wear, renewing parts as necessary. Do not attempt to straighten a bent control arm.

Refitting

7 Refitting is the reverse of removal. Tighten all of the nut/bolts to the torque values listed in this Chapter's Specifications. **Note:** *Before tightening the pivot bolt (and the pivot nut on the rear of the control arm, if you're working on a 2000 or earlier model), raise the outer end of the control arm with a hydraulic jack to simulate normal ride height.*
8 Fit the wheel and nuts, lower the vehicle and tighten the nuts to the torque listed in the Specifications.
9 It's a good idea to have the front wheel alignment checked and, if necessary, adjusted after this job has been performed.

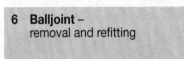

6 Balljoint – removal and refitting

Removal

1 Loosen the wheel nuts, raise the vehicle and support it securely on axle stands. Remove the wheel.
2 Remove the split pin from the balljoint stud and loosen the nut (but don't remove it yet).
3 Separate the balljoint from the steering knuckle with a balljoint separator **(see illustration)**. Remove the balljoint stud nut. The clearance between the balljoint stud and the CV joint is very tight. To remove the stud

nut, you'll have to alternately back off the nut a turn or two, pull down the stud, turn the nut another turn or two, etc, until the nut is off.
4 Remove the bolt and nuts securing the balljoint to the control arm. Separate the balljoint from the control arm with a lever **(see illustration 5.2b)**.

Refitting

5 To refit the balljoint, insert the balljoint stud through the hole in the steering knuckle and fit the nut, but don't tighten it yet. Don't push the balljoint stud all the way up into and through the hole; instead, thread the nut onto the stud as soon as the stud protrudes through the hole, then turn the nut to draw the stud up through the hole.
6 Attach the balljoint to the control arm and fit the bolt and nuts, tightening them to the torque listed in this Chapter's Specifications.
7 Tighten the balljoint stud nut to the torque listed in this Chapter's Specifications and fit a new split pin. If the split pin hole doesn't line up with the slots on the nut, tighten the nut additionally until it does line up – don't loosen the nut to insert the split pin.
8 Fit the wheel and nuts. Lower the vehicle and tighten the nuts to the torque listed in the Specifications.

7 Steering knuckle and hub – removal and refitting

⚠️ **Warning: Dust created by the brake system is harmful to your health. Never blow it out with compressed air and don't inhale any of it. Do not, under any circumstances, use petroleum-based solvents to clean brake parts. Use brake system cleaner only.**

Removal

1 Remove the wheel cover and loosen, but don't remove, the driveshaft/hub nut. Loosen the wheel nuts, raise the vehicle and support it securely on axle stands, then remove the wheel.
2 Remove the brake caliper (don't disconnect the hose) and the brake disc (see Chapter 9), and disconnect the brake hose from the strut.

6.3 Separate the balljoint from the steering knuckle with a balljoint separator

Hang the caliper from the coil spring with a piece of wire – don't let it hang by the brake hose.
3 If the vehicle is equipped with ABS, remove the wheel speed sensor (see Chapter 9).
4 Mark the relationship of the strut to the steering knuckle. Loosen, but don't remove the strut-to-steering knuckle nuts and bolts (see Section 2).
5 Separate the tie-rod end from the steering knuckle arm (see Section 16).
6 Remove the balljoint-to-lower arm bolt and nuts **(see illustrations 5.2a and 5.2b)**.
7 Remove the driveshaft/hub nut and push the driveshaft from the hub as described in Chapter 8. Support the end of the driveshaft with a piece of wire.
8 Using a balljoint removal tool **(see illustration)** or a small puller, remove the balljoint from the steering knuckle. **Note:** *If you're removing the steering knuckle to renew*

7.8 Use a balljoint removal tool or small puller to force the balljoint stud from the steering knuckle

9.2 To detach a rear stabiliser bar link from the stabiliser bar, remove this nut (arrowed) and pivot the link out of the way

the hub bearings, and the balljoint is in good condition, the balljoint can remain attached.

9 The strut-to-knuckle bolts can now be removed.

10 Carefully separate the steering knuckle from the strut.

Refitting

11 Guide the knuckle and hub assembly into position, inserting the driveshaft into the hub.

12 Push the knuckle into the strut flange and fit the bolts and nuts, but don't tighten them yet.

13 If you removed the balljoint from the old knuckle, and are planning to use it with the new knuckle, connect the balljoint to the knuckle and tighten the balljoint stud nut to the torque listed in this Chapter's Specifications. Fit a new split pin.

14 Attach the balljoint to the control arm, but don't tighten the bolt and nuts yet.

15 Attach the tie-rod to the steering knuckle arm (see Section 16). Tighten the strut bolt nuts, the balljoint-to-control arm bolt and nuts and the tie-rod nut to the torque listed in this Chapter's Specifications.

16 Place the brake disc on the hub and refit the caliper as outlined in Chapter 9.

17 Refit the driveshaft/hub nut and tighten it securely, but not completely yet.

18 Refit the wheel and nuts. Lower the vehicle and tighten the nuts to the torque listed in the Specifications.

19 Tighten the driveshaft/hub nut to the torque

10.3a Remove the trim cover, unscrew the two upper shock mounting nuts, then remove the retainers and bushing; this is a 2000 or earlier model . . .

9.3 To detach the rear stabiliser bar from the vehicle body, remove the bolts (arrowed) from the bushing clamps

listed in the Chapter 8 Specifications. Refit the wheel cover.

20 Have the front-end alignment checked and, if necessary, adjusted.

8 Hub and bearing assembly (front) – removal and refitting

Due to the special tools and expertise required to press the hub and bearing from the steering knuckle, this job should be left to a professional mechanic. However, the steering knuckle and hub may be removed and the assembly taken to a garage or other qualified repair facility equipped with the necessary tools. See Section 7 for the steering knuckle and hub removal procedure.

9 Stabiliser bar and bushings (rear) – removal and refitting

Note: This procedure applies to 2001 and later models only.

Removal

1 Raise the rear of the vehicle and support it securely on axle stands. Block the front wheels to prevent the vehicle from rolling.

2 Remove the stabiliser bar-to-link nut (see illustration). If the ball-stud turns with the nut, use a spanner to hold the stud.

3 Unbolt the stabiliser bar bushing clamps from the body (see illustration).

10.3b . . . and this is a 2001 or later model

4 The stabiliser bar can now be removed from the vehicle. Pull the retainers off the stabiliser bar (if they haven't fallen off already) using a rocking motion.

5 Check the bushings for wear, hardness, distortion, cracking and other signs of deterioration, renewing them if necessary.

6 Check the stabiliser bar links for wear as described in Section 4.

7 Using a wire brush, clean the areas of the bar where the bushings ride. Fit the bushings on the bar with the slits facing down. Also, the bushings must be fitted to the inside of the paint line on the bar. If necessary, use a light coat of vegetable oil to ease bushing and U-bracket refitting (don't use petroleum-based products or brake fluid, as these will damage the rubber).

Refitting

8 Refitting is the reverse of removal. Tighten the nut/bolts to the torque listed in this Chapter's Specifications.

10 Shock absorber (rear) – removal, inspection and refitting

Removal

1 Loosen the wheel nuts, raise the vehicle and support it securely on axle stands. Block the front wheels to prevent the vehicle from rolling. Remove the wheel.

2 Support the rear end of the trailing arm with a hydraulic jack. Raise the jack slightly to take the spring pressure off the shock absorber lower mounting.

⚠️ **Warning: The jack must remain in this position throughout the entire procedure.**

3 Working inside the vehicle, remove the trim cover for access to the shock absorber upper mounting nuts. Remove the nuts, upper retainer, bushing and lower retainer (see illustrations).

4 Unscrew the shock absorber lower mounting bolt, then pull the shock off the mounting pin (see illustration). Note how the retainers are positioned.

Inspection

5 Mount the shock absorber upright in a vice.

10.4 Shock absorber lower mounting bolt

11.2 Suspension arm-to-trailing arm mounting points – 2000 and earlier models

11.3 Upper suspension arm outer pivot bolt – 2001 and later models

11.4 Upper suspension arm inner pivot bolt

Fully depress the rod, then pull it up fully. The piston rod must move smoothly over its complete length. If not, or if there is excessive resistance, renew the shock absorber.

Refitting

6 Refitting is the reverse of the removal procedure. Tighten the mounting nut/bolts to the torque listed in this Chapter's Specifications.

11 Suspension arms (rear) – removal and refitting

1 Loosen the wheel nuts, raise the vehicle and support it securely on axle stands. Block the front wheels to prevent the vehicle from rolling. Remove the wheel.

Upper suspension arm

2 If you're working on a 2000 or earlier model, remove the split pin and nut from the ball-stud at the outer end of the arm **(see illustration)**, then separate the arm from the boss on the trailing arm. If the ball-stud sticks in its boss, a two-jaw puller or balljoint removal tool can be used to force it out.
3 If you're working on a 2001 or later model, remove the nut and bolt securing the arm to the bracket on the trailing arm **(see illustration)**.
4 Remove the nut and pivot bolt from the inner end of the arm **(see illustration)**. Remove the arm from the vehicle.
5 Check the arm for bending and cracks, and the bushing for wear, hardness or deterioration. On 2000 and earlier models, also check the ball-stud for excessive wear. To check it, flip the balljoint stud side-to-side five or six times, then fit the nut. Using a lbf in torque wrench, turn the nut continuously one turn every two to four seconds and note the torque reading on the fifth turn **(see illustration 4.4)**. It should be no less than 7 lbf in. If it is, it's too loose and the arm should be renewed.
6 Refitting is the reverse of removal. Tighten the nut/bolts to the torque listed in this Chapter's Specifications. **Note:** *Before tightening the pivot bolt nuts, use a hydraulic jack to raise the trailing arm to simulate normal ride height. If you're working on a 2000 or earlier model, fit new split pins.*

Lower suspension arm

7 If you're working on a 2001 or later model, detach the stabiliser bar link from the lower suspension arm.
8 Refer to Paragraphs 2 to 6 for the removal, check and refitting procedures, but note that the camber adjusting cam at the inner end of the arm must be marked to preserve wheel alignment **(see illustration)**.
9 Have the rear wheel alignment checked and, if necessary, adjusted.

Trailing arm

10 Remove the coil spring (see Section 12).
11 Unbolt the brake hose and brake line brackets from the trailing arm. Unbolt the handbrake cable brackets from the trailing arm.
12 If equipped, remove the ABS wheel speed sensor and unbolt the harness brackets from the trailing arm (see Chapter 9).
13 Remove the hub and bearing assembly (see Section 13). Separate the brake backing plate/brake shoe assembly from the trailing arm and suspend it out of the way with a piece of wire or string.
14 Mark the relationship of the toe adjusting cam to the trailing arm mounting bracket **(see illustration)**.
15 Unscrew the pivot bolt and separate the trailing arm from the vehicle.
16 Inspect the trailing arm pivot bushing for signs of deterioration. If it is in need of renewal, take the trailing arm to a garage to have the bushing renewed.

11.8 Mark the relationship of the camber adjusting cam to the suspension crossmember

17 Refitting is the reverse of removal, noting the following points:
a) Align the marks on the toe adjusting cam and the mounting bracket.
b) Before fully-tightening the trailing arm pivot bolt, raise the rear end of the trailing arm with a hydraulic jack to simulate normal ride height.
c) Tighten all nut/bolts to the correct torque specifications.
d) It won't be necessary to bleed the brakes unless a hydraulic fitting was loosened.
e) Have the rear wheel alignment checked and, if necessary, adjusted.

12 Coil spring (rear) – removal and refitting

⚠️ **Warning: Always renew the springs as a set – never renew just one of them.**

Removal

1 Loosen the wheel nuts, raise the vehicle and support it securely on axle stands. Block the front wheels to prevent the vehicle from rolling. Remove the wheel.
2 If you're working on a 2001 or later model, detach the stabiliser bar link from the lower suspension arm.
3 Support the trailing arm with a hydraulic jack.
4 Detach the lower end of the shock absorber from the trailing arm **(see illustration 10.4)**.

11.14 Mark the relationship of the toe adjusting cam to the trailing arm mounting bracket

12.5 Removing the coil spring out from between the trailing arm and the upper mount

5 Slowly lower the hydraulic jack, pull the trailing arm down and remove the coil spring **(see illustration)**.

6 Check the spring for cracks and chips, renewing the springs as a set if any defects are found. Also check the upper insulator for damage and deterioration, renewing it if necessary.

Refitting

7 Refitting is the reverse of removal. Be sure to position the lower end of the coil spring in the depressed area of the trailing arm. Tighten all nut/bolts to the correct torque specifications.

13 Hub and bearing assembly (rear) – removal and refitting

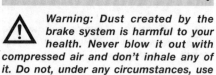

Warning: Dust created by the brake system is harmful to your health. Never blow it out with compressed air and don't inhale any of it. Do not, under any circumstances, use petroleum-based solvents to clean brake parts. Use brake system cleaner only.
Note: *Due to the special tools required to renew the bearing, the hub and bearing assembly should not be disassembled by the home mechanic. The assembly can be removed, however, and taken to a garage to have the bearing renewed.*

Removal

1 If you're working on a 4WD model, loosen the rear driveshaft/hub nut (see Chapter 8).

14.2 Loosen the Torx screws until the airbag module is free, but don't try to remove them from the screw case

2 Loosen the wheel nuts, raise the vehicle and support it securely on axle stands. Block the front wheels to prevent the vehicle from rolling. Remove the wheel.

3 Remove the brake drum (see Chapter 9). If you're working on a 1996 or 1997 2WD model, or a 2000 or earlier 4WD model, remove the brake shoes, detach the handbrake cable from the brake backing plate and disconnect the brake line from the wheel cylinder (see Chapter 9).

4 If you're working on a 4WD model, remove the rear driveshaft (see Chapter 8).

5 Remove the four hub-to-trailing arm bolts (2000 and earlier models) or nuts (2001 and later models), accessible by turning the hub flange so that the large circular cut-out exposes each bolt **(see illustration)**.

6 Remove the hub and bearing assembly. If you're working on a 1996 or 1997 2WD model, or a 2000 or earlier 4WD model, the brake backing plate is removed along with the hub and bearing. If you're working on a 1998 to 2000 2WD model, refit one of the bolts to hold the brake backing plate in place.

7 On 1996 or 1997 2WD models, or 2000 and earlier 4WD models, the rear axle hub can be removed from the bearing to allow removal of the bearing. Due to the special tools required to do this, you'll have to take the hub and bearing assembly to a specialist and have the old bearing pulled off the hub and a new bearing pressed on (you can re-use the hub itself, as long as it's in good condition). On all other models, the entire assembly must be renewed as a unit. **Note:** *If you're working on a 2001 or later 2WD model with ABS, remove the wheel speed sensor from the old hub and fit it on the new one (see Chapter 9).*

Refitting

8 Position the hub and bearing assembly on the trailing arm. Refit the bolts or nuts. After all four bolts or nuts have been fitted, tighten them to the torque listed in this Chapter's Specifications.

9 If you're working on a 1996 or 1997 2WD model, or a 2000 or earlier 4WD model, refit the brake shoes and connect the brake line to the wheel cylinder (see Chapter 9).

10 If you're working on a 4WD model, refit the driveshaft (see Chapter 8).

14.3a Lift the airbag module off the steering wheel . . .

13.5 To remove the four bolts or nuts which secure the hub and bearing assembly, rotate the hub flange and align one of the holes in the flange with each of the bolts or nuts

11 Refit the brake drum and the wheel.

12 If you're working on a 1996 or 1997 2WD model, or a 2000 or earlier 4WD model, bleed the brakes (see Chapter 9).

13 Lower the vehicle and tighten the nuts to the torque listed in the Specifications. If you're working on a 4WD model, tighten the driveshaft/hub nut to the torque listed in the Chapter 8 Specifications, then fit a new split pin.

14 Steering wheel – removal and refitting

Warning 1: These models are equipped with a Supplemental Restraint System (SRS), more commonly known as airbags. Always disable the airbag system before working in the vicinity of any airbag system component to avoid the possibility of accidental deployment of the airbag(s), which could cause personal injury (see Chapter 12).

Warning 2: Do not use a memory saving device to preserve the PCM or radio memory when working on or near airbag system components.

Removal

1 Turn the ignition key to Off, then disconnect the cable from the negative terminal of the battery. Wait at least two minutes before proceeding.

2 Turn the steering wheel so the wheels are pointing straight-ahead. If you're working on a 1996 or 1997 model, lever off the covers on either side of the steering wheel. On all models, loosen the Torx screws that attach the airbag module to the steering wheel **(see illustration)**. Loosen each screw until the groove in the circumference of the screw catches on the screw case.

3 Pull the airbag module off the steering wheel **(see illustration)**, disengage the connector lock and disconnect the module electrical connector **(see illustration)**. Set the airbag module in a safe, isolated area.

14.3b ... then disengage the connector lock and unplug the electrical connector – 1998 and later model shown; slide the connector lock in the direction of the arrow. On earlier models the connector lock must be flipped up

14.4 Unplug the electrical connectors for the horn and cruise control switches

⚠ *Warning: Carry the airbag module with the trim side facing away from you, and set the airbag module down with the trim side facing up. Don't place anything on top of the airbag module.*

4 Unplug the electrical connector for the horn and, if equipped, the cruise control switch **(see illustration)**.

5 Remove the steering wheel retaining nut, then mark the relationship of the steering shaft to the hub (if marks don't already exist or don't line up) to simplify refitting and ensure steering wheel alignment **(see illustration)**.

6 Use a puller to disconnect the steering wheel from the shaft **(see illustration)**.

⚠ *Warning: Do not hammer on the shaft or the puller in an attempt to loosen the wheel from the shaft. Also, don't allow the steering shaft to turn with the steering wheel removed. If the shaft turns, the airbag spiral cable will become off-centre, which may cause the wire inside to break when the vehicle is returned to service.*

7 If it is necessary to remove the airbag spiral cable, unplug the electrical connector, then remove the four screws (2000 and earlier models) or disengage the three claws (2001 and later models) and detach it from the combination switch **(see illustration)**.

Refitting

8 Make sure that the front wheels are facing straight-ahead, then centre the spiral cable. Turn the hub of the spiral cable anti-clockwise by hand until it stops (but don't force it, as the cable could break). Rotate the hub clockwise about 2½ turns and align the two pointers **(see illustration)**.

9 To refit the wheel, align the mark on the steering wheel hub with the mark on the shaft and slip the wheel onto the shaft. Fit the nut and tighten it to the torque listed in this Chapter's Specifications.

10 Plug in the cruise control and horn connectors.

11 Plug in the electrical connector for the airbag module and close the locking device.

12 Make sure the airbag module electrical connector is positioned correctly and that the wires don't interfere with anything, then refit the airbag module and tighten the retaining screws to the torque listed in this Chapter's Specifications.

13 Connect the negative battery cable.

14.5 After removing the steering wheel nut, mark the relationship of the steering wheel to the shaft before removing the wheel

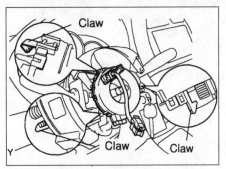

14.7 On 2001 and later models, the airbag spiral cable is retained by three claws

15 Steering column – removal and refitting

Removal

1 Park the vehicle with the wheels pointing straight-ahead. Disconnect the cable from the negative terminal of the battery.

2 Remove the steering wheel (see Section 14),

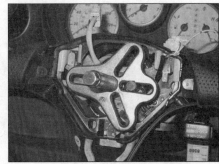

14.6 If the steering wheel is difficult to remove from the shaft, use a steering wheel puller to remove it

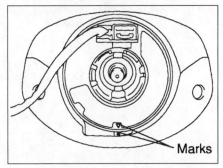

14.8 After properly centring the spiral cable as described, make sure the pointers are aligned – location of pointers may vary

15.6 Mark the U-joint to the steering shaft, then remove the pinch-bolt

15.7a Steering column mounting bolts (bolt indicated by lower right arrow not visible) – 2001 and later models

then turn the ignition key to the Lock position to prevent the steering shaft from turning. *Caution: If this is not done, the airbag clock spring could be damaged.*

3 Remove the lower finish panel under the column and the knee bolster behind it (see Chapter 11).

4 Remove the steering column covers (see Chapter 11).

5 Disconnect the electrical connectors for the steering column harness.

6 Mark the relationship of the U-joint to the steering shaft, then remove the pinch-bolt **(see illustration)**.

7 Remove the steering column mounting nut/

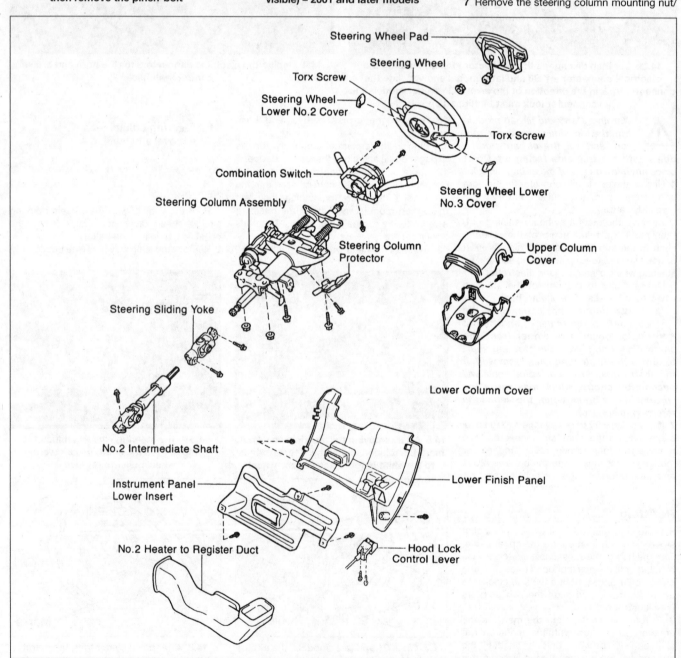

15.7b Steering column mounting details – 2000 and earlier models

bolts **(see illustrations)**, lower the column and pull it to the rear, making sure nothing is still connected. Separate the intermediate shaft from the steering shaft and remove the column.

Refitting

8 Guide the steering column into position, connect the intermediate shaft, then fit the mounting nut/bolts, but don't tighten them yet.
9 Tighten the column mounting nut/bolts securely.
10 Refit the pinch-bolt, tightening it securely.
11 The remainder of refitting is the reverse of removal.

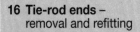
16 Tie-rod ends –
removal and refitting

Removal

1 Loosen the wheel nuts. Apply the handbrake, raise the front of the vehicle and support it securely on axle stands. Remove the front wheel.
2 Remove the split pin **(see illustration)** and loosen the nut on the tie-rod end stud.
3 Hold the tie-rod with a pair of locking pliers or spanner and loosen the locknut enough to mark the position of the tie-rod end in relation to the threads **(see illustrations)**.
4 Disconnect the tie-rod from the steering knuckle arm with a puller **(see illustration)**. Remove the nut and detach the tie-rod.
5 Unscrew the tie-rod end from the tie-rod.

Refitting

6 Thread the tie-rod end on to the marked position and insert the tie-rod stud into the steering knuckle arm. Tighten the lock nut securely.
7 Refit the castle nut on the stud and tighten it to the torque listed in this Chapter's Specifications. Install a new split pin. If the hole for the split pin doesn't line up with one of the slots in the nut, tighten the nut an additional amount until it does.
8 Refit the wheel and nuts. Lower the vehicle and tighten the nuts to the torque listed in the Specifications.
9 Have the alignment checked and, if necessary, adjusted.

17 Steering gear boots –
renewal

1 Loosen the nuts, raise the vehicle and support it securely on axle stands. Remove the wheel.
2 Remove the tie-rod end and lock nut (see Section 16).
3 Remove the outer steering gear boot clamp with a pair of pliers **(see illustration)**. Cut off the inner boot clamp with a pair of diagonal cutters **(see illustration)**. Slide off the boot.
4 Before fitting the new boot, wrap the threads

16.2 Remove the split pin from the castle nut and loosen, but don't remove, the nut

16.3b . . . then mark the position of the tie-rod end in relation to the threads

and serrations on the end of the steering rod with a layer of tape so the small end of the new boot isn't damaged.
5 Slide the new boot into position on the steering gear until it seats in the groove in the steering rod and fit new clamps.
6 Remove the tape and refit the tie-rod end (see Section 16).
7 Refit the wheel and nuts. Lower the vehicle and tighten the nuts to the torque listed in the Specifications.

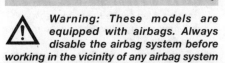
18 Steering gear –
removal and refitting

⚠ *Warning: These models are equipped with airbags. Always disable the airbag system before working in the vicinity of any airbag system*

17.3a The outer ends of the steering gear boots are secured by band-type clamps; they're easily released with a pair of pliers

16.3a Loosen the locknut . . .

16.4 Disconnect the tie-rod end from the steering knuckle arm with a puller

component to avoid the possibility of accidental deployment of the airbag(s), which could cause personal injury (see Chapter 12).

Removal

1 Disconnect the cable from the negative terminal of the battery.
2 Remove the steering wheel (see Section 14).
Note: *This will prevent the spiral cable from being damaged in the event the steering gear is not centred when it is refitted.*
3 Loosen the front wheel nuts, raise the front of the vehicle and support it securely on axle stands. Apply the handbrake and remove the wheels. Remove the engine under covers.
4 Place a drain pan under the steering gear. Detach the power steering pressure and return lines **(see illustration)** and cap the ends to prevent excessive fluid loss and contamination.

17.3b The inner ends of the steering gear boots are retained by boot clamps which must be cut off and discarded

18.4 Disconnect the power steering line fittings (arrowed)

18.5a Remove the universal joint cover . . .

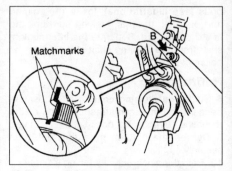

18.5b . . . then mark the relationship of the universal joint to the steering gear input shaft and remove the U-joint pinch-bolt (B)

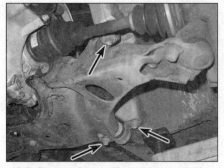
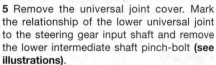

18.9 Suspension crossmember mounting bolts – 2000 and earlier models (left side shown)

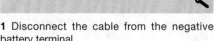

18.10 Steering gear mounting bolt – 2001 and later LHD models (left side shown, right side similar)

2001 and later models

10 Remove the steering gear mounting bolts (see illustration). Separate the intermediate shaft from the steering gear input shaft, then remove the steering gear.

Refitting

11 Refitting is the reverse of removal, noting the following points:

a) When connecting the steering gear input shaft to the intermediate shaft U-joint, be sure to align the marks.

b) Tighten all nut/bolts to the torque values listed in this Chapter's Specifications.

c) Set the front wheels in the straight-ahead position, then centre the spiral cable and refit the steering wheel and airbag module (see Section 14).

d) Fill the power steering fluid reservoir with the recommended fluid (see 'Weekly

5 Remove the universal joint cover. Mark the relationship of the lower universal joint to the steering gear input shaft and remove the lower intermediate shaft pinch-bolt (see illustrations).

6 Separate the tie-rod ends from the steering knuckle arms (see Section 16).

2000 and earlier models

7 Disconnect the balljoints from the control arms (see illustrations 5.2a and 5.2b).

8 Remove the front section of the exhaust system (see Chapter 4A or 4B).

9 Support the suspension crossmember with a hydraulic jack. Unbolt the suspension crossmember (see illustration) and lower it along with the control arms (separate the intermediate shaft from the steering gear input shaft as it is being lowered) steering gear and stabiliser bar. The steering gear can now be unbolted from the crossmember

checks'). Bleed the steering system (see Section 20).

19 Power steering pump – removal and refitting

1 Disconnect the cable from the negative battery terminal.

2 Using a large syringe, suck as much fluid out of the power steering fluid reservoir as possible. Place a drain pan under the vehicle to catch any fluid that spills out when the hoses are disconnected.

2000 and earlier models

Removal

3 Raise the front of the vehicle and support it securely on axle stands. Remove the right-side engine under-cover.

4 Remove the front portion of the exhaust pipe (see Chapter 4A or 4B).

5 Disconnect the balljoints from the control arms (see Section 5), unbolt the steering gear from the crossmember (see Section 18), then unbolt and remove the suspension crossmember (see illustration 18.9).

6 Loosen the pivot bolt and pinch-bolt, then remove the auxiliary drivebelt (see illustration).

7 Loosen the clamp and disconnect the fluid return hose from the pump.

8 Using a flare-nut wrench, unscrew the pressure line fitting from the pump (see illustration).

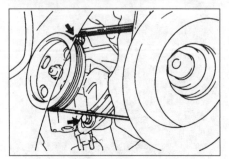

19.6 Loosen these bolts, push the pump towards the engine, then remove the drivebelt – 2000 and earlier models

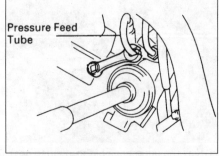

19.8 Unscrew the pressure line fitting from the pump – 2000 and earlier models

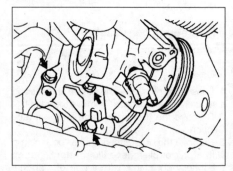

19.10 Power steering pump bracket-to-engine bolts – 2000 and earlier models

19.17 Unscrew the lower mounting bolt (B), loosen the upper mounting bolt (A) and slide the pump out of its mounting bracket – 2001 and later models

9 Detach the two vacuum lines from the pump.
10 Unbolt the pump bracket from the engine block **(see illustration)** and lower the assembly from the engine compartment.
11 The pump can now be separated from the bracket. If necessary, the pulley can be removed by unscrewing the nut; prevent the pulley from turning by holding the pulley with a pin spanner or by inserting a long punch through one of the holes in the pulley.

Refitting

12 Refitting is the reverse of removal, noting the following points:
a) *Tighten all nut/bolts to the torque listed in this Chapter's Specifications.*
b) *Adjust the auxiliary drivebelt tension following the procedure described in Chapter 1A or 1B.*
c) *Top-up the fluid level in the reservoir (see 'Weekly checks') and bleed the system (see Section 20).*

2001 and later models

Removal

13 Remove the auxiliary drivebelt (see Chapter 1A or 1B). Loosen the right front wheel nuts, raise the front of the vehicle and support it securely on axle stands. Remove the wheel and the right-side engine under-cover
14 Unplug the electrical connector from the power steering fluid pressure switch.
15 Unscrew the pressure line-to-pump union bolt and detach the line from the pump. Discard the sealing washers from either side of the line fitting (they are attached to each other); new ones should be used during refitting.
16 Loosen the hose clamp and detach the return hose from the pump.
17 Unscrew the lower mounting bolt, loosen the upper mounting bolt and detach the pump from the engine **(see illustration)**. **Note:** *The upper bolt can't be removed; loosening it will allow the pump to slide from its mounting bracket.*

Refitting

18 Refitting is the reverse of removal. Be sure to tighten the mounting bolts and the pressure line union bolt to the torque listed in this Chapter's Specifications.
19 Refit the engine under-cover, wheel and nuts. Lower the vehicle and tighten the nuts to the torque listed in the Specifications.
20 Refit the auxiliary drivebelt (see Chapter 1A or 1B).
21 Top-up the fluid level in the reservoir (see *Weekly checks*) and bleed the system (see Section 20).

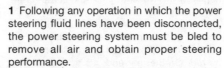

20 Power steering system – bleeding

1 Following any operation in which the power steering fluid lines have been disconnected, the power steering system must be bled to remove all air and obtain proper steering performance.
2 With the front wheels in the straight-ahead position, check the power steering fluid level and, if low, add fluid until it reaches the Cold mark on the dipstick.
3 Start the engine and allow it to run at fast idle. Recheck the fluid level and add more if necessary to reach the Cold mark on the dipstick.
4 Bleed the system by turning the wheels from side-to-side, without hitting the stops. This will work the air out of the system. Keep the reservoir full of fluid as this is done.
5 When the air is worked out of the system, return the wheels to the straight-ahead position and leave the vehicle running for several more minutes before shutting it off.
6 Road test the vehicle to be sure the steering system is functioning normally and noise free.
7 Recheck the fluid level to be sure it is up to the Hot mark on the dipstick while the engine is at normal operating temperature. Add fluid if necessary (see *Weekly checks*).

21 Wheel studs – removal and refitting

Note: *This procedure applies to both the front and rear wheel studs.*

Removal

1 Loosen the wheel nuts, raise the vehicle and support it securely on axle stands. Remove the wheel.
2 Remove the brake disc or drum (see Chapter 9).
3 Fit a nut part way onto the stud being renewed. Push the stud out of the hub flange with a press tool **(see illustration)**.

Refitting

4 Insert the new stud into the hub flange from the rear and fit some flat washers and a nut on the stud **(see illustration)**.
5 Tighten the nut until the stud is seated in the flange.

21.3 Use a press tool to push the stud out of the flange

1 Hub flange   2 Wheel nut on stud   3 Press tool

21.4 Install a spacer and a wheel nut on the stud, then tighten the nut to draw the stud into place

1 Hub flange   2 Spacer

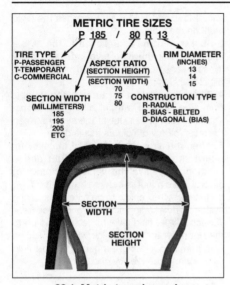

22.1 Metric tyre size code

6 Refit the brake drum or disc. Refit the wheel and nuts. Lower the vehicle and tighten the nuts to the torque listed in the Specifications.

22 Wheels and tyres –
general information

1 All vehicles covered by this manual are equipped with metric-sized radial tyres **(see illustration)**. Use of other size or type of tyres may affect the ride and handling of the vehicle. Don't mix different types of tyres, such as radials and bias belted, on the same vehicle as handling may be seriously affected. It's recommended that tyres be renewed in pairs on the same axle, but if only one tyre is being renewed, be sure it's the same size, structure and tread design as the other.
2 Because tyre pressure has a substantial effect on handling and wear, the pressure on all tyres should be checked at least once a month or before any extended trips (see *Weekly checks*).
3 Wheels must be renewed if they are bent, dented, leak air, have elongated bolt holes, are heavily rusted, out of vertical symmetry or if the nuts won't stay tight. Wheel repairs that use welding are not recommended.
4 Tyre and wheel balance is important in the overall handling, braking and performance of

the vehicle. Unbalanced wheels can adversely affect handling and ride characteristics as well as tyre life. Whenever a tyre is fitted on a wheel, the tyre and wheel should be balanced by a garage with the proper equipment.

23 Wheel alignment –
general information

A wheel alignment refers to the adjustments made to the wheels so they are in proper angular relationship to the suspension and the ground. Wheels that are out of proper alignment not only affect vehicle control, but also increase tyre wear. The front end angles normally measured are camber, castor and toe-in **(see illustration)**. Toe-in and camber are adjustable; if the castor is not correct, check for bent components. Rear camber and toe-in are also adjustable.
Getting the proper wheel alignment is a very exacting process, one in which complicated and expensive machines are necessary to perform the job properly. Because of this, you should have a technician with the proper equipment perform these tasks. We will, however, use this space to give you a basic idea of what is involved with a wheel alignment so you can better understand the process and deal intelligently with the garage that does the work.
Toe-in is the turning in of the wheels. The purpose of a toe specification is to ensure parallel rolling of the wheels. In a vehicle with zero toe-in, the distance between the front edges of the wheels will be the same as the distance between the rear edges of the wheels. The actual amount of toe-in is normally only a fraction of an inch. On the front end, toe-in is controlled by the tie-rod end position on the tie-rod. On the rear end, it's controlled by a cam at the front of the suspension trailing arm. Incorrect toe-in will cause the tyres to wear improperly by making them scrub against the road surface.
Camber is the tilting of the wheels from vertical when viewed from one end of the vehicle. When the wheels tilt out at the top, the camber is said to be positive (+). When the wheels tilt in at the top the camber is negative (-). The amount of tilt is measured in degrees from vertical and this measurement is called the camber angle. This angle affects the amount of tyre tread which contacts the

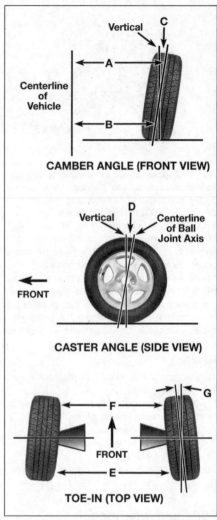

23.1 Camber, castor and toe-in angles

road and compensates for changes in the suspension geometry when the vehicle is cornering or travelling over an undulating surface. On the front end it is adjusted using special camber adjusting bolts, which alter the relationship between the strut and the steering knuckle. At the rear end camber is adjusted by a cam at the inner end of the lower suspension arm.
Castor is the tilting of the front steering axis from the vertical. A tilt toward the rear is positive castor and a tilt toward the front is negative castor.

Chapter 11
Body

Contents

	Section number
Back door – removal, refitting and adjustment	21
Back door lock, lock cylinder and handle – removal and refitting	22
Body – maintenance	2
Body repair – major damage	6
Body repair – minor damage	5
Bonnet – removal, refitting and adjustment	9
Bonnet lock and release cable – removal and refitting	10
Bumpers – removal and refitting	11
Centre console – removal and refitting	23
Cowl cover and vent tray – removal and refitting	14
Door – removal, refitting and adjustment	16
Door lock, lock cylinder and handles – removal and refitting	17
Door trim panels – removal and refitting	15
Door window glass – removal and refitting	18
	Section number
Door window glass regulator – removal and refitting	19
Facia trim panels	24
Front wing – removal and refitting	12
General information	1
Hinges and locks – maintenance	7
Instrument panel – removal and refitting	26
Mirrors – removal and refitting	20
Radiator grille – removal and refitting	13
Seats – removal and refitting	27
Steering column covers – removal and refitting	25
Sunroof – adjustment	28
Upholstery and carpets – maintenance	4
Vinyl trim – maintenance	3
Windscreen and fixed glass – removal and refitting	8

Degrees of difficulty

Easy, suitable for novice with little experience	**Fairly easy,** suitable for beginner with some experience	**Fairly difficult,** suitable for competent DIY mechanic	**Difficult,** suitable for experienced DIY mechanic	**Very difficult,** suitable for expert DIY or professional

1 General information

Warning: The front seat belts on some models are equipped with pretensioners, which are pyrotechnic (explosive) devices designed to retract the seat belts in the event of a collision. On models equipped with pretensioners, do not remove the front seat belt retractor assemblies, and do not disconnect the electrical connectors leading to the assemblies. Problems with the pretensioners will turn on the SRS (airbag) warning light on the dash. If any pretensioner problems are suspected, take the vehicle to a dealer service department.

These models feature a 'unibody' layout, using a floorpan with integral side frame rails which support the body components, front and rear suspension systems and other mechanical components.

Certain components are particularly vulnerable to accident damage and can be unbolted and repaired or renewed. Among these parts are the body mouldings, bumpers, front wings, the bonnet and boot lid, doors and all glass.

Only general body maintenance practices and body panel repair procedures within the scope of the do-it-yourselfer are included in this Chapter.

2 Body – maintenance

1 The condition of your vehicle's body is very important, because the resale value depends a great deal on it. It's much more difficult to repair a neglected or damaged body than it is to repair mechanical components. The hidden areas of the body, such as the wheel wells, the frame and the engine compartment, are equally important, although they don't require as frequent attention as the rest of the body.
2 Once a year, or every 12,000 miles, it's a good idea to have the underside of the body steam-cleaned. All traces of dirt and oil will be removed and the area can then be inspected carefully for rust, damaged brake lines, frayed electrical wires, damaged cables and other problems.
3 At the same time, clean the engine and the engine compartment with a steam cleaner or water-soluble degreaser.
4 The wheel wells should be given close attention, since undercoating can peel away and stones and dirt thrown up by the tires can cause the paint to chip and flake, allowing rust to set in. If rust is found, clean down to the bare metal and apply an anti-rust paint.
5 The body should be washed about once a week. Wet the vehicle thoroughly to soften the dirt, then wash it down with a soft sponge and plenty of clean soapy water. If the surplus dirt

is not washed off very carefully, it can wear down the paint.
6 Spots of tar or asphalt thrown up from the road should be removed with a cloth soaked in paraffin. Scented lamp oil is available in most hardware stores and the smell is easier to work with than straight paraffin.
7 Once every six months, wax the body and chrome trim. If a chrome cleaner is used to remove rust from any of the vehicle's plated parts, remember that the cleaner also removes part of the chrome, so use it sparingly. On any plated parts where chrome cleaner is used, use a good paste wax over the plating for extra protection.

3 Vinyl trim – maintenance

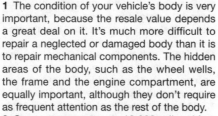

Don't clean vinyl trim with detergents, caustic soap or petroleum-based cleaners. Plain soap and water works just fine, with a soft brush to clean dirt that may be ingrained. Wash the vinyl as frequently as the rest of the vehicle.

After cleaning, application of a high quality rubber and vinyl protector will help prevent oxidation and cracks. The protector can also be applied to weather stripping, vacuum lines and rubber hoses, which often fail as a result of chemical degradation, and to the tyres.

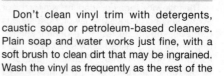

4 Upholstery and carpets – maintenance

1 Every three months remove the floor mats and clean the interior of the vehicle (more frequently if necessary). Use a stiff whisk broom to brush the carpeting and loosen dirt and dust, then vacuum the upholstery and carpets thoroughly, especially along seams and crevices.

2 Dirt and stains can be removed from carpeting with basic household or automotive carpet shampoos available in spray cans. Follow the directions and vacuum again, then use a stiff brush to bring back the 'nap' of the carpet.

3 Most interiors have cloth or vinyl upholstery, either of which can be cleaned and maintained with a number of material-specific cleaners or shampoos available in auto supply stores. Follow the directions on the product for usage, and always spot-test any upholstery cleaner on an inconspicuous area (bottom edge of a backseat cushion) to ensure that it doesn't cause a colour shift in the material.

4 After cleaning, vinyl upholstery should be treated with a protector. **Note:** *Make sure the protector container indicates the product can be used on seats – some products may make a seat too slippery.*

Caution: Do not use protector on steering wheels.

5 Leather upholstery requires special care. It should be cleaned regularly with saddlesoap or leather cleaner. Never use alcohol, petrol, nail polish remover or thinner to clean leather upholstery.

6 After cleaning, regularly treat leather upholstery with a leather conditioner, rubbed in with a soft cotton cloth. Never use car wax on leather upholstery.

7 In areas where the interior of the vehicle is subject to bright sunlight, cover leather seating areas of the seats with a sheet if the vehicle is to be left out for any length of time.

5 Body repair – minor damage

Flexible plastic body panels

The following repair procedures are for minor scratches and gouges. Repair of more serious damage should be left to a dealer service department or qualified body shop. Below is a list of the equipment and materials necessary to perform the following repair procedures on plastic body panels. Although a specific brand of material may be mentioned, it should be noted that equivalent products from other manufacturers may be used instead.

Wax, grease and silicone removing solvent.
Cloth-backed body tape.
Sanding discs.
Drill motor with three-inch disc holder.
Hand sanding block.
Rubber squeegees.
Sandpaper.
Non-porous mixing palette.
Wood paddle or putty knife.
Curved-tooth body file.
Flexible parts repair material.

1 Remove the damaged panel, if necessary or desirable. In most cases, repairs can be carried out with the panel *in situ*.

2 Clean the area(s) to be repaired with a wax, grease and silicone removing solvent applied with a water-dampened cloth.

3 If the damage is structural, that is, if it extends through the panel, clean the back of the panel area to be repaired as well. Wipe dry.

4 Sand the rear surface about 40 mm beyond the break.

5 Cut two pieces of fibreglass cloth large enough to overlap the break by about 40 mm. Cut only to the required length.

6 Mix the adhesive from the repair kit according to the instructions included with the kit, and apply a layer of the mixture approximately 1/8-inch thick on the back of the panel. Overlap the break by at least 40 mm.

7 Apply one piece of fibreglass cloth to the adhesive and cover the cloth with additional adhesive. Apply a second piece of fibreglass cloth to the adhesive and immediately cover the cloth with additional adhesive in sufficient quantity to fill the weave.

8 Allow the repair to cure for 20 to 30 minutes at room temperature.

9 If necessary, trim the excess repair material at the edge.

10 Remove all of the paint film over and around the area(s) to be repaired. The repair material should not overlap the painted surface.

11 With a drill motor and a sanding disc (or a rotary file), cut a V along the break line approximately 12 mm wide. Remove all dust and loose particles from the repair area.

12 Mix and apply the repair material. Apply a light coat first over the damaged area; then continue applying material until it reaches a level slightly higher than the surrounding finish.

13 Cure the mixture for 20 to 30 minutes at room temperature.

14 Roughly establish the contour of the area being repaired with a body file. If low areas or pits remain, mix and apply additional adhesive.

15 Block sand the damaged area with sandpaper to establish the actual contour of the surrounding surface.

16 If desired, the repaired area can be temporarily protected with several light coats of primer. Because of the special paints and techniques required for flexible body panels, it is recommended that the vehicle be taken to a paint shop for completion of the body repair.

Steel body panels

Repair of minor scratches

17 If the scratch is superficial and does not penetrate to the metal of the body, repair is very simple. Lightly rub the scratched area with a fine rubbing compound to remove loose paint and built-up wax. Rinse the area with clean water.

18 Apply touch-up paint to the scratch, using a small brush. Continue to apply thin layers of paint until the surface of the paint in the scratch is level with the surrounding paint. Allow the new paint at least two weeks to harden, then blend it into the surrounding paint by rubbing with a very fine rubbing compound. Finally, apply a coat of wax to the scratch area.

19 If the scratch has penetrated the paint and exposed the metal of the body, causing the metal to rust, a different repair technique is required. Remove all loose rust from the bottom of the scratch with a pocket knife, then apply rust inhibiting paint to prevent the formation of rust in the future. Using a rubber or nylon applicator, coat the scratched area with glaze-type filler. If required, the filler can be mixed with thinner to provide a very thin paste, which is ideal for filling narrow scratches. Before the glaze filler in the scratch hardens, wrap a piece of smooth cotton cloth around the tip of a finger. Dip the cloth in thinner and then quickly wipe it along the surface of the scratch. This will ensure that the surface of the filler is slightly hollow. The scratch can now be painted over.

Repair of dents

20 When repairing dents, the first job is to pull the dent out until the affected area is as close as possible to its original shape. There is no point in trying to restore the original shape completely as the metal in the damaged area will have stretched on impact and cannot be restored to its original contours. It is better to bring the level of the dent up to a point which is about 1/8-inch below the level of the surrounding metal. In cases where the dent is very shallow, it is not worth trying to pull it out at all.

21 If the back of the dent is accessible, it can be hammered out gently from behind using a soft-face hammer. While doing this, hold a block of wood firmly against the opposite side of the metal to absorb the hammer blows and prevent the metal from being stretched.

22 If the dent is in a section of the body which has double layers, or some other factor makes it inaccessible from behind, a different technique is required. Drill several small holes through the metal inside the damaged area, particularly in the deeper sections. Screw long, self-tapping screws into the holes just enough for them to get a good grip in the metal. Now the dent can be pulled out by pulling on the protruding heads of the screws with locking pliers.

23 The next stage of repair is the removal

of paint from the damaged area and from an inch or so of the surrounding metal. This is easily done with a wire brush or sanding disk in a drill motor, although it can be done just as effectively by hand with sandpaper. To complete the preparation for filling, score the surface of the bare metal with a screwdriver or the tang of a file and drill small holes in the affected area. This will provide a good grip for the filler material. To complete the repair, see the Section on filling and painting.

Repair of rust holes or gashes

24 Remove all paint from the affected area and from an inch or so of the surrounding metal using a sanding disk or wire brush mounted in a drill motor. If these are not available, a few sheets of sandpaper will do the job just as effectively.

25 With the paint removed, you will be able to determine the severity of the corrosion and decide whether to renew the whole panel, if possible, or repair the affected area. New body panels are not as expensive as most people think and it is often quicker to fit a new panel than to repair large areas of rust.

26 Remove all trim pieces from the affected area except those which will act as a guide to the original shape of the damaged body, such as headlight shells, etc. Using metal snips or a hacksaw blade, remove all loose metal and any other metal that is badly affected by rust. Hammer the edges of the hole in to create a slight depression for the filler material.

27 Wire brush the affected area to remove the powdery rust from the surface of the metal. If the back of the rusted area is accessible, treat it with rust inhibiting paint.

28 Before filling is done, block the hole in some way. This can be done with sheet metal riveted or screwed into place, or by stuffing the hole with wire mesh.

29 Once the hole is blocked off, the affected area can be filled and painted. See the following subsection on filling and painting.

Filling and painting

30 Many types of body fillers are available, but generally speaking, body repair kits which contain filler paste and a tube of resin hardener are best for this type of repair work. A wide, flexible plastic or nylon applicator will be necessary for imparting a smooth and contoured finish to the surface of the filler material. Mix up a small amount of filler on a clean piece of wood or cardboard (use the hardener sparingly). Follow the manufacturer's instructions on the package, otherwise the filler will set incorrectly.

31 Using the applicator, apply the filler paste to the prepared area. Draw the applicator across the surface of the filler to achieve the desired contour and to level the filler surface. As soon as a contour that approximates the original one is achieved, stop working the paste. If you continue, the paste will begin to stick to the applicator. Continue to add thin layers of paste at 20-minute intervals until the level of the filler is just above the surrounding metal.

32 Once the filler has hardened, the excess can be removed with a body file. From then on, progressively finer grades of sandpaper should be used, starting with a 180-grit paper and finishing with 600-grit wet-or-dry paper. Always wrap the sandpaper around a flat rubber or wooden block, otherwise the surface of the filler will not be completely flat. During the sanding of the filler surface, the wet-or-dry paper should be periodically rinsed in water. This will ensure that a very smooth finish is produced in the final stage.

33 At this point, the repair area should be surrounded by a ring of bare metal, which in turn should be encircled by the finely feathered edge of good paint. Rinse the repair area with clean water until all of the dust produced by the sanding operation is gone.

34 Spray the entire area with a light coat of primer. This will reveal any imperfections in the surface of the filler. Repair the imperfections with fresh filler paste or glaze filler and once more smooth the surface with sandpaper. Repeat this spray-and-repair procedure until you are satisfied that the surface of the filler and the feathered edge of the paint are perfect. Rinse the area with clean water and allow it to dry completely.

35 The repair area is now ready for painting. Spray painting must be carried out in a warm, dry, windless and dust-free atmosphere. These conditions can be created if you have access to a large indoor work area, but if you are forced to work in the open, you will have to pick the day very carefully. If you are working indoors, dousing the floor in the work area with water will help settle the dust which would otherwise be in the air. If the repair area is confined to one body panel, mask off the surrounding panels. This will help minimise the effects of a slight mismatch in paint colour. Trim pieces such as chrome strips, door handles, etc, will also need to be masked off or removed. Use masking tape and several thickness of newspaper for the masking operations.

36 Before spraying, shake the paint can thoroughly, then spray a test area until the spray painting technique is mastered. Cover the repair area with a thick coat of primer. The thickness should be built-up using several thin layers of primer rather than one thick one. Using 600-grit wet-or-dry sandpaper, rub down the surface of the primer until it is very smooth. While doing this, the work area should be thoroughly rinsed with water and the wet-or-dry sandpaper periodically rinsed as well. Allow the primer to dry before spraying additional coats.

37 Spray on the top coat, again building-up the thickness by using several thin layers of paint. Begin spraying at the top of the repair area and then, using a side-to-side motion, work down until the whole repair area and about two inches of the surrounding original paint is covered. Remove all masking material 10 to 15 minutes after spraying on the final coat of paint. Allow the new paint at least two

weeks to harden, then use a very fine rubbing compound to blend the edges of the new paint into the existing paint. Finally, apply a coat of wax.

6 Body repair – major damage

1 Major damage must be repaired by a body shop specifically equipped to perform unibody repairs. These body shops have the specialised equipment required to do the job properly.

2 If the damage is extensive, the body must be checked for proper alignment or the vehicle's handling characteristics may be adversely affected and other components may wear at an accelerated rate.

3 Due to the fact that some of the major body components (bonnet, wings, doors, etc) are separate and renewable units, any seriously damaged components should be renewed rather than repaired. Sometimes the components can be found in a wrecking yard that specialises in used vehicle components, often at considerable savings over the cost of new parts.

7 Hinges and locks – maintenance

Once every 3000 miles, or every three months, the hinges and lock assemblies on the doors and bonnet should be given a few drops of light oil or lock lubricant. The door lock strikers should also be lubricated with a thin coat of grease to reduce wear and ensure free movement. Lubricate the door locks with spray-on graphite lubricant.

8 Windscreen and fixed glass – removal and refitting

Removal and refitting of the windscreen and fixed glass requires the use of special fast-setting adhesive/caulk materials and some specialised tools and techniques. These operations should be left to a dealer service department or a body shop specialising in glass work.

9 Bonnet – removal, refitting and adjustment

Note: *The bonnet is somewhat awkward to remove and refit, at least two people should perform this procedure.*

Removal

1 Open the bonnet, then place blankets or pads over the wings and windscreen cowl

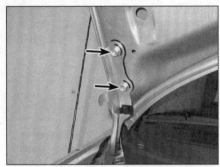

9.3 Draw alignment marks around the bonnet hinges to ensure proper alignment of the bonnet when it's refitted – arrows indicate the hinge-to-bonnet retaining bolts

area of the body. This will protect the body and paint as the bonnet is lifted off.

2 Disconnect any cables or wires that will interfere with removal. Disconnect the windscreen washer tubing from the nozzles on the bonnet.

3 Make marks around the bonnet hinge to ensure proper alignment during refitting **(see illustration)**.

4 Have an assistant support one side of the bonnet. Take turns removing the hinge-to-bonnet bolts and lift off the bonnet.

Refitting

5 Refitting is the reverse of removal. Align

9.10a To adjust the vertical height of the leading edge of the bonnet so that it's flush with the wings, turn each edge cushion (arrow indicates one) clockwise (to lower the bonnet) or anti-clockwise (to raise the bonnet)

9.10b On 2001 and later models, there are also bonnet adjusting bumpers located on the bonnet

9.9 To adjust the bonnet lock horizontally or vertically, loosen these bolts (arrows)

the hinge bolts with the marks made in Paragraph 3.

Adjustment

6 Fore-and-aft and side-to-side adjustment of the bonnet is done by moving the hinge plate slot after loosening the bolts or nuts. **Note:** *The factory bolts are 'centring' type that will not allow adjustment. To adjust the bonnet in relation to the hinges, these bolts must be replaced with standard bolts with flat washers and lock washers.*

7 Mark around the entire hinge plate so you can determine the amount of movement.

8 Loosen the bolts and move the bonnet into correct alignment. Move it only a little at a time. Tighten the hinge bolts and carefully lower the bonnet to check the position.

9 If necessary after refitting, the entire bonnet lock assembly can be adjusted up-and-down as well as from side-to-side on the radiator support so the bonnet closes securely and flush with the wings. Scribe a line or mark around the bonnet lock mounting bolts to provide a reference point, then loosen them and reposition the lock assembly, as necessary **(see illustration)**. Following adjustment, retighten the mounting bolts.

10 Finally, adjust the bonnet bumpers on the radiator support so the bonnet, when closed, is flush with the wings **(see illustrations)**.

11 The bonnet lock assembly, as well as the hinges, should be periodically lubricated with white, lithium-base grease to prevent binding and wear.

10.2 Lever out the cable retainer from the rear of the bonnet lock assembly, then disengage the cable

10 Bonnet lock and release cable – removal and refitting

Warning: The models covered by this manual are equipped with Supplemental Restraint systems (SRS), more commonly known as airbags. Always disable the airbag system before working in the vicinity of any airbag system component to avoid the possibility of accidental deployment of the airbag, which could cause personal injury (see Chapter 12).

Lock

Removal

1 Scribe a line around the lock to aid alignment when refitting, then remove the retaining bolts securing the bonnet lock to the radiator support **(see illustration 9.9)**. Remove the lock.

2 Disconnect the bonnet release cable by disengaging the cable from the lock assembly **(see illustration)**.

Refitting

3 Refitting is the reverse of removal. **Note:** *Adjust the lock so the bonnet engages securely when closed and the bonnet bumpers are slightly compressed.*

Cable

Removal

4 Working in the passenger compartment, remove the left-hand side kick panel.

5 Lift the bonnet release handle lever upward, then pull down on the cable housing end and disengage the cable from the bonnet release lever handle. If the handle lever needs to be renewed simply pull outward on the handle retaining tab and push downward to release it from the instrument panel **(see illustration)**.

6 Attach a piece of thin wire or string to the end of the cable.

7 Working in the engine compartment, disconnect the bonnet release cable from the

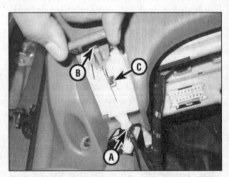

10.5 Lift upward on the handle and pull the cable housing end (A) from the base of the handle, then detach the cable end (B) from the lever

C Indicates the handle retaining tab

lock assembly as described in Paragraphs 1
and 2. Unclip all the cable retaining clips on
the radiator support and the inner wheel arch.
8 Pull the cable forward into the engine
compartment until you can see the wire or
string. then remove the wire or string from the
old cable and fasten it to the new cable.

Refitting

9 With the new cable attached to the wire
or string, pull the wire or string back through
the bulkhead until the new cable reaches the
inside handle.
10 Working in the passenger compartment,
fit the new cable into the bonnet release lever,
making sure the cable housing fits snugly into
the notch in the handle bracket. **Note:** *Pull on
the cable with your fingers from the passenger
compartment until the cable stop seats in the
grommet on the bulkhead.*
11 The remainder of the refitting is the reverse
of removal.

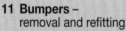
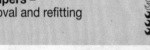

11 Bumpers –
removal and refitting

⚠ *Warning: The models covered by
this manual are equipped with
Supplemental Restraint systems
(SRS), more commonly known as airbags.
Always disable the airbag system before
working in the vicinity of any airbag
system component to avoid the possibility
of accidental deployment of the airbag,
which could cause personal injury (see
Chapter 12).*

Front bumper

Removal

1 Apply the handbrake, raise the vehicle and
support it securely on axle stands.
2 Disconnect the negative battery cable,
then the positive battery cable and wait
two minutes before proceeding any further.
Working below the vehicle remove the lower
splash shields.
3 On 2000 and earlier models, detach the
screws securing the top, bottom and sides
of the bumper cover. Pull the cover outward
slightly and disconnect the connectors from
the front turn signal lights. Remove the cover
from the vehicle **(see illustrations)**.
4 On 2001 and later models, remove the
radiator grille (see Section 13) and the headlight filler panel **(see illustrations)**. Remove
the bumper cover retaining bolts **(see
illustrations)**. **Note:** *Use a small screwdriver
to pop the centre button up on the plastic
fasteners, but do not try to remove the centre
buttons. They stay in the ferrules.* Pull the
cover outward slightly and disconnect the
connectors from the front turn signal lights.
Remove the cover from the vehicle.

Refitting

5 Refitting is the reverse of removal. Make
sure the tabs (if equipped) on the back of

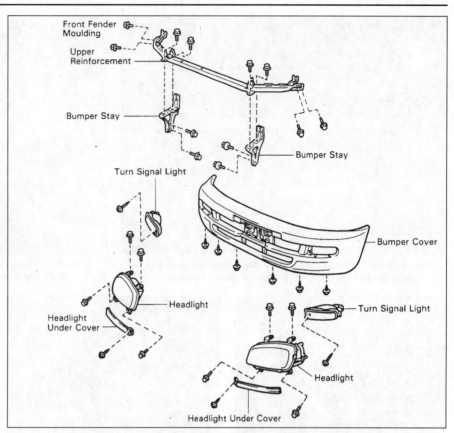

11.3a Exploded view of the front bumper – 1996 and 1997 models

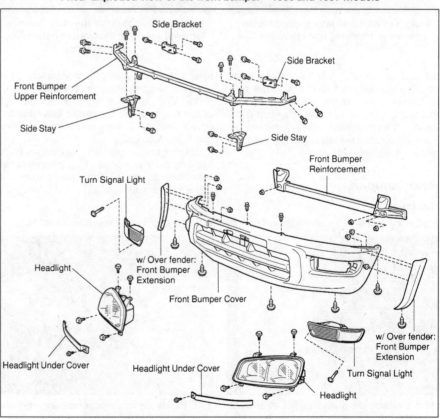

11.3b Exploded view of the front bumper – 1998 through 2000 models

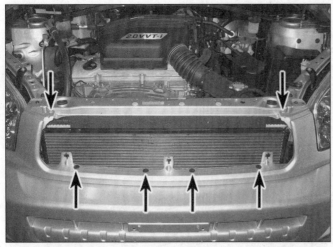

11.4a Remove the two screws at the top (upper arrows) and the push pins at the centre of the panel (lower arrows) . . .

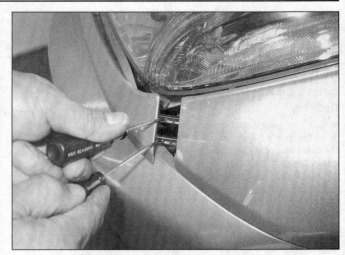

11.4b . . . then depress the tabs securing the ends of the headlight filler panel and remove it from the vehicle

11.4c On 2001 and later models remove the lower retaining bolts (arrows) . . .

11.4d . . . then remove the lower screws (arrows) securing the front of both inner wheel arch liners

11.4e Peel back the front of the inner wheel arch liners and remove the screw (arrow) securing the bumper cover to the wing

the bumper cover fit into the corresponding clips on the body before attaching the bolts and screws. An assistant would be helpful at this point. If the bumper reinforcement beam needs to be removed, simply unscrew the bolts, disconnect the horns (if applicable) and remove it from the vehicle.

Rear bumper

Removal

6 Working in the rear wheel arch, detach the

plastic clips and the upper bolt securing the edge of the bumper cover **(see illustration)**. **Note:** *Use a small screwdriver to pop the centre button up on the plastic fasteners, but do not try to remove the centre buttons. They stay in the ferrules.*
7 Open the back door and remove the bolts securing the inside edge of the bumper cover **(see illustration)**. Pull the bumper cover out and away from the vehicle.

Refitting

8 Refitting is the reverse of removal.

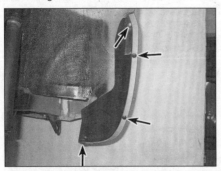

11.6 Remove the push pins (lower arrows) and the upper bolt (upper arrow) from the rear wheel arch

11.7 Inside the back door opening, remove the two bolts securing the inner edge of the rear bumper cover

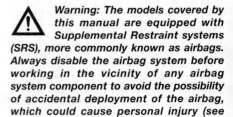

12 Front wing – removal and refitting

Warning: The models covered by this manual are equipped with Supplemental Restraint systems (SRS), more commonly known as airbags. Always disable the airbag system before working in the vicinity of any airbag system component to avoid the possibility of accidental deployment of the airbag, which could cause personal injury (see Chapter 12).

Removal

1 Loosen the front wheel nuts. Raise the vehicle, support it securely on axle stands and remove the front wheel.
2 Open the bonnet.
3 On 2000 and earlier models, remove the finish panel below the headlight housing.
4 On 2001 and later models, remove the radiator grille (see Section 13).
5 Remove the front bumper cover (see Section 11).
6 Remove the headlight housing (see Chapter 12).

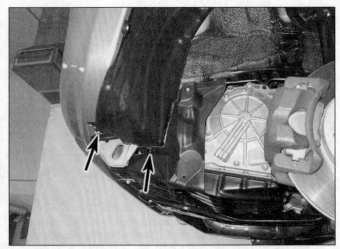

12.7a Remove the bolt and push pins (arrows) at the front lower portion of the inner liner

12.7b Detach the main portion of the inner liner, secured by bolts, screws and plastic clips (arrows)

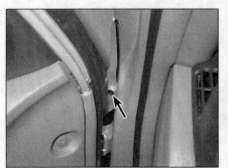

12.9 Remove the upper wing bolt (arrow) with the door open

12.10 Remove the bottom bolt (arrow) retaining the wing

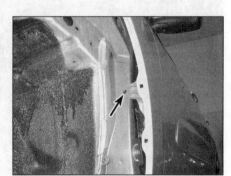

12.11a Remove the bolt in the wheel arch opening (arrow)

7 Detach the inner wheel arch push pins, then remove the inner wheel arch liner **(see illustrations)**.

8 If you're removing the right-hand side wing, remove the radio aerial (see Chapter 12). If you're removing the left-hand side wing, remove the bonnet support rod and hold the bonnet open in a safe position.

9 Open the front door, and remove the upper wing-to-body bolt **(see illustration)**.

10 Remove the lower wing-to-body bolt **(see illustration)**.

11 Remove the remaining wing mounting bolts **(see illustrations)**.

12 Lift off the wing. It's a good idea to have an assistant support the wing while it's being moved away from the vehicle to prevent damage to the surrounding body panels.

Refitting

13 Refitting is the reverse of removal. Check the alignment of the wing to the bonnet and front edge of the door before final tightening of the wing fasteners.

13 Radiator grille –
removal and refitting

Removal

1 Open the bonnet.

2 On 2000 and earlier models, the grille is mounted to the bonnet. Working from the back of the bonnet, remove the nuts securing the grille to the bonnet **(see illustration)**. Using

12.11b Remove the front wing-to-brace bolt (arrow) – the upper bolt in this photo is the bumper cover bolt which would already have been removed with the bumper cover

12.11c Remove the three bolts (arrows) along the top of the wing

13.2 Radiator grille fasteners – 2000 and earlier models

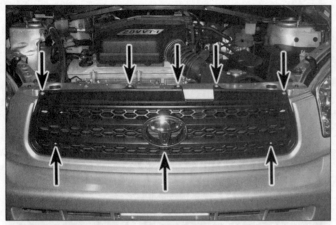

13.3 Remove the screws at the top and disengage the clips at the bottom – 2001 and later models

14.2a Use a small screwdriver to pop the centre button up on the plastic fasteners, but do not try to remove the centre buttons (they stay in the ferrules) – 2001 and later models shown

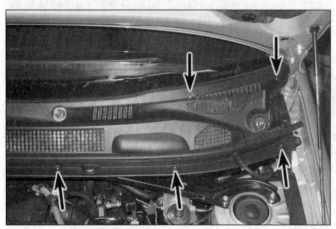

14.2b Driver's side cowl cover fasteners – 2001 and later LHD models

14.3 Vent tray mounting bolts – 2001 and later LHD models (passenger side shock absorber bolts not shown in this photo)

a pair of pliers squeeze the plastic retaining clips and detach the grille from the bonnet.

3 On 2001 and later models, remove screws along the top of the grille **(see illustration)**. Pull the top of the grille out slightly and disengage the retaining clips with a screwdriver. The retaining clips can be disengaged by simply pressing downward on the tabs.

4 Once the retaining clips are disengaged, pull the grille out and remove it.

Refitting

5 Refitting is the reverse of removal.

14 Cowl cover and vent tray – removal and refitting

Removal

1 Remove the wiper arms (see Chapter 12).

2 Remove the push pin fasteners securing the cowl cover **(see illustrations)**.

3 If the vent tray on 2001 and later models needs to be removed, first remove the wiper motor linkage assembly as described in Chapter 12, then remove the vent tray mounting bolts **(see illustration)**.

Refitting

4 Refitting is the reverse of removal.

15 Door trim panels – removal and refitting

Removal

Front and rear doors

1 On manual window models, remove the window crank handle **(see illustration)**.

2 On power window models, lever up the window switch plate to access one panel mounting screw underneath **(see illustration)**.

3 Lever out the outside mirror cover **(see illustration)**.

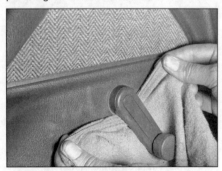

15.1 On models with manual windows, remove the window crank handle by working a cloth behind it to release the clip

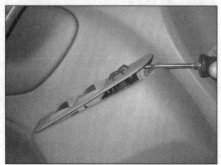

15.2 Lever up the power window switch plate, disconnect the electrical connectors

4 On 2001 and later models lever out the door grip trim cover **(see illustration)**.

5 Remove the door trim panel retaining screws and the inside door handle trim cover, then carefully lever the panel out until the clips disengage **(see illustration)**. Work slowly and carefully around the outer edge of the trim panel until it's free. **Note:** *The rear doors only use three screws to secure the door trim panels, two at the door grip and one at the inside handle bezel.*

6 Once all of the clips are disengaged, pull the trim panel up from the door, unplug any wiring harness connectors and remove the panel.

7 For access to the door outside handle or the door window regulator inside the door, raise the window fully, then carefully peel back the plastic membrane **(see illustration)**.

Back door

8 Open the back door.

9 Using a screwdriver or trim removal tool lever out the clips and remove the trim panel from the back door **(see illustration)**. On 2000 and earlier models use a small screwdriver to pop the centre button up on the plastic fasteners, but do not try to remove the centre buttons.

10 For access to other components inside the door, carefully peel back the plastic membrane **(see illustration 15.7)**.

Refitting

11 Prior to refitting of the door trim panel, be sure to refit any clips in the panel which may have come out when you removed the panel.

12 Position the wire harness connectors for the power door lock switch and the power window switch (if equipped) through the hole in the door trim panel, then place the panel in position in the door. Press the door panel into place until the clips are seated.

13 The remainder of the refitting is the reverse of removal.

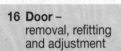
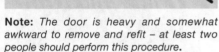

16 Door –
removal, refitting
and adjustment

Note: *The door is heavy and somewhat awkward to remove and refit – at least two people should perform this procedure.*

Removal

1 Raise the window completely in the door and disconnect the negative cable from the battery.

2 Open the door all the way and support it from the ground on jacks or blocks covered with rags to prevent damaging the paint.

3 Remove the door trim panel and membrane as described in Section 15.

4 Disconnect all electrical connections, earth wires and harness retaining clips from the door. **Note:** *It is a good idea to label all connections to aid the reassembly process.*

15.3 Lever off the mirror trim cover

5 From the door side, detach the rubber conduit between the body and the door. Then pull the wiring harness through the conduit hole and remove it from the door.

6 Remove the door stop strut bolt(s) **(see illustration)**.

7 Mark around the door hinges with a pen or a scribe to facilitate realignment during reassembly.

8 With an assistant holding the door, remove the hinge-to-door bolts **(see illustrations)** and lift the door off. **Note:** *Draw a reference line around the hinges before removing the bolts.*

Refitting

9 Refitting is the reverse of removal.

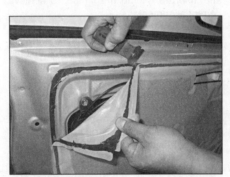

15.7 Carefully peel back the plastic membrane for access to the inner door

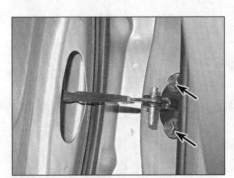

16.6 Remove the bolt(s) retaining the door stop strut (arrows)

15.4 On 2001 and later models lever out the trim cover on the door grip

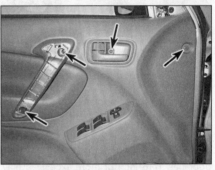

15.5 Door trim panel retaining screws (arrows) – 2001 and later model shown, 2000 and earlier models have two extra screws in the storage compartment area of the front door

15.9 The trim panel for the back door can be removed by simply levering out the clips

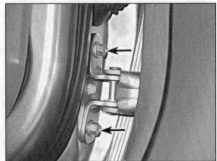

16.8a Remove the door hinge bolts with the door supported (arrows indicate bolts for the bottom hinge, top hinge similar)

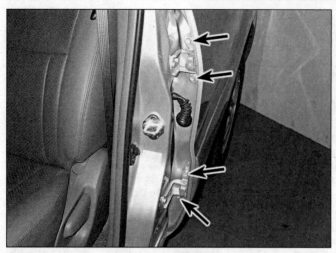

16.8b Open the front door to access the rear door hinge-to-body bolts (arrows)

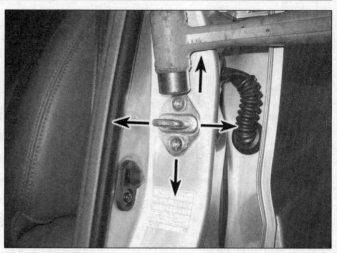

16.13 Adjust the door lock striker by loosening the mounting screws and gently tapping the striker in the desired direction (arrows)

Adjustment

10 Having proper door-to-body alignment is a critical part of a well-functioning door assembly. First check the door hinge pins for excessive play. Fully open the door and lift up-and-down without lifting the body. If a door has 1/16-inch or more excessive play, the hinges should be renewed.

17.2 Detach the plastic clips on the actuating rods leading to the outside handle and the door lock cylinder

11 Door-to-body alignment adjustments are made by loosening the hinge-to-body bolts or hinge-to-door bolts and moving the door. Proper body alignment is achieved when the top of the doors are parallel with the roof section, the front door is flush with the wing, the rear door is flush with the rear quarter panel and the bottom of the doors are aligned with the lower sill panel. If these goals can't be reached by adjusting the hinge-to-body or hinge-to-door bolts, body alignment shims may have to be purchased and inserted behind the hinges to achieve correct alignment.

12 To adjust the door-closed position, scribe a line or mark around the striker plate to provide a reference point, then check that the door lock is contacting the centre of the lock striker. If not adjust the up-and-down position first.

13 Finally adjust the lock striker sideways position, so that the door panel is flush with the centre pillar or rear quarter panel and provides positive engagement with the lock mechanism **(see illustration)**.

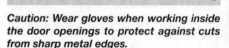

17 Door lock, lock cylinder and handles – removal and refitting

Caution: Wear gloves when working inside the door openings to protect against cuts from sharp metal edges.

Door lock

Removal

1 Raise the window, then remove the door trim panel and membrane (see Section 15).

2 Working through the large access hole, disengage the outside door handle-to-lock rod, outside door lock-to-lock rod, and the inside handle-to-lock rod **(see illustration)**.

3 All door lock rods are attached by plastic clips. The plastic clips can be removed by unsnapping the portion engaging the connecting rod and then pulling the rod out of its locating hole. On models with power door locks, disconnect the electrical connectors at the lock.

4 Remove the screws securing the lock to the door **(see illustrations)**. Remove the lock

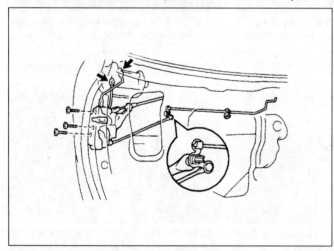

17.4a Door lock mounting details – 2000 and earlier models

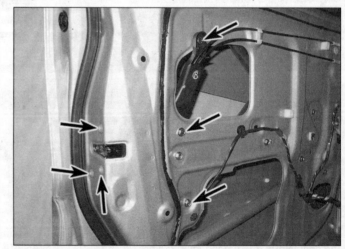

17.4b Door lock mounting details – 2001 and later models

17.9a Remove the plug from the end of the door to access the door lock cylinder retaining bolt – 2001 and later models

17.9b Removing the door lock cylinder on a 2002 model

17.9c Outside door handle retaining bolts (arrows) – 2001 and later models shown, 2000 and earlier similar except that there is no handle frame

assembly through the door opening. On 2001 and later models, it will be necessary to remove the inside handle retaining bolt, then detach the handle from the door and remove the inside handle and the lock as an assembly.

Refitting

5 Refitting is the reverse of removal.

Outside handle and door lock cylinder

Removal

6 To remove the outside handle and lock cylinder assembly, raise the window and remove the door trim panel and membrane (see Section 15).
Caution: Take care not to scratch the paint on the outside of the door. Wide masking tape applied around the handle opening before beginning the procedure can help avoid scratches.
7 Working through the access hole, disengage the plastic clips that secure the outside door lock-to-lock rod and the outside door handle-to-lock rod **(see illustration 17.2)**.
8 On 2000 and earlier models, remove the handle retaining bolts and withdraw the handle and lock cylinder as an assembly from the vehicle. The lock cylinder can be removed from the handle assembly by removing a clip.
9 On 2001 and later models, Remove the plug from the end of the door and remove the lock cylinder retaining screw. Withdraw the lock cylinder from the door, and disconnect the electrical connector if equipped. Unbolt the handle from the inside of the door and remove the handle and the handle frame **(see illustrations)**.

Refitting

10 Refitting is the reverse of removal.

Inside door handle

Removal

11 Remove the door trim panel (see Section 15).
12 Remove the handle retaining screw(s) and disengage the handle from the door **(see illustration)**.
13 Disengage the handle-to-lock rod on 2000 and earlier models or the handle-to-lock

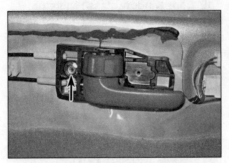

17.12 Inside handle retaining bolt (arrow) – 2001 and later model shown, 2000 and earlier models have two screws securing the handle

cables on 2001 and later models and remove the handle from the door **(see illustration)**.

Refitting

14 Refitting is the reverse of removal.

18 Door window glass – removal and refitting

Caution: Wear gloves when working inside the door openings to protect against cuts from sharp metal edges.

Front door glass

Removal

1 Remove the door trim panel and the plastic membrane (see Section 15).
2 Lower the window glass all the way down.

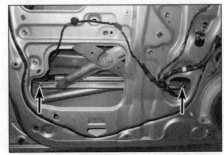

18.3 Raise the window to access the glass retaining bolts (arrows) through the holes in the door frame

17.13 Removing the cables from the inside handle – 2001 and later models

3 Raise the window just enough to access the window retaining bolts through the holes in the door frame **(see illustration)**.
4 Place a rag over the glass to help prevent scratching the glass and remove the two glass mounting bolts.
5 Remove the glass by pulling it up and out.

Refitting

6 Refitting is the reverse of removal.

Rear door glass

Removal

7 Remove the door panel and membrane (see Section 15).
8 Lower the window glass all the way down.
9 Remove the outer weatherstrip. Lever upward on the clips to release it from the door **(see illustration)**.
10 Remove the bolt and screw securing the

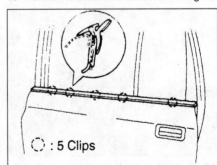

○ : 5 Clips

18.9 Outer weatherstrip clip locations – rear door

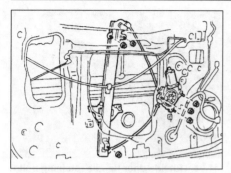

19.4 Front window regulator mounting bolts – 2000 and earlier models

division bar to the door frame, then remove the division bar and the fixed glass.

11 Raise the window just enough to access the window retaining bolts through the holes in the door frame.

12 Place a rag over the glass to help prevent scratching the glass and remove the two glass mounting bolts.

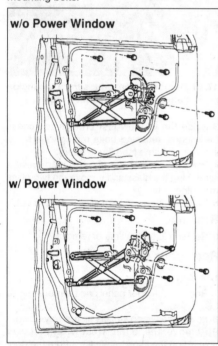

19.5 Front window regulator mounting bolts – 2001 and later models

20.4 Remove the three mirror mounting bolts (upper arrows) – on power mirrors, disconnect the connector (lower arrows)

13 Remove the glass by pulling it up and out.

Refitting

14 Refitting is the reverse of the removal procedure.

Back door glass

15 Removal and refitting of the back door glass requires the use of special fast-setting adhesive/caulk materials and some specialised tools and techniques. These operations should be left to a dealer service department or a body shop specialising in glass work.

19 Door window glass regulator – removal and refitting

Caution: Wear gloves when working inside the door openings to protect against cuts from sharp metal edges.

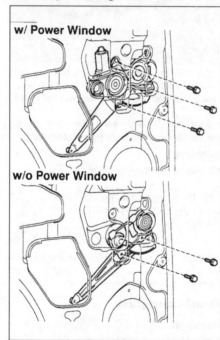

19.11 Rear window regulator mounting bolts – all models

20.6 While pulling up on the inside mirror, push a screwdriver into the slot in the bottom of the base to release it

Front

Removal

1 Remove the door trim panel and the plastic membrane (see Section 15).

2 Remove the window glass (see Section 18).

3 On power-operated windows, disconnect the electrical connector from the window regulator motor.

4 On 2000 and earlier models, remove the regulator/motor assembly mounting bolts **(see illustration)**.

5 On 2001 later models, the regulator assembly is a scissors-type. Before removing the bolts, mark the position of the upper roller guide. Remove the bolts holding the window regulator/motor to the door **(see illustration)**.

6 Pull the equaliser arm and regulator assemblies through the service hole in the door frame to remove it.

Refitting

7 Refitting is the reverse of removal. Lubricate the rollers and wear points on the regulator with white grease before refitting.

Rear

Removal

8 Remove the door trim panel and the plastic membrane (see Section 15).

9 Remove the window glass assembly (see Section 18).

10 On power-operated windows, disconnect the electrical connector from the window regulator motor.

11 Remove the regulator/motor assembly mounting bolts **(see illustration)**.

12 Remove the equaliser bar and raise the regulator assembly through the service hole in the door frame to remove it.

Refitting

13 Refitting is the reverse of removal. Lubricate the rollers and wear points on the regulator with white grease before refitting.

20 Mirrors – removal and refitting

Outside mirrors

Removal

1 Lever off the mirror trim cover on the inside of the door.

2 On power mirror equipped models, remove the door trim panel and peel back the plastic membrane if necessary (see Section 15).

3 Disconnect the electrical connector from the mirror (if equipped).

4 Remove the three mirror retaining bolts and detach the mirror from the vehicle **(see illustration)**.

Refitting

5 Refitting is the reverse of removal.

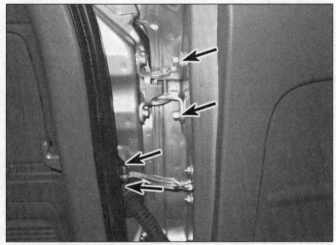

21.8 Back door-to-hinge bolts (upper arrows indicate bolts for the top hinge, bottom hinge similar) – lower arrows are the door stop strut retaining bolts

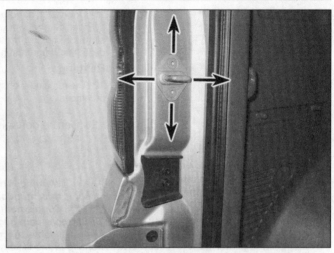

21.13 Adjust the door lock striker by loosening the mounting screws and gently tapping the striker in the desired direction (arrows)

Inside mirror

Removal

6 Lever between the mirror mounting and the notch in the base of the mirror stalk with a screwdriver tip covered with tape **(see illustration)**. There is a hairpin-type spring holding the mirror stalk in the base. Push the screwdriver in about 3/4-inch to release the spring.

Refitting

7 To refit the mirror, reinsert the spring if it was removed earlier. Insert the mirror stalk's lug into the mounting, pushing downward until the mirror is secured.

21 Back door –
removal, refitting and adjustment

Note: *The back door is heavy and somewhat awkward to remove and refit – at least two people should perform this procedure.*

Removal

1 Disconnect the negative cable from the battery. Remove the spare tyre from the back door.
2 Open the door all the way and support it from the ground on jacks or blocks covered with rags to prevent damaging the paint.
3 Remove the door trim panel and membrane as described in Section 15.
4 Disconnect all electrical connections, earth wires and harness retaining clips from the door. **Note:** *It is a good idea to label all connections to aid the reassembly process.*
5 From the door side, detach the rubber conduit between the body and the door. Then pull the wiring harness through the conduit hole and remove it from the door.
6 Remove the door stop strut bolt(s).
7 Mark around the door hinges with a pen or a scribe to facilitate realignment during reassembly.

8 With an assistant holding the door, remove the hinge-to-door bolts **(see illustration)** and lift the door off. **Note:** *Draw a reference line around the hinges before removing the bolts.*

Refitting

9 Refitting is the reverse of removal.

Adjustment

10 Having proper door-to-body alignment is a critical part of a well-functioning door assembly. First check the door hinge pins for excessive play. Fully open the door and lift up-and-down without lifting the body. If a door has 1/16-inch or more excessive play, the hinges should be renewed.
11 Door-to-body alignment adjustments are made by loosening the hinge-to-body bolts or hinge-to-door bolts and moving the door. Proper body alignment is achieved when the top of the door is parallel with the roof section and the sides of the door are flush with the rear quarter panels and the bottom of the door is aligned with the lower door sill. If these goals can't be reached by adjusting the hinge-to-body or hinge-to-door bolts, body alignment shims may have to be purchased and inserted behind the hinges to achieve correct alignment.
12 To adjust the door-closed position, scribe a line or mark around the striker plate to

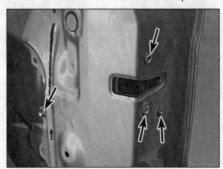

22.5 Back door lock fasteners (arrows)

provide a reference point, then check that the door lock is contacting the centre of the lock striker. If not adjust the up-and-down position first.
13 Finally adjust the lock striker sideways position, so that the door panel is flush with the rear quarter panel and provides positive engagement with the lock mechanism **(see illustration)**.

22 Back door lock, lock cylinder and handle – removal and refitting

Back door lock

Removal

1 Disconnect the negative cable from the battery.
2 Open the back door and remove the door trim panel and membrane as described in Section 15.
3 Working through the large access hole, disengage the outside door handle-to-lock rod and the outside door lock-to-lock rod.
4 All door lock rods are attached by plastic clips. The plastic clips can be removed by unsnapping the portion engaging the connecting rod and then pulling the rod out of its locating hole. On models with power door locks, disconnect the electrical connectors at the lock.
5 Remove the screws securing the lock to the door **(see illustration)**. Remove the lock assembly through the door opening. On 2000 and earlier models, lever out the four plastic plugs and remove the screws.

Refitting

6 Refitting is the reverse of removal.

Back door lock cylinder and outside handle

Removal

7 Open the back door and remove the door

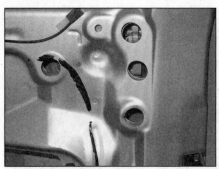

22.10 The outside handle retaining bolts can be accessed through the holes in the door frame

trim panel and membrane as described in Section 15.

8 Working through the large access hole, disengage the outside door handle-to-lock rod and the outside door lock-to-lock rod.

9 All door lock rods are attached by plastic clips. The plastic clips can be removed by unsnapping the portion engaging the connecting rod and then pulling the rod out of its locating hole.

10 Remove the handle retaining bolts through the holes in the door frame and detach the handle and lock assembly from the back door **(see illustration)**.

23.4 Removing the shift lever bezel on an automatic transmission vehicle – 2001 and later models shown

11 Once the handle is removed the lock cylinder can be removed from the handle by simply removing the retaining screw(s) and detaching it from the handle.

Refitting

12 The remainder of the refitting is the reverse of removal.

23 Centre console – removal and refitting

⚠ *Warning: The models covered by this manual are equipped with Supplemental Restraint systems (SRS), more commonly known as airbags. Always disable the airbag system before working in the vicinity of any airbag system component to avoid the possibility of accidental deployment of the airbag, which could cause personal injury (see Chapter 12).*

Removal

1 Disconnect the negative cable from the battery.

2 Raise the handbrake handle.

3 If the vehicle is equipped with manual transmission, unscrew the shift lever knob and remove the shift lever boot.

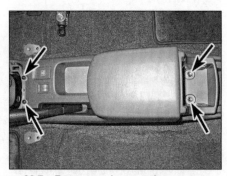

23.7a Rear console mounting screws (arrows) – 2001 and later models

4 If the vehicle is equipped with an automatic transmission, remove the shift lever bezel **(see illustration)**.

5 On 2001 and later models, remove the screws then lever the lower centre finish panel off the instrument panel (see Section 24). Be sure to tape the tip of the screwdriver tip to prevent scratching the panels.

6 On 2000 and earlier models, remove the screws at the front and centre of the console, then remove the screw at the rear in the cup holder. Pull the console up and back to remove it from the vehicle.

7 On 2001 and later models, remove the retaining screws and detach the rear half of the console from the vehicle **(see illustration)**. Also remove the trim covers at the front of the console **(see illustration)**.

8 Remove the front console screws and lift the console up and over the shift lever **(see illustration)**. Disconnect any electrical connections and remove the console from the vehicle.

Refitting

9 Refitting is the reverse of removal.

24 Facia trim panels

⚠ *Warning: The models covered by this manual are equipped with Supplemental Restraint systems (SRS), more commonly known as airbags. Always disable the airbag system before working in the vicinity of any airbag system component to avoid the possibility of accidental deployment of the airbag, which could cause personal injury (see Chapter 12).*

1 Disconnect the negative cable from the battery.

Instrument cluster bezel

2 If equipped with a tilt steering column, tilt the column all the way down.

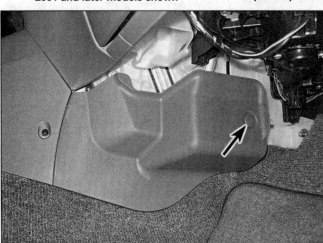

23.7b Console front trim cover – 2001 and later models

23.8 Front console mounting screws – 2001 and later models (the two lower left side screws are not visible in this photo)

3 On 2000 and earlier models, remove the screw at the top of the instrument cluster bezel **(see illustration)**. Grasp the bezel with both hands and pull straight out to disengage the bezel from the instrument panel.

4 On 2001 and later models simply grasp the bezel with both hands and pull straight out to disengage the bezel from the instrument panel **(see illustration)**.

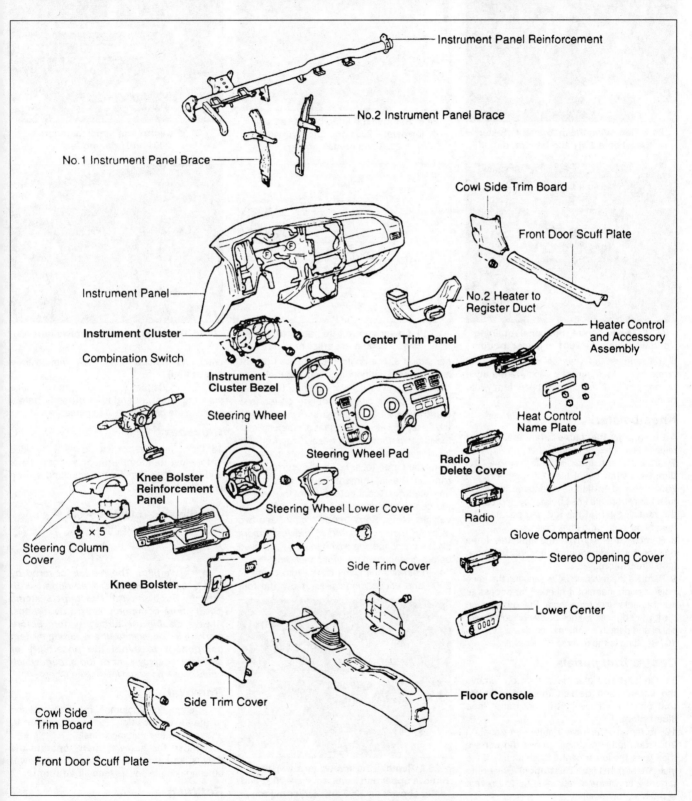

Instrument Panel Reinforcement

No.2 Instrument Panel Brace

No.1 Instrument Panel Brace

Cowl Side Trim Board

Front Door Scuff Plate

Instrument Panel

No.2 Heater to Register Duct

Instrument Cluster

Center Trim Panel

Heater Control and Accessory Assembly

Combination Switch

Instrument Cluster Bezel

Heat Control Name Plate

Steering Wheel

Steering Wheel Pad

Radio Delete Cover

Knee Bolster Reinforcement Panel

Steering Wheel Lower Cover

Radio

Glove Compartment Door

Steering Column Cover

× 5

Side Trim Cover

Stereo Opening Cover

Knee Bolster

Lower Center

Side Trim Cover

Floor Console

Cowl Side Trim Board

Front Door Scuff Plate

**24.3 Instrument panel and related components –
2000 and earlier models**

24.4 Removing the instrument cluster bezel on a 2001 and later model

24.8 Remove the knee bolster screws (arrows) – 2001 and later shown, 2000 and earlier similar

24.11 Centre trim panel fasteners – 2001 and later models

24.12 Lower centre trim panel retaining screws (arrows) – 2001 and later models

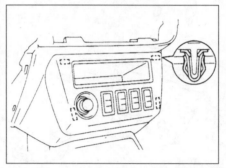

24.14 Lower centre trim panel retaining clips – 2000 and earlier models

24.16 Glovebox retaining screws (arrows)

5 Refitting is the reverse of the removal procedure. Make sure the clips are engaged properly before pushing the bezel firmly into place.

Knee bolster

6 Disengage the cable from the bonnet release lever (see Section 10).

7 On 2001 and later models, remove the dimmer switch bezel (see Chapter 12). On 2000 and earlier models disengage the small fuse panel from the knee bolster by depressing the retaining tab at the top and pushing the fuse panel out of the knee bolster.

8 Remove the screws and pull the knee bolster out to disengage the clips behind it **(see illustration)**.

9 Remove the retaining bolts securing the knee bolster reinforcement if needed for access to components under the facia. Pull outward on the lower edge of the knee bolster reinforcement panel and detach it from the vehicle.

10 Refitting is the reverse of removal.

Centre trim panels

11 On 2001 and later models, simply remove the screws and detach the upper centre trim panel from the instrument panel **(see illustration)**.

12 To remove the lower centre trim panel on 2001 and later models, remove the screws then lever the lower centre finish panel off the instrument panel **(see illustration)**. Be sure to tape the tip of the screwdriver tip to prevent scratching the panels,

13 On 2000 and earlier models, remove the instrument cluster bezel as described in

paragraph 3. Then pull off the knobs from the heating/air conditioning control panel. Also remove the lower screws securing the stereo opening cover or radio delete cover **(see illustration 24.3)**. Using a screwdriver with the tip taped with masking tape, carefully lever the lower portion of the bezel away from the instrument panel until the clips are released. Take care not to scratch the surrounding trim on the instrument panel. Disconnect any electrical connectors from the rear of the centre trim panel and remove it from the vehicle. **Note:** *Some models may have two retaining screws located in the instrument cluster bezel opening which must be removed before disengaging the trim panel clips.*

14 To remove the lower centre trim panel on 2000 and earlier models, lever out the four

25.2 Remove the screws (arrows), then remove upper and lower covers – 2001 and later shown; on 2000 and earlier models, one more screw secures the upper cover, accessible after the lower cover is removed

clips and remove it from the vehicle **(see illustration)**.

15 Refitting is the reverse of removal. Make sure the clips are engaged properly before pushing the bezel firmly into place.

Glovebox

16 Open the glovebox and squeeze the sides in to allow the compartment to come back and down, then remove the mounting screws **(see illustration)**.

25 Steering column covers – removal and refitting

⚠️ *Warning: The models covered by this manual are equipped with Supplemental Restraint systems (SRS), more commonly known as airbags. Always disable the airbag system before working in the vicinity of any airbag system component to avoid the possibility of accidental deployment of the airbag, which could cause personal injury (see Chapter 12).*

Removal

1 On tilt steering columns, move the column to the lowest position. Refer to Chapter 10 and remove the steering wheel.

2 Remove the screws, then separate the halves and remove the upper and lower steering column covers **(see illustration)**.

Refitting

3 Refitting is the reverse of the removal procedure.

26 Instrument panel – removal and refitting

Warning: The models covered by this manual are equipped with Supplemental Restraint systems (SRS), more commonly known as airbags. Always disable the airbag system before working in the vicinity of any airbag system component to avoid the possibility of accidental deployment of the airbag, which could cause personal injury (see Chapter 12).

Removal

1 Disconnect the negative battery cable.
2 Remove the facia trim panels (see Section 24) and the centre floor console (see Section 23).
3 Remove the instrument cluster (see Chapter 12) .
4 Disconnect the electrical connector from the passenger's side airbag and on 2001 and later models, remove it (see Chapter 12).
5 Remove the audio unit from the centre of the facia (see Chapter 12).
6 Remove the air conditioning control panel (see Chapter 3).

7 Remove the driver's knee bolster and reinforcement panel (see Section 24). Then unscrew the bolts securing the steering column and lower it away from the instrument panel (see Chapter 10).
8 A number of electrical connectors must be disconnected in order to remove the instrument panel. Most are designed so that they will only fit on the matching connector (male or female), but if there is any doubt, mark the connectors with masking tape and a marking pen before disconnecting them **(see illustration). Note:** *On 2000 and earlier models, disconnect the main connectors*

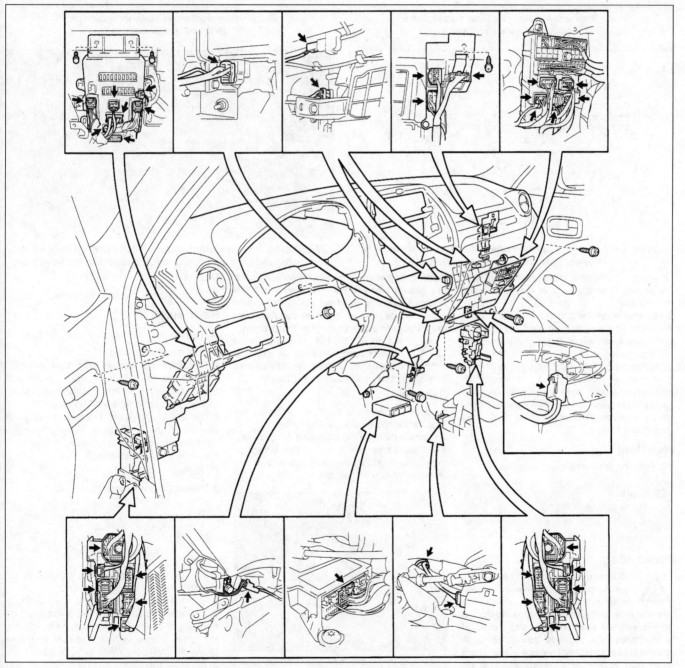

26.8a Instrument panel fastener and electrical connections – 2001 and later models

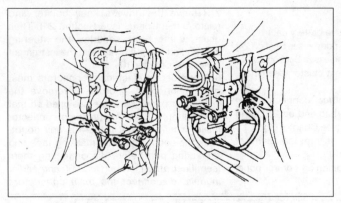

**26.8b Instrument panel electrical connections –
2000 and earlier models**

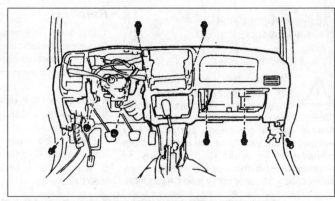

**26.9a Instrument panel fastener locations –
2000 and earlier models**

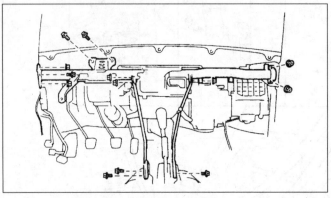

**26.9b Cross beam mounting bolts – 2000 and earlier models
shown, 2001 and later models similar**

**27.2 Typical front seat track retaining bolts (arrows indicate the
rear bolts; slide the seat to the rear for access to the front bolts**

on each side of the instrument panel and the two earth straps bolts at the centre (see illustration).

9 Remove all of the fasteners (bolts, screws and nuts) holding the instrument panel to the body (see illustration). Once all are removed, lift the panel then pull it away from the windscreen and take it out through the driver's door opening. **Note:** This is a two-person job, and you may also have to remove the bolts to the instrument panel reinforcement tube for complete removal of the instrument panel (see illustration).

Refitting

10 Refitting is the reverse of removal.

27 Seats –
removal and refitting

Front seat

⚠️ **Warning 1: The front seat belts on some models are equipped with pretensioners, which are pyrotechnic (explosive) devices designed to retract the seat belts in the event of a collision. On models equipped with pretensioners, do not remove the front seat belt retractor assemblies, and do not disconnect the electrical connectors**

leading to the assemblies. Problems with the pretensioners will turn on the SRS (airbag) warning light on the dash. If any pretensioner problems are suspected, take the vehicle to a dealer service department.

⚠️ **Warning 2: On models with side-impact airbags, be sure to disarm the airbag system before beginning this procedure (see Chapter 12).**

Removal

1 Lever out the plastic covers to access the seat tracks and their mounting bolts.
2 Remove the retaining bolts (see illustration).
3 Tilt the seat upward to access the underside, then disconnect any electrical connectors and lift the seat from the vehicle.

**27.7 Lift up on the lock bar to disengage
the rear seat from the pivots on the floor**

Refitting

4 Refitting is the reverse of removal.

Rear seat

Removal

5 Fold the seat forward.
6 On 2000 and earlier four-door models, remove the two hinge retaining bolts and detach the seat from the vehicle. On two-door models the seat is retained by four bolts.
7 On 2001 and later models, simply lift upward on the locking bar to disengage the hook from the pivot and remove the seat from the vehicle (see illustration).

Refitting

8 Refitting is the reverse of removal.

28 Sunroof –
adjustment

1 The position of the glass panel can be adjusted in the following manner.
2 Operate the sunroof until it is tilted open.
3 The side-to-side adjustment is achieved by removing the sunroof drive motor and moving the drive cable until the cable-to-frame alignment marks are even on both sides.
4 Remove the glass retaining screws and remove the glass (see illustration).

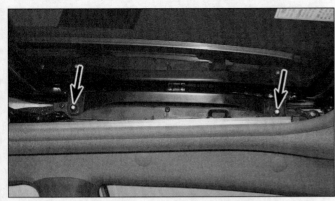

28.4 Sunroof glass retaining bolts (arrows indicate two of four bolts)

28.5a Lever out the interior light lens, lower the compartment door and remove the overhead console screws

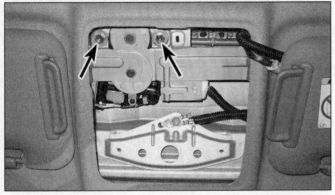

28.5b Remove the drive motor retaining bolts (arrows) and disengage the drive motor gear from the drive cable

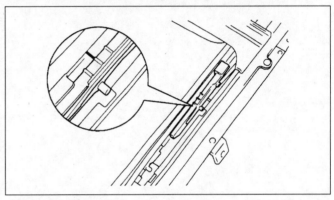

28.5c Working up in the sunroof opening, move the cable end until the cable-to-frame alignment marks are even on both sides

5 Remove the sunroof drive motor **(see illustrations)**. Move the drive cable end until the cable alignment marks are even with the marks on the frame on each side.

6 When the adjustment is correct, refit the drive motor and the sunroof glass.
7 The final adjustment is the forward and rearward adjustment. This is achieved by loosening the glass retaining screws and moving the glass the amount necessary to allow proper sealing with the front and rear edge.

Chapter 12
Chassis electrical system

Contents

Section number

Aerial – removal and refitting 13
Airbag system – general information 26
Bulb renewal. 19
Circuit breakers – general information 4
Cruise control system – description. 21
Daytime Running Lights (DRL) – general information. 25
Electric side mirrors – description 20
Electrical troubleshooting – general information 2
Fuses and fusible links – general information 3
General information 1
Headlight bulb – renewal 15
Headlight housing – removal and refitting 17
Headlights – adjustment. 16
Heated rear window second – check and repair 14

Section number

Horn – check, removal and refitting 18
Ignition switch and lock cylinder – removal and refitting 8
Instrument cluster – removal and refitting 10
Instrument panel switches – removal and refitting. 9
Power door lock system – description. 23
Power sunroof – description 24
Power window system – description 22
Radio and speakers – removal and refitting. 12
Relays – general information and testing. 5
Steering column switches – removal and refitting 7
Turn signal and hazard flasher – check, removal and refitting 6
Wiper motor – check, removal and refitting 11
Wiring diagrams – general information. 27

Degrees of difficulty

Easy, suitable for novice with little experience	**Fairly easy,** suitable for beginner with some experience	**Fairly difficult,** suitable for competent DIY mechanic	**Difficult,** suitable for experienced DIY mechanic	**Very difficult,** suitable for expert DIY or professional

1 General information

The electrical system is a 12 volt, negative earth type. Power for the lights and all electrical accessories is supplied by a lead-acid type battery which is charged by the alternator.

This Chapter covers repair and service procedures for the various electrical components not associated with the engine. Information on the battery, alternator, distributor and starter motor can be found in Chapter 5.

It should be noted that when portions of the electrical system are serviced, the cable should be disconnected from the negative battery terminal to prevent electrical shorts and/or fires.

2 Electrical troubleshooting – general information

A typical electrical circuit consists of an electrical component, any switches, relays, motors, fuses, fusible links or circuit breakers related to that component and the wiring and connectors that link the component to both the battery and the chassis. To help you pinpoint an electrical circuit problem, wiring diagrams are included at the end of this Chapter.

Before tackling any troublesome electrical circuit, first study the appropriate wiring diagrams to get a complete understanding of what makes up that individual circuit. Trouble spots, for instance, can often be narrowed down by noting if other components related to the circuit are operating properly. If several components or circuits fail at one time, chances are the problem is in a fuse or earth connection, because several circuits are often routed through the same fuse and earth connections.

Electrical problems usually stem from simple causes, such as loose or corroded connections, a blown fuse, a melted fusible link or a failed relay. Visually inspect the condition of all fuses, wires and connections in a problem circuit before troubleshooting the circuit.

If test equipment and instruments are going to be utilised, use the diagrams to plan ahead of time where you will make the necessary connections in order to accurately pinpoint the trouble spot.

The basic tools needed for electrical

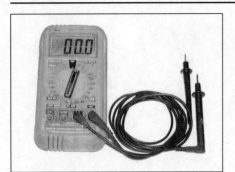

2.5a The most useful tool for electrical troubleshooting is a digital multimeter that can check volts, amps and test continuity

troubleshooting include a circuit tester or voltmeter (a 12 volt bulb with a set of test leads can also be used), a continuity tester, which includes a bulb, battery and set of test leads, and a jumper wire, preferably with a circuit breaker incorporated, which can be used to bypass electrical components **(see illustrations)**. Before attempting to locate a problem with test instruments, use the wiring diagram(s) to decide where to make the connections.

Voltage checks

Voltage checks should be performed if a circuit is not functioning properly. Connect one lead of a circuit tester to either the negative battery terminal or a known good earth. Connect the other lead to a connector in the circuit being tested, preferably nearest to the battery or fuse **(see illustration)**. If the bulb of the tester lights, voltage is present, which means that the part of the circuit between the connector and the battery is problem-free. Continue checking the rest of the circuit in the same fashion. When you reach a point at which no voltage is present, the problem lies between that point and the last test point with voltage. Most of the time the problem can be traced to a loose connection. **Note:** *Keep in mind that some circuits receive voltage only when the ignition key is in the Accessory or Run position.*

2.6 In use, a basic test light's lead is clipped to a known good earth, then the pointed probe can test connectors, wires or electrical sockets – if the bulb lights, the circuit being tested has battery voltage

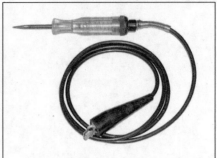

2.5b A simple test light is a very handy tool for testing voltage

Finding a short

One method of finding shorts in a live circuit is to remove the fuse and connect a test light in place of the fuse terminals (fabricate two jumper wires with small spade terminals, plug the jumper wires into the fusebox and connect the test light). There should be voltage present in the circuit. Move the suspected wiring harness from side-to-side while watching the test light. If the bulb goes off, there is a short to earth somewhere in that area, probably where the insulation has rubbed through.

Earth check

Perform a earth test to check whether a component is properly earthed. Disconnect the battery and connect one lead of a continuity tester or multimeter (set to the ohms scale), to a known good earth. Connect the other lead to the wire or earth connection being tested. If the resistance is low (less than 5 ohms), the earth is good. If the bulb on a self-powered test light does not go on, the earth is not good.

Continuity check

A continuity check is done to determine if there are any breaks in a circuit – if it is passing electricity properly. With the circuit off (no power in the circuit), a self-powered continuity

2.9 With a multimeter set to the ohms scale, resistance can be checked across two terminals – when checking for continuity, a low reading indicates continuity, a high reading or infinity indicates lack of continuity

tester or multimeter can be used to check the circuit. Connect the test leads to both ends of the circuit (or to the 'power' end and a good earth), and if the test light comes on the circuit is passing current properly **(see illustration)**. If the resistance is low (less than 5 ohms), there is continuity; if the reading is 10,000 ohms or higher, there is a break somewhere in the circuit. The same procedure can be used to test a switch, by connecting the continuity tester to the switch terminals. With the switch turned On, the test light should come on (or low resistance should be indicated on a meter).

Finding an open circuit

When diagnosing for possible open circuits, it is often difficult to locate them by sight because the connectors hide oxidation or terminal misalignment. Merely wiggling a connector on a sensor or in the wiring harness may correct the open circuit condition. Remember this when an open circuit is indicated when troubleshooting a circuit. Intermittent problems may also be caused by oxidised or loose connections.

Electrical troubleshooting is simple if you keep in mind that all electrical circuits are basically electricity running from the battery, through the wires, switches, relays, fuses and fusible links to each electrical component (light bulb, motor, etc) and to earth, from which it is passed back to the battery. Any electrical problem is an interruption in the flow of electricity to and from the battery.

Connectors

Most electrical connections on these vehicles are made with multiwire plastic connectors. The mating halves of many connectors are secured with locking clips moulded into the plastic connector shells. The mating halves of large connectors, such as some of those under the instrument panel, are held together by a bolt through the centre of the connector.

To separate a connector with locking clips, use a small screwdriver to lever the clips apart carefully, then separate the connector halves. Pull only on the shell, never pull on the wiring harness as you may damage the individual wires and terminals inside the connectors. Look at the connector closely before trying to separate the halves. Often the locking clips are engaged in a way that is not immediately clear. Additionally, many connectors have more than one set of clips.

Each pair of connector terminals has a male half and a female half. When you look at the end view of a connector in a diagram, be sure to understand whether the view shows the harness side or the component side of the connector. Connector halves are mirror images of each other, and a terminal shown on the right side end-view of one half will be on the left side end view of the other half.

3.1a The interior fuse box is located on the dashboard, to the left of the steering column – 2001 and later model shown

3.1b The main engine compartment fuse/relay box on a 2001 and later model

3 Fuses and fusible links – general information

Fuses

The electrical circuits of the vehicle are protected by a combination of fuses, circuit breakers and fusible links. Fuse blocks are located under the instrument panel and in the engine compartment depending on the model year of the vehicle **(see illustrations)**.

Each of the fuses is designed to protect a specific circuit, and the various circuits are identified on the fuse panel cover.

Miniaturised fuses are employed in the fuse blocks. These compact fuses, with blade terminal design, allow fingertip removal and refitting. If an electrical component fails, always check the fuse first. The best way to check a fuse is with a test light. Check for power at the exposed terminal tips of each fuse. If power is present on one side of the fuse but not the other, the fuse is blown. A blown fuse can also be confirmed by visually inspecting it **(see illustration)**.

Be sure to renew blown fuses with the correct type. Fuses of different ratings are physically interchangeable, but only fuses of the proper rating should be used. Renewing a fuse with one of a higher or lower value than specified is not recommended. Each electrical circuit needs a specific amount of protection. The amperage value of each fuse is moulded into the fuse body.

If the renewed fuse immediately fails, don't renew it again until the cause of the problem is isolated and corrected. In most cases, this will be a short circuit in the wiring caused by a broken or deteriorated wire.

Fusible links

Some circuits are protected by fusible links. The links are used in circuits which are not ordinarily fused, such as the ignition circuit, or which carry high current.

Cartridge type fusible links are located in the engine compartment fusible link box and are similar to a large fuse. After disconnecting the negative battery cable, simply unplug and renew a fusible link of the same amperage.

2000 and earlier models are equipped with a fusible link box located near the battery. 2001 and later models locate the fusible link box near the right side shock absorber in the engine compartment.

4 Circuit breakers – general information

Circuit breakers protect certain circuits, such as the power windows or heated seats. Depending on the vehicle's accessories, there may be one or two circuit breakers, located in the fuse/relay box in the engine compartment **(see illustration 3.1b)**.

Because the circuit breakers reset automatically, an electrical overload in a circuit-breaker-protected system will cause the circuit to fail momentarily, then come back on. If the circuit does not come back on, check it immediately. **Note:** *Some circuit breakers must be reset manually.*

For a basic check, pull the circuit breaker

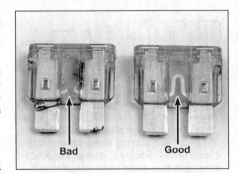

3.3 When a fuse blows, the element between the terminals melts

Bad   Good

up out of its socket on the fuse panel, but just far enough to probe with a voltmeter. The breaker should still contact the sockets.

With the voltmeter negative lead on a good chassis earth, touch each end prong of the circuit breaker with the positive meter probe. There should be battery voltage at each end. If there is battery voltage only at one end, the circuit breaker must be renewed.

5 Relays – general information and testing

General information

1 Several electrical circuits in the vehicle, such as the fuel injection system, horns, starter, and foglights use relays to transmit the electrical signal to the component. Relays use a low-current circuit (the control circuit) to open and close a high-current circuit (the power circuit). If the relay is defective, that component will not operate properly. Most relays are mounted in the engine compartment fuse/relay boxes, with some specialised relays located above the interior fuse box under the dash **(see illustrations)**. If a faulty relay is suspected, it can be removed and tested using the procedure below or by a dealer

5.1a The covers of the engine compartment relay boxes have a printed key to identify the relays

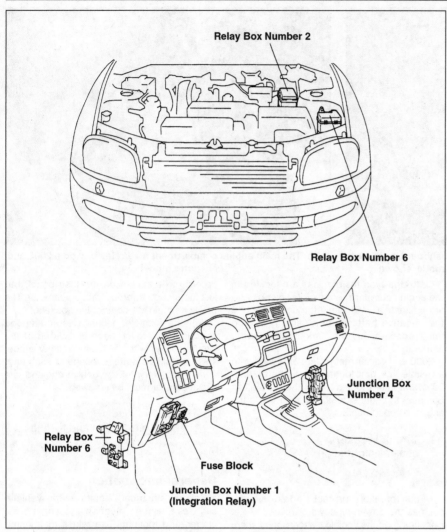

5.1b Relay box and junction box locations on 2000 and earlier LHD models

service department or garage. Defective relays must be renewed as a unit.

Testing

2 Refer to the wiring diagrams for the circuit to determine the proper connections for the relay you're testing. If you can't determine the correct connection from the wiring diagrams, however, you may be able to determine the test connections from the information that follows.

3 There are four basic types of relays used on these models (see illustrations). Some are normally open type and some normally closed, while others include a circuit of each type.

4 On most relays, two of the terminals are the relay control circuit (they connect to the relay coil which, when energised, closes the large contacts to complete the circuit). The other terminals are the power circuit (they are connected together within the relay when the control-circuit coil is energised).

5 Some relays may be marked as an aid to help you determine which terminals are the control circuit and which are the power circuit. If the relay is not marked, refer to the wiring diagrams at the end of this Chapter to determine the proper hook-ups for the relay you're testing.

6 To test a relay, connect an ohmmeter across the two terminals of the power circuit, continuity should not be indicated (see illustration). Now connect a fused jumper wire between one of the two control circuit terminals and the positive battery terminal. Connect another jumper wire between the other control circuit terminal and earth. When the connections are made, the relay should click and continuity should be indicated on the meter. On some relays, polarity may be critical, so, if the relay doesn't click, try swapping the jumper wires on the control circuit terminals.

7 If the relay fails the above test, renew it.

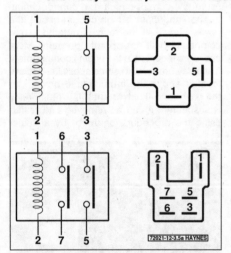

5.3a These two relays are typical normally open types; the one above completes a single circuit (terminal 5 to terminal 3) when energised – the lower relay type completes two circuits (6 and 7, and 3 and 5) when energised

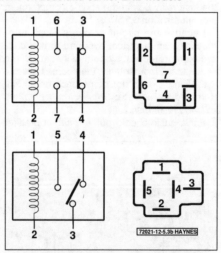

5.3b These relays are normally closed types, where current flows though one circuit until the relay is energised, which interrupts that circuit and completes the second circuit

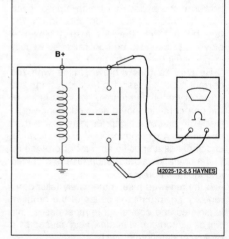

5.6 To test a typical four-terminal normally open relay, connect an ohmmeter to the two terminals of the power circuit – the meter should indicate continuity with the relay energised and no continuity with the relay not energised

6 Turn signal and hazard flasher – check, removal and refitting

⚠ **Warning:** *The models covered by this manual are equipped with Supplemental Restraint Systems (SRS), more commonly known as airbags. Always disable the airbag system before working in the vicinity of any airbag system components to avoid the possibility of accidental deployment of the airbags, which could cause personal injury (see Section 26).*

Check

1 The turn signal and hazard flasher is a single combination unit.
2 When the flasher unit is functioning properly, an audible click can be heard during its operation. If the turn signals fail on one side or the other and the flasher unit does not make its characteristic clicking sound, or if a bulb on one side of the vehicle flashes much faster than normal but the bulb at the other end of the vehicle (on the same side) doesn't light at all, a faulty turn signal bulb may be indicated.
3 If both turn signals fail to blink, the problem may be due to a blown fuse, a faulty flasher unit, a defective switch or a loose or open connection. If a quick check of the fusebox indicates that the turn signal fuse has blown, check the wiring for a short before installing a new fuse.

Removal

4 To renew the flasher, disconnect the electrical connector and remove the flasher unit from its mounting bracket located under the instrument panel to the right of the steering column **(see illustrations)**.
5 Make sure that the new unit is identical to the original. Compare the old one to the new one before installing it.

Refitting

6 Refitting is the reverse of removal.

7 Steering column switches – removal and refitting

⚠ **Warning:** *The models covered by this manual are equipped with Supplemental Restraint Systems (SRS), more commonly known as airbags. Always disable the airbag system before working in the vicinity of any airbag system components to avoid the possibility of accidental deployment of the airbags, which could cause personal injury (see Section 26).*

Removal

1 Disconnect the cable from the negative terminal of the battery.

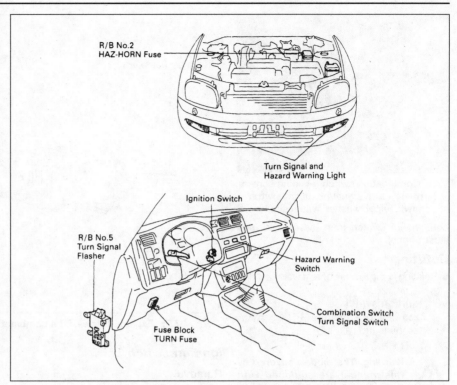

6.4a Location of the turn signal and hazard flasher on 2000 and earlier LHD models

2 Remove the steering wheel (see Chapter 10).
3 Remove the steering column covers (see Chapter 11).
4 Unplug the electrical connectors from the combination switch.
5 Remove the retaining screws and pull the

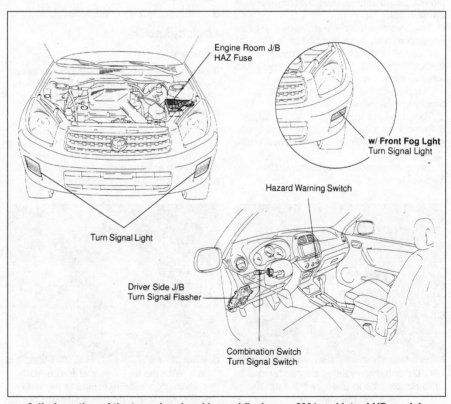

6.4b Location of the turn signal and hazard flasher on 2001 and later LHD models

7.5a Combination switch retaining screws (arrows) – turn signal/headlight switch shown, wiper/washer switch similar

combination switch from the column (see illustrations).

Refitting

6 Refitting is the reverse of removal.

8 Ignition switch and key lock cylinder – removal and refitting

⚠ **Warning: The models covered by this manual are equipped with Supplemental Restraint Systems (SRS), more commonly known as airbags. Always disable the airbag system before working in the vicinity of any airbag system components to avoid the possibility of accidental deployment of the airbags, which could cause personal injury (see Section 26).**

Note: *These models are equipped with an integration relay (see illustration 5.1b). The integration relay works in conjunction with the ignition switch to activate the key unlock warning system and anti-theft system.*

1 Disconnect the cable from the negative terminal of the battery.
2 Place the ignition key in the ACC position.
3 Remove the steering wheel (see Chapter 10).
4 Remove the steering column covers (see Chapter 11).
5 Remove the steering column switches (see Section 7).

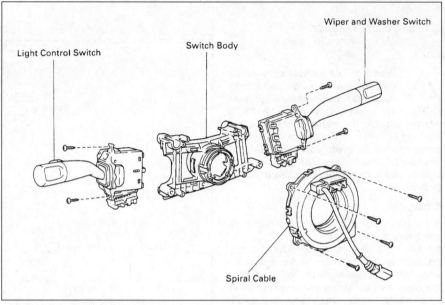

7.5b Exploded view of the combination switch and wiper/washer switch

Ignition switch

Removal

6 Unplug the ignition switch wiring harness connectors.
7 Remove the switch retaining screws (see illustration) then pull the switch from the lock cylinder housing.

Refitting

8 Refitting is reverse of the removal.

Lock cylinder

Removal

9 Use a small screwdriver or punch to depress the lock cylinder retaining pin (see illustration).
10 Pull straight out on the lock cylinder assembly to remove it from the housing.

Refitting

11 To refit the lock cylinder, depress the retaining pin and guide the lock cylinder into the housing until the retaining pin extends itself back into the locating hole in the housing.

12 The remainder of the refitting is the reverse of removal.

9 Instrument panel switches – removal and refitting

⚠ **Warning: The models covered by this manual are equipped with Supplemental Restraint Systems (SRS), more commonly known as airbags. Always disable the airbag system before working in the vicinity of any airbag system components to avoid the possibility of accidental deployment of the airbags, which could cause personal injury (see Section 26).**

Hazard warning switch

2000 and earlier models

1 Carefully lever the switch (see illustration) from the centre cluster finish panel.

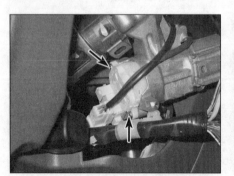

8.7 Detach the retaining screws (arrows) to remove the ignition switch from the steering column housing

8.9 With the lock cylinder in the ACC position, depress the retaining pin with a small screwdriver, then pull straight out to remove the lock cylinder

9.1 Carefully lever the switch housing out using a flat-bladed screwdriver

9.2 Remove the hazard switch and disconnect the harness connector

9.5 Remove the mounting bolts (arrows) from the heater control assembly

2 Disconnect the electrical connector at the rear of the switch **(see illustration)**. Depress the tab and remove the switch from the housing.
3 Refitting is the reverse of the removal procedure.

2001 and later models

4 Carefully remove the centre cluster finish panel from the instrument panel.
5 Remove the mounting bolts from the heater control assembly **(see illustration)** and pull the assembly out until you can disconnect the electrical connector at the rear of the switch. Depress the tab and remove the switch from the bezel.
6 Refitting is the reverse of the removal procedure.

Power mirror control switch

2000 and earlier models

7 Carefully lever the switch from the instrument panel.
8 Disconnect the electrical connector **(see illustration)** and remove the switch.
9 Refitting of the is the reverse of the removal procedure.

2001 and later models

10 Carefully lever the number one switch hole base from the instrument panel **(see illustration)**, using tape on the screwdriver tip to prevent scratching the instrument panel.
11 Disconnect the electrical connector and remove the switch.
12 Refitting is the reverse of the removal procedure.

Heated rear window switch

2000 and earlier models

13 Carefully lever the switch from the centre cluster finish panel.
14 Disconnect the electrical connector at the rear of the switch. Depress the tab and remove the switch from the housing.
15 Refitting is the reverse of the removal procedure.

9.8 Remove the power mirror switch from the instrument panel

2001 and later models

16 Carefully remove the centre cluster finish panel from the instrument panel.
17 Remove the mounting bolts from the heater control assembly **(see illustration 9.5)** and pull the assembly out until you can disconnect the electrical connector at the rear of the switch. Depress the tab and remove the switch from the bezel.
18 Refitting is the reverse of the removal procedure.

Instrument panel light control switch

2000 and earlier models

19 Remove the instrument panel (see Chapter 11).
20 Disconnect the electrical connector and remove the switch.
21 Refitting is the reverse of the removal procedure.

2001 and later models

22 Carefully lever the number one switch hole base from the instrument panel **(see illustration 9.10)**, using tape on the screwdriver tip to prevent scratching the instrument panel.
23 Disconnect the electrical connector **(see illustration)** and remove the switch.

9.10 Lever the number one switch hole base from the instrument panel

24 Refitting is the reverse of the removal procedure.

10 Instrument cluster – removal and refitting

⚠️ *Warning: The models covered by this manual are equipped with Supplemental Restraint Systems (SRS), more commonly known as airbags. Always disable the airbag system before working in the vicinity of any airbag system components to avoid the possibility of*

9.23 Disconnect the instrument panel light control switch harness

10.3a Remove the instrument cluster mounting screws – 2000 and earlier models shown . . .

accidental deployment of the airbags, which could cause personal injury (see Section 26).

Removal

1 Disconnect the negative battery cable.
2 Remove the instrument cluster trim panel (see Chapter 11).

10.3b . . . then guide the cluster out from between the instrument panel and steering wheel – 2001 and later models shown

3 Remove the cluster mounting screws **(see illustrations)** and pull the instrument cluster towards the steering wheel.
4 Disconnect any electrical connectors that would interfere with removal.
5 Cover the steering column with a cloth to protect the trim covers, then remove the instrument cluster from the vehicle.

Refitting

6 Refitting is the reverse of removal.

11 Wiper motor – check, removal and refitting

Wiper motor circuit check

Note: *Refer to the wiring diagrams for wire colours and locations in the following checks. When checking for voltage, probe an earthed 12 volt test light to each terminal at a connector until it lights; this verifies voltage (power) at the terminal. If the following checks fail to locate the problem, have the system diagnosed by a dealer service department or other properly-equipped repair facility.*

1 If the wipers work slowly, make sure the battery is in good condition and has a strong charge (see Chapter 5). If the battery is in good condition, remove the wiper motor (see below) and operate the wiper arms by hand. Check for binding linkage and pivots. Lubricate or repair the linkage or pivots as necessary. Refit the wiper motor. If the wipers still operate slowly, check for loose or corroded connections, especially the earth connection. If all connections look OK, renew the motor.
2 If the wipers fail to operate when activated, check the fuse **(see illustration)**. If the fuse is OK, connect a jumper wire between the wiper motor's earth terminal and earth, then retest. If the motor works now, repair the earth connection. If the motor still doesn't work, turn the wiper switch to the HI position and check for voltage at the motor. **Note:** *The cowl cover will have to be removed (see Chapter 11) to access the electrical connector.*
3 If there's voltage at the connector, remove the motor and check it off the vehicle with fused jumper wires from the battery. If the motor now works, check for binding linkage (see Paragraph 1). If the motor still doesn't work, renew it. If there's no voltage to the motor, check for voltage at the wiper control relays. If there's voltage at the wiper control relays and no voltage at the wiper motor, have the switch tested. If the switch is OK, the wiper control relay is probably bad. See Section 5 for relay testing.
4 If the interval (delay) function is inoperative, check the continuity of all the wiring between the switch and wiper control module.
5 If the wipers stop at the position they're in when the switch is turned off (fail to park), check for voltage at the park feed wire of the wiper motor connector when the wiper switch is off but the ignition is on. If no voltage is present, check for an open circuit between the wiper motor and the fuse panel.

Removal and refitting

6 Disconnect the negative cable from the battery.
7 Mark the positions of the wiper arm(s) on the windshield, then remove the wiper arm(s)

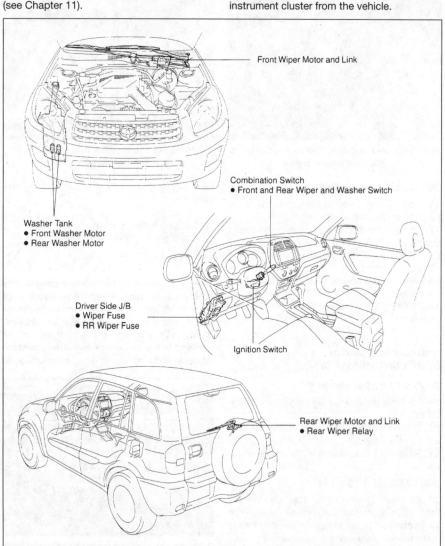

11.2 Details of a typical front and rear wiper motor system

11.7a Lift the end cap to access the wiper arm nut

11.7b Rear wiper arm mounting details

11.9 Location of the wiper linkage mounting bolts (arrows)

(see illustrations). Note: *Disconnect the washer hose from the wiper arm.*

Front wiper motor

8 Remove the windshield cowl cover (see Chapter 11).
9 Disconnect the wiper motor harness connector and remove the windshield wiper motor/linkage assembly mounting nuts (see illustration).
10 Lift the windshield wiper motor assembly from the cowl area.
11 Remove the wiper motor mounting nuts and separate the motor from the assembly (see illustration).
12 Refitting is the reverse of removal.

Rear wiper motor

13 Remove the back door trim board from the hatch area (see Chapter 11).
14 Remove the service hole cover, if equipped.
15 Disconnect the wiper motor harness connector and remove the windshield wiper motor mounting bolts (see illustration).
16 Lift the windshield wiper motor assembly from the hatch area.
17 Refitting is the reverse of removal.

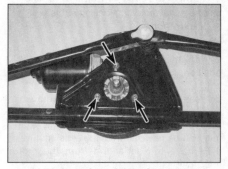

11.11 Location of the wiper motor mounting bolts (arrows)

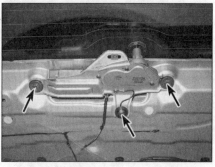

11.15 Rear wiper motor mounting bolts (arrows)

(SRS), more commonly known as airbags. Always disable the airbag system before working in the vicinity of any airbag system components to avoid the possibility of accidental deployment of the airbags, which could cause personal injury (see Section 26).
1 Disconnect the negative battery cable.

Radio

Removal

2 Access the radio by removing the dash panel surrounding the radio.
  a) On 2000 and earlier models, remove the centre cluster finish panel (see illustration).
  b) On 2001 and later models, remove the instrument cluster trim panel (see Chapter 11).
3 Remove the retaining screws and pull

the radio outward to access the back, then disconnect the electrical connectors and the aerial lead (see illustrations).

Refitting
4 Refitting is the reverse of removal.

Door speakers
Removal
5 Remove the door trim panel (see Chapter 11). All models have speakers in both front and rear doors. Rear door speakers are mounted similarly to the front door speakers.
6 Remove the speaker rivets. Drill out the rivets using the correct size drill bit. Disconnect the electrical connector and remove the speaker from the vehicle (see illustration).
Refitting
7 Refitting is the reverse of removal.

12 Radio and speakers – removal and refitting

 Warning: The models covered by this manual are equipped with Supplemental Restraint Systems

12.2 Remove the centre cluster finish panel mounting screws (arrows) – 2000 and earlier models

12.3a Remove the radio mounting screws (arrows)

12.3b Pull the radio out, then disconnect the aerial lead and the electrical connector

Tweeters

Removal

8 In addition to the standard door and rear speakers, some models are equipped with tweeters for improved high-range sound **(see illustration)**. Mounted in the front doors just ahead of the window glass, they can be removed by drilling out the rivets using the correct size drill bit. Pull the tweeter out and disconnect the electrical connector.

Refitting

9 Refitting is the reverse of removal.

13 Aerial – removal and refitting

Warning: The models covered by this manual are equipped with Supplemental Restraint Systems (SRS), more commonly known as airbags. Always disable the airbag system before working in the vicinity of any airbag system components to avoid the possibility of accidental deployment of the airbags, which could cause personal injury (see Section 26).

Removal

Fixed aerial

1 Separate the aerial from the vehicle body.
 a) *On top-mounted aerials, remove the mounting screws* **(see illustration)**.
 b) *On wing-mounted aerials, unscrew the aerial rod* **(see illustration)** *and remove*

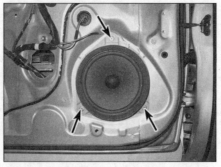

12.6 Remove the speaker rivets (arrows) and disconnect the electrical connector to remove the speaker from the vehicle

 the aerial mounting locking nut **(see illustration)**.

Power aerial

2 With the ignition switch in the LOCK position, loosen the aerial mounting locking nut.
3 Press the AM buttons on the radio while simultaneously turning the ignition switch to the ACC position. The aerial rod will extend fully and be released from the aerial motor.
4 Remove the aerial rod from the motor assembly.

All models

5 On wing-mounted aerials, raise the vehicle and secure it on axle stands.
6 On wing-mounted aerials, remove the front wheel.
7 Remove the aerial assembly from the vehicle body.

12.8 Location of the tweeter (arrow) near front door mirror mount

 a) *On top-mounted aerials, remove the left-hand side door pillar trim to access the aerial cable.*
 b) *On wing-mounted aerials, working in the wheel arch area, remove the aerial mounting bolt* **(see illustration)**.
8 On wing-mounted aerials, push the aerial mounting into the wing to separate the assembly from the grommet.
9 Remove the radio (see Section 12) and disconnect the aerial cable **(see illustration)**.
10 On wing-mounted aerials, remove the glovebox (see Chapter 11) and pull the cable from behind the dash **(see illustration)**.
11 On automatic aerials, disconnect the aerial cable from the motor.

Refitting

Fixed aerial

12 On top-mounted aerials, Refit the aerial

13.1a Remove the mounting screws (arrows) on top-mounted aerials

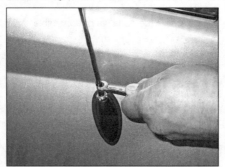

13.1b On wing-mounted aerials, unscrew the aerial rod from the base

13.1c Remove the aerial mount locking nut

13.7 Remove the aerial bolt (arrow) working in the wheel arch

13.9 Disconnect the aerial cable from the radio

13.10 Working behind the glovebox, feed the aerial cable through the dash area

onto the vehicle body and refit the mounting bolts.
13 On wing-mounted aerials, refit the mounting bolt inside the wheel arch and the aerial mounting locking nut.
14 On wing-mounted aerials, refit the aerial rod.

Power aerial
15 Refit the aerial into the wheel arch area and refit the mounting bolt.
16 Refit the aerial rod into the mast assembly with the cable teeth facing the front of the vehicle (see illustration).
17 Turn the ignition to the LOCK position to retract the aerial rod.
18 Refit the aerial mounting locking nut and carefully tighten the nut until the aerial rod is seated fully inside the mast assembly.

All models
19 Working in the dash area, feed the aerial cable behind the glovebox and into the radio.
20 Refit the radio (see Section 12).
21 Refit the glovebox (see Chapter 11).
22 Refitting is the reverse of removal.

14 Heated rear window – check and repair
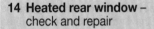

1 The rear window defogger consists of a number of horizontal elements baked onto the glass surface.
2 Small breaks in the element can be repaired without removing the rear window.

Check
3 Turn the ignition switch and defogger system switches to the On position. Using a voltmeter, place the positive probe against the defogger grid positive terminal and the negative probe against the earth terminal. If battery voltage is not indicated, check the fuse, defogger switch and related wiring. If voltage is indicated, but all or part of the defogger doesn't heat, proceed with the following tests.
4 When measuring voltage during the next two tests, wrap a piece of aluminium foil around the tip of the voltmeter positive probe and press the foil against the heating element with your finger (see illustration). Place the negative probe on the defogger grid earth terminal.
5 Check the voltage at the centre of each heating element (see illustration). If the voltage is 5 or 6 volts, the element is okay (there is no break). If the voltage is 0 volts, the element is broken between the centre of the element and the positive end. If the voltage is 10 to 12 volts the element is broken between the centre of the element and earth. Check each heating element.
6 Connect the negative lead to a good body earth. The reading should stay the same. If it doesn't, the earth connection is bad.
7 To find the break, place the voltmeter negative probe against the defogger earth

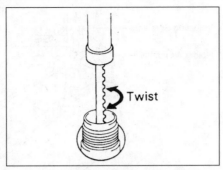

13.16 The cable teeth must face toward the front of the vehicle

terminal. Place the voltmeter positive probe with the foil strip against the heating element at the positive terminal end and slide it toward the negative terminal end. The point at which the voltmeter deflects from several volts to zero is the point at which the heating element is broken (see illustration).

Repair
8 Repair the break in the element using a repair kit specifically recommended for this purpose, available at most car accessory shops. Included in this kit is plastic conductive epoxy.
9 Prior to repairing a break, turn off the system and allow it to cool off for a few minutes.
10 Lightly buff the element area with fine steel wool, then clean it thoroughly with rubbing alcohol.

14.4 Wrap a piece of aluminium foil around the positive probe of the voltmeter and press the foil against the wire with your finger

14.7 Finding the break

11 Use masking tape to mask off the area being repaired.
12 Thoroughly mix the epoxy, following the instructions provided with the repair kit.
13 Apply the epoxy material to the slit in the masking tape, overlapping the undamaged area about 3/4-inch on either end (see illustration).
14 Allow the repair to cure for 24 hours before removing the tape and using the system.

15 Headlight bulb – renewal

⚠ *Warning: Halogen gas filled bulbs are under pressure and may shatter if the surface is scratched or the bulb is dropped. Wear eye protection and handle the bulbs carefully, grasping only the base whenever possible. Do not touch the surface of the bulb with your fingers because the oil from your skin could cause it to overheat and fail prematurely. If you do touch the bulb surface, clean it with methylated spirit.*

1 Reach behind the headlight assembly and unplug the electrical connector.
2 Remove the rubber insulator (see illustration).
3 Grasp the bulbholder securely and rotate it anti-clockwise to remove it from the housing (see illustration).

14.5 To determine if a heating element has broken, check the voltage at the centre of each element

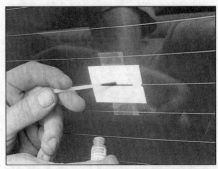

14.13 To use a demister repair kit, apply masking tape to the inside of the window at the damaged area, then brush on the special conductive coating

15.2 Remove the rubber insulator from the back of the headlight housing

15.3 Rotate bulbholder anti-clockwise – remove the bulb from the holder to renew it

4 Pull straight on the bulb to remove from it from the bulbholder. Without touching the glass with your bare fingers, insert the new bulb assembly into the headlight housing.
5 Plug in the electrical connector.

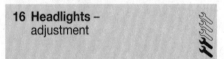

16 Headlights – adjustment

Note: *The headlights must be aimed correctly. If adjusted incorrectly they could blind the driver of an oncoming vehicle and cause a serious accident or seriously reduce your ability to see the road. The headlights should be checked for proper aim every 12 months and any time a new headlight is fitted or front end body work is performed. It should be emphasised that the following procedure is*

16.2 Use a cross-head screwdriver to rotate the gear-drive mechanism on 2001 and later models

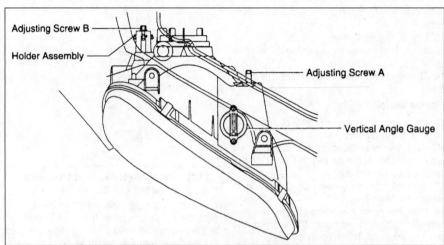

16.1 Location of the headlight adjustment screws on 1996 and 1997 models

only a temporary measure which will provide preliminary adjustment until the headlights can be adjusted by a properly-equipped garage.

1996 and 1997 models

1 These models have two adjustment screws located on the back of each headlight housing **(see illustration)**.

1998 and later models

2 These models have one adjustment screw located on the back of each headlight housing. On 1998 through 2000 models a spanner or socket can be used to turn the screw. On 2001 and later models, insert a cross-head screwdriver into the gear-drive mechanism to turn the screw **(see illustration)**.

All models

3 There are several methods of adjusting the headlights. The simplest method requires masking tape, a blank wall and a level floor.
4 Position masking tape vertically on the wall in reference to the vehicle centreline and the centrelines of both headlights **(see illustration)**.

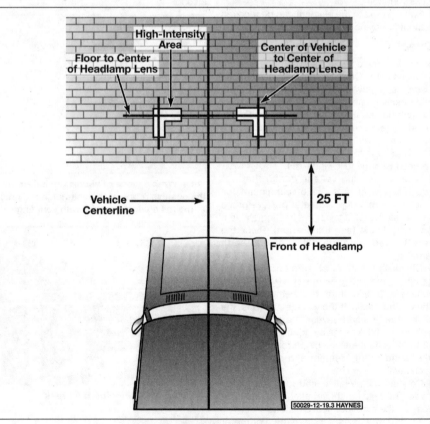

16.4 Headlight adjustment details

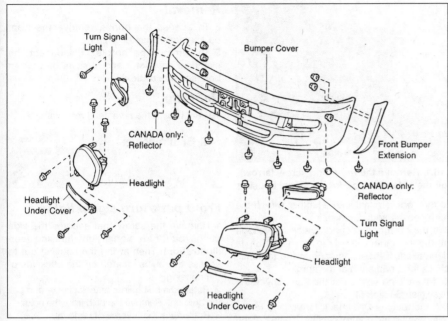

17.3a Exploded view of the headlight housing and surrounding components on 2000 and earlier models

5 Position a horizontal tape line in reference to the centreline of all the headlights. **Note:** *It may be easier to position the tape on the wall with the vehicle parked only a few inches away.*

6 Adjustment should be made with the vehicle parked 25 feet from the wall, sitting level, the gas tank half-full and no unusually heavy load in the vehicle.

7 Starting with the low beam adjustment, position the high intensity zone so it is two inches below the horizontal line and two inches to the side of the headlight vertical line, away from oncoming traffic. Adjustment is made by turning the vertical adjusting screw to raise or lower the beam. The horizontal adjusting screw should be used in the same manner to move the beam left or right. **Note:**

1998 and later models are designed to adjust the vertical position only.

8 With the high beams on, the high intensity zone should be vertically centred with the exact centre just below the horizontal line. **Note:** *It may not be possible to position the headlight aim exactly for both high and low beams. If a compromise must be made, keep in mind that the low beams are the most used and have the greatest effect on driver safety.*

9 Have the headlights adjusted by a dealer service department or service station at the earliest opportunity.

17 Headlight housing – removal and refitting

⚠ *Warning: Some vehicles are equipped with halogen gas-filled headlight bulbs which are under pressure and may shatter if the surface is damaged or the bulb is dropped. Wear eye protection and handle the bulbs carefully, grasping only the base whenever possible. Do not touch the surface of the bulb with your fingers because the oil from your skin could cause it to overheat and fail prematurely. If you do touch the bulb surface, clean it with methylated spirit.*

Removal

1 Remove the headlight bulb (see Section 15).
2 Access the headlight housing lower mounting bolts.
  a) On 2000 and earlier models, remove the headlight under cover panel.
  b) On 2001 and later models, remove the radiator/bumper support panel and the front bumper (see Chapter 11).
3 Remove the retaining bolts, detach the housing and withdraw it from the vehicle **(see illustrations)**.

Refitting

4 Refitting is the reverse of removal. Be sure to check headlight adjustment (see Section 16).

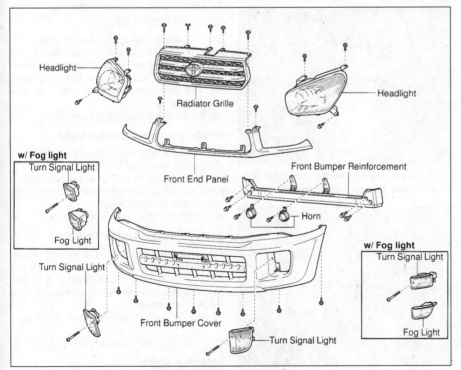

17.3b Exploded view of the headlight housing and surrounding components on 2001 and later models

17.3c Use a screwdriver to separate the clips from the base of the headlight housing

18.9 Location of the horn mounting bolts (arrows)

18 Horn –
check, removal and refitting

⚠️ *Warning: The models covered by this manual are equipped with Supplemental Restraint Systems (SRS), more commonly known as airbags. Always disable the airbag system before working in the vicinity of any airbag system components to avoid the possibility of accidental deployment of the airbags, which could cause personal injury (see Section 26).*

Check

Note: *Check the fuses before beginning electrical diagnosis.*

1 Disconnect the electrical connector from the horn.
2 To test the horn, connect battery voltage

19.8 Remove the access panel inside the trunk side compartment

19.12 Rotate the bulbholder and remove it from the high-mounted brake light assembly

19.1 Remove the mounting screw (arrow) on the side of the park/turn signal housing

to the horn terminal with a jumper wire. If the horn doesn't sound, renew it.
3 If the horn does sound, check for voltage at the terminal when the horn button is depressed. If there's voltage at the terminal, check for a bad earth at the horn.
4 If there's no voltage at the horn, check the relay (see Section 5).
5 If the relay is OK, check for voltage to the relay power and control circuits. If either of the circuits is not receiving voltage, inspect the wiring between the relay and the fuse panel.
6 If both relay circuits are receiving voltage, depress the horn button and check the circuit from the relay to the horn button for continuity to earth. If there's no continuity, check the circuit for an open. If there's no open circuit, renew the horn button.
7 If there's continuity to earth through the horn button, check for an open or short in the circuit from the relay to the horn.

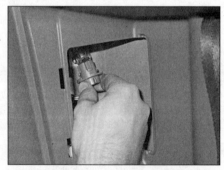

19.9 Rotate the bulbholder and remove it from the tail light assembly

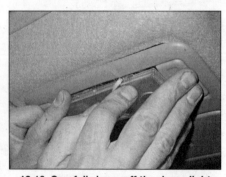

19.16 Carefully lever off the dome light lens using a flat-bladed screwdriver

Removal

8 To access the horns, remove the front bumper (see Chapter 11).
9 To remove the horn(s), disconnect the electrical connector and remove the bracket bolt (see illustration).

Refitting

10 Refitting is the reverse of removal.

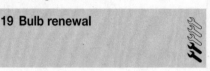

19 Bulb renewal

Front park/turn signal lights

1 Remove the screw that secures the side of the park/turn signal light housing (see illustration). Then swing the housing out to access the bulbs located on the backside of the housing.
2 Rotate the bulbholder anti-clockwise and pull the bulb out. Remove the bulb from the holder.
3 Refitting is the reverse of removal.

Rear tail/brake/turn signal light

2000 and earlier models

4 To remove the tail light assembly for bulb renewal, remove the taillight assembly under-cover panel to access the mounting screws.
5 Remove the two mounting screws and detach the tail light assembly.
6 Rotate the bulb holders anti-clockwise and pull the bulbs out to remove them. Remove the bulb from the holder.
7 Refitting is the reverse of removal.

2001 and later models

8 To access the tail light bulbs, working in the luggage area, remove the inspection covers (see illustration) and remove the access panel.
9 Rotate the bulb holders anti-clockwise and pull the bulbs out to remove them (see illustration).
10 Refitting is the reverse of removal.

High-mounted brake light

11 Open the boot and unclip the plastic cover for the high-mounted brake light.
12 Twist the bulb holder anti-clockwise to remove it, then pull the bulb straight out of the holder (see illustration).
13 Refitting is the reverse of removal.

Instrument cluster lights

13 To gain access to the instrument cluster illumination bulbs, the instrument cluster will have to be removed (see Section 10). The bulbs can then be removed and renewed from the rear of the cluster.
14 Rotate the bulb anti-clockwise to remove it.
15 Refitting is the reverse of removal.

Interior light

16 Lever the interior lens off the interior light housing (see illustration).

19.17 Remove the bulb

17 Detach the bulb from the terminals **(see illustration)**. It may be necessary to lever the bulb out – if this is the case, lever only on the

ends of the bulb (otherwise the glass may shatter).
18 Refitting is the reverse of removal.

Number plate light

19 Press the two release clips **(see illustration)** and remove the number plate bulb sockets from the back door **(see illustration)**. Remove the bulbs.
20 Refitting is the reverse of removal.

Foglight

21 Raise the vehicle and secure it on axle stands.
22 Remove the front wheels and remove the inner wheel arch covers to access the foglight assembly **(see illustration)**.
23 Twist the bulbholder from the housing and renew the bulb.

19.19a Press the mounting clips from the side of the number plate bulb sockets

19.19b Rotate the number plate light bulbholder

19.22 Location of the foglight bulbholder (arrow)

20 Electric side mirrors – description

1 Most electric rear view mirrors use two motors to move the glass; one for up-and-down adjustments and one for left-right adjustments **(see illustration)**.
2 The control switch has a selector portion which sends voltage to the left or right side mirror. With the ignition on but the engine off, roll down the windows and operate the mirror control switch through all functions (left-right and up-down) for both the left and right side mirrors.
3 Listen carefully for the sound of the electric motors running in the mirrors.

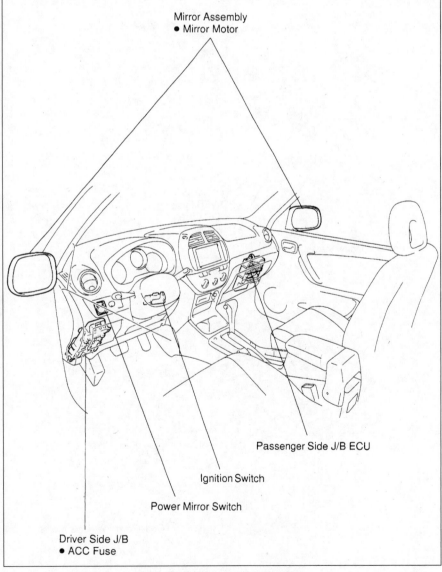

20.1 Typical power mirror system

21.5 Lift the cover from the cruise control actuator to examine the cables

4 If the motors can be heard but the mirror glass doesn't move, there's a problem with the drive mechanism inside the mirror. Remove and disassemble the mirror to locate the problem.
5 If the mirrors do not operate and no sound comes from the mirrors, check the fuse (see Section 3).
6 If the fuse is OK, remove the mirror control switch from the dashboard. Have the switch continuity checked by a dealership service department or other qualified automobile repair facility.
7 Test the earth connections. Refer to the wiring diagrams at the end of the Chapter.
8 If the mirror still doesn't work, remove the mirror and check the wires at the mirror for voltage.
9 If there's no voltage in each switch position, check the circuit between the mirror and control switch for opens and shorts.
10 If there's voltage, remove the mirror and test it off the vehicle with jumper wires. Renew the mirror if it fails this test.

21 Cruise control system – description

1 The cruise control system maintains vehicle speed with a electrically-operated motor located in the engine compartment, which is connected to the accelerator pedal by a cable. The system consists of the cruise control unit, brake switch, control switches and vehicle speed sensor. Some features of the system require special testers and diagnostic procedures which are beyond the scope of this manual. Listed below are some general procedures that may be used to locate common problems.
2 Check the fuses (see Section 3).
3 Have an assistant operate the brake lights while you check their operation (voltage from the brake light switch deactivates the cruise control).
4 If the brake lights don't come on or stay on all the time, correct the problem and retest the cruise control.
5 Visually inspect the control cable between cruise control motor and the throttle linkage for free movement **(see illustration)**. Renew it if necessary.
6 The cruise control system uses inputs from the Vehicle Speed Sensor (VSS). Refer to Chapter 6A or 6B for more information on the VSS.
7 Test drive the vehicle to determine if the cruise control is now working. If it isn't, take it to a dealer service department or an automotive electrical specialist for further diagnosis.

22 Power window system – description

1 The power window system operates electric motors, mounted in the doors, which lower and raise the windows. The system consists of the control switches, relays, the motors, regulators, glass mechanisms and associated wiring **(see illustration)**.
2 The power windows can be lowered and raised from the master control switch by the driver or by remote switches located at the individual windows. Each window has a separate motor that is reversible. The position of the control switch determines the polarity and therefore the direction of operation.
3 The circuit is protected by a fuse and a circuit breaker. Each motor is also equipped

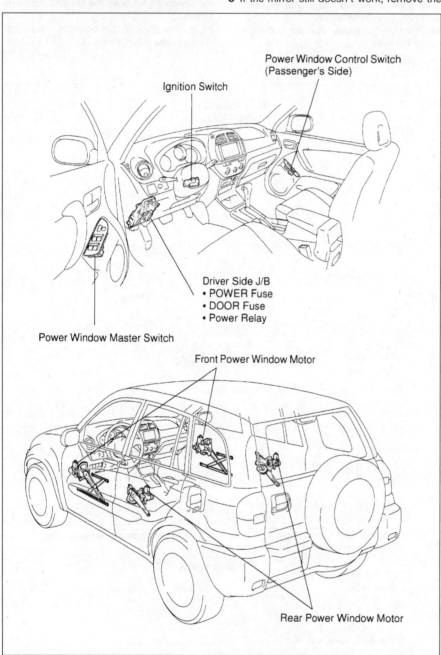

Power Window Control Switch
(Passenger's Side)

Ignition Switch

Driver Side J/B
• POWER Fuse
• DOOR Fuse
• Power Relay

Power Window Master Switch

Front Power Window Motor

Rear Power Window Motor

22.1 Typical power window system

with an internal circuit breaker; this prevents one stuck window from disabling the whole system.

4 The power window system will only operate when the ignition switch is on. In addition, many models have a window lockout switch at the master control switch that, when activated, disables the switches at the rear windows and, sometimes, the switch at the passenger's window also. Always check these items before troubleshooting a window problem.

5 These procedures are general in nature, so if you can't find the problem using them, take the vehicle to a dealer service department or other properly-equipped repair facility.

6 If the power windows won't operate, always check the fuse and circuit breaker first.

7 If only the rear windows are inoperative, or if the windows only operate from the master control switch, check the rear window lockout switch for continuity in the unlocked position. Renew it if it doesn't have continuity.

8 Check the wiring between the switches and fuse panel for continuity. Repair the wiring, if necessary.

9 If only one window is inoperative from the master control switch, try the other control switch at the window. **Note:** *This doesn't apply to the driver's door window.*

10 If the same window works from one switch, but not the other, check the switch for continuity. Have the switch checked at a dealer service department or other qualified automobile repair facility.

11 If the switch tests OK, check for a short or open in the circuit between the affected switch and the window motor.

12 If one window is inoperative from both switches, remove the trim panel from the affected door and check for voltage at the switch and at the motor while the switch is operated.

13 If voltage is reaching the motor, disconnect the glass from the regulator (see Chapter 11). Move the window up-and-down by hand while checking for binding and damage. Also check for binding and damage to the regulator. If the regulator is not damaged and the window moves up-and-down smoothly, renew the motor. If there's binding or damage, lubricate, repair or renew parts, as necessary.

14 If voltage isn't reaching the motor, check the wiring in the circuit for continuity between the switches and motors. You'll need to consult the wiring diagram for the vehicle. If the circuit is equipped with a relay, check that the relay is earthed properly and receiving voltage.

15 Test the windows after you are done to confirm proper repairs.

23 Power door lock system – description

1 A power door lock system operates the

door lock actuators mounted in each door **(see illustration)**. The system consists of the switches, actuators, a control unit and associated wiring. Diagnosis can usually be limited to simple checks of the wiring connections and actuators for minor faults that can be easily repaired.

2 Power door lock systems are operated by bi-directional solenoids located in the doors. The lock switches have two operating positions: Lock and Unlock. When activated, the switch sends a earth signal to the door lock control unit to lock or unlock the doors. Depending on which way the switch is activated, the control unit reverses polarity to the solenoids, allowing the two sides of the circuit to be used alternately as the feed (positive) and earth side.

3 Some vehicles may have an anti-theft system incorporated into the power locks. If you are unable to locate the trouble using the following general Paragraphs, consult a dealer service department or other qualified garage.

4 Always check the circuit protection first. Some vehicles use a combination of circuit breakers and fuses.

5 Operate the door lock switches in both directions (Lock and Unlock) with the engine off. Listen for the click of the solenoids operating.

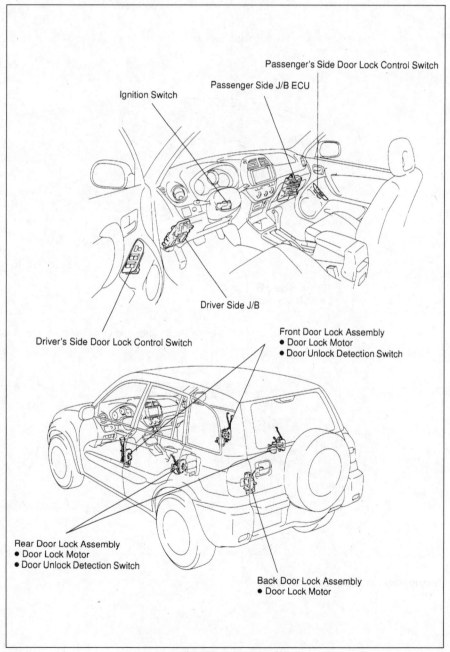

23.1 Typical power door lock system

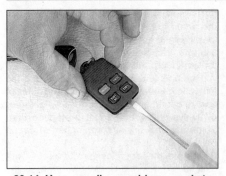

23.14 Use a small screwdriver or coin to separate the transmitter halves

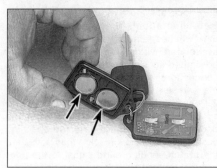

23.15 Renew the lithium batteries with the same type as used originally

6 Test the switches for continuity. Remove the switches and have them checked by a dealer service department or other qualified automobile repair facility.

7 Check the wiring between the switches, control unit and solenoids for continuity. Repair the wiring if there's no continuity.

8 Check for a bad earth at the switches or the control unit.

9 If all but one lock solenoids operate, remove the trim panel from the affected door (see Chapter 11) and check for voltage at the solenoid while the lock switch is operated. One of the wires should have voltage in the Lock position; the other should have voltage in the Unlock position.

10 If the inoperative solenoid is receiving voltage, renew the solenoid.

11 If the inoperative solenoid isn't receiving voltage, check the circuit between the lock solenoid and the control unit. **Note:** *It's common for wires to break in the portion of the harness between the body and door (opening and closing the door fatigues and eventually breaks the wires).*

Keyless entry system

12 The keyless entry system consists of a remote control transmitter that sends a coded infrared signal to a receiver which then operates the door lock system. On models so equipped, the transmitter may also engage the alarm system and provide a 'panic' button which flashes the lights and blows the horn for emergencies.

13 Renew the transmitter batteries when the red LED light on the case doesn't light when the button is pushed. As the batteries deteriorate with age, the distance at which the remote transmitter operates will diminish.

14 Use a coin or small screwdriver to carefully separate the case halves for battery removal and refitting **(see illustration)**.

15 Renew the two lithium batteries with the same type as originally fitted, observing the polarity diagram on the case **(see illustration)**.

16 Snap the case halves together.

24 Power sunroof – description

1 The power sunroof or sliding roof system consists of the control switch, the module, the roof motor and the glass and track mechanism **(see illustration)**. The sunroof switch is located in a panel in the headliner, above the rear view mirror. For information on roof panel adjustment details, see Chapter 11.

25 Daytime Running Lights (DRL) – general information

The Daytime Running Lights (DRL) system used in certain territories illuminates the

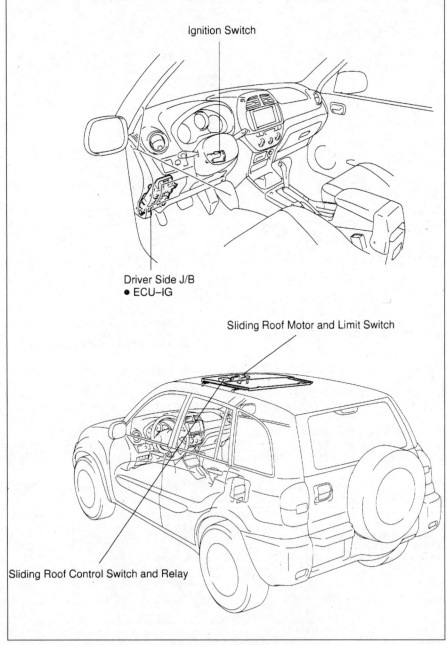

Ignition Switch

Driver Side J/B
● ECU–IG

Sliding Roof Motor and Limit Switch

Sliding Roof Control Switch and Relay

24.1 Typical power roof system

headlights whenever the engine is running **(see illustration)**. The only exception is with the engine running and the handbrake engaged. Once the handbrake is released, the lights will remain on as long as the ignition switch is on, even if the handbrake is later applied.

The DRL system supplies reduced power to the headlights so they won't be too bright for daytime use, while prolonging headlight life.

26 Airbag system – general information

All models are equipped with a Supplemental Restraint System (SRS), more commonly known as an airbag. This system is designed to protect the driver, and the front seat passenger, from serious injury in

the event of a head-on or frontal collision. It consists of airbag sensors mounted on the front underbody frame members and a sensing/diagnostic module mounted in the centre of the vehicle, near the floor console. **Note:** *1996 and 1997 models are not equipped with the airbag sensors mounted up front but instead operate only with the console mounted airbag sensor/diagnostic module.*

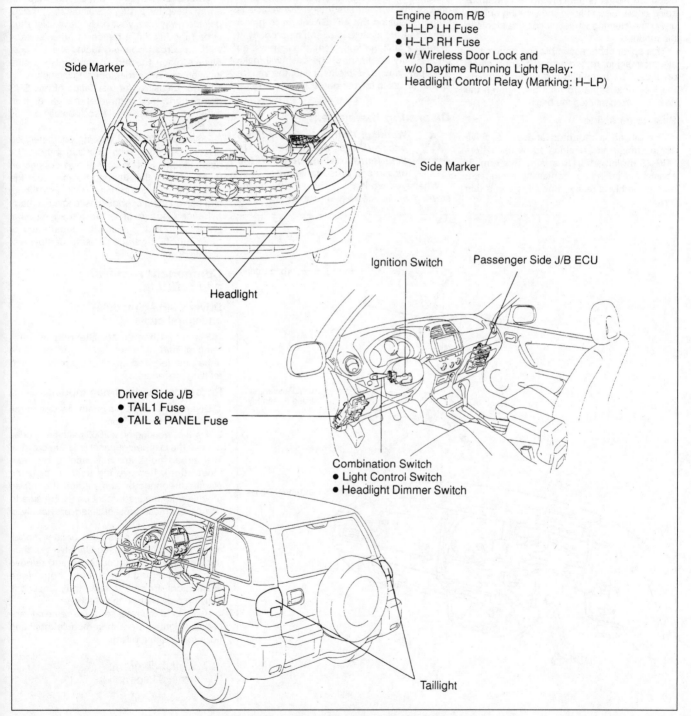

25.1 Typical headlight and daytime running light system

Airbag module

Driver's side

The airbag inflator module contains a housing incorporating the cushion (airbag) and inflator unit, mounted in the centre of the steering wheel The inflator assembly is mounted on the back of the housing over a hole through which gas is expelled, inflating the bag almost instantaneously when an electrical signal is sent from the system. A spiral cable assembly on the steering column under the steering wheel carries this signal to the module.

This spiral cable assembly can transmit an electrical signal regardless of steering wheel position. The trigger in the airbag converts the electrical signal to heat and ignites the powder, which inflates the bag.

Passenger's side

The airbag is mounted above the glove compartment and designated by the letters SRS (Supplemental Restraint System). It consists of an inflator containing a trigger, a bag assembly, a reaction housing and a trim cover.

The airbag is considerably larger than the steering wheel-mounted unit and is supported by the steel reaction housing. The trim cover is textured and painted to match the instrument panel and has a moulded seam which splits when the bag inflates.

Sensing and diagnostic module

The sensing and diagnostic module supplies the current to the airbag system in the event of the collision, even if battery power is cut off. It checks this system every time the vehicle is started, causing the AIR BAG light to go on then off, if the system is operating properly. If there is a fault in the system, the light will go on and stay on, flash, or the dash will make a beeping sound. If this happens, the vehicle should be taken to your dealer immediately for service.

Disarming the system

 Warning: Failure to follow these precautions could result in accidental deployment of the airbag and personal injury.

Whenever working in the vicinity of the steering wheel, steering column or any of the other SRS system components, the system must be disarmed. To disarm the system:
a) Point the wheels straight-ahead and turn the key to the Lock position.
b) Disconnect the cable from the negative battery terminal, then the positive cable.
c) Wait at least two minutes for the back-up power supply to be depleted.

Precautions

Whenever handling an airbag module, always keep the airbag opening (the trim side) pointed away from your body. Never place the airbag module on a bench of other surface with the airbag opening facing the surface. Always place the airbag module in a safe location with the airbag opening facing up.

Never measure the resistance of any SRS component. An ohmmeter has a built-in battery supply that could accidentally deploy the airbag.

Never use electrical welding equipment on a vehicle equipped with an airbag without first disconnecting the yellow airbag connector, located under the steering column near the combination switch connector (driver's airbag) and behind the glovebox (passenger's airbag).

Never dispose of a live airbag module. Return it to a dealer service department or other qualified garage for safe deployment and disposal.

Component removal and refitting

Driver's airbag module and spiral cable

Refer to Chapter 10, Steering wheel – removal and refitting, for the driver's side airbag module and spiral cable removal and refitting procedures.

Passenger's side airbag module

1 Disarm the airbag system as describes previously in this Section.
2 If you're working on a 2000 or earlier model, remove the instrument panel (see Chapter 11). The airbag bolts are now accessible **(see illustration)**. Remove the bolts, unplug the electrical connector and detach the airbag module from the instrument panel. Be sure to heed the precautions outlined previously in this Section.
3 If you're working on a 2001 or later model, remove the glovebox (see Chapter 11), then unplug the electrical connector and remove the airbag module mounting bolts **(see illustration)**. Be sure to heed the precautions outlined previously in this Section.
4 Refitting is the reverse of the removal procedure. Tighten the airbag module mounting bolts to 15 lbf ft (20 Nm).

27 Wiring diagrams – general information

Airbag Door

Front Passenger Airbag Assembly

Instrument Panel

26.2 Passenger's side airbag details – 2000 and earlier LHD models

Since it isn't possible to include all wiring

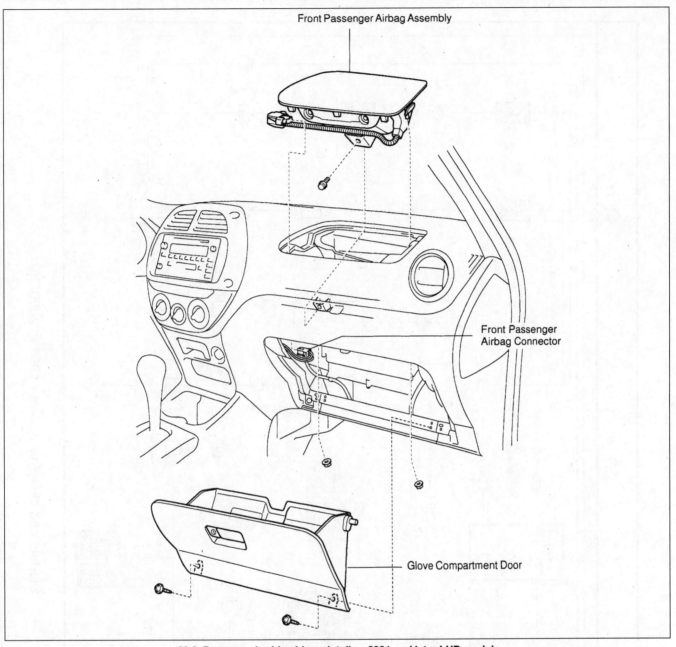

Front Passenger Airbag Assembly

Front Passenger
Airbag Connector

Glove Compartment Door

26.3 Passenger's side airbag details – 2001 and later LHD models

diagrams for every year covered by this manual, the following diagrams are those that are typical and most commonly needed **(see illustration)**.

Prior to troubleshooting any circuits, check the fuse and circuit breakers (if equipped) to make sure they're in good condition. Make sure the battery is properly charged and check the cable connections.

When checking a circuit, make sure that all connectors are clean, with no broken or loose terminals. When unplugging a connector, do not pull on the wires. Pull only on the connector housings themselves.

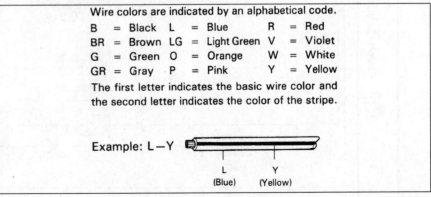

Wire colors are indicated by an alphabetical code.

B	=	Black	L	=	Blue	R	=	Red
BR	=	Brown	LG	=	Light Green	V	=	Violet
G	=	Green	O	=	Orange	W	=	White
GR	=	Gray	P	=	Pink	Y	=	Yellow

The first letter indicates the basic wire color and the second letter indicates the color of the stripe.

Example: L—Y

L
(Blue)

Y
(Yellow)

27.1 Wiring diagram colour code chart

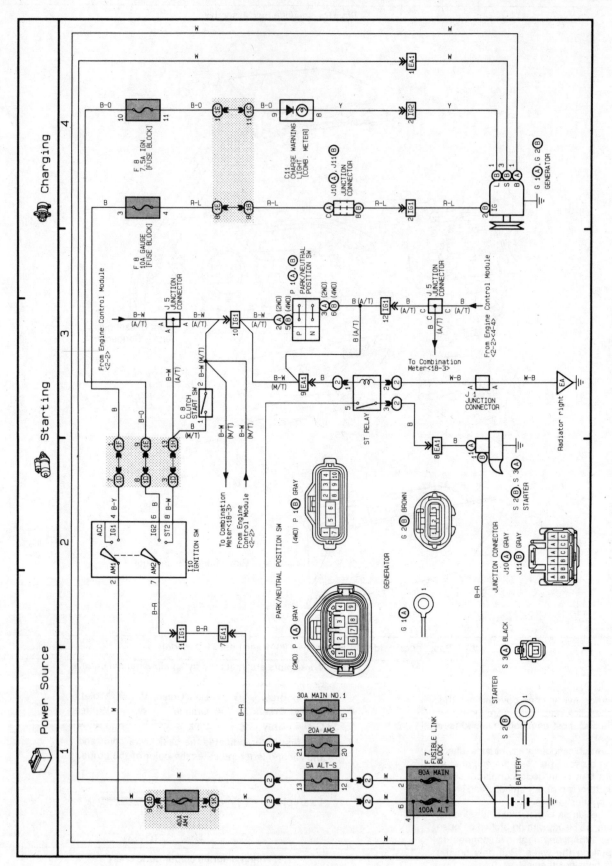

Starting and charging system - 1996 to 2000

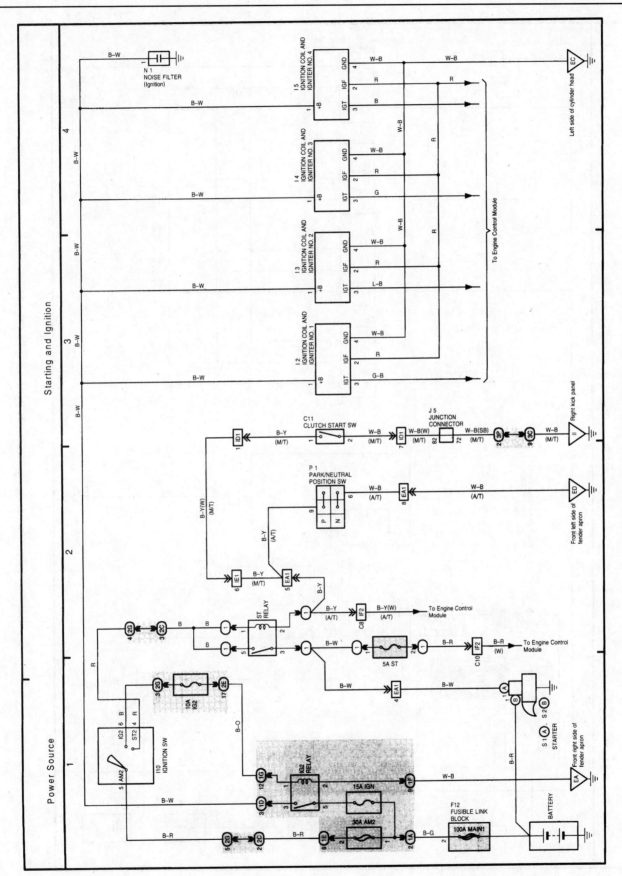

Starting and Ignition

Power Source

Starting system - 2001 to 2002

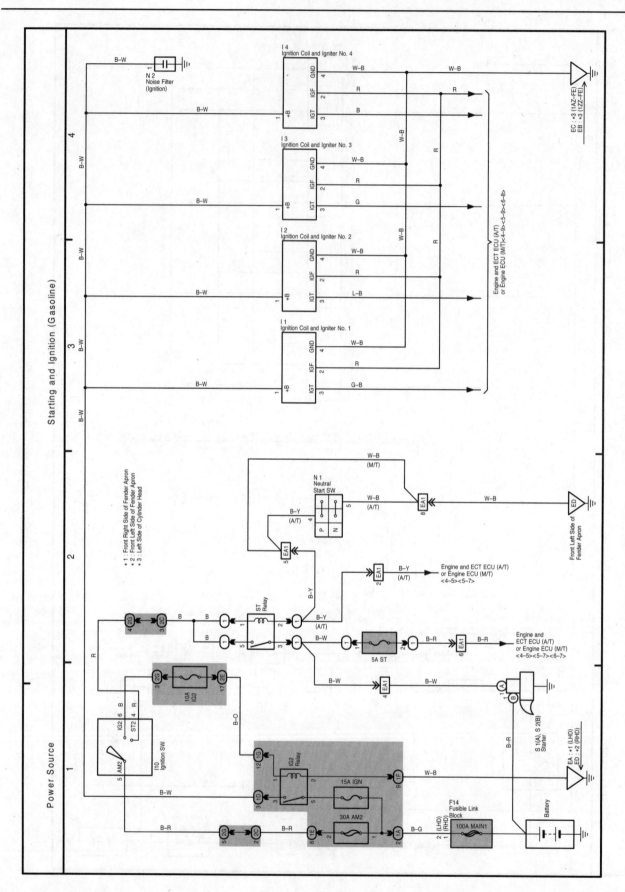

Starting and Ignition (Gasoline)

Power Source

Starting system and ignition (petrol) - 2003 onwards

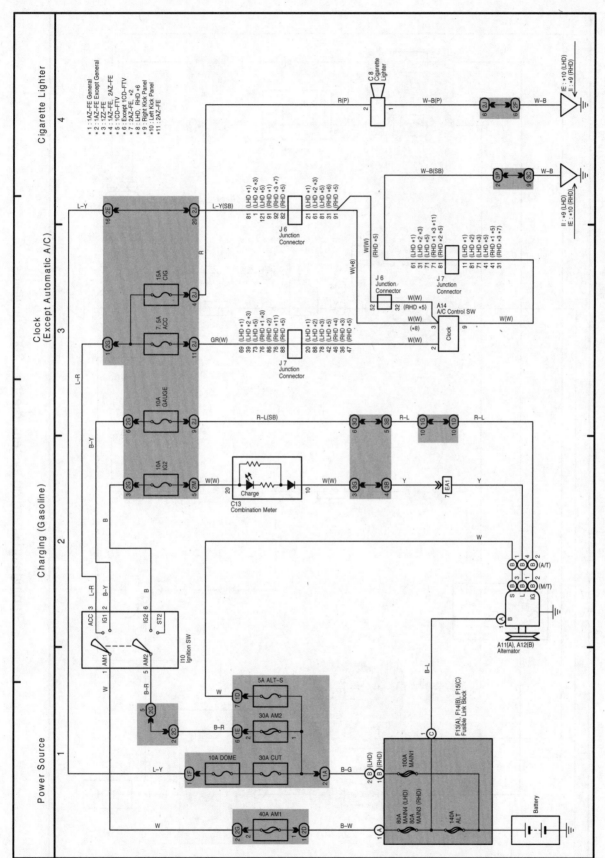

Charging system (petrol), clock and cigar lighter - 2003 onwards

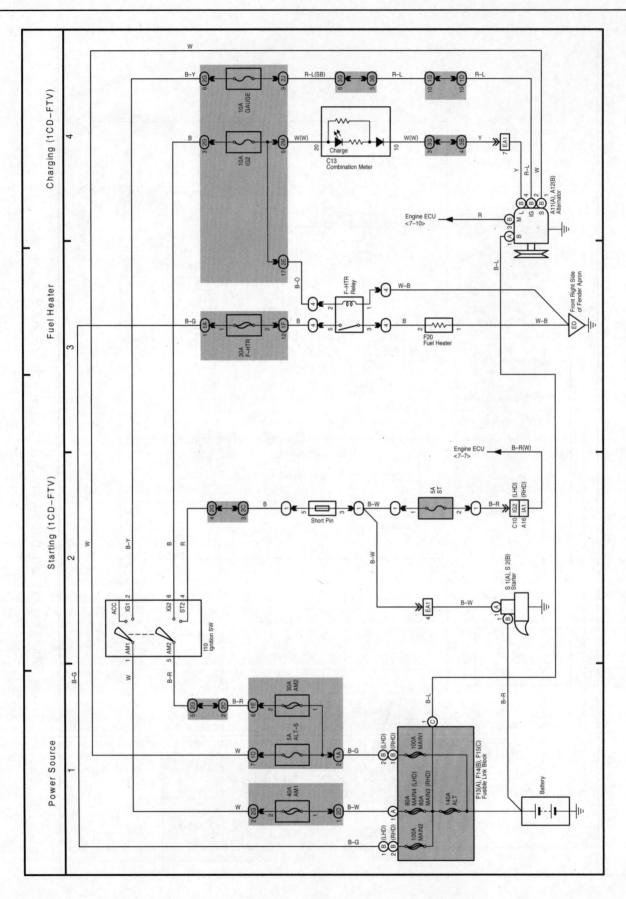

Starting and charging system (diesel) - 2003 onwards

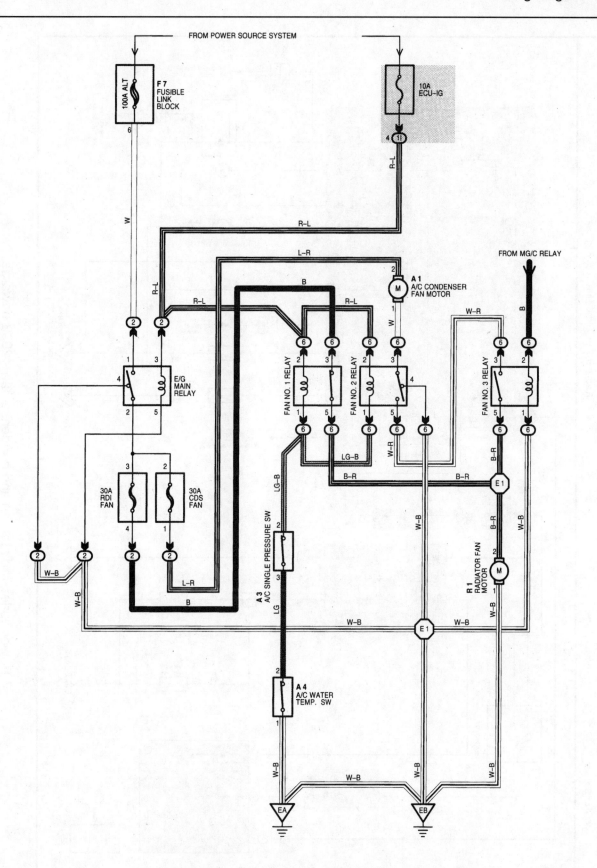

Radiator and condenser fan system - 2000 and earlier

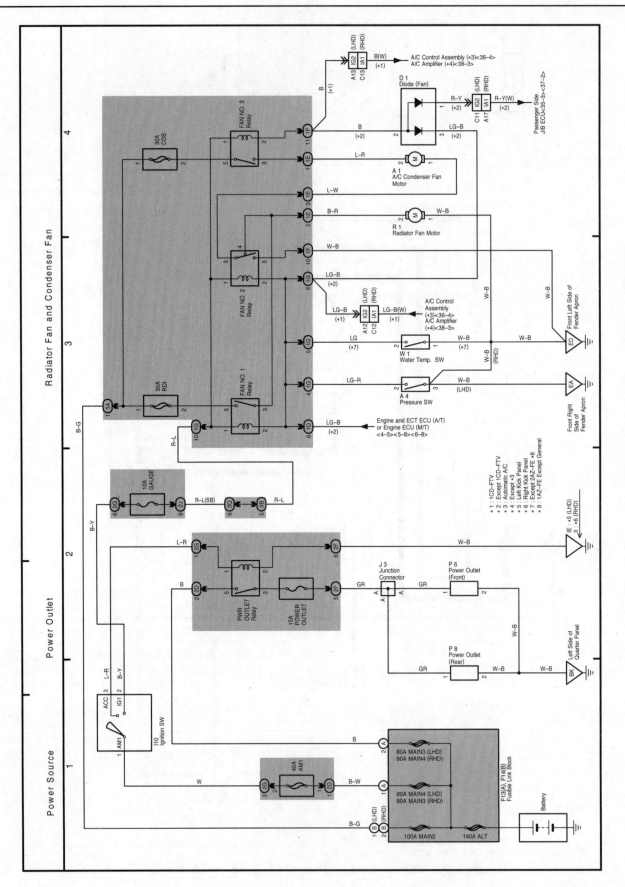

Power outlet, radiator fan and condenser fan - 2003 onwards

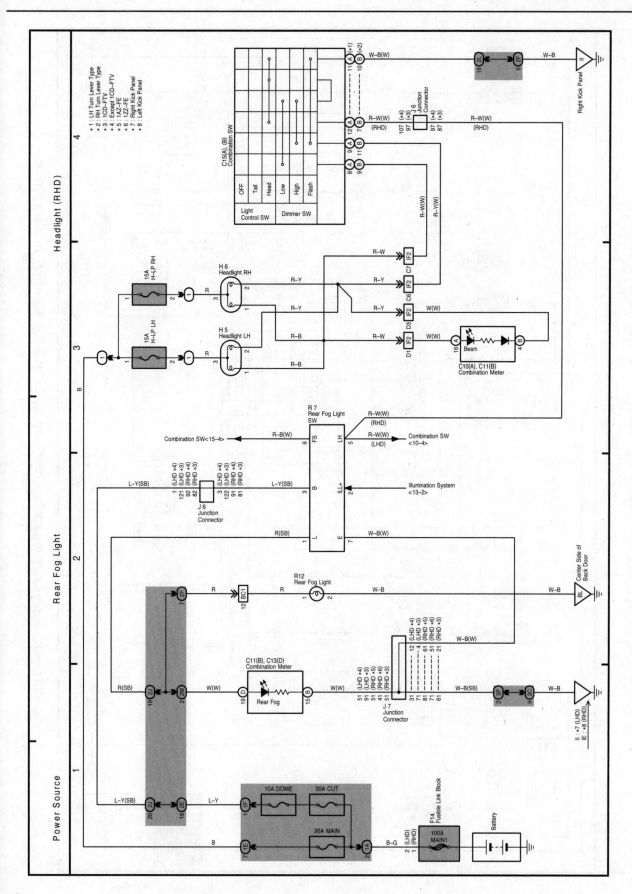

Rear fog light and headlight system - 2003 onwards (2001 and 2002 similar)

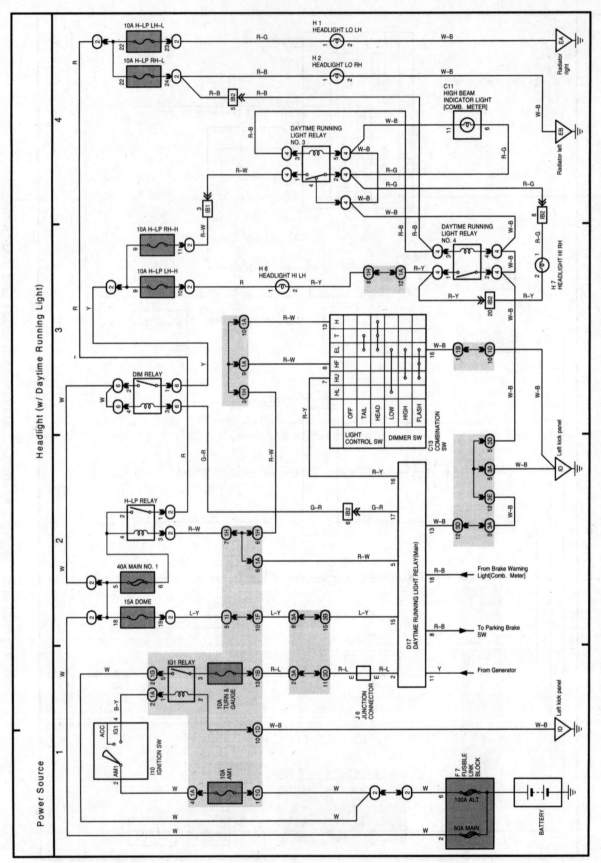

Headlights with daytime running lights – 1998 through 2000 (1996 and 1997 models similar)

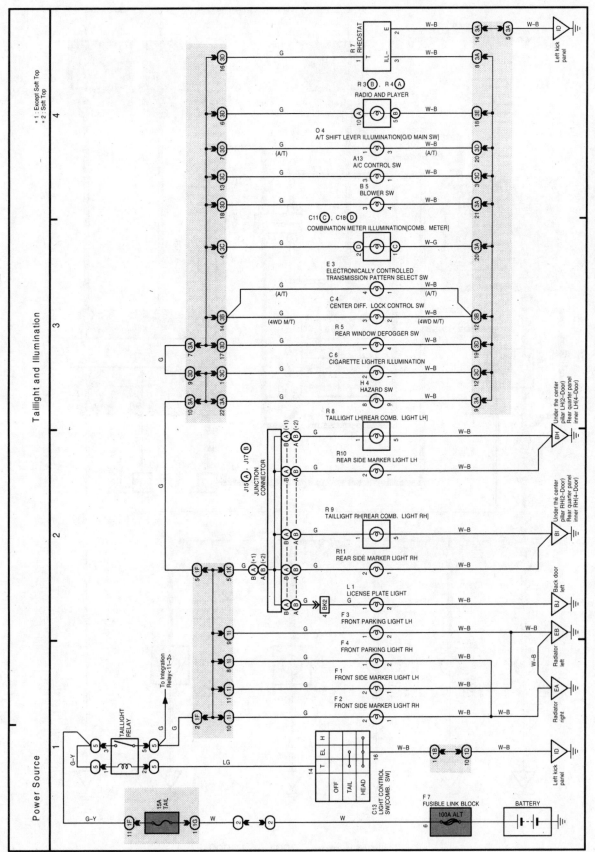

Taillight system and instrument illumination - 1998 through 2000 (1996 and 1997 models similar)

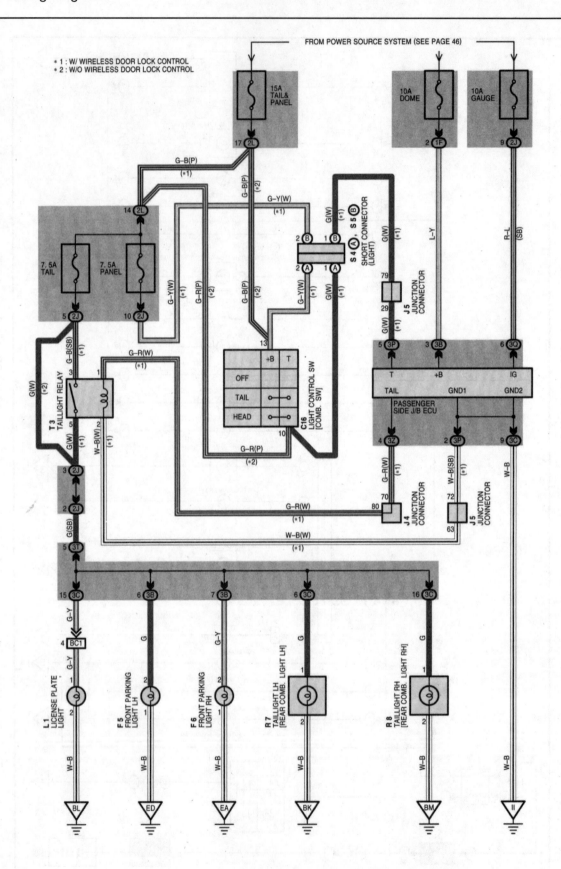

Taillight system - 2001 and 2002

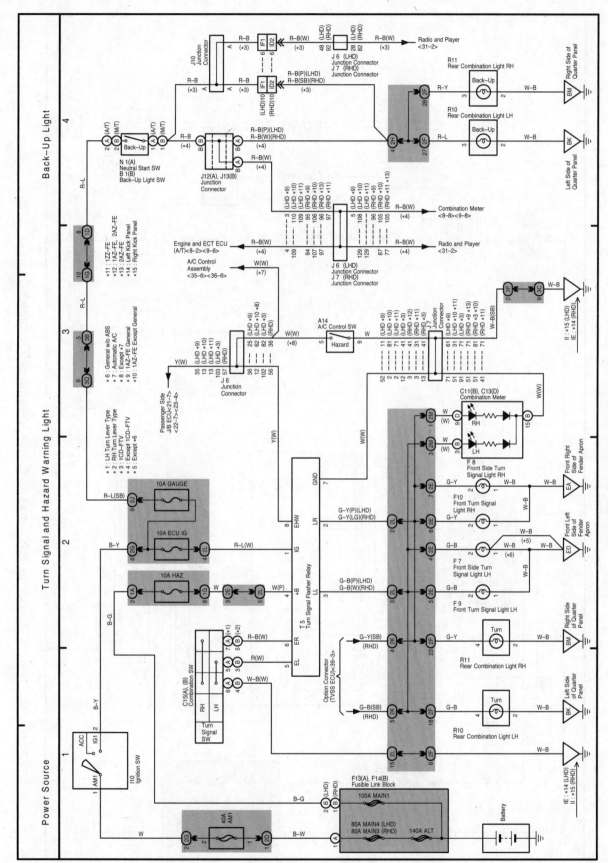

Taillight system - 2003 onwards

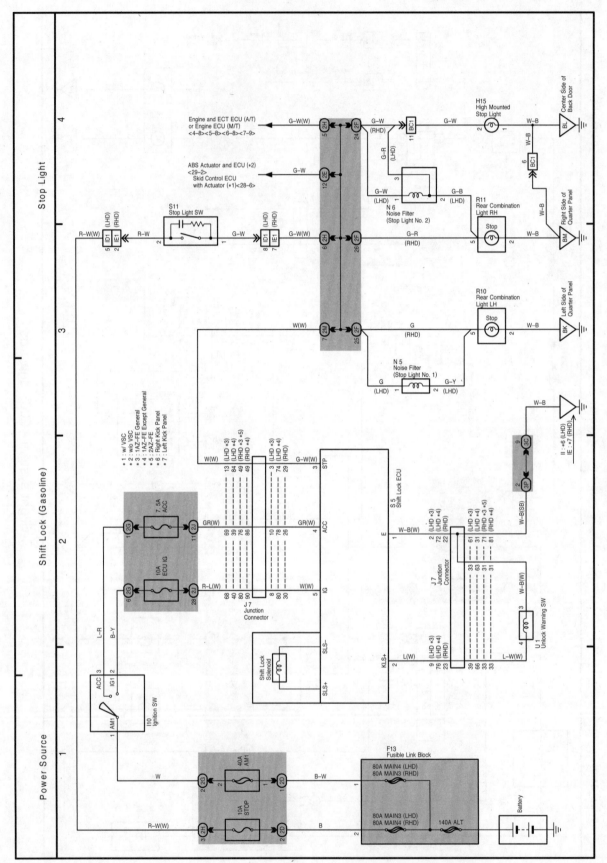

Brake lights and shift lock (petrol) – 2003 onwards

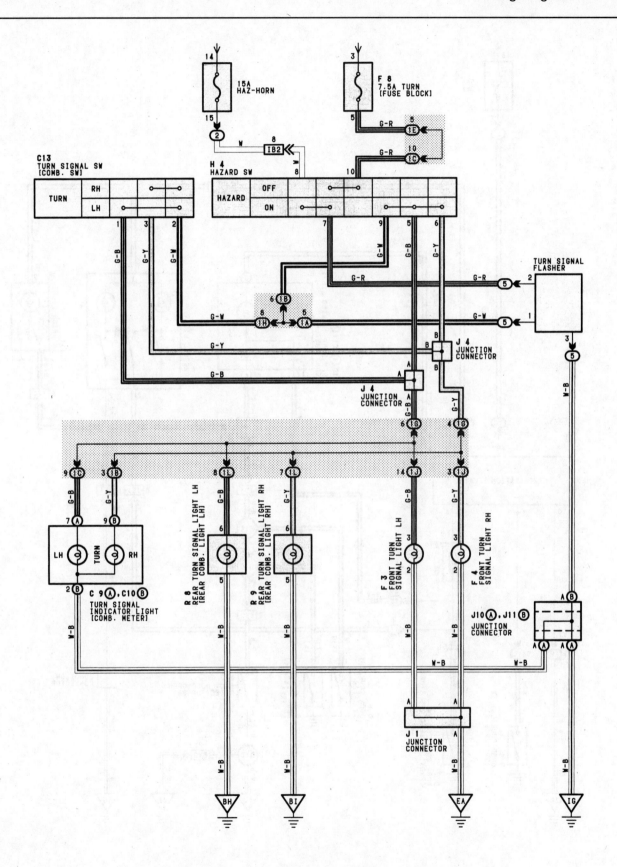

Turn signals and hazard warning system - 2000 and earlier

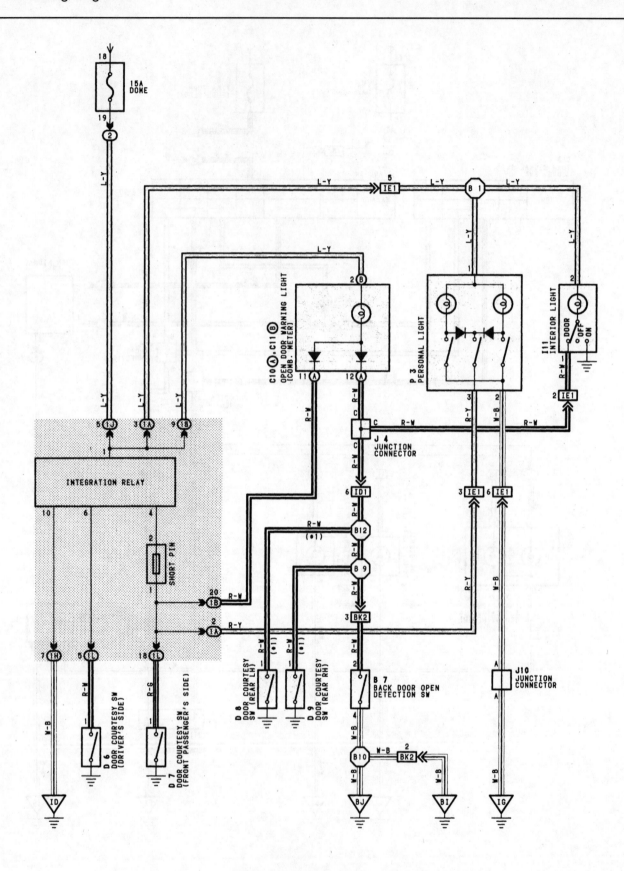

Interior lighting system - 1996 to 1997

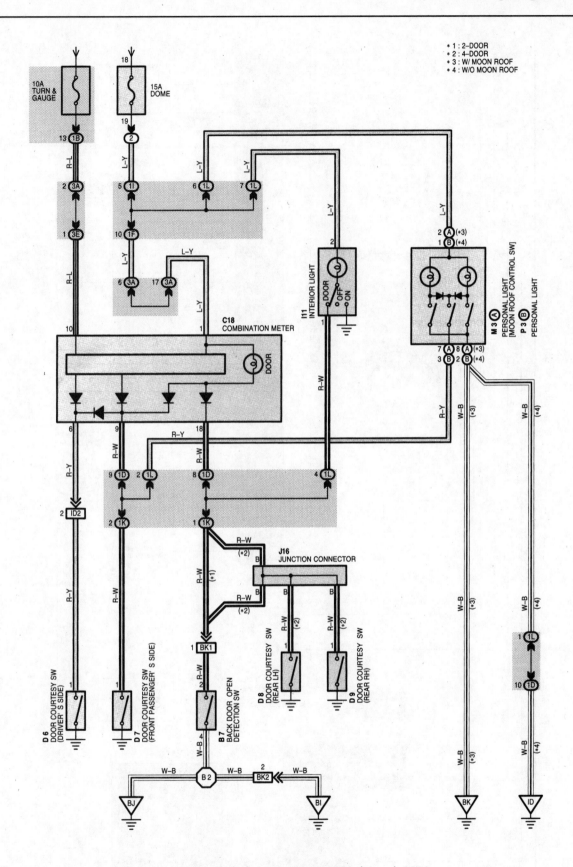

* 1 : 2–DOOR
* 2 : 4–DOOR
* 3 : W/ MOON ROOF
* 4 : W/O MOON ROOF

Interior lighting system - 1998 through 2000

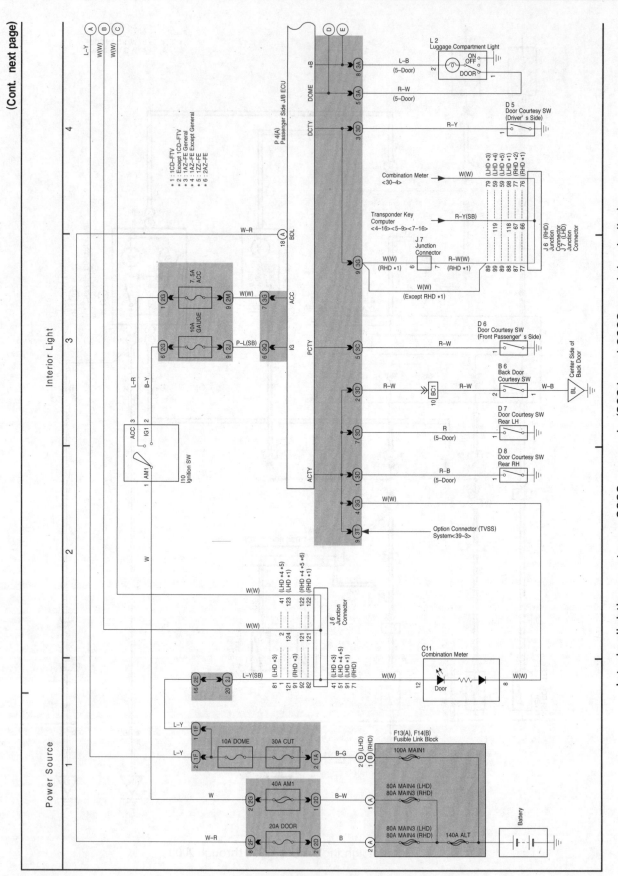

Interior lighting system - 2003 onwards (2001 and 2002 models similar)

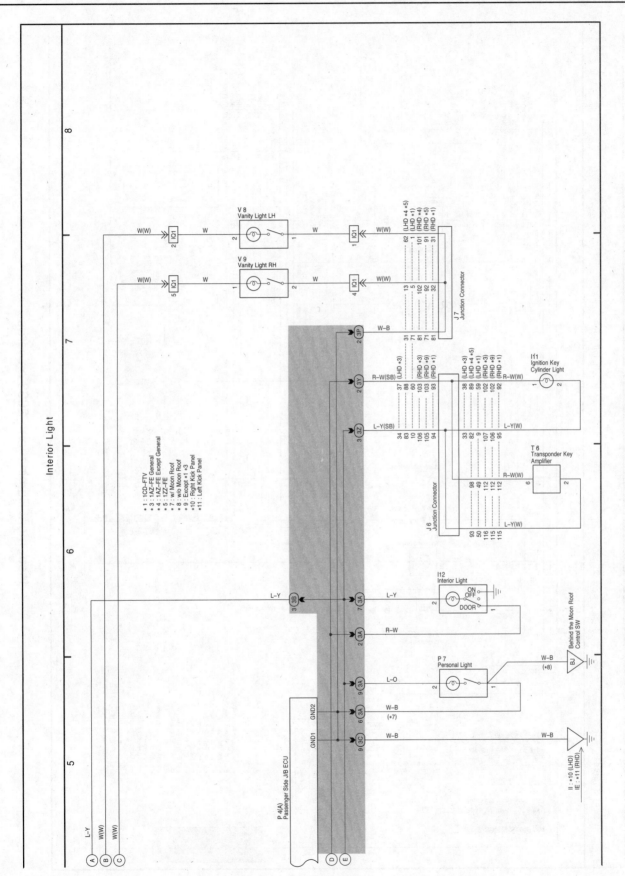

Interior lighting system – 2003 onwards (2001 and 2002 models similar)

(Cont. next page)

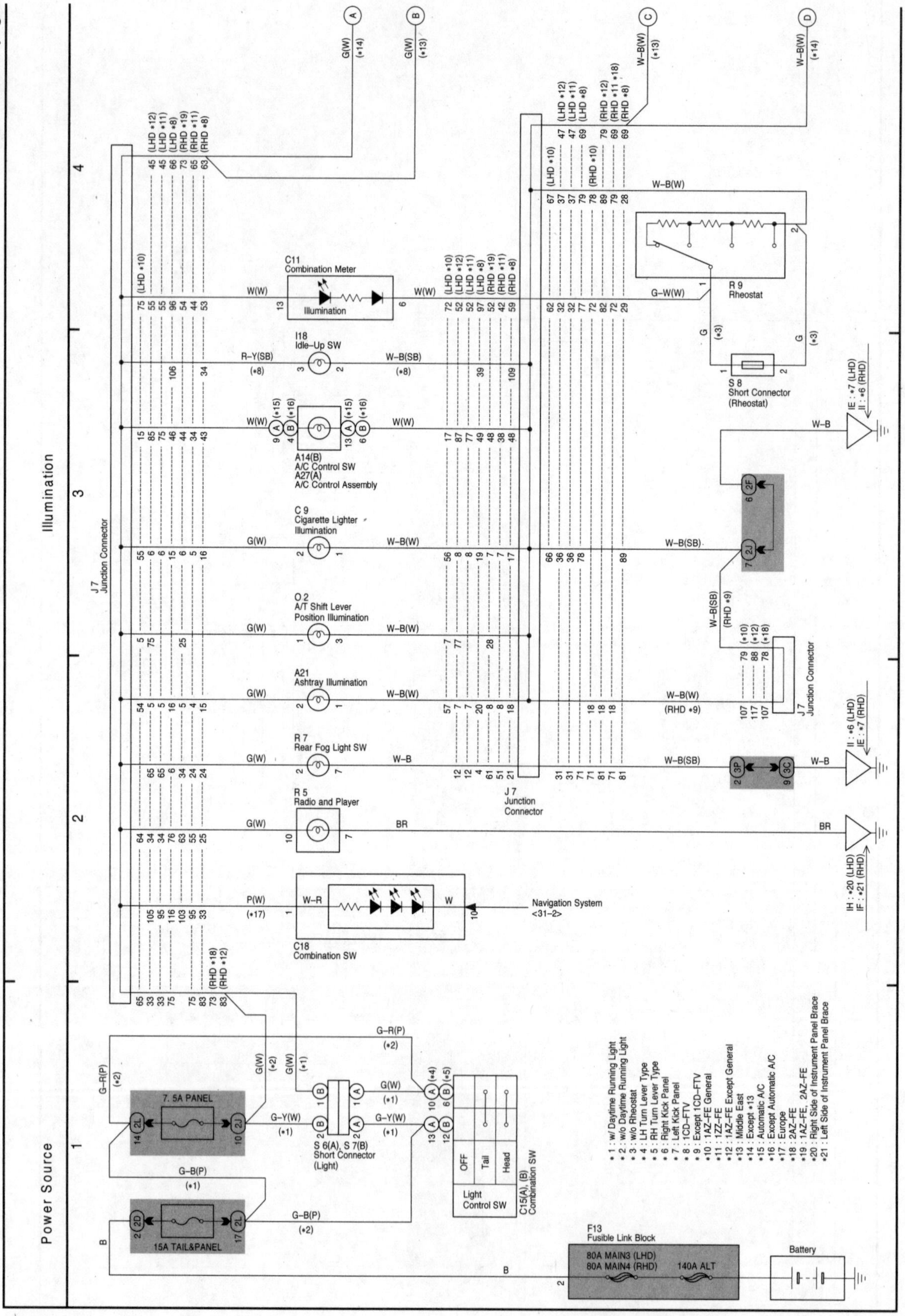

Instrument illumination – 2003 onwards

Illumination

A G(W) (*14)
B G(W) (*13)
C W–B(W) (*13)
D W–B(W) (*14)

C11 Combination Meter
W(W) — Illumination — W(W)

I18 Idle-Up SW
R–Y(SB) (*8) W–B(SB) (*8)

A14(B) A/C Control SW
A27(A) A/C Control Assembly
W(W) W(W)

C9 Cigarette Lighter Illumination
G(W) W–B(W)

O.2 A/T Shift Lever Position Illumination
G(W) W–B(W)

A21 Ashtray Illumination
G(W) W–B(W)

R7 Rear Fog Light SW
G(W) W–B

R5 Radio and Player
G(W) BR

C18 Combination SW
P(W) (*17) W–R W
Navigation System <31–2>

R9 Rheostat
W–B(W)
G–W(W)

S8 Short Connector (Rheostat)

J7 Junction Connector

2F
2J

3P 3C

IE : *7 (LHD)
JI : *6 (RHD)

II : *6 (LHD)
IE : *7 (RHD)

IH : *20 (LHD)
IF : *21 (RHD)

J7 Junction Connector

Power Source

7. 5A PANEL
15A TAIL&PANEL

S6(A), S7(B) Short Connector (Light)

C15(A), (B) Combination SW
Light Control SW
OFF / Tail / Head

F13 Fusible Link Block
80A MAIN3 (LHD)
80A MAIN4 (RHD)
140A ALT

Battery

*1 : w/ Daytime Running Light
*2 : w/o Daytime Running Light
*3 : w/o Rheostat
*4 : LH Turn Lever Type
*5 : RH Turn Lever Type
*6 : Right Kick Panel
*7 : Left Kick Panel
*8 : Except 1CD–FTV
*9 : 1CD–FTV
*10 : Except 1CD–FTV
*11 : 1AZ–FE General
*12 : 1AZ–FE Except General
*13 : Middle East
*14 : Except *13
*15 : Automatic A/C
*16 : Except Automatic A/C
*17 : Europe
*18 : 2AZ–FE
*19 : 1AZ–FE, 2AZ–FE
*20 : Right Side of Instrument Panel Brace
*21 : Left Side of Instrument Panel Brace

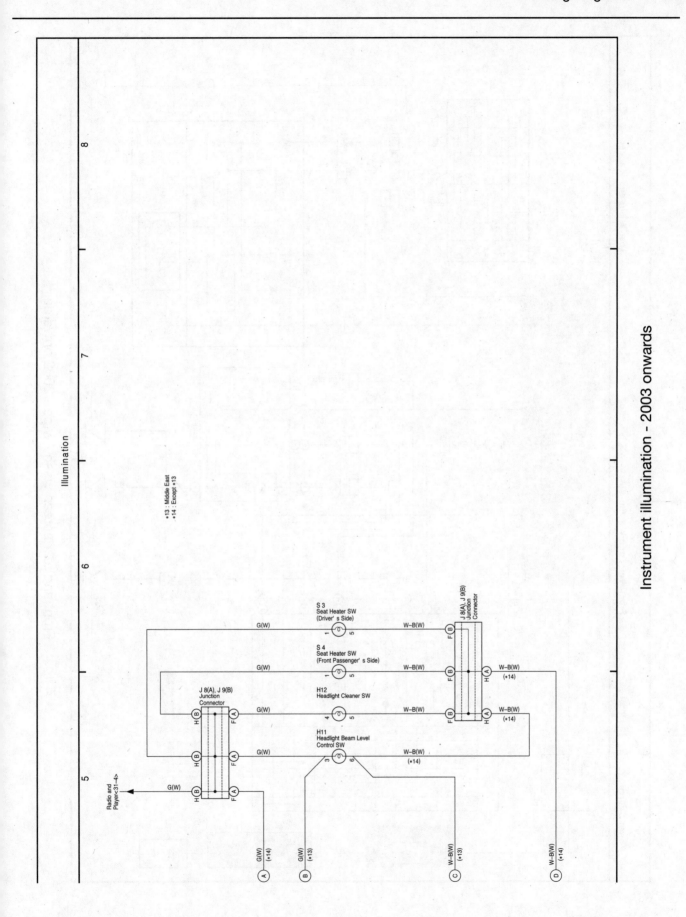

Illumination

*13 : Middle East
*14 : Except *13

Instrument illumination - 2003 onwards

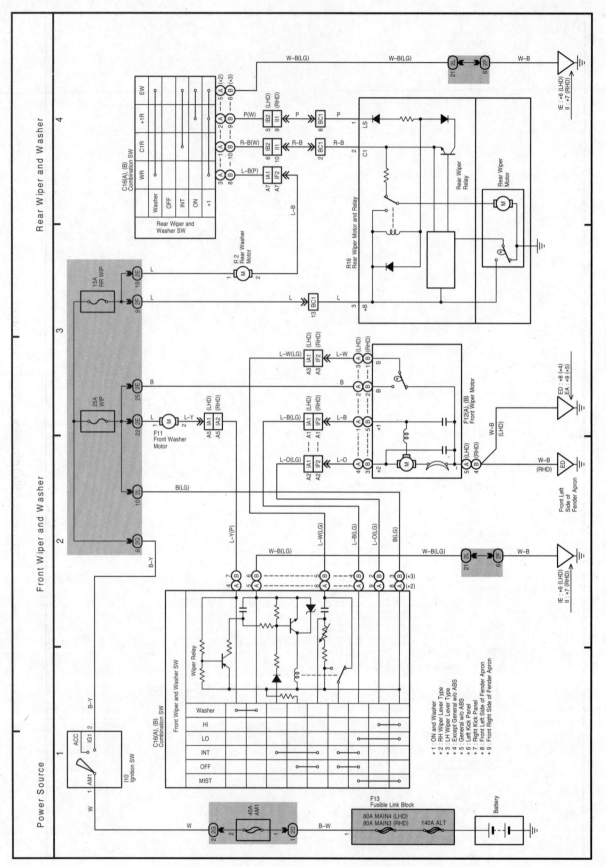

Front and rear screen wash / wipe - 2003 onwards

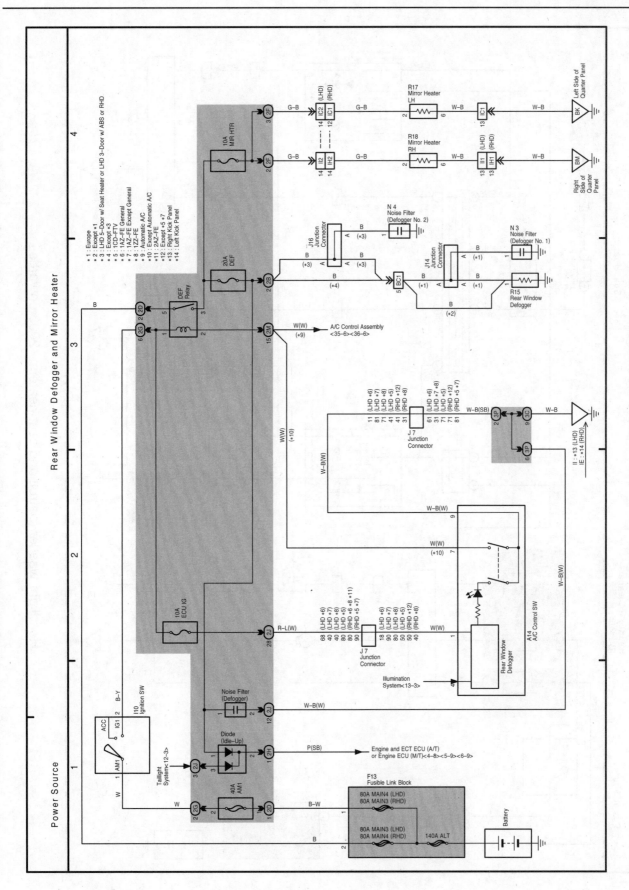

Rear Window Defogger and Mirror Heater

Rear screen heater and mirror heaters - 2003 onwards

Power Source

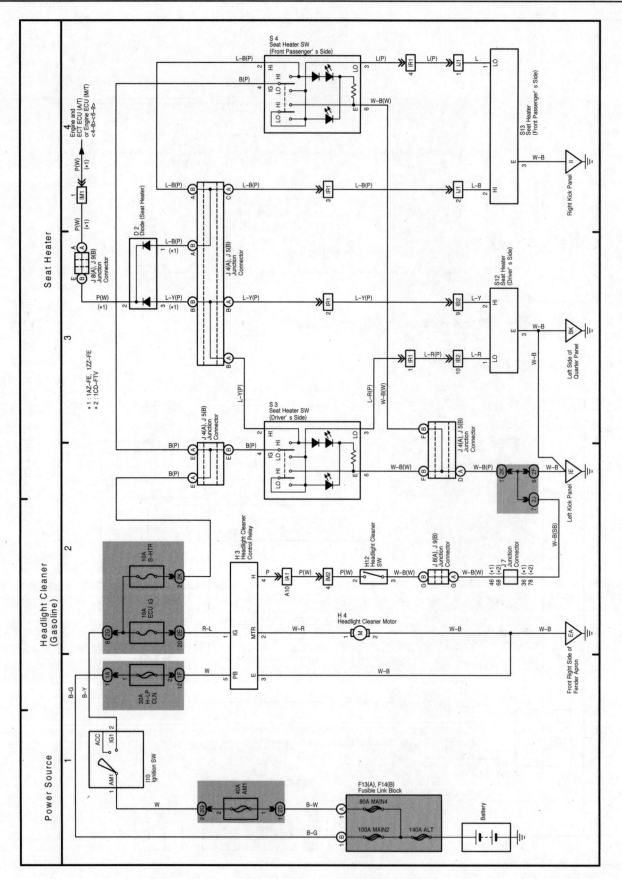

Headlight washer (petrol) and seat heaters - 2003 onwards

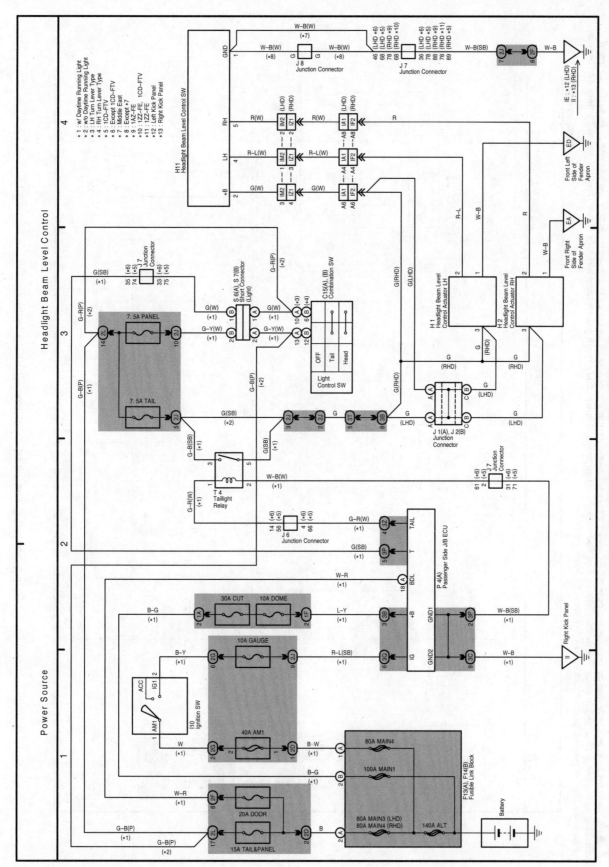

Headlight levelling - 2003 onwards

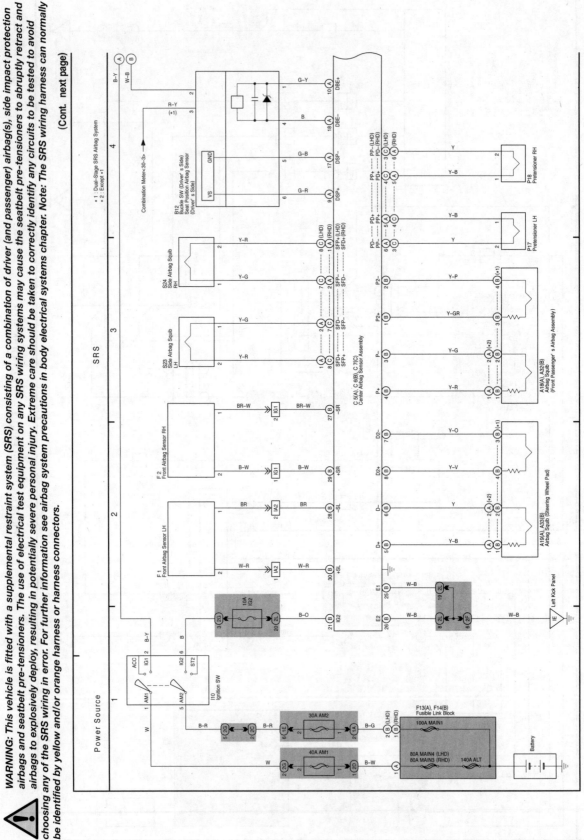

WARNING: This vehicle is fitted with a supplemental restraint system (SRS) consisting of a combination of driver (and passenger) airbag(s), side impact protection airbags and seatbelt pre-tensioners. The use of electrical test equipment on any SRS wiring systems may cause the seatbelt pre-tensioners to abruptly retract and airbags to explosively deploy, resulting in potentially severe personal injury. Extreme care should be taken to correctly identify any circuits to be tested to avoid choosing any of the SRS wiring in error. For further information see airbag system precautions in body electrical systems chapter. Note: The SRS wiring harness can normally be identified by yellow and/or orange harness or harness connectors.

(Cont. next page)

Supplemental restraint system - 2003 onwards

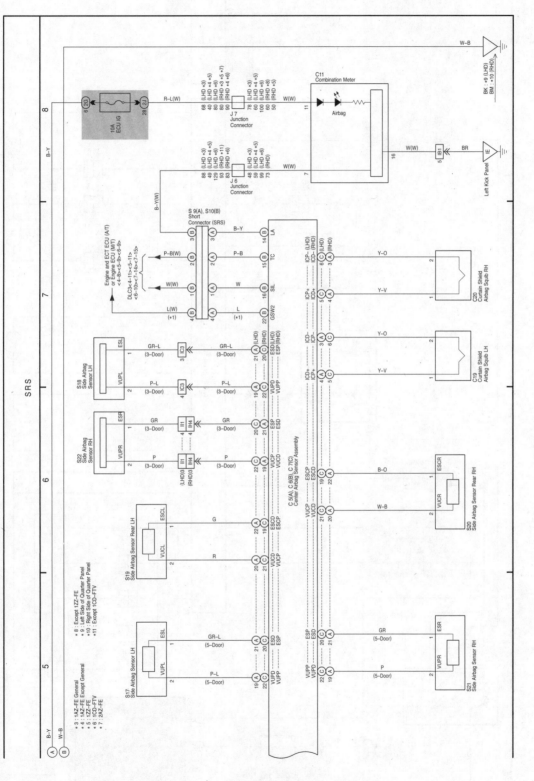

Supplemental restraint system – 2003 onwards

WARNING: This vehicle is fitted with a supplemental restraint system (SRS) consisting of a combination of driver (and passenger) airbag(s), side impact protection airbags and seatbelt pre-tensioners. The use of electrical test equipment on any SRS wiring systems may cause the seatbelt pre-tensioners to abruptly retract and airbags to explosively deploy, resulting in potentially severe personal injury. Extreme care should be taken to correctly identify any circuits to be tested to avoid choosing any of the SRS wiring in error. For further information see airbag system precautions in body electrical systems chapter. Note: The SRS wiring harness can normally be identified by yellow and/or orange harness or harness connectors.

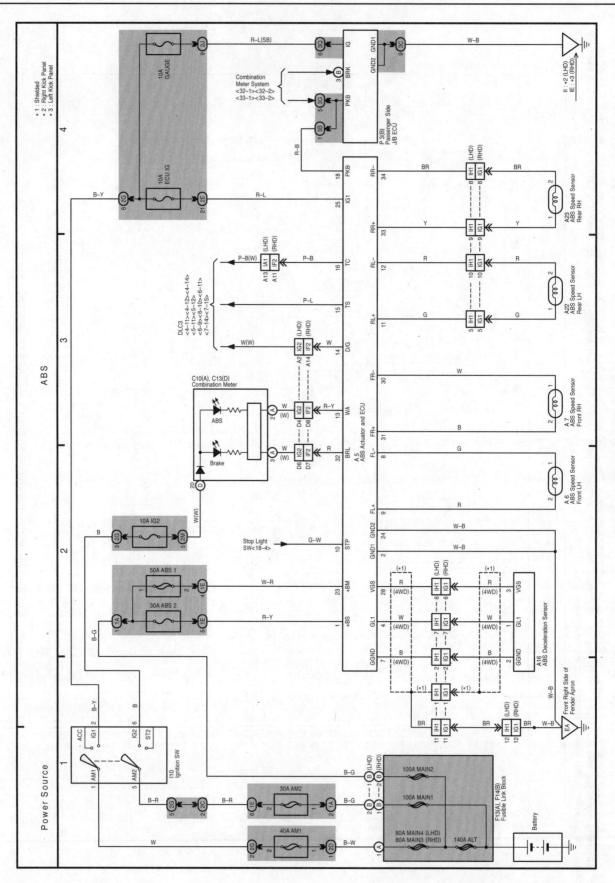

ABS system - 2003 onwards

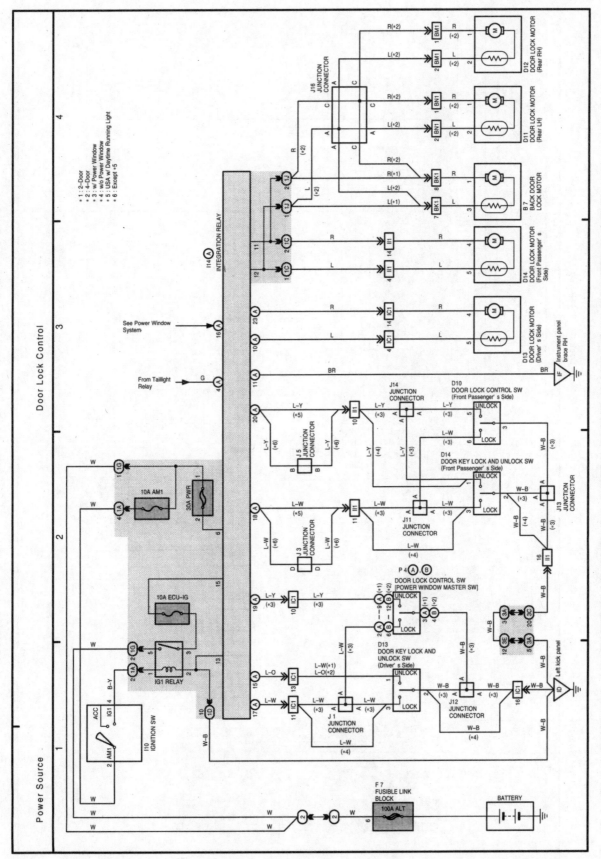

Central locking system – 1998 to 2000 (1996 and 1997 models similar)

(Cont. next page)

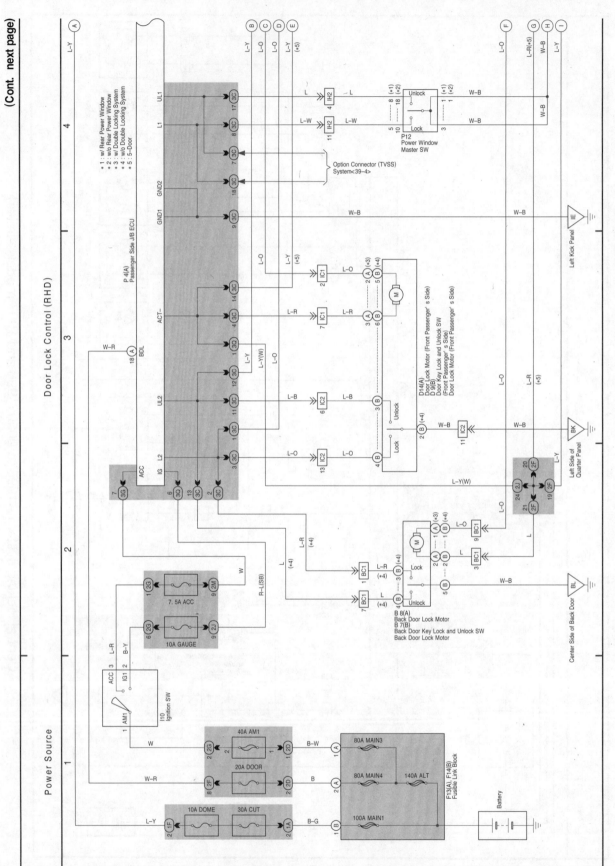

Central locking system - 2003 onwards (2001 and 2002 models similar)

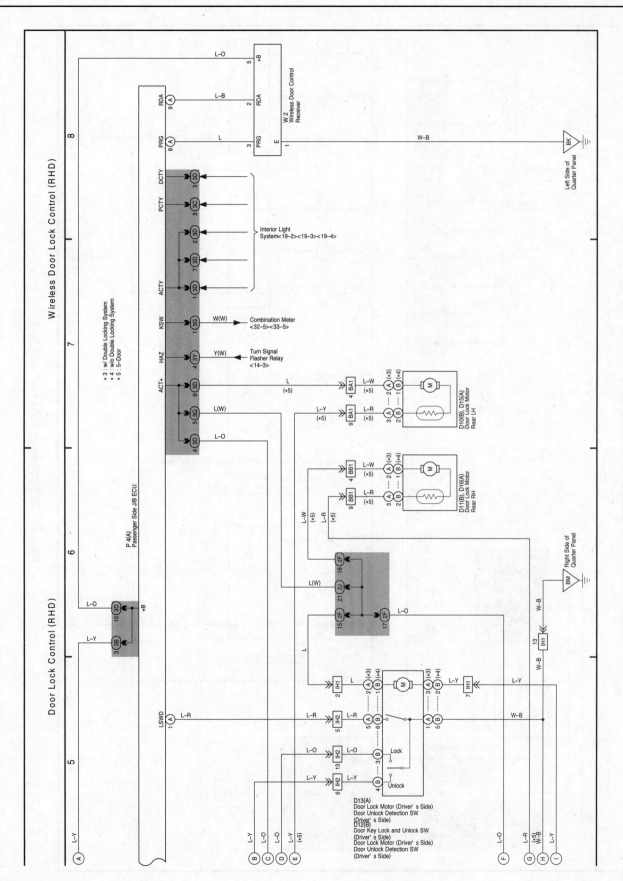

Central locking system - 2003 onwards (2001 and 2002 models similar)

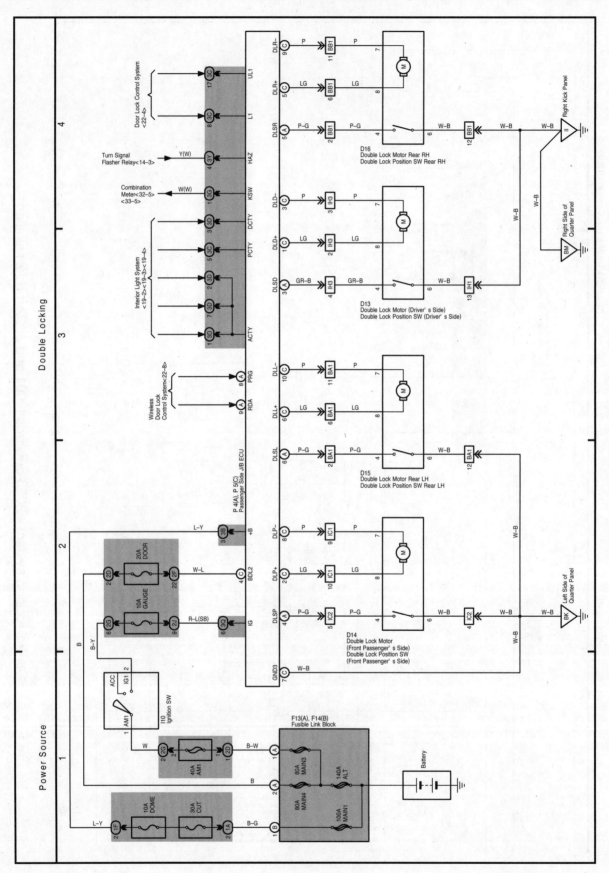

Dead lock system - 2003 onwards

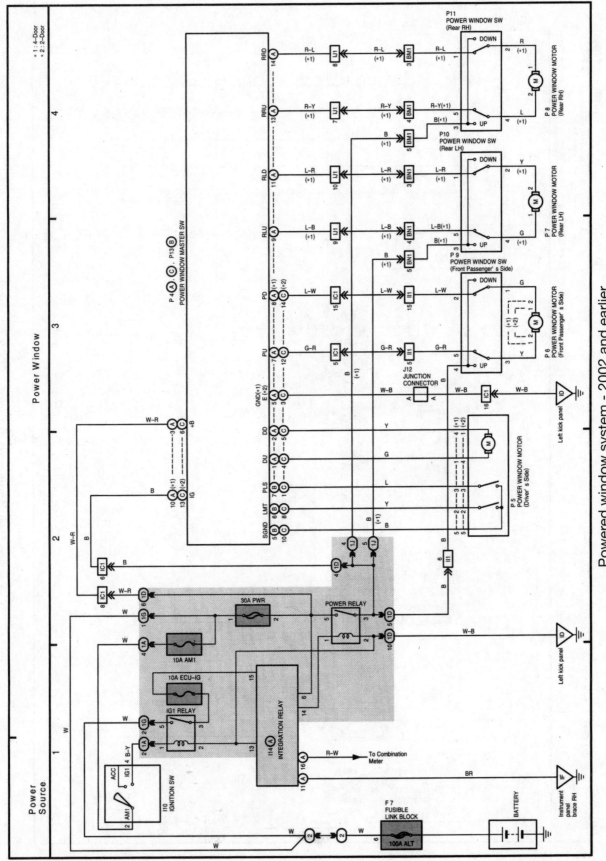

Powered window system - 2002 and earlier

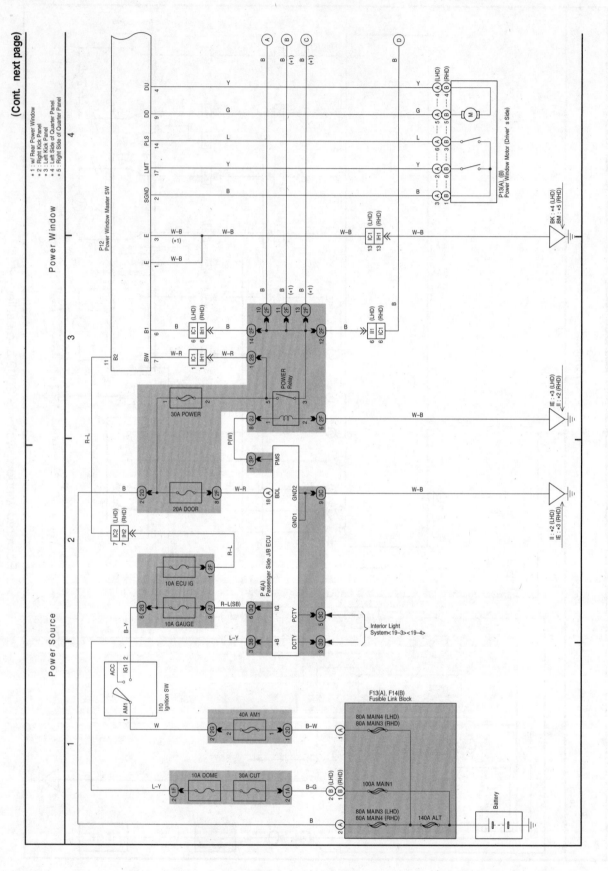

Powered windows and sunroof - 2003 onwards

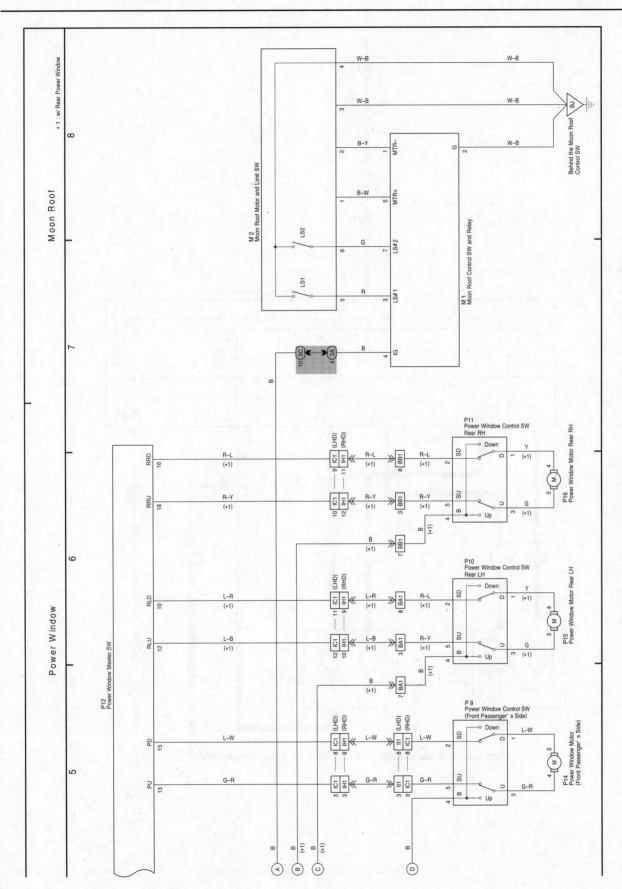

Powered windows and sunroof - 2003 onwards

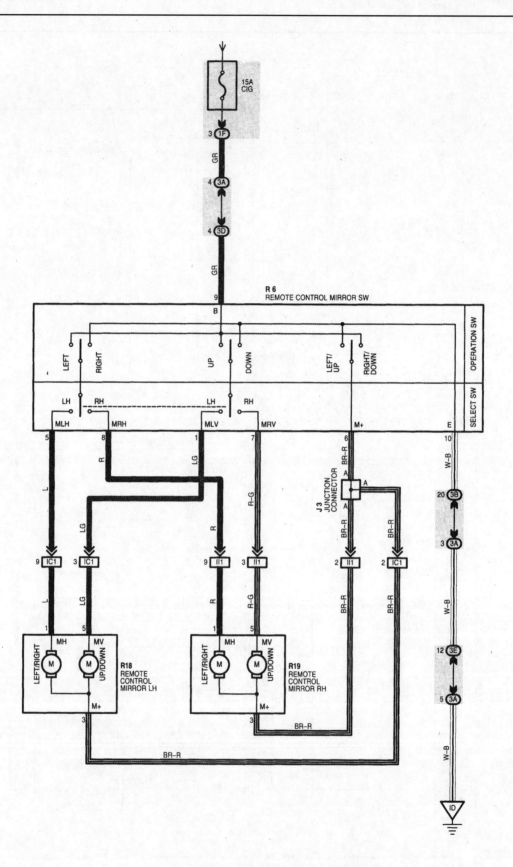

Powered mirrors - 2002 and earlier

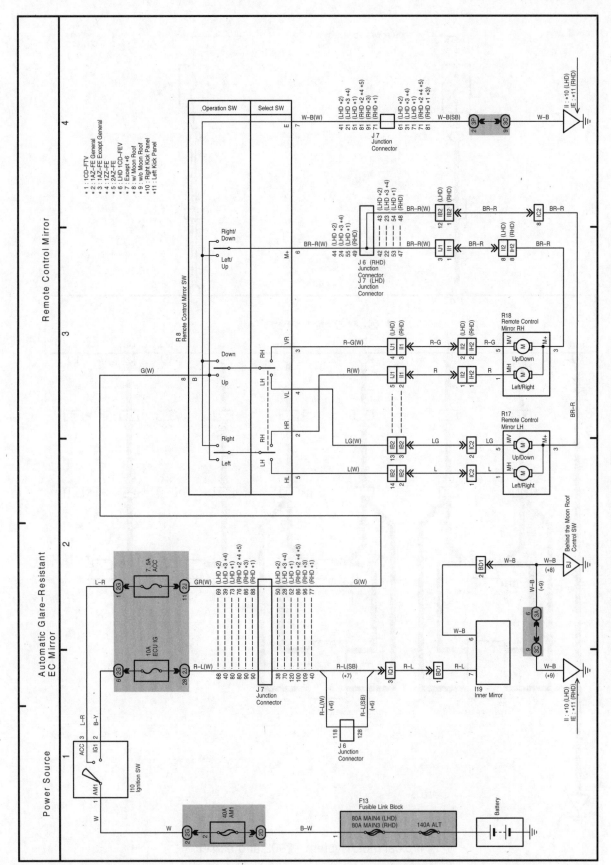

Powered mirrors and auto anti-glare rear view mirror - 2003 onwards

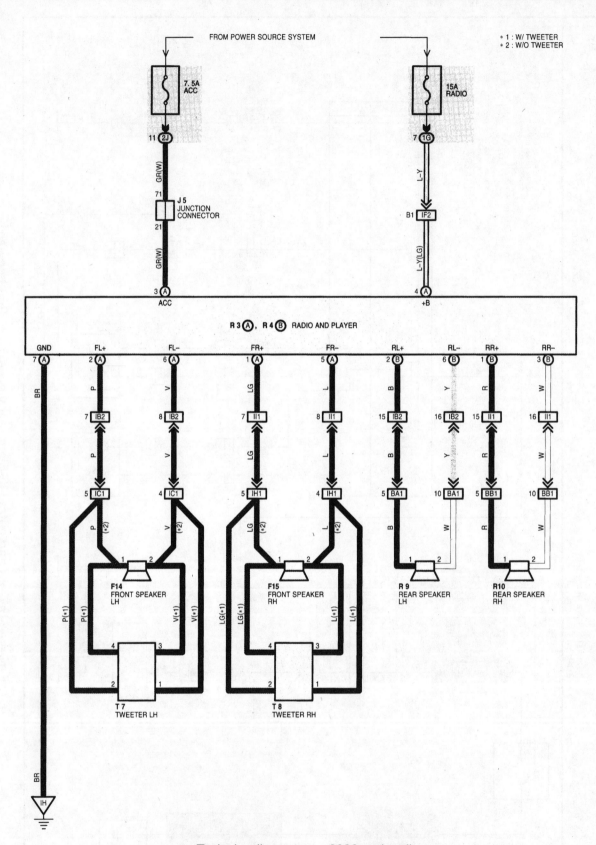

Typical radio system - 2002 and earlier

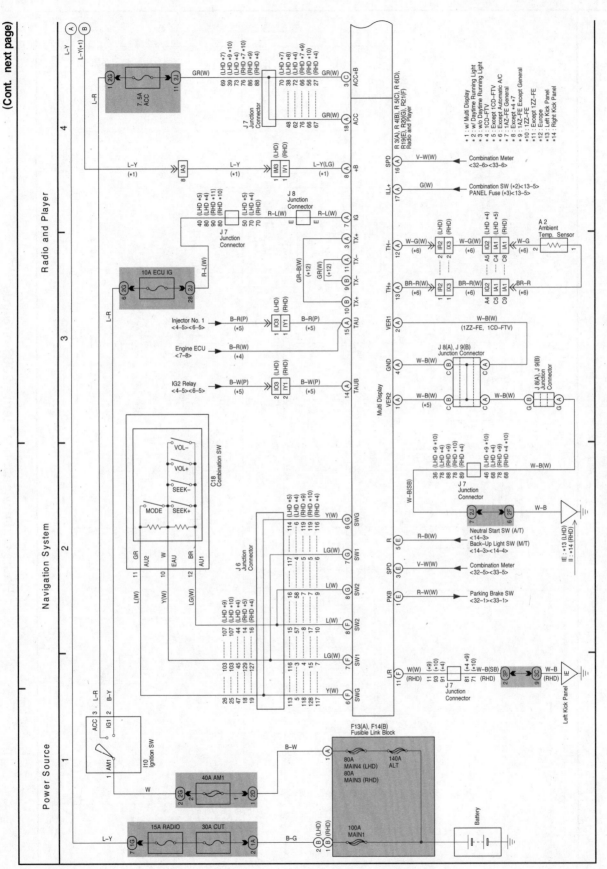

Radio and navigation system - 2003 onwards

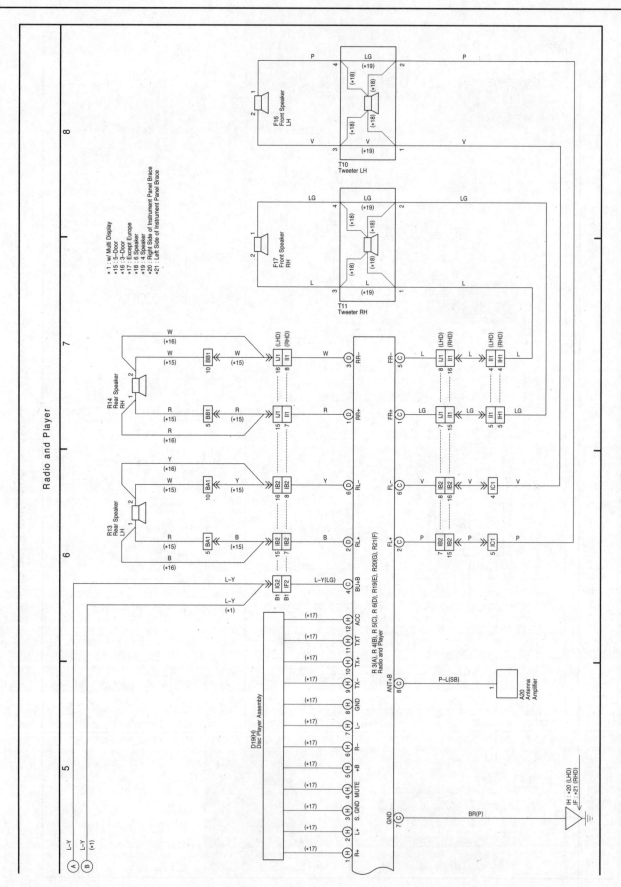

Radio and Player

Radio and navigation system - 2003 onwards

*1 : w/ Multi Display
*15 : 5-Door
*16 : 3-Door
*17 : Except Europe
*18 : 6 Speaker
*19 : 4 Speaker
*20 : Right Side of Instrument Panel Brace
*21 : Left Side of Instrument Panel Brace

F16 Front Speaker LH
T10 Tweeter LH

F17 Front Speaker RH
T11 Tweeter RH

R14 Rear Speaker RH

R13 Rear Speaker LH

D19(H) Disc Player Assembly

R 3(A), R 4(B), R 5(C), R 6(D), R19(E), R20(G), R21(F)
Radio and Player

A20 Antenna Amplifier

IH : *20 (LHD)
IF : *21 (RHD)

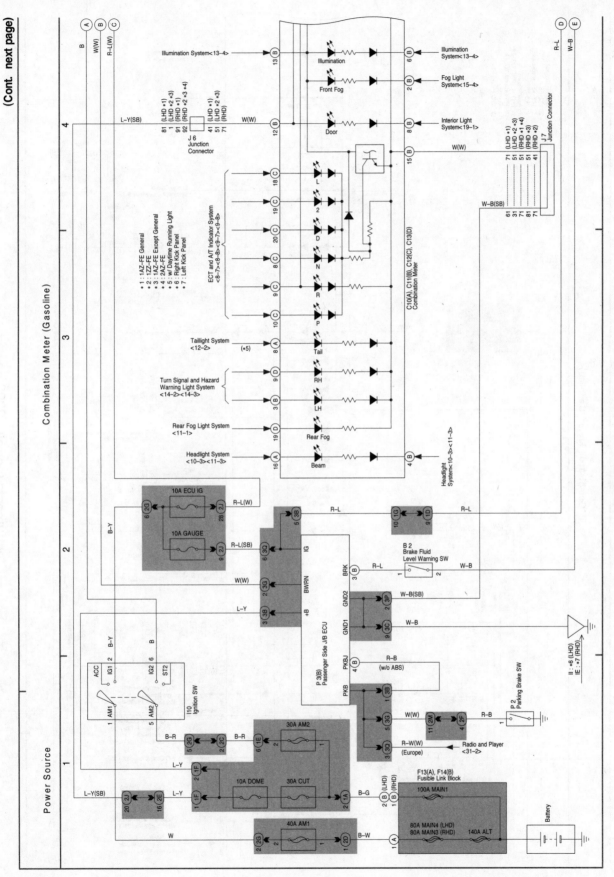

Instruments (petrol) - 2003 onwards

Combination Meter (Gasoline)

Power Source

(Cont. next page)

(Cont. next page)

*1 : 1AZ-FE General
*2 : 1ZZ-FE
*3 : 1AZ-FE Except General
*4 : 2AZ-FE
*8 : Automatic A/C
*9 : LHD *1, RHD 1ZZ-FE
*10 : RHD Except 1ZZ-FE
*11 : Europe
*12 : LHD Except *1

8

C10(A), C11(B), C12(C), C13(D)
Combination Meter

CRUISE — 12 C — Cruise Control System<8–6>

A/T OIL TEMP — 3 C

O/D OFF — 16 C — ECT and A/T Indicator System <8–7><9–7>

Check Engine — 2 C — Engine Control System<4–7><5–6><6–7>

Oil Pressure — 1 C

L–W(W) (*10)
L–W(W) (*1)(*3)(*4)
127 126
117 116
J 6 Junction Connector
L–W(W) (*1)(*3)(*4)
L–W(W) (*10)
L–W(W) (*9)

9 IF1 (LHD)
9 ID2 (RHD)

L–W(SB) (LHD *12) 1 IM5 L–W(SB) (RHD *12)

O 1 Oil Pressure SW
1

L–W

7

10A IG2
3 2G
5 2M
W(W)

Combination Meter (Gasoline)

B

20 D — Charge — 10 D — Charging System<2–2>

16 B — W (W) — 5 IB1 — BR — IE Left Kick Panel

Brake

ABS — 18 B

W(W)

Airbag — 3 A — W(W) (w/o ABS) — D4 IG2 (LHD) / D7 IF2 (RHD) — W–B (w/o ABS)

Fuel — 2 A — (w/ ABS) — ABS System<29–2><29–3> VSC System<28–12>

Driver's Side Seat Belt — W(W) (w/o ABS) — D6 IG2 (LHD) / D8 IF2 (RHD) — W–B (w/o ABS) — EA Front Right Side of Fender Apron

7 B — SRS System<27–8> — W–B

R–L(W)
68 (LHD *1)
40 (LHD *2 *3)
80 (RHD *1 *2 *4)
90 (RHD *3)

78 (LHD *1)
60 (LHD *1 *3 *4)
60 (RHD *3)
50 (RHD *2)

W(W)

11 B

J 7 Junction Connector

5 A — W (W) — 4 IB1 — BR–W — F18 Fuel Sender 3

15 A — W (W) — 3 IB1 — Y–B — Y–R — F19 Fuel Sender (Sub) 1 2

J 6 (LHD *2 *3)
Junction Connector
J 7 (LHD *1, RHD)
Junction Connector

V–W(W)
IM1
V–W(W) (LHD *11)

Radio and Player <31–2><31–4>

V–W (RHD *11)

Temp.

6 A — W (W) — D5 IA1 (LHD) / D5 IF2 (RHD) — R–Y — 9 EA1 — R–Y — SE — V 2 Vehicle Speed Sensor (Combination Meter) 2

112
74
64

V–W(W)

Fuel

123
85
73

V–W(W)

4 A — W (W) — D6 IA1 (LHD) / D4 IF2 (RHD) — L–B — 3 EA1 — L–B — SI / IG+ 3 1

Engine and ECT ECU (A/T) or Engine ECU (M/T)<4–10> <5–9><6–9>

93
102
93
104
94
104

V–W(W)

Tachometer

9 B — Key Reminder and Light Reminder Buzzer System<30–4>

Speedometer

10 B — W(W) — Engine and ECT ECU (A/T) or Engine ECU (M/T) <4–10><4–13> <5–10><5–11> <6–9><6–10>

5 C — GR(W)

63 (LHD *1)
122 (LHD *2 *3)
74 (LHD *4)
84 (RHD *1)
74 (RHD *4)
74 (RHD *4)

V–W(W)

W (W)

26 2J
6 2M

1 B

15 C — G(W) (*8) — A/C Control Assembly<35–5>

A/C Control Assembly <35–6>

W(W) (*8)

16 2M

18 A — Seat Belt Warning System<30–4>

17 A

Seat Belt Warning System<30–3>

9 A

20 B — W(W) — Passenger Side J/B ECU <21–7><22–7><23–4>

19 B — Key Reminder and Light Reminder Buzzer System<30–3>

Buzzer

A — B
B — W(W)
C — R–L(W)

D — R–L
E — W–B

Instruments (petrol) – 2003 onwards

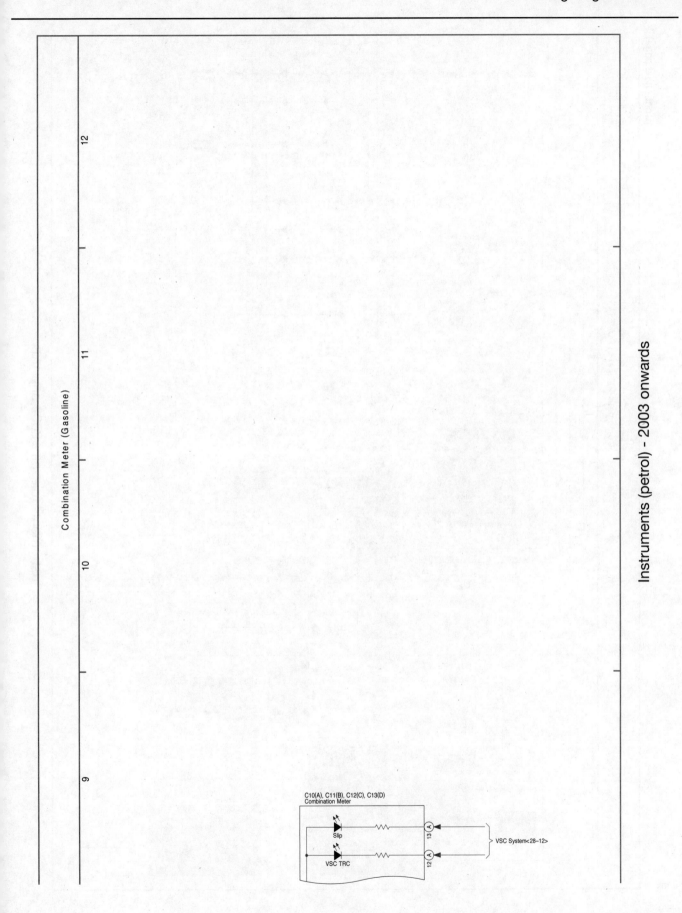

Combination Meter (Gasoline)

Instruments (petrol) - 2003 onwards

C10(A), C11(B), C12(C), C13(D)
Combination Meter

Slip

VSC TRC

13 A

12 A

VSC System<28–12>

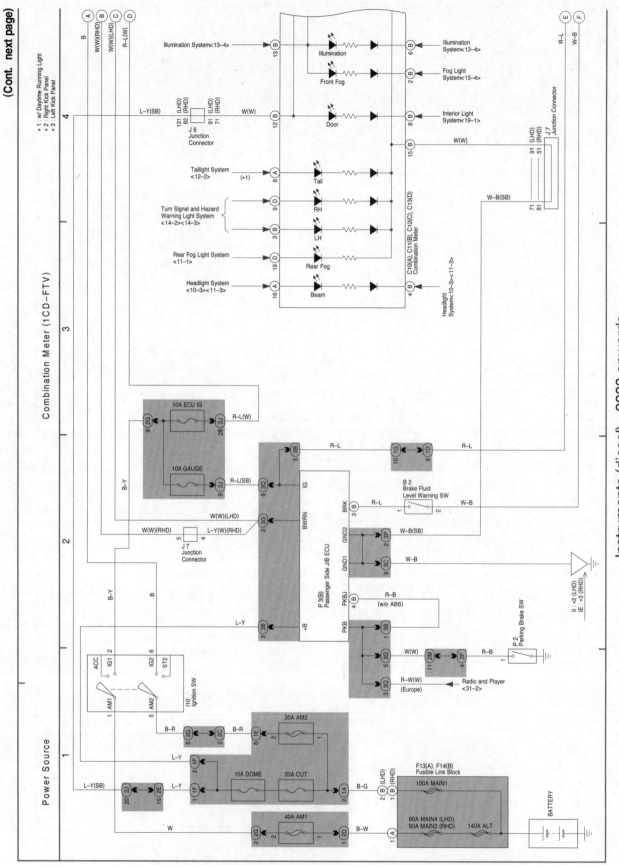

Instruments (diesel) - 2003 onwards

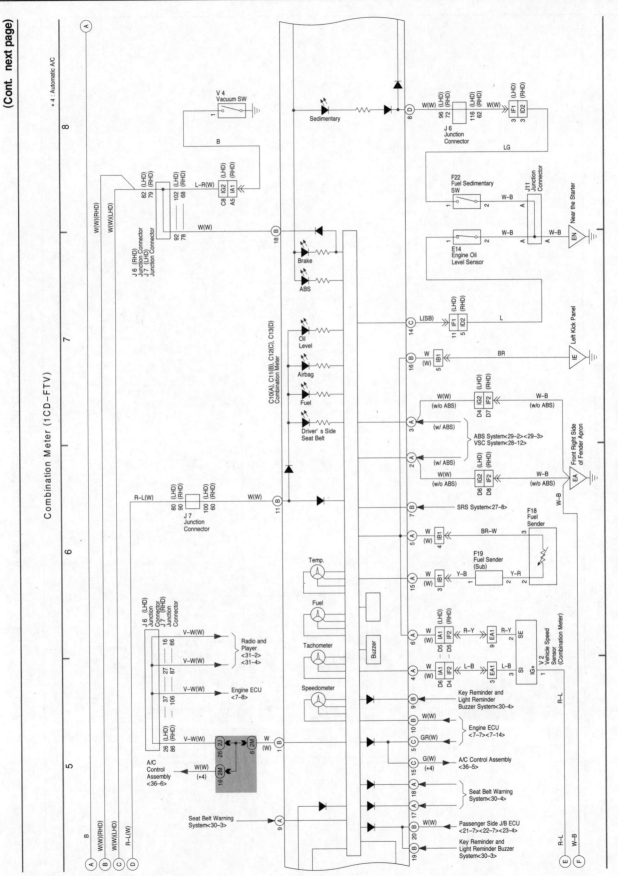

Instruments (diesel) - 2003 onwards

Combination Meter (1CD-FTV)

(Cont. next page)

*4 : Automatic A/C

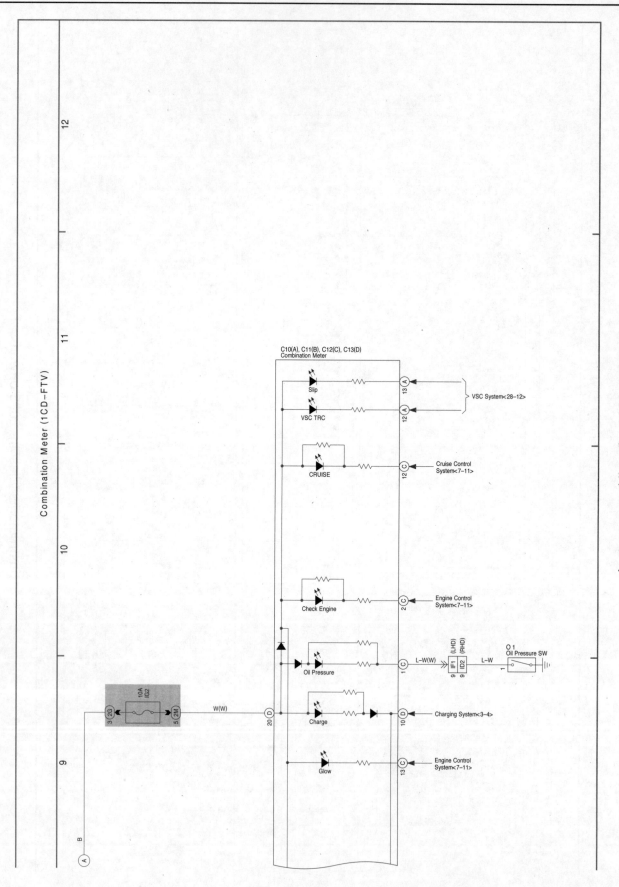

Combination Meter (1CD–FTV)

C10(A), C11(B), C12(C), C13(D)
Combination Meter

Slip

VSC TRC

CRUISE

Check Engine

Oil Pressure

Charge

Glow

VSC System<28–12>

Cruise Control
System<7–11>

Engine Control
System<7–11>

Engine Control
System<7–11>

Charging System<3–4>

(LHD)
(RHD)

O 1
Oil Pressure SW

L–W(W)

L–W

10A
IG2

W(W)

Instruments (diesel) - 2003 onwards

Dimensions and weights . . . . **REF•1**
Conversion factors . . . . **REF•2**
General repair procedures . . . . **REF•3**
Vehicle identification numbers . . . . **REF•4**
Buying spare parts . . . . **REF•5**

Jacking and vehicle support . . . . **REF•5**
Tools and working facilities . . . . **REF•6**
MOT Test Checks . . . . **REF•8**
Troubleshooting . . . . **REF•12**
Index . . . . **REF•19**

Dimensions and weights

Note: *All figures and dimensions are approximate and may vary according to model. Refer to manufacturer's data for exact figures.*

Overall length
3-door models	3870 mm
5-door models	4265 mm

Overall width
All models	1785 mm

Overall height (unladen)
3-door models:
Two-wheel drive models	1685 mm
Four-wheel drive models	1695 mm

5-door models:
Two-wheel drive models	1705 mm
Four-wheel drive models	1715 mm

Wheelbase
3-door models	2280 mm
5-door models	2490 mm

Weights*

Gross Vehicle Mass (GVM)

3-door models:
Petrol models	1685 kg
Diesel models	1785 kg

5-door models:
Petrol models	1825 kg
Diesel models	1930 kg

* Exact kerb weights depend upon model and specification – details are given in the owner's handbook.

Maximum roof rack load
All models	75 kg

Maximum towing weights	**Unbraked trailer**	**Braked trailer**
1.8 litre petrol engine models	500 kg	1000 kg
2.0 litre petrol engine models	640 kg	1500 kg
Diesel engine models	640 kg	1500 kg

* Exact kerb and towing weights depend upon model and specification – details are given in the owner's handbook.

Conversion factors

Length (distance)

Inches (in)	x 25.4	= Millimetres (mm)	x 0.0394	= Inches (in)
Feet (ft)	x 0.305	= Metres (m)	x 3.281	= Feet (ft)
Miles	x 1.609	= Kilometres (km)	x 0.621	= Miles

Volume (capacity)

Cubic inches (cu in; in³)	x 16.387	= Cubic centimetres (cc; cm³)	x 0.061	= Cubic inches (cu in; in³)
Imperial pints (Imp pt)	x 0.568	= Litres (l)	x 1.76	= Imperial pints (Imp pt)
Imperial quarts (Imp qt)	x 1.137	= Litres (l)	x 0.88	= Imperial quarts (Imp qt)
Imperial quarts (Imp qt)	x 1.201	= US quarts (US qt)	x 0.833	= Imperial quarts (Imp qt)
US quarts (US qt)	x 0.946	= Litres (l)	x 1.057	= US quarts (US qt)
Imperial gallons (Imp gal)	x 4.546	= Litres (l)	x 0.22	= Imperial gallons (Imp gal)
Imperial gallons (Imp gal)	x 1.201	= US gallons (US gal)	x 0.833	= Imperial gallons (Imp gal)
US gallons (US gal)	x 3.785	= Litres (l)	x 0.264	= US gallons (US gal)

Mass (weight)

Ounces (oz)	x 28.35	= Grams (g)	x 0.035	= Ounces (oz)
Pounds (lb)	x 0.454	= Kilograms (kg)	x 2.205	= Pounds (lb)

Force

Ounces-force (ozf; oz)	x 0.278	= Newtons (N)	x 3.6	= Ounces-force (ozf; oz)
Pounds-force (lbf; lb)	x 4.448	= Newtons (N)	x 0.225	= Pounds-force (lbf; lb)
Newtons (N)	x 0.1	= Kilograms-force (kgf; kg)	x 9.81	= Newtons (N)

Pressure

Pounds-force per square inch (psi; lbf/in²; lb/in²)	x 0.070	= Kilograms-force per square centimetre (kgf/cm²; kg/cm²)	x 14.223	= Pounds-force per square inch (psi; lbf/in²; lb/in²)
Pounds-force per square inch (psi; lbf/in²; lb/in²)	x 0.068	= Atmospheres (atm)	x 14.696	= Pounds-force per square inch (psi; lbf/in²; lb/in²)
Pounds-force per square inch (psi; lbf/in²; lb/in²)	x 0.069	= Bars	x 14.5	= Pounds-force per square inch (psi; lbf/in²; lb/in²)
Pounds-force per square inch (psi; lbf/in²; lb/in²)	x 6.895	= Kilopascals (kPa)	x 0.145	= Pounds-force per square inch (psi; lbf/in²; lb/in²)
Kilopascals (kPa)	x 0.01	= Kilograms-force per square centimetre (kgf/cm²; kg/cm²)	x 98.1	= Kilopascals (kPa)
Millibar (mbar)	x 100	= Pascals (Pa)	x 0.01	= Millibar (mbar)
Millibar (mbar)	x 0.0145	= Pounds-force per square inch (psi; lbf/in²; lb/in²)	x 68.947	= Millibar (mbar)
Millibar (mbar)	x 0.75	= Millimetres of mercury (mmHg)	x 1.333	= Millibar (mbar)
Millibar (mbar)	x 0.401	= Inches of water (inH₂O)	x 2.491	= Millibar (mbar)
Millimetres of mercury (mmHg)	x 0.535	= Inches of water (inH₂O)	x 1.868	= Millimetres of mercury (mmHg)
Inches of water (inH₂O)	x 0.036	= Pounds-force per square inch (psi; lbf/in²; lb/in²)	x 27.68	= Inches of water (inH₂O)

Torque (moment of force)

Pounds-force inches (lbf in; lb in)	x 1.152	= Kilograms-force centimetre (kgf cm; kg cm)	x 0.868	= Pounds-force inches (lbf in; lb in)
Pounds-force inches (lbf in; lb in)	x 0.113	= Newton metres (Nm)	x 8.85	= Pounds-force inches (lbf in; lb in)
Pounds-force inches (lbf in; lb in)	x 0.083	= Pounds-force feet (lbf ft; lb ft)	x 12	= Pounds-force inches (lbf in; lb in)
Pounds-force feet (lbf ft; lb ft)	x 0.138	= Kilograms-force metres (kgf m; kg m)	x 7.233	= Pounds-force feet (lbf ft; lb ft)
Pounds-force feet (lbf ft; lb ft)	x 1.356	= Newton metres (Nm)	x 0.738	= Pounds-force feet (lbf ft; lb ft)
Newton metres (Nm)	x 0.102	= Kilograms-force metres (kgf m; kg m)	x 9.804	= Newton metres (Nm)

Power

Horsepower (hp)	x 745.7	= Watts (W)	x 0.0013	= Horsepower (hp)

Velocity (speed)

Miles per hour (miles/hr; mph)	x 1.609	= Kilometres per hour (km/hr; kph)	x 0.621	= Miles per hour (miles/hr; mph)

Fuel consumption*

Miles per gallon, Imperial (mpg)	x 0.354	= Kilometres per litre (km/l)	x 2.825	= Miles per gallon, Imperial (mpg)
Miles per gallon, US (mpg)	x 0.425	= Kilometres per litre (km/l)	x 2.352	= Miles per gallon, US (mpg)

Temperature

Degrees Fahrenheit = (°C x 1.8) + 32   Degrees Celsius (Degrees Centigrade; °C) = (°F - 32) x 0.56

It is common practice to convert from miles per gallon (mpg) to litres/100 kilometres (l/100km), where mpg x l/100 km = 282

Whenever servicing, repair or overhaul work is carried out on the car or its components, observe the following procedures and instructions. This will assist in carrying out the operation efficiently and to a professional standard of workmanship.

Joint mating faces and gaskets

When separating components at their mating faces, never insert screwdrivers or similar implements into the joint between the faces in order to prise them apart. This can cause severe damage which results in oil leaks, coolant leaks, etc upon reassembly. Separation is usually achieved by tapping along the joint with a soft-faced hammer in order to break the seal. However, note that this method may not be suitable where dowels are used for component location.

Where a gasket is used between the mating faces of two components, a new one must be fitted on reassembly; fit it dry unless otherwise stated in the repair procedure. Make sure that the mating faces are clean and dry, with all traces of old gasket removed. When cleaning a joint face, use a tool which is unlikely to score or damage the face, and remove any burrs or nicks with an oilstone or fine file.

Make sure that tapped holes are cleaned with a pipe cleaner, and keep them free of jointing compound, if this is being used, unless specifically instructed otherwise.

Ensure that all orifices, channels or pipes are clear, and blow through them, preferably using compressed air.

Oil seals

Oil seals can be removed by levering them out with a wide flat-bladed screwdriver or similar implement. Alternatively, a number of self-tapping screws may be screwed into the seal, and these used as a purchase for pliers or some similar device in order to pull the seal free.

Whenever an oil seal is removed from its working location, either individually or as part of an assembly, it should be renewed.

The very fine sealing lip of the seal is easily damaged, and will not seal if the surface it contacts is not completely clean and free from scratches, nicks or grooves. If the original sealing surface of the component cannot be restored, and the manufacturer has not made provision for slight relocation of the seal relative to the sealing surface, the component should be renewed.

Protect the lips of the seal from any surface which may damage them in the course of fitting. Use tape or a conical sleeve where possible. Lubricate the seal lips with oil before fitting and, on dual-lipped seals, fill the space between the lips with grease.

Unless otherwise stated, oil seals must be fitted with their sealing lips toward the lubricant to be sealed.

Use a tubular drift or block of wood of the appropriate size to install the seal and, if the seal housing is shouldered, drive the seal down to the shoulder. If the seal housing is unshouldered, the seal should be fitted with its face flush with the housing top face (unless otherwise instructed).

Screw threads and fastenings

Seized nuts, bolts and screws are quite a common occurrence where corrosion has set in, and the use of penetrating oil or releasing fluid will often overcome this problem if the offending item is soaked for a while before attempting to release it. The use of an impact driver may also provide a means of releasing such stubborn fastening devices, when used in conjunction with the appropriate screwdriver bit or socket. If none of these methods works, it may be necessary to resort to the careful application of heat, or the use of a hacksaw or nut splitter device.

Studs are usually removed by locking two nuts together on the threaded part, and then using a spanner on the lower nut to unscrew the stud. Studs or bolts which have broken off below the surface of the component in which they are mounted can sometimes be removed using a stud extractor. Always ensure that a blind tapped hole is completely free from oil, grease, water or other fluid before installing the bolt or stud. Failure to do this could cause the housing to crack due to the hydraulic action of the bolt or stud as it is screwed in.

When tightening a castellated nut to accept a split pin, tighten the nut to the specified torque, where applicable, and then tighten further to the next split pin hole. Never slacken the nut to align the split pin hole, unless stated in the repair procedure.

When checking or retightening a nut or bolt to a specified torque setting, slacken the nut or bolt by a quarter of a turn, and then retighten to the specified setting. However, this should not be attempted where angular tightening has been used.

For some screw fastenings, notably cylinder head bolts or nuts, torque wrench settings are no longer specified for the latter stages of tightening, "angle-tightening" being called up instead. Typically, a fairly low torque wrench setting will be applied to the bolts/nuts in the correct sequence, followed by one or more stages of tightening through specified angles.

Locknuts, locktabs and washers

Any fastening which will rotate against a component or housing during tightening should always have a washer between it and the relevant component or housing.

Spring or split washers should always be renewed when they are used to lock a critical component such as a big-end bearing retaining bolt or nut. Locktabs which are folded over to retain a nut or bolt should always be renewed.

Self-locking nuts can be re-used in non-critical areas, providing resistance can be felt when the locking portion passes over the bolt or stud thread. However, it should be noted that self-locking stiffnuts tend to lose their effectiveness after long periods of use, and should then be renewed as a matter of course.

Split pins must always be replaced with new ones of the correct size for the hole.

When thread-locking compound is found on the threads of a fastener which is to be re-used, it should be cleaned off with a wire brush and solvent, and fresh compound applied on reassembly.

Special tools

Some repair procedures in this manual entail the use of special tools such as a press, two or three-legged pullers, spring compressors, etc. Wherever possible, suitable readily-available alternatives to the manufacturer's special tools are described, and are shown in use. In some instances, where no alternative is possible, it has been necessary to resort to the use of a manufacturer's tool, and this has been done for reasons of safety as well as the efficient completion of the repair operation. Unless you are highly-skilled and have a thorough understanding of the procedures described, never attempt to bypass the use of any special tool when the procedure described specifies its use. Not only is there a very great risk of personal injury, but expensive damage could be caused to the components involved.

Environmental considerations

When disposing of used engine oil, brake fluid, antifreeze, etc, give due consideration to any detrimental environmental effects. Do not, for instance, pour any of the above liquids down drains into the general sewage system, or onto the ground to soak away. Many local council refuse tips provide a facility for waste oil disposal, as do some garages. If none of these facilities are available, consult your local Environmental Health Department, or the National Rivers Authority, for further advice.

With the universal tightening-up of legislation regarding the emission of environmentally-harmful substances from motor vehicles, most vehicles have tamperproof devices fitted to the main adjustment points of the fuel system. These devices are primarily designed to prevent unqualified persons from adjusting the fuel/air mixture, with the chance of a consequent increase in toxic emissions. If such devices are found during servicing or overhaul, they should, wherever possible, be renewed or refitted in accordance with the manufacturer's requirements or current legislation.

OIL CARE
FOLLOW THE CODE
OIL BANK LINE
0800 66 33 66
www.oilbankline.org.uk

Note: *It is antisocial and illegal to dump oil down the drain. To find the location of your local oil recycling bank, call this number free.*

Modifications are a continuing and unpublicised process in vehicle manufacturing. Since spare parts manuals and lists are compiled on a numerical basis, the individual vehicle numbers are essential to correctly identify the component required.

Vehicle Identification Number (VIN)

This very important identification number is stamped on the bulkhead in the engine compartment and, on 1997 and later models, on a plate attached to the facia inside the windscreen on the left-hand side of the

vehicle. It is also stamped in the bodywork beneath a flap under the right-hand front seat. The Manufacturer's Certification Label appears on the driver's side door pillar **(see illustrations)**.

VIN model year code

Counting from the left, the model year code letter designation is the 10th character. On all models covered by this manual the model year codes are:

T 1996
V 1997
W 1998
X 1999

Y 2000
1 2001
2 2002
3 2003
4 2004
5 2005
6 2006

Engine number

The engine code number is stamped into a machined pad on the right end of the engine on 2000 and earlier models. On 2001 and later models, it can be found on a pad on the front (radiator) side of the cylinder block **(see illustrations)**.

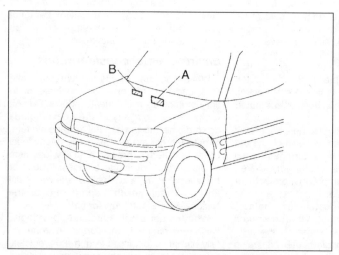

Location of the Manufacturer's Plate (A) and the Vehicle Identification Number (VIN) (B) on 1996 models

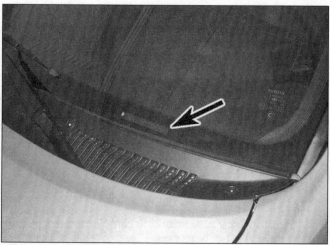

Location of the Vehicle Identification Number (VIN) which is visible through the left-hand side of the windscreen on 1997 and later models

The Manufacturer's Certification Label is on the door pillar on 1997 and later models

Location of the engine identification number – 2000 and earlier models

Location of the engine identification number – 2001 and later models

Spare parts are available from many sources, including maker's appointed garages, accessory shops, and motor factors. To be sure of obtaining the correct parts, it will sometimes be necessary to quote the vehicle identification number. If possible, it can also be useful to take the old parts along for positive identification. Items such as starter motors and alternators may be available under a service exchange scheme – any parts returned should be clean.

Our advice regarding spare parts is as follows.

Officially appointed garages

This is the best source of parts which are peculiar to your car, and which are not otherwise generally available (eg, badges, interior trim, certain body panels, etc). It is also the only place at which you should buy parts if the vehicle is still under warranty.

Accessory shops

These are very good places to buy materials and components needed for the maintenance of your car (oil, air and fuel filters, light bulbs, drivebelts, greases, brake pads, touch-up paint, etc). Components of this nature sold by a reputable shop are usually of the same standard as those used by the car manufacturer.

Besides components, these shops also sell tools and general accessories, usually have convenient opening hours, charge lower prices, and can often be found close to home. Some accessory shops have parts counters where components needed for almost any repair job can be purchased or ordered.

Motor factors

Good factors will stock all the more important components which wear out comparatively quickly, and can sometimes supply individual components needed for the overhaul of a larger assembly (eg, brake seals and hydraulic parts, bearing shells, pistons, valves). They may also handle work such as cylinder block reboring, crankshaft regrinding, etc.

Tyre and exhaust specialists

These outlets may be independent, or members of a local or national chain. They frequently offer competitive prices when compared with a main dealer or local garage, but it will pay to obtain several quotes before making a decision. When researching prices, also ask what extras may be added – for instance fitting a new valve and balancing the wheel are both commonly charged on top of the price of a new tyre.

Other sources

Beware of parts or materials obtained from market stalls, car boot sales or similar outlets. Such items are not invariably sub-standard, but there is little chance of compensation if they do prove unsatisfactory. In the case of safety-critical components such as brake pads, there is the risk not only of financial loss, but also of an accident causing injury or death.

Second-hand components or assemblies obtained from a car breaker can be a good buy in some circumstances, but this sort of purchase is best made by the experienced DIY mechanic.

Jacking and vehicle support

⚠️ **Warning: The jack supplied with the vehicle should only be used for changing a wheel. Never work under the vehicle or start the engine while this jack is being used as the only means of support.**

The vehicle should be on level ground. Place the gear lever in Park, if you have an automatic, or Reverse if you have a manual transmission. Apply the handbrake.

Position the jack under the vehicle beneath the appropriate jacking point. The front lifting point is accessed from behind the front wheel – on 2000 and earlier models, it is beneath the front suspension control arm rear mounting bush, and on 2001 and later models, it is beneath the control arm rear mounting bolt. The rear lifting point is beneath the rear suspension trailing arm, and is accessed from in front of the rear wheel **(see illustrations)**.

Raise the jack until the wheels clear the ground. Axle stands must also be positioned beneath the jacking points, by raising one side of the vehicle until the axle stand can be positioned beneath the jacking point on the other side.

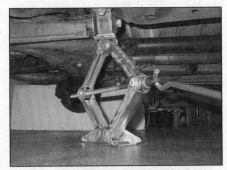

Front jacking point (place the jack under the control arm rear mounting bush) – 2000 and earlier models

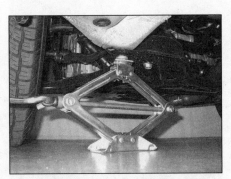

Front jacking point (place the jack under the control arm rear mounting bolt) – 2001 and later models

Rear jacking point (place the jack under the rear trailing arm) – all models

Introduction

A selection of good tools is a fundamental requirement for anyone contemplating the maintenance and repair of a motor vehicle. For the owner who does not possess any, their purchase will prove a considerable expense, offsetting some of the savings made by doing-it-yourself. However, provided that the tools purchased meet the relevant national safety standards and are of good quality, they will last for many years and prove an extremely worthwhile investment.

To help the average owner to decide which tools are needed to carry out the various tasks detailed in this manual, we have compiled three lists of tools under the following headings: *Maintenance and minor repair, Repair and overhaul*, and *Special*. Newcomers to practical mechanics should start off with the *Maintenance and minor repair* tool kit, and confine themselves to the simpler jobs around the vehicle. Then, as confidence and experience grow, more difficult tasks can be undertaken, with extra tools being purchased as, and when, they are needed. In this way, a *Maintenance and minor repair* tool kit can be built up into a *Repair and overhaul* tool kit over a considerable period of time, without any major cash outlays. The experienced do-it-yourselfer will have a tool kit good enough for most repair and overhaul procedures, and will add tools from the *Special* category when it is felt that the expense is justified by the amount of use to which these tools will be put.

Maintenance and minor repair tool kit

The tools given in this list should be considered as a minimum requirement if routine maintenance, servicing and minor repair operations are to be undertaken. We recommend the purchase of combination spanners (ring one end, open-ended the other); although more expensive than open-ended ones, they do give the advantages of both types of spanner.

☐ *Combination spanners:*
  Metric - 8 to 19 mm inclusive
☐ *Adjustable spanner - 35 mm jaw (approx.)*
☐ *Spark plug spanner (with rubber insert) - petrol models*
☐ *Spark plug gap adjustment tool - petrol models*
☐ *Set of feeler gauges*
☐ *Brake bleed nipple spanner*
☐ *Screwdrivers:*
  Flat blade - 100 mm long x 6 mm dia
  Cross blade - 100 mm long x 6 mm dia
  Torx - various sizes (not all vehicles)
☐ *Combination pliers*
☐ *Hacksaw (junior)*
☐ *Tyre pump*
☐ *Tyre pressure gauge*
☐ *Oil can*
☐ *Oil filter removal tool*
☐ *Fine emery cloth*
☐ *Wire brush (small)*
☐ *Funnel (medium size)*
☐ *Sump drain plug key (not all vehicles)*

Repair and overhaul tool kit

These tools are virtually essential for anyone undertaking any major repairs to a motor vehicle, and are additional to those given in the *Maintenance and minor repair* list. Included in this list is a comprehensive set of sockets. Although these are expensive, they will be found invaluable as they are so versatile - particularly if various drives are included in the set. We recommend the half-inch square-drive type, as this can be used with most proprietary torque wrenches.

The tools in this list will sometimes need to be supplemented by tools from the *Special* list:

☐ *Sockets (or box spanners) to cover range in previous list (including Torx sockets)*
☐ *Reversible ratchet drive (for use with sockets)*
☐ *Extension piece, 250 mm (for use with sockets)*
☐ *Universal joint (for use with sockets)*
☐ *Flexible handle or sliding T "breaker bar" (for use with sockets)*
☐ *Torque wrench (for use with sockets)*
☐ *Self-locking grips*
☐ *Ball pein hammer*
☐ *Soft-faced mallet (plastic or rubber)*
☐ *Screwdrivers:*
  Flat blade - long & sturdy, short (chubby), and narrow (electrician's) types
  Cross blade – long & sturdy, and short (chubby) types
☐ *Pliers:*
  Long-nosed
  Side cutters (electrician's)
  Circlip (internal and external)
☐ *Cold chisel - 25 mm*
☐ *Scriber*
☐ *Scraper*
☐ *Centre-punch*
☐ *Pin punch*
☐ *Hacksaw*
☐ *Brake hose clamp*
☐ *Brake/clutch bleeding kit*
☐ *Selection of twist drills*
☐ *Steel rule/straight-edge*
☐ *Allen keys (inc. splined/Torx type)*
☐ *Selection of files*
☐ *Wire brush*
☐ *Axle stands*
☐ *Jack (strong trolley or hydraulic type)*
☐ *Light with extension lead*
☐ *Universal electrical multi-meter*

Sockets and reversible ratchet drive

Brake bleeding kit

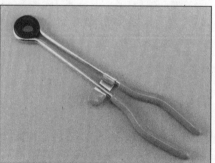
Hose clamp

Angular-tightening gauge

Torx key, socket and bit

Special tools

The tools in this list are those which are not used regularly, are expensive to buy, or which need to be used in accordance with their manufacturers' instructions. Unless relatively difficult mechanical jobs are undertaken frequently, it will not be economic to buy many of these tools. Where this is the case, you could consider clubbing together with friends (or joining a motorists' club) to make a joint purchase, or borrowing the tools against a deposit from a local garage or tool hire specialist. It is worth noting that many of the larger DIY superstores now carry a large range of special tools for hire at modest rates.

The following list contains only those tools and instruments freely available to the public, and not those special tools produced by the vehicle manufacturer specifically for its dealer network. You will find occasional references to these manufacturers' special tools in the text of this manual. Generally, an alternative method of doing the job without the vehicle manufacturers' special tool is given. However, sometimes there is no alternative to using them. Where this is the case and the relevant tool cannot be bought or borrowed, you will have to entrust the work to a dealer.

- ☐ Angular-tightening gauge
- ☐ Valve spring compressor
- ☐ Valve grinding tool
- ☐ Piston ring compressor
- ☐ Piston ring removal/installation tool
- ☐ Cylinder bore hone
- ☐ Balljoint separator
- ☐ Coil spring compressors (where applicable)
- ☐ Two/three-legged hub and bearing puller
- ☐ Impact screwdriver
- ☐ Micrometer and/or vernier calipers
- ☐ Dial gauge
- ☐ Stroboscopic timing light
- ☐ Dwell angle meter/tachometer
- ☐ Fault code reader
- ☐ Cylinder compression gauge
- ☐ Hand-operated vacuum pump and gauge
- ☐ Clutch plate alignment set
- ☐ Brake shoe steady spring cup removal tool
- ☐ Bush and bearing removal/installation set
- ☐ Stud extractors
- ☐ Tap and die set
- ☐ Lifting tackle
- ☐ Trolley jack

Buying tools

Reputable motor accessory shops and superstores often offer excellent quality tools at discount prices, so it pays to shop around.

Remember, you don't have to buy the most expensive items on the shelf, but it is always advisable to steer clear of the very cheap tools. Beware of 'bargains' offered on market stalls or at car boot sales. There are plenty of good tools around at reasonable prices, but always aim to purchase items which meet the relevant national safety standards. If in doubt, ask the proprietor or manager of the shop for advice before making a purchase.

Care and maintenance of tools

Having purchased a reasonable tool kit, it is necessary to keep the tools in a clean and serviceable condition. After use, always wipe off any dirt, grease and metal particles using a clean, dry cloth, before putting the tools away. Never leave them lying around after they have been used. A simple tool rack on the garage or workshop wall for items such as screwdrivers and pliers is a good idea. Store all normal spanners and sockets in a metal box. Any measuring instruments, gauges, meters, etc, must be carefully stored where they cannot be damaged or become rusty.

Take a little care when tools are used. Hammer heads inevitably become marked, and screwdrivers lose the keen edge on their blades from time to time. A little timely attention with emery cloth or a file will soon restore items like this to a good finish.

Working facilities

Not to be forgotten when discussing tools is the workshop itself. If anything more than routine maintenance is to be carried out, a suitable working area becomes essential.

It is appreciated that many an owner-mechanic is forced by circumstances to remove an engine or similar item without the benefit of a garage or workshop. Having done this, any repairs should always be done under the cover of a roof.

Wherever possible, any dismantling should be done on a clean, flat workbench or table at a suitable working height.

Any workbench needs a vice; one with a jaw opening of 100 mm is suitable for most jobs. As mentioned previously, some clean dry storage space is also required for tools, as well as for any lubricants, cleaning fluids, touch-up paints etc, which become necessary.

Another item which may be required, and which has a much more general usage, is an electric drill with a chuck capacity of at least 8 mm. This, together with a good range of twist drills, is virtually essential for fitting accessories.

Last, but not least, always keep a supply of old newspapers and clean, lint-free rags available, and try to keep any working area as clean as possible.

Micrometers

Dial test indicator ("dial gauge")

Strap wrench

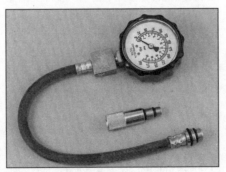

Compression tester

Fault code reader

This is a guide to getting your vehicle through the MOT test. Obviously it will not be possible to examine the vehicle to the same standard as the professional MOT tester. However, working through the following checks will enable you to identify any problem areas before submitting the vehicle for the test.

It has only been possible to summarise the test requirements here, based on the regulations in force at the time of printing. Test standards are becoming increasingly stringent, although there are some exemptions for older vehicles.

An assistant will be needed to help carry out some of these checks.

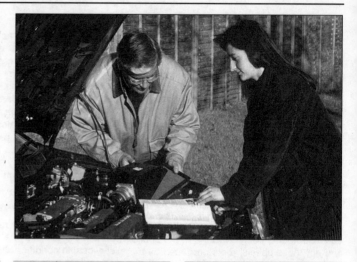

The checks have been sub-divided into four categories, as follows:

1 Checks carried out **FROM THE DRIVER'S SEAT**

2 Checks carried out **WITH THE VEHICLE ON THE GROUND**

3 Checks carried out **WITH THE VEHICLE RAISED AND THE WHEELS FREE TO TURN**

4 Checks carried out on **YOUR VEHICLE'S EXHAUST EMISSION SYSTEM**

---

1 Checks carried out **FROM THE DRIVER'S SEAT**

Handbrake

☐ Test the operation of the handbrake. Excessive travel (too many clicks) indicates incorrect brake or cable adjustment.

☐ Check that the handbrake cannot be released by tapping the lever sideways. Check the security of the lever mountings.

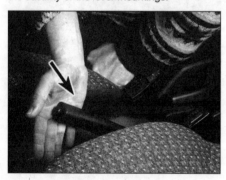

Footbrake

☐ Depress the brake pedal and check that it does not creep down to the floor, indicating a master cylinder fault. Release the pedal, wait a few seconds, then depress it again. If the pedal travels nearly to the floor before firm resistance is felt, brake adjustment or repair is necessary. If the pedal feels spongy, there is air in the hydraulic system which must be removed by bleeding.

☐ Check that the brake pedal is secure and in good condition. Check also for signs of fluid leaks on the pedal, floor or carpets, which would indicate failed seals in the brake master cylinder.

☐ Check the servo unit (when applicable) by operating the brake pedal several times, then keeping the pedal depressed and starting the engine. As the engine starts, the pedal will move down slightly. If not, the vacuum hose or the servo itself may be faulty.

Steering wheel and column

☐ Examine the steering wheel for fractures or looseness of the hub, spokes or rim.

☐ Move the steering wheel from side to side and then up and down. Check that the steering wheel is not loose on the column, indicating wear or a loose retaining nut. Continue moving the steering wheel as before, but also turn it slightly from left to right.

☐ Check that the steering wheel is not loose on the column, and that there is no abnormal

movement of the steering wheel, indicating wear in the column support bearings or couplings.

Windscreen, mirrors and sunvisor

☐ The windscreen must be free of cracks or other significant damage within the driver's field of view. (Small stone chips are acceptable.) Rear view mirrors must be secure, intact, and capable of being adjusted.

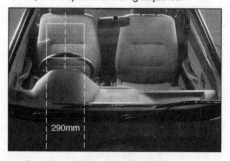

290mm

☐ The driver's sunvisor must be capable of being stored in the "up" position.

Seat belts and seats

Note: *The following checks are applicable to all seat belts, front and rear.*

☐ Examine the webbing of all the belts (including rear belts if fitted) for cuts, serious fraying or deterioration. Fasten and unfasten each belt to check the buckles. If applicable, check the retracting mechanism. Check the security of all seat belt mountings accessible from inside the vehicle.

☐ Seat belts with pre-tensioners, once activated, have a "flag" or similar showing on the seat belt stalk. This, in itself, is not a reason for test failure.

☐ The front seats themselves must be securely attached and the backrests must lock in the upright position.

Doors

☐ Both front doors must be able to be opened and closed from outside and inside, and must latch securely when closed.

2 Checks carried out WITH THE VEHICLE ON THE GROUND

Vehicle identification

☐ Number plates must be in good condition, secure and legible, with letters and numbers correctly spaced – spacing at (A) should be at least twice that at (B).

☐ The VIN plate and/or homologation plate must be legible.

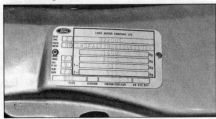

Electrical equipment

☐ Switch on the ignition and check the operation of the horn.

☐ Check the windscreen washers and wipers, examining the wiper blades; renew damaged or perished blades. Also check the operation of the stop-lights.

☐ Check the operation of the sidelights and number plate lights. The lenses and reflectors must be secure, clean and undamaged.

☐ Check the operation and alignment of the headlights. The headlight reflectors must not be tarnished and the lenses must be undamaged.

☐ Switch on the ignition and check the operation of the direction indicators (including the instrument panel tell-tale) and the hazard warning lights. Operation of the sidelights and stop-lights must not affect the indicators - if it does, the cause is usually a bad earth at the rear light cluster.

☐ Check the operation of the rear foglight(s), including the warning light on the instrument panel or in the switch.

☐ The ABS warning light must illuminate in accordance with the manufacturers' design. For most vehicles, the ABS warning light should illuminate when the ignition is switched on, and (if the system is operating properly) extinguish after a few seconds. Refer to the owner's handbook.

Footbrake

☐ Examine the master cylinder, brake pipes and servo unit for leaks, loose mountings, corrosion or other damage.

☐ The fluid reservoir must be secure and the fluid level must be between the upper (A) and lower (B) markings.

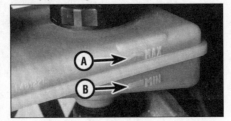

☐ Inspect both front brake flexible hoses for cracks or deterioration of the rubber. Turn the steering from lock to lock, and ensure that the hoses do not contact the wheel, tyre, or any part of the steering or suspension mechanism. With the brake pedal firmly depressed, check the hoses for bulges or leaks under pressure.

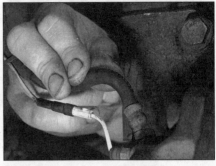

Steering and suspension

☐ Have your assistant turn the steering wheel from side to side slightly, up to the point where the steering gear just begins to transmit this movement to the roadwheels. Check for excessive free play between the steering wheel and the steering gear, indicating wear or insecurity of the steering column joints, the column-to-steering gear coupling, or the steering gear itself.

☐ Have your assistant turn the steering wheel more vigorously in each direction, so that the roadwheels just begin to turn. As this is done, examine all the steering joints, linkages, fittings and attachments. Renew any component that shows signs of wear or damage. On vehicles with power steering, check the security and condition of the steering pump, drivebelt and hoses.

☐ Check that the vehicle is standing level, and at approximately the correct ride height.

Shock absorbers

☐ Depress each corner of the vehicle in turn, then release it. The vehicle should rise and then settle in its normal position. If the vehicle continues to rise and fall, the shock absorber is defective. A shock absorber which has seized will also cause the vehicle to fail.

Exhaust system

☐ Start the engine. With your assistant holding a rag over the tailpipe, check the entire system for leaks. Repair or renew leaking sections.

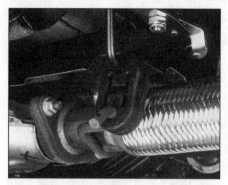

3 Checks carried out
WITH THE VEHICLE RAISED AND THE WHEELS FREE TO TURN

Jack up the front and rear of the vehicle, and securely support it on axle stands. Position the stands clear of the suspension assemblies. Ensure that the wheels are clear of the ground and that the steering can be turned from lock to lock.

Steering mechanism

☐ Have your assistant turn the steering from lock to lock. Check that the steering turns smoothly, and that no part of the steering mechanism, including a wheel or tyre, fouls any brake hose or pipe or any part of the body structure.
☐ Examine the steering rack rubber gaiters for damage or insecurity of the retaining clips. If power steering is fitted, check for signs of damage or leakage of the fluid hoses, pipes or connections. Also check for excessive stiffness or binding of the steering, a missing split pin or locking device, or severe corrosion of the body structure within 30 cm of any steering component attachment point.

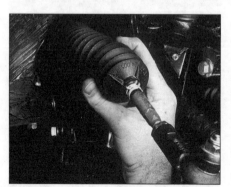

Front and rear suspension and wheel bearings

☐ Starting at the front right-hand side, grasp the roadwheel at the 3 o'clock and 9 o'clock positions and rock gently but firmly. Check for free play or insecurity at the wheel bearings, suspension balljoints, or suspension mountings, pivots and attachments.
☐ Now grasp the wheel at the 12 o'clock and 6 o'clock positions and repeat the previous inspection. Spin the wheel, and check for roughness or tightness of the front wheel bearing.

☐ If excess free play is suspected at a component pivot point, this can be confirmed by using a large screwdriver or similar tool and levering between the mounting and the component attachment. This will confirm whether the wear is in the pivot bush, its retaining bolt, or in the mounting itself (the bolt holes can often become elongated).

☐ Carry out all the above checks at the other front wheel, and then at both rear wheels.

Springs and shock absorbers

☐ Examine the suspension struts (when applicable) for serious fluid leakage, corrosion, or damage to the casing. Also check the security of the mounting points.
☐ If coil springs are fitted, check that the spring ends locate in their seats, and that the spring is not corroded, cracked or broken.
☐ If leaf springs are fitted, check that all leaves are intact, that the axle is securely attached to each spring, and that there is no deterioration of the spring eye mountings, bushes, and shackles.

☐ The same general checks apply to vehicles fitted with other suspension types, such as torsion bars, hydraulic displacer units, etc. Ensure that all mountings and attachments are secure, that there are no signs of excessive wear, corrosion or damage, and (on hydraulic types) that there are no fluid leaks or damaged pipes.
☐ Inspect the shock absorbers for signs of serious fluid leakage. Check for wear of the mounting bushes or attachments, or damage to the body of the unit.

Driveshafts (fwd vehicles only)

☐ Rotate each front wheel in turn and inspect the constant velocity joint gaiters for splits or damage. Also check that each driveshaft is straight and undamaged.

Braking system

☐ If possible without dismantling, check brake pad wear and disc condition. Ensure that the friction lining material has not worn excessively, (A) and that the discs are not fractured, pitted, scored or badly worn (B).

☐ Examine all the rigid brake pipes underneath the vehicle, and the flexible hose(s) at the rear. Look for corrosion, chafing or insecurity of the pipes, and for signs of bulging under pressure, chafing, splits or deterioration of the flexible hoses.
☐ Look for signs of fluid leaks at the brake calipers or on the brake backplates. Repair or renew leaking components.
☐ Slowly spin each wheel, while your assistant depresses and releases the footbrake. Ensure that each brake is operating and does not bind when the pedal is released.

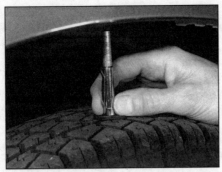

☐ Examine the handbrake mechanism, checking for frayed or broken cables, excessive corrosion, or wear or insecurity of the linkage. Check that the mechanism works on each relevant wheel, and releases fully, without binding.

☐ It is not possible to test brake efficiency without special equipment, but a road test can be carried out later to check that the vehicle pulls up in a straight line.

Fuel and exhaust systems

☐ Inspect the fuel tank (including the filler cap), fuel pipes, hoses and unions. All components must be secure and free from leaks.

☐ Examine the exhaust system over its entire length, checking for any damaged, broken or missing mountings, security of the retaining clamps and rust or corrosion.

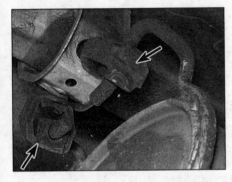

Wheels and tyres

☐ Examine the sidewalls and tread area of each tyre in turn. Check for cuts, tears, lumps, bulges, separation of the tread, and exposure of the ply or cord due to wear or damage. Check that the tyre bead is correctly seated on the wheel rim, that the valve is sound and properly seated, and that the wheel is not distorted or damaged.

☐ Check that the tyres are of the correct size for the vehicle, that they are of the same size

and type on each axle, and that the pressures are correct.

☐ Check the tyre tread depth. The legal minimum at the time of writing is 1.6 mm over at least three-quarters of the tread width. Abnormal tread wear may indicate incorrect front wheel alignment.

Body corrosion

☐ Check the condition of the entire vehicle structure for signs of corrosion in load-bearing areas. (These include chassis box sections, side sills, cross-members, pillars, and all suspension, steering, braking system and seat belt mountings and anchorages.) Any corrosion which has seriously reduced the thickness of a load-bearing area is likely to cause the vehicle to fail. In this case professional repairs are likely to be needed.

☐ Damage or corrosion which causes sharp or otherwise dangerous edges to be exposed will also cause the vehicle to fail.

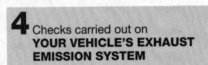

4 Checks carried out on **YOUR VEHICLE'S EXHAUST EMISSION SYSTEM**

Petrol models

☐ The engine should be warmed up, and running well (ignition system in good order, air filter element clean, etc).

☐ Before testing, run the engine at around 2500 rpm for 20 seconds. Let the engine drop to idle, and watch for smoke from the exhaust. If the idle speed is too high, or if dense blue or black smoke emerges for more than 5 seconds, the vehicle will fail. Typically, blue smoke signifies oil burning (engine wear); black smoke means unburnt fuel (dirty air cleaner element, or other fuel system fault).

☐ An exhaust gas analyser for measuring carbon monoxide (CO) and hydrocarbons (HC) is now needed. If one cannot be hired or borrowed, have a local garage perform the check.

CO emissions (mixture)

☐ The MOT tester has access to the CO limits for all vehicles. The CO level is measured at idle speed, and at 'fast idle' (2500 to 3000 rpm). The following limits are given as a general guide:
  At idle speed – Less than 0.5% CO
  At 'fast idle' – Less than 0.3% CO
  Lambda reading – 0.97 to 1.03
☐ If the CO level is too high, this may point to poor maintenance, a fuel injection system problem, faulty lambda (oxygen) sensor or catalytic converter. Try an injector cleaning treatment, and check the vehicle's ECU for fault codes.

HC emissions

☐ The MOT tester has access to HC limits for all vehicles. The HC level is measured at 'fast idle' (2500 to 3000 rpm). The following limits are given as a general guide:
  At 'fast idle' – Less then 200 ppm
☐ Excessive HC emissions are typically caused by oil being burnt (worn engine), or by a blocked crankcase ventilation system ('breather'). If the engine oil is old and thin, an oil change may help. If the engine is running badly, check the vehicle's ECU for fault codes.

Diesel models

☐ The only emission test for diesel engines is measuring exhaust smoke density, using a calibrated smoke meter. The test involves accelerating the engine at least 3 times to its maximum unloaded speed.

Note: *On engines with a timing belt, it is VITAL that the belt is in good condition before the test is carried out.*

☐ With the engine warmed up, it is first purged by running at around 2500 rpm for 20 seconds. A governor check is then carried out, by slowly accelerating the engine to its maximum speed. After this, the smoke meter is connected, and the engine is accelerated quickly to maximum speed three times. If the smoke density is less than the limits given below, the vehicle will pass:
  Non-turbo vehicles: 2.5m-1
  Turbocharged vehicles: 3.0m-1
☐ If excess smoke is produced, try fitting a new air cleaner element, or using an injector cleaning treatment. If the engine is running badly, where applicable, check the vehicle's ECU for fault codes. Also check the vehicle's EGR system, where applicable. At high mileages, the injectors may require professional attention.

Engine

- ☐ Engine will not rotate when attempting to start
- ☐ Engine rotates but will not start
- ☐ Engine hard to start when cold
- ☐ Engine hard to start when hot
- ☐ Starter motor noisy or excessively rough in engagement
- ☐ Engine starts but stops immediately
- ☐ Oil puddle under engine
- ☐ Engine 'lopes' while idling or idles erratically
- ☐ Engine misses at idle speed
- ☐ Engine misses throughout driving speed range
- ☐ Engine stumbles on acceleration
- ☐ Engine surges while holding accelerator steady
- ☐ Engine stalls
- ☐ Engine lacks power
- ☐ Engine backfires
- ☐ Pinking or knocking engine sounds during acceleration or uphill
- ☐ Engine runs with oil pressure light on
- ☐ Engine continues to run after switching off

Engine electrical system

- ☐ Battery will not hold a charge
- ☐ Alternator light fails to go out
- ☐ Alternator light fails to come on when key is turned on

Fuel system

- ☐ Excessive fuel consumption
- ☐ Fuel leakage and/or fuel odour

Cooling system

- ☐ Overheating
- ☐ Overcooling
- ☐ External coolant leakage
- ☐ Internal coolant leakage
- ☐ Coolant loss
- ☐ Poor coolant circulation

Clutch

- ☐ Pedal travels to floor – no pressure or very little resistance
- ☐ Unable to select gears
- ☐ Clutch slips (engine speed increases with no increase in vehicle speed)
- ☐ Grabbing (juddering) as clutch is engaged
- ☐ Transmission rattling (clicking)
- ☐ Noise in clutch area
- ☐ Clutch pedal stays on floor
- ☐ High pedal effort

Manual transmission

- ☐ Knocking noise at low speeds
- ☐ Noise most pronounced when turning
- ☐ Clunk on acceleration or deceleration
- ☐ Clicking noise in turns
- ☐ Vibration
- ☐ Noisy in neutral with engine running
- ☐ Noisy in one particular gear
- ☐ Noisy in all gears
- ☐ Slips out of gear
- ☐ Leaks lubricant
- ☐ Hard to gearchange

Automatic transmission

- ☐ Fluid leakage
- ☐ Transmission fluid brown or has burned smell
- ☐ General selector mechanism problems
- ☐ Transmission will not downshift with accelerator pedal pressed to the floor
- ☐ Engine will start in gears other than Park or Neutral
- ☐ Transmission slips, shifts roughly, is noisy or has no drive in forward or reverse gears

Driveshafts

- ☐ Clicking noise in turns
- ☐ Shudder or vibration during acceleration
- ☐ Vibration at motorway speeds

Brakes

- ☐ Vehicle pulls to one side during braking
- ☐ Noise (high-pitched squeal when the brakes are applied)
- ☐ Brake roughness or chatter (pedal pulsates)
- ☐ Excessive pedal effort required to stop vehicle
- ☐ Excessive brake pedal travel
- ☐ Dragging brakes
- ☐ Grabbing or uneven braking action
- ☐ Brake pedal feels spongy when depressed
- ☐ Brake pedal travels to the floor with little resistance
- ☐ Handbrake does not hold

Suspension and steering systems

- ☐ Vehicle pulls to one side
- ☐ Abnormal or excessive tyre wear
- ☐ Wheel makes a thumping noise
- ☐ Shimmy, shake or vibration
- ☐ Hard steering
- ☐ Poor self-centring
- ☐ Abnormal noise at the front end
- ☐ Wander or poor steering stability
- ☐ Erratic steering when braking
- ☐ Excessive pitching and/or rolling around corners or during braking
- ☐ Suspension bottoms
- ☐ Excessive tyre wear on outside edge
- ☐ Excessive tyre wear on inside edge
- ☐ Tyre tread worn in one place
- ☐ Excessive play or looseness in steering system
- ☐ Rattling or clicking noise in steering gear

Introduction

This section provides an easy reference guide to the more common problems that may occur during the operation of your vehicle. These problems and their possible causes are grouped under headings denoting various components or systems, such as Engine, Cooling system, etc. They also refer you to the chapter and/or section that deals with the problem.

Remember that successful troubleshooting is not a mysterious black art practised only by professional mechanics. It is simply the result of the right knowledge combined with an intelligent, systematic approach to the problem. Always work by a process of elimination, starting with the simplest solution and working through to the most complex – and never overlook the obvious. Anyone can run the fuel tank dry or leave the lights on overnight, so don't assume that you are exempt from such oversights.

Finally, always establish a clear idea of why a problem has occurred and take steps to ensure that it doesn't happen again. If the electrical system fails because of a poor connection, check the other connections in the system to make sure that they don't fail as well. If a particular fuse continues to blow, find out why – don't just renew one fuse after another. Remember, failure of a small component can often be indicative of potential failure or incorrect functioning of a more important component or system.

Diesel engine troubleshooting

The majority of starting problems on small diesel engines are electrical in origin. The mechanic who is familiar with petrol engines but less so with diesel may be inclined to view the diesel's injectors and pump in the same light as the spark plugs and distributor, but this is generally a mistake.

When investigating complaints of difficult starting for someone else, make sure that the correct starting procedure is understood and is being followed. Some drivers are unaware of the significance of the preheating warning light – many modern engines are sufficiently forgiving for this not to matter in mild weather, but with the onset of winter, problems begin.

As a rule of thumb, if the engine is difficult to start but runs well when it has finally got going, the problem is electrical (battery, starter motor or preheating system). If poor performance is combined with difficult starting, the problem is likely to be in the fuel system. The low-pressure (supply) side of the fuel system should be checked before suspecting the injectors and high-pressure pump. The most common fuel supply problem is air getting into the system, and any pipe from the fuel tank forwards must be scrutinised if air leakage is suspected. Normally the pump is the last item to suspect, since unless it has been tampered with, there is no reason for it to be at fault.

Engine

Engine will not rotate when attempting to start

- [ ] Battery terminal connections loose or corroded (Chapters 1A or 1B).
- [ ] Battery discharged or faulty (Chapters 1A or 1B).
- [ ] Automatic transmission not completely engaged in Park (Chapter 7B) or clutch pedal not completely depressed (Chapter 8).
- [ ] Broken, loose or disconnected wiring in the starting circuit (Chapters 5 and 12).
- [ ] Starter motor pinion jammed in flywheel ring gear (Chapter 5).
- [ ] Starter solenoid faulty (Chapter 5).
- [ ] Starter motor faulty (Chapter 5).
- [ ] Ignition switch faulty (Chapter 12).
- [ ] Starter pinion or flywheel teeth worn or broken (Chapter 5).

Engine rotates but will not start

- [ ] Fuel tank empty.
- [ ] Battery discharged (engine rotates slowly) (Chapter 5).
- [ ] Battery terminal connections loose or corroded (Chapters 1A or 1B).
- [ ] Leaking fuel injector(s), faulty fuel pump, pressure regulator, etc (Chapter 4A or 4B).
- [ ] Broken or stripped timing belt (Chapter 2A or 2C).
- [ ] Ignition components damp or damaged (Chapter 5).
- [ ] Worn, faulty or incorrectly gapped spark plugs (Chapter 1A).
- [ ] Broken, loose or disconnected wiring in the starting circuit (Chapter 5).
- [ ] Broken, loose or disconnected wires at the ignition coils or faulty coils (Chapter 5).
- [ ] Defective MAF sensor (see Chapter 6A or 6B).
- [ ] Defective fuel injection pump or fuel injector (diesel) (Chapter 4B).
- [ ] Contaminated fuel.

Engine hard to start when cold

- [ ] Battery discharged or low (Chapters 1A or 1B).
- [ ] Malfunctioning fuel system (Chapter 4A or 4B).
- [ ] Faulty coolant temperature sensor or intake air temperature sensor (Chapter 6A or 6B).
- [ ] Injector(s) leaking (Chapter 4B).
- [ ] Faulty ignition system (Chapter 5).
- [ ] Defective MAF sensor (see Chapter 6A or 6B).
- [ ] Defective fuel injection pump or fuel injector (diesel) (Chapter 4B).

Engine hard to start when hot

- [ ] Air filter clogged (Chapters 1A or 1B).
- [ ] Fuel not reaching the fuel injection system (Chapter 4A or 4B).
- [ ] Corroded battery connections, especially ground (Chapters 1A or 1B).
- [ ] Faulty coolant temperature sensor or intake air temperature sensor (Chapter 6A or 6B).
- [ ] Low cylinder compression (Chapter 2D).
- [ ] Defective fuel pump or fuel injector (diesel) (Chapter 4B).

Starter motor noisy or excessively rough in engagement

- [ ] Pinion or flywheel/driveplate gear teeth worn or broken (Chapter 5).
- [ ] Starter motor mounting bolts loose or missing (Chapter 5).

Engine starts but stops immediately

- [ ] Loose or faulty electrical connections at distributor, coil or alternator (Chapter 5).
- [ ] Insufficient fuel reaching the fuel injector(s) (Chapters 1A or 1B and 4A or 4B).
- [ ] Vacuum leak at the gasket between the intake manifold and throttle body (Chapters 1A or 1B and 4A or 4B).
- [ ] Intake air leaks, broken vacuum pipes (see Chapter 4A or 4B).
- [ ] Defective fuel pump or fuel injector (diesel) (Chapter 4B).
- [ ] Contaminated fuel.

Oil puddle under engine

- [ ] Sump gasket and/or sump drain bolt washer leaking (Chapter 2A, 2B or 2C).
- [ ] Oil pressure sending unit leaking (Chapter 2A, 2B or 2C).
- [ ] Valve covers leaking (Chapter 2A, 2B or 2C).
- [ ] Engine oil seals leaking (Chapter 2A, 2B or 2C).
- [ ] Oil pump housing leaking (Chapter 2A, 2B or 2C).

Engine 'lopes' while idling or idles erratically

- [ ] Vacuum leakage (Chapters 2A, 2B or 2C and 4A or 4B).
- [ ] Leaking EGR valve (Chapter 6A or 6B).
- [ ] Air filter clogged (Chapters 1A or 1B).
- [ ] Fuel pump delivering insufficient fuel to the fuel injection system (Chapter 4A or 4B).
- [ ] Leaking head gasket (Chapter 2A, 2B or 2C).
- [ ] Timing belt and/or sprockets worn (Chapter 2A or 2C).
- [ ] Camshaft lobes worn (Chapter 2A, 2B or 2C).
- [ ] Defective fuel pump or fuel injector (diesel) (Chapter 4B).

Engine misses at idle speed

- [ ] Spark plugs worn or not gapped properly (Chapter 1A).
- [ ] Faulty HT leads (Chapter 1A).
- [ ] Vacuum leaks (Chapters 2A, 2B or 2C and 4A or 4B).
- [ ] Uneven or low compression (Chapter 2D).
- [ ] Problem with the fuel injection system (Chapter 4A or 4B).
- [ ] Faulty ignition coils (Chapter 5).
- [ ] Defective fuel pump or fuel injector (diesel) (Chapter 4B).

Engine (continued)

Engine misses throughout driving speed range

- ☐ Fuel filter clogged and/or impurities in the fuel system (Chapters 1A or 1B).
- ☐ Low fuel output at the fuel injector(s) (Chapter 4A or 4B).
- ☐ Faulty or incorrectly gapped spark plugs (Chapter 1A).
- ☐ Defective HT leads (Chapters 1A or 5).
- ☐ Faulty emission system components (Chapter 6A or 6B).
- ☐ Low or uneven cylinder compression pressures (Chapter 2D).
- ☐ Weak or faulty ignition system (Chapter 5).
- ☐ Vacuum leak in fuel injection system, throttle body, intake manifold or vacuum hoses (Chapter 4A or 4B).
- ☐ Defective fuel pump or fuel injector (diesel) (Chapter 4B).

Engine stumbles on acceleration

- ☐ Spark plugs fouled (Chapter 1A).
- ☐ Problem with fuel injection system (Chapter 4A or 4B).
- ☐ Fuel filter clogged (Chapters 1A or 1B and 4A or 4B).
- ☐ Intake manifold leak (Chapters 2A, 2B or 2C and 4A or 4B).
- ☐ EGR system malfunction (Chapter 6A or 6B).

Engine surges while holding accelerator steady

- ☐ Intake air/vacuum leak (Chapter 4A or 4B).
- ☐ Problem with fuel injection system (Chapter 4A or 4B).
- ☐ Problem with the emissions control system (Chapter 6A or 6B).

Engine stalls

- ☐ Idle speed incorrect (Chapter 4A or 4B).
- ☐ Fuel filter clogged and/or water and impurities in the fuel system (Chapters 1A or 1B and 4A or 4B).
- ☐ Faulty emissions system components (Chapter 6A or 6B).
- ☐ Faulty or incorrectly gapped spark plugs (Chapter 1A).
- ☐ Faulty HT leads (Chapter 1A).
- ☐ Vacuum leak in the fuel injection system, intake manifold or vacuum hoses (Chapters 2A, 2B or 2C and 4A or 4B).
- ☐ Defective fuel pump or fuel injector (diesel) (Chapter 4B).

Engine lacks power

- ☐ Faulty HT leads or coils (Chapters 1A and 5).
- ☐ Faulty or incorrectly gapped spark plugs (Chapter 1A).
- ☐ Problem with the fuel injection system (Chapter 4A or 4B).

- ☐ Plugged air filter (Chapter 1A or 1B).
- ☐ Brakes binding (Chapter 9).
- ☐ Automatic transmission fluid level incorrect (Chapter 1A or 1B).
- ☐ Clutch slipping (Chapter 8).
- ☐ Fuel filter clogged and/or impurities in the fuel system (Chapters 1A or 1B and 4A or 4B).
- ☐ Emission control system not functioning properly (Chapter 6A or 6B).
- ☐ Low or uneven cylinder compression pressures (Chapter 2D).
- ☐ Obstructed exhaust system (Chapters 2A, 2B or 2C and 4A or 4B).
- ☐ Defective fuel pump or fuel injector (diesel) (Chapter 4B).
- ☐ Defective turbocharger or wastegate (diesel) (Chapter 4B).

Engine backfires

- ☐ Emission control system not functioning properly (Chapter 6A or 6B).
- ☐ Faulty spark plug lead or coils (Chapters 1A and 5).
- ☐ Problem with the fuel injection system (Chapter 4A or 4B).
- ☐ Vacuum leak at fuel injector(s), intake manifold, air control valve or vacuum hoses (Chapters 2A, 2B or 2C and 4A or 4B).
- ☐ Valves sticking (Chapter 2A, 2B or 2C).

Pinking or knocking engine sounds during acceleration or uphill

- ☐ Incorrect grade of fuel.
- ☐ Ignition timing incorrect (Chapter 5).
- ☐ Fuel injection system faulty (Chapter 4A or 4B).
- ☐ Improper or damaged spark plugs or leads (Chapter 1A).
- ☐ EGR valve not functioning (Chapter 6A or 6B).
- ☐ Vacuum leak (Chapters 2 and 4A or 4B).
- ☐ Knock sensor malfunctioning (Chapter 6A).

Engine runs with oil pressure light on

- ☐ Low oil level (Chapter 1A or 1B).
- ☐ Idle rpm below specification (Chapter 4A or 4B).
- ☐ Short in wiring circuit (Chapter 12).
- ☐ Faulty oil pressure sender (Chapter 2).
- ☐ Worn engine bearings and/or oil pump (Chapter 2).

Engine continues to run after switching off

- ☐ Excessive engine operating temperature (Chapter 3).
- ☐ Excessive carbon deposits on valves and pistons (Chapter 2).
- ☐ Fuel shut-off valve malfunctioning (diesel) (Chapter 4B).

Engine electrical system

Battery will not hold a charge

- ☐ Auxiliary drivebelt defective or not adjusted properly (Chapter 1A or 1B).
- ☐ Battery electrolyte level low (*Weekly checks*).
- ☐ Battery terminals loose or corroded (Chapter 1A or 1B).
- ☐ Alternator not charging properly (Chapter 5).
- ☐ Loose, broken or faulty wiring in the charging circuit (Chapter 5).
- ☐ Short in vehicle wiring (Chapter 12).
- ☐ Internally defective battery (Chapter 1A or 1B and 5).

Alternator light fails to go out

- ☐ Faulty alternator or charging circuit (Chapter 5).
- ☐ Auxiliary drivebelt defective or out of adjustment (Chapter 1A or 1B).
- ☐ Alternator voltage regulator inoperative (Chapter 5).

Alternator light fails to come on when key is turned on

- ☐ Warning light bulb defective (Chapter 12).
- ☐ Fault in the printed circuit, dash wiring or bulb holder (Chapter 12).

Fuel system

Excessive fuel consumption

- ☐ Dirty or clogged air filter element (Chapter 1A or 1B).
- ☐ Engine management problem (Chapter 6A or 6B).
- ☐ Emissions system not functioning properly (Chapter 6A or 6B).
- ☐ Fuel injection system not functioning properly (Chapter 4A or 4B).
- ☐ Low tyre pressure or incorrect tyre size (*Weekly checks*).

Fuel leakage and/or fuel odour

- ☐ Leaking fuel feed or return pipe (Chapter 1A or 1B and 4A or 4B).
- ☐ Tank overfilled.
- ☐ Problem with the evaporative emissions control system (Chapters 6).
- ☐ Problem with the fuel injection system (Chapter 4A or 4B).

Cooling system

Overheating

- [ ] Insufficient coolant in system (Chapter 1A or 1B).
- [ ] Water pump defective (Chapter 3).
- [ ] Radiator core blocked or grille restricted (Chapter 3).
- [ ] Thermostat faulty (Chapter 3).
- [ ] Electric coolant fan inoperative or blades broken (Chapter 3).
- [ ] Expansion tank cap not maintaining proper pressure (Chapter 3).
- [ ] Blown head gasket (Chapter 2A, 2B, or 2C).
- [ ] Coolant temperature sender inoperative (Chapter 3)

Overcooling

- [ ] Faulty thermostat (Chapter 3).
- [ ] Inaccurate temperature gauge sender unit (Chapter 3)

External coolant leakage

- [ ] Deteriorated/damaged hoses; loose clamps (Chapter 1A or 1B and 3).

- [ ] Water pump defective (Chapter 3).
- [ ] Leakage from radiator core or coolant reservoir tank (Chapter 3).
- [ ] Cylinder head gasket leaking (Chapter 2A, 2B, or 2C).

Internal coolant leakage

- [ ] Leaking cylinder head gasket (Chapter 2A, 2B, or 2C).
- [ ] Cracked cylinder bore or cylinder head (Chapter 2A, 2B, or 2C).

Coolant loss

- [ ] Too much coolant in system (Chapter 1A or 1B).
- [ ] Coolant boiling away because of overheating (Chapter 3).
- [ ] Internal or external leakage (Chapter 3).
- [ ] Faulty expansion tank cap (Chapter 3).

Poor coolant circulation

- [ ] Defective water pump (Chapter 3).
- [ ] Restriction in cooling system (Chapter 1A or 1B and 3).
- [ ] Thermostat sticking (Chapter 3).

Clutch

Pedal travels to floor – no pressure or very little resistance

- [ ] Hydraulic release system leaking or air in the system (Chapter 8).
- [ ] Broken release bearing or fork (Chapter 8).

Unable to select gears

- [ ] Faulty transmission (Chapter 7).
- [ ] Faulty clutch disc or pressure plate (Chapter 8).
- [ ] Faulty release lever or release bearing (Chapter 8).
- [ ] Faulty gearchange lever assembly or cables (Chapter 8).
- [ ] Faulty clutch release system.

Clutch slips (engine speed increases with no increase in vehicle speed)

- [ ] Clutch plate worn (Chapter 2A, 2B, or 2C and 8).
- [ ] Clutch plate is oil soaked by leaking rear main seal (Chapter 2A, 2B, or 2C and 8).
- [ ] Clutch plate not seated (Chapter 8).
- [ ] Warped pressure plate or flywheel (Chapter 8).
- [ ] Weak diaphragm spring in pressure plate (Chapter 8).
- [ ] Clutch plate overheated. Allow to cool.
- [ ] Piston stuck in bore of clutch slave cylinder, preventing clutch from fully engaging (Chapter 8).

Grabbing (juddering) as clutch is engaged

- [ ] Oil on clutch plate lining, burned or glazed facings (Chapter 8).
- [ ] Worn or loose engine or transmission mounts (Chapters 2 and 7).
- [ ] Worn splines on clutch plate hub (Chapter 8).
- [ ] Warped pressure plate or flywheel (Chapter 8).
- [ ] Burned or smeared resin on flywheel or pressure plate (Chapter 8).

Transmission rattling (clicking)

- [ ] Release fork loose (Chapter 8).
- [ ] Low engine idle speed.

Noise in clutch area

- [ ] Faulty bearing (Chapter 8).

Clutch pedal stays on floor

- [ ] Broken release bearing or fork (Chapter 8).
- [ ] Hydraulic release system leaking or air in the system (Chapter 8).

High pedal effort

- [ ] Piston binding in bore of slave cylinder (Chapter 8).
- [ ] Pressure plate faulty (Chapter 8).

Manual transmission

Knocking noise at low speeds

- [ ] Worn driveshaft constant velocity (CV) joints (Chapter 8).

Noise most pronounced when turning

- [ ] Differential gear noise (Chapter 7A).*

Clunk on acceleration or deceleration

- [ ] Loose engine or transmission mountings (Chapters 2 and 7A).
- [ ] Worn differential pinion shaft in case.*
- [ ] Worn or damaged driveshaft inboard CV joints (Chapter 8).

Clicking noise in turns

- [ ] Worn or damaged outboard CV joint (Chapter 8).

Vibration

- [ ] Rough wheel bearing (Chapter 10).
- [ ] Damaged driveshaft (Chapter 8).
- [ ] Out-of-round tyres (Weekly checks).

- [ ] Tyre out of balance (Chapter 1A or 1B and 10).
- [ ] Worn CV joint (Chapter 8).

Noisy in neutral with engine running

- [ ] Damaged input gear bearing (Chapter 7A).*
- [ ] Damaged clutch release bearing (Chapter 8).

Noisy in one particular gear

- [ ] Damaged or worn constant mesh gears (Chapter 7A).*
- [ ] Damaged or worn synchronisers (Chapter 7A).*
- [ ] Bent reverse fork (Chapter 7A).*
- [ ] Damaged fourth speed gear or output gear (Chapter 7A).*
- [ ] Worn or damaged reverse idler gear or idler bush (Chapter 7A).*

Noisy in all gears

- [ ] Insufficient lubricant (Chapter 7A).
- [ ] Damaged or worn bearings (Chapter 7A).*
- [ ] Worn or damaged input gear shaft and/or output gear shaft (Chapter 7A).*

Manual transmission (continued)

Slips out of gear

- ☐ Worn or improperly adjusted linkage (Chapter 7A).
- ☐ Transmission loose on engine (Chapter 7A).
- ☐ Gearchange linkage does not work freely, binds (Chapter 7A).
- ☐ Input gear bearing retainer broken or loose (Chapter 7A).*
- ☐ Worn gearchange fork (Chapter 7A).*

Leaks lubricant

- ☐ Driveshaft seals worn (Chapter 7A).
- ☐ Excessive amount of lubricant in transmission (Chapter 1A or 1B and 7A).
- ☐ Loose or broken input gear shaft bearing retainer (Chapter 7A).*

- ☐ Input gear bearing retainer O-ring and/or lip seal damaged (Chapter 7A).*
- ☐ Selector rod seal leaking (Chapter 7A).
- ☐ Vehicle speed sensor O-ring leaking (Chapter 7A).

Hard to gearchange

- ☐ Gearchange cable(s) worn (Chapter 7A).

*Although the corrective action necessary to remedy the symptoms described is beyond the scope of this manual, the above information should be helpful in isolating the cause of the condition so that the owner can communicate clearly with a professional mechanic.

Automatic transmission

Note: *Due to the complexity of the automatic transmission, it is difficult for the home mechanic to properly diagnose and service this component. For problems other than the following, the vehicle should be taken to a dealer or transmission specialist.*

Fluid leakage

- ☐ Automatic transmission fluid is a deep red colour. Fluid leaks should not be confused with engine oil, which can easily be blown onto the transmission by air flow.
- ☐ To pinpoint a leak, first remove all built-up dirt and grime from the transmission housing with degreasing agents and/or steam cleaning. Then drive the vehicle at low speeds so air flow will not blow the leak far from its source. Raise the vehicle and determine where the leak is coming from. Common areas of leakage are:
  a) *Sump (Chapter 1A or 1B and 7B).*
  b) *Dipstick tube (Chapters 1A or 1B and 7B).*
  c) *Transmission oil pipes (Chapter 7B).*
  d) *Speed sensor (Chapter 7B).*
  e) *Driveshaft oil seals (Chapter 7B).*

Transmission fluid brown or has a burned smell

- ☐ Transmission fluid overheated (Chapter 1A or 1B).

General gearchange mechanism problems

- ☐ Chapter 7, Part B, deals with checking and adjusting the gearchange cable on automatic transmissions. Common problems that may be attributed to poorly adjusted cable are:
  a) *Engine starting in gears other than Park or Neutral.*

b) *Indicator on selector lever pointing to a gear other than the one actually being used.*
c) *Vehicle moves when in Park.*
- ☐ Refer to Chapter 7B for the gearchange cable adjustment procedure.

Transmission will not downshift with accelerator pedal pressed to the floor

- ☐ The transmission is electronically controlled. This type of problem – which is caused by a malfunction in the control unit, a sensor or solenoid, or the circuit itself – is beyond the scope of this book. Take the vehicle to a dealer service department or a competent automatic transmission specialist.

Engine will start in gears other than Park or Neutral

- ☐ Transmission Range (TR) switch malfunctioning (Chapter 7B).

Transmission slips, shifts roughly, is noisy or has no drive in forward or reverse gears

- ☐ There are many probable causes for the above problems, but the home mechanic should be concerned with only one possibility – fluid level. Before taking the vehicle to a garage, check the level and condition of the fluid as described in Chapter 1A or 1B. Correct the fluid level as necessary or change the fluid and filter if needed. If the problem persists, have a professional diagnose the cause.

Driveshafts

Clicking noise in turns

- ☐ Worn or damaged outboard CV joint (Chapter 8).

Shudder or vibration during acceleration

- ☐ Excessive toe-in (Chapter 10).
- ☐ Incorrect spring heights (Chapter 10).
- ☐ Worn or damaged inboard or outboard CV joints (Chapter 8).
- ☐ Sticking inboard CV joint assembly (Chapter 8).

Vibration at motorway speeds

- ☐ Out-of-balance front wheels and/or tyres (Chapters 1A or 1B and 10).
- ☐ Out-of-round front tyres (Chapters 1A or 1B and 10).
- ☐ Worn CV joint(s) (Chapter 8).

Brakes

Note: *Before assuming that a brake problem exists, make sure that:*
a) *The tyres are in good condition and properly inflated (Weekly checks).*
b) *The front end alignment is correct (Chapter 10).*
c) *The vehicle is not loaded with weight in an unequal manner.*

Vehicle pulls to one side during braking

- [ ] Incorrect tyre pressures (*Weekly checks*).
- [ ] Front end out of alignment (have the front end aligned).
- [ ] Front, or rear, tyre sizes not matched to one another.
- [ ] Restricted brake pipes or hoses (Chapter 9).
- [ ] Malfunctioning caliper assembly (Chapter 9).
- [ ] Loose suspension parts (Chapter 10).
- [ ] Loose calipers (Chapter 9).
- [ ] Excessive wear of pad material or disc on one side.

Noise (high-pitched squeal when the brakes are applied)

- [ ] Front and/or rear disc brake pads/shoes worn out (Chapter 9).

Brake roughness or chatter (pedal pulsates)

- [ ] Excessive lateral runout (Chapter 9).
- [ ] Uneven pad wear (Chapter 9).
- [ ] Defective disc (Chapter 9).

Excessive brake pedal effort required to stop vehicle

- [ ] Malfunctioning brake servo (Chapter 9).
- [ ] Partial system failure (Chapter 9).
- [ ] Excessively worn pads (Chapter 9).
- [ ] Piston in caliper stuck or sluggish (Chapter 9).
- [ ] Brake pads contaminated with oil or grease (Chapter 9).
- [ ] Brake disc grooved and/or glazed (Chapter 1A or 1B).

- [ ] New pads fitted and not yet seated. It will take a while for the new material to seat against the disc or drum.
- [ ] Vacuum pump not operating properly (diesel) (Chapter 9).

Excessive brake pedal travel

- [ ] Partial brake system failure (Chapter 9).
- [ ] Insufficient fluid in master cylinder (Chapters 1A or 1B and 9).
- [ ] Air trapped in system (Chapters 1A or 1B and 9).

Dragging brakes

- [ ] Master cylinder pistons not returning correctly (Chapter 9).
- [ ] Restricted brakes pipes or hoses (Chapters 1A or 1B and 9).
- [ ] Incorrect handbrake adjustment (Chapter 9).
- [ ] Seized caliper (Chapter 9).

Grabbing or uneven braking action

- [ ] Malfunction of proportioning valve (Chapter 9).
- [ ] Malfunction of brake servo unit (Chapter 9).
- [ ] Binding brake pedal mechanism (Chapter 9).

Brake pedal feels spongy when depressed

- [ ] Air in hydraulic pipes (Chapter 9).
- [ ] Master cylinder mounting bolts loose (Chapter 9).
- [ ] Master cylinder defective (Chapter 9).

Brake pedal travels to the floor with little resistance

- [ ] Little or no fluid in the master cylinder reservoir caused by leaking caliper piston(s) (Chapter 9).
- [ ] Malfunctioning master cylinder (Chapter 9).
- [ ] Loose, damaged or disconnected brake pipes (Chapter 9).

Handbrake does not hold

- [ ] Handbrake linkage improperly adjusted (Chapters 1A or 1B and 9).

Suspension and steering systems

Note: *Before attempting to diagnose the suspension and steering systems, perform the following preliminary checks:*
a) *Tyres for wrong pressure and uneven wear.*
b) *Steering universal joints from the column to the rack-and-pinion for loose connectors or wear.*
c) *Front and rear suspension and the rack-and-pinion assembly for loose or damaged parts.*
d) *Out-of-round or out-of-balance tyres, bent rims and loose and/or rough wheel bearings.*

Vehicle pulls to one side

- [ ] Mismatched or uneven tyres (Chapter 10).
- [ ] Broken or sagging springs (Chapter 10).
- [ ] Wheel alignment out of specifications (Chapter 10).
- [ ] Front brake dragging (Chapter 9).

Abnormal or excessive tyre wear

- [ ] Wheel alignment out of specifications (Chapter 10).
- [ ] Sagging or broken springs (Chapter 10).
- [ ] Tyre out-of-balance (Chapter 10).
- [ ] Worn strut damper or shock absorber (Chapter 10).
- [ ] Overloaded vehicle.

Wheel makes a thumping noise

- [ ] Blister or bump on tyre (Chapter 10).
- [ ] Improper strut damper or shock absorber action (Chapter 10).

Shimmy, shake or vibration

- [ ] Tyre or wheel out-of-balance or out-of-round (Chapter 10).
- [ ] Loose or worn wheel bearings (Chapters 1A or 1B, 8 and 10).
- [ ] Worn track rod ends (Chapter 10).
- [ ] Worn balljoints (Chapters 1A or 1B and 10).
- [ ] Excessive wheel runout (Chapter 10).
- [ ] Blister or bump on tyre (Chapter 10).

Hard steering

- [ ] Defective balljoints, track rod ends or rack-and-pinion assembly (Chapter 10).
- [ ] Front wheel alignment out of specifications (Chapter 10).
- [ ] Low tyre pressure(s) (Chapters 1A or 1B and 10).
- [ ] Power steering system defective (Chapter 10).

Poor self-centring

- [ ] Defective balljoints or track rod ends (Chapter 10).
- [ ] Binding in steering gear or column (Chapter 10).
- [ ] Lack of lubricant in steering gear assembly (Chapter 10).
- [ ] Front wheel alignment out of specifications (Chapter 10).

Abnormal noise at the front end

- [ ] Defective balljoints or track rod ends (Chapters 1A or 1B and 10).
- [ ] Damaged strut mounting (Chapter 10).
- [ ] Worn control arm bushings or track rod ends (Chapter 10).
- [ ] Loose stabiliser bar (Chapter 10).
- [ ] Loose wheel bolts (Chapter 1A or 1B).
- [ ] Loose suspension bolts (Chapter 10).

Suspension and steering systems (continued)

Wander or poor steering stability

- ☐ Mismatched or uneven tyres (Chapter 10).
- ☐ Defective balljoints or track rod ends (Chapters 1A or 1B and 10).
- ☐ Worn strut assemblies (Chapter 10).
- ☐ Loose stabiliser bar (Chapter 10).
- ☐ Broken or sagging springs (Chapter 10).
- ☐ Wheels out of alignment (Chapter 10).

Erratic steering when braking

- ☐ Wheel bearings worn (Chapter 10).
- ☐ Broken or sagging springs (Chapter 10).
- ☐ Defective caliper (Chapter 10).
- ☐ Warped discs (Chapter 10).
- ☐ Front end alignment incorrect.

Excessive pitching and/or rolling around corners or during braking

- ☐ Loose stabiliser bar (Chapter 10).
- ☐ Worn strut dampers, shock absorbers or mountings (Chapter 10).
- ☐ Broken or sagging springs (Chapter 10).
- ☐ Overloaded vehicle.
- ☐ Front end alignment incorrect.

Suspension bottoms

- ☐ Overloaded vehicle.
- ☐ Worn strut dampers or shock absorbers (Chapter 10).
- ☐ Incorrect, broken or sagging springs (Chapter 10).

Excessive tyre wear on outside edge

- ☐ Inflation pressures incorrect (*Weekly checks*).
- ☐ Excessive speed in turns.
- ☐ Front end alignment incorrect (excessive toe-in). Have professionally aligned.
- ☐ Suspension arm bent or twisted (Chapter 10).

Excessive tyre wear on inside edge

- ☐ Inflation pressures incorrect (*Weekly checks*).
- ☐ Front end alignment incorrect (toe-out). Have professionally aligned.
- ☐ Loose or damaged steering components (Chapter 10).

Tyre tread worn in one place

- ☐ Tyres out-of-balance.
- ☐ Damaged wheel. Inspect and renew if necessary.
- ☐ Defective tyre (*Weekly checks*).

Excessive play or looseness in steering system

- ☐ Wheel bearing(s) worn (Chapter 10).
- ☐ Track rod end loose or worn (Chapter 10).
- ☐ Steering gear loose or worn (Chapter 10).
- ☐ Worn or loose steering intermediate shaft (Chapter 10).
- ☐ Rattling or clicking noise in steering gear
- ☐ Steering gear loose or worn (Chapter 10).

Note: *References throughout this index are in the form "***Chapter number***" • "***Page number***"*. So, for example, 2C•15 refers to page 15 of Chapter 2C.*

A

About this manual – 0•6
Accelerator cable – 4A•11
Accelerator Pedal Position (APP) sensor – 6A•18, 6B•3, 6B•6
Accessory shops – REF•5
Acknowledgements – 0•6
Actuator assembly (ABS) – 9•3, 9•4
Aerial – 12•10
Air conditioning system – 3•2, 3•11
    compressor – 3•13
    condenser – 3•14
    control assembly – 3•9
    odours – 3•12
    receiver/drier – 3•13
Air control valve – 6A•5, 6A•14
Air filter – 1A•16, 1B•14, 1B•20, 4A•8, 4B•3
Air intake system – 4A•12
Air temperature sensor – 6A•9, 6B•3, 6B•5
Air/fuel sensor – 6A•4, 6A•11
Airbags – 0•5, 12•19
Airflow meter – 6B•3, 6B•5
Airflow sensor – 6A•4, 6A•9
Alternator – 5•8
Antifreeze – 0•12, 0•16, 3•2
Anti-lock Brake System (ABS) – 9•2
Anti-roll bar and bushings – 10•6, 10•8
Asbestos – 0•5
Automatic transmission – 7B•1 *et seq*
    fluid – 0•14, 0•16, 1A•23, 1B•18
    fluid leaks – 7B•2
    oil seals – 7B•2, 7B•3
    troubleshooting – REF•16
Auxiliary drivebelt – 1A•11, 1B•10

B

Back door – 11•13
Balljoint – 10•7
Battery – 0•5, 1A•9, 1B•8, 5•3, 5•4
    disconnection – 5•2
    electrolyte – 0•13
Big-end bearings – 2D•15
Bleeding
    brake hydraulic system – 9•16
    clutch hydraulic system – 8•3
    power steering – 10•15
Blower motor – 3•9
Body – 11•1 *et seq*
    corrosion – REF•11
    panels – 11•2
Bonnet – 11•3, 11•4
Boots
    driveshaft – 1A•18, 1B•15
    steering gear – 10•13
Brakes – 9•1 *et seq*, REF•8, REF•9, REF•10
    check – 1A•15, 1B•12
    fluid – 0•13, 0•16, 1A•19, 1B•17
    lights – 12•14
    troubleshooting – REF•17
    vacuum servo – 1A•16, 1B•13
Bulbs – 12•11, 12•14
Bumpers – 11•5
Burning – 0•5
Buying spare parts – REF•5

C

Cables
    accelerator – 4A•11
    automatic transmission shift – 7B•5
    battery – 5•4
    bonnet release – 11•4
    gearchange – 7A•3
    handbrake – 9•18
    heater/air conditioning control – 3•9
    Throttle Valve (TV) – 7B•3
Calipers – 9•9
Camshafts – 2A•8, 2B•9, 2C•11
    Camshaft Position (CMP) sensor – 6A•4, 6A•10, 6B•3, 6B•6
    oil seal – 2A•8, 2C•11
Carpet maintenance – 11•2
Catalytic converter – 6A•17
Central locking system – 12•17
Centre console – 11•14
Centre support bearing – 8•9
Centre trim panels – 11•16
Charcoal canister – 6A•17
Charging – 1A•11, 1B•9, 5•7
Chassis electrical system – 12•1 *et seq*
Check Engine light – 6B•3
Circuit breakers – 12•3
Circuit check – 12•8
Clutch and driveshafts – 8•1 *et seq*
    clutch fluid – 0•13, 0•16
    clutch pedal freeplay – 1A•9, 1B•8
    clutch troubleshooting – REF•15
Coil module – 5•5, 5•6
Coil spring – 10•9
Common rail – 4B•6
Compression check – 2D•4
Compressor – 3•13
Computer (ABS) – 9•3
Condenser – 3•14
Connecting rods – 2D•11, 2D•14, 2D•18
Connectors – 12•2
Console – 11•14
Continuity check – 12•2
Control arm – 10•6
Conversion factors – REF•2
Coolant – 0•12, 0•16, 3•2
    pump – 3•6
    reservoir/expansion tank – 3•6
    temperature sending unit – 3•8
    temperature sensor – 6A•4, 6A•9, 6B•3, 6B•5
Cooling fans – 3•4
Cooling, heating and air conditioning systems – 1A•14, 1A•21, 1B•11, 1B•17, 3•1 *et seq*
    troubleshooting – REF•15
Courtesy light – 12•14
Cowl cover and vent tray – 11•8
Crankcase ventilation system – 6A•14, 6B•7
Crankshaft – 2D•12, 2D•15, 2D•16
    oil seal – 2A•8, 2A•16, 2B•15, 2B•17, 2C•10, 2C•20
    Crankshaft Position (CKP) sensor – 6A•4, 6A•10, 6B•3, 6B•6
    pulley/vibration damper – 2B•14
Cruise control system – 12•16
Crushing – 0•5
Cylinder block – 2D•13
Cylinder compression check – 2D•4
Cylinder head – 2A•11, 2B•13, 2C•13, 2D•9, 2D•10, 2D•11

*Note: References throughout this index are in the form "**Chapter number**" • "**Page number**". So, for example, 2C•15 refers to page 15 of Chapter 2C.*

D

Daytime Running Lights (DRL) – 12•18
Deceleration sensor (ABS) – 9•3, 9•6
Dents – 11•2
Diagnostic checks – 2D•5
 ABS – 9•3
 tool information – 6A•4, 6B•3
 Trouble Codes – 6A•5, 6B•4
Diesel engines – 2C•1 *et seq*
 troubleshooting – REF•13
Diesel injection equipment – 0•5
Differential – 8•11
 oil – 0•16, 1A•18, 1A•24, 1B•15, 1B•19
 oil seals – 8•10
Dimensions – REF•1
Disc brakes – 1A•15, 1B•13
 discs – 9•9
Distributor – 5•7
 cap – 1A•20
Distributorless Ignition System – 5•5
Doors – 11•8, 11•9, 11•10, 11•11, 11•12, 11•13, REF•9
 Power lock system – 12•17
Drivebelt – 1A•11, 1B•10
Driveplate – 2A•15, 2B•17, 2C•20
Driveshafts – 8•6, REF•10
 boot – 1A•18, 1B•15, 8•7
 oil seals – 7B•2, 8•10
 troubleshooting – REF•16
Drum brakes – 1A•15, 1B•13
 shoes – 9•10

E

Earth check – 12•2
EFI main relay – 6A•4
EGR vacuum modulator filter – 6A•15
EGR valve – 6A•15, 6B•7
Electric shock – 0•5
Electric window system – 12•16
Electrical equipment – REF•9
 troubleshooting – 12•1
Electrolyte – 0•13
Electronic Driving Unit – 6B•6
Electronic fuel Injection system – 4A•2, 4A•12
Electronic ignition – 5•4
Emission system – REF•11
Emissions and engine control systems – diesel engine – 6B•1 *et seq*
Emissions and engine control systems – petrol engines – 6A•1 *et seq*
Engine Control Module (ECM) fuel system – 6A•6, 6B•7
Engine Coolant Temperature (ECT) sensor – 6A•4, 6A•9
Engine electrical systems – 5•1 *et seq*
 troubleshooting – REF•14
Engine number – REF•4
Engine oil – 0•11, 0•16, 1A•7, 1B•6
Engine removal and overhaul procedures – 2D•1 *et seq*
Engine troubleshooting – REF•13, REF•14
Environmental considerations – REF•3
Evaporative emissions control (EVAP) system – 1A•22, 6A•16
 Vacuum Switching Valve (VSV) – 6A•5
Exhaust Gas Recirculation – 6A•15, 6B•7
Exhaust manifold – 2A•4, 2B•12, 2C•5
Exhaust specialists – REF•5
Exhaust system – 1A•23, 1B•18, 4A•2, 4A•16, 4B•11, REF•10, REF•11
Expansion tank – 3•6
Extension housing oil seal – 7B•3

F

Facia trim panels – 11•14
Fans – 3•4
 switch – 3•8
Filling – 11•3
Filter
 air – 1A•16, 1B•14, 1B•20, 4A•8, 4B•3
 automatic transmission fluid – 1A•23, 1B•18
 EGR vacuum modulator – 6A•15
 fuel – 1A•19, 1B•19, 1B•21, 4B•4
 oil – 1A•7, 1B•6
 pollen – 1A•18, 1B•16
Fire – 0•5
Fixed glass – 11•3
Flexible hoses – 4A•4
Fluids – 0•16
Flywheel – 2A•15, 2B•17, 2C•20
Foglight – 12•15
Followers – 2A•8, 2B•9, 2C•11
Fuel and exhaust systems – diesel engine – 4B•1 *et seq*
Fuel and exhaust systems – petrol engines – 4A•1 *et seq*
Fuel delivery system – 4A•12
Fuel filter – 1A•19, 1B•19, 1B•21, 4B•4
Fuel heater – 4B•4
Fuel hose – 1A•14, 1B•11
Fuel injection main relay – 6A•4
Fuel Injection system – 4A•2, 4A•12
Fuel injectors – 4A•14, 4B•7, 6A•4
Fuel level sending unit – 4A•7, 4B•3
Fuel lines – 4A•2, 4A•4, 4B•2, 4B•6
Fuel pressure limiter – 6B•7
Fuel pressure regulator – 4A•6
Fuel pressure relief – 4A•2
Fuel pressure sensor – 6B•3, 6B•6
Fuel pulsation damper – 4A•14
Fuel pump – 4A•2, 4A•3, 4A•4, 4B•5
Fuel rail and injectors – 4A•14
Fuel sensor – 6A•4, 6A•11
Fuel system – 1A•17, 1B•14, REF•11
 troubleshooting – REF•14
Fuel tank – 4A•7, 4A•8, 4B•3
Fuel temperature sensor – 6B•3, 6B•5
Fume or gas intoxication – 0•5
Fuses – 12•3
Fusible links – 12•3

G

Gaiters
 driveshaft – 1A•18, 1B•15, 8•7
 steering gear – 10•13
Garages – REF•5
Gashes – 11•3
Gaskets – REF•3
 leaks – 7B•2
Gearchange
 cables – 7A•3
 lever – 7A•3
General repair procedures – REF•3
Glass – 11•3, 11•11, 11•12
Glovebox – 11•16
Glow plugs – 5•10, 6B•3
Grille – 11•7

Note: *References throughout this index are in the form "**Chapter number**" • "**Page number**". So, for example, 2C•15 refers to page 15 of Chapter 2C.*

H

Handbrake – 1A•16, 1B•14, 9•2, 9•17, 9•18, REF•8
   shoes – 9•19
Handles
   back door – 11•13
   doors – 11•10
Hazard flasher – 12•5
   switch – 12•6
Headlights – 12•11, 12•12, 12•13
Heated rear window – 12•11
   switch – 12•7
Heating system – 3•2, 3•12
   blower motor – 3•9
   control assembly – 3•9
   matrix – 3•10
High-mounted brake light – 12•14
High-pressure common rail – 4B•6
High-pressure fuel lines – 4B•6
High-pressure fuel pump – 4B•5
Hinges maintenance – 11•3
Holes – 11•3
Horn – 12•14
Hoses – 1A•13, 1A•24, 1B•11, 1B•19, 4A•4, 9•15
Hubs and bearing – 10•8, 10•10
Hydraulic system – 9•2
Hydrofluoric acid – 0•5

I

Identification numbers – REF•4
Identifying leaks – 0•10
Idle Air Control (IAC) valve – 6A•5, 6A•14
Ignition system – 5•4, 5•5
   coils – 5•6
   module – 5•5, 5•6, 6A•5
   switch – 12•6
Indicators – 12•5, 12•14
Information sensors – 6A•4, 6B•3
Injectors – 4A•14, 4B•7, 6A•4
Inlet system – 4B•3
Instrument cluster – 12•7
   bezel – 11•14
   lights – 12•14
Instrument panel – 11•17
   light control switch – 12•7
Instrument panel switches – 12•6
Intake Air Temperature (IAT) sensor – 6A•4, 6A•9, 6B•3, 6B•5
Intake manifold – 2A•3, 2B•11, 2C•5
Intercooler – 4B•11
Interior light – 12•14

J

Jacking and vehicle support – REF•5
Joint mating faces – REF•3
Jump starting – 0•8

K

Key interlock solenoid – 7B•7
Key lock cylinder – 12•6
Keyless entry system – 12•18
Knee bolster – 11•16
Knock sensor – 6A•13

L

Leaks – 0•10, 7B•2
Limited slip differential oil seal – 8•10
Locknuts, locktabs and washers – REF•3
Locks
   back door – 11•13
   bonnet – 11•4
   central locking system – 12•17
   doors – 11•10, 12•17
   key – 12•6
   maintenance – 11•3
Lubricants and fluids – 0•16

M

Main bearings – 2D•15
Maintenance
   carpets – 11•2
   hinges – 11•3
   locks – 11•3
   trim – 11•1
   upholstery – 11•2
   vinyl trim – 11•1
Manifold Absolute Pressure (MAP) sensor – 6A•4, 6A•8
Manifolds – 2A•3, 2A•4, 2B•11, 2B•12, 2C•5
Manual transmission – 7A•1 *et seq*
   oil – 0•16, 1A•17, 1A•24, 1B•14, 1B•19
   oil cooler – 7A•6
   troubleshooting – REF•15, REF•16
Mass Airflow Sensor (MAF) – 6A•4, 6A•9
Master cylinder
   brake – 9•14
   clutch – 8•3
Matrix – 3•10
Metal lines – 1A•14, 1B•11
Mirrors – 11•12, 12•15, REF•8
   control switch – 12•7
MOT test checks – REF•8 *et seq*
Motor factors – REF•5
Mountings – 2A•16, 2B•17, 2C•20

N

Number plate light – 12•15

O

Oil cooler (manual transmission) – 7A•6
Oil
   differential – 0•16, 1A•18, 1A•24, 1B•15, 1B•19
   engine – 0•11, 0•16, 1A•7, 1B•6
   manual transmission – 0•16, 1A•17, 1A•24, 1B•14, 1B•19
   transfer case – 0•16, 1A•17, 1A•24, 1B•14, 1B•19
Oil filter – 1A•7, 1B•6
Oil pressure check – 2D•4
Oil pump – 2A•14, 2B•16, 2C•17
Oil seals – REF•3
   automatic transmission – 7B•2, 7B•3
   camshaft – 2A•8, 2C•11
   crankshaft – 2A•8, 2A•16, 2B•15, 2B•17, 2C•10, 2C•20
   differential – 8•10
   driveshaft – 7B•2, 8•10
   extension housing – 7B•3
   limited slip differential – 8•10
   pinion – 8•10
   torque-sensing limited slip differential – 8•10

Note: *References throughout this index are in the form* "**Chapter number**" • "**Page number**". *So, for example, 2C•15 refers to page 15 of Chapter 2C.*

On-Board Diagnostic (OBD) system – 6A•4, 6B•3
Open circuit – 12•2
Output actuators – 6B•3
Oxygen sensors (O_2) – 6A•4, 6A•11

P

Pads – 9•6
Painting – 11•3
Park/Neutral Position (PNP) switch – 7B•6
Park/turn signal lights – 12•14
Parts – REF•5
Pedals
  accelerator position sensor – 6A•18, 6B•3, 6B•6
  brake – 9•18
  clutch – 1A•9, 1B•8
Petrol engines – 2000 and earlier – 2A•1 et seq
Petrol engines – 2001 and later – 2B•1 et seq
Pinion oil seal – 8•10
Pipes – 1A•14, 1B•11, 4A•4, 9•15
Piston rings – 2D•17
Pistons – 2D•11, 2D•14, 2D•18
Plastic body panels – 11•2
Poisonous or irritant substances – 0•5
Pollen filter – 1A•18, 1B•16
Positive Crankcase Ventilation (PCV) valve – 1A•24, 1B•19, 6A•14
Power door lock system – 12•17
Power steering
  fluid – 0•14, 0•16
  pressure switch – 6A•4
  pump – 10•14
Power window system – 12•16
Propeller shaft – 8•9
Puncture repair – 0•9

R

Radiator – 3•5
  fan switch – 3•8
  grille – 11•7
Radio – 12•9
Rear window – 12•11
  switch – 12•7
Receiver/drier – 3•13
Regulator (window glass) – 11•12
Relays – 12•3
  EFI – 6A•4
Release bearing and lever – 8•5
Repair procedures – REF•3
Reversing light switch – 7A•3
Roadside repairs – 0•7 et seq
Rotor – 1A•20
Routine maintenance and servicing – diesel models – 1B•1 et seq
Routine maintenance and servicing – petrol models – 1A•1 et seq
Running lights – 12•18

S

Safety first! – 0•5
Scalding – 0•5
Scratches – 11•2
Screw threads and fastenings – REF•3
Seat belts – 1A•15, 1B•12
Seats – 11•18
Sequential Electronic Fuel Injection system – 4A•2
Servo – 1A•16, 1B•13, 9•2, 9•16
Shift lock system – 7B•6
  cable – 7B•5
  control computer – 7B•8
  control switch – 7B•8
Shock absorbers – 10•8, REF•9, REF•10
Shoes – 9•10
  handbrake – 9•19
Short circuit – 12•2
Slave cylinder (clutch) – 8•3
Spare parts – REF•5
Spark plugs – 1A•19, 5•5
  lead – 1A•20
Speakers – 12•9
Speed sensor – 6A•4, 6A•14, 6B•3
  ABS – 9•3, 9•4
  O-ring – 7B•3
Spring – 10•4, 10•9, REF•10
Sprockets – 2A•5, 2B•5, 2C•6
Stabiliser bar and bushings – 10•6, 10•8
Start switch – 8•6
Starting system – 5•9
  motor – 5•9, 5•10
Start-up after reassembly – 2D•19
Steel body panels – 11•2
Steel pipes – 4A•4
Steering – 1A•17, 1B•15, REF•9, REF•10
Steering column – 10•11, REF•8
  covers – 11•16
  switches – 12•5
Steering gear – 10•13
  gaiters – 10•13
Steering knuckle and hub – 10•7
Steering pressure switch – 6A•4
Steering pump – 10•14
Steering wheel – 10•10, REF•8
Strut (suspension) – 10•4
Sump – 2A•13, 2B•15, 2C•17
Sunroof – 11•18, 12•18
Suspension and steering systems – 1A•17, 1B•15, 10•1 et seq, REF•9, REF•10
  troubleshooting – REF•17, REF•18
Switches
  brake light – 9•19
  hazard warning – 12•6
  heated rear window – 12•7
  ignition – 12•6

Note: *References throughout this index are in the form* **"Chapter number"** • **"Page number"**. *So, for example, 2C•15 refers to page 15 of Chapter 2C.*

instrument panel – 12•6
instrument panel light control – 12•7
mirror control – 12•7
park/neutral position (PNP) – 7B•6
radiator fan – 3•8
reversing light – 7A•3
shift lock control – 7B•8
start (clutch) – 8•6
steering column – 12•5

T

Tail lights – 12•14
Tappets – 2A•8, 2B•9, 2C•11
Temperature gauge sending unit – 3•8
Temperature sensor – 6A•4, 6A•9, 6B•3, 6B•5
Thermostat – 3•3
Throttle body – 4A•13, 4B•9
Throttle Position Sensor (TPS) – 6A•4, 6A•8
Throttle Valve (TV) cable – 7B•3
Tie-rod ends – 10•13
Timing belt and sprockets – 2A•5, 2C•6
Timing chain and sprockets – 2B•5
Tools and working facilities – REF•3, REF•6 *et seq*
Top Dead Centre (TDC) for number one piston location – 2A•3, 2B•3, 2C•3
Torque-sensing limited slip differential oil seal – 8•10
Towing – 0•10
Toyota RAV4 – 0•6
Trailing arm – 10•9
Transfer case oil – 0•16, 1A•17, 1A•24, 1B•14, 1B•19
Transmission sensors – 6A•4
Trim panels – 11•8, 11•14, 11•16
    maintenance – 11•1
Trouble codes – 6A•5, 6B•3
Troubleshooting – REF•12 *et seq*
    automatic transmission – REF•16
    brakes – REF•17
    clutch – REF•15
    cooling system – REF•15
    diesel engine – REF•13
    driveshafts – REF•16
    electrical system – 12•1
    engine – REF•13, REF•14
    engine electrical system – REF•14
    fuel system – REF•14
    manual transmission – REF•15, REF•16
    suspension and steering systems – REF•17, REF•18
Turbo pressure sensor – 6B•3, 6B•6
Turbocharger – 4B•9
    wastegate regulator valve – 6B•3
Turn signal indicators – 12•5, 12•14
Tyres – 10•16, REF•11
    checks – 0•15
    rotation – 1A•14, 1B•12
    specialists – REF•5

U

Underbonnet hoses – 1A•13, 1A•24, 1B•11, 1B•19
Upholstery maintenance – 11•2

V

Vacuum gauge diagnostic checks – 2D•5
Vacuum hoses – 1A•13, 1B•11
Vacuum pump – 9•21
Vacuum regulating valve – 6B•7
Vacuum servo – 1A•16, 1B•13
Vacuum Switching Valve (VSV) – 6A•5, 6A•15
Valve cover – 2A•3, 2B•3, 2C•3
Valve lifters – 2A•8, 2B•9, 2C•11
Valve timing system – 2B•4
Valves – 2D•10, 2D•11
    clearances – 1A•25, 1B•16
Vapour pressure sensor – 6A•4
Variable Valve Timing (VVT) system – 2B•4
Vehicle identification numbers – REF•4, REF•9
Vehicle Speed Sensor (VSS) – 6A•4, 6A•14, 6B•3
Vehicle support – REF•5
Vent tray – 11•8
Vibration damper – 2B•14
VIN model year code – REF•4
Vinyl trim maintenance – 11•1
Voltage checks – 12•2

W

Washer fluid – 0•13
Wastegate regulator valve – 6B•3
Water pump – 3•6
Weekly checks – 0•11 *et seq*
Weights – REF•1
Wheels – 10•16, REF•11
    alignment – 10•16
    bearings – 10•8, 10•10, REF•10
    changing – 0•9
    studs – 10•15
Wheel cylinder – 9•14
Wheel speed sensor (ABS) – 9•4
Window glass – 11•11
    regulator – 11•12
Windscreen – 11•3, REF•8
Windscreen washer fluid – 0•13
Windscreen wiper blade – 1A•9, 1B•7
Wing – 11•6
Wiper blade – 1A•9, 1B•7
Wiper motor – 12•8
    circuit check – 12•8
Wiring diagrams – 12•20 *et seq*
Working facilities – REF•7

Preserving Our Motoring Heritage

< The Model J Duesenberg
Derham Tourster.
Only eight of these
magnificent cars were
ever built – this is the
only example to be found
outside the United States
of America

Almost every car you've ever loved, loathed or desired is gathered under one roof at the Haynes Motor Museum. Over 300 immaculately presented cars and motorbikes represent every aspect of our motoring heritage, from elegant reminders of bygone days, such as the superb Model J Duesenberg to curiosities like the bug-eyed BMW Isetta. There are also many old friends and flames. Perhaps you remember the 1959 Ford Popular that you did your courting in? The magnificent 'Red Collection' is a spectacle of classic sports cars including AC, Alfa Romeo, Austin Healey, Ferrari, Lamborghini, Maserati, MG, Riley, Porsche and Triumph.

A Perfect Day Out

Each and every vehicle at the Haynes Motor Museum has played its part in the history and culture of Motoring. Today, they make a wonderful spectacle and a great day out for all the family. Bring the kids, bring Mum and Dad, but above all bring your camera to capture those golden memories for ever. You will also find an impressive array of motoring memorabilia, a comfortable 70 seat video cinema and one of the most extensive transport book shops in Britain. The Pit Stop Cafe serves everything from a cup of tea to wholesome, home-made meals or, if you prefer, you can enjoy the large picnic area nestled in the beautiful rural surroundings of Somerset.

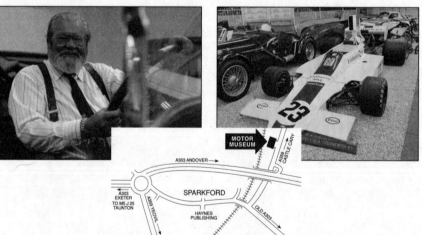

John Haynes O.B.E.,
Founder and
Chairman of the
museum at the wheel
of a Haynes Light 12. >

< Graham Hill's Lola
Cosworth Formula 1
car next to a 1934
Riley Sports.

The Museum is situated on the A359 Yeovil to Frome road at Sparkford, just off the A303 in Somerset. It is about 40 miles south of Bristol, and 25 minutes drive from the M5 intersection at Taunton.

Open 9.30am - 5.30pm (10.00am - 4.00pm Winter) 7 days a week, *except Christmas Day, Boxing Day and New Years Day*

Special rates available for schools, coach parties and outings Charitable Trust No. 292048